Guns 360

Guns 360

Differing Perspectives and Common-Sense Approaches to Firearms in America

Edited by
Eric S. See
Christopher M. Bellas
Sarah A. See

ROWMAN & LITTLEFIELD
Lanham • Boulder • New York • London

Published by Rowman & Littlefield
An imprint of The Rowman & Littlefield Publishing Group, Inc.
4501 Forbes Boulevard, Suite 200, Lanham, Maryland 20706
www.rowman.com

86-90 Paul Street, London EC2A 4NE, United Kingdom

British Library Cataloguing in Publication Information Available

Library of Congress Cataloging-in-Publication Data

Names: See, Eric S., 1968– editor. | Bellas, Christopher M., 1974– editor. | See, Sarah A., 1972– editor.

Title: Guns 360 : differing perspectives and common-sense approaches to firearms in America / edited by Eric S. See, Christopher M. Bellas, Sarah A. See.

Other titles: Guns three-sixty

Description: Lanham : Rowman & Littlefield, [2022] | Includes bibliographical references and index. | Summary: "Guns 360 takes a comprehensive, interdisciplinary, and common-sense approach to some of the most difficult issues facing not only the criminal justice system but also society as a whole: firearm possession, regulation, and control"—Provided by publisher.

Identifiers: LCCN 2021053619 (print) | LCCN 2021053620 (ebook) | ISBN 9781538140673 (cloth) | ISBN 9781538140680 (epub)

Subjects: LCSH: Gun control—United States. | Firearms—Law and legislation—United States.

Classification: LCC HV7436 .G8767 2022 (print) | LCC HV7436 (ebook) | DDC 363.3/3/0973—dc23/eng/20220125

LC record available at https://lccn.loc.gov/2021053619

LC ebook record available at https://lccn.loc.gov/2021053620

™ The paper used in this publication meets the minimum requirements of American National Standard for Information Sciences—Permanence of Paper for Printed Library Materials, ANSI/NISO Z39.48-1992.

Contents

Preface

It would be remiss not to open this book with a brief reflection upon the year in which it was written. Firearms are a controversial issue every year, but thankfully every year is not like 2020. Although most Americans tend to debate firearms in terms of the Second Amendment and on a federal, constitutional level, most firearm laws and regulations are made on the state level. In a similar manner, much of the pandemic response of 2020 occurred on the state level as well. Various forms of lockdown and stay-at-home orders were passed. Many states saw protests of these orders, and in some cases, most notably in Michigan, firearms were brought to these protests. As a result of the various lockdowns and stay-at-home orders, several states reduced or halted the processing of carry-conceal permits and/or ordered the closing of gun stores. Then came the killing of George Floyd and civil unrest.

While protests of police brutality occurred in towns big and small all across the country, Portland, Oregon, became the epicenter where protests have currently been in progress for more than five months with no sign of letting up. In Seattle, protestors took over a six-block area of downtown and renamed it the Capitol Hill Autonomous Zone or "Chaz." Similar protests, riots, and "occupations" occurred across the country. Weapons were reported to have been displayed and used by those seeking to protest police violence as well as by Antifa and counterprotesters. Fears of the pandemic, violence, rioting, and looting appeared to have widened the gap between those who favor gun ownership and those who condemn it. People who have never held a gun before have been submitting applications for concealed carry permits and purchasing guns out of fear for their safety, while there are others who believe that gun ownership is not necessary if the United States can just unite against inequality.

During a normal election, firearm initiatives on the ballot and Second Amendment concerns have the ability to drive people to the polls. No one will ever accuse 2020 of being a normal time. As noted, a global pandemic and levels of social unrest not witnessed since the 1960s guaranteed that. All of this occurred before the presidential election of 2020. Many states do not prohibit the presence of weapons at campaign stops and rallies or at voting locations. This patchwork of state, local laws, and regulations added to the general sense of apprehension felt by many as they prepared to cast their ballots and guaranteed that firearms would remain a central issue in this country regardless of the outcome of the election. Both loved and hated, President Trump polarized the American public; however, his administration had very little impact on federal firearm laws in this country over the course of a single, four-year term. The election of President Biden capped off a chaotic and hectic 2020 and promised a reexamination of many existing firearm laws and policies, resulting in additional uncertainty and anxiety regarding the topic of firearm ownership and use.

This book provides a wide range of information on various aspects pertaining to the world of firearms. In addition to chapters written by criminologists and experts in criminal justice, it also includes the work of experts in the areas of economics, psychology, sociology, religion, political science, communications, management, forensics, public health, medicine, and digital forensics. This book adds to the literature by providing an academic analysis of issues critical to our democracy.

The authors in the book represent not only academic excellence and expertise, but practical expertise as well. Experts who have worked in law enforcement in the military and civilian world, along with a current chief of police, are included. Subject-matter experts in forensics and digital forensics offer their insights. All of this skill, knowledge, and experience has been brought together to aid students in learning about firearms. This book, however, goes one step further. It does not talk at students; it talks to them and with them. One chapter in this book was written exclusively by undergraduate students from Methodist University, and another chapter was written by undergraduate and graduate students at Youngstown State University. Students talking to students adds a unique perspective to this book not found or replicated in other works. Firearms will never disappear from our society, nor will the controversy surrounding firearms suddenly turn into agreement. What can be accomplished, however, is an increased knowledge, understanding, and discussion of the complex topics of firearms.

Acknowledgments

To our children, Cameron, Lauren, and Stephanie.

—Eric S. See and Sarah A. See

I would like to thank my family who has been very supportive of me throughout my academic journey over these many years. Their patience and understanding were deeply appreciated. I could not have come this far without their encouragement. I would also like to thank my friends and colleagues outside of YSU for always lending their reassurance to whatever projects I undertake and for always rooting for my success.

—Christopher M. Bellas

A very special thanks to Ms. Rebecca King, MFA. This book would not have been possible without her hard work and dedication and the role of the Methodist University Writing Center.

In Memory of Elke Weinbrenner, My Loving Sister. Dedicated to Learning the Truth!

—Karla Weinbrenner

Part I

AN INTRODUCTION TO FIREARM TYPES, MARKETS, AND OWNERSHIP

1

Gadget Guns

A Legal and Ethical Examination of a Unique Portion of the Firearms Market

Eric S. See and Sarah A. See

What's the image that comes to mind when thinking about a firearm? For most people, the image is that of a handgun, a rifle, or a shotgun. This makes sense given the current reality; the United States has more firearms than citizens. According to 2017 data, 30 percent of American adults own a firearm. Among that subset, 66 percent own more than one firearm, 72 percent own a handgun, 62 percent own a rifle, and 54 percent own a shotgun (Gramlich & Schaeffer, 2020).

Most firearm debates and discussions in this country currently focus around a few key areas, including the definition of assault rifles, the prevalence of handguns, the requirements for concealed carry, large-capacity magazines, and the number of homicides or suicides committed with a firearm each year. While all of these topics are worthy of extended debate and research, a unique segment of the firearms market referred to as gadget guns has been neglected.

Gadget guns are firearms or accessories manufactured to allow the owner options and a level of flexibility not found in conventional weapons. They are often not what they appear to be. Many are designed to hide in plain sight. They may be made out of unconventional materials, change calibers in mere seconds, be worn on the body as though they are part of a decorative outfit, or appear as if they are another tool altogether. Some gadget guns have been mass produced, while others are still in the concept stage. Gadget guns can also be purchased in the form of a kit that allows the user to make a handgun or AR-15–style rifle at home. While some of these weapons have come to the attention of law enforcement, many have not been a part of the public dialogue of firearms in America.

For many, when thinking of gadget guns, images of a zip gun, a cane gun, or a gun used by a spy might come to mind. Traditionally, zip guns have been relatively simple, if not crude, handmade, single-shot weapons. While designs vary, common items such as a nail for a firing pin, a hollow tube, and rubber bands to fire a single round at a time (Koffler, 1970). While zip guns were perhaps more popular in the 1950s, they are still being made today. Another image of a gadget gun might be that of an antique cane gun. Antique cane guns are valued by collectors and have been reproduced in recent times. While a rifle disguised as a cane certainly qualifies as a gadget gun, the practicality of finding a safe, operable antique cane gun is not very good, and the modern reproductions have never become popular or easy to find. Gadget guns have evolved from the simple modification of a pipe or the golden gun from the imagination of James Bond.

From one at a time and one-of-a-kind guns forged on a garage workbench to mass production by leading companies, gadget guns have changed with the times. This chapter will explore variations of modern gadget guns, and when possible, identify particular manufacturers, concepts, and styles. Pros and cons of the weapons will also be addressed, and the relevant ethical and legal concerns will be presented. The author is neither endorsing nor condemning any of the firearms or accessories provided in this chapter. They are simply used to illustrate a small portion of the variety seen in the marketplace today. The variations covered here are by no means exhaustive. The purpose of this chapter is to familiarize the reader with these types of items and to explore the particular legal, ethical, and moral challenges they provide to criminal justice personnel and the criminal justice system.

THE LEGALITY OF OWNING GUNS AND GADGET GUNS

The general public, let alone legal scholars, have never agreed on American's rights to own firearms. Exactly who can own a firearm and what type of firearm may be owned has been the source of consistent litigation. Only relatively recently has the Supreme Court clarified the general legal right of a private citizen to own a firearm. The right was clearly established in the District of Columbia v. Heller 554 U.S. 570 (2008).

> While this was not the first nor the last Supreme Court decision dealing with the Second Amendment, it is the controlling case on this issue. This decision makes clear that private individuals have a right to own and carry a weapon in their homes for self-defense, unrelated to military service. This right is not without limits however. Felons and the mentally ill can be excluded, and certain unusual

> and dangerous weapons can be excluded. However, this does not end the legal or moral discussion. (See, Bellas, & See, 2021, p. 99)

The concept of "unusual" weapons" is of interest here. What does it mean? How unusual does a weapon have to be for it to be illegal? It is legal to own guns in general, but are gadget guns legal? In addition to the legal issues presented by firearm ownership, there are moral issues to consider as well. Is it moral to own a gun? Turning to morals, in order to understand firearm ownership from a moral and ethical perspective, the moral intentions of the individual must be examined. Why does the individual wish to own a firearm? Is ownership sought for the purposes of good or evil?

> Owning a firearm to further the rights of self-preservation and self-defense satisfies an inquiry on ethical grounds. The decision to own a firearm for the purposes of self-preservation and self-defense is therefore an ethical decision. (See, Bellas, & See, 2021, p. 102)

Establishing a general legal and ethical framework for firearms is important, but does this same framework apply across the board to all types of firearms, or could there be exceptions? Are there firearms or accessories that might be legal to own yet unethical? Or perhaps ethical, yet illegal? An examination of various types of gadget guns is necessary to address these important questions.

3-D PRINTED GUNS

For the most part, gadget guns are perfectly legal. The major exception to this rule concerns 3-D printed guns. Not only is the legality of these firearms in question, but there are legal issues surrounding the mere possession and distribution of the digital or CAD files used to "print" the weapons.

The first 3-D printer was created in the early 1980s, and the machines needed for the process could cost $100,000 or more (Hoffman, 2020). These printers use a digital file to lay down very thin layers of plastic or metal to create, manufacture, or "print" a particular object. Today, these machines are commonplace, and inexpensive models can be purchased for a few hundred dollars. These printers can be used to make everyday items, but they can also be used to make firearms.

Ethical/Moral Issues

Early designs were often single use or provided a few uses at best. While the technology is improving, 3-D guns are typically single-shot weapons. As designs and materials improve, multiple-use weapons are more likely. Traditionally, these guns have been entirely made of plastic, needing only a nail for a firing pen. With the firing pen removed, these weapons can easily slip through metal detectors. All schools, churches, courthouses, hospitals, airports, and other gun-free zones would be at risk.

Some 3-D guns have been printed using metal, which may ease the fear of sneaking the weapon past a metal detector; however the weapon would still be lacking a serial number. Without a serial number, these guns, plastic or metal, would be virtually impossible to trace. In addition, once the CAD file becomes widely available, there is no way to determine the motives of the individual who downloads the file. Single-use weapons lacking serial numbers that can avoid metal detectors and other conventional security measures raise serious ethical and moral questions. The rights of self-defense and self-preservation can easily be achieved by an alternate weapon that does not pose as many risks to the legitimate safety and security aims of society as a whole.

Legal Issues

In 2013, a company by the name of Defense Distributed designed the plans for a 3-D printed handgun and put the plans on their website. The plans were free to download, and in fact were, approximately a million times. A series of legal battles ensued at both the federal and state level about the legality of distributing the plans. Initially, the US Department of State blocked the distribution of the digital files. Eventually a settlement was reached in which Defense Distributed would once again be allowed to post the files online. Before the settlement deadline, however, twenty-one state's attorneys general filed suit to block the settlement agreement. The final result is still pending (Baldwin, 2020).

An additional legal issue is presented by the Undetectable Firearms Act (GovTrack.us, 2020). This act was passed in 1988 and has been amended and extended a number of times. Simply put, the intent of the law is to make it illegal to import, possess, sell, or receive a firearm that does not contain enough metal to activate a metal detector. While this seems to apply directly to 3-D printed guns, keep in mind that most need a metal firing pin to function. Attempts have been made to amend the act and require that specified amounts of metal be added to various components of a weapon to make them legal. Thus far, these amendments have not been successful.

At this point, the legal status of 3-D printed firearms remain unclear. Also unclear is the legal status of those who own and/or distribute the CAD files necessary to print such a weapon, and legal uncertainty over 3-D firearm printing is unlikely to become clear anytime soon. Once these files are widely available, there is simply no mechanism to prevent children, felons, and the mentally disturbed from printing a weapon when they could not legally buy a traditional weapon from a licensed firearm dealer.

BUMP STOCKS

Bump stocks are an accessory that can be added to an existing weapon. It replaces the traditional butt stock of the weapon and operates by using the natural recoil created when a semiautomatic weapon is fired. Natural recoil moves the weapon back, and the bump stock "bumps" the weapon forward against the trigger finger. This process is repeated as long as the operator keeps his or her finger on the trigger. The result is a semiautomatic weapon that fires nearly as fast as a fully automatic machine gun. How is this legal? Because the bump stock does not alter the mechanical function of the weapon, it had remained legal. That all changed after the 2017 mass shooting in Las Vegas, and the intervention of President Trump.

Ethical Issues

A bump stock is not a weapon, does not fire rounds, nor does it alter the mechanical operation of an existing weapon. It is a piece of plastic, an accessory that can be added to an existing weapon. There is nothing inherently unethical about a piece of plastic. When used to replace the stock of an AR-15, however, the semiautomatic weapon is transformed into a weapon capable of nearing fully automatic fire rates. It would take an examination of the motivations of the individual to determine if owning and using a bump stock were an ethical issue. There are certainly no ethical issues if the owner of the bump stock wants to have fun at a firing range and fire as many rounds as possible as quickly as possible at a safe target. It is a vastly different situation if the owner of the bump stock wants to increase the speed and quantity of rounds fired to kill more victims in a planned attack.

Legal Issues

Bump stocks have been in existence, in one form or another, for approximately twenty years. During that time, the Bureau of Alcohol, Tobacco, and Firearms (ATF) ruled a number of times that bump stocks were merely a firearm part, and thus not subject to regulation. The mass shooting in Las Vegas prompted many, including President Trump, to take another look. In February 2018, he signed a memorandum instructing the Attorney General to regulate the use of bump stocks. Effective March 26, 2019, a new Department of Justice rule amended existing ATF regulations and officially classified bump stocks as machine guns.

> The Department of Justice is amending the regulations of the Bureau of Alcohol, Tobacco, Firearms, and Explosives (ATF) to clarify that bump-stock-type devices—meaning "bump fire" stocks, slide-fire devices, and devices with certain similar characteristics—are "machineguns" as defined by the National Firearms Act of 1934 and the Gun Control Act of 1968 because such devices allow a shooter of a semiautomatic firearm to initiate a continuous firing cycle with a single pull of the trigger. Specifically, these devices convert an otherwise semiautomatic firearm into a machinegun by functioning as a self-acting or self-regulating mechanism that harnesses the recoil energy of the semiautomatic firearm in a manner that allows the trigger to reset and continue firing without additional physical manipulation of the trigger by the shooter. Hence, a semiautomatic firearm to which a bump-stock-type device is attached is able to produce automatic fire with a single pull of the trigger. (*Bump-Stock-Type Devices*, 2018, para.1)

With the passage of this law, bump stocks became illegal to manufacture, own, or possess. There was no grandfather provision allowed. Anyone who owned a bump stock after the new law went into effect was ordered to either destroy it or turn it in to the proper authorities. Possession of a bump stock may be punished the same as possession of a machine gun.

GHOST GUNS

There have always been individuals interested in making or building their own firearms. Traditionally, these people were highly skilled, forged their own components, and used extra parts to build and modify weapons. In recent years, however, this dynamic has changed. What started as a hobby among a small group of gun enthusiasts and builders has turned into a full-fledged market designed to allow individuals to buy and complete the assembly of weapons that will be "off the books" and lacking a serial number. These weapons are referred to as ghost guns.

Ghost guns are a category of firearms that are unserialized. The lack of a serial number means these guns are untraceable. When found at a crime scene, the history, ownership, and records of the weapon are impossible to determine (Owen, 2019). It is in fact a ghost. While the lack of a serial number also applies to 3-D printed guns and zip guns, ghost guns are generally far more reliable and efficient. They are not designed to be crude weapons. They are not single-use guns with a limited amount of firing ability and practicality. In fact, they are most often manufactured by leading gun companies. These ghost guns are often referred to as 80 percent guns because they are sold to the customer approximately 80 percent assembled. Sold as is, because they are inoperable, they require the user to complete the manufacturing process, which can include drilling a couple of holes or putting components together. This allows them to be sold without a serial number.

Ethical/Moral Issues

How difficult is it to complete a ghost gun? According to ATF Agent Carlos Canino, “If you can put Ikea furniture together, you can make one of these. They could make one thousand or ten thousand of these. Nobody would know” (Stephens, 2019, para. 7). The ability for a company to sell what will be a fully functional firearm with no serial number certainly presents ethical issues, as does the ability for a private citizen to buy, own, or sell a weapon with no serial number. In addition, it becomes difficult if not impossible to track or return lost or stolen weapons without a serial number.

Legal Issues

Like 3-D printed guns, there are no simple answers with 80 percent guns. In fact, even the term “80 percent” can be misleading. “80 percent receiver,” “80 percent finished,” “80 percent complete,” “unfinished receiver” are all terms referring to an item that some may believe has not yet reached a stage of manufacture that meets the definition of firearm frame or receiver found in the Gun Control Act of 1968 (Gun Control Act). Although the variations of the term 80 percent guns have developed a clear meaning to gun buyers, these are not statutory terms or terms the ATF employs or endorses.

The ATF has a statement on their website that indicates that while the terms and variations of “80 percent” may be commonly used, they are not terms acknowledged and recognized by the ATF (What Is an “80%” or “Unfinished” Receiver?, 2020). As a result, there is no unified common or legal definition. It is gun buyers and sellers who have created these terms. Lacking standardization, it may be impossible to apply the terms consistently industry wide.

Instead of terms like 80 percent finished or unfinished receiver, the ATF instead refers to “receiver blanks” (Are “80%” or “Unfinished” Receivers

Illegal?, 2020). "Receiver blanks that do not meet the definition of a 'firearm' are not subject to regulation under the GCA. The ATF has long held that items such as receiver blanks, 'castings,' or 'machined bodies' in which the fire-control cavity area is completely solid and un-machined have not reached the 'stage of manufacture' which would result in the classification of a firearm per the GCA."

The ATF is explaining what classifies as a firearm and what does not. The website contains additional explanations as well as photographs to help clarify the issues involved. While confusion certainly exists, as well as legal and ethical issues, for now unfinished receivers or 80 percent complete firearms are legal, widely advertised, and available for purchase. They have been used in mass shootings and are turning up at crime scenes across the country.

DERRINGERS AND MINIATURE BELT BUCKLE GUNS

The two most common types of handguns are revolvers and semiautomatic pistols. Selection of one over the other is often a highly personal decision and dependent on the needs and preferences of the owner. Derringers and miniature revolvers are different. The term derringer is generally used to refer to a small handgun that is neither a revolver nor a semiautomatic. What is it then? Typically, a derringer is a small weapon that usually fires one or two rounds, each from a separate barrel. The barrels may be side by side or one on top of the other. While antique variations with three and often several more barrels exist, they are rare and often lacking in practicality. A miniature revolver is just as it sounds. It is a fully functional firearm, only very small. How small? The barrel length can be as short as 1⅛ inches, and it can hide in plain sight.

DERRINGERS

As noted above, a derringer is simply a small handgun that is not a revolver or a semiautomatic. The weapon was created by Henry Deringer in 1825. A deringer was used to assassinate President Lincoln, and a misspelling of the name deringer by a reporter forever named these types of weapons as derringers (Encyclopedia Britannica, 2020). Derringers have a long and rich history and have been produced and come in a variety of calibers and barrel configurations. While there are a number of derringers on the market today, perhaps the most interesting are made by Bond Arms (Bond Arms, 2020).

Bond Arms produces derringers in a variety of calibers, and all feature two barrels, one on top of the other. The barrels fire one at a time, and the order depends upon the placement of the firing pin. What makes the Bond Arms derringer unique, however, is not the variety of calibers available in its barrels, but the ability to swap multiple barrels on the same platform. The barrels on a Bond Arms derringer flip up. Each weapon comes with an Allen wrench that can be used to remove the barrels from the frame of the weapon. New barrels can be added. A Bond Arms derringer that fires two rounds of nine millimeter ammo can be changed in mere seconds to a weapon that fires 357 or 38 rounds. Another quick barrel change and the weapon now fires 410 shotgun shells or 45 long colt.

The Bond Arms derringer is by no means the first or only weapon that makes barrel and caliber changes an option. Dan Wesson and others produced a much more practical version of a barrel-changing handgun that fired more than two shots in the 1960s (Fitzpatrick, 2018; Boddington, 2017). There are many other examples in history. Bond Arms stands out because of the modern production of their weapons, the quality and versatility they offer, and the popularity of their product.

Ethical Issues

Ethical issues for any weapon that easily changes calibers comes back to the identification of a particular weapon in a particular crime. While not impossible, it is certainly more difficult if the authorities are trying to match a 45 caliber round yet find a weapon with a nine millimeter barrel. This is simply another aspect that is often overlooked in the world of firearms and makes the Bond Arms derringer, and any weapon that can change barrels and calibers, unique.

Legal Issues

The only legal issues of note with the Bond Arms Derringer revolves around the ability of the weapon to fire 410 shotgun shells. A provision of California law makes it illegal to have a handgun that can chamber shotgun shells (State of California Department of Justice). The provision makes this particular version of the Bond Arms derringer illegal in California, as well as other popular revolvers that can fire shotgun shells. Bond Arms does produce derringers that comply with, and can be owned by, residents of California.

MINIATURE GUNS, BELT BUCKLE OPTIONAL!

If the idea of a miniature derringer designed to be worn as a belt buckle sounds familiar or sounds like a toy, there is good reason. Beginning in the 1950s, Mattel produced the Shooting Shell Buckle Gun. It was a child's toy and allowed the toy derringer to be worn in plain sight as a piece of jewelry. What began as a toy, however, would soon be turned into a real-life, fully operational handgun.

With production beginning in the late 1970s, Freedom Arms produced a five shot pistol with a 1½ inch barrel that could be slipped into a pocket or could fit into a belt buckle, allowing the owner to wear a fully loaded minirevolver capable of firing 22 long rifle rounds (Taffin, 2019). Additional variations were produced in 22 short and 22 WMR. Freedom Arms made these mini revolvers until around 1990, at which time the company sold the design to North American Arms (Eger, 2013). They produce these weapons to this day.

Ethical/Moral Issues

The ethical issues with the minirevolvers are different and center on the manufacture of a fully functional handgun that closely resembles a child's toy. Children and many adults not familiar with firearms simply would not think that the weapon is real. This leads to an increased opportunity for misuse and accidental firing. An additional concern centers on the fact that people are generally not looking for miniature firearms and not closely examining belt buckles, which makes it easier to bring this weapon into a restricted area. With a barrel length of 1⅛ inches and a total length of just 3.63 inches, this weapon is easy to conceal in any number of ways.

Legal Issues

The legal issues for this weapon center on open and concealed carry. A resident in an open-carry state could legally carry this weapon in a belt buckle. However, if their shirt or jacket were to cover the belt buckle, the weapon would now be concealed.

DOUBLE BARRELED, BUT NOT A DERRINGER

S333 Thunderstruck

The S333 Thunderstruck is a unique handgun chambered to fire 22 magnum rounds (Standard Mfg. Co. LLC. *S333 Thunderstruck*™). It is a double-barreled handgun with the two barrels side by side as opposed to barrels that are on top of one another or in an over-under design common with derringers. Unlike a derringer that fires first one barrel and then the other, the Thunderstruck fires from both barrels at the same time. The revolvers hold eight rounds and could be emptied very quickly through four squeezes of the double trigger. While not the first handgun to fire from more than one barrel at the same time, it is rare to see such a design in modern handguns.

Ethical/Moral Issues

Anytime a weapon goes against the norm or does not operate in a conventional manner, ethical issues are potentially raised. Eight rounds can be fired from this weapon very rapidly. The same holds true for semiautomatic pistols and rifles, however, which often fire a much more destructive round than the Thunderstruck. While this weapon does not raise any glaring ethical issues, its practicality has been questioned. Like the derringer, this weapon would be most effective for self-defense in situations in which the target was in very close range. Accuracy would decrease rapidly as the distance to the target increased.

Legal Issues

Because this weapon fires two rounds from two separate barrels, it is legal and is not considered a machine gun. Were the two rounds to come from the same barrel with a single trigger pull, the weapon would be illegal. While the gun is legal in California, the manufacturer conceded that it is illegal in Massachusetts and Maryland (Standard Mfg. Co. LLC. *S333 Thunderstruck*™).

CELL PHONE GUNS

One of the primary reasons people choose to carry a concealed weapon centers on the element of surprise. The individual wants to blend in and does not want to advertise that they are carrying a weapon. A firearm can be concealed in a number of ways including in one's pocket, in a purse, in a waistband holster, or simply covered up with a shirt or jacket. A weapon worn on the holster strapped to one's side or clipped to a belt makes the weapon visible to all and is a key element of open carry. Unless of course things are not what they appear to be. A relatively new firearm has completely flipped the concept of open and concealed carry.

Introduced in 2018, Ideal Conceal brought the double barreled .380 caliber "cell phone" pistol to the market (*Double Barreled .380 Caliber*. Ideal). This pistol operates just like the derringers that have been discussed, with one barrel over the other, firing one round at a time. It is designed to be clipped onto a belt and worn in plain sight. A simple release of the safety reveals the trigger and readies the weapon to fire. This weapon allows for an open carry option, while still keeping the true nature of the weapon concealed.

Ethical/Moral Issues

With this particular weapon, ethical and legal issues quickly become intertwined. In theory, there is nothing unethical or illegal about this weapon. It is simply a two-shot derringer marketed as a pistol. Many of the weapons discussed in this chapter are more powerful and cheaper. If an adult owns this weapon and follows all applicable laws, there are no concerns. As criminal justice professionals, however, we must ask additional questions, and imagine additional scenarios.

Similar to belt buckle guns, this weapon is designed to hide in plain sight. It is not difficult to imagine the cell phone gun being worn on a belt and easily being carried into a gun-free zone. Who is going to check a cell phone at a high school football game or in a church? What about a courthouse? A metal detector would find the gun though, right? Many times, people place their keys and cell phones into a dish that is specifically not put through a metal detector. How closely are the hundreds or thousands of cell phones that pass through these locations in a day examined? Without an X-ray machine on site or the close examination of all cell phones by a trained officer or employee, this weapon could easily slip past security.

This weapon only fires two rounds. Often times only one is needed. Of course, anyone can misuse a firearm and decide to violate a firearm law. A weapon that so easily blends in, however, raises special concerns not only for law enforcement, but also for any one in an official capacity who is tasked with keeping firearms from a designated location. It would be easy to imagine this weapon being worn on the belt of an individual and brought into a courtroom, police station, school, church, or any setting in which an individual can bring a cell phone. Flipping the question, in what locations are cell phones banned? Not simply required to be silenced, but specifically banned? When considered in those terms, it becomes easier to imagine all of the places that a handgun that passes as a cell phone could be transported and used.

FOLDING CARD GUN

Entering the market in 2017, the LifeCard 22 caliber single-shot folding handgun was released by Trailblazer Firearms (Trailblazer Firearms LLC). This weapon is unique even in a category of unique weapons. The handgun has an approximate height of 2.1 inches, a length of 3.4 inches, and a width of .5 inch. The total weight of the weapon is only seven ounces and is often compared in visual terms to a stack of a few credit cards. While a typical derringer is limited to two shots, the LifeCard is limited to one. Pressing a release allows the weapon to be unfolded. Once unfolded a handle grip and a trigger are revealed. The weapon can be carried with one round chambered, and a few additional rounds can be stored in the grip of the weapon. The weapon cannot be fired while folded. Once unfolded, the user can cock the firing pin and then fire the weapon. A pin is then released allowing the user to lift the barrel, remove the fired round, and load another round to fire.

The functionality of this weapon is extremely limited. To that point, it was never designed to be a practical weapon. It was designed to be a last-ditch emergency self-defense weapon and a fun weapon to fire. It is relatively inexpensive and not common style handgun.

Ethical/Legal Issues

The ethical and legal issues surrounding this weapon are nearly identical to those presented by the cell phone gun. The LifeCard is a deadly weapon that it specifically designed not to look like one. Placed on a table with everyday, ordinary objects, only an individual with specific knowledge of these specific weapons would have the ability to pick them out as firearms.

There is nothing inherently illegal about this weapon, though it could easily pass unnoticed into a gun-free zone. There is nothing inherently unethical about this weapon, though it could easily be used for unethical purposes. In the final analysis, both the cell phone gun and the LifeCard gun are products, and the ethics of owning them depends upon the motivations and ethics of their owners.

CONCLUSIONS AND RECOMMENDATIONS

This chapter introduced the concept of gadget guns and demonstrated that the materials involved, the design, the manufacturing process, or the appearance of the weapon were some of the criteria that can make a weapon a gadget gun. After establishing the ethics and legality of gun ownership in general, an examination of the legality and ethics of gadget guns was conducted. For the most part, the weapons explored in this chapter are all legal at this time. The major exception pertains to 3-D printed guns and bump stocks. Laws, of course, change. As was also noted, not all of the weapons discussed here are legal in all fifty states. Some require specific modifications to be legal in some states, and others, like the Thunderstruck, are illegal in select states.

Ethical issues are a separate, yet often intertwined concern. There is nothing inherently unethical about a weapon that looks different than other weapons. There is nothing inherently unethical about a weapon that functions differently from other weapons. As was established, the ethics of gun ownership can be connected to the ethics of the gun owner. Just as the vast majority of gun owners in this country are law-abiding citizens, the majority of those who own gadget guns have no unethical intentions. Nevertheless, several of the guns discussed in this chapter are designed to be made without a serial number. They are designed to blend in and avoid detection. The very elements that set these weapons apart make them ideal for use in criminal misconduct or for unethical purposes.

The Second Amendment clearly lays out the right to bear arms, and to date, the Supreme Court has protected that right. The amendment, however, lists the term "arms." The exact definition of arms has been left to the people, the legislators, and the courts to determine. The firearms market is enormous. Gadget guns make up an extremely small percentage of the 13 to 15 million firearms sold a year. Those yearly totals add to the approximately 270 million firearms Americans already own. Although the sales of gadget guns are small in numbers, the ethical and legal issues created by them are large. Those in the field need to take the time necessary to educate themselves about this unique category of weapons and the special problems they create.

BIBLIOGRAPHY

Are "80%" or "Unfinished" Receivers Illegal? Bureau of Alcohol, Tobacco, Firearms and Explosives. (2020). https://www.atf.gov/firearms/qa/are-%E2%80%9C80%E2%80%9D-or-%E2%80%9Cunfinished%E2%80%9D-receivers-illegal.

Baldwin, L. (2020, September 28). *Are Downloadable Plans for 3D Printed Guns Legal?* www.criminaldefenselawyer.com. https://www.criminaldefenselawyer.com/resources/are-downloadable-plans-for-3d-printed-guns-legal.html.

Boddington, C. (2017, November 16). *Thompson/Center Contender Just Turned 50 and Is Still Going Strong.* Guns and Ammo. https://www.gunsandammo.com/editorial/thompsoncenter-contender-just-turned-50-and-is-still-going-strong/248000.

Bond Arms. (2020). https://www.bondarms.com/.

Bump-Stock-Type Devices 83(246). (2018). https://www.federalregister.gov/documents/2018/12/26/2018-27763/bump-stock-type-devices.

District of Columbia v. Heller 554 U.S. 570 (2008).

Double Barreled .380 Caliber. Ideal Conceal. https://www.idealconceal.com/product/double-barreled-380-caliber/.

Eger, C. (2013, September 10). *NAA Mini Revolvers: Five Rounds of 'Get Off Me!' (VIDEO)*. Guns.com. https://www.guns.com/news/2013/09/10/naa-mini-revolvers-five-rounds-mousegun-fun-video.

Encyclopedia Britannica (Ed.). (2020, October 22). *Henry Deringer*. Encyclopedia Britannica. https://www.britannica.com/biography/Henry-Deringer.

Fitzpatrick, B. (2018, November 13). *Dan Wesson Brings Back Its Legendary Switch-Barrel Revolver*. Handguns. https://www.handgunsmag.com/editorial/dan-wesson-brings-back-its-legendary-switch-barrel-revolver/327992.

GovTrack.us. (2020). H.R. 4445 (100th Congress): Undetectable Firearms Act of 1988. Retrieved from https://www.govtrack.us/congress/bills/100/hr4445.

Gramlich, J., and Schaeffer, K. (2020, May 30). 7 Facts about Guns in the U.S. https://www.pewresearch.org/fact-tank/2019/10/22/facts-about-guns-in-united-states/.

Gun Control Act. Bureau of Alcohol, Tobacco, Firearms and Explosives. https://www.atf.gov/rules-and-regulations/gun-control-act.

Hoffman, T. (2020, July 1). *3D Printing: What You Need to Know*. PCMAG. https://www.pcmag.com/news/3d-printing-what-you-need-to-know.

Koffler, B. B. (1970). Zip Guns and Crude Conversions: Identifying Characteristics and Problems. *The Journal of Criminal Law, Criminology, and Police Science* 61(1), 115. https://doi.org/10.2307/1142105.

Owen, T. (2019, December). *Everytown Is Going After the ATF for Not Regulating Untraceable 'Ghost Guns'*. https://www.vice.com/en/article/m7qqpy/everytown-is-going-after-the-atf-for-not-regulating-untraceable-ghost-guns.

See, E. S., Bellas, C. M., and See, S. A. (2021). The Firearm Debate: The Legality, Morality, and Ethics of Ownership. In *Society, Ethics, and the Law: A Reader* (pp. 93–103). Article, Jones & Bartlett Learning.

Standard Mfg. Co. LLC. *S333 Thunderstruck™*. Standard Manufacturing. https://stdgun.com/s333-thunderstruck/.

State of California Department of Justice. Office of Attorney General. Title 11, Division 5, Chapter 7, Dangerous Weapons. https://oag.ca.gov/sites/all/files/pdfs/firearms/regs/chapter7.pdf.

Stephens, A. (2019, December 9). *Ghost Guns Are Everywhere in California*. The Trace. https://www.thetrace.org/2019/05/ghost-gun-california-crime/.

Taffin, J. (2019, September 11). *The Legacy of Wayne Baker Founder of Freedom Arms*. American Handgunner. https://americanhandgunner.com/our-experts/the-legacy-of-wayne-baker-founder-of-freedom-arms/.

Trailblazer Firearms LLC. (2020, August 25). Trailblazer Firearms LifeCard .22LR. https://www.trailblazerfirearms.com/products/.

What Is an "80%" or "Unfinished" Receiver? Bureau of Alcohol, Tobacco, Firearms and Explosives. (2020). https://www.atf.gov/firearms/qa/what-%E2%80%9C80%E2%80%9D-or-%E2%80%9Cunfinished-receiver.

2

Regulating the American Firearms Market

Understanding the Economics of Guns

Josiah R. Baker

BACKGROUND

In 2019, the U.S. Department of Justice estimated that American gun ownership varies from 31 to 49 percent of all households and that 21 to 38 percent of adults own guns. Moreover, in recent years, multiple surveys and sources show that these percentages have risen and seemingly are continuing to increase. The market demand for personal firearms in the United States is primarily driven by two factors: first, the universal human need for physical safety, and second, the recreational and practical needs for guns (usually in semi-rural and rural areas) mainly for hunting and target practice. There is also a sizable collectible market for guns, but most of it consists of antique weapons that are rarely used and, therefore, play an insignificant role within the sphere of the public debate involving gun ownership. Resting near the foundation of Abraham Maslow's hierarchy of needs, only immediate physiological needs (i.e., food, water, and shelter from the elements) supersedes safety (Maslow, 1943). For many Americans, gun ownership (and the access to personalized, self-defense weapons) fulfills that deep-seated human need to feel safe.

Although explicitly addressed and supported in the constitution, James Madison and other contributing authors did not create or inject the idea of gun ownership into what became a greater part of American culture and its public consciousness. Instead, owning firearms became enshrined in the fundamentals of American law because it already reflected the perspective, spirit, and challenging physical conditions that contributed to forming the new country (and a revolutionary form of governance). Early American leaders were risktakers who had successfully colonized Great Britain's claimed overseas territories and then boldly ridded themselves of imperial governance, primarily by using firearms. From a historical perspective, guns symbolize freedom from tyranny for traditionalist Americans. Thus, Madison and other federalists viewed guns not only as personal safety tools but also as the means to create a new, rebellious, cutting-edge state (Satia, 2019).

This circumstance of widespread colonial-era firearms ownership was not accidental nor due to a lack of oversight or negligence from London. Gun ownership, from a British perspective, furthered and enabled the expansion and survival of their colonial ambitions (Satia, 2019). Therefore, gun ownership encapsulates a conceptual and practical function in understanding traditional America. This chapter examines and reviews the overall economic-political landscape of the American firearms market. This analysis includes an emphasis of two conflicting factions: one supporting regulatory attempts to restrict the private gun market and the other resisting these initiatives because it represents the unique, yet indispensable role that gun ownership has within the hearts and minds of traditionalist Americans and their culture.

INELASTICITY AND GUN OWNERSHIP

Why do people own guns? In 2019, a Gallup Poll revealed the top three reasons cited by people who own guns: 63 percent cited protection against crime, 40 percent for hunting, and 15 percent for recreation or target shooting (Saad, 2019). Given these responses, most gun owners perceive their guns as necessities. In economics, elasticity is a way of measuring how consumers and producers respond to price fluctuations. For example, if products or services are perceived as luxuries or as nonnecessities, they are considered to be elastic, meaning that consumers can dramatically change their spending habits or producers may also greatly adjust their production plans in response to market price changes. Inelastic goods, however, represent goods that exhibit less change in consumption despite price hikes because they are perceived as necessities.

Over recent decades, an abundance of economic studies have repeatedly shown that whenever governments try restricting access to inelastic goods and services (those that are interpreted as necessities), people will inevitably seek and resort to participating in illegal transactions (Baker, 2004). In the case of the American firearms market, the perceived necessity of gun ownership also hinders regulatory efforts. The inelastic relationship of demand for weapons means that price hikes or lack of easy access may not hamper sales and that regulations designed to prevent ownership might simply drive participants and their transactions into a black market. For example, how many convicted felons are arrested for committing a crime using or possessing a gun? Also, consider how often people with restraining orders, designed to prevent them for having guns, still obtain and use weapons.

Controlling an inelastic good such as guns is a similar challenge to another decades-long governmental campaign, often showcased in the media as a "war" or a "battle." Since the early 1970s, the United States has struggled with its purported "war on drugs." Yet, after tens of millions of arrests, convictions, and hundreds of billions spent, the quantity for the market demand for illegal drugs in America has not changed (U.S. Department of Justice, Bureau of Alcohol, Tobacco, Firearms, and Explosives, 2019). In effect, the government has lost this "war" because regulatory efforts consistently pursued suppliers or drug dealers rather than strongly addressing the inherent problem of needing to curb the inelastic demand for consuming illicit drugs (Pew Center, 2016).

Guns and drugs market interactions, particularly because of their inelasticities (Baker, 2006), have a considerable overlap. For example, guns are frequently shipped along similar trade channels used by other contraband items such as rhino horn, fur, ivory, and drugs (Baker, 2008). Guns, a well-known common tool in the drug dealing and trafficking trades, serve a dual function as a pragmatic tool and as a tradable commodity. Federal law enforcement agents and their Department of Justice leaders have also recognized the practical and commercial linkages between illicit drugs and arms (Baker, 2004). Consequently these two goods are frequently shipped together, illustrating the exceptionally strong inelasticity of demand.

Flea markets and well-publicized gun shows (or gun exhibitions) sprinkled throughout the United States represent just two of many manifestations of the strong inelasticity demand for guns which fulfill a need for self-protection and may also overlap with specific needs in conducting legal or illegal businesses. In 2018, a Small Arms global survey indicated that the United States has the highest number of privately held firearms in the world with 120.5 guns per 100 people (Karp, 2018). This survey also cited an increasing demand for guns, showing an additional 122 million guns were officially purchased between 2006 and 2017. The Small Arms survey notes the difficulty of obtaining precise numbers. For example, illegally purchased guns which likely involve millions of additional sales each year (in the United States alone) are generally excluded.

Aside from safety, much of this inelasticity of demand, for some people, is a reflection of the belief that possessing firearms reinforces and enhances their perception of personal autonomy. Rather than remaining dependent upon or relying on government services, weapons enhance one's ability to exercise one's personal sense of responsibility and freedom. Women, for example, who carry guns do so as a means to feel more confident when traveling on highways or driving around town alone (U.S. Department of Justice, Bureau of Alcohol, Tobacco, Firearms, and Explosives, 2019). Beginning in the 1980s, increased female gun ownership (particularly in southern states as noted by the Pew Center) reflected a form of female empowerment that is often ignored in the mainstream media. This example, and others, demonstrate that the perceived safety from gun ownership validates some people's sense of individuality by helping them assert their will and self-confidence in their daily lives (Pew Center, 2016).

Since personal values and expectations of the government are not uniform throughout the vast expanses of the fifty United States and its territories, there is considerable variation in interpreting the importance of self-reliance in one's life. For example, people living in somewhat isolated areas possess different circumstances than those in closer proximity to government services. Also, people who perceive themselves as "fiercely independent" may have an elevated sense of self-reliance. Last, some gun owners might distrust the effectiveness of their local, state, and federal governments in offering protection, so they resort to protecting themselves with guns (Wintemute, 2002).

HISTORICAL MARKET REGULATORY EFFORTS

Today, the highly regulated, heavily taxed American firearms market is under considerable political pressure for further restrictions. Modern governmental efforts to restrict gun ownership began with President Franklin D. Roosevelt's "New Deal for Crime," which was in response to "public concern with crime and criminals . . . to the machine-gun-toting interstate gangster personified by John Dillinger" (Zimring, 1975, p. 137). During the Great Depression era (1929–1941), radio broadcasts (which peaked in popularity during this period; nearly every family in America would sit around a radio resting as a centerpiece in their living room—and attentively listen) and newspapers continually ran sensational stories about terrifying acts of crime often personified by sordid, scary stories of gangsters. By capitalizing on their audience's collective fears, media companies captured more attention which meant increases in copy sales (for newspapers and magazines) and advertisement revenue.

The media then, as now, greatly influenced and set an agenda for the public to demand a governmental response. Zimring (1975) notes that FDR, who previously advocated banning machine guns as governor of New York State, was more than willing to take the initiative (Zimring, 1975). First, there was the National Firearms Act of 1934, which levied a restrictive $200 tax on the manufacture or sale of machine guns and sawed-off shotguns. In addition, all sales were to be recorded in a national registry. Franklin Roosevelt's second effort was the National Firearms Act of 1938, which required licensing all interstate gun dealers, who also had to record their sales (Zimring, 1975). This law also prohibited selling to individuals under indictment or convicted of violent crimes.

However, most of the current federal regulations are directly traced to the Gun Control Act of 1968 and the Omnibus Crime Control and Safe Streets Act of 1968 signed by President Lyndon B. Johnson (*Washington Post*, 2012). Proponents for this legislation were responding to rapid increases in violent crime. For example, FBI statistics indicated that between 1962 and 1973 "gun killings increased from 2.5 per 100,000 to 6.2 per 100,000" (Pew Center, 2016). These laws prohibited all convicted felons, drug users, and the mentally ill from buying guns; raised the age to purchase handguns from a federally licensed dealer from generally eighteen to twenty-one; expanded the licensing requirements to include more gun dealers; and required more detailed record-keeping of transactions (Wintemute, 2002).

THOSE WHO SUPPORT FURTHER REGULATIONS OF THE PRIVATE GUNS MARKET

Opposition to personal gun ownership is rooted in a firm belief and trust in governmental protections primarily promoted by people who proclaim themselves, and are often identified by the mainstream media, as progressives. Since its formation mainly from Protestant Christian origins in the late nineteenth century (D'Antonio et al., 2013), the progressive movement seeks to support and nurture an ever-evolving governmental apparatus that will play a much greater role in everyday society than previously imagined to be possible. Hence, a more regulated, truncated domestic arms market is a consequential goal of moralistic governmental intentions. If successful, the gun industry would largely become incorporated into an expanded public sector much like the monopsony market of defense contractors. If curbing gun control efforts are unsuccessful, it will be largely due to the influential efforts of the National Rifle Association of America (NRA) and other lobbyist organizations who seek to expand or preserve individual access to the firearms market.

The struggle, or conflict, between individual rights and freedoms versus the influence and effects of an expansive government is not new. For example, in 1651, English political philosopher Thomas Hobbes (1588–1679) in his famous book, *Leviathan*, observed that without government people live in what he called "the state of nature," which would result in a "solitary, poor, nasty, brutish, and short" life. In other words, with unlimited freedoms due to an absence of government, Hobbes feared a "war of all against all" would ensue (Hobbes, 1651). Therefore, government protects people from themselves by offering a social mechanism that involves sacrificing natural freedoms in exchange for protection (mainly from other people). In effect, Hobbes proposed that an effective social contract persists between the individual and the state; although Jean-Jacques Rousseau (1712–1778) coined the concept of a "social contract" in his 1762 book "*Du contrat social; ou Principes du droit politique*" (Rousseau, 1762). This simplistic but compelling arrangement helps explains why some people believe in and completely accept and trust the government's authority in ensuring their personal safety and would perceive no need for privately owned handguns. American progressivism, with its moralistic, highly regulatory intentions, represents a continuation of the traditions of Hobbesian thinking.

Today, operating under the guise of "anti-violence," much support for the ongoing regulatory efforts to restrict gun ownership is reinforced by many educators, entertainers, pundits in the mainstream media, public health officials, and some medical professionals (Pew Center, 2016). Their collective rejection of private gun ownership reflects a denial, lack of appreciation, and in some cases an ignorance of history preventing them from acknowledging (or comprehending) America's traditional postcolonial cultural values. The purported progressive mind-set, a perspective that clutches onto a moralistic view of governance, arguably negates and dismisses much of the need for self-protection. This moralistic perspective views government as noble, competent, and efficient (Baker, 2008). Thus, the notion of needing an armed revolt seems absurd and antiquated because of embracing a bias that refuses to ever doubt the government's capability of effectively protecting its populace. This is reinforced by the assumption that well-funded moralistic governments will diligently apply their vast resources and expertise to effectively address whatever interior social ills and exterior threats that might generate a need for personal gun ownership (D'Antonio et al., 2013).

UNDERSTANDING DEMAND IN THE PERSONAL GUN MARKET: WHY BUY ONE?

In a safety-focused society where people often now customarily tell each other "stay safe" or "be safe," it should be unsurprising that many believe that guns not only symbolize but also provide an ultimate sense of safety. Beyond a lack of faith and disbelief in a moralistic government, there is an obvious consequential motivation involved in securing one's own safety as well as protecting their loved ones or property (Malcolm & Swearer, 2018). In localities with lengthy histories of inadequate or incompetent governmental services (usually large heavily urbanized areas governed by a political monopoly), it is likely quite difficult to convince legal (or illegal) gun owners that their weapons are unnecessary and represent a greater cost than a benefit (Williams, 2019). Autonomy and nurturing a desire for feeling safe generate a strong demand for obtaining guns by any means (Malcolm & Swearer, 2018). Thus, possessing firearms reinforces and enhances one's personal independence while also offering a feeling of freeing one from perpetual fears of vulnerability.

Within the American historical context, firearms represent self-sufficiency in that they helped people defend their homes from enemies and wild animals (Abramowitz & Saunders, 2008). Another factor that encourages widespread gun ownership is that most people can easily learn how to use and maintain them. As such, guns served as a primary tool for survival. Removing guns from the pre-revolutionary American colonists and during the eighteenth- and nineteenth-century pioneer period of the United States would have meant depriving them of a primary means for sustenance (Saad, 2019). Living in the isolated, far-flung frontier lands often meant surviving on limited or scarce resources and needing protection from other people and sometimes wildlife.

Early American life, particularly within those frontier lands of the Wild West, was disconnected from well-established society and only slowly became integrated with the modern industrialized world. Later, well into the twentieth century, hunting (and fishing) still represented a major source of sustenance for lower income rural people (Baker, 2017). Firearms helped bring home much needed protein, especially during tough times. In the twentieth century, during harsh economic times especially in the worst years of the Great Depression, many impoverished families in Appalachia and throughout other rural regions survived by using guns to hunt animals for food. Many American families, if they search their fairly recent history, will uncover these common stories. Although those days seemingly are gone, the memories of the usefulness of guns linger deep within the rural American psyche (Brady & Hahrie, 2006).

SUPPORTERS OF A PRIVATE GUNS MARKET

Pressures to defend and sustain a vibrant private gun market are backed by traditionalists of different sorts. In particular, pro-gun advocates tend to embrace customs, traditions, and an independent lifestyle (especially rural inhabitants) which continues to resonate with much of the general public. Intertwined with twenty-first-century capitalism and contemporary interpretations of individualism, guns rights proponents have emerged as a potent populist political force that transcends socioeconomic classes, resulting in a friction with the purported progressive faction (Baker, 1993). In 2016, Gallup polls showed the percentage of gun ownership for the following groups: male 43 percent, female 17 percent, white 35 percent, nonwhite 34 percent, Republican 45 percent, Independent 32 percent, and Democrat 16 percent (Pew Center, 2016).

ORIGINS OF THE ARGUMENT: A DIVIDED SOCIETY

Not until the late 1960s with the rapid expansion of the federal government's involvement in American life (particularly the Gun Control Act of 1968) did firearms become a highly debated, controversial public issue. During that tumultuous time, young adults (the Baby Boomer generation) ideologically split (Dionne, 2006) and began pushing the country toward greater political polarization (Satia, 2019). Protests that erupted into riots during the 1968 Democratic Convention in Chicago epitomized the growing division (Mann, 2006) between generations as well as ideas. Since that time, political moderates in Congress, particularly those members who self-identified as Mainline Protestants, diminished in numbers while more dogmatic leaders replaced them in both parties (Pew Center, 2016). For this study, Mainline Protestants were defined as self-identifying (according to the *Congressional Record*) as having a membership to a Protestant church established before 1800 (Pew Center, 2016). Political polarization as a dividing force behind congressional legislative and voting behavior will be addressed in more detail later in this chapter.

Well into the twenty-first century, the consequences of the Baby Boomers' ideological split continue influencing and affecting how the general public perceive gun ownership. For example, in August 2016, the Pew Center published a series of survey results indicating that opinions relating to gun control had never been so disparate between Republicans and Democrats (since 2000, when they began conducting those surveys). For example, in 2000 when asked if it was "more important to control gun ownership than to protect gun rights" a 20 percent gap separated supporters of the Democratic candidate Al Gore from those of the Republican candidate George W. Bush. In 2012, during the President Barack Obama's reelection campaign, the gap had increased to 41 percent. Returning to 2016, the Pew Center cited a 70 percent discrepancy between Clinton and Trump supporters. Since then, plenty of other evidence points to a continued increasing divide between the two parties regarding firearms ownership (Pew Center, 2016). Thus, these polling gaps illustrate a highly polarized political environment often dominated by high emotions, strong beliefs, and raw outrage from the dozens of well-publicized and intensely visual personal tragedies in recent decades.

With its agenda-setting powers, the mainstream media heavily influence the public dialogue (by largely dictating its content and the perspective of such content) pertaining to whether guns should be restricted or not. These dramas portrayed by the mainstream media mar pragmatic decision-making and escalate growing tensions between the pro-gun ownership faction and those who demand restricting or abolishing privately owned firearms.

Yet a disbelief, even a strong distrust in the government and the mainstream media persists. Tens of millions of Americans possess guns of many sorts for many reasons, but above all, for the sake of safety. Much of what some social scientists may call a "gun culture" is based on a society that, for a variety of reasons, has been less affected by the influence of progressive ideology and its perspective of a noble, moralistic government. Such a limited exposure to the doctrine of progressivism is evident in that three-quarters of Americans lack a college degree (Barone et al., vols. 1972, 1974, 1976, 1978, 1980, 1982, 1984, 1986, 1988, 2000, 2002, 2004, 2006, 2008, 2010, 2012, 2014). Reinforcing the durability of this non-college-educated population is the persistent fact that a mere 25 percent of newly created jobs in the American economy require a college degree. In 2016, the Pew Center's surveys noted that only "adults with postgraduate degrees" resulted in a majority (59 percent) that believed that "gun ownership does more to put people's safety at risk than to protect people from crime" (Pew Center, 2016, p. 1). Thus, the less educated the person, the more likely they will perceive a gun as a necessity that will protect them.

Aside from the lack of a postsecondary educational influence, the country's size and most notably its varying population density results in a variation of perceived personal safety needs and standards. When considering the inconsistent living conditions between urban and rural dwellers, gun owners frequently feel justified in seeking their own personal protection. Consider also that not all cities are perceived as safe and almost all urban areas have perceived unsafe or high-crime districts or areas. Regarding rural life, often government services (i.e., the police or emergency personnel) are located too far away from peoples' homes to reach them within a reasonable response time because of sheer distances in the countryside. If it takes twenty, thirty, forty, or more minutes for help to arrive, possessing a gun for personal protection makes more sense than if one lives in highly densely populated localities such as Washington, DC, or New York City, where in some areas police officers patrol nearly every corner. The geographic proximity of governmental services thus creates a variation of needs which can easily justify needing to provide for one's own personal protection.

DISTRUST IN GOVERNMENT SERVICES

Universal support of a moralistic, progressive gun control agenda is hindered by the much of the public because of their doubts in the ability of all local governments to consistently provide a sense of personal safety. Furthermore, as mentioned before, there is a persistent and distinct lack of faith, or a disbelief, in the variability of capacity and competency in local governments for protecting its citizens. For example, FBI crime statistics, U.S. census data, and economic information from the Bureau of Labor Statistics clearly show a wide spectrum of living conditions which infers that some cities simply offer better services than others. Although difficult to quantify, for most Americans it is evident enough that they will frequently relocate to better communities (if they have the means to move).

The lack of trust and reliance in government, regarding the protection of one's life and property, is thwarted by innumerable circumstances that make it impossible for regulators to predict and plan the needs of all people (Baker, 2006). Furthermore, people do not possess a uniform sense of dependency upon government services. Given such wide variations involving local law enforcement problems, it is hardly realistic to assume that consistent policing strategies can be applied throughout the country's more than 3,000 counties.

In essence, gun owners question or doubt the government's competency in protecting their lives, loved ones, and personal property. Lack of faith in government protection is reinforced by the varying quality of local services between different cities but also within the same municipality. Any casual observer in almost all of America's major cities can easily detect conspicuous differences between "*good*" and "*bad*" parts of town. Ironically, those who often champion gun regulations and restrictions rarely live within these conspicuously undesirable areas where violence is geographically concentrated. For example, according to the Crime Prevention Research Center (Lott, 2017), over 50 percent of all murders occur in only 2 percent of all counties. Glancing at the U.S. Census Bureau's zip code–based data shows that a supermajority of well-paid professionals, bureaucrats, educators, and influential members of the mainstream media dwell in low-crime, high-service areas of cities or within exceptionally peaceful affluent suburbs with highly responsive local governments. To better illustrate this disparity in the quality of American life, in 2014, 54 percent of America's 3,142 counties had *zero* murders (Pew Center, 2016).

RECENT MARKET REGULATORY EFFORTS

The anonymity of black and gray market transactions makes calculating a precise market involving the quantity of demand for guns impossible. Legislative efforts to restrict and control gun ownership are also hindered by the durability of these weapons (U.S. Department of Justice, Bureau of Alcohol, Tobacco, Firearms, and Explosives, 2019) (unlike perishable or somewhat potentially perishable contraband goods, guns do not decay or have expiration dates) and the interpersonal nature of guns transactions (e.g., friends frequently sell and trade guns with each other). Made mainly of metal, guns are far more durable than most other potential contraband such as narcotics. Weapons caches, hidden for legal or safety reasons, routinely fail to be disclosed. This durability enables guns to be hidden for lengthy periods of time and in many more places. People can secretly stash guns for many years, even decades (Baker, 2008).

Unregistered, or unaccounted for, weapons can remain hidden for later use as a trading or sales commodity. Since no one other than the owners knows the locations or existence of these hidden weapons, there is little reason to sacrifice a potentially profitable, quite useful resource (Baker, 2008). For example, when the Soviet Union collapsed in December 1991, guns that had been hidden since at least the Second World War (including some from before the October 1917 Bolshevik Revolution) began recirculating from private hands. Most of those older weapons were modernized or sold to private collectors. Aside from their use, like wine and coins, antique guns can be highly valued as a collectible commodity (Baker, 2008). Also, legally purchased and registered guns are frequently hidden (sometimes for safety purposes). Therefore, as many surveys and researchers acknowledge, difficulties arise in trying to compute or account for a quantity of demand or an exact quantity of guns in the American firearms market.

CONGRESSIONAL VOTES ON REGULATING THE GUNS MARKET

As mentioned earlier, in recent times, Democrats and Republicans have become increasingly divided over firearms issues. Political divisions (D'Antonio et al., 2013) involving regulating the guns markets are based on the vastly different cultural and political cleavages (Baker, 1993) stemming from often gerrymandered (Barone, et al., 2013) if not already politically skewed congressional districts where there is little incentive for cooperating or compromising with competing or other political interests (Baker, 2008). Since the United States holds no national elections or referendums, congressional representatives are winners of political contests fought at the state level (for the Senate) or are usually within relatively small, local, highly urbanized or suburbanized areas (for the House of Representatives) (Dionne, 2006). Please note that a geographical exception for House members exists among the least populated states, where one district is designated as "at-large" and does represent an entire state.

Given the limited geographic scope of most congressional House districts, most of them are socially and politically shaped by the practice of homophily (Americans often form communities around a single or related ethnicities such as "Chinatowns") or a self-selecting separation in the form of de facto segregation (Dionne, 2006). Regarding the House of Representatives with few exceptions, members are elected in specific geographically drawn districts which are usually manipulated to yield "safe" results (as mentioned in the previous paragraph, states with the lowest populations are constitutionally guaranteed a single "at-large" district). Gerrymandering, also mentioned earlier, is one of the most common manipulative methods of packing certain groups of people into specific districts, and is encouraged by both parties because it promotes stability and produces a pool of reliable representatives favored by party leaders (e.g., more Democrat blacks and socially conservative Republicans are elected) (Barone et al., vols. 1972, 1974, 1976, 1978, 1980, 1982, 1984, 1986, 1988, 2000, 2002, 2004, 2006, 2008, 2010. 2012, 2014).

Gerrymandering's electoral success record for increasing the reelection chances of incumbents is clearly evident. In recent decades, congressional election outcome data shows that House incumbents have over a 90 percent chance of being reelected (Baker, 2013). Although the dominant political party can, through the nomination process, push out an internally unpopular candidate, often elected House members will retain their seats for many election cycles with little or no serious opposition. Due to this lack of turnover, members of Congress are growing older and since the 1970s voting results are becoming more polarized (D'Antonio et al., 2013).

An occasional, but persistent exception to this trend of perpetual incumbents in recent decades is that increasing political polarization forces out moderates. For example, in the House, in 2018 Democratic Socialist candidate Alexandria Ocasio-Cortez defeated a more moderate Democrat, Rep. Joe Crowley, in the primary election and then easily won and later defended her seat in 2020 (*Congressional Record*, 2020). Also, in the Senate during the 2006 election Joe Lieberman (D-Connecticut), a politically moderate Democratic vice presidential candidate in 2000 had lost his party nomination and had to run as an Independent to retain his Senate seat (Layman et al., 2010).

Since President Lyndon B. Johnson's Gun Control Act of 1968, Congress has continually battled between either deregulating some of its provisions or expanding its original mandate. Note, congressional Republicans have never made a consolidated effort to completely repudiate the Gun Control Act of 1968 (Zimring, 1975). Meanwhile, at the state and local levels, restrictions for buying and selling guns also have become more divided. Some states have liberated their weapons markets through deregulatory efforts (e.g., Florida, North Carolina, and Texas) while others have tightened them with stricter regulations (e.g., New York, California, and Illinois). To better understand the key issues and problems addressed in these legislative conflicts, a list showing the general issues related to regulating the firearms markets is provided here:

General Issues Related to Regulating the Firearms Market (Zimring, 1975)

- *Controlling Demand (Access)*: age restrictions, mental competency rules, convicted felons, recipients of restraining orders, mandatory waiting periods.
- *Use of guns*: gun locks rules, storage requirements, portability (conceal and carry rules), general licensing requirements and fees.
- *Transaction*: background checks, gun show purchase rules, gun registration requirements, rules for recording sales.
- *Controlling Supply*: limiting ammunition purchases, legal liability for manufacturers, limiting types of guns (plastic guns, assault weapon bans, semi-automatic and automatic weapons bans), permits for manufacturing weapons, political and social media pressures on retailers or companies (i.e., Walmart) not to sell guns.

Although these regulatory efforts carry financial or economic repercussions (i.e., legal liability issues), gun control advocates have also applied considerable social and political pressure on retailers not to sell ammunition or guns. For example, in 2019, the largest retailer in the United States, Walmart, finally succumbed to many years of pressure and stopped selling guns and ammunition. Social media and the mainstream media by exercising their agenda-setting power (e.g., purposefully focusing on gun violence stories) have amplified their influential efforts of applying social pressure (awareness) to favor restricting gun sales and also to deter people from carrying guns (i.e., not allowing patrons into stores, restaurants, or shopping malls if they carry guns) (Zimring, 1975).

Throughout the country public schools, universities, and many government buildings also have either created anti-gun rules or posted signs and warnings on their websites and entrances reminding people not to bring guns onto the premises. When comparing enforcement tactics used against drugs, along with sharing a similar timeline (President Richard Nixon's "war on drugs" began in 1970 just two years after President Lyndon Johnson's Gun Control Act), an arguable "war" on guns exists (Zimring, 1975).

Next, is the methodological section which explains in further detail how gun-related votes in Congress, like the rest of the country, have become more polarized over time.

Methodology of Congressional Voting Data

In the book *Religion, Politics, and Polarization*, D'Antonio et al. (2013) explain that the origins of increasing voting polarization in Congress are rooted in the increased religious diversity of its members. Most notably, the decline of Mainline Protestants with an increase of Catholics, Jews, and Conservative Protestants contributed to less legislative cooperation and compromise. Jews and Catholics represented a strong leftward shift, while Conservative Protestants and Catholics reflected a solid rightward shift in the House and Senate (Baker, 2013). Regarding Catholics, although Democrat and Republican Catholics shared common values, they vastly differed over how to address political and social issues (Barone et al., vols. 1972, 1974, 1976, 1978, 1980, 1982, 1984, 1986, 1988, 2000, 2002, 2004, 2006, 2008, 2010, 2012, 2014). American Catholics, thus, were split (Rohter, 1991) between diverging left and right factions (Mann, 2006). This split continued through the 2020 election.

Measuring polarization began by determining which members belonged to a specific ideological group, their religious identity, and then by tracking changes in the religious affiliation of members of Congress from 1959 to 2013. The authors used several sources including the *Almanac of American Politics*, the *Congressional Quarterly*, individual websites, and newspaper and magazine articles to create a compilation of a dataset that included the name, political party, self-identified religious affiliation, and the district (and state) that they represented—for every member of Congress over this time period. The analysis selected key votes retrieved from dozens of editions of Michael Barone's *Almanac of American Politics* (Vol. 1972, 1974, 1976, 1978, 1980, 1982, 1984, 1986, 1988, 2000, 2002, 2004, 2006, 2008, 2010, 2012, 2014), which is widely considered by social scientists as a benchmark reference for U.S. legislative records. Most of the roll call votes were then processed as SPSS-data, which showed votes for each member of Congress beginning in 1969 and ending with the Health Care Bill of 2009–2010. Note,

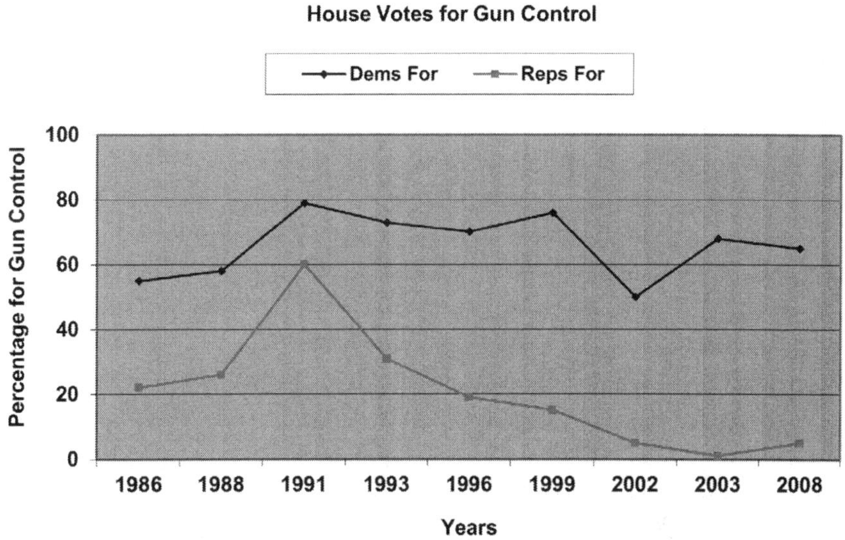

Figure 2.1. U.S. House of Representatives: Votes to Further Regulate the Firearms Market. ***Created by Josiah R. Baker, first published in*** **Religion, Politics, and Polarization: How Religiopolitical Conflict Is Changing Congress and American Democracy,** ***Rowman & Littlefield, 2013. Data from*** **The Almanac of American Politics,** ***1968–2010 editions.***

after 2010, a few votes were added to the tables. These were not from the SPSS database but were directly taken from Barone's *Almanac*.

Regarding the attempts to regulate the firearms market (or gun control) for the House of Representatives, the voting behavior of parties was less polarized in the 1970s than in the 1990s (D'Antonio et al., 2013). Polarization has continued (Mann, 2006) and arguably deepened into the twenty-first century. Overall, following the traditions of Presidents Franklin Roosevelt and Lyndon Johnson, House Democrats were always much more likely to support gun control-related bills than House Republicans. Figure 2.1 shows the House of Representatives' votes to further regulate the firearms market.

In the House of Representatives, as expected and explained earlier, Democrats always supported gun control bills more than Republicans. As mentioned earlier, the Democratic Party started the modern gun control movement. However, Republican support for gun control legislation temporarily increased in the late 1980s and early 1990s compared to earlier or later years due to widespread violence associated with illegal trade involving crack cocaine and other illicit drugs (Baker, 2013). Violent crime, as a proportion to the overall population, was much higher than in later years. Consequently, strong public pressure persisted to address the surging crime wave. By 1996,

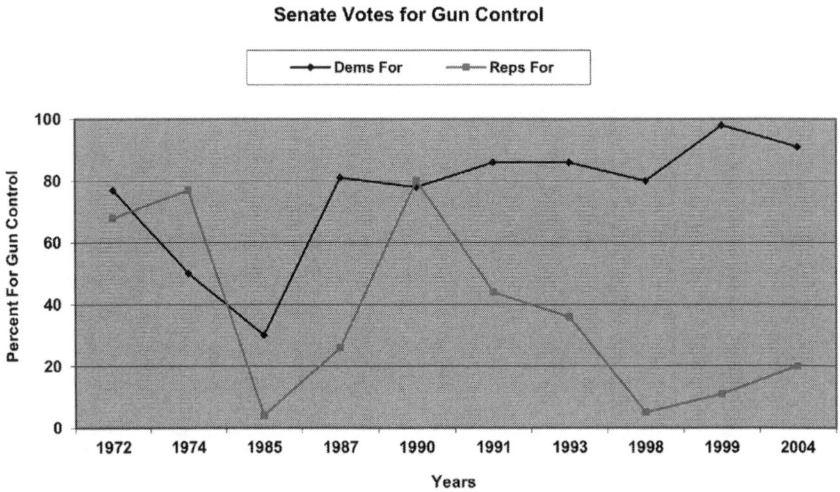

Figure 2.2. U.S. Senate: Votes to Further Regulate the Firearms Market. ***Created by Josiah R. Baker, first published in*** **Religion, Politics, and Polarization: How Religiopolitical Conflict Is Changing Congress and American Democracy*****, Rowman & Littlefield, 2013. Data from*** **The Almanac of American Politics*****, 1968–2010 editions.***

with crime rates plummeting, and after Representative Newt Gingrich's ascent to becoming the first Republican Speaker of the House in more than forty years, Republican support for gun control slipped below 20 percent (Rohter, 1991). While Republicans briefly increased their proportional support of gun control, Democrats also initially increased by 20 percent and then remained nearly consistent at that level of support for gun control legislation afterward. Consequently, after Speaker Gingrich, a broader divergence or polarization happened. Figure 2.2 illustrates the voting pattern in the U.S. Senate for regulating the firearms market.

Referring to figure 2.2, compared to their colleagues in the House of Representatives, Republican Senators were more proportionally supportive of gun control while Democratic Senators were less proportionally supportive of gun control until the early 1990s. For the Senate, the first substantial polarization occurred in 1985 with S.49 to ease gun control restrictions. The Senate voted 79 (Aye) to 15 (Nay) with 30 Democrats and 49 Republicans voting in favor and 13 Democrats and only 2 Republicans voting against (Baker, 2013). Also, Senate bill 49 (1985) intended to revise the Gun Control Act of 1968 by easing licensing requirements for gun collectors, removing the ban on interstate sales of guns, and ending inspections of gun dealers without prior notice. Afterward, support among Republican senators for gun control rapidly declined while Democrats increased their overall support resulting in a voting polarization pattern that was consistent and more similar to behavior of the House of Representatives.

D'Antonio et al. (2013) note that the initial reduced polarization was partially attributed to longer terms for Senators (six years instead of two) and their representing a different, broader constituency (entire states, which included rural areas instead of more urbanized districts). Their research noted that Mainline Protestant Senate Republicans voted more independently than other Senate Republicans during the earlier congressional sessions (91st to 104th). When the proportion of Mainline Protestant Republicans declined, the polarization and independent voting diminished. For example, in the 86th Congress (1959–1961), Mainline Protestant Republicans represented 28 of 35 total Republicans or 80 percent (Barone et al., Vol. 1972, 1974, 1976, 1978, 1980, 1982, 1984, 1986, 1988, 2000, 2002, 2004, 2006, 2008, 2010, 2012, 2014). By the 111th Congress (2009–2011), Mainline Protestant Republicans represented 17 of 41 total Republicans or about 40 percent (Baker, 2013). With a proportional decline of roughly 50 percent, the influence of Mainline Protestant moderation clearly declined.

For further details, see tables 2.1 and 2.2 which provide a list of key congressional gun control bills, including the votes from each party and the degree of polarization (*Congressional Record*, 2020).

CONCLUSION

In conclusion, although advocates for further regulating the firearms market are energized and regulatory attempts continue at the federal and state levels, these efforts are met with considerable resistance. The economics involving the inelasticity of demand for guns continues to stymie various legislative attempts to regulate the American firearms market. In addition, centuries of cultural and historical preexisting conditions for needing firearms were present when gun control legislation began in 1968 under President Lyndon Johnson, contributing to the formation of almost instant black markets.

The taste and desire for personal guns had long since become embedded into the American psyche. Thus, any regulatory effort was poised to cause an almost sudden creation of black and gray markets which carry negative effects and represent an externality, or an unintended consequence of policy-making (Baker, 2006). In 2020, at the time of this writing, gun control was an election issue this year and remains a highly polarizing issue in the public and within the United States Congress. Divisions between different values and lifestyles reinforce and perpetuate this unresolved conflict within modern America's consciousness (Baker, 2013). Thus, firearms, especially the

Table 2.1. Examples of Specific Gun Control Votes in the U.S. House of Representatives

Year	*Bill*	*Polarity*	*YEA*	*NAY*	*total*	*% for*	*% against*	*House Democrats FOR*	*House Democrats AGAINST*	*total*	*% for*	*% against*	*House Republicans FOR*	*House Republicans AGAINST*	*Notes*
1986	HR 4332	41.9	176	248	246	55.00	45	136	110	178	22	78	40	138	Retain Gun Control
1988	HR 5210	50.9	228	182	238	42.00	58	101	137	172	74	26	127	45	Handgun Sales
1991	HR 7	35.4	239	185	262	68.00	32	179	83	162	37	63	60	102	Handgun Wait
1993	HR 1025	X	238	188	253	73.00	27	184	69	173	31	69	54	119	Brady Handgun Purchase
1996	HR 125	73.1	219	172	186	30.00	70	56	130	225	81	19	183	42	Repeal Assault Weapons Ban
1999	HR 2122	64.4	192	235	208	76.00	24	159	49	219	15	85	33	186	Gun Show Background Checks
2002	HR 4635	60.7	308	113	204	50.00	50	102	102	217	95	5	206	11	Arm Commercial Pilots
2003	HR 1036	70.7	284	140	200	32.00	68	63	137	224	99	1	221	3	Restrict Gun Liability
2008	HR 6842	62.1	260	160	233	35.00	65	82	151	187	95	5	178	9	Repeal DC Gun Law

Source: Created by Josiah R. Baker, first published in *Religion, Politics, and Polarization: How Religiopolitical Conflict Is Changing Congress and American Democracy*, Rowman & Littlefield, 2013. Data from *The Almanac of American Politics*, 1968–2010 editions.

Table 2.2. Examples of Specific Gun Control Votes in the U.S. Senate

YEAR	*BILL*	*Polarity*	*YEA*	*NAY*	*total*	*% for*	*% against*	*Senate Democrats FOR*	*Senate Democrats AGAINST*	*Abstain*	*total*	*% for*	*% against*	*Senate Republicans FOR*	*Abstain*	*Senate Republicans AGAINST*	*Notes*
1972	S 2507	0.7	67	25	48	77	23	37	11		43	68	32	29		14	Gun Control
1974	S 1401	18.8	54	33	50	50	50	25	25		35	77	23	27		8	Handgun Licenses
1985	S 49	84.5	79	15	43	70	30	30	13		51	96	4	49		2	Ease Gun Control
1987	S 9	33.0	47	42	46	26	74	12	34		43	81	19	35		8	Ban Plastic Guns
1990	S 1970	82.3	48	51	55	22	78	12	43		45	80	20	36		9	Strike Firearms Ban
1991	S 1241	44.4	71	26	57	79	18	45	10	2	43	60	37	26	1	16	Handgun Wait
1993	HR 1025	X	63	36	55	86	14	47	8		44	36	64	16		28	Brady Handgun Purchase
1998	S 2260	68.6	61	39	45	20	80	9	36		55	95	5	52		3	Table Child Gun Locks
1999	S 254	81.4	50	50	45	98	2	44	1		55	11	89	6		49	Gun Show Background Checks
2004	S 1805	69.1	51	47	47	91	9	41	6		51	20	80	10		41	Assault Weapons Ban

Source: Created by Josiah R. Baker, first published in *Religion, Politics, and Polarization: How Religiopolitical Conflict Is Changing Congress and American Democracy*, Rowman & Littlefield, 2013. Data from *The Almanac of American Politics*, 1968–2010 editions.

private ownership of guns, symbolically and literally represent a widening chasm between two conflicting ideological factions who are competing to define the relationship between the individual and government in twenty-first-century America.

REFERENCES

Abramowitz, Alan I., and Kyle L. Saunders. 2008. "Is Polarization a Myth?" *The Journal of Politics* 70(2): 542–55.

Baker, Josiah R. 1993. An Analysis of Economic and Political Reform in Command Economies: The Polish Case. University of Central Florida, Orlando, Florida: Undergraduate Honors Thesis. Dec. 1. http://stars.library.ucf.edu/honors theses1990-2015/30/.

Baker, Josiah R. 2004, November 28. "Coca Leaf Crop Transforms Destitute Nation." *Orlando Sentinel*. http://articles.orlandosentinel.com/2004-11-28/news/0411270106_1_coca-bolivia-growing.

Baker, Josiah R. 2006. *Macroeconomics: Theories, Principles, and Issues: Basic Text for Macroeconomic Related Courses.* London: Pearson Publishing.

Baker, Josiah R. 2008. "Arms Trafficking." In the *Encyclopedia of Africa and the Americas*, 124–25. Santa Barbara, CA: ABC-CLIO, Inc. Publications.

Baker, Josiah R. 2013a. *The Influence of Religious Affiliation on Welfare Spending in the American House of Representatives.* Presented paper. Sweden's Network for Welfare Policy Annual Conference, Sigtuna, Sweden. November.

Baker, Josiah R. 2013b. *Religion, Politics, and Polarization: How Religiopolitical Conflict is Changing Congress and American Democracy.* Appendix A. Online publication for Rowman and Littlefield Publications. June.

Baker, Josiah R. 2017. *Religion: Past, Present, and Future Perspectives.* Chapter 3, "Evangelical Christianity as a Populist Political Force: The Case of Donald Trump's Unlikely Victory," edited by Stephen D. Mills, 67–100. New York: Nova Science Publishers. May.

Barone, Michael, and Grant Ujifusa et al. *Almanac of American Politics.* Volumes 1972, 1974, 1976, 1978, 1980, 1982, 1984, 1986, 1988, 2000, 2002, 2004, 2006, 2008, 2010, 2012, 2014. Washington, DC: National Journal Group.

Brady, David W., and C. Han Hahrie. 2006. "Polarization Then and Now: A Historical Perspective." In *Red and Blue Nation? Characteristics and Causes of America's Polarized Politics*, edited by Pietro S. Nivola and David W. Brady, vol. 1, 119–151. Washington, DC: The Brookings Institution.

Congressional Record, 2020.

D'Antonio, W., S. Tuch, and J. Baker. 2013. *Religion, Politics, and Polarization: How Religiopolitical Conflict Is Changing Congress and American Democracy.* Lanham, MD: Rowman and Littlefield Publications.

Dionne, E. J., Jr. 2006. "Polarized by God? American Politics and the Religious Divide." *Red and Blue Nation: Characteristics and Causes of America's Polarized*

Politics, edited by Pietro S. Nivola and David W. Brady. Washington, DC: The Brookings Institution.

Hobbes, T. 1651. *Leviathan*.

Karp, A. 2018. Estimating Global Civilian-Held Firearms Numbers. Briefing Paper. *Small Arms Survey*. http://www.smallarmssurvey.org/fileadmin/docs/T-Briefing-Papers/SAS-BP-Civilian-Firearms-Numbers.pdf. June.

Layman, G. C., T. M. Carsey, J. C. Green, R. Herrera, and R. Cooperman. 2010. "Activists and Conflict Extension in American Party Politics." *American Political Science Review* 104, no. 2: 324–46. http://journals.cambridge.org/action/displayAbstract?fromPage=online&aid=7793127.

Lott, John R. 2017, April 25. "Murders in US Very Concentrated: 54% of US Counties in 2014 Had Zero Murders, 2% of Counties Have 51% of the Murders." Crime Prevention Research Center. https://crimeresearch.org/2017/04/number-murders-county-54-us-counties-2014-zero-murders-69-1-murder/.

Malcolm, John, and Amy Swearer. 2018, March 14. "Here Are 8 Stubborn Facts on Gun Violence in America." The Heritage Foundation.

Mann, Thomas E. 2006. "Polarizing the House of Representatives: How Much Does Gerrymandering Matter?" In *Red and Blue Nation: Characteristics and Causes of America's Polarized Politics*, edited by Pietro S. Nivola and David W. Brady. Washington, DC: The Brookings Institution.

Maslow, A. H. 1943. "A Theory of Human Motivation." *Psychological Review* 50 (4): 370–96.

Pew Center. 2016, August 26. Gun Policy and the 2016 Campaign. https://www.pewresearch.org/politics/2016/08/26/opinions-on-gun-policy-and-the-2016-campaign/.

Rohter, L. 1991, August 12. "In the Shady World of Illegal Arms, Miami Is Hot." *International Herald Tribune*.

Rousseau, J. 1762. "*Du contrat social; ou Principes du droit politique*."

Saad, Lydia. 2019, August 14. "What Percentage of Americans Own Guns?" Gallup.

Satia, P. 2019. "What Guns Meant in Eighteenth Century Britain." *Palgrave Communications* 5, 104.

U.S. Department of Justice, Bureau of Alcohol, Tobacco, Firearms, and Explosives. 2019. *Report*: "Firearms Commerce in the United States Annual Statistical Update 2019." www.atf.gov. August 8.

Washington Post. 2012, December 22. "National: History of Gun Control Legislation." https://www.washingtonpost.com/national/history-of-gun-control-legislation/2012/12/22/80c8d624-4ad3-11e2-9a42-d1ce6d0ed278_story.html.

Williams, W. 2019. Gun Grabbers Misleading Us. *Creators*. https://www.creators.com/read/walter-williams/10/19/gun-grabbers-misleading-us.

Wintemute, G. 2002. "Where the Guns Come From: The Gun Industry and Gun Commerce." *The Future of Children*. 12 (2) 55–71. doi:10.2307/1602738.

Zimring, F. 1975. Firearms and Federal Law: The Gun Control Act of 1968. *The Journal of Legal Studies* 4 (1), 133–98.

3

The International Guns Market

Josiah R. Baker[1]

INTRODUCTION

Despite the American media's overwhelming focus on domestic gun issues, there persists a flourishing international firearms market. An expanding global market driven by technological innovations in communications and transportation has resulted in increases of commercial interconnectivity that feeds an ever-growing appetite for weapons, particularly within developing countries (Schroeder, 2016). For example, firearms are commonly traded in tandem with illicit narcotics or other contraband and are frequently imported into a designated country in similarly not so transparent manners. In this regard, Schroeder (2016) observed that traffickers use a "wide array of additional smuggling tactics and techniques" (p. 11), which included providing false or misleading information on shipping documents such as: "calling weapons 'metal hunting tools,' 'steel blocks,' and 'toy parts;' using aliases and false shipping addresses; and purposely undervaluing the contents of shipments" (Schroeder, 2016, p. 11).

The Smalls Arms Survey also reports that other evasive tactics used by traffickers involved "mailing shipments under false names, writing false descriptions of firearms parts on customs forms, generating invoices with false descriptions of shipped items, packing items to avoid detection by X-ray machines or other screening devices; shipping manuals and weapons separately, minimizing personal interactions with the staff of shipping services, and shipping items from several different locations" (Schroeder, 2016, p. 12). Last, traffickers may also resort to "recruiting intermediaries who then can receive partial shipments, repack their contents, and then illicitly reship weapons to a third location as a means of circumventing detection from customs." In doing so, some traffickers can "better shield their identity" while also "enabling their ability to acquire controlled items from law abiding retailers" (Schroeder, 2016, p. 11).

Furthermore, legal U.S. firearms manufacturers actively and quite visibly participate in these flourishing markets by exporting their products to embattled places throughout the world, particularly in Latin America, the Middle East, and Africa. Media coverage typically focuses on official government-to-government agreements and transactions often due to politicians seeking or promoting certain foreign policies and/or international relations (Van Kesteren, 2014). Such stories are also usually less controversial, easy to report, and carry almost no investigative costs.

The portion of the market constituting private firearms sales is generally neglected, underrated, or underestimated by many scholars (Schroeder, 2016). For several reasons, research on this relationship is methodologically difficult. First, a dearth of reliable data exists for both gun ownership and violent incidents between civilians (Schroeder, 2016). Especially in countries where gun ownership is highly restricted (e.g., most countries in Europe and some in East Asia), official ownership statistics inevitably include estimates of "ample dark numbers" (Schroeder, 2016). Complications involving the inclusion of illegal firearms also negatively affects the reliability of recording the numbers of committed violent crimes (Schroeder, 2016). Furthermore, these numbers recorded by the police are frequently heavily influenced by unreliable, if not inconsistent reporting methods. Regarding empirical analysis, unreliable analyses are commonplace because often data is obtained from small, underrepresented parts of a country's population (Schroeder, 2016). Underreporting is effectively encouraged due to the internal political relationships between central governments and their ever-dependent local leaders who strive to portray their localities under the brightest, most optimistic lights (Schroeder, 2016). Therefore, many official nationwide statistics for gun ownership and violent crime are invariably distorted, even outright unreliable at the aggregate level (Schroeder, 2016).

The resulting inaccurate figures deflate the harsh conditions at the local level. Microlevel studies (e.g., specific cities, especially if not among the largest urban areas in a country) become impossible to accurately measure or to make comparative analyses (Schroeder, 2016). For example, Van Kesteren (2014) concluded that international evidence on the link between firearms ownership and total homicide is less conclusive. Critics against gun ownership argue that it becomes a vicious circle of violence because citizens seek guns to protect themselves from the existing gun violence and as a result ordinary citizens become involuntarily drawn into the very culture of violence they wish to defend themselves against by owning guns (Masanzu, 2006).

Although other countries (e.g., the United States, Canada, the United Kingdom, Peru, and Indonesia) are mentioned, this chapter primarily aims to present and examine the general market conditions found in three regions of the world: Latin America, Africa, and East Asia. A wide spectrum of regulations, varying degrees of enforcement, distinct geographically specific demands for weapons, and other key influential factors will be addressed in this analysis with the goal of demonstrating the magnitude and complexities of these underreported yet widespread private firearms markets. In brief, are restrictions effective in achieving their purported goals of harnessing the demand for privately owned firearms?

INTERPRETING THE SCOPE AND SCALE OF THE INTERNATIONAL FIREARMS MARKET

> *"There are over 550 million firearms in worldwide circulation. That's one firearm for every 12 people on the planet. The only question is: How do we arm the other 11?"*
>
> (Niccol, *Lord of War*, 2005)

Country-specific factors of demand complicate and add to the complexities involving accurate assessments in analyzing how the international firearms market operates, especially in matters of measuring and assessing its overall size and its buyer and seller-based dynamics, all of which demand adopting a multifaceted approach. First, the global market for firearms can be examined by dividing its activities within two sectors: (1) government-based or -related transactions, and (2) nongovernmental or private market sales. Second, a further distinction of a market's scope is important: (A) imported firearms, and (B) domestically manufactured firearms. Last, within the domestic sector related to weapons, manufacturing can be subdivided into either large-scale commercial operations (i.e., factories), which are usually easily identifiable, or handcrafted work sites or cottage industries typically manned by small groups of workers or individuals, which are often quite difficult if not impossible to detect much less fully assess. The perceived, yet persistent and compelling demand for weapons around the world contribute to these varying manners by which people, often desperate, impoverished, and facing stunningly scarce resources, resort to sometimes extreme efforts to obtain much-needed firearms.

For the purpose of this chapter, the term "small arms" adheres to a broader definition offered by Schroeder in that they refer to the following items: revolvers and self-loading pistols; rifles and carbines; shotguns; sub-machine guns; and light machine guns (Schroeder, 2016). In most cases, this chapter will distinguish between long guns (i.e., rifles, other guns with long barrels) and handguns (Van Kesteren, 2014). Van Kesteren (2014) notes that hunting is the most commonly cited reason for owning any firearm in all surveyed countries. Most hunting firearms are typically long guns (referring to the length of their barrels). However, hunting is usually the second-most common reason for owning handguns (after personal defense). The popularity of target shooting as a sport also contributes to more handgun and long gun ownership. A fourth cited reason for owning a gun is that it belongs to a collection (or has always been in the family). Last, Van Kesteren (2014) cites a fifth common reason for gun ownership is because of occupational obligations (i.e., a household member works for the police, as an armed security guard, or in the armed forces). Regarding job-related purposes, some scholars argue that gun ownership might also be a proxy for a high-risk lifestyle (Small Arms Survey, 2018).

As mentioned earlier, most academic research relies upon easily observed, and commonly perceived as more reliable, official governmental arms deals involving government-to-government transactions (Small Arms Survey, 2018); although, there is also a secondary concentration on government-to-nongovernmental organizational sales (which may include paramilitary groups or revolutionaries directly or indirectly aiding the cause of those who arm them). The popularity of these official firearms deals studies is largely a consequence attributed to the difficulty of determining, often even estimating, the volume of private market sales due to secrecy, legal culpability, or the hidden nature of person-to-person sales (Baker, 2008). In lesser developed economies, for example, barter transactions thrive due to a lack of access to hard currencies (often caused by low income and the prevalence of informal market operations and conditions) (Baker, 2008). At the street level, private firearms transactions may or may not be easily observable or commonplace, but often even those that can be detected are still not officially tracked by the respective national governments or nongovernmental organizations. Also, successful uses of guns (i.e., warding off potential or real violence) by the threat of using a gun are underreported (Schroeder, 2016).

Indeed, analysts originating from developed, higher-income economies with the support from well-organized and -funded governmental agencies may falsely assume or accept that written laws are acknowledged, observed, and effectively enforced (Masanzu, 2006). Often, outsiders interacting within these foreign settings are embedded with considerably different factors and features that render a firearms market environment that counters most, if not nearly all, of these preconceived assumptions (Masanzu, 2006). In other words, officially strict handgun laws may become meaningless if they are rarely enforced and flagrantly violated throughout most of the country. At times, reliable enforcement of law may be consistent within small geographic areas or pockets of control (i.e., within the capital city or select inner-city areas of larger cities) but then quickly dissipates and even vanishes in lesser populated, remote, or rural areas (Masanzu, 2006). Last, in some cases, the most-restrictive countries cause people to resort to making their own weapons. For example, in the U.K., which is among the most restrictive in the world, about 80 percent of all guns used in crimes in 2011 and 2012 were improvised, craft-produced, or converted (Small Arms Survey, 2018).

A further disconnect between "what is" and "what should be" profoundly persists within countries challenged by geopolitical fractures or civil uprisings. Aside from existential threats, the failures of local governments to protect their citizens frequently prompts many households, particularly men, to actively acquire and maintain their own form of protection for themselves and their loved ones (National Public Radio, June 28, 2019). Crime statistics in such arduous conditions can become irrelevant or nearly impossible to accurately gauge or interpret, which also underscores the disparity between what a functionally compromised government may report to international authorities versus what is actually occurring (Mills, 1993). If in doubt, such semi-competent or incompetent regimes will seek to cultivate a more favorable, positive public image, that also contributes to a resulting underestimation of the volume and widespread distribution of legally or illegally purchased weapons (Mills, 1993). These kinds of behavior are pervasively evident in countries with established, good reputations (and intentions to keep it) such as Japan and for places that may not want to soften or reduce the negative consequences of breaking the law when they already are widely known for conveying an incomplete picture of their less than stellar law enforcement practices (e.g., Mexico, Brazil, Nigeria, South Africa, and the Philippines) (Mills, 1993).

Capability or capacity of these more dysfunctional, operationally challenged governments to register, collect, and enforce taxes from private sales also contributes to knowledge deficits (Small Arms Survey, 2018). Another predominant feature in the guns market that inhibits collecting reliable data is the manner in which many sales are conducted. Sometimes there are swaps, or barters, executed either among distributors or for sales to individuals, or as transactions strictly between discrete individuals who are often friends or relatives (Small Arms Survey, 2018). This chapter attempts to describe these underlying market conditions, with a particular focus on existing regulations and restrictions for private firearms ownership while also presenting evidence that indicates their effectiveness toward curbing the demand for privately owned guns. Given the highly regulated nature of firearms, an abundance of black and gray market arrangements populate this spectrum of the market, making exact estimates or figures impossible (Baker, 2006). Since empirical evidence is obviously incomplete, or less than sufficiently reliable, this chapter focuses on describing, explaining, and to some extent comparing the market and law enforcement dynamics between the purported restrictions and regulations with the circumstances and motivations for those who participate in the private market of these selected countries within three global regions: Mexico and Brazil (Latin America), Nigeria and South Africa (Africa), and Japan and the Philippines (Asia).

THE OFFICIAL GOVERNMENTAL ROLE IN INTERNATIONAL FIREARMS SALES

From an American perspective, often it is difficult to imagine the many differences in how firearms markets operate within lesser developed, law enforcement–challenged economies. Aside from obvious social structural, financial, and institutional distinctions, varying unique elements—including the breadth or scope of firearms sales within isolated, more traditionalist communities especially inside impoverished countries—challenge many outside presumptions. Yet, for many firearms manufacturers, transactions within these underdeveloped states may constitute a significant revenue source (Schroeder, 2016). For example, from 2002 through 2018 the United States sold over $200 billion in major conventional weapons to 169 countries (Schroeder, 2016). Of those countries, 31 of them officially purchased at least $1 billion in firearms (Schroeder, 2016). By 2018, the United States extended its dominance as the leading exporter of weapons with a 36 percent share of the global market (compared to Russia with 21 percent and 6.8 percent for France, the second- and third-ranked exporters) (Schroeder, 2016). These sums reflect mere estimates largely involving direct, official, and primary market sales. An overall more accurate estimation of the financial impact stemming from American weapons makers would need to include secondary, indirect, and black-market sales (Brayton, 1983). Such sums of money and potential political implications of U.S. involvement with the global firearms export market has attracted the attention of American lawmakers, the entertainment industry, and the mainstream media.

BACKGROUND OF U.S. GOVERNMENTAL INVOLVEMENT

To some degree, the United States like most other countries has engaged in sanctioned or official arms dealing throughout almost all of its history (Baker, 2008). However, the scale and scope of such deals, along with widespread publicity, did not emerge as a consistently dominant world-market participant until after winning the Second World War. Afterward, although the struggle with Japanese imperialism and German fascism had succeeded, the remaining and lingering threat of Soviet-style communism stemming from the globalist ambitions of Josef Stalin and his KGB international network resumed its campaign for world dominance which ignited and sustained the long-term American foreign policy of containment against Soviet aggression (Baker, 2008). The following decades yielded a Cold War (1945–1991) which eventually engulfed the vast majority of Latin American, African, and Asian countries. Civil uprisings, military coups, and armed incursions from communist-influenced neighbors and trained revolutionaries fueled ongoing efforts to officially sell arms or to traffic them as a means to service what were perceived as American causes while these Soviet proxy conflicts continued (Baker, 2008).

Starting in the 1980s, but especially after the Soviet Union's collapse in 1991, economic developmental successes in some Asian countries tempered and harnessed arms dealing in that part of the world (Shaw & Gastrow, 2001). However, many African and Latin American countries did not experience marked declines in the demand for firearms (Shaw & Gastrow, 2001). Even after the demise of the Soviet Union, African and Latin American arms trafficking involved supplying ongoing conflicts that struggled to overturn or enforce disputed governing bodies (e.g., Liberia, Sierra Leone, South Sudan, Colombia, and Venezuela) and also in the pursuit of sectarian and tribal animosities (Baker, 2008). For the purpose of this study, the term "trafficking" is synonymous for "smuggling" and refers to the transfer of illicit weapons across international boundaries.

During the 2000s, many Hollywood-produced popular films (e.g., *Traffic*, *Blood Diamond*, and *Lord of War*) depicted well-known circumstances that involved different facets of the international firearms market, while also demonstrating clear commercial linkages to First World economies. These notorious exogenous import-export activities typically served two distinct forms of conflict: (1) internal, with regional fighting specific to a single territory or state; or (2) external powers acting out proxy warfare. In many cases, due to civil wars, expedited changes in government, and civil and military uprisings, the difference between governmental and private arms transactions became blurred and nearly impossible to clearly distinguish (Shaw &

Gastrow, 2001). As such, some of the arguments and observations in this chapter overlap and apply to both the governmental and private sector as they relate to transactions, market conditions, and general business practices in the trading of firearms.

U.S. LEGISLATIVE EFFORTS

Stemming from the surging unpopularity of the latter years of the Vietnam War (1945–1975) and nearby conflicts in other Southeastern Asian countries (e.g., Laos, Cambodia, and Burma), consistent, highly vocal critics and opponents of America's flourishing firearms export market have continually pressed for greater oversight and accountability. Regarding international arms dealings, most American legislative efforts have focused on official governmental weapons trades (Thrall et al., 2020). For example, in 1976 Congress passed the Arms Export Control Act, (Baker, 2013) which required the executive branch to conduct a risk assessment *before* approving any major arms sales to ensure that it "would not contribute to an arms race, aid in the development of weapons of mass destruction, support international terrorism, increase the possibility of outbreak or escalation of conflict, or prejudice the development of bilateral or multilateral arms control or nonproliferation agreements or other arrangements" (Thrall et al., 2020, p. 101). Much later, in 1997, Congress passed the first version of the Leahy Law, designed to prohibit security assistance—including arms transfers—to military units for which there was credible information implicating them in committing gross violations of human rights (Thrall et al., 2020). The Leahy Law has since been expanded, becoming a permanent part of the Foreign Assistance Act in 2008 (Thrall et al., 2020).

Yet political support persists for exporting weapons especially in support of certain countries (especially in the Middle East) partly because it coincides with foreign policy prerogatives (Thrall et al., 2020). Presidents and members of Congress are also keenly aware that firearms sales represent jobs and rake in corporate profits for Americans and their respective companies. In recent years, President Donald Trump has repeatedly echoed this rationale publicly. Reflecting on a major deal with Saudi Arabia, he stated, "It will create hundreds of thousands of jobs, tremendous economic development, and much additional wealth for the United States" (Thrall et al., 2020, p. 101). President Trump's desire to generate income from firearms sales has been more transparent or explicit than most, but every president since Bill Clinton has made clear in their policy documents that economic benefits are a key consideration for governmental approval (Thrall et al., 2020). From a political perspective, every arms sale is thus a calculated gamble in that the expected strategic and economic benefits will outweigh the potential costs.

Since 2002, in a post-September 11 world aimed at combating terrorism, American arms exports have ranged between $15 and $75 billion per year, representing as much as 4 to 5 percent of America's total annual exports (Thrall et al., 2020). Powerful allies for arms dealers are found within the defense industry, which spends a great deal of time and money lobbying Washington's policy makers to keep arms sales flowing. Lobbyists' efforts include funding millions into campaign contributions and funneling other soft-money contributions to both parties (Thrall et al., 2020). Executive and legislative scrutiny over pending arms transactions are generally minimal or inconsequential because preventing such sales harms the interests of some of their most financially supportive constituents (i.e., arms suppliers) while also going against reliable customers and political allies (i.e., the recipients) (Thrall et al., 2020). The threat of losing potential profits can also harm access to strategic resources (i.e., precious metals and energy sources) which also aid a less critical approach toward evaluating the impact of sanctioned weapons sales. A portion of these sales, again, are not government to government. Regarding indirect sales stemming from these initiatives, these agreements also facilitate the ease of increasing private sales that have little or nothing to do with the government's agreement to commence (Thrall et al., 2020).

Success in tabulating the total numbers of sales, much less tracing them to their final destinations, remains elusive. The unruly environment of the remote, conflicted locations of these final points of sale often disregards formal accounting processes making the assessment of the existing physical reserves of weapons systems, arms, and munitions a cumbersome, if not an insurmountable task (Baker, 2008). Even in cases where the recipient country is well organized and makes their best intentions known, the process of uncovering and tabulating the actual amount of traded and stored weapons remains excruciatingly difficult. For example, in estimating any existing situation involving an armed conflict, weapons caches, hidden for strategic reasons during times of conflict, routinely fail to be disclosed (Baker, 2008). Secret owners of these reserves fail to be accounted for because their weapons can remain hidden for later use as a trading or sales commodity, or for committing violence (for defensive or offensive purposes). Since no one else knows the locations or existence of such hidden weapons, unofficial owners have little reason to sacrifice a potentially profitable, invaluable, inelastic resource (Baker, 2008). Finally, there is a general fear that collected weapons will not be properly handled in that they may be sold or worse, used to harm political opponents (especially those who had recently surrendered their weapons).

Trust becomes an indispensable, yet intangible element that may be impossible to secure, especially within a matter of a few years. Many of these war-torn nations have long histories of betrayals (especially in the Middle East) and centuries of tribal warfare (especially in Africa) where loyalties lie with their given localities rather than the country (Baker, 2008). Given that two or three generations have elapsed since European colonialism ended (and can no longer be directly blamed), still many of these countries continue struggling with these same internal issues. Correcting these kinds of embedded difficulties will likely take many generations (Baker, 2008).

SAMPLES OF DOMESTIC FIREARMS REGULATIONS AND RULES GOVERNING THE GUN MARKET

Around the world, legal requirements for gun ownership and the complexities of firearms ownership regulations vary considerably, reflecting a broad spectrum ranging from easy to follow and understand to the nearly impossible to follow or the unreasonably expensive compliance costs (Van Kesteren, 2014). Van Kesteren (2014) wrote that the key assumption "behind the strict regulation of gun ownership in most European countries" (p. 53) is the belief that guns facilitate violence. Government programs aimed at decreasing the availability or supply of guns in Brazil, Canada, Columbia, Mexico, South Africa, and parts of the United States also adhered to such a notion (Van Kesteren, 2014). Enforcement and compliance to such proposed restrictions vary considerably—from seemingly nearly perfect obedience coupled with possessing a high capacity to enforce existing rules in politically stable, high income countries (i.e., Japan and Canada) who carry consistent, predictable legal consequences whenever a wrongdoing is identified—to nonexistent enforcements and a lack of capacity to exercise governmental authority (i.e., Mexico and Nigeria). As already mentioned earlier in this chapter a brief review of two sampled countries from three regions of the world, including Latin America (Mexico and Brazil), Africa (Nigeria and South Africa), and Asia (Japan and the Philippines), will help highlight regulatory differences and domestic conditions between these markets.

What are the most common ways to restrict access to firearms? In more economically developed countries (particularly in Europe), usually safety tests or courses are required, and for some occasions a specific reason is necessary for a gun permit. Usually the recipient must be of "good character," meaning having no prior criminal convictions or documented mental health issues (Canadian Library of Congress, December 30, 2020). For example, in Canada, firearms licensing requires the following: (1) be eighteen years old,

(2) must pass the Canadian Firearms Safety Course; and (3) for "restricted firearms," non-hunting or sport, one "must pass the Canadian Restricted Firearms Safety Course (CRFC) tests." In addition, all restricted firearms must be registered. Since nonrestricted may not, these firearms may be owned in Canada without registration. However, if one owns a prohibited firearm knowingly without registration, the maximum penalty is ten years in prison (Canadian Library of Congress, December 30, 2020). Despite such stringent regulations and its reputation as a law-abiding and orderly society, Canada has roughly 2.1 million registered firearms, with another 10.7 million unregistered, resulting in an estimated 34.7 firearms per 100 people. In other words, approximately 83.6 percent of weapons remain unregistered (Tasker, 2020). The majority of the estimated number of unregistered guns are categorized by the Canadian government as unrestricted, which are not required to be registered.

In 2020, in response to a serial shooting in the province of Nova Scotia, Canadian Prime Minister Justin Trudeau pushed steeper restrictions aimed at having a much greater proportion registering all weapons, including banning 1,500 types of "assault-style" firearms (Tasker, 2020). Consequently, Canadian media reported that an estimated 105,000 firearms currently classified as "restricted" will become classified as "prohibited."(Tasker, 2020). Examples of these new "prohibited" weapons include semi-automatic rifles such as: the M16, AR-10, AR-15, and the M4 carbine. John Paul Tasker of CBC News points out that critics of Prime Minister Trudeau's executive order argue that it targets licensed gunowners rather than criminals, "who often turn to the black market to procure firearms to commit crimes" (Tasker, 2020). Opponents, such as Rod Giltaca, CEO of the Canadian Coalition for Firearm Rights, argued, "The only people that will lose their guns in this action are licensed gun owners. No criminals will register or turn in a single rifle" (Tasker, 2020). An indicator that Prime Minister Trudeau's executive order may be misdirected is cited by the Canadian Broadcast Center who estimated that illegal firearms from the United States are used in 70 to 90 percent of all gun-related crimes in Canada. Andrew Scheer, Canada's Conservative Leader, also disagreed with Prime Minister Trudeau's initiative, saying it "does nothing to target smugglers or those who illegally modify firearms" (i.e., adjusting a weapon from semi-automatic to automatic) (Tasker, 2020).

UNDERSTANDING THE INTERNATIONAL MARKET

Since few countries engage in a wholly deregulated private arms market, accurately examining how a free market for private firearms (beyond theoretical assumptions) would function abroad becomes impossible. The persistence of nearly or virtual autarkic trade regimes in so many countries (e.g., the State Department must give permission for U.S. citizens to travel to North Korea) who officially highly restrict or prohibit firearms sales heightens the sense of scarcity for weapons, thus indirectly encouraging widespread inflated black-market prices accompanied by inevitable shortages of demanded weapons (Small Arms Survey, 2018). Such excess demand for firearms contributes to desperate measures to counter what firearms consumers may perceive as unreasonable conditions. Trading in contraband such as firearms weapons behaves as an act of substitution when such transactions are conducted within an informal market setting absent of or in violation of governmental sanctions (Rohter, 1991). *Black markets*, or informal markets, exist whenever governmental restrictions prevent people from obtaining their perceived needs. Therefore, shortages of many goods persist, which further fuels thriving black markets. Driven by a personal quest for safety and fear of violence, many millions of people who feel vulnerable go through desperate measures to find ways to circumvent unreasonable restrictions imposed by the state. If given the choice of obedience to the law with a consequential increased likelihood of death, physical harm, or loss of property or breaking the rules and acquiring what is demanded via the informal market, individuals will repeatedly seek alternative means to buy what they believe to be necessary (Rohter, 1991).

LATIN AMERICA: A DISCONNECTION BETWEEN POLICIES AND REALITIES

Since governments frequently cite the relationship between gun ownership with higher crime rates as a reason for regulating the firearms market, it is critical to understand how crimes are reported and whether potential gun owners feel justified in seeking ways to enhance their personal protection. As mentioned previously, for lesser developed countries, governmental statistics can be unreliable for a variety of reasons. For example, regarding Latin American countries which often have strict gun ownership regulations, Van Kesteren argues that official statistics are unreliable and "cannot be reliably used for cross-country comparisons" (Van Kesteren, 2014, p. 53). If gun ownership and gun-related crimes are underreported, what then causes these widely deflated statistics? According to Muggah and Tobon, in 2018, "citizens simply do not trust the police" (p. 22). Victimization surveys consistently result in much higher rates of crime than the national statistic offices reported. In Peru, for example, the official incidence of robbery is 217 events per 100,000 or 64,000 incidents, yet victimization surveys suggest that 23 percent of Peruvians were robbed or roughly 6.8 million potential incidents which is over 100 times of the official robbery rate (Muggah & Tobon, 2018).

Publicly available data indicates that Latin America exhibits the highest homicide rates in the world (Muggah & Tobon, 2018). Although the region is home to only 8 percent of the world's population, 33 percent of all reported murders happen in Latin America. Thus, the regional homicide rate based on official data is 21.5 per 100,000, which is over three times the global murder rate of 7 per 100,000. For example, in 2015, there were roughly 154,000 murders in Latin American. From 2000 to 2016, over 2.5 million people died of homicide. As noted with the Peruvian example in the previous paragraph, these statistics are almost certainly markedly *under* counted, especially when one considers the prevalence of so many disappearances throughout the region (Muggah & Tobon, 2018).

According to Muggah and Tobon (2018), many observers have characterized homicide levels in countries such as Brazil, Colombia, El Salvador, Guatemala, Honduras, Mexico, some Caribbean countries, and Venezuela as epidemic, and even exceeding war-time levels (which are defined by WHO as 30 per 100,000) (Muggah & Tobon, 2018). Typically, poverty is cited as a primary culprit for increased violence, but paradoxically during the 2000s, significant reductions of poverty occurred (e.g., greater than 80 million people rose above the poverty line from 2003 to 2012), declines in income inequality happened (over fourteen countries experienced drops in their Gini coefficient, which is a commonly used measure in illustrating the distribution of societal income), and the Latin American middle class expanded (Muggah & Tobon, 2018). While such economic strides were accomplished, at this same time, the prevalence of violence also rose in most countries. Rising standards of living accompanied by increasing reported violence contradicts conventional wisdom (Muggah & Tobon, 2018).

As a result of this crisis of confidence and contradictory conditions, Latin Americans increasingly relied on private rather than public services such as hiring private security guards as an effort to bolster general safety conditions (Muggah & Tobon, 2018). By 2018, Latin America averaged a higher ratio of security guards than police, resulting in a total of 3.8 million private guards versus 2.6 million police officers. In some countries (i.e., Guatemala) the security-to-police ratio was even more extreme (a total of only 19,900 police officers compared to 120,000 private security guards). Indeed, Muggah cited that the "share of public expenditures on law enforcement and private security as a function of total spending in Latin America is double that of OECD countries" (Muggah & Tobon, 2018, p. 39).

MEXICAN REGULATIONS AND RESTRICTIONS: A CONTRADICTORY STATE OF RIGHTS AND REGULATIONS

Mexico, on its surface, projects a contradictory circumstance for potential gun owners. Although the Mexican constitution (Article 10) explicitly protects and permits gun ownership for household personal security, firearms are extensively regulated by its federal penal code (Gun Policy, 2020). For example, Title Two of Mexico's Federal Law on Firearms and Explosives includes a national firearms registry that "requires all firearms to be registered with the Secretariat of National Defense in the Federal Arms Registry" (Gun Policy, 2020). In addition, only firearms on a federal approval list are considered potentially legal. Furthermore, specific calibers of weapons also demand a compelling explanation or functional purpose for approval of ownership.

In 2020, Mexico had only 3.1 million registered firearms, with roughly another 13.7 million unregistered, or 12.9 firearms per 100 people (Gun Policy, 2020). This sum means that approximately 81.4 percent of all weapons are unregistered which partially explains why the infamous Mexican cartels and miscellaneous, scattered gangs across the country easily acquire and trade firearms despite their federal government's restrictions. Unlike Canada, it is illegal to leave any firearm off the Mexico's national registry. Penalties for not registering a firearm are fairly steep. Per article 162 of the Federal Penal Code, possessing an unregistered firearm could result in up to three years of imprisonment with between 180 and 360 days of the criminal's net income as a fine (Canadian Library of Congress, December 30, 2020).

Like Canada, many illegal firearms circulating in the Mexican black markets are originally from the United States (Canadian Library of Congress, December 30, 2020). Schroeder (2016, p. 3) observed that other studies have revealed that firearms parts are sometimes illicitly shipped abroad where they are then secretly assembled into functional weapons (Schroeder, 2016). For example, in 2012, in Corpus Christi, Texas, law enforcement authorities arrested numerous people involved in an illicit firearms manufacturing operation (Canadian Library of Congress, December 30, 2020). In this situation, these participants bought kits of firearms from the internet and also at nearby gun shops and then assembled the kits into AK-style rifles and eventually sold the rifles to a trafficker located near the Mexico border.

BRAZILIAN REGULATIONS AND RESTRICTIONS: STEEP REGULATIONS, LAX RULES, POOR ENFORCEMENT

Brazil, as South America's most populous country and its largest firearms market, has a detailed (and sometimes contradictory or confusing elements) list of regulations. All firearms "manufactured, imported, sold" as well as all privately owned, must be registered. Potential owners must be twenty-five years old and then must meet the following rules to own a "permitted firearm" by providing: (1) "evidence of suitability" (meaning no criminal record or have a history of criminal investigations), (2) documented evidence of a lawful place of residence to store the firearm (may also include workplace), (3) evidence of psychological and technical capacity to handle firearms, (4) proof that the potential owner will not expose "children to firearms" (meaning the weapons must not be stored near children), and last, (5) all approved weapons must then be registered with the Brazilian army command (Canadian Library of Congress, December 30, 2020).

Additional firearms restrictions include the inability to transport firearms (which requires additional licensing) and then usually only to permitted places of work or if given a specifically defined exception (Canadian Library of Congress, December 30, 2020). Furthermore, in Brazil, possessing an unregistered firearm within a home or workplace can result in a maximum of three years in prison (same as Mexico) and an indeterminate fine. Also, possessing a firearm in any other setting (such as in a car) can result in up to four years in prison and a fine. Last, if the firearm and its ammunition has been found to be deliberately concealed, the punishment is up to imprisonment for six years (Canadian Library of Congress, December 30, 2020).

Despite so many restrictive efforts, in 2020 according to the Library of Canada, Brazil has just over 8 million registered firearms yet another estimated 9.4 million unregistered guns (or roughly 53.9 percent of all known firearms are unregistered with a total of 8.3 firearms per 100 people) (Canadian Library of Congress, December 30, 2020). Like Mexico, and unlike Canada, in Brazil it is illegal to leave any firearm unregistered. Also, in 2019, National Public Radio reported that among all guns used in crimes and seized by Brazilian authorities, only 1 percent in São Paulo were from improvised and craft-produced small arms, meaning that almost all of these confiscated weapons originated as factory-made imports or from industrialized domestic production sites—which strongly contradicts the idea of an allegedly tightly controlled market (National Public Radio, June 28, 2019).

Unlike Canada, Brazil cannot blame a particular neighbor as the common point of origin of its illegal weapons. Brazil's increasing global trading relations complicate controlling access to their domestic market. Regarding the difficulties of monitoring the inflow of foreign firearms, Schroeder observed that "the sheer volume of goods that pass through air- and seaports every day" make it "impossible for customs and border officers to detect all illicit small arms shipments on their own" (Schroeder, 2016, p. 13). Such an abundance of unregistered manufactured weapons likely indicates that many arrive in a variety of ways (in ports and on land). The widespread inflow of illegal handguns and long guns is not necessarily true for all firearms. Regarding some semi-automatic weapons, illegally imported guns seemingly do not meet domestic demand. For example, among the seized submachine guns in Brazil, National Public Radio reported that roughly 48 percent of those were homemade or handcrafted modifications (National Public Radio, June 28, 2019). The preponderance of these informally made lethal weapons is evidence of consumers taking matters in their own hands and sidestepping existing laws.

NIGERIA: LAX LAWS, LAX ENFORCEMENT

According to the Small Arms Survey in 2020, the Nigerian government was estimated to have had 350 million, or roughly 70 percent, of West Africa's 500 million illegal firearms (National Public Radio, June 28, 2019). While the Nigerian constitution does not legally guarantee the right to own firearms, anyone over age seventeen (with the proper licensure) may own a gun. Some restrictions exist such as the prohibition of certain firearms (i.e., machine-guns and military rifles) (National Public Radio, June 28, 2019). Yet some of the rules are inconsistent. For example, while a background check is required, there is no legal stipulation that demands that the results of the said check can determine whether a license is granted. In addition, no kind of firearms training is required. Next, licenses only grant the firearm owner possession of the specific firearm on an annual basis, meaning that they are supposed to be renewed each year. Although all firearms manufactured and owned must be registered, guns may be carried openly, yet it is illegal to conceal them in public places (Vanguard Nigeria, 2016).

Nigerian firearms (other than submachine guns), unlike those typically found in South America, and like much of sub-Saharan Africa, are usually repaired older weapons and sometimes entirely handcrafted (Nowak & Gsell, 2018). These informally manufactured or produced firearms, which consist of used parts of older guns (sometimes many decades old) with handcrafted augmentations are called "Dane" guns (named from the massive influx of Danish-produced weapons during the European colonial era in the nineteenth century) (Nowak & Gsell, 2018). In the Small Arms Survey, a Nigerian blacksmith explained, "The production and repair of firearms is [*sic*] not about income for me, but for protection from incessant attacks for [*sic*] Fulani militia, and defence from armed robbers" (Nowak, & Gsell, 2018, p. 7). Okoli also notes that Nigerian cattle rustlers who are armed with "sophisticated weapons" are typically destructive and violent, and "operate with immense criminal efficiency and brutality" (Okoli, 2019, p. 57). The demand for homemade weaponry persists in rural areas where people clash over cattle and control of land, but also inside politically unstable urban areas where the need for personal protection is not satisfactorily met by inept, often corrupt or heavily conflicted local government officials (USIP, 2017).

Also, the Survey cited sources that explained: "Owners of licenced guns often came to the aid of neighbours by shooting to scare robbers when their neighbourhood was under attack. . . . Rural communities also had vigilante groups that used Dane guns to protect lives and property" (Alternative Africa, 2019). These examples of a lack of local protection underscore a dire need for acquiring firearms for personal protection that may be difficult for citizens in predictably lawful countries such as Japan and Canada to imagine. The maximum punishment for unlawful possession of any firearm is five years in prison. However, additional punishments for additional illicit activities can be doled out by local authorities (Vanguard Nigeria, 2016).

What are the consequences of Nigeria's strict firearms regulations? Although the Nigerian government estimates that there are roughly only 6.1 million firearms in Nigeria, UN officials in UNREC believe that over 350 million firearms are in circulation (Vanguard Nigeria, 2016). Experts believe that many such guns are likely primitive "Daneguns," or handcrafted weapons. These numbers vary wildly, depending upon the source. Yet it is illegal to possess an unregistered firearm in Nigeria (USIP, 2017). A similar sub-Saharan Africa case is found in Sudan which has *only* 6,724 registered firearms yet over 2.76 million unregistered firearms at least in circulation (Alternative Africa, 2019).

SOUTH AFRICA: HIGH CRIME RATES

In South Africa, firearms can only be possessed under very specific circumstances, which may include: (1) self-defense, in which case the applicant must demonstrate a need "for a weapon and an inability to achieve protection through other means," (2) for sport, meaning that the prospective owner "must be a member of an accredited hunting association." In both of these cases additional demands are involved: (A) the prospective buyer must complete a firearms training and safety course and (B) submit a consequential competency certificate; (C) the applicant must prove that "the applicant does not have a proclivity for violence or a substance-abuse problem," and (D) if they receive a permit to purchase a firearm, it must be on a governmental regulated non-restricted list. In some cases, certain restricted firearms can be allowed conditionally (e.g., for museums or for collectors with collector licenses). Next, (E) all firearms must be safely stored (i.e., inside a safe), and (F) all firearms transaction must be registered by the buyer and seller. Last, (G) licenses must be renewed every five years (Juta Law, January 31, 2015).

Just as in Mexico, Brazil, and Nigeria, it is illegal to possess an unregistered firearm in South Africa. However, the punishment of serving up to fifteen years in prison for the unlawful possession of a firearm or failure to satisfy any of the requirements of legal ownership is more severe than in Nigeria, Brazil, or Mexico (Alternative Africa, 2019). Despite these restrictive efforts South Africa claims that there are approximately 3 million registered firearms and another 2.4 million unregistered, resulting in an estimated 43.9 percent of all firearms being unregistered, with a total of 9.7 firearms per person (Alternative Africa, 2019).

Unique security concerns persist in South Africa because it appears to have more serious levels of violent crime than countries that have a comparable socioeconomic status, such as Brazil or Argentina. For example, Interpol data throughout the 1990s and 2000s showed that South African statistics revealed that they had among the highest murder rates in the world (at 121.67 murders and attempted murders per 100,000 citizens in 1997) (Masanzu, 2006). Concerns for personal safety according to Shaw and Gastrow (2001) continue to dominate every facet of South African life. High walls, barbed wire, and omnipresent security guards serve as reminders of the general public's fears (Shaw & Gastrow, 2001).

For many years, academics and journalists have been quite critical of South Africa's official crime statistics by claiming that the South African Police Service provides a poor indication of actual crime rates in the country. Critics do not believe official statistics because for many years they never seem to match the personal experiences of citizens (and their friends and neighbors), and because crime statistics are often, unsurprisingly, manipulated to serve political purposes (Masanzu, 2006). In particular, South African whites view government at the very least as evasive when it comes to confronting crime (Masanzu, 2006). For example, the majority of citizens in the country's capital city, Pretoria, when asked whether they believed government and police statistics about changing crime levels, showed little hesitation in answering in the negative (Shaw & Gastrow, 2001).

The ominous threat of victimization fuels much of the need for seeking a gun for personal protection. In South Africa (as is the case for every country) the likelihood of being a victim of a crime is determined by where people live, work, and how they live their daily lives. White residents of the city were more likely than others to express their skepticism of governmental enforcement against crime (Shaw & Gastrow, 2001). Furthermore, South Africa's recent history and apartheid legacy mar the capability of examining past crime statistics with the present because before 1990, the majority of the country's citizens experienced the police as instruments of repression. Consequently, before apartheid ended in 1994, reporting crimes had a diminished purpose (Shaw & Gastrow, 2001).

JAPAN: ISOLATED, RESTRICTED, AND UNIQUE

The well-publicized allegedly tiny Japanese private firearms market is a consequence of long-standing traditions including centuries-old restrictions (gun regulations began in 1629) (Shaw & Gastrow, 2001), geographic isolation (it is a Pacific Ocean nation of islands), and among the world's most restrictive rules for acquiring a legal gun. By any measure, in Japan it is extremely difficult to legally purchase and own any firearm. Civilians are only permitted to own rifles or shotguns after proving a purpose or need for them, and then only after meeting extensive criteria which include the following: (1) Must be older than eighteen years, (2) no bankruptcy declarations, (3) no existing or perceived risks of losing mental health (including dementia), (4) no current or past addictions to any substance, (5) cannot be declared "feebleminded," (6) cannot be "without a fixed abode" or homeless, (7) have previously lost a gun license, (8) have previously been imprisoned, (9) have previously violated firearms-related laws, (10) have stalked somebody and received a legal warning or restraining order, (11) have behaved violently, (12) been recognized as a member of a violent group, and last (13) be reasonably expected to harm someone else or themselves (Shaw & Gastrow, 2001).

Additional provisions must be met, including (A) completing courses on the use, the safety, and the storage of firearms (and finish all three courses), (B) take and pass skills tests by successfully also completing a shooting class, (C) only receiving rifles if the person is a professional hunter or has a specific extermination need (usually in the countryside), (D) renewing all gun licenses every three years, (E) registering all guns, (F) only discharging a firearm with their licensed purpose, (G) never keeping a gun loaded, (H) transporting all guns inside a case, and (I) always allow a police inspection at any time. Last, ammunition must be purchased using a separate license, which also cannot be stored in the same container (Shaw & Gastrow, 2001).

Japan's geographic isolation and long history of strict gun controls does result in an extremely low proportion of 0.3 firearms per 100 people. Yet there are 175,221 registered firearms, with another 201,779 unregistered, meaning that approximately 53.5 percent of firearms are unregistered even though it is illegal to possess an unregistered firearm in Japan (Quimpo, 2007). This is another example of evidence that high inelasticity of demand for firearms supersedes legal constraints. Purported obedience aside, Japanese consumers still seek and obtain guns despite the law's intentions to prevent widespread gun ownership. Japan is often lauded for its success in keeping gun-related deaths so low. However, statistical results are not always transparent or transferable. Differences of outcome can be caused by using different samples within a country (Van Kesteren, 2014).

THE PHILIPPINES: RULE BY KLEPTOCRACY

There is no legal guarantee to own a firearm. However, certain firearms can be purchased after an applicant acquires a license and registers the firearm. This process includes passing a firearms course, stating a purpose for acquiring the firearm, and registering the firearm purchased, as well as reapplying and requalifying for the license every two years (Quimpo, 2007). Licensed firearm owners may only possess up to fifteen firearms and fifty rounds of ammunition. Open carrying of firearms is prohibited; however, concealed carry licenses are available. Unlawful possession of a firearm in the Philippines can result in up to ten years in prison. Further associated crimes with an unregistered firearm can increase time in prison and fines (Gun Policy, 2020). In the Philippines, it is estimated that 53.9 percent of all firearms (over 1.7 million are registered, with just over another 2 million unregistered) are unregistered. Also, it is illegal to possess an unregistered firearm in the Philippines. Officially, there are only 3.6 firearms per 100 people, although most experts doubt this estimate (Quimpo, 2007).

Since its independence from the United States just after the Second World War (1946), an oligarchic elite has persistently dominated Philippine politics. Quimpo (2007) notes that Paul Hutchcroft described the Philippines as "having a patrimonial oligarchic state, a weak state preyed upon and plundered by different factions of the elite, who take advantage of, and extract privilege from, a largely incoherent bureaucracy" (Quimpo, 2007, p. 282). Embedded institutional corruption is another way of characterizing its postcolonial political environment. It is not just the presidents and their cronies but, according to Hutchcroft, "the oligarchic elite as a whole that engages in plunder" (Quimpo, 2007, p. 278). Among its many postcolonial presidents, Ferdinand Marcos (in office from 1965 to 1986) was its most notorious kleptocrat, having effectively stolen an estimated

$5 to $10 billion from the government during his autocratic presidency (Quimpo, 2007).

Postauthoritarian Philippines, which is defined as the years following the forced ending and subsequent exile of President Marcos's regime (since 1986), has experienced ongoing violence and increased, overt corrupt practices (which has been noted by many domestic and international political pundits) (Quimpo, 2007). Transparency International, a global corruption nongovernmental organization, lists the Philippines "among the countries with severe corruption problems" (Quimpo, 2007, p. 283). For example, since 2003 the Corruption Perception Index which has a 1 to 10 scale (with 10 as the least corrupt), the Philippines has consistently scored less a 3.0. The *Economist* magazine's Intelligence Unit has estimated that corruption accounts for roughly 20 to 30 percent of its national budget (Quimpo, 2007). Quimpo (and others, including the Hong Kong-based Political and Economic Risk Consultancy Ltd., or PERC) have portrayed the level of corruption and violence as having "reached . . . staggering proportions." Thus, a kind of "booty capitalism" has hindered the Philippines's economic development, placing it in a "developmental bog" (Quimpo, 2007, p. 282). According to Quimpo, within the Southeast Asia region, only Indonesia has been consistently characterized as being more corrupt. Incidentally, in 2013, in Indonesia, 98 percent of guns confiscated from robbery suspects were homemade (Quimpo, 2007).

CONCLUSION

With the exception of Japan, each country sampled or presented in this study has experienced persistent problems and perennial setbacks in regulating their private firearms market. In almost every case, huge proportions of guns acquired and owned in these countries are not registered or are owned by unknown individuals. In many cases, rules and penalties on paper for infractions may not take effect or they lack the means to inhibit ownership. Furthermore, just as gun registration and regulations are managed differently from country to country, that is usually the case within different parts of each country, as well. In all cases, with the possible exception of Japan, the total number of privately owned firearms far exceeded the official numbers of those that are registered (Quimpo, 2007). Lesser developed, politically unstable countries also lack the capacity and the means to accurately estimate gun ownership, much less exert substantial control over the private markets (legal or illegal) within their jurisdictional boundaries. Sources cited throughout this chapter have continually claimed that the number of illegally purchased or illegally manufactured guns is likely to be higher than many estimates. The harsh, impoverished circumstances in parts of many of these countries coincide with a lack of government resources, redirected priorities, and an insufficient or distracted political will to rigidly enforce firearms restrictions and regulations.

Lang (2016) noted that accurate firearms data throughout much of the world remains sparse. Inaccurate surveys relating to gun ownership are limited because of geographic, time, and sample size constraints. Many gun ownership surveys, due to the controversial nature of firearms, contain significant biases. Consequently, many researchers resort to using proxy measures (e.g., sophisticated estimates involving magazine subscriptions, suicide fractions, and stolen gun reports) for assessing the total numbers of gun ownership while attempting to link guns and crime. Furthermore, a variety of conclusions are shaped by varying methodological differences.

Today, increasing evidence shows that small arms trafficking from the United States defies common assumptions about the illicit arms trade because more illicit guns arrive in smaller quantities, using mundane methods often hidden among legal goods "in 20-foot shipping containers owned by legitimate companies" (Schroeder, 2016, p. 14). This side of the illicit arms trade defies many stereotypes of what people expect and, in some ways, is more challenging to stop than the multi-ton shipments arranged by organized crime (Schroeder, 2016).

Traffickers have complicated small arms smuggling by shipping parts and accessories (Lang, 2016). After arriving to their destination, those receivers of these illicit firearms parts and accessories will quickly either assemble the pieces into fully functional weapons or will circulate them into a broader geographic area where others will assemble them. As demonstrated throughout this chapter, there is a massive global black firearms market that extends to nearly every region of the world.

While the segment of the firearms market pertaining to collecting is generally insignificant and inconsequential to public policy concerns, typically weapons used for hunting purposes also draw less criticism due to the global popularity for hunting game (for sustenance) and also as a defensive or practical tool in managing livestock or performing other agrarian-related lines of work (Lang, 2016). Firearms used for criminal and civil uprising activities hold the most concern, especially in markets of developing countries. Although much information on the gun-violence link is available from publications such as the Small Arms Surveys on individual countries, the regions of Africa and Latin America lack good-quality, reliable quantitative cross-sectional and time-series studies. As noted earlier, Japan is a special case due to its unique geographical, historical, and cultural factors which make it difficult to compare and impossible to emulate.

Last, when all else fails in matters of receiving an affordable, cheap supply of weapons, people tend to improvise by making their guns or restoring old, even antique ones to make them useful. These acts of market substitution are found in lower income sub-Saharan African states but also in wealthy, restrictive countries such as the United Kingdom. In conclusion, for many people of varying backgrounds and circumstances, firearms are extraordinarily useful tools that can be used for offensive and defensive purposes. Safety and security drive the defensive market. Aggression, poverty, and greed drive the offensive market. Regulators around the world have struggled and largely failed to control these two general impulses because they are endemic to humanity. Who doesn't want to feel safe? Are aggression and greed indelible parts of human nature? Such basic, instinctive features of the human psyche continue to fuel these markets, whether they are legal or not.

NOTE

1. The author would like to acknowledge Samuel J. Baker for his help with this chapter.

BIBLIOGRAPHY

Alternative Africa. 2019, May 5. "Nigerian Reps Urge President Buhari to Reverse Executive Order Revoking Guns." https://alternativeafrica.com/2019/05/30/nigerian-reps-urge-president-buhari-to-reverse-executive-order-revoking-gun-license/.

Baker, Josiah R. 2006. *Macroeconomics: Theories, Principles, and Issues: Basic Text for Macroeconomic Related Courses.* Pearson Publishing.

Baker, Josiah R. 2008. "Arms Trafficking." In *The Encyclopedia of Africa and the Americas*, 124–25. Santa Barbara, CA: ABC-CLIO, Inc. Publications.

Baker, Josiah R. 2013. *Religion, Politics, and Polarization: How Religiopolitical Conflict Is Changing Congress and American Democracy.* Appendix A. Online publication for Rowman and Littlefield Publications. June.

Brayton, A. 1983, March. "The Politics of Arms Limitations in Africa." *African Studies Review*, *26*(1).

Canadian Library of Congress. 2020. "Firearms Control." https://www.loc.gov/law/help/firearmscontrol/index.php.

Gun Policy. 2020. "Firearms by Region: Mexico." https://www.gunpolicy.org/firearms/region/mexico.

Juta Law. 2015. "Firearms Control Act 60 of 2000." South African Government Documents. https://www.saps.gov.za/resource_centre/acts/downloads/juta/firearms_control_act_2000_a_0060.pdf.

Karp, A. 2018, June. *Estimating Global Civilian-Held Firearms Numbers*. Briefing Paper. Small Arms Survey. http://www.smallarmssurvey.org/fileadmin/docs/T-Briefing Papers/SAS-BP-Civilian-Firearms-Numbers.pdf.

Lang, M. 2016. "State Firearm Sales and Criminal Activity: Evidence from Firearm Background Checks." *Southern Economic Journal, 83*(1), 45–68. doi:10.2307/26632325.

Lord of War. 2005. Film. Directed by Andrew Niccol. Saturn Films.

Masanzu, K. 2006. "'Of Guns and Laws': A South African Perspective in Light of United Kingdom and United States Gun Laws." *The Comparative and International Law Journal of Southern Africa, 39*(1), 131–151. http://www.jstor.org/stable/23253015.

Mills, G. 1993. *Small Arms Control and Southern Africa*. Defense Analysis.

Muggah, R., and Tobón, K. 2018. *Citizen Security in Latin America: Facts and Figures* (pp. 22–46, Rep.). Igarape Institute. http://www.jstor.org/stable/resrep19172.6.

National Public Radio. 2019, June 28. "U.S. Agents Announce Thousands of Weapons Seized in Operation Patagonia Express." https://www.npr.org/2019/06/28/737041530/u-s-agents-announce-thousands-of-weapons-seized-in-operation-patagonia-express.

Nowak, M., and Gsell, A. 2018. Small Arms Survey. "Nigerian Craft Weapons." http://www.smallarmssurvey.org/fileadmin/docs/T-Briefing-Papers/SAS-BP-Nigeria-craft-weapons.pdf.

Okoli, A. 2019. "Cows, Cash and Terror: How Cattle Rustling Proceeds Fuel Boko Haram Insurgency in Nigeria." *Africa Development / Afrique Et Développement, 44*(2), 53–76. doi:10.2307/26873429.

Quimpo, N. 2007. "THE PHILIPPINES: Political Parties and Corruption." *Southeast Asian Affairs,* 277–294. http://www.jstor.org/stable/27913337.

Rohter, L. 1991, August 12. "In the Shady World of Illegal Arms, Miami Is Hot." *International Herald Tribune*.

Schroeder, M. 2016. (Rep.). Small Arms Survey. http://www.jstor.org/stable/resrep10641.

Shaw, M., and Gastrow, P. 2001. "Stealing the Show? Crime and Its Impact in Post-Apartheid South Africa." *Daedalus, 130*(1), 235–258. http://www.jstor.org/stable/20027686.

Small Arms Survey. 2018. U-Reports. "SAS-improvised Craft Weapons Report." http://www.smallarmssurvey.org/fileadmin/docs/U-Reports/SAS-improvised-craft-weapons-report.pdf.

Tasker, John Paul. 2020, May 1. "Trudeau Announces Ban on 1,500 types of 'Assault-Style' Firearms—Effective Immediately." Canadian Broadcast Center (CBC). https://www.cbc.ca/news/politics/trudeau-gun-control-measures-ban-1.5552131.

Thrall, A., Cohen, J., and Dorminey, C. 2020. "Power, Profit, or Prudence? US Arms Sales since 9/11." *Strategic Studies Quarterly, 14*(2), 100–126. doi:10.2307/26915279.

USIP. 2017, April. "Nigeria's New Threat: Guns, Cows, and Clashes over Land." https://www.usip.org/blog/2017/04/nigerias-new-threat-guns-cows-and-clashes-over-land.

Van Kesteren, J. 2014. "Revisiting the Gun Ownership and Violence Link: A Multilevel Analysis of Victimization Survey Data." *The British Journal of Criminology, 54*(1), 53–72. http://www.jstor.org/stable/23640288.

Vanguard Nigeria. 2016, August."Nigeria Accounts for 70 Percent of Illicit Weapons in West Africa." https://www.vanguardngr.com/2016/08/nigeria-accounts-70-illicit-weaponswafrica/.`

4

A Critique of Some Phenomenological Studies on Guns and Gun Ownership

Michael Potts

Some recent phenomenological studies on guns and gun ownership focus on the alleged effect a gun has on a person's identity. Examples include the claim that owning a gun is associated with greater aggressiveness and a sense of aggrandizement and power. It has also been claimed that gun owners are fearful of "the other," the person from a different race and/or social class. Although admitting some validity to these studies' claims, this chapter argues against a naïve acceptance of such claims in favor of a more cautious approach. After a section examining the root of the critiques, Martin Heidegger's phenomenology of "equipment," the second section summarizes the arguments of phenomenologists on gun ownership. The final section presents three critiques of phenomenological accounts of gun ownership. First, it argues that the phenomenological method is limited in its accuracy given that it is can easily degenerate into a subjective analysis in the guise of an objective study of human experience as a whole. Second, there is a critique of the anti-essentialism, nominalism, and social constructivism of such studies. Finally, there is a defense of libertarian free will against the view that gun ownership determines a person's behavior (or significantly limits a person's freedom) to act as (s)he pleases.

THE GROUNDWORK: MARTIN HEIDEGGER'S PHENOMENOLOGICAL METHOD AND THE CONCEPT OF "EQUIPMENT"

Phenomenology is a method of philosophy pioneered first by Charles Sanders Peirce in the United States and by Edmund Husserl in Germany; however, it is Husserl's method that influenced later European phenomenologists and existentialists. In this method, a person removes any pretense of discovering the ultimate nature of things and attempts to describe the concrete human experience of the world. Martin Heidegger used this method in his discussion of *Dasein*, his term for the human being acting in the world. His concept of "equipment" is part of his discussion of the "everyday world" (Käufer & Chemero, 2015).

Heidegger focuses on human beings' use of objects in the world for particular purposes; that is, human beings use objects with an end in mind. Heidegger's goal is to understand human beings in terms of "those entities which we encounter as closest to us" (Heidegger, 1962). These are objects that are "used," "what gets produced" (Heidegger, 1962). Such objects "become accessible when we put ourselves into the position of concerning ourselves with them in such way" (Heidegger, 1962, p. 96). It is at the point at which we are concerned with them that Heidegger labels "equipment" (*das Zeug*). Equipment is used "in order to"—that is, it is used with a particular goal or set of goals in mind. For example, if someone uses a hammer, he usually uses it to drive nails into wood or some other material. Someone can use a computer to type a paper (as I am now) or to play a game or to program. Whenever we use equipment, it becomes an extension of the phenomenal self. Equipment is always used in a larger context; for example, hammering a nail might be part of the larger task of building an attic, which is part of the larger context of building a house. The "environment" is not neutral but is shaped by objects of our concern (objects that are "ready-to-hand," "equipment"). Such objects make up the world that is "familiar" to us (Heidegger, 1962). When we engage in practical tasks using equipment, we do not usually consciously think in terms of rule-following or a series of discrete steps. For example, driving a car is a kind of skill knowledge that drivers know; if a driver thought of driving in terms of following rules, as she did when learning how to drive, most likely she would be a much poorer driver.

Most skills are social skills, having to do with our relationships to other people (Heidegger, 1962). Activities such as cooking, driving to work, building, playing a game, running a business, medical practice, and so forth all involve relationships with others, and each activity affects relationships to certain people in particular ways. For example, if someone sees a doctor for the flu, and the doctor diagnoses pneumonia and the proper treatment for it, this gives that particular patient knowledge of what to do to cure her illness as well as the medicines to help.

For Heidegger, equipment shapes us as much as we shape equipment. Equipment becomes an extension of the self into the world. If I hold a hammer in my hand to nail down a two-by-four, the hammer becomes an extension of my body. It shapes me—I will use the correct part of the hammer to drive the nail. If I use the wooden handle to drive the nail, that is ineffective due to the nature and purpose of the hammer. Equipment can shape our identity in the sense that it constrains us within a particular world governed by its rules and not ours. It can shape attitudes and emotions. Someone with a good-quality ax who sells firewood can have greater confidence due to the reliability of his equipment. Using the axe consistently can lead to greater physical strength in which the person can take pride. It may also affect him if he goes to a bar and there gets into a fight—he may think that having a strong arm gives him an advantage. All these are possibilities that can arise due to the use of a particular item of equipment, in this case, an axe.

PHENOMENOLOGICAL ACCOUNTS OF GUN OWNERSHIP

B. D. McClay offers a phenomenological account of the gun, which she argues is a kind of tool. Now tools are used to perform particular tasks which are done for particular reasons. For example, a hammer is used to drive nails into wood or some other appropriate material to work toward a given task, such as putting up a new roof. Regarding the purpose of guns, they are "meant to kill something" (McClay, 2014). She points out that hunting is one clear purpose for using guns, a purpose encased in a system of morality and law. However, she also notes that private citizens and law enforcement officers own guns that have only one purpose: to kill another human being. McClay alleges that this use of guns is not encased in law or a particular moral code. She further claims that when a gun is used to kill a human being, "the only ethical guide available to consult at the moment is the user's fear. If you're sufficiently afraid, you can shoot a woman through a door. If you're sufficiently afraid, you can shoot a man at a traffic stop for no reason at all, or a child who is doing nothing but playing outside" (McClay, 2014).

While I shall present a general critique of her approach and others' later, here more specific criticisms come to mind. At the legal level, there are legal guidelines covering the boundary between legitimate and illegitimate shootings in the laws of all U.S. states. They differ somewhat from state to state, but no state would support the legality of a shooting in which someone at a traffic stop is murdered only because his murderer says, "I was afraid."

Context matters here. If someone pulls a toy gun that looks real on a person, then that person might understandably shoot back with a real gun, even if the "shooter" is a child. In a case in which a person or persons shot were doing nothing to raise fear, then any DA following state law would prosecute unless the DA has an ethical problem. Other scenarios could be brought up, but the key point is that overall situational context makes a difference in whether a law regarding guns was violated. That is not necessarily the fault of the state's laws, and if a law is ambiguous, then the state legislature has a moral obligation to amend it.

McClay also claims, without justification, that "the history of gun control is . . . frequently racist" (McClay, 2014). She might be referring to California's response to the Black Panther's protest "on the steps of the California statehouse," in which members carried ".357 Magnums, 12-gauge shotguns and .45-caliber pistols" in an attempt to get the legislature to support blacks arming themselves. Out of fear that they were trying to arm themselves against police officers, Governor Ronald Reagan supported legislation that banned open carry of loaded weapons (Morgan, 2018). However, such legislation may not have passed as a result of fear of African Americans per se as much as fear of the reputation of the Black Panthers and concern that they would turn their guns on police officers.

McClay is correct regarding the reciprocal relationship between rights and responsibilities; owning a gun may be a right under the Second Amendment, but all rights imply responsibilities. But she goes on to say that many Americans focus only on the right of owning a gun, not the responsibility to use the gun in an appropriate manner. That may be correct, though it would require empirical evidence from psychological and sociological studies for verification.

For her own part, McClay says she bought a gun so she could be afraid, so she could "transform the world around me into a series of potential threats" (McClay, 2014). Thus, she says that her gun changed her initial wary attitude toward people she met that she perceived as behaving in an intimidating or threatening manner. Instead, after buying a gun she perceived them as "unreal [i.e., not human, M.P.] targets of [her own] potential violence" (McClay, 2014).

Johnnie Spraggins takes a postmodern approach to male gun ownership, using gender theory, feminism, social construction, deconstruction, and reconstruction (Spraggins, 1995). Spraggins used a field study approach, joining "a shooting club, observed a handgun intervention program in Detroit, observed in a gun shop and shooting ranges," and held interviews with various people who interacted with guns. He concluded that white men "were socialized into gun use" in the family, while black men were socialized via "peer groups or alone" (Spraggins, 1995). He claims that guns are symbols of "valued masculinities." He notes the emphasis by male gun owners on "physical and emotional control of the body" as well as "the texture and quality of the guns themselves" (Spraggins, 1995).

Evan Sellinger attacks the defense of guns that states, "Guns don't kill people; people kill people" (Sellinger, 2012). He does not deny that some gun owners are well-trained and responsible, nor does he deny that there is cultural variance among gun owners. Guns are a particular kind of technology, so Sellinger turns to general views of technology. One which he criticizes is the instrumentalist view, which holds that while the goals of technology may be subject to moral criticism, the technology itself is "value-neutral." Applied to guns, instrumentalism holds that guns are value-neutral in themselves, and it is people who put them to good or evil uses. Such a view is expressed, according to Sellinger, in the NRA's position that "Guns don't kill people. People kill people." He goes on to say that the NRA slogan "aptly expresses the folk psychology that underlies moral and legal norms" (Sellinger, 2012)

Although the term "folk psychology" refers to the psychology held implicitly in common by most people in a culture, it has a pejorative tinge to it. The term "folk" has the connotations of "common," "ordinary," "primitive," and "unreflective" as opposed to a more sophisticated neutral term, and Sellinger does not need to use it for his general argument.

Sellinger wishes to apply a phenomenological analysis of gun possession, focusing on Don Idhe's view of "lived experience." That is, such analysis "focus[es] on what it is like for a flesh-and-blood human to actually be in possession of a gun" (Sellinger, 2012). He begins with the point that technology functions like a tool, and that a specific tool can be used in different ways. This constrains the use of a tool outside its accustomed contexts. For example, it makes little sense to use a hammer to flatten dough, while it makes perfect sense to hammer roofing nails to secure new roof tiles. Guns are, like a hammer, "multistable" in the sense that their structure is compatible with a limited number of ends. Thus, Sellinger (2012) states that "*A gun's excellence simply lies in its capacity to quickly fire bullets that can reliably pierce targets*" (italics his) (Sellinger, 2012). Thus, the design of guns is oriented toward "accomplishing radical and life-altering action at a distance with minimal physical exertion on the part of the shooter" (Sellinger, 2012). Sellinger (2012) says it is "difficult to imagine" the utility of guns used for other ends.

This is not strictly the case. Gun collectors might keep a large number of guns just to have them without having the goal of firing them, regardless of their original purpose. Antique dealers desire to sell a gun to someone whose goals may not include shooting it, and museums can house guns in their displays for their historic interest. In addition, some people enjoy target shooting and have no intention of using a gun for any other purpose. At such events as "Turkey Shoots," a person who does not own a gun can borrow one to shoot at a moving target to have a chance to win a turkey in a drawing. With that said, one must grant McClay the point that the primary purpose of a gun's structure/design is to maim or kill an animal organism.

Following Heidegger, McClay believes that tools, including guns, transform human beings who use them. Thus, the world appears in a different form to the person holding a gun than to someone who does not. There are now potential targets (animals and/or human beings) that were not potential targets before the person got the gun. In addition, Sellinger (2012) asserts that "gun possession makes it easy to be bold, even hotheaded. Physically weak, emotionally passive, and psychologically introverted people will be inclined to experience shifts in demeanor." In addition, Sellinger (2012) states that the number of objects perceived dangerous is reduced for the one holding a gun, and the number of objects "perceived as calling for the subject to respond with violence" are increased.

In a related series of claims regarding shooting sprees, Robert McInerney affirms that "things compel us and move us toward different feelings and moods, levels of intensity, intention, and involvement" (McInerney, 2014, 46). Following Heidegger, he believes that "the thing is in some way inseparable from the human being experiencing it" (McInerney, 2014, 46). In this case, McInerney argues that the gun becomes inseparable from the person holding the gun; there is a fusion of identities in some sense that erases boundaries between person and thing. He admits that if someone holds a rapid-fire gun, this act will not have a significant effect on her identity. The issue for him is someone owns a gun so long that "it recedes into the everydayness of our lives" (McInerney, 2014, 48).

In such cases, McInerney believes that holding the rapid-fire gun can affect a person's emotions in a radical way. He says it leads to an emotional "rush" and refers to the etymology of the word "rapid": "hurried and rushed . . . as well as seizing and grasping," and he says that the word is associated with "rape" and "rapture" (McInerney, 2014, 50). The gun creates a fascination with its power and lessens the subjective distance to the mass murder of other people. In a vulnerable person, such an emotional rush can lead to mass murder using the rapid-fire gun.

However, McInerney should take into account the fact that there are some mass shootings that might fit into this category, such as the man who is fired and comes back to his workplace the same day to shoot as many people as possible. Others are carefully planned, as was the Columbine shootings by Eric Harris and Dylan Klebold. Mass killing can be cold and "rational" and not due to the gun's influence on emotions.

A CRITIQUE OF SOME PHENOMENOLOGICAL ACCOUNTS OF GUN OWNERSHIP

There are three major problems with such phenomenological accounts of gun ownership that paint it in a negative light due to the effects the gun has on the gun owner. The first lies in the phenomenological method itself. Originally Husserl took it as operating without presuppositions and describing everyday experience in order to find the "essences" of that experience. However, no one has used the phenomenological method without presuppositions, at least presuppositions about subjective human experience, and no one could. The philosopher at least assumes that a phenomenological method is possible, that it can accurately describe the nature of particular human experiences without making reality claims, and, at least in Husserl's version of phenomenology, that there are Platonic-like essences of human experience. Heidegger focused on humans as users of "equipment," emphasizing humans as primarily tool-using beings. That focus is to sneak in ideological presuppositions (Tonso, 2004). Phenomenologists make a similar mistake when they put the worst light on the phenomenal features of owning or carrying a gun by focusing on how it makes a person feel more powerful and lessens her inhibitions against murder.

Walter Kirn provides his own phenomenological analysis of gun ownership from the standpoint of a person who has owned six guns. In many rural communities in the United States, owning a gun is a "coming of age" event, "the proper acknowledgement of oncoming adulthood" (Kirn, 2013). He argues that the phenomenological experience of guns is different for those who grew up around guns and those who did not. When he heard about the Aurora, Colorado, movie theater shooting that left twelve dead, he did not feel guilty for owning or using a gun. Instead, he deplored "a depraved, unbalanced culture of splatter-fest games and other dark entertainments" (Kirn, 2013). The issue he brings up is that there may be other factors involved in motivations to murder than feeling powerful because of a gun. Even from a phenomenological point of view, a person may feel fear when handling a gun as much as power. Even feeling the gun as powerful may not motivate to kill; it may motivate someone to respect that power and use the gun responsibly. As Kirn puts it, "When I shoot at the range, I don't feel personally powerful but like the custodian of something powerful. I feel like a successful disciplinarian of something radically alien and potent" (Kirn, 2013). It may invoke a fear of harming or killing someone. If guns themselves make people more likely to kill, why did an Army historian conclude that only 15–20 percent of U.S. Army World War II soldiers fired their weapons during combat (Grossman, 2009)? That is why the Army adopted the policy of dehumanizing the enemy in training. Additionally, round targets were replaced by human-shaped targets in order to desensitize the soldiers.

Phenomenological analyses of gun ownership and use can go both ways. The phenomenologist who asserts his interpretation of the experience of owning and handling a gun is the correct one can be opposed by someone with a radically different phenomenological analysis. A good question to ask is whether the phenomenologist himself owns a gun. If not, how can the phenomenalist generalize about the nature of the experience of owning a gun for everybody? Often phenomenology seems more like amateur psychology than a philosophical method to better understand human experience. A better way of understanding the phenomenology of gun ownership is to survey a random sample of gun owners and interview them. Although psychologists can also have ideological biases that enter into studies, there are empirical checks on their studies.

Phenomenology seems to work best when analyzing situations in which every person or almost every person involved in such a situation would agree that the analysis faithfully reflects the experience. Heidegger's phenomenological analysis of tool use in general seems true to the experience. A hammer has a clear use in different social contexts, so the experience of using a hammer can be subjected to a true-to-life phenomenological analysis. With guns, however, there are multiple uses under the primary use of killing—one can hunt and kill animals, one can avoid killing altogether in target shooting and skeet shooting, or one can kill a human being. Even killing a human being is not necessarily a bad goal in cases of self-defense or in a just war (assuming just war theory is sound).

In addition, the phenomena of gun possession and ownership differ from culture to culture. In Switzerland, all adult males own a military weapon since they each undergo military training and are in the Swiss Army. The experience of owning such a gun is different than someone without military training owning one—or the experience of one who uses a gun often in full-time military work in training and/or combat. In places where sheep are raised, the shepherd might carry a gun to protect the flock. In some Arab cultures firing guns in the air is a form of celebration. Most phenomenological experience of guns is culturally situated.

A second issue with current phenomenological analyses of gun possession and ownership is the tendency to assume nominalism (universal terms do not refer to anything objective in extramental reality but in terms of what human beings group together in terms of their own interests). This takes away the notion that real natures in things constrain our use of language and thus is a kind of anti-essentialism. Reality is constructed by human interests and the artifacts of human culture, as well as by race, class, sexual identity, and sexual orientation.

This trend is an ironic twist on the philosophy of Immanuel Kant (1724–1804). Kant assumed that human beings constructed the general structures of reality based on universal forms of sensibility (space and time) and categories of the understanding (such as cause and effect). These structures are the same in all human beings, and thus there is one world that humans perceive (Kant, 1965/1781). With the breakdown of the view in the eighteenth-century Enlightenment of a universal humanity common to all and a universal human reason, construction of reality was relegated to smaller and smaller components: society, race, class, gender, sexual identity and orientation, and in the case of Heidegger, "equipment." Now Heidegger himself believes there is sufficient human freedom for some to transcend the ordinary world of equipment and attain a kind of self-transcendence in "authentic existence." Once that option is gone, then the factors mentioned above control us, mold us, shape us into the particular individuals we are. Thus, if guns function in the way that some contemporary phenomenologists suggest, the alleged sense of power and sense of ease in killing a person will change a person's reality to the reality molded by the gun. If social constructivism shifts to social determinism, or in this case "equipment determinism," the gun and its associated aggressive values necessarily become part of the person owning it. At the very least, it provides temptations to use the gun to kill a person in ways that were not previously present.

However, those claims run into the critique presented earlier, that there is no one gun culture, that the response to guns is psychologically complex and differs from person to person, that heredity (is a person born with more than average aggressive personality traits vs. someone who is born with fewer aggressive traits, for instance) and environment play a role in the reaction to owning a gun as does the common biological and psychological features humans universally share regardless of culture. The complex factors involved go beyond any simple notion of "I own a gun. Therefore, I feel powerful and know how easy it would be to kill a person." This is a fundamental issue with some phenomenological analyses of guns; they oversimplify the complex.

The issue of free will vs. determinism is an ancient one that will probably not be resolved to everyone's satisfaction. It is clear that heredity, environment, social background, family background, state of physical health, and psychological temperament as well as the context in which a person uses a gun affects the choices made by a gun owner. Now on the issue of free will vs. determinism, I follow Aristotle (Aristotle, 1999) and Thomas Aquinas (2017) in holding that human beings choose on the basis of what they perceive to be good. That is, the intellect suggests a potential good, and the will consents. All intentional actions have reasons; the notion of total chance making up the nature of choice is nonsense, since that would only yield chaos. The will is free to assent or withhold assent from a particular good; for example, someone may perceive the good of going fishing in the morning, but when the weather forecast predicts dangerous thunderstorms, the person does not consent to that good since a higher good, preserving one's life, overrides it. While in a technical sense one could say reasons determined the will, the person still has libertarian free will to assent or refuse to assent to a perceived good at a particular time.

Suppose someone (Person A) believes it would be good if his obnoxious neighbor (Person B), who roughs up local children, threatens the neighbors, throws beer cans over the fence, and constantly disputes the property line, was dead (since the neighbor clearly has no plans to move). Now Person A owns a gun, let's say a .45 caliber pistol, that he uses for target practice at the local range. If Person A picks up the pistol, does it make him more likely to kill Person B? Admittedly that is possible, but it does not determine Person A to shoot Person B even if the thought comes into his mind that killing Person B is a possible good for consideration. But if Person A deliberates, he finds possible evils, such as prison, leaving his wife without a husband present and children without a father, that outweigh the perceived good of killing Person B. Given free will, the person can choose either way, and even if the gun decreases the emotional distance of killing someone, Person A does not have to consent to kill.

Consider a different scenario, in which Person A carries the gun everywhere, and Person A has a bad temper that is made worse by drinking alcohol. Then freedom is compromised, as Aristotle recognized, due to the influence of alcohol. That is a dangerous situation, and if Person A has a gun, he may feel powerful and, while under the influence, kill Person B.

Granting that, however, does not justify some of the phenomenological analyses of gun ownership in the scholarly literature. There are numerous things to consider in this case; the irresponsibility of drinking alcoholic beverages by someone who knows they make him hot-tempered and lose judgment is one. Another thing to consider applies to both scenarios: phenomenologically, is there anything qualitatively or quantitatively different between the experience of owning or possessing a gun and the experience of owning or possessing a sword or a switchblade knife? There was an incident in my own family in which a man tried to murder his brother who was attempting to seduce the man's wife. The man took a sword he picked up as a souvenir in World War II and tried to murder his brother (who outran him and was not harmed). Is it not possible that the experience of possessing a sword in that case and the experience of possessing a gun would be nearly equivalent in the two cases? One could make the same argument about switchblade knives in tough 1950s neighborhoods.

The most one could legitimately claim is that owning and possessing a gun can tilt the intellect toward the possibility of killing a person, but the will does not have to act on that possibility. Such a possibility can also make a person cautious and careful with a gun so that she does not harm or kill a person by accident (or intentionally). There will always be people who will misuse their free will and use guns to intentionally wound and/or kill the innocent. The same is true for people with knives or people with martial arts skills. Sauce for the goose is sauce for the gander.

CONCLUSION

Most contemporary phenomenological approaches appear to be more ideologically driven; that is, they seem to reflect a prior bias against guns and gun owners that is reflected in their analysis. Given the complexity of the cultural and individual factors involved in the phenomenology of gun possession and ownership, it is more reasonable to say that the experience of owning and/or possessing a gun differs from society to society and from person to person. While in a sense it is true that guns, like other tools, can work as extensions of the body and can have an effect on the psyche, to say that such phenomena only have negative effects on a person rather than positive effects goes beyond current available evidence. Phenomenological approaches to gun ownership must (1) avoid as much as is humanly possible the prior biases of the researcher, (2) keep in mind the nature of the human being, of particular societies, and of the individuals who own guns vs. those who do not. In order to do so, sound psychological studies should lay the groundwork for the philosophical method of phenomenology to avoid its becoming lost in a subjective morass.

BIBLIOGRAPHY

Aquinas, St. Thomas. (2017). *Summa theologica*. Second and revised edition. Fathers of the English Dominican Province. Online edition prepared by Kevin Knight. Retrieved May 12, 2020, from newadvent.org/summa.

Aristotle. (1999). *Nicomachean ethics*. Second edition. Terence Irwin (trans.). Indianapolis: Hackett Publishing Company.

Grossman, David. (2009). *On killing: The psychological costs of learning to kill in war and society*. New York: Back Bay Books.

Heidegger, Martin. (1962). *Being and time*. John Macquarrie and Edward Robinson (trans.). Oxford: Blackwell.

Kant, Immanuel. (1965/1781). *Critique of pure reason.* Norman Kemp Smith (trans.). New York: St. Martin's Press.

Käufer, Stephan, and Anthony Chemero. (2015). *Phenomenology: An introduction.* Hoboken, NJ: Wiley.

Kirn, Walter. (2013). What gun owners really want. *The New Republic* (January 30). Retrieved May 7, 2020, from https://newrepublic.com/article/112194/walter-kirn-gun-owners.

McClay, B. D. (2014). Phenomenology of the gun. Retrieved April 2, 2020, from www.commonwealmagazine.org/phenomenology-gun.

McInerney, Robert G. (2014). A phenomenological account of the shooting spree. *Janus Head* 13(2), 45–59. Retrieved May 20, 2021, from http://janushead.org/wp-content/uploads/2020/07/McInerney-1.pdf.

Morgan, Thad. (2018). The NRA supported gun control when the Black Panthers had the weapons. Retrieved April 6, 2020, from https://www.history.com/news/black-panthers-gun-control-nra-support-mulford-act.

Sellinger, Evan. (2012). The philosophy of the technology of the gun. *The Atlantic* (July 23). Retrieved April 2, 2020, from https://www.theatlantic.com/technology/archive/2012/07/the-philosophy-of-the-technology-of-the-gun/260220/.

Spraggins, Johnnie David. (1995). Body and soul: The sociology of the bodies and emotions of male gun owners. PhD dissertation, University of Michigan. Abstract retrieved April 2, 2020, from https://deepblue.lib.umich.edu/handle/2027.42/104708.

Tonso, William R. (2004). How sociology textbooks address gun control. *Academic questions* 17 (Spring): 67–79.

Part II

FIREARMS AND THE PUBLIC

Messages from the Media, and the Police, and the NRA

5

Media Message on Guns

It's Complicated

Kevin Swift

There is a conversation I frequently have with students, conference guests, and friends in law enforcement. "Tell me if this sounds familiar," I insist. Something happens, anything, a shooting, an arrest gone awry, or any other potentially controversial incident that someone captures a short video of on their smart phone. Within minutes it ends up on social media and often goes viral. Shortly after, a statement is made by law enforcement, an attorney, or those involved. Sometimes an apology, sometimes a denial, or an attempt at a clarifying statement claiming the picture or video was taken out of context. Anyone who has worked in a newsroom understands that at this point, news organizations are involved, whether they want to cover the story or not. The official statement is news, and context must be given to what was being referenced. This has had a dramatic effect on newsrooms across America in the last decade. Having control of the coverage, the narrative or, as theorists might argue, setting the agenda, is largely lost.

We see examples of a changing landscape across news platforms in many ways. One such instance is in regard to an unwritten rule that has existed for decades in news, when dealing with graphic images. "Does the public NEED to see this?" It has been a general rule of thumb for decades, especially in broadcast news. Do the graphic depictions advance the story? If not, we don't need them. Cases such as Bud Dwyer committing suicide during a news conference in 1986 are still the topic of discussion and university lesson plans in journalism ethics classes across America. Three television news affiliates existed in Pittsburgh, Pennsylvania, at the time (WTAE, KDKA, WPXI), each showing a different amount of graphic video to their audiences. Of the three stations, only WPXI, the NBC affiliate, chose to show the full video of the suicide. WTAE, the ABC affiliate (my future employer from 1999–2001), and KDKA, the CBS affiliate, showed Dwyer waiving the gun as he pulled it from an envelope, but stopped the video of him pulling the trigger (Matviko, 1988). The discussion sparks debate to this day as to how much video the audience should have been shown. Did the public have the right to know? Was it too gruesome? Was it simply not necessary in order to inform the audience of what happened? The debate will likely continue.

Fast forward to the age of social media. If an elected official committed suicide in public with a .357 Magnum today, the video would likely go viral before the news organizations made it to their next newscast. No discussion of protecting viewers, children, or veterans with PTSD, who may be triggered or traumatized by the video. The example of Bud Dwyer has now gone the way of competition with social media for many newsrooms (McCabe & Britzky, 2018).

As the American public is inundated with media from a countless and ever-growing number of sources, the message on serious and important topics such as guns becomes increasingly complicated. As we will explore, the general public often doesn't understand what they are watching and reading, they are reinforcing existing and self-serving beliefs, and the message from each form of media is evolving and somewhat different, due to the nature of the medium's format, if nothing else.

THE PUBLIC

As navigating "media" in the twenty-first century becomes increasingly difficult, the need for media literacy is ever more important. Any attempt at understanding the media's message on guns and the public's comprehension of it must include a look at where the public stands on their decoding of those media messages and what the inconsistency might mean to them.

Often, when presenting lectures on media literacy, whether it be to a group of academics or a public forum, I begin by boldly exclaiming, "The general public has no idea what they are watching and reading." Full disclosure, this is done to get the attention of the audience. What I am referring to, for those discussions, is the polarization of the public due to misunderstandings of what they are reading and watching on television. Often, arguments are put forth that journalists are liberal or conservative because they shared their opinion on a "newscast." Only to find out through probing that the individual was watching a cable news program that is actually a talk show, with a panel of guests who were asked to share their opinions. Comments are also made about "the media" showing no respect for people, trespassing on their property to get photographs, and harassing them as they move from place to place. A few simple questions usually unveil that the reference is to paparazzi (who function as freelancers and routinely ignore rules that unionized news practitioners are required to follow) and not a professional news photographer or reporter.

It is not, however, without research and long-argued theory that back up my claim. We can look back nearly a century to Walter Lippmann's seminal study from 1922 for evidence of concern over the public's comprehension (Lippmann, 1921). The first chapter of Lippman's classic, *Public Opinion*, is titled "The World Outside and the Pictures in Our Heads." Lippman compares the public to a "deaf spectator" sitting in the back row (Lippmann, 1921). The author and newspaper columnist was expressing concern over the public's ability to manage media messages, recognize propaganda, and gain an accurate understanding of what was actually happening in their lives, communities, and with global issues. He was concerned that readers, and the growing popularity of radio news, would leave citizens so traumatized that they couldn't navigate their daily lives. He further admitted that journalism, being prone to sensationalism, made the situation worse (Lippmann, 1921). While this was a full century ago, the sentiment holds true that the public perception of their reality may be significantly shaped by pieces of information that don't necessarily add up to a realistic view of society.

Evidence of public confusion is nearly never-ending. The famous media theorist George Gerbner looked deeply into the media's role in society. He based it on a theory called Cultivation Analysis, in which the public is nurtured to believe certain things that are untrue, or exaggerated, about society through various news sources and prime time television viewing (further explained in theory section). Gerbner and his colleagues comprised a list of questions to test public perception of violence:

1. In any given week, what are the chances that you will be involved in some kind of violence? The answers given ranged from 1 in 10 to 1 in 100. The actual answer is 0.41 percent, or less than 1 in 200. In prime time television, however, more than 64 percent of all characters are involved in violence.
2. What percentage of all working males in the United States toil in law enforcement and crime detection? Answers ranged from 1 to 5 percent. The actual answer is around 1 percent. On television, it is 12 percent.
3. Of all of the crimes that occur in the Unites states each year, what proportion is violent crime, like murder, rape, robbery, and assault? Answers ranged from 15 to 25 percent. The *Statistical Abstract of the United States* lists the answer at 10 percent. On television . . . 77 percent of all major characters who commit crimes commit violent crimes. (Baran & Davis, 2015)

While this study focuses on television, it is interesting to note that the perception of "reality" by the public is closer in line with entertainment television than any actual statistical data of the Unites States. Gerbner's research points to the public developing a false sense of reality based on what they are watching. He argued that our own views of the society we live in may be skewed by the media we are taking in.

As for an understanding of news, studies also point to public misperception. A project by the American Press Institute in 2018 revealed several disturbing statistics regarding the public and their understanding of what they are watching and reading:

- 50% are not sure what an op-ed is.
- 43% do not know what the term "attribution" means.
- 42% do not understand how anonymous sourcing works.
- Most adults ages 18–29 say news is fairly inaccurate.
- Most adults age 30 and above consider news fairly accurate.

Journalists and the public do agree on certain aspects of news that would increase trust.

- 68% of people say the news media should offer more information about sources.
- 66% of journalists agree.
- 48% of people say journalists should explain how a story was reported.
- 42% of journalists agree.
- 44% say news organizations should explain their sources better.
- 48% of journalists agree. (American Press, 2014)

Whether the public would actually follow along with these explanations is rather a dubious proposition. The main form of writing a basic news story for over a century has been the inverted pyramid. This is a form in which the main facts are summarized at the top of the story and additional details are pushed to the bottom. Journalists (originally newspapers) use this concept because the belief, through their own research, is that readers scan stories and don't read the whole piece. With this in mind, it is very questionable as to whether the general public would be interested in detailed explanations of sources and story building (Harrower, 2013). Furthermore, television stations, especially after deregulation laws allowed expansion of corporate ownership, have long relied on media consultants to help build a newscast that will grow ratings. The overwhelming trend among consultants over the last twenty years is higher story count and shorter stories, to keep the public, and their short attention span, engaged (Swift, 2013). This is partially due to social media and viewers' ability to read and view stories on phones instead of sitting in front of a television.

As far as knowledge of current events goes, the public does not fare well. A *Newsweek* study conducted a national survey based on the American citizenship test. The results were staggering:

- 29% could not name the sitting vice president.
- 73% could not explain why we fought the Cold War.
- 44% did not know what the Bill of Rights was. (Baran & Davis, 2015)

These statistics lead to the question, Do Americans lack the knowledge or intelligence to be truly informed or understand media messages? Political writer Lee Harris doesn't think so. In his essay, "Are Americans Too Dumb for Democracy?" Harris stated, "The challenge we face is one we all face together—it stems from the maddening complexity and relentless perversity of the world we live in" (Harris, 2012). With media sources ever expanding in the twenty-first century, it stands to reason that this complexity will only continue to grow. Perhaps the only hope for the public is an expansion of media literacy.

THEORIES

To take a legitimate look at the media message on guns, we must examine what the effects of various forms of media might be. If there is a message, or messages, how might media consumers take that information in and be affected by it? We know from significant research that the intended message (encoding) is not always how the consumer identifies and makes sense of those messages (decoding). Statistical evidence given would suggest that the intended meaning is working in that the worldview of consumers reflects what they are watching and reading. Many theories apply, but some are clearly more applicable.

As mentioned previously, cultivation analysis plays a major role in this discussion. A theory developed by George Gerbner, it now represents a significant body of research by many theorists. The term describes "an underlying process of 'acculturation', meaning that people gradually come to accept the view of the world as portrayed on television (in particular) as a true representation of reality and adapt their hopes, fears, and understandings accordingly" (Baran & Davis, 2015). Gerbner and his colleagues further developed their Cultural Indicators Project, which moved beyond the violence index and examined how television cultivated views of reality in both adults and children (Baran & Davis, 2015). Through the process of their research, the Gerbner team made five assumptions:

1. *Television is essentially and fundamentally different that other forms of mass media.*
   Gerbner noted that television is in nearly 100 percent of American homes, is largely free, does not require literacy, combines pictures and words, and is the only medium in history that an individual can interact with from birth to death.
2. *The medium (television) is the "central, cultural arm" of American society.*
   The argument was that television is so accessible to everyone that it is responsible for creating synthetic cultural patterns.
3. *The substance of the consciousness cultivated by TV is not so much specific attitudes and opinions as more basic assumptions about the "facts" of life and standards of judgement on which conclusions are based.*
   This assumption flows from the second and is self-explanatory.
4. *Television's major cultural function is to stabilize social patterns, to cultivate resistance to change.*
   This was seen as a theoretically fiduciary relationship with advertisers. Gerbner and associates called the repetitive messages and images a form of socialization and enculturation.
5. *The observable, measurable, independent contributions of television to the culture are relatively small.*
   (Baran & Davis, 2015)

While this assumption (5) was controversial at the time, it is now regarded as significant and more widely accepted. Gerber was not arguing that the effects of television are small, but that while its contribution to society may appear small, its constant, pervasive influence is crucial. This has been referred to as Gerbner's "ice-age" analogy.

Long before cable news programing targeted audiences with a specific political ideology, Marshall McLuhan saw this trend developing. He described the effects of cultivation as a "retribalizing" (McQuail, 2000) of audiences in that they draw identities from messages that they watch, hear, and read through mass media. This is thought to happen through a systematic and selective view of society (McQuail, 2000).

With respect to both Gerbner and McLuhan's perspectives, we can point to current times and see that the process of deregulating the television industry (lifting of ownership rules, elimination of the Fairness Doctrine, and loosening of public interest requirements, etc.) has allowed more focused and centralized programming aimed at specific audiences. Long before these famous theorists could have seen what was coming, they discovered theories that apply directly to a television market dominated by cable programming geared at specific political, ideological, and personal interests. If television programming was ritualistic affirmation before, it could be much more powerful in doing so with a polarized and specific audience.

There are certain theories that become pervasive. This means the theories move beyond the theorists and the graduate school discussions and into the mainstream. One of those theories is Agenda Setting. Agenda setting, introduced by Maxwell McCombs and Donald Shaw (McQuail, 2000), is the concept that "the media" (often news oriented) are not telling people what to think, but what to think about. By "stacking" news rundowns, placing stories in a specific order, and offering extended words or time to a specific story, they are increasing its importance. Therefore, news professionals are, in turn, setting the agenda for what the audience should think about, debate over, and see as a point of concern.

When considering a media message on guns, agenda setting must be considered and is often thrown around loosely by members of the public. Far-left media consumers might accuse conservative channels of setting the agenda for the NRA and at the same time far-right media consumers might accuse liberal channels of being anti–Second Amendment and setting the agenda for gun regulation. While the media message on guns is complicated, so too is the theory of agenda setting. We must consider whose agenda is being set, if it is possible, and the differences between types of news programming.

When considering the news media, the clearest evidence of agenda setting is in cable news programming. Aside from live, breaking news, cable news programming revolves largely around talk show–style content. A typical hour-long program is usually begun by stating the topics of the day and introducing a panel to discuss those topics and share opinions. While this is often confused with biased journalism, this style of broadcast is very popular and falls most closely into the definition of agenda setting. Many cable shows openly lean left or right of the political spectrum and like-minded viewers and listeners follow along. Helping those tuning in to decide what the important issues of the day might be then becomes quite simple. Clearly, an hour-long program cannot discuss every current affairs topic, but it is the producers of the show who decide what makes the short list.

Local news of all formats is a much more complex discussion. Debate has existed for decades between news professionals and theorists. Professionals argue that something has to go first in a broadcast or a newspaper headline and something has to go last. While a certain amount of decision making goes into the process, the question then becomes, whose agenda is being served? Everett Rogers and James Dearing add that there are at least three different agendas to consider: those of the media, those of the public, and those of policy (McQuail, 2000). The job of local news professionals is to deliver content that is of concern and importance to the market area. In a situation where a producer might think a story is important, a decision could be overridden by a more senior member of the staff who suggests that another story is more important to their particular viewers. Furthermore, broadcast professionals must deal with technical limitations as well. For example, if a decision is made to lead the newscast with a live shot regarding an NRA rally, the transmission signal could fail and the story would then be moved to later in the newscast. Professionals are also often asked to relocate by law enforcement due to safety concerns. This results in significant delay preparation for a live stand-up.

While agenda setting is often mentioned and results in significant criticism of the news media, it is obvious that it is a very complex theory, with many considerations. If a cable news program or national newscast leads with a story about guns (positive or negative), is it network policy to promote a particular view? On the other hand, if a local newscast or print publication leads with the same story, is it agenda setting or an effort to serve the local/regional public who might have a particular concern over that issue? Agenda setting is important to consider, but not as cut and dry as some would describe it. The debate over whether agenda setting theories provide sufficient evidence for a causal relationship has continued for decades (Baran & Davis, 2015).

Finally, we must consider that audiences are active participants (Baran & Davis, 2015). Early research into mass communication focused on media effects on audiences. Beginning in the 1940s theorists began to consider an "active, gratifications-seeking audience" (Baran & Davis, 2015). In laymen's terms, this means that audiences are not simply victims of the mass media, absorbing information like helpless sponges, but are actively participating in and seeking out the information they receive. Much consideration is given to cognitive consistency (consciously working to preserve existing beliefs) and cognitive dissonance (the discomfort created by information that runs counter to existing beliefs). These theories can be viewed, however, as more of a starting-off point than a final conclusion.

Long before social media and smart phones allowed individuals to choose the information they receive, Leon Festinger began researching the theory of selectivity (Baran & Davis, 2015). Selective exposure (audiences exposing themselves to information consistent with their preexisting beliefs) and selective retention (audience members remembering the information they find most meaningful) remain as significant theories in mass communication. This has moved into a more complex approach to research called uses and gratifications (Baran & Davis, 2015). This research looks deeper into satisfactions derived from audience members and their media use, further making the connection between media effects and their consistency with audience needs (Baran & Davis, 2015).

Many theories can be applied to a study of the media message on guns. What's important, in looking at these particular theories, is to understand that there is no silver bullet answer. Various forms of media, through influence by corporations, advertisers, and political agendas, may be cultivating beliefs of audience members. Newscasts and news programming may be setting an agenda of issues and attitudes to raise interest and concern among audience members. However, the audience also plays a role in the process by choosing content for personal reasons. The changing and complex message on guns becomes more intricate as we delve deeper into the issue.

SOCIAL MEDIA

Every generation or so a new medium tends to shift the landscape of how people get news and information. Early newspapers, largely expensive, slow to produce and in magazine format, had to reinvent themselves due to the influence of the penny press. The modernized press had to learn to deal with the immediacy of radio news. Television, while slow to move into the news business, brought film. And with these moving pictures, America would eventually see riots, protests, the assassination of a president, the Vietnam War, man landing on the moon, a shift in politics to a much stronger focus on appearance, Olympics, sports championships from all over the world, and countless other events over the last seventy years. These massive changes are, perhaps, less significant than the seismic shift brought by the internet, social media, smart phones, and file sharing. For the first time in history, news and media outlets of all sorts have major competition for the delivery of information, pictures, and video—from the general public. Taking pictures and video (previously film, followed by videotape and digital files), once a job for a small number of highly skilled and well-trained professionals, is now a common practice among nearly every member of society old enough to operate a smart phone. Long story short, social media is a game changer.

What makes social media so different, as mentioned in the open, is its unchecked immediacy. As smart phone users gather pictures and video, the ability to upload that video to social media sites becomes more readily available. Growing distrust of American news media only helps shocking videos uploaded to social media sites go viral (Schudson, 2019). This has put professional media in unchartered territory as a viral video itself becomes news. Regardless of validity or completeness, when video of a possible crime event goes viral, it is news. News organizations, once proud of taking the time to get stories correct, increased live shots in the race to be first, but were then largely criticized for the immediacy of the twenty-four-hour news cycle. These same news sites now find themselves playing catch up and drawn into stories not yet verified.

Social media could also be viewed as a "wild west" situation. Rules for posting video are changing day by day. Facebook and Instagram (owned by Facebook) do not allow advertisements by gun manufacturers. However, social media "influencers" are free to promote themselves and gain unlimited followers promoting a lifestyle that includes guns (Tiffany, 2019). Because manufacturers cannot advertise guns on these social media websites, they support influencers (usually attractive females) who can (Tiffany, 2019). "Firearm manufacturers use social media to attract audiences to websites that sell firearms: 14.1% of Twitter posts, 53.6% of YouTube videos, and 89.5% of YouTube influencer videos link to websites that facilitate sales" (Jordan et al., 2020). While rules change, clearly social media remains one step ahead. Furthermore, personal videos taken at crime scenes and events do not violate advertising rules, thus the ability to go viral remains.

PROFESSIONAL MEDIA

As for professional news media (local, national, cable, print, broadcast, and their online versions), the research shows a series of misrepresentations. First and foremost is of guns and gun owners themselves. Gun ownership in America is quite common. Pew Research Center statistics show more than four in ten Americans live in a gun-owning household. In rural areas that number jumps to six in ten and around 45 percent throughout the south (Gramlich & Schaeffer, 2019). However, while most gun owners are male, middle aged, and rural, they are often portrayed in news media as living in cities and using their guns for crime (Parker et al., 2017). While this could reflect the location of news outlets, it misrepresents the largest demographic, which is the rural south, 58 percent of whom say they use their guns at ranges and 37 percent of whom use them for hunting (Gramlich & Schaeffer, 2019).

As for actual guns, journalist Ben Hallman explains that reporters are often confused, "The most common mistakes concern how firearms function. Journalists confuse magazines, essentially a spring-loaded box that pushes ammunition up into a gun's chamber, with clips, small metal parts that hold rounds together in place without any moving parts. They misunderstand the effectiveness of silencers, which make gunfire less loud, but not at all quiet" (Hallman, 2017). Hallman continues to say that reporters are often confused about the legality of automatic weapons and the technicalities involved in owning one (automatic weapons produced before 1986 are legal, but rare and expensive).

Perhaps the most pronounced misrepresentation of guns in America is of mass shootings. Six of the ten deadliest shootings have occurred in the last decade. However, this only represents 2 percent of all gun deaths (Hallman, 2017). A fifty-year study shows that while school shootings and lone-wolf-style mass homicides comprised 32 percent of all mass public shootings, they received 75 percent to 80 percent of the *New York Times*'s total coverage of mass shootings. Conversely, disgruntled employee and rampage shootings make up a combined 68 percent of all mass public shootings but received only 15 percent to 20 percent of the news coverage (Silva & Capellan, 2018a). Further research shows that school shootings, those with a high death toll, attacks linked to ideological extremism, and those perpetrated by people of Middle Eastern descent get more coverage (Silva & Capellan, 2018b).

With regard to mass shootings, an undue focus also tends to be put on violent crime and serious mental illness (SMI). While approximately 3 percent to 5 percent of all violent crimes in the United States were attributed to mental illness, a two-decade study indicates that 38 percent of news stories about mental illness focused on violence (Silva & Capellan, 2018).

Previous research has indicated five facts often not mentioned in news coverage:

1. People with SMI are often stigmatized;
2. Negative public attitudes about SMI can lead to reluctance to seek treatment among persons with SMI;
3. Negative public attitudes about SMI can lead to public desire for social distance (e.g., reluctance to live near or work with) persons with SMI;
4. Most people with SMI are not violent; and
5. Predicting violence among persons with SMI is difficult. (Skeem & Mulvey, 2019)

It should come as no surprise with this misrepresentation that 63 percent of Americans surveyed said they believe public mass shootings in the United

States are the result of mental health issues (Silva & Capellan, 2018). Furthermore, Mental Health America reports that 95 percent to 97 percent of homicidal gun violence in America is not carried out by those with mental illness and that a person's history of violence is the only evidence-based predictor of future violence (Skeem & Mulvey, 2019).

The results of this misrepresentation of mass shootings can be seen in several areas. A study conducted at Arizona State University concluded that evidence showed significant signs of contagion (copycat) in high-profile cases with at least four killings (Chatterjee, 2019). Families of victims can be further traumatized and there can be increased prejudice and stigmatization of those living with mental health issues (Recommendations for Reporting, n.d.). Evidence of public concern and fear for safety over the coverage can be seen in consistent spikes in gun purchases in the weeks following the incident. A study by the American Medical Association shows that handgun purchases rose 21 percent of the time after coverage of a mass shooting (Henray, 2019). The question then becomes whether those purchasing handguns are experienced and properly trained. Health organizations and research groups overwhelmingly support the news media using incidents of mass shooting to paint a broader picture of overall gun violence and violent crime in America and highlighting what is or is not representative of the country.

QUESTIONS AND DISCUSSION

So, what's the difference? Those getting their information from television are facing a two-pronged information stream, both of which are delivering unrealistic views of gun use and violent crime. On one hand, television news is focusing on mass shootings. As we have seen, mass shootings constitute only a small percentage of gun violence in America. However, in a world of for-profit media, mass shootings meet nearly all of the elements on the "what makes for a good news story" checklist: Timelines, prominence, proximity, drama, conflict, impact, uniqueness. News professionals hope that a story touches on one or more of these elements. A mass shooting touches on at least five. For this reason alone, television will not likely lose its interest in covering mass shootings any time soon. On the other hand, entertainment television is offering up a much-skewed view of overall violent crime in America. A disproportionate number of prime-time characters are involved in violent crime, often with guns involved. In both cases, the attention to the actions being shown and gun involvement do not align with statistics.

In the case of print media, the message is similar, but one could argue, takes a long view. Instead of television's immediate and sometimes nonstop coverage, newspapers will offer feature coverage that will continue over a longer period of time. The *New York Times* has published nearly 500 articles about Columbine as of 2019 (Goldstone & Partan, 2019). As we have seen, the bias toward mass shootings still exists. The slower, longer approach to the coverage does offer the potential for a broader scope and more realistic view of the big picture.

The message on guns from social media is a fragmented one. For those Americans getting their information through social media and online sources, messages can be not only disproportionate, in terms of focus, but also downright inaccurate. Brief video clips of violence or mass shootings can fail to offer accuracy even within a single story. Members of the public display partial and often personally biased information. While viewing multiple viewpoints and clips from professional news organizations and various online stories may provide a full picture of an incident, the method requires a level of media literacy that, as we have seen, the general public is largely lacking.

The widespread influence of social media makes us ask, Is the tail wagging the dog? With influencers promoting a pro-gun lifestyle, gun manufacturers linking to websites, and everyday users of social media posting videos of shootings, arrests, shocking videos, often involving firearms, there appears to be no consistent message. And with professional media drawn into stories of violence and alleged misconduct, often without the rigors that once existed in journalism, is social media consequently watering down or helping to deteriorate quality in the news media?

Media literacy begs the question: Should Americans have to have a PhD to understand what they are watching and reading? Gaining a full understanding of a news story in the twenty-first century, especially about guns or gun activity, requires an understanding of what one is watching and reading. This requires a level of media literacy not shared by the general public. News professionals and PhDs can surely find the full story through multiple, trusted sources and weed out the nonsense, fake news, and doctored clips. Can we expect the public to do this? It's not likely at this point. A glimmer of hope does exist in the push for starting media literacy at a young age (Herbst, 2019). A graduate professor of mine suggested in 1998 that children should begin learning media literacy in kindergarten. It sounded ridiculous at the time. In a world of countless and growing forms of mass media, however, it does not.

Finally, can we even expect news professionals to offer the full scope? After all, guns in America is a very complicated topic. Violent crime is down, but mass shootings are up (Schmidt, 2014).

The majority of gun owners live in the south, are nonviolent, and have no serious mental health issues. But mass shootings cannot be ignored, especially with the immediate and lasting impact on communities. However, if we are going to expect the public to gain media literacy, through education and researching a multitude of sources, they will surely argue that we can expect professionals to offer a broader and more balanced picture.

CONCLUSIONS

The media message on guns is a fragmented one. Ultimately, the message is that guns are bad, and mostly used for mass shootings by people with serious mental health disorders. The evidence does not support this. It is further complicated by personal bias, lack of public media literacy, and an unrealistic portrayal put forth by various forms of media. The public and professionals face difficult challenges in order to gain a clear understanding of a realistic picture. With ever-expanding forms of media and accessibility to them, the public needs to be educated on a continuing basis. The news media also face challenges. Covering mass shootings is important and will continue. However, not offering a full scope and perspective of guns, gun owners, and violent crime in America, the news media are actually missing a story that would benefit them to fully report. With the difficult demands of the news cycle, an opportunity exists to provide a full picture. It is important to get an accurate message on guns to the American public. But as with all other aspects surrounding the situation, it will be quite complicated.

BIBLIOGRAPHY

American Press Institute. (2014). *How Americans Get Their News*. Reston, VA.

Baran, S. J., and Davis, D. K. (2015). *Mass Communication Theory: Foundations Ferment and Future* (7th ed.). Stamford, CT: Cengage Learning.

Chatterjee, R. (2019). Mass Shootings Can Be Contagious, Research Shows. Radio Interview. Retrieved from https://www.npr.org/sections/health-shots/2019/08/06/748767807/mass-shootings-can-be-contagious-research-shows#mainContent.

Goldstone, H., and Partan, E. (2019). How Mass Media Shapes Perceptions of Mass Shootings. Radio Interview. Retrieved from https://www.capeandislands.org/post/how-mass-media-shapes-perceptions-mass-shootings#stream/0.

Gramlich, J., and Schaeffer, K. (2019). *7 facts about guns in the U.S.* Pew Research Center. Retrieved from https://www.pewresearch.org/fact-tank/2019/10/22/facts-about-guns-in-united-states/.

Hallman, B. (2017). A Gun-Focused News Outlet on What It Takes to Cover Firearms Credibly. *Columbia Journalism Review*. Retrieved from https://www.cjr.org/united_states_project/las-vegas-guns-media-coverage.php.

Harris, L. (2012). Are Americans Too Dumb for Democracy? Retrieved from https://www.aei.org/articles/are-americans-too-dumb-for-democracy/.

Harrower, T. (2013). *Inside Reporting: A Practical Guide to the Craft of Journalism* (3rd ed.). New York: McGraw-Hill.

Henray, T. A. (2019). When Mass Shootings Get Big Media Play, Firearm Purchases Often Rise. American Medical Association. Retrieved from https://www.ama-assn.org/delivering-care/public-health/when-mass-shootings-get-big-media-play-firearm-purchases-often-rise.

Herbst, M. (2020). How to Raise Media-Savvy Kids in the Digital Age. Retrieved from https://www.wired.com/story/kids-digital-media-literacy-tips/.

Jordan, L., Kalin, J., and Dabrowski, C. (2020). Characteristics of Gun Advertisements on Social Media: Systematic Search and Content Analysis of Twitter and YouTube Posts. *Journal of Medical Internet Research*. Retrieved from https://www.ncbi.nlm.nih.gov/pmc/articles/PMC7148552/#:~:text=social%20media%20platforms.-,Results,to%20websites%20that%20facilitate%20sales.

Lippmann, W. (1921). *Public Opinion*. Retrieved from https://wps.pearsoncustom.com/wps/media/objects/2429/2487430/pdfs/lippmann.pdf.

Matviko, John (1988, April). How Far Do You Go and How Much Do You Show: Pittsburgh Television News Media and the R. Budd Dwyer Suicide. Retrieved from https://eric.ed.gov/?id=ED294257.

McCabe, D., and Britzky, H. (2018, March). Social Media under the Microscope for Role in Gun Violence. Retrieved from https://www.axios.com/republicans-social-media-guns-1520969224-b09783d0-60b2-4b56-af94-d3ad6d5de6e1.html.

McQuail, D. (2000). *McQuail's Mass Communication Theory* (4th Ed.). London: SAGE Publications LTD.

Mental Health America. Gun Deaths, Violence and Mental Health. Retrieved from https://www.mhanational.org/gun-deaths-violence-and-mental-health.

Parker, K., Horowitz, J. M., Igielnik, R., Oliphant, J. B., and Brown, A. (2017). America's Complex Relationship with Guns. Retrieved from https://www.pewsocialtrends.org/2017/06/22/americas-complex-relationship-with-guns/.

Recommendations for Reporting on Mass Shootings. Retrieved from https://www.reportingonmassshootings.org/

Schmidt, M. (2014, 9/24). F.B.I. Confirms a Sharp Rise in Mass Shootings since 2000. *New York Times*. Retrieved from file:///C:/Users/Kevin%20Swift/Desktop/F.B.I.%20Confirms%20a%20Sharp%20Rise%20in%20Mass%20Shootings%20Since%202000%20-%20The%20New%20York%20Times.html.

Schudson, M. (2019). The Fall, Rise and Fall of Media Trust. Retrieved from https://www.cjr.org/special_report/the-fall-rise-and-fall-of-media-trust.php.

Silva, J., and Capellan, J. (2018a). A Comparative Analysis of Media Coverage of Mass Public Shootings: Examining Rampage, Disgruntled Employee, School, and Lone-Wolf Terrorist Shootings in the United States. Retrieved from https://journals.sagepub.com/doi/full/10.1177/0887403418786556.

Silva, J., and Capellan, J. (2018b). The Media's Coverage of Mass Public Shootings in America: Fifty Years of Newsworthiness. Retrieved from https://www

.tandfonline.com/doi/abs/10.1080/01924036.2018.1437458?needAccess=true&journalCode=rcac20&.

Skeem, J., and Mulvey, E. (2019). What Role Does Serious Mental Illness Play in Mass Shootings, and How Should We Address it? Retrieved from https://onlinelibrary.wiley.com/doi/full/10.1111/1745-9133.12473.

Swift, K. (2013). *The Changing Landscape of Television News at a Time of Deregulation: A Case Study of Practitioners in Three Major Markets*. Ann Arbor, MI: ProQuest.

Tiffany, K. (2019). The Hired Guns of Instagram. Retrieved from https://www.vox.com/features/2019/6/19/18644129/instagram-gun-influencers-second-amendment-tactical-community.

6

Guns, Maps, and Media

Silencers and Loud Reports

Dan Trigoboff

Public records are "the property of the people," North Carolina law says. Such records are to be provided to the people of the state "at minimal cost" (NC Code 132-1, n.d.).

Tell that to the *Cherokee Scout.*

When *Scout* editor Robert Horne, in 2013, asked the Cherokee county sheriff for a list of local residents who had applied for or had been granted a gun permit, he and his newspaper paid a heavy price. And they never even got the records.

Editor Horne's request for the information was denied on grounds that were at best, at the time, legally questionable. And after rejecting the request, Sheriff Keith Lovin made it public, leading to threats of violence against newspaper staff and their families, and the further threat to the newspaper of financial ruin (Elliston, 2013; Farhi, 2013).

The ensuing controversy demonstrated the long-standing tension among media, gun owners, agencies, and legislators that has been exacerbated by the quicker and greater access to information brought by the internet. The Murphy-based North Carolina newspaper is one of several media organizations around the nation that sought gun permit information from public records, sometimes following mass shootings, and got a lot more in response than anticipated (Farhi, 2013).

Emotional, potentially dangerous responses came from those who believe gun ownership is a private matter, even when such records were expressly designated for public access, and exacerbated conflicts about government transparency typically brought by news organizations in agencies and courtrooms for decades. Ultimately, state and local gun records have become less accessible than ever (Elliston, 2013).

And in the case of the *Cherokee Scout* in North Carolina, where the information requested was considered public record at the time, despite the rejection of its lawful request it was left apologizing humbly, humiliatingly, in the opinions of media commentators. The newspaper apologized to the local community and thanked it for making it see the error of its ways. The *Scout* even thanked the sheriff who hung the target on the newspaper and its employees. And amid all that, Robert Horne, the editor who made the request, lost his job. So much for "minimal cost" (NC Code 132-1, n.d.).

The North Carolina's legal code at §132-1 defines "public records" as "all documents, papers, letters, maps, books, photographs, films, sound recordings, magnetic or other tapes, electronic data-processing records, artifacts, or other documentary material, regardless of physical form or characteristics, made or received pursuant to law or ordinance in connection with the transaction of public business by any agency of North Carolina government or its subdivisions." *Scout* editor Horne cited that law when he asked Cherokee County Sheriff Keith Lovin for a list of "all Cherokee County residents who have applied for and/or received a concealed carry permit." Lovin quickly rejected Horne's request on February 19, 2013. In his response, though, the sheriff did not address Horne's citation of the state's public records law. He cited instead §14-403, which dealt with issuance, form, and expiration of gun permits under the heading, "Permit issued by sheriff; form of permit; expiration of permit" (N.C. Code, n.d.).

The sheriff wrote that "[t]here is nothing within the statue that makes the information contained therein a public record," referring to §14-403, which does not address access to public records. "The mere fact that it is information gathered by this office, in and of itself, is not enough," he said. In an editorial, the *Scout* said it had no plan to publish the list. But the county's decision to suppress, Horne said, alarmed him (Elliston, 2013).

Numerous public officials had acknowledged prior to the Cherokee County controversy that gun permit information at the time was not confidential under the law at the time. Four Republican state representatives, in fact, had introduced a bill to change the law and expressly exclude such information from public access. A similar bill was introduced in the state Senate. Cherokee was among several North Carolina counties where leaders felt a need to separate gun permit information from accessible public records under then-current law, adopting a resolution "To Request Legislation to Exempt Certain Records of the Sheriffs' Office from the Public Records Act." And among the speakers in support of the resolution to exempt gun permit information from public records going forward was Cherokee County Sheriff Keith Lovin—*the same* Sheriff Lovin who ignored *the same* Public Records Act in his response to Horne (Elliston, 2013, para. 7).

After the sheriff denied the request for public records, he decided public access to government documents was important, at least sometimes, and made Horne's request public. Lovin posted both Horne's letter and his own response on the sheriff's Facebook page. "As the Sheriff of Cherokee County," Lovin told his social media friends and followers, "I feel that it is my responsibility to provide for the safety of all citizens of Cherokee County. My Office will continue to support the constitution [*sic*] and all amendments including the Second Amendment. I will continue to uphold my Oath of Office and serve the Citizens of Cherokee County" (Elliston, 2013, para. 18).

What one local journalist called "a firestorm of comments" ensued, mostly in support of Lovin and in opposition to Horne and the *Scout*, which was reportedly inundated with complaints, subscription cancellations, and, according to staff, threats. Commenters suggested a boycott and that the newspaper "be run out of town" (Elliston, 2013).

The *Scout* responded, at first with a mix of conciliation and contrition. "The readers have spoken, and the *Cherokee Scout* has heard you—loud and clear," the statement began. In fact, the statement was released in the names of publisher David Brown and Sheriff Lovin. Following the apparent opening capitulation, there was a suggestion of defiance. "We should have expected Sheriff Keith Lovin's posting of his correspondence with Editor Robert Horne, because he knows he can't win in a court of law but wants to win in the court of public opinion" (Elliston, 2013, para. 21).

"However," the statement continued, "despite the fact that the Scout likely would win a lawsuit, we have no intention of taking it to court." The statement also lamented that Horne, "a U.S. Marine and a veteran of Operation Desert Storm who instructed members of the military on the firing range during his service" was also "a Marine who actually has been threatened today by near-hysterical residents as a result of the sheriff's actions" (Elliston, 2013, para. 22).

"We must be vigilant in maintaining the public's right to know," the statement continued. "We cannot give away our rights to access to public records. If we do, soon there will be no way to hold government officials accountable for their actions, which will lead to that dystopian future so many gun advocates dread."

The statement closed largely the way it opened. "Our readers have spoken," the statement said, "and we always listen to you. We are retracting our request, and the matter is closed" (Elliston, 2013, para. 24). But as much as the newspaper wanted to put it behind it, the matter was not closed to the public. Its anger did not abate. Brown issued another statement, this time under his name, and with a tone far more conciliatory, one which drew the ire of media commentators:

"The *Cherokee Scout* made a tremendous error in judgement this week, and thanks to our readers we learned a tough lesson. As publisher of your local newspaper, I want to apologize to everyone we unintentionally upset with our request for a list of those who have or have applied for a concealed carry permit. We had no idea the reaction it would cause" (Elliston, 2013, para. 26).

"Sheriff Keith Loven [*sic*] had the best interests of the people of Cherokee County at heart when he denied our request. The Scout would like to offer him an apology as well." The *Scout* praised Lovin and his staff for quickly responding to the threats made against Horne—threats that followed Lovin's posting and rejecting Horne's request without addressing the state's public records law. The newspaper also noted that the sheriff "graciously" accepted Horne's invitation for a sit-down (Elliston, 2013).

Brown had cited Horne's military service, and now cited his own local Murphy, North Carolina, roots, and Horne's rural background: "As for myself, I attended Murphy High School, I was married and baptized here, and three of my children are proud Bulldogs," he wrote (Elliston, 2013, para 28).

"Many of you have asked where Horne is from. He is from a small town in South Georgia—Cairo, Ga., to be exact. It is a rural area much like Murphy, and his roots are helping him better understand this community" (Reeve, 2013, para. 11). Brown was assuring his readers, *Atlantic* writer Elspeth Reeve wrote, with some sarcasm, that Horne was "no big-city gun-grabber" (Reeve, 2013).

But only days after Horne's initial request, Brown sent out another statement, which said: "Robert Horne has resigned, effective immediately, as editor of the *Cherokee Scout* and *Andrews Journal*, . . . Horne is leaving the local newspapers to pursue other opportunities as well as relocate closer to family. We wish Robert well in all his future endeavors," said David Brown, publisher of the *Scout* and *Journal*. "He's a good man who has done a lot of positive things for the area that should be remembered" (Hutchins, 2013, para. 1).

Horne said he enjoyed his time working at the *Cherokee Scout* and *Andrews Journal*, where he had worked since 2005. "I have learned a lot from David and the staff here. I will take what I have learned here and use it in my future endeavors. I wish the *Scout* and *Journal* all the best moving forward" (Hutchins, 2013, para. 2).

In an interview, Horne said he was leaving both the newspaper and the area for "the safety of my family. I could not put my wife through this" (Farhi, 2013, para. 6).

Brown told the *Columbia Journalism Review*, which had followed the story, that he preferred not to comment further. "Everything's still pretty raw right now," he said. "Anything I might say would only add fuel to the fire" (Hutchins, 2013, para. 13).

Judgment came swiftly and harshly from media peers. The *Atlantic* called Brown's apology "absolutely groveling" (Reeve, 2013). Media blogger Jim Romenesko called Brown's later note to readers the "most incredible newspaper apology ever" (Reeve, 2013). In a commentary, the *Philadelphia Daily News*'s Will Bunch called Brown's apology "embarrassing" and "sniveling" and dubbed Murphy, North Carolina, "Where American Journalism Went to Die" (Bunch, 2013).

"So let's think about that," Bunch wrote. "[T]he publisher is apologizing to the people who made threats against one of his employees. How low can you go?" (Bunch, 2013, para. 7).

Bunch said, "Alleged publisher David Brown is the worst person in American journalism . . . at this moment," and concluded that "[i]f a newspaper publisher won't defend the 1st Amendment rights of a free media," Bunch said, "then America is doomed. Get out of the business . . . now" (Bunch, 2013, para. 11).

The *Burlington* (N.C.) *Times* gave a slightly more positive diagnosis than Will Bunch. It suggested American journalism was on "life support." Essentially, said the *Times*, "the newspaper apologized to readers for seeking a public record it was entitled to by law" (Taylor, 2013, para. 7). The *Scout* editor, it noted, resigned in terror, not disgust. And the sheriff, to whom the newspaper apologized, and praised, violated the law and "enflamed the public to hysterical levels." Staff at the *Scout*, the *Times* said, "got scared. As well they should. There are a handful of unhinged people out there in the land where Olympic bomber Eric Rudolph went to hide" (Taylor, 2013, para. 10). Eric Rudolph, sometimes called the Olympic Park Bomber, was convicted for a series of politically motivated bombings which killed two people and injured more than 100 others. He was arrested in Murphy, North Carolina, in 2003 after hiding for five years in western North Carolina. In June 2020, the imprisoned Rudolph released a handwritten appeal over his conviction (Robinson, 2020).

Cecil Bothwell, a former investigative reporter for the western North Carolina *Mountain Xpress*, recognized local challenges and offered a more charitable perspective. Bothwell said sheriffs in the area had enormous power, and that his newspaper commonly faced intimidation and threats when he reported on the sheriff in another western North Carolina county. He said vans with dark windows sometimes parked outside the homes of newspaper staff. Bothwell, who had become a city councilman in Asheville, North Carolina, said deputies had told him of threats Sheriff Bobby Medford made against him. Although nothing came of the threats, Bothwell acknowledged being frightened, and said he took evasive measures that included disguises and borrowing friends' cars. Medford was sent to prison in 2008 on public corruption and extortion charges and died in custody in June 2020 (Hutchins, 2013).

Margaret Williams, news editor of the *Mountain Xpress*, was also more sympathetic than many in the more distant press. "I doubt it's fair for fellow journalists to judge Cherokee Scout publisher David Brown so harshly," she wrote. "Few people likely know the whole story" (Hutchins, 2013, para. 27).

"More worrisome," Williams wrote, "is what the [Cherokee County] sheriff's reaction says about the state of law enforcement and the understanding about public-records law" (Hutchins, 2013, para. 27).

The *Cherokee Scout*, journalist and teacher Corey Hutchins noted in the *Columbia Journalism Review*, "is a small, western North Carolina newspaper. But the *Scout*'s story is larger than that, part of a saga about guns and newspapers and public records that is not likely to end soon" (Hutchins, 2013, para. 34).

The North Carolina General Assembly enacted legislation the following year to exclude from records accessible to the public concealed handgun permit information given to sheriff's departments. Records of permits denied continue to be public records. Dealers must keep records of all sales, but the records maintained by dealers are not public records (K. Gun Permits, n.d.). In 2019, Cherokee County was among the first eastern U.S. areas to declare itself a "Gun Sanctuary," that would resist stricter state or federal gun control measures (Eldridge, 2019; Price, 2019).

The "saga about guns and newspapers and public records" to which Corey Hutchins referred had been around for quite a while. In 1999, Michigan's Supreme Court closed access to records of registered handguns. The following year, Michigan's Court of Appeals upheld a lower court ruling that denied the *Detroit Free Press* access to the names of state legislators on concealed gun permit applications, allowing the newspaper to see only permit applications with the names removed. The Michigan courts cited privacy rights, and said that the requirement to show a need for the carry permit indicated disclosure could jeopardize safety. Moreover, the appeals court said, applying for a concealed weapon permit a "potentially embarrassing detail of one's private life" (Court Denies Newspaper, 2000, para. 2).

The RCFP monitored numerous states taking steps to exempt gun records from public access, sometimes following clashes over the use of the records, in the early years of the twentieth century, and the challenges they presented for journalists. Indiana reporters writing a story about increases in requests for silencers, permits, and automatic weapons found much of the information they sought from public records sealed. A reporter with the *Indianapolis Star* believed state law changed to keep the information secret following an investigative story that found 450 felons were illegally granted concealed carry permits by State Police (Reporting on Gun Permit Data).

The most notorious use of gun permit data by a media organization came not in North Carolina, but in White Plains, New York. In late 2012, following the horrific mass shooting at the Sandy Hook elementary school in Newtown, Connecticut, the *Journal News* posted on its website an interactive map, compiled from available records, that included the names and addresses of handgun-permit owners in New York's Westchester and Rockland counties. The map contained thousands of dots; clicking on each identified the name and address of the handgun permit holders at that location (Horowitz, 2012).

The newspaper said it believed informing people about legal weapons in their neighborhoods was a public service. *Journal News* President and Publisher Janet Hasson said the information about gun ownership provided on the map allowed parents to make informed decisions about their children's safety. "Frequently," Hasson wrote, "the work of journalists is not popular. One of our roles is to report publicly available information on timely issues, even when unpopular. We knew publication of the database (as well as the accompanying article providing context) would be controversial, but we felt sharing information about gun permits in our area was important in the aftermath of the Newtown shootings." She declined a request to elaborate, the *Post* reported (Goodman, 2013).

But gun owners expressed outrage. In response, some individuals targeted the *Journal News*'s publisher, editors, and reporters by publishing private details about them online, including home phone numbers, addresses, and pictures of their homes. Employees were threatened, including executives at parent group Gannett, targeted by their home addresses and phone numbers (Horowitz, 2012). Armed security guards were hired (Goodman, 2013).

Area political leaders also took note. Local State Senator Greg Ball said, "This is clearly a violation of privacy and needs to be corrected immediately." Ball called the newspaper's editors "asinine" (Trotter, 2013, para. 1) and said they "have gone out of their way to place a virtual scarlet letter on law-abiding firearm owners throughout the region" (Seller, 2012, para. 5). Ball later said the interactive map might have been responsible for a White Plains burglary in which guns were targeted (Silverman, 2013).

Local officeholders noted that many public records laws were enacted before technology like social media and Google maps. Others noted the high number of retired police officers, among other responsible professionals, who held gun permits and did not want their personal information released (Goodman, 2013).

Lawmakers in New York and other states moved quickly to block public access to gun records following the *Journal News*'s publication of its map. As of March 2013, only five states—including North Carolina—gave unfettered access to information about holders of concealed carry permits, and those laws—including North Carolina's—proved fragile (Malewitz, 2013).

After passage of the New York law, the newspaper decided to take down the map. As a news organization, it said, it constantly defended the public's right to know, and insisted the newspaper wasn't caving to public pressure or intimidation.

"We know our business is a controversial one, and we do not cower," she said (Beaujon, 2013, para. 2). Nor, the newspaper said, was it acknowledging a mistake, and it cited praise from some members of the community. The publisher said that the database had been up for twenty-seven days and had been viewed 1.2 million times. Eventually the information would be dated. She also acknowledged that many, including legislators, favored making such information private, and said "we are not deaf to voices" calling for new rules (New York newspaper, 2013, para. 9).

Wrote publisher Hasson:

> While the new law does not require us to remove the data, we believe that doing so complies with its spirit. For the past four weeks, there has been vigorous debate over our publication of the permit data, which has been viewed nearly 1.2 million times by readers. One of our core missions as a newspaper is to empower our readers with as much information as possible on the critical issues they face, and guns have certainly become a top issue since the massacre in nearby Newtown, Conn. Sharing as much public information as possible provides our readers with the ability to contribute to the discussion, in any way they wish, on how to make their communities safer. . . . We remain committed to our mission of providing the critical public service of championing free speech and open records. (Beaujon, 2013, para 10)

Washington Post media critic Erik Wemple called the response "cowardly."

Media critics met the news with mixed sentiments. Journalist and educator Jeff Jarvis said he "struggled with this matter." But, he said, "I would hate to see news organizations being condemned for trafficking in public information. I would also hate to see journalists end up campaigning to make *less* information public. Journalists of all people should be fighting to make *more* information public" (Jarvis, 2013 para. 2).

Government today, Jarvis argued, "is secret by default and transparent by force when it must become transparent by default and secret by necessity. There are," he acknowledged, "necessary secrets regarding security, criminal investigation, and citizens' privacy" (Jarvis, 2013, para. 2). He added:

> There is a public interest in this information being available and accessible. It allows the public, journalists and neighbors included, to keep watch on the

> process of government issuing permits. It enables the public, news organizations and others, to correlate data about permits with data about crime and safety. At a personal level, it enables me as a parent to know whether the homes where my children go play have arms, and to be able to discuss with the parents there whether their weapons are safely secured. These are matters of public safety, of public interest. . . . [T]here's no half-pregnant, . . . In the net age, there's no slightly public. (Jarvis, 2013, para. 1)

New York Times media writer David Carr said his initial "reflex" as an absolutist on matters of open data, public records need to be public, "and as agents of transparency, news media outlets should help cast sunlight on those records. In that context, data is not good or bad, right or wrong; it is information that should be there for the asking, taking or publishing." Regarding the White Plains map, "I followed a simple logic: the records were open, the public interest was high and journalism that blends both those things makes sense" (Carr, 2013, para. 2).

"But on reflection, was it really journalism? Not so much. The accompanying article was about whether gun permits should be public, but the newspaper seemed to have all but decided that debate by publishing the map. More problematic was the closeness in time to the Newtown massacre, which served to cast suspicion and guilt in tendentious ways. By dropping the records into the maelstrom of a mass shooting, was *The Journal News* merely putting data-driven link bait out there?" (Carr, 2013, para. 3).

The job of journalists, Carr said, is to draw attention, to create context, provide analysis and insight. "Simply pointing out that something is public as the sole reason for republishing it is not a sufficient justification," he said. "It is one thing to have a public database available that lets me look up whether the neighbor I am feuding with might have a gun permit. It is quite another to publish the names and addresses of all my neighbors who own guns. The decision lacked a rationale. It was what we in the business call 'b matter' in search of a 'lead'" (Carr, 2013).

Leonard Downie Jr., former executive editor of the *Washington Post*, now an educator at Arizona State University's Walter Cronkite School of Journalism and Mass Communication, commented, "You have to have a very high standard when you publish the addresses of people to begin with, even though those are public" (Carr, 2013, para. 6).

Not long after the controversies in Murphy and White Plains, the state of Louisiana passed laws making it a crime to made public the name or address of a concealed gun permit holder or applicant. The law contained exceptions, as permission to publish the name of someone charged with a felony. But journalists and media lawyers nonetheless argued that the law was unconstitutional as a prior restraint on legally obtained information (Louisiana Criminalizes, 2013).

Obviously not all gun owners opposing gun permit information as public record made angry threats instead of arguments. The Electronic Privacy Information Center asserted that "the disclosure of gun ownership records could provide a potential road map for criminals in search of firearms, as well as potential for neighborhood gossip" (Gutierrez, n.d., para. 1). Gun ownership advocates, including the National Rifle Association's Institute for Legislative Action, argue that publication serves no public purpose, and exposes "responsible gun owners and their families to a heightened risk of crimes and fear of harassment," NRA-ILA said as recently as 2020 (Gun Licenses, 2020, para. 11). "Given the amount of information already available online, enterprising criminals or anti-gun doxxers will have little trouble in identifying some licensees using a full name and zip code" (Gun Licensees, 2020, para. 11). The NRA claimed in 2004 that research showed "the principle reason right-to-carry laws deter crime is that criminals do not know who is armed" (Penrod, 2004, para. 18).

Years earlier, NRA-ILA suggested a clash of constitutional rights. When Virginia's *Roanoke Times*, in 2007, "made the irresponsible and dangerous choice to post a searchable database of Virginia's Right-to-Carry permit holders on its website," albeit temporarily, and then said it would no longer accept advertising for gun shows, NRA-ILA said, "A 'Pillar' Of The First Amendment Discriminates Against The Second" (Gun Licensees, 2020).

EPIC said that gun ownership advocates "believe it is their legal right to own and use a firearm, and that anonymity is critically linked this ownership" (Gutierrez, n.d., para. 1).

Constitutional claims may be a stretch in either direction. The Second Amendment expressly mentions "[a] well regulated militia," which does not indicate secrecy or anonymity (A "Pillar," 2007). But neither does constitutional jurisprudence recognize a clear right of journalists to gather information. Media law scholars and media advocates contend that a right to gather and report information is inherent in the First Amendment.

"A people who mean to be their own governors must arm themselves with the power which knowledge gives," founding father James Madison wrote in 1822 to W. T. Barry, at various times a congressman, U.S. senator, Kentucky secretary of state and lieutenant governor, and U.S. Postmaster General. Madison said, "A popular Government, without popular information, or the means of acquiring it, is but a Prologue to a Farce or a Tragedy; or, perhaps both. Knowledge will forever govern ignorance" (United States Constitution, Amendment II).

For all Madison's unparalleled influence over the nation's cornerstone document, a constitutional right to gather information is not as clear as the right to publish information, which has developed over a century of jurisprudence.

The Records Act of 1789 (the year the Constitution took effect), signed by George Washington, directed federal departments to set up their own procedures and policies for keeping and sharing documents (Letter from James Madison, 1822).

The Supreme Court has limited its endorsement, recognizing that newsgathering is important to advancing First Amendment interests, but not clearly defining a First Amendment right of access to government information. Numerous appeals courts also have found no explicit right to gather government information, or limited rights at best (1 Stat 68, 1789).

The Supreme Court has found a broader constitutional right of access to courts, but other records, federal, state, and local, are regulated largely by federal and state "freedom of information" statutes, sometimes called "sunshine laws," which are subject to change and often require time and the intervention of a judge (Chemerinsky, 2000). Future Supreme Court Justice Louis Brandeis famously wrote in 1913 that "sunlight is said to be the best of disinfectants." Brandeis's comment was considered an important endorsement of open government in a democracy (Kraft, 2009). Yet that same Louis Brandeis is also credited as a pioneer in privacy law, advocating a right of privacy earlier, although he acknowledged exceptions for matters of public interest (Brandeis, 1914).

University of Arizona journalism professor David Cuillier wondered if the public wouldn't be better off with no law than with flawed statutes. "Public record statutes in a lot of ways give government officials the ability to legally delay releasing information, to deny information on often questionable reasoning," he said, almost channeling Sheriff's Lovin's response to Robert Horne. "They will just pick an exemption—personnel, or it's under investigation, or prejudicial discussions. The law allows those pegs to hang those denials on" (Dyer, 2016, para. 17).

"We need to make access to information a constitutional right in this country," Cuillier says. "We need to make it a human right, like it is in Europe, like having clean water and not being tortured" (Dyer, 2016, para. 57).

Craig, Ketterer, and Yousuf noted in 2017 the relatively small body of academic literature regarding the ethics of "data journalism" which, they said, was not clearly defined, but appeared to have grown and expanded from such earlier designations as "computer assisted reporting," "computational journalism," and "precision journalism." "The fundamental difference between data and traditional journalism," they concluded, "is the analysis involves digitized data. Journalists traditionally conducted investigations using paper records and analyzed the resulting data using mathematical techniques. With the advent of personal computers and the increased availability of government databases, the analysis is now often conducted using statistical programs that require specialized knowledge to interpret." Computer analysis, they noted, set a new standard in investigative journalism, allowing more precise data even when reporters continue to use traditional journalism techniques.

"Internet technology allows journalists to post data to media websites," they noted, "making it easier for the public to access the information and to assess it." Among the tools for communicating data broadly, they said, were interactive graphics such as Google Maps. "These changes in journalism are occurring during an unprecedented increase in the volume of data collected by private industry and government, including personal data, and an equally unprecedented expansion of computing power and storage necessary to process and analyze data in new ways." But although an abundance of data can produce excellent journalism, they said, data collection can lead to concerns about truthfulness, harm, and privacy (Craig et al., 2017).

University of Ottawa law professor Teresa Scassa found that some information "which had been acceptably public when contained in a register accessible only through a government office or an access to information request, was unacceptably public" when displayed graphically and more accessibly the internet (Scassa, 2014, p. 404).

Access to some public records raised issues of privacy and potential dangers even before the wider distribution channels and expanded access brought by digital media and the Internet. In 1989, the murder of actress-model Rebecca Schaeffer brought attention to information seemingly harmless as a name and address on a driver's license.

An obsessed fan had written the twenty-one-year old actress and attempted to meet her at the studio where she starred in the television show *My Sister Sam*. He later paid a private data broker for her home address in Los Angeles—information gained from California motor vehicle records. Schaeffer was shot to death at the door of her apartment.

Similar stories of women stalked, threatened, and attacked by former husbands or boyfriends followed the news of Schaeffer's death (Barnett, 2001). California and other states passed numerous "anti-stalking" laws, which included restrictions on public access to addresses gleaned from driving records. Barbara Boxer, the U.S. Senator from California, included an amendment to the Violent Crime Control Act of 1994 barring state employees from releasing such information as names, addresses, phone numbers, social security numbers, and photographs from motor vehicle records (Barnett, 2001).

Only one senator took up the journalists' position, that such limitations on public access to information would harm newsgathering. Utah Republican Orrin Hatch voiced concerns from his state's chapter of the Society of Professional Journalists, which cited numerous examples of important journalism that resulted from the use of driver's license records. Those stories included one from Rhode Island's *Providence Journal*, which used public records to identify school bus drivers with dangerous driving records, and another that used public driving records to reveal airline pilots who were flying despite losing driving privileges over alcohol-related offenses (Barnett, 2001).

Such information, accessed by journalists, can also be used to tell meaningful stories, the Reporter's Committee for Freedom of the Press (RCFP), a journalists' association, said in an editorial on its website. Those stories may include "whether home invasions, burglaries, or even accidental shootings are higher or lower in areas with a lot of homeowners who have guns." Computer-assisted reporting, it said, while relatively new can nonetheless allow statistical analyses of data to report or compare communities regarding "health care, education, crime and much more, or just report how their citizens are being served by government or affected by trends and other factors" (Bulk Data, n.d., para. 10).

RCFP has reported as far back as 2000 on state and local efforts to keep gun permit information from public access. It advocated keeping such records available to the public and not subject to legislators' determination regarding what could be "categorically exempt from disclosure, regardless of the fact that this data represents the documentation of exactly what our governments are doing and for whom" (Bulk Data, n.d., para. 4).

"When we let this data be closed, the end result is . . . governments granting certain privileges to individuals in secret, which runs counter to our country's democratic principles. The process of giving out gun permits is a state licensing scheme; it's not only newsworthy, but journalists can keep tabs on whether the system is working and keeping guns out of dangerous individuals' hands" (Bulk Data, n.d., para. 5).

For gun rights advocates, notably the NRA, battling public record-keeping regarding gun ownership has been a priority. But private organizations keeping records—even without subjects' consent—may be a different matter. News website *Buzzfeed* reported in 2013 that the NRA itself cast a wide net, building a massive database through years of acquiring the same gun permit lists from state and county offices purchased—or attempted—as newspapers, as well as lists of attendees from gun shows, from students of NRA-certified gun training, hunting permit lists, subscribers to gun-oriented publications, and more. Numerous state and local officials confirmed requests from NRA representatives for information. Experts said the information-gathering process was highly sophisticated, similar to high-tech strategies used in two successful presidential campaigns by Barack Obama. A former NRA lobbyist told *Buzzfeed* the database likely covered tens of millions. The NRA declined to discuss the database, its assembly, or its use, *Buzzfeed* said (Friess, 2013).

Information gathered by an advocacy organization for likely recruiting and shaping messages, even beyond gun issues, clearly serves a different purpose than identifying gun owners by name and/or address, even if both arguably advance agendas and both give discretion to the information holder. People surrender personal information every day, and not only to the NRA. Media scholar Neil Postman wrote in 1985, years before the internet became both a major disseminator and collector of information, that while the year 1984 passed without George Orwell's vision of an "externally imposed oppression," an equally chilling dystopic vision was overlooked. In Aldous Huxley's *Brave New World*, Postman wrote, "No Big Brother is required to deprive people of their autonomy, maturity and history. As he saw it, people will come to love their oppression, to adore the technologies that undo their capacities to think" (Postman, 1985, foreword).

Citing numerous data security compromises, the Brookings Institution, considered a liberal think tank, said in 2018 that "[m]ore and more data about each of us is being generated faster and faster from more and more devices, and we can't keep up" (Kerry, 2018, para. 2).

Yet for all the fear of Big Brother, the Reporters Committee notes that exempting gun records from public access leaves the information entirely in the hands of government. Governments, noted RCFP, in an editorial, "will always try and restrict or prohibit public access or force those seeking it to justify their request." Some restrictions make sense, RCFP acknowledged. "But ultimately, it has to be left up to the journalists who want to make use of public information how they will keep it and relay it to the public. Anything less," RCFP said, is "simply a decision to vest the power of public knowledge with the government, which may sometimes be truly looking out for the interests of citizens, but often is simply trying to avoid the accountability that comes with meaningful access to records" (Bulk Data, n.d., para. 12).

And so far, as the stories indicate, it's been the media held most accountable.

BIBLIOGRAPHY

1 Stat. 68. (1789).

A "pillar" of the First Amendment discriminates against the Second. (2007, October 26). NRA-ILA. Retrieved from https://www.nraila.org/articles/20071026/a-pillar-of-the-first-amendment-discr.

Barnett, Brooke. (2001). Use of public record databases in newspaper and television newsrooms. *Federal Communications Law Journal*: Vol. 53: Iss. 3, Article 7.

Beaujon, A. (January 18, 2013). Journal News removes gun map. Poynter. Retrieved from https://www.poynter.org/reporting-editing/2013/journal-news-removes-gun-map/.

Brandeis, L. (1914). *Other people's money and how the bankers use it.* New York: Frederick A. Stokes. Retrieved from: https://archive.org/stream/otherpeoplesmone00bran#page/n5/mode/2up.

Bulk data—whether gun records or anything else—must remain accessible. Reporters Committee for Freedom of the Press. Retrieved from: https://www.rcfp.org/journals/bulkdata-whether-gun-recor/.

Bunch, W. (February 25, 2013). Murphy, N.C., is where American journalism went to die. *Philadelphia Enquirer*. Retrieved from https://www.inquirer.com/philly/blogs/attytood/Murphy-NC-is-whereAmericanjournalism-went-to-die.html.

Carr, D. (January 13, 2013). Guns, maps and data that disturb. *New York Times*. Retrieved from https://www.nytimes.com/2013/01/14/business/media/guns-maps-and-disturbingdata.html.

Chemerinsky, E. (2000). Protect the press: A First Amendment standard for safeguarding aggressive newsgathering, *Richmond L. Rev.* 1143.

Court denies newspaper access to concealed gun permits. (November 15, 2000). Retrieved from https://www.rcfp.org/court-denies-newspaper-access-concealed-gun-permits/.

Craig, D., Ketterer, S., and Yousuf, M. (March 1, 2017). To post or not to post: Online discussion of gun permit mapping and the development of ethical standards in data journalism. *Journalism & Mass Communication Quarterly*. 94(1): 168–188.

Dyer, J. (January 12, 2016). Fifty years of FOIA: As the Freedom of Information Act turns 50, journalists are innovating new ways to use the law. Retrieved from https://nieman.harvard.edu/articles/fiftyyears-of-foia/.

Eldridge, D. (March 18, 2019). Locked and loaded: Cherokee County becomes "gun sanctuary county" in WNC. *Trappalachia.* Retrieved from https://trappalachia.com/index.php/2019/03/18/locked-and-loaded-cherokee-countybecomes-gun-sanctuary-county-in-wnc/.

Elliston, J. (March 1, 2013). Request for gun-permit info puts local newspaper in a crossfire. *Carolina Public Press*. Retrieved from https://carolinapublicpress.org/13853/request-forgun-permit-info-puts-local-newspaper-in-a-crossfire/.

Farhi, P. (February 27, 2013). Newspapers face death threats over requests for public records on gun ownership. *Washington Post.* Retrieved from https://www.washingtonpost.com/lifestyle/style/2013/02/27/49e935b6-8117-11e2-b99e6baf4ebe42df_story.html.

Friess, S. (August 20, 2013). How the NRA built a massive secret database of gun owners. *Buzzfeed*. Retrieved from https://www.buzzfeednews.com/article/stevefriess/how-the-nrabuilt-a-massive-secret-database-of-gun-owners.

Goodman, J. (January 3, 2013). Newspaper that put gun permit map online hires armed guards. *New York Times.* Retrieved from https://www.nytimes.com/2013/01/03/nyregion/putnamofficials-keep-gun-permit-records-from-journal-news.html.

Gun Licensees and Privacy in the Empire State. (August 3, 2020). NRA-ILA. Retrieved from https://www.nraila.org/articles/20200803/gun-licensees-and-privacy-in-the-empire-state.

Gutierrez, E. Gun owners' privacy. Electronic Privacy Information Center. Retrieved from https://www.epic.org/privacy/firearms/.

Horowitz, J. (December 26, 2012). N.Y. newspaper posts gun permit map, starts nasty online battle. *Washington Post.* Retrieved from https://www.washingtonpost.com/politics/nynewspaper-posts-gun-permit-map-starts-nasty-online-battle/2012/12/26/747ae7d6-4fb011e2-950a-7863a013264b_story.html.

Hutchins, C. (February 26, 2013). Guns and public records: The *Cherokee Scout*'s saga (UPDATED). Retrieved from https://archives.cjr.org/united_states_project/guns_and_public_records_the_cherokee_scuts_saga.php.

Jarvis, J. (January 24, 2013). Public is public . . . except in journalism? Retrieved from https://buzzmachine.com/2013/01/14/public-is-public-except-in-journalism/.

K. Gun Permits. Reporter's Committee for Freedom of the Press. Retrieved from https://www.rcfp.org/open-government-sections/k-gun-permits/.

Kerry, C. F. (July 12, 2018). Why protecting privacy is a losing game today—and how to change the game. Brookings Institute. Retrieved from https://www.brookings.edu/research/whyprotecting-privacy-is-a-losing-game-today-and-how-to-change-the-game/.

Kraft, E. S. (2009). Access to courtrooms. *The First Amendment Encyclopedia.* Retrieved from https://www.mtsu.edu/first-amendment/article/1547/access-to-courtrooms.

Letter from James Madison to W. T. Barry (August 4, 1822), in *The Writings of James Madison* (Gaillard Hunt ed.).

Louisiana criminalizes publishing gun permit information. (June 24, 2013). Reporters Committee for Freedom of the Press. Retrieved from https://www.rcfp.org/louisiana-criminalizespublishing-gun-permit-information/.

Malewitz, J. (March 7, 2013). Lawmakers move swiftly to block release of gun permit records. Pew. https://www.pewtrusts.org/en/research-andanalysis/blogs/stateline/2013/03/07/lawmakers-move-swiftly-to-block-release-of-gunpermit-records.

N.C. Code. §132-1 Public Record Defined.

N.C. Code §14-403.

New York newspaper takes down gun owner details from website. January 18, 2013. https://www.reuters.com/article/usa-guns-newspaper/refile-new-york-newspaper-takes-down-gun-owner-details-from-website-idINL1E9CJ09G20130119.

Penrod, G. (2004). Gunning for access. *The News Media & The Law*. Spring. p. 27.

Postman, N. (1985). *Amusing Ourselves to Death: Public Discourse in the Age of Show Business*. New York: Penguin Books.

Price, M. (March 15, 2019). 'Gun Sanctuary' movement spreads to NC as county adopts plan to thwart gun control. *Charlotte Observer*. Retrieved from https://www.charlotteobserver.com/news/local/article227784574.html.

Reeve, E. (February 25, 2013). Local paper very, very sorry for asking questions about guns. *The Atlantic*. Retrieved from https://www.theatlantic.com/politics/archive/2013/02/localpaper-very-very-sorry-askingquestions-about-guns/317991/.

Reporting on gun permit data. RCFP.org. Retrieved from https://www.rcfp.org/journals/reporting-gun-permit-data/.

Robinson, C. (June 25, 2020). Serial bomber Eric Robert Rudolph wants out of prison. Retrieved from https://www.al.com/news/birmingham/2020/06/serial-bomber-ericrobert-rudolph-wants-out-of-prison.html.

Scassa, T. (2014). Privacy and open government. *Future Internet, 6*(2): 397–413. Retrieved from http://dx.doi.org.prox.lib.ncsu.edu/10.3390/fi6020397.

Seller, C. (December 26, 2012). Ball scolds Journal News for posting permit data. *Times Union.* Retrieved from https://blog.timesunion.com/capitol/archives/174488/ball-scolds-journal-news-for-posting-permit-data/.

Silverman, A. (January 13, 2013). Gun permit map to blame for White Plains burglary? WCBSNews. Retrieved from https://newyork.cbslocal.com/2013/01/13/gun-permit-list-toblamefor-white-plains-burglary/.

Taylor, M. (March 1, 2013). Journalism resuscitation. *Burlington* (N.C.) *Times-News*. Retrieved from https://www.thetimesnews.com/20130301/journalism-resuscitation/303019789.

Trotter, J. K. (January 2, 2013). Local government refuses to give local newspaper data for its gun-owner map. *The Atlantic*.

U.S. Constitution Amendment II.

7

Guns in America

Public Opinion, Research, and the Role of the NRA

Paul Knudson

Debates over firearms, gun rights, and gun ownership go as far back as the founding of the country itself. The federalists and anti-federalists debated the drafting and the interpretation of the Second Amendment at the Constitutional Convention beginning in 1787. Lawmakers also wrestled with the salience of state constitutions versus the federal constitution with regard to gun rights (Briggs, 2017). Debates continued through the eighteenth, nineteenth, and twentieth centuries and proceed to this day. The disputes surrounding gun rights are unsurprising given that Americans own more firearms than any other society on earth. Some 300 million guns populate the country, about one firearm for every man, woman, and child in America.

The mainstream media, particularly cable television, tends to frame gun issues in simplistic terms, and this contributes to lack of productive debate and dialogue surrounding the issue. For example, although mass shootings—defined as those that include more than five victims—devour most of the airtime, America's core gun violence problem is linked to domestic violence and acquaintance-to-acquaintance interactions that escalate into the use of deadly force (Planty & Truman, 2013). The intent of this statement is not to minimize the immensely real suffering and socially deleterious effects of mass shootings (which occur almost daily), but rather to point out that if these events dictate the policy response of lawmakers, such measures will not adequately reduce gun violence.

These brief introductory points illustrate the intent of this chapter. The aim of this reading is to present hard data and facts regarding guns and gun violence in this country. My aim is to provide a well-reasoned and dispassionate analysis of this issue that will assist in the understanding of this topic. The layout of the chapter is as follows: Part 1 examines the current state of national public opinion on guns. The data presented comes from research institutions that use high-quality, scientific polling techniques. The data suggest that most Americans support gun rights but also favor restrictions of gun use. Part 2 examines the different rates of gun ownership by state along with firearm deaths. It also explores the varying gun regulations by state and describes the outcomes in those states in terms of gun deaths. The data show that states with more firearms regulations tend to have fewer gun deaths. This raises the question of why specific gun regulations have been so elusive on the national level. Part 3 begins to answer this question by taking a closer look at some of the specific political organizations in America that are central in the gun debate. This section, in particular, provides a brief overview of the National Rifle Organization (NRA) and how this group has become such a powerful force in the United States. The political activities of the NRA explain much of the lack of political action to reduce American gun violence. Finally, Part 4 explores some of the political reforms that could be pursued that would open up the US political system to a broader dialogue and discussion over guns. These reforms could also make compromise and reforms surrounding firearms more achievable.

THE CURRENT GUN DEBATE

What is the current state of public opinion in America on guns? To measure public opinion, research organizations use what social scientists call probability sampling. A sample is a segment of people chosen to represent a larger group or population. Probability samples are designed to prevent bias in the selection of people included in the sample. They are designed so that everyone in the population has an equal likelihood or probability of being selected. For example, probability samples ensure that the people selected to be studied mirror their proportions in the larger population in regard to race, ethnicity, gender, age, income, education, and other important social variables. Sophisticated statistical techniques are also used to account for any discrepancies in the data. For instance, if people with higher levels of education are more likely to respond to research surveys than people with lower levels of education, mathematical modeling techniques, including "weighting," are used to make any necessary adjustments.

The way in which questions are asked also affects the responses survey participants will offer. This is why readers must be careful when examining information. The best way to ensure that audiences and readers will obtain accurate information is to examine multiple high-quality studies that explore the same question. Pew Research is one of the premier global research organizations that conducts public opinion studies. They use scientific and methodologically sound practices in their collection of social data.

According to Pew's recent data, about 60 percent of Americans in 2019 wanted stricter gun laws. Eleven percent wanted fewer restrictions of guns, while 28 percent said current gun laws were adequate. Support for stricter gun laws has grown since 2017 when only 52 percent of Americans felt that way. Not surprisingly, attitudes toward gun laws vary by social and demographic characteristics. More women than men want stricter gun laws (64% to 55%), college graduates are more likely than non-college graduates (72% to 55%) to favor stricter gun laws, and most notably Democratic voters favor tighter gun laws than Republican voters (86% to 31%) (Gramlich & Schaeffer, 2019).

Gallup is another preeminent research institution that uses high-quality probability sampling and other scientific research methodologies. Gallup provides us with very nuanced data regarding Americans' views on guns. In 2018, they recorded that 60 percent of Americans wanted tighter gun laws (very similar to Pew's data), but in 2017, 67 percent answered yes to that question. The drop of 7 percent, however, may or may not reflect a real shift in public opinion, and again, this is why audiences must be careful. First, the drop could be the result of a slightly different sample of Americans from the 2018 study. Second, a shift of 7 percent is only three points outside the survey's margin of error. All probability samples include what social scientists call a standard error. The standard error is the difference between a population mean or average (if we were to collect data from every single American adult) and the sample mean or average—the data that were collected from the sample of Americans (Reinhart, 2018).

Gallup's data include responses that go back to 1992. To the surprise of many, Americans' support for tighter gun restrictions have waned since 1992, when 78 percent of Americans favored stricter gun laws. However, the 60 percent of Americans who said they wanted tighter gun laws in 2018 is far higher than in 2012 when support bottomed out at 43 percent. The data suggest a couple of points. First, public mood and sentiment surrounding guns is fairly unstable, and second, over a near thirty-year period, the majority of Americans still tended to favor stricter gun laws. Nonetheless, the reasons for the changing sentiments are unclear, and therefore we are left to only speculate. For instance, homicides and overall violent crime in the early 1990s in America were actually significantly higher than they are today (Zimring, 2008). Most of the homicides were committed by people using firearms. Perhaps that explains the public's higher support for stricter gun regulations in the early 1990s. Other factors could be at work as well. Support for tighter firearm laws over the last twenty-five years has remained constant among Democrats but weakened substantially for Republican voters (Parker et al., 2017).

Indeed, over the last twenty-five years, the Democratic Party has increasingly become a party of city and suburban dwellers. These voters, regardless of party, tend to favor greater firearms restrictions. Meanwhile, the Republican Party has lost city and suburban voter support and increasingly relies on voters who live in rural areas and in the "exurbs," which are low-population density subdivisions and communities built outside the older, existing suburban core of metropolitan areas. Rural and exurban residents, regardless of party, tend to favor less restrictive firearm measures (Parker et al., 2017).

Findings from the Gallup data continue to be more nuanced than the television media's discussions and framing of firearms. Only 28 percent of Americans want handguns to be banned, compared to 71 percent who oppose such a ban. It should be noted that neither Democratic nor Republican Party platforms include legislation that would ban handguns. Although there are differences once more by gender, political affiliation and actual gun ownership, majorities of all groups oppose an outright ban on handguns. Interestingly, support for the prohibition of handguns has declined substantially since Gallup began asking the question in 1959. Back then, 60 percent of Americans favored a ban on handguns. Conversely, American's views on handguns are very different from their views of so-called assault weapons. Gallup reported that 61 percent of Americans supported a ban on the manufacturing, sale, and possession of semiautomatic weapons (Reinhart, 2018).

Finally, Johns Hopkins University conducted a study using similar research methodologies as Gallup and Pew. The questions they asked, however, were more specific. Social scientists favor survey questions that are both as specific as possible but also as straightforward or clear as possible in order to minimize confusion for survey respondents. Johns Hopkins found very high levels of public support for gun regulations when Americans were asked very specific questions. For example, 77 percent favored a policy that required gun buyers to purchase a license to own a gun; 88 percent favored universal background checks on handgun purchases. Substantial support also existed for risk-mitigation policies known as "red flag" laws. Seventy-six percent of those surveyed supported the authorization of law enforcement officers to temporarily remove guns from people deemed to pose "an immediate threat of self-harm or harm to others." Sixty-six percent of *gun owners* supported these measures, whereas support among non-gun owners stood at 88 percent (Barry et al., 2019).

Overall, high-quality social science research suggests two main points. With the exception of semiautomatic weapons, the majority of Americans believe that people should be able to purchase and own guns. Simultaneously, majorities of Americans want tighter laws and regulations surrounding firearms. This is even more apparent when people are given the opportunity to respond to very specific questions related to detailed policies regarding firearms. Perhaps very surprisingly to nearly all parties, the majority of gun owners actually supported certain gun safety and regulatory measures. Indeed, a Harvard study suggested that a majority of gun owners were willing to purchase a child-proof gun. The study also suggested that a majority of NRA members (albeit not NRA leadership) supported a mandatory waiting period for purchasing guns as well as mandatory registration of handguns (Wolfson et al., 2016).

Most Americans who watch Fox News, CNN, or any other major media outlet probably are not aware of a growing national consensus that gun rights should be respected but should come with responsibilities, restrictions, and safeguards. This nuance is lost in the public discussion. This is somewhat perplexing and unfortunate. Some of the division may be a result of NRA messaging. The NRA leadership has often equated measured gun regulations with gun confiscation. Indeed, after the election of Barack Obama in 2008, gun purchases soared and rhetoric about Obama "coming for your guns" escalated. This came despite gun confiscation being nowhere in the platform of the Democratic Party (Sharockman, 2012). Yet the media hyperbole is surprising given that the majority of NRA members support specific and measured gun regulations, according to the Harvard study.

The extreme rhetoric coming from some in the gun rights movement may be more a sign or a product of high-stakes partisan politics when political power in the country is so closely divided between Democratic and Republican majorities. The smallest of margins exist between Democratic and Republican victories throughout the country in elections at every level of government. This includes gubernatorial and state legislative races all the way to national elections for the US Senate, House of Representatives, and even the presidency, which in 2016 was decided by about 70,000 votes (out of roughly 120 million total votes cast) over three important states in the Electoral College. The near-50/50 partisan makeup of the United States tends to encourage both parties to play to more extreme elements within their bases as a way to encourage excitement and election turnout. Over the last thirty years, this tendency, however, has been more visible in the Republican Party than in the Democratic Party (Mann & Ornstein, 2016).

CURRENT GUN STATISTICS AND POLICY RESEARCH

The lack of nuance reported by television media in regard to public opinion is also apparent in their unwillingness to inform the American public about the effects of firearm regulations on public safety. America is not one country when it comes to the issue of firearms. Gun regulations and gun ownership vary widely by state. Similarly, although the United States recorded approximately 40,000 gun-related deaths in 2017, death rates widely vary by state (Gramlich, 2019). Table 7.1 displays gun deaths by state from highest to lowest (National Center, 2020).

Table 7.1. Firearm Deaths per 100,000 Total Population by State

State	*Deaths per 100,000 total population*	*State*	*Deaths per 100,000 total population*
Mississippi	22.9	Michigan	12.9
Alabama	21.8	Florida	12.9
Wyoming	21.5	Vermont	12.8
Missouri	21.5	Pennsylvania	12.5
Louisiana	21.4	Texas	12.2
Alaska	21	Virginia	11.8
New Mexico	20.7	Oregon	11.7
Arkansas	18.9	Maryland	11.7
West Virginia	18.2	Delaware	11.6
Nevada	17.9	North Dakota	11.5
Tennessee	17.8	Illinois	10.9
South Carolina	17.6	New Hampshire	10.8
Montana	17.3	Washington	10.4
Kentucky	16.9	Maine	10.3
Oklahoma	16.8	Wisconsin	10.1
Idaho	16.6	Nebraska	9
Georgia	15.7	Iowa	8.7
Arizona	15.3	Minnesota	7.8
Colorado	15.2	California	7.5
Kansas	14.8	Connecticut	4.9
Indiana	14.7	New Jersey	4.8
South Dakota	13.6	New York	4.1
North Carolina	13.3	Hawaii	4
Utah	13.2	Massachusetts	3.5
Ohio	13.1	Rhode Island	3.3

Gun deaths tend to be highest in the poor southern and western states of the United States. As shown in table 7.2, many of these states also have very high rates of gun ownership among their populations. In contrast, in addition to Hawaii, gun ownership is lowest in New England and in more urbanized and wealthy parts of the northeast. Gun deaths are the lowest in these states as well. Calculating the correlation coefficient between these two variables gives us a correlation of 0.686 which is a very strong relationship. Correlation coefficients lie between 0 and 1 and 0 and -1. A value of 1 or -1 is a perfect correlation, but this never exists in real life as other variables exist that influence an outcome. Because the sign on our correlation coefficient is positive 0.686 not -0.686, this means that the two variables move in the same direction. In this case, as gun ownership increases, gun deaths increase. To be sure, this is correlational, not causative, but the statistical association between gun ownership rates and gun death rates is quite strong.

Table 7.2. Gun Ownership by State

State	*Ownership Rate %*	*State*	*Ownership Rate %*
Alaska	61.7	Kansas	32.2
Arkansas	57.9	Utah	31.9
Idaho	56.9	Georgia	31.6
West Virginia	54.2	Oklahoma	31.2
Wyoming	53.8	Virginia	29.3
Montana	52.3	Vermont	28.8
New Mexico	49.9	Michigan	28.8
Alabama	48.9	North Carolina	28.7
North Dakota	47.9	Washington	27.7
Hawaii	45.1	Missouri	27.1
Louisiana	44.5	Pennsylvania	27.1
South Carolina	44.4	Oregon	26.6
Mississippi	42.8	Illinois	26.2
Kentucky	42.4	Maine	22.6
Tennessee	39.4	Massachusetts	22.6
Nevada	37.5	Maryland	20.7
Minnesota	36.7	California	20.1
Texas	35.7	Nebraska	19.8
South Dakota	35	Ohio	19.6
Colorado	34.3	Connecticut	16.6
Wisconsin	34.7	New Hampshire	14.4
Indiana	33.8	New Jersey	11.3
Iowa	33.8	New York	10.3
Florida	32.5	Rhode Island	5.8
Arizona	32.3	Delaware	5.2

Kiersz, A., & LoGiurato, B. (2015). Heres where youre most likely to own a gun. *Business Insider*. July 3. Retrieved February 19, 2020 (https://www.businessinsider.com/gun-ownership-by-state-2015–7).

This basic correlational analysis is illustrated by a scatterplot in figure 7.1. The data show that for every 1 percent increase in state gun ownership, state gun death rates increase by 0.264 units.

My simple analysis here is very basic. I did not statistically control for any other factors that might influence gun deaths like the state poverty rate or alcohol consumption. However, the overwhelming majority of recent studies that use much more sophisticated statistics suggest that state-level gun deaths are associated with greater levels of gun ownership and looser gun

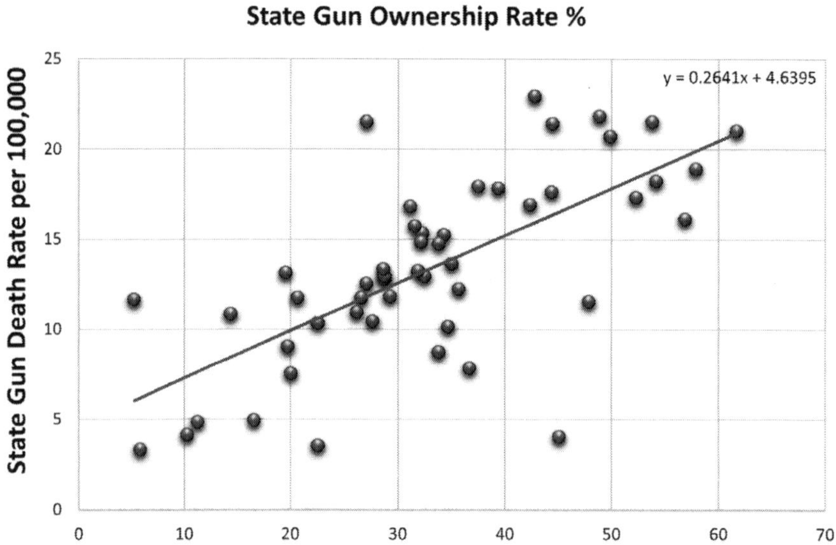

State Gun Ownership Rate %. ***Figure created by Paul Knudson with data from: National Center for Health Statistics (2020).*** **Firearm Mortality by State.** ***Centers for Disease Control and Prevention. Retrieved February 19, 2020. https://www.cdc.gov/nchs/pressroom/sosmap/firearm_mortality/firearm.htm.***

regulations and restrictions (Briggs, 2017). The various studies examine different sets of laws and different types of deaths. Yet most suggest that gun regulatory measures like universal background checks and gun registries have a modest but statistically significant effect on reducing gun violence and gun deaths. In contrast, loosely regulated states, including states that allow for "concealed carrying" of certain firearms, have higher rates of gun deaths (Briggs, 2017). To be sure, this is a very complex issue with numerous other factors that also affect gun violence outcomes. But it is quite clear that there are strong links between gun safety laws and lower gun deaths and violence.

The first set of studies examines the outcome of gun registries. Gun registration laws require those purchasing firearms to register them with the appropriate law enforcement agency in their state or locality. These laws help assist police and other law enforcement officials to identify, disarm, and prosecute violent criminals and those who are in illegal possession of such firearms. As noted earlier, strong public support exists for firearm registries, even by a majority of gun owners and NRA members. There, however, is no federal law that requires registration. Only certain states have registration policies and requirements (Briggs, 2017).

One recent study published in the *American Journal of Public Health* examined the association between state-level registry laws and gun homicide rates. The authors used injury statistics from the Centers for Disease Control (CDC). Meanwhile, existing literature reviews on laws regulating firearm dealers and other measurements of each state's regulatory status allowed the researchers to test this hypothesis. Overall, states that had three or more laws regulating the use of firearms had lower homicide rates. Such laws included licensing and allowed firearm inspections. Laws that required theft reporting, however, were not associated with lower homicide levels (Irvin et al., 2014).

Similar results appeared in a study published in the same journal that examined the impact of gun registries in the state of Connecticut. The study uses some of the most sophisticated statistical techniques of all current studies on firearms. In 1995, Connecticut began a Permit-to-Purchase (PTP) law. These laws mandate that buyers of handguns must first obtain a permit or license in person at a local police department. Licensing is predicated on the ability to first pass a background check. The law applies to both firearm retailers and private sellers. Connecticut's law also raised the legal age for purchasing a handgun from eighteen to twenty-one. Finally, buyers in Connecticut—as in neighboring Massachusetts—must undergo eight hours of approved safety training for handguns (Rudolph et al., 2015).

This study used a sophisticated statistical methodology known as the synthetic control method which essentially tests varying outcomes based on different policy scenarios. Their findings suggested that without Connecticut's 1995 PTP law, the state would have experienced 40 percent more gun-related homicides from 1995 to 2005 than what actually transpired. The results, however, suggested that non-gun-related homicides would have remained the same. Still, given that the majority of homicides are committed by people using guns, the PTP most likely contributed to a significant advancement in public safety and public health.

Most states do not have the comprehensive gun safety legislative environment of liberal Connecticut or Massachusetts, but research suggests that considerable variance still exists by states. These include the levels of injuries and death—from both homicides and suicides. A study published in the *Journal of Family Violence* found that firearms are the most common cause of death for individuals in domestic violence incidents. This included homicide-suicide cases, incidents in which children were killed first before the parent (usually the mother), and homicides and suicides that occurred when children were not present (Sillito & Salari, 2011). Another study (Anestis et al., 2017) found that suicide rates are lower in states that employ compulsory waiting periods and universal background checks for handguns relative to states that lack these laws. Moreover, states with *both* mandatory waiting periods and universal background checks had lower suicide rates than those with only one of these restrictions. However, "open-carry" restrictions and regulations regarding gun locks and storage had no statistically significant effect on suicide rates.

A study in the *American Journal of Economics and Sociology* (Kwon & Baack, 2005) adds further evidence to this trend. The study divided states into comprehensive and lax firearm regulation states. They ranked states using six measures: registration of firearms, mandatory safety training, regulation of firearm sales (including waiting periods and types of background checks), safe storage and accessibility, owner licensing, and litigation and preemption. The litigation variable either entails state restrictions or places outright bans on litigation aimed at the firearms industry. The preemption variable means that the state in question can preempt any or all local/municipal laws aimed at regulating firearms. The authors found stark contrasts between lax and comprehensive regulation states. After statistically controlling for numerous other variables including racial composition, percent of residents in poverty, age of residents, percent urban, and unemployment rates, states with comprehensive gun regulations had significantly lower rates of gun-related deaths compared to their lax-state counterparts.

Finally, another study published in the same journal (Kwon et al., 1997) backs up the findings laid out in the prior studies. The researchers hypothesized that states with some type of firearms restrictions and regulations would experience lower gun-related deaths than states without similar regulations. The study controlled for eight other variables including the racial and ethnic makeup of the population, age of the population, unemployment rates, poverty rates, percent urban, and alcohol consumption rates. Even after controlling for these variables, states with more firearm regulations had lower gun death rates than states with fewer restrictions. Social factors, however, played a greater role in predicting gun-related deaths than firearm laws: higher poverty rates and alcohol consumption are associated with increased gun-related deaths more than lax gun regulations are. Yet we might deduce from this that a combination of economic desperation, heavy alcohol consumption, and household gun ownership is a dangerous mix.

These studies suggest that the issue surrounding firearms is complex and that numerous social factors influence gun violence and gun deaths. It is quite clear, however, that state-level gun regulations make a difference in firearm death outcomes. The question then becomes, if public opinion in America generally favors more safety measures, regulations, and restrictions on firearms, and if systematic research suggests that these regulations reduce injuries and deaths, why has comprehensive gun regulation been so elusive in this country?

POLITICAL ORGANIZATIONS DEVOTED TO THE GUN ISSUE

As with everything else, there is not a simplistic answer to this question. However, existing sociological and historical research suggests that one of the main impediments to comprehensive firearm safety legislation is the political power of the NRA. Even though the majority of Americans favor more firearm regulations, the vast majority of these people are not politically involved in the issue. Generally left-of-center and affiliated with the Democratic Party, these voters tend to favor tighter gun restrictions. Yet this issue is only one of many—including healthcare, education, the environment, and worker's rights—that is considered important to this set of voters. Furthermore, gun politics is generally not the most important issue to these voters (Drutman, 2019). On the right-of-center side, however, gun rights are a central and top issue. Indeed, the Republican Party's core base of supporters includes three constituencies: evangelical Christians, economic conservatives, including big and small business, and gun rights activists. Moreover, all three constituencies favor the advancement of "small government," at least as it concerns restrictions on "religious liberty," private enterprise, and gun ownership (Newport, 2009).

The NRA has four million members who pay dues to the organization. Unlike other gun owners in America, NRA members specifically believe that gun rights are "under attack," and the NRA has portrayed any attempt by lawmakers to regulate firearms as "confiscation." The NRA's severe rhetoric is spread widely with its sizable budget. In 2009, the organization had annual revenue of more than $200 million (Melzer, 2009). In the 2016 election cycle, the NRA spent more than $3 million on lobbying efforts directed at the nation's lawmakers. Furthermore, political action committees (PACs) tied to the NRA spent a total of more than $54 million on political campaigns, with nearly every dollar raised advancing Republican candidates (Open Secrets Center for Responsive Politics, 2020b). Beyond the NRA's financial clout are the everyday, informal actions of NRA members. The NRA distributes political literature to its millions of members, organizes letter-writing campaigns to officials at all levels of government, orchestrates grassroots voter turnout measures, raises consciousness at local and national rallies, teaches self-defense courses, provides firearms training, and holds an annual meeting that attracts tens of thousands of members.

Conversely, the gun safety and regulatory movement is far less organized, and its members lack the fervor of the right-wing gun rights movement. The Brady Campaign to Prevent Gun Violence is an important group on the gun regulation side, yet they are outmatched at every level by the NRA and other gun rights groups. Michael Bloomberg's Everytown for Gun Safety is arguably the only pro-gun regulation group that has major financial and political resources. In 2016, its budget stood at $36 million, but this figure is still dwarfed by the NRA's (Open Secrets Center for Responsive Politics, 2020a). Everytown, however, has contributed to races in which its preferred candidates have won major victories, especially in the 2018 midterm elections in which the Democratic Party witnessed a significant surge in voter support. Still, Everytown and the Brady Campaign have not cultivated what amounts to a distinct culture, identity, and lifestyle that the NRA has been propagating in its members for well over forty years. The intensity and fervor of the gun rights groups are still unmatched.

In the 1970s, gun hard-liners took control of the NRA from the moderate old guard. In 1977, Harlon Carter was elected as NRA president. With support by hard-liners, Carter transformed the organization from what had been a relatively small group focused on promoting marksmanship and recreational shooting to what the NRA is today, a full-fledged national political organization fully committed to advancing the right-wing political movement as well as cultivating among its members a distinctive gun culture, lifestyle, and identity (Open Secrets, 2020a).

The NRA's transformation came in the midst of drastic changes in American society and law. After the assassination of John F. Kennedy, Robert Kennedy, and Martin Luther King Jr., there was mounting pressure in Washington to enact stronger gun regulations. This came in the form of the Gun Control Act of 1968 which regulated interstate firearm purchasing and licensing (Parker et al., 2017). But other changes were happening as well. The major civil rights victories in the 1960s which opened up advancement for people of color, women, and gay and lesbian individuals was met in the 1970s by a strong conservative political backlash. The right-wing was especially troubled by advancements in social safety-net programs and threat of the passage of the Equal Rights Amendment (ERA) which would legislate equal treatment for Americans regardless of gender or sex (Hedges, 2010). ERA passed both houses of Congress and was signed by President Jimmy Carter. The amendment, however, required ratification by thirty-eight states and failed to achieve this goal by the mandated deadline.

According to the right-wing, progressive legislation in America is an affront to Christianity, capitalism, the traditional family, and the male breadwinner. The hard-liners who took control of the NRA in the late 1970s positioned the group into the middle of the new conservative insurgency of this era, and these political values continue to be cultivated today. The NRA, through its vast literature, seeks to cultivate what its own leadership refers to as "frontier masculinity." Sociologist Scott Melzer defines for us this concept. "Characterized by rugged individualism, hard work, protecting and providing for families, and self-reliance, frontier masculinity is the mythologized dominant version of manhood from America's frontier past" (Melzer, 2009, p. 16).

The NRA, therefore, has become more than simply a gun rights organization. It is a group that has cultivated and nourished a comprehensive social movement and personal identity that is religious in its devotion. It is an identity that is committed to opposing feminism, gay rights, and the government's social safety net. Do note that these issues are considered centrist and not leftist in every other Western industrialized country. However, NRA members are instructed to fear that "liberals are plotting to take away their gun rights and give women, gays, and people of color not equal but 'special' rights. The gun-owning, rural, conservative, straight, white man is the new victim of discrimination, the new minority, they believe" (Melzer, 2009, p. 11).

In contrast, there is no "story" or "myth" that has been created by the American left, including those who favor tighter firearm restrictions. This reality handicaps policy that would lead to greater firearm regulations. The mainstream media, desiring ever higher ratings, is also loath to portray the gun debate in more reasoned terms that emphasize the findings of important studies in the social sciences. Instead, they prefer the appearance of conflict and a false "two-sides-only" simplification of the issue. As long as the gun issue is framed in these overly simplistic and conflict-ridden terms, the American public will continue to be misinformed, and public policy solutions to the gun violence problem will not be achieved.

THE POTENTIAL OF POLITICAL REFORMS

Progress, however, could be made on the political front in a few ways, but these changes would not come easily. This section will discuss two important political reforms that could help lead to a greater national consensus on gun issues: the end of gerrymandering and campaign finance reform. The practice of gerrymandering is one of the reasons why politics has become increasingly polarized in America. Many Americans may not realize that in most states, the political party in power draws the local, state, and national legislative district maps. This is done at the beginning of each new decade following updated population statistics collected from the US Census. Most states do not use an independent commission to accomplish this task. Because the political party in power has the authority to draw legislative districts, it benefits that party to draw districts in such a way to dilute the power of the opposition, while designing maps that bolster the power of their party. Parties do this in a couple of ways. First, they use powerful mapping software to identify where voters of the opposition party tend to live and draw district boundaries in such a way as to pack that group of voters into a small, lopsided district that is heavily made up of the voters of that party. Therefore, the opposition does receive representation in certain strangely drawn districts, but they are shut out of every other district that is drawn in the state. The vast majority of districts are drawn to favor the party in power.

Second, by sorting voters in the opposition party into strangely drawn districts that pack those voters into a very few districts, the party in power ensures that the remaining districts contain a vast majority of the voters of that party. Therefore, both sets of districts become lopsided politically. In states governed by Republicans, lawmakers pack likely Democratic voters into a few districts that tend to be clustered around central cities and university towns, while the vast remaining geography of the state becomes Republican districts. The opposite of this is done in many states that are governed by Democrats. Overall, gerrymandering creates districts that either tilt heavily Republican or heavily Democratic. Few or no competitive districts exist with gerrymandered maps and districts. In essence, gerrymandering allows the politicians to pick their voters rather than voters selecting their political representatives. Because gerrymandering creates uncompetitive districts, Republican incumbents, for example, do not worry about competing against a Democratic candidate in the general election. Their main goal is to win their district's Republican Party primary. Candidates tend to win their party primaries by appealing to the core base of the party which consists of the party's most loyal voters. The base of each party, moreover, tends to be more extreme politically than marginal party voters. For example, the most loyal Democratic voters tend to be more liberal than marginal Democratic voters. The most loyal Republican voters tend to be more conservative than marginal Republican voters (McGann et al., 2016).

Because gerrymandering only makes the party primary elections relevant, incumbents in either party are not incentivized to appeal to a wide range of voters. Republican candidates only have to appeal to very conservative voters and Democrats only have to appeal to left-leaning and liberal voters. Because of this, more extreme positions, including positions on firearms, are taken by political candidates. These positions tend not to reflect broad public opinion. Election reforms that grant power to independent commissions to draw legislative districts would result in many fewer districts in which one political party or the other had a lopsided advantage. Legislative districts would be drawn that would allow for more competitive elections. Candidates would be forced to appeal to a broad slice of the electorate, and their positions on policies, including gun policy, would likely become more moderated (Klein, 2020).

Campaign finance reforms would also improve the chances for action to be taken on firearm regulation and safety measures. Right now, wealthy sectors of the society can donate unlimited sums of money to PACs. PACs are formed to benefit certain political parties, candidates, and issues. Unlimited donations to PACs connected to the NRA have allowed for tens of millions of dollars of largely unregulated or "dark money" to flow into the political system. For example, if a specific Republican lawmaker decided to support a popular gun regulatory measure, a PAC connected to the NRA might begin running nonstop television ads against that lawmaker. This PAC would, perhaps, demand that Republican voters in the next Republican primary replace this lawmaker in question with a more hard-line candidate who is more supportive of unfettered gun rights.

Campaign finance reform would limit the power and activities of these largely unregulated, wealthy PACs, entities that do not represent the interests or concerns of the vast majority of voters (Nader, 2014). Indeed, as we saw earlier in this chapter, even a majority of NRA members support some specific regulations over firearms. Yet this does not show up in the PAC that supports NRA leadership and other right-wing policies. Reforms could be made that limit or altogether ban PAC contributions in the political sphere. The public financing of state and national elections would also limit the power of wealthy, narrow interests in our political system and allow a broader slice of the American electorate to be heard in the current political debate surrounding guns and other important issues.

CONCLUSION

The democratization of our political dialogue and of the overall political process would assist gun reform measures. Although the majority of Americans believe that basic rights to own a firearm ought to be respected, majorities also believe that those rights should come with restrictions and safeguards. As reviewed in this chapter, numerous regulations such as licensing, registration, universal background checks, red-flag laws, and mandated gun safety training, are popular with the general public and are shown to make a difference in saving lives. These findings should be encouraging to both gun owners and gun enthusiasts, as well as those who are pressing for gun safety measures. There is more consensus in the nation than what we see in our current partisan politics and in our mass media. The broad public wants gun rights to be respected, but for those rights to come with important responsibilities.

BIBLIOGRAPHY

Anestis, M., Anestis, J., and Butterworth, S. (2017). Handgun legislation and changes in statewide overall suicide rates. *American Journal of Public Health, 107*(4): 579–581.

Barry, C., Stone, E., Crifasi, C., Vernick, J., Webster, D., and McGinty, E. (2019). Trends in public opinion on US gun laws: Majorities of gun owners and non-gun owners support a range of measures. *Health Affairs, 38*(10).

Briggs, W. (2017). *How America got its guns: A history of the gun violence crisis.* Albuquerque: University of New Mexico Press.

Drutman, L. (2019, August). Opposing forces: Issues dividing voters ahead of election 2020. Democracy Fund. Retrieved February 20, 2020 (https://www.voterstudygroup.org/publication/opposing-forces).

Gramlich, J. (2019, August 16).What the data says about gun death in the U.S. Pew Research Center. Retrieved March 22, 2020 (https://www.pewresearch.org/fact-tank/2019/08/16/what-the-data-says-about-gun-deaths-in-the-u-s/).

Gramlich, J., and Schaeffer, K. (2019). Facts about guns in the U.S. Pew Research Center. Retrieved February 22, 2020 (https://www.pewresearch.org/fact-tank/2019/10/22/facts-about-guns-in-united-states/).

Hedges, C. (2010). *Death of the liberal class.* New York: Bold Type Books.

Irvin, N., Rhodes, K., Cheney, R., and Wiebe, D. (2014). Evaluating the effect of state regulation of federally licensed firearm dealers on firearm homicide. *American Journal of Public Health, 104*(8): 1384–1386.

Klein, E. (2020). *Why we're polarized.* New York: Simon and Schuster.

Kwon, I., and Baack, D. (2005). The effectiveness of legislation controlling gun usage. *The American Journal of Economics and Sociology, 64*(2): 533–547.

Kwon, I., Scott, B., Safranski, S., and Bae, M. (1997). The effectiveness of gun control laws: Multivariate statistical analysis. *American Journal of Economics and Sociology, 56*(1): 41–50.

Mann, T., and Ornstein, N. (2016). *It's even worse than it looks: How the American constitutional system collided with the new politics of extremism.* New York: Basic Books.

McElwee, S. (2018, August 23). Data for politics #14: Who Is Trump's base? Data for Progress. Retrieved February 2, 2020 (https://www.dataforprogress.org/blog/2018/8/21/data-for-politics-14-who-is-trumps-base).

McGann, A., Smith, C. A., and Latner, M. (2016). *Gerrymandering in America: The House of Representatives, the Supreme Court, and the future of popular sovereignty.* Cambridge, UK: Cambridge University Press.

Melzer, S. (2009). *Gun crusaders: The NRA's culture war.* New York: New York University Press.

Nader, R. (2014). *UnStoppable: The emerging left-right alliance to dismantle the corporate state.* New York: Bold Type Books.

National Center for Health Statistics. (2020). Firearm mortality by state. Centers for Disease Control and Prevention. Retrieved February 19, 2020 (https://www.cdc.gov/nchs/pressroom/sosmap/firearm_mortality/firearm.htm).

Newport, F. (2009, June 1). Republican base heavily white, conservative, religious. Gallup Research. Retrieved February 2, 2020 (https://news.gallup.com/poll/118937/republican-base-heavily-white-conservative-religious.aspx).

Open Secrets Center for Responsive Politics. 2020a. Everytown for Gun Safety. Retrieved March 18, 2020 (https://www.opensecrets.org/orgs/summary.php?id=D000067401).

Open Secrets Center for Responsive Politics. 2020b. National Rifle Assn. Retrieved March 18, 2020 (https://www.opensecrets.org/orgs/summary.php?id=d000000082&cycle=2016).

Parker, K., Horowitz, J., Igielnik, R., Oliphant, B., and Brown, A. (2017, June 22). America's complex relationship with guns. Pew Research Center. Retrieved March 3, 2020 (https://www.pewsocialtrends.org/2017/06/22/views-on-gun-policy/).

Planty, M., and Truman, J. (2013). Firearm violence, 1993–2011. US Department of Justice. Bureau of Justice Statistics. May. Retrieved March 1, 2020 (https://bjs.gov/content/pub/pdf/fv9311.pdf).

Reinhart, R. (2018). 6 in 10 Americans support stricter gun laws. Gallup Research. Retrieved February 22, 2020 (https://news.gallup.com/poll/243797/six-americans-support-stricter-gun-laws.aspx).

Rudolph, K., Stuart, E., Vermick, J., and Webster, D. (2015). Association between Connecticut's permit-to-purchase handgun law and homicides. *American Journal of Public Health, 105*(8): 49–54.

Sharockman, A. (2012, June 15). Is the NRA right that Obama is 'coming for our guns?' Politifact. Retrieved February 13, 2020 (https://www.politifact.com/article/2012/jun/15/nra-right-obama-coming-our-guns/).

Sillito, C., and Salari, S. (2011). Child outcomes and risk factors in U.S. homicide-suicide cases 1999–2004. *Journal of Family Violence,* 26: 285–297.

Wolfson, J., Teret, S., Frattaroli S., Miller M., and Azrael, D. (2016). The US public's preference for safer guns. *American Journal of Public Health,* 106: 411–413.

Zimring, F. (2008). *The great American crime decline.* New York: Oxford University Press.

8

What Every Civilian Needs to Know from Professional Law Enforcement Firearms Instructors

David Wulff and Joseph Binns

Today the politics of guns gets in the way of how we view the world and the political parties in our country. Most people continue to narrow their focus and concerns for gun rights to one specific issue: their constitutional right to own and possess a weapon. They spend more time worrying about what weapon to purchase and when to purchase it but give no thought whatsoever about training with the new weapon. This lack of practical training puts everyone at risk. As we have over sixty years of law enforcement firearms training, we have seen mistakes that officers make due to lack of training all the time. One of the most common errors made is to keep your finger off the trigger until you plan to shoot. Officers will then have something happen that startles them and next thing you know the trigger is pulled by accident. Recently, I was assigned a civil case where the suspect who was wanted for a very serious charge jumped out of the side window of a house, right into an officer covering that portion of the house, but the officer had his finger on the trigger, negligently fired his weapon, killing the suspect. This is not what anyone wanted to happen, but it comes from not being attentive to your training.

I remember attending the North Carolina Firearms Instructor's Annual Conference back in the 1990s and the guest speaker was Col. Jeff Cooper (*History of Lt*, 2020). Of the many things he discussed with us that day, he spent some time talking about choosing weapons for our respective agencies. This was during the time where most agencies were switching over from revolvers to semi-automatic handguns. What he said has stuck with me to this day. He stated that "the very best handgun on the market, and the very best round for that handgun, was the one in your hand." Of course, he knew that most of us being low-ranking officers did not have the power to choose the weapon carried at our agencies, but we had to train our officers to use that handgun to the very best of their abilities to save their life, or the life of others. He understood and made us understand that our handgun is just an extension of our will.

ARE YOU YELLOW OR BLACK?

What Col. Cooper was famous for was a simple to remember Color Code of Awareness Levels (OPSGEAR, 2018). Condition White, Condition Yellow, Condition Orange, Condition Red, and Condition Black. Many people live their lives existing in Condition White which is a state of complete unawareness of conditions around them. They are not looking for anything to occur, because nothing has ever occurred before. Nothing will ever happen to me; it is always the "other guy" syndrome. If a critical situation/threat were to occur in Condition White you are most likely to become a victim.

Condition Yellow is a person who has trained themselves to look out for trouble. You can stay in this condition indefinitely and simply pay attention to your surroundings. You evaluate your surrounds and assess any changes as they happen. This is not a consistent state of fear, but a state of awareness.

Condition Orange means that you have identified a threat, or at least the possibility of a threat. An example might be that in Condition Yellow when at home and you hear a knock at the door that is not expected, you think about any potential concerns that this may mean, but in Condition Orange it may be a pounding at the door late at night. This is completely unexpected, but since you are always aware of your situation it is an easy transition from Condition Yellow to the next level and are developing a plan.

Condition Red is the mode of reaction. You are aware of your surroundings, have identified a threat, developed a plan, and now you are reacting to the plan. A person cannot stay in Condition Orange or Condition Red for an extended period of time but can sustain Condition Yellow indefinitely.

Condition Black was added to the chart years later and just identifies a complete breakdown of ability to react. Imagine a serious incident threat occurred when your mindset was in Condition White. You would be completely unprepared to act and react, causing a breakdown. In your panic, you would transition to Condition Black where you are basically frozen and unable to react to the incident. In Condition Black, there is no fighting back, no reacting, or even seeking cover. No one wants to ever end up in Condition Black.

Situational awareness/Condition Yellow is a whole new way of thinking. If you can keep yourself in Condition Yellow, you find yourself not sitting in a restaurant with your back to the door. You sit in the back of the restaurant or other building so that you can watch who comes in and out of the business. You are more aware of your surroundings, being careful when leaving a public restroom because things may have changed while you were inside. When you are looking for a parking space at the store, you find yourself looking for spaces that are closer to the store in well-lighted conditions. If the only available space is far away in a dark area, you move on to the next place, or shop another day. It is all about having the right mindset. After all, if it is too dangerous to go to some place unarmed, why are you going there to begin with? This is all about total commitment, a new responsibility that you must take seriously.

As you can see, a majority of the thought process for being armed is mindset. Carrying a firearm is not a hobby; it is a real change of lifestyle that needs to be taken seriously. Carrying a firearm needs to be consistent, so that it is something that you do every day. After all, you never know when that day may come when you will need your firearm to protect yourself or a loved one. If you knew the day you were going to need your firearm, that is the only day you would need to carry it. Unfortunately, none of us is psychic, so any day could be the one that you need the gun. The only way to be prepared is to carry every day. It means keeping your wallet, keys, and carry gun all together so that whenever you leave the house it comes with you.

To this point, I remember hearing a story in the news about a woman who always carried her handgun in her purse. On one Sunday afternoon, she met her daughter at a local restaurant for lunch. She decided to leave her purse in her car when she went into the business. About halfway through the lunch, an irate armed employee came into the store and started shooting customers and employees. All she could think about was that she had left her gun in her purse in the car. Having a weapon does no good if you do not have it with you when you need it.

We know for certain that the more you train in realistic scenarios the better you will perform in a real-life scenario. The problem is that now, when we go to our local ranges, the civilian range rules get in the way of appropriate training. We are prohibited from shooting fast, shooting multiple rounds, shooting from a draw, shooting while moving, practicing malfunction drills, and a variety of other training exercises needed in order to protect ourselves properly and be proficient at handling the weapon we carry. Finding appropriate training facilities and training courses that allow this type of shooting is essential to learning to be effective in handling a firearm. There are schools available, but they are difficult to find and can be extremely costly depending on what they offer. Finding a training facility/school that offers the ability to practice shooting from various positions as well as other mechanics such as moving, reloading, and simply drawing the weapon can be the most important thing to look for in a training class. Conversely, we have seen special weapons and tactics teams that only train for speed and not accuracy. While they may be able to draw and fire very quickly, during an actual event where accuracy is just as important, they are lacking in the appropriate training to accurately hit their target. Every firearms owner is ultimately responsible for the resting place of the round they fire from their weapon. If they hit an innocent person, they are responsible for that round. As you can see, both speed and accuracy are both extremely important and both only come with the proper training.

As law enforcement firearms instructors, we have been fortunate to have been in professionally sponsored schools that provide the techniques needed to survive a deadly force encounter. Unfortunately, the general public does not have these same opportunities to take these advanced-skills classes without spending an inordinate amount of money. These schools are out there, but they may not be an option for most people who own firearms.

In this chapter, we will discuss various options on where to carry a firearm as a civilian, whether extra ammunition should be carried and where. We will also discuss training, equipment, escalation of force, use of deadly force, cover vs. concealment, revolvers vs. semi-automatics, ammunition, weapon retention, and unfortunately, we would be remiss if we did not bring out suicide as an issue as well. In our experience in teaching both civilian and professional law enforcement officers, we see that this is an area that needs to be reviewed.

ESCALATION OF FORCE

The escalation of force is the increase in the level of force based on the force being used against you. Everyone who carries a deadly weapon needs to be aware of this continuum. Each situation is different, and you can go directly to the use of deadly force (U.S. Department of Justice, 2009), but these considerations do need to take place:

- Physical Presence—your mere presence can work to deter criminal activity. Most criminals are there for a crime of opportunity and do not want confrontation.
- Verbal—by using calm commands, telling the person to get away will generally work and if at all possible, should be attempted.
- Soft Hands—if necessary, you can grab the person and direct them away from you.
- Hard Hands—if necessary and all lower levels of force have failed, you can punch or kick the suspect who is trying to harm you.

- Chemical (Mace, OC Spray, & Electrical)—pepper spray or controlled energy devices can be used to get the suspect to stop their threatening behavior.
- Impact Weapons (Stick or Club)—an impact weapon such as a baton, stick, bat, or club can also deter a suspect from hurting you. The use of any weapon along these lines would be considered deadly force if used against the head.
- Deadly Force—the last resort on the continuum, and only if all else has failed.

It is not always necessary to use each of these steps, although if possible, you should. If a suspect starts out at a higher level of force because they have a gun, you do not have to go through the steps, you can go straight to deadly force. Generally, though, you are better of having tried some lower level of force first.

Unless there is an immediate threat to your life, you always have a duty to retreat. That does not always mean running away but may mean an attempt to use a lower level of force such as pepper spray, or soft hands. If you look at any police officer's duty gear you will see pepper spray, a baton of some sort, and generally a controlled energy device, so they are prepared to retreat where necessary.

USE OF DEADLY FORCE

Each state has its own laws and rules, but as a general rule these are safe guidelines to follow:

a. The citizen actually believes deadly force is necessary to prevent an imminent threat of death, great bodily harm, or sexual assault, and
b. The facts and circumstances prompting that belief would cause a person of ordinary firmness to believe deadly force was necessary to prevent an imminent threat of death, great bodily harm, or sexual assault, and
c. The person using deadly force was not an instigator or aggressor who voluntarily provoked, entered, or continued the conflict leading to deadly force, and
d. Force used was not excessive—greater than reasonably needed to overcome the threat posed by a hostile aggressor.

What is listed in (a) through (d) is North Carolina Common Law on Use of Deadly Force (North Carolina, n.d.). Each state will have variations, but generally if you follow these guidelines, you will be safe from criminal prosecution. It is best to visit the Attorney General's website in the state you reside to be sure of any variables in the law.

TRAINING

In all aspects of firearms training, mindset is extremely important. You must have made up your mind under no uncertain terms that you can use deadly force to protect yourself, or others from a deadly attack. In other words, could you take a human life in order to protect your own life, or the life of another? If the answer is no, then carrying a firearm is not for you.

In order to get a concealed handgun permit in most states the training is minimal. Most of the process surrounds your legal right to possess a firearm, criminal record, mental health record, and so on. Very little time is spent shooting with the expectation that you already know how to shoot before you attend the class. In many cases, though, the first time a person shoots a handgun is just before, or the day of the class. This shooting is very basic at best and more training needs to be done by the shooter/student to be skilled enough to carry a firearm.

In order to learn, you need to find a place to practice that will allow you to train. We need to look for courses that teach the fundamentals of the draw from a concealed carry, malfunction drills, shooting while moving, reloading techniques, trigger control techniques, and more. One way you can hone your skills is to get involved in competition. One of the best places to start is with the International Defensive Pistol Association (IDPA) Competitions (2020). These are set up to be practical and use the skills you need to have in order to safely carry a firearm for self-defense. By involving yourself in these matches, you do not have to set your sights on becoming a National Champion but come out to learn and hone your skills. You can see how others go through the drills and improve. You generally do not have to go far to find a local match and maybe meet some nice people in your area with similar interests. There are online courses available; although not ideal for handling skills, they go a long way to help mindset.

As you begin training with your new firearm, the best way to start is by working on the draw and trigger pull. Remember, if you are carrying your handgun concealed, then you must first be able to reach the weapon quickly before drawing it. This puts you already at a disadvantage as there is a barrier in place that prevents you from easily reaching the weapon. The goal is to practice the draw and trigger pull so that you can quickly access the weapon and use it should you need to. Carrying a gun does not do you any good should you not be able to get to it quickly in an emergency.

Some weapon systems have more difficult triggers than others. You always start any training session with the weapon unloaded and the magazine out of the weapon. You look to verify the magazine is out and feel with a finger to verify the weapon is unloaded, with the slide back for semi-automatic weapons and safety on (if it comes with one). After verifying both physically and visually that the weapon is unloaded, you face in a safe direction and practice your draw and fire. You want to make sure you come out of the holster "smooth and fast" and that your trigger pull is smooth. You must be careful not to jerk the trigger as this will cause the barrel to move off of target. You should practice one-handed draws, strong and support handed. If your strong hand were to become incapacitated, could you still reach your weapon with your support hand? That could make the difference between life and death. Practice drawing and pulling the trigger twice as you draw your weapon. Again, all this before you ever get to an open range to actually fire the weapon.

COVER VS. CONCEALMENT

When involved in a gunfight the person involved will revert to their training. If a person has had no training, they will revert to Condition Black as discussed earlier, where they are in a state of panic. Knowing what to do and when to do it is important. A key element that could make the difference between being a victim and being a survivor is knowing the difference between seeking cover and finding concealment. While operating in Condition Yellow, you should be thinking about objects that provide cover versus objects that only provide concealment. An object that provides cover is something that you can physically get behind that will provide protection from an assailant by stopping a bullet. Examples of an object that provides cover would be the engine block on a car or possibly a solid metal door or table. Concealment is really just the opposite. It is simply something that hides you from view but does not provide any specific protection from an assailant's bullet. An example of an item that provides concealment is possibly hiding behind an interior wall or even behind some brush if outside. You cannot be seen, but a bullet can go right through it. The takeaway from this is while walking around, you should pay attention to the things around you that you can quickly identify as items that provide the cover you would want should you find yourself in a life-threatening situation.

With the increasing number of mass shootings coming to crowded locations like houses of worship and shopping malls, everyone should be observant in identifying items that provide cover versus concealment. In many cases, there may not be any way to run away from the area so you will find yourself having to shelter in place. Will a church pew provide cover or concealment? Where in a mall will you find the most protection for you and your family? Where do you run toward or go to in the event of an active shooter? Twenty years ago, this was not an issue like it is today.

REVOLVER VS. SEMI-AUTOMATIC

Most revolvers that are compact enough for concealed carry hold five or six rounds of ammunition. Most semi-automatic pistols hold at least six rounds with some holding up to twelve or more depending on the model. Capacity of the weapon is seen as a big advantage when it comes to choosing a weapon to carry. In reality, however, the key is not the number of rounds your weapon holds but how reliable it is and how quickly you can access it to fire a round off. A semi-automatic handgun must be kept in pristine condition, being cleaned and well oiled to protect against malfunctions. All semi-automatic handguns are prone to malfunctions at one time or another. These malfunctions could include double-feeds, stovepipe, failure to feed, or even failure to fire. As you can see, there are many points of failure in the semi-automatic handgun. Revolvers generally are much more reliable and tend to rarely malfunction unless there is a problem with the round itself. If someone tells you they have never had a malfunction with a semi-automatic pistol, they are lying to you. It just happens.

A common problem with training is that once a skill is learned, it must be continually practiced in order to maintain that skill. In reality, most people, once they have been trained and pass qualification on the weapon, never train again. This is problematic, especially for those who carry and use a semi-automatic handgun. If you do not train repeatedly on how to clear a malfunctioning weapon, you will never remember how to do it when under stress. Police typically train at least eight to sixteen hours each year on their handgun. This training covers these skills and more. Civilians may only train once on the weapon. If they have a semi-automatic handgun, they will never be able to function in a crisis event. Therefore, we do not suggest a semi-automatic pistol for the novice that has no interest in spending time to learn with their equipment.

Revolvers work very well and have a serious advantage in that they are very simple to use, reload, and clear. This is unlike the semi-automatic where you must train on reloads and malfunction drills regularly to stay safe. Knowing what type of malfunction (*How to Identify*, 2019; Christian, 2018) and how to clear one of several types of malfunctions is key to the responsibility of carrying a semi-automatic pistol. Training on these malfunctions is what will save you in the event it happens in real life.

EQUIPMENT

You will rarely ever see a law enforcement officer with a firearm and no means to reload that firearm. Whether it be a spare magazine, or a speed loader/speed strip it is vital to have that extra insurance. Carrying an extra loading device is not always because you will need extra ammo as the average gunfight is less than three rounds for law enforcement officers. Actual statistics are very difficult to obtain for civilian shootings, but one can deduce from reading cases that it is at least as low for civilians. Law enforcement, however, keeps these statistics, and we find the average is three rounds (FBI, 2017; Michalowski, 2019). So, if so few rounds are fired, why do we need to carry extra ammo? The main reason is malfunctions. If a malfunction occurs with a semi-automatic pistol, most likely the problem can be solved quickly with a magazine change. How you carry spare ammunition is also up to the user. If a semiautomatic is carried, a spare magazine should be carried on the opposite side of your primary shooting hand. This way you can draw the extra magazine out with your support hand to reload. In the event you use a revolver, then the speed loader is on the same side you carry the gun.

How you carry your firearms is also very important. We always try to stay consistent as someone is learning the skills. In other words, one day you carry a shoulder holster, then the next day a strong side draw holster, or a pocket holster, and so on. Stay consistent in what you do so that when you need the weapon your hand goes to the right place. The holster needs to be able to hold the weapon in place while doing a series of exercises like jumping jacks. No matter what system you use, make sure the weapon is carried on your body. By no means should you use a purse/backpack-style carry system that is not attached to the body. It is so easy to set down an item and next thing you know it is stolen from you. Remember that you have added this additional responsibility to your life and it is important to take it seriously.

Women make up the fastest growing portion of gun owners today and therefore many new items are coming available for women to carry today. Do your research and find the weapon and carry system that works best for you. There are a great deal of clothes available today that have built-in holsters, belly bands, leggings, shirts. Always remember that the key is concealment.

Just because you have the weapon covered does not mean that your clothes won't cause an imprint of the weapon, making it obvious what you are doing. Several things affect the ability to identify a bulge as a gun. The location where you have the gun on your body, how tight is the clothing over top of the gun, and the angle you have the gun. The carry system also needs to be comfortable, or you won't use it.

AMMUNITION

Ammunition is a key component of any weapons system and needs to be taken very seriously. Making a decision about the best round to carry is difficult. A great deal of information is available from SAAMI (Sporting Arms and Ammunition Manufacturers' Institute, n.d.). What you are trying to achieve is fifteen inches of penetration (Vista Outdoor, n.d.) on a gelatin test through a variety of mediums. The material used is automobile glass, wallboard, steel, heavy clothing, and plywood. Accurate information is available to help you make these decisions. Generally, you want to use the ammo that will perform best in the gun that you are using.

Ammunition should also be inspected before you carry it. This is generally done by the disassembly of your gun, using only the barrel. You place each round in the barrel, making sure the round does not hang up and is free of defects. Occasionally the case has a bur, or the primer is raised. This will cause a malfunction when you do not need one. In the decades we have been teaching law enforcement firearms, we have only seen this on a handful of occasions, but the point is that it does happen. This only needs to be done with the ammo you are carrying for defense. Range ammo is just that—if you have a malfunction, it is the perfect opportunity to practice malfunction drills.

In the event you are carrying a revolver, you would do the same test. Place the rounds in the cylinder, and before closing the cylinder, you examine that the rounds fit into the cylinder and that all the primers are flush with the back of the case. If there is a high primer, the cylinder will not rotate and the revolver will not function.

Ammunition that is carried on you for defense should only be carried for a year. This ammo is exposed to a variety of climates, perspiration, oil, and so on, and should be replaced at the end of each year. You certainly can use it for the range, but do not trust your life on it. While discussing just this issue with a sheriff's deputy friend, he confided in me that he was carrying the same ammo in his gun that he was issued when he graduated from the academy. That was about seven years prior to this conversation. I made a bet with him for a steak dinner that it would not fire. We went to a secluded place to test my theory. The first round did fire, but lodged halfway down his barrel. I lost the bet on a technicality, but most likely saved his life as he was involved in a shooting a few weeks later where he needed his handgun to actually work.

Many people unload their gun when they come home and then reload before they go back out. If this is what you do, then make sure you rotate that first round of ammunition around so that it is not always the same round being chambered. The consistent slamming of that round into the barrel up the feed ramp will eventually close the hollow point, causing the bullet to overpenetrate when it is needed most.

Cleaning your firearm is very important and carrying a clean gun is vital as well. Making sure your gun does not rust means the use of a good quality oil, but being careful not to have too much lubrication that will drip onto and damage your ammunition is also a key element. Oils can penetrate your rounds, killing the gun powder and damaging the primer as well. It is important to make sure that you keep your gun dry yet well lubricated.

Carrying a clean gun is important for a variety of reasons. One of the main reasons it is recommended for law enforcement is if an on-duty shooting occurs and you are not involved, it is easy to show a clean gun. Imagine this being the same case in the civilian world and found in a shooting. You having a weapon that is nice and clean would go a long way in showing you were not involved.

We are often asked how often you need to clean your weapon (Lexipol, 2020). Generally, it is recommended that every six months, or anytime you fire your weapon it should be cleaned. There are variables that change this. If you get caught out in rain, or in the heat and you perspire a lot, it is a good idea to clean and oil your weapon. Some of the military branches require the weapons be cleaned every month, or after every exercise, or operation. The important thing is to know how your gun functions and stay on top of the maintenance.

IMPORTANCE OF WEAPON RETENTION

While the feeling of being safe because of having a gun readily available can be comforting, there are many dangers that go along with possessing a weapon. Just as in law enforcement, every encounter someone has who is carrying a concealed weapon involves that weapon. Whether the perpetrator has a weapon or not, there is a weapon involved in the incident. Police officers train frequently on gun retention skills because there is always the likelihood that someone will try and take their weapon away. For most departments however, the officers' handgun is in a holster that provides some protection.

Depending on the threat level, also known as retention level of the holster, there are actually specific movements that must be completed to draw the gun from the holster (Wood, 2015). Most concealed carry holsters do not have these protections, so the threat of the bad guy getting hold of your gun is much greater.

If you make the decision to carry a concealed weapon, you must prepare for the possibility that the perpetrator will attempt to get your gun away from you. How are you going to react? What are you going to do to keep this from happening? If the bad guy does try and take your weapon away from you, then that is certainly a deadly force encounter. Are you willing to shoot someone who is attempting to get your gun? Have you practiced how-to gun-retention skills so that you can reach quickly and effectively?

Protecting yourself is really all about maintaining or creating distance between you and your attacker. It's not about being able to "stand your ground." It should be used as a defensive weapon only, as a means of not just protecting yourself and your loved ones, but also providing the necessary time to create distance and move to a safe location to get help. If you pull that weapon, then distance should be your primary goal. Understand that if you are too close or extend your arms out to fire the weapon, there is the possibility that the perpetrator can grab your gun and then you both become involved in a life-or-death struggle for the gun. Should you lose your handgun in the scuffle, you would more than likely be the victim of a deadly shooting. It is imperative that you learn to shoot with the weapon up close, tucked in so that it provides the maximum amount of protection from the attacker grabbing the weapon. Officers learn all day to shoot from what we call a combat stance where the weapon remains tucked unless they are extending to fire.

If the situation presents itself where you feel that your life or the life of someone is in danger, draw the weapon from whatever location you have it concealed. As you are drawing the weapon, go with a two-hand hold on the weapon for maximum control. Keep the weapon tucked as you are moving to an area away from the threat. If you need to fire, then fire as you are extending your arms toward the target, look to verify that you have struck your target, but continuing to move to a safe location. Follow the first rounds fired with additional rounds if necessary if the threat continues toward you.

Understand again that if you allow the offender to grab your gun, then you are in a fight for your life. Pull the weapon in close to your body as you continue to try and pull the weapon away. Depending on where the barrel of the gun is pointing, you can pull the trigger in an attempt to make the offender release the weapon. Having it tucked close to your body provides additional strength from your core whereas the offender is using arm strength alone. This gives you a tactical advantage. As you are tucking the weapon, turn to your side and use your body as a wedge to force the offender to release their grip. Again, as they release their grip, your objective is to continue moving to a safe location but should provide some distance between you and your attacker so that you can again be prepared to fire.

SUICIDE

While carrying a concealed handgun is great for protection, the leading cause of violent death in the United States is suicide, and most suicides are gun related. In the United States today, we are "experiencing a suicide epidemic." Suicide by gun is one of the most underreported incidents in the United States. The media will report all day on homicides by guns and accidental shootings. But when it comes to suicides, they frequently do not put that information on their newscasts. It is therefore out of the public eye and most people do not realize how big of a problem it actually is. There are still a lot of issues with people who have been diagnosed with a mental illness who have violent tendencies being able to purchase guns. Many of the loopholes have been closed if purchasing from a retailer but many people buy weapons from personal sellers or at gun shows. Here, there are no background checks to see if someone has been committed to an institution or diagnosed with a mental health disorder that would otherwise keep them from gun ownership. When purchasing from private sellers, no permits are obtained so the seller has no idea about the personal character of the buyer or how mentally stable they are. In areas where people have this easy access to guns, the death rate by suicide is triple what it is in other places.

When people make the decision to take their own life, many times they plan out their own demise over and over in their head, down to the smallest detail. In a lot of cases, however, the decision is based on a major life event such as a divorce or losing their job. In these cases, when a firearm is easily accessed, there is an increased risk of completing the actual suicide (Gramlich, 2022). The time difference between the decision to take their own life and the attempt is typically short, especially when there is a lethal force option available.

Each year, there are more than 1,000 children and teen deaths by guns alone (Maloney, n.d.). This makes it imperative that gun owners secure their handguns while they are not carrying them. Many states have enacted laws that require gun owners to secure their weapons and keep them out of the reach of children. These laws come with hefty penalties for any violators. As a best practice, firearms should be kept in a locked safe, something that is either opened by biometrics or some combination. Too many times, kids find the keys to the gun safe and out of curiosity, go into the safe and play with the guns inside. Not having been trained in how to safely handle a gun, kids are more likely to mistake an unloaded gun for a loaded gun. This reality too often results in the death or severe injury of a child. Given the numbers of kids who commit suicide, it is even more imperative that they are unable to easily access firearms.

SUMMARY

Carrying a weapon is not just a right given to us by the Constitution, it is a choice that each gun owner must make every day they leave their house. The overall decision to own and carry a handgun should not be taken lightly. There is a big difference between the individual who carries a weapon and trains with it and the untrained civilian who just carries it with them to make themselves feel better or safer. The untrained individual is just as much a threat to themselves as they are to everyone around them. It ultimately comes down to whether or not you are committed to carrying a weapon and whether you believe you would use it if you had to. There is a big difference between drawing the weapon and pulling the trigger while pointing at another human being. If you are not prepared for that possible outcome, you are better off not carrying a gun at all.

You are responsible for every round that comes out of your weapon. Far too many people are injured or killed every year by accidental gunfire. I can remember countless calls as a police officer where civilians have accidentally shot a family member or themselves while "playing with the gun" and "didn't realize it was loaded." They have shot through their hands or legs while cleaning the gun because they forgot to check the chamber for a live round. These are not toys, so they must be treated as if loaded all the time. The decision to own and carry a handgun must be taken seriously along with the commitment to train with that weapon so that you will be proficient and safe should the need arise to use it.

After deciding on which gun to purchase, there are so many other decisions that have to be made. A decision has to be made about what holster to use, where to carry the concealed weapon to provide for maximum access, what type of ammunition to purchase, and how often and how much training you need to be competent. There are decisions about what other equipment must be purchased, where to train, and where to store the weapon when at home.

There is not a book out there that can cover every detail a person can think of to protect you in every instance. If you are going to take the carrying of a handgun seriously, you need to spend time learning the details spoken about in this chapter and beyond. Get together with friends of like mind and talk through scenarios. Study what has happened in various cases when you hear about them and consider what could have been done better or differently. By all means, please take this topic seriously, or leave it alone.

BIBLIOGRAPHY

Christian, C. (2018, May 30). *4 Handgun Malfunction Causes & Clearance Drills*. Shooting Illustrated. https://www.shootingillustrated.com/articles/2018/5/30/4-handgun-malfunction-causes-clearance-drills/.

FBI. (2017). *2017 Law Enforcement Officers Killed & Assaulted*. UCR. https://ucr.fbi.gov/leoka/2017/tables/table-106.xls.

Gramlich, J. (2022, February 3). *What the Data Says About Gun Deaths in the U.S.* https://www.pewresearch.org/fact-tank/2022/02/03/what-the-data-says-about-gun-deaths-in-the-u-s/.

History of Lt Col Jeff Cooper. Gunsite Academy. (2020, July 29). https://www.gunsite.com/about-lt-col-jeff-cooper/.

How to Identify and Clear Pistol Malfunctions. NSSF Let's Go Shooting. (2019, January 8). https://www.letsgoshooting.org/articles/how-to-identify-and-clear-pistol-malfunctions/.

International Defensive Pistol Association. (2020, October 29). https://www.idpa.com/.

Lexipol. (2020, January 21). *How to Maintain Your Carry Ammo*. Police1. https://www.police1.com/police-products/firearms/accessories/ammunition/articles/how-to-maintain-your-carry-ammo-h6YlR5T4tgOTiNRL/.

Maloney, C. (n.d.). Guns and Suicide. United States Congress. https://www.jec.senate.gov/public/_cache/files/e4c6a3e3-a170-4cee-8218-0167fe4311e9/jec2019-gunsandsuicide-final.pdf.

Michalowski, K. (2019, February 25). *The Statistically Perfect Gunfight*. USCCA. https://www.usconcealedcarry.com/blog/the-statistically-perfect-gunfight/.

North Carolina General Assembly. (n.d.). G.S. 14-51.3. https://www.ncleg.net/EnactedLegislation/Statutes/PDF/BySection/Chapter_14/GS_14-51.3.pdf.

OPSGEAR (DP Creations LLC). (2018, December 18). *Color Code of Mental Awareness & Combat Mindset*. OPSGEAR (DP Creations LLC). https://www.opsgear.com/blogs/opsgear%C2%AE-blog/color-code-of-mental-awareness-combat-mindset.

Sporting Arms and Ammunition Manufacturers' Institute. (n.d.). SAAMI. https://saami.org/.

U.S. Department of Justice. (2009, August 3). *The Use-of-Force Continuum*. National Institute of Justice. https://nij.ojp.gov/topics/articles/use-force-continuum.

Vista Outdoor Operations LLC. (n.d.). *Wound Ballistics—Load Comparison*. Law Enforcement Ammunition and Accessories. https://le.vistaoutdoor.com/wound_ballistics/load_comparison/load_comparison.aspx.

Wood, M. (2015). *What Cops Need to Know About "Levels" of Holster Retention.* https://www.police1.com/police-products/firearms/accessories/articles/what-cops-need-to-know-about-levels-of-holster-retention-FYon6lo6B1TJ8qHl/.

Part III

ECONOMICS, PSYCHOLOGY, POLITICS, AND RACE

9

The Use and Misuse of Gun Data

Matthew Dobra

The United States has some of the highest rates of gun ownership, violent crime, and gun crime among developed countries. Many argue that these facts imply that guns are not simply involved in a significant amount of violence in America, but rather are the cause of the significant amount of violence in America. This is not the only perspective, however; those who stand in opposition to this view argue that the availability of guns simply leads to criminals choosing to use them more often than other weapons in crimes they would commit anyway, and guns used defensively by private citizens actually reduce crime.

These competing perspectives have been a ubiquitous part of the American political landscape for decades, particularly after the events at Columbine High School on April 20, 1999. The Columbine massacre marked a watershed moment in American history. Since Columbine, mass shootings have become increasingly more common in America, as seen in figure 9.1. Figure 9.1 displays FBI data on active shooter incidents by year in the United States between 2000 and 2018 (Federal Bureau, 2020). The top panel shows a clear increase in the number of active shooter incidents over this time period, and the middle panel displays an increase in casualties (both deaths and injuries) from those incidents. The spike in casualties in 2017 was driven by the shooting at the Route 91 Harvest country music festival in Las Vegas, which makes the time trend somewhat difficult to see in the middle panel. The bottom panel of figure 9.1 omits the casualties from the Las Vegas shooting for the sole purpose of showing that the rise in casualties is not simply the result of a single outlier event, but rather that there is a clear trend of increasing severity over this time period.

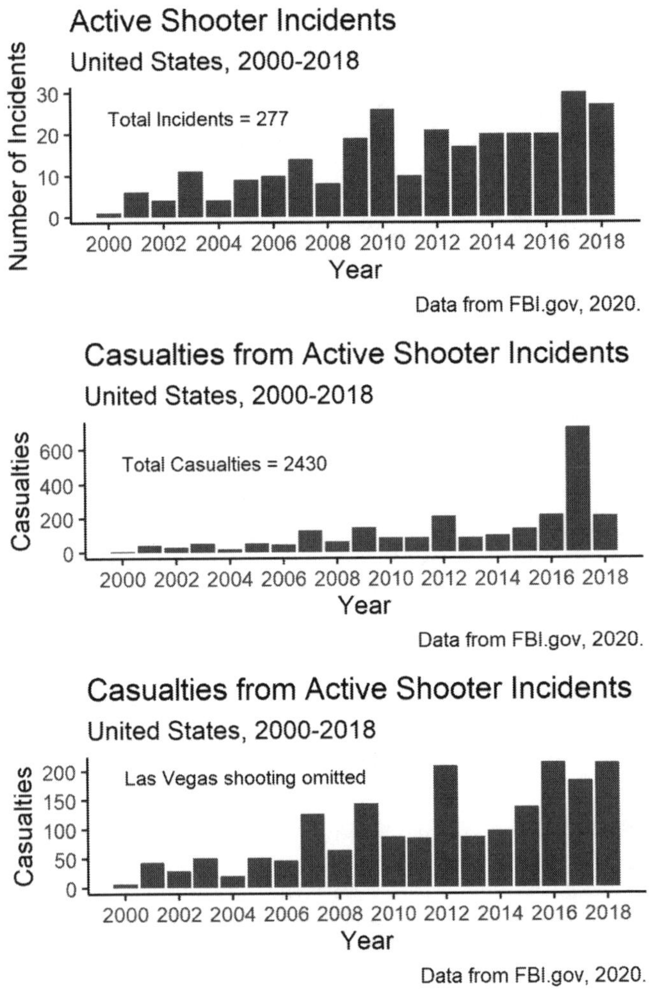

Figure 9.1. Active Shooter Incidents. ***Data from FBI.gov.***

Those who believe that guns are the cause of violence often point to the rise in mass shootings in their calls for gun control measures. While the sensational headlines and evocative graphics that are splashed across all forms of media following shootings generate sympathy and awareness for the issue, these shootings typically disappear into the news cycle within a few days, so the calls are rarely sustained for long. Gun proponents, on the other hand, seem to be capable of more sustained support for their cause. As a result, despite frequent agitation for more stringent regulation on the ownership of guns in the United States, there has been relatively little change in federal gun laws this century.

What is the relationship between gun ownership and crime rates? The answer to this question is the "holy grail" of gun literature. As discussed above, for some, the answer is that higher gun ownership rates are the cause of higher crime rates. To others, the answer is that guns actually reduce crime. Knowing the answer, and building gun policy based on that answer, should be the government's ultimate goal. But which of these answers is correct? This chapter does not seek to answer this question; rather, this chapter will look at the issue of *how* to answer this question and why most answers given are unsatisfactory, as many claims of a causal relationship between guns and crime are less convincing than they appear at first glance.

This chapter will advance four primary arguments. While claims regarding the relationship between guns and crime are often built on emotion or logic, this chapter will (1) demonstrate that this question cannot be resolved without careful data analysis. Moreover, many of the data-driven claims mistake correlation with causation. Establishing causation is very tricky, particularly in the case of the relationship between guns and crime, and this chapter will (2) illustrate why this question is indeed so tricky (with as little actual math and statistics and as much intuition as possible), (3) identify common statistical mistakes made when attempting to answer this question, and (4) provide guidance on how to evaluate the validity of the data-based evidence deployed in this research.

THE NEED FOR CAREFUL DATA ANALYSIS

The empirical research around guns typically starts with a deceptively simple question: what is the relationship between rates of gun ownership and crime? This question is necessarily empirical; the answer cannot be deduced logically because there are a variety of avenues by which gun ownership might affect crime rates. In other words, because there are some mechanisms by which the prevalence of guns might *increase* crime, and other mechanisms by which the prevalence of guns might *decrease* crime, the *net* effect of all these mechanisms has to be teased out from the data. The various avenues by which the prevalence of firearms might impact crime can be sorted into three broad categories: *criminal technology*, *self-defense*, and *deterrence* (Kovandzic et al., 2013).

The extent to which higher rates of firearm prevalence might be expected to result in higher crime rates owes primarily to the fact that guns are a potential criminal technology. Guns, simply put, increase the practicality of criminal behavior. If guns make crimes easier to commit and/or increase the likelihood of success from a given criminal act, areas where guns are more prevalent should see higher crime rates. Moreover, if guns increase the profitability of criminal activity relative to legal activity, then higher rates of gun ownership might result in more people being drawn into criminal behavior. Finally, even if there is no effect on the amount of criminal behavior, the use of guns in criminal acts may increase the severity and lethality of any given crime.

While the criminal technology mechanism implies that higher rates of gun ownership should increase crime rates, the effect of the self-defense and deterrence mechanisms should push in the other direction. The self-defense mechanism implies that the more guns are prevalent within a society, the higher the likelihood that a crime might be thwarted by either an armed would-be victim or onlooker, thereby reducing the crime rate; the crime does not occur because it is simply stopped in the process. The deterrence effect suggests that criminals view committing a crime against an armed victim, or in the presence of a gun-wielding onlooker, as being a relatively more dangerous exercise than committing a crime in the absence of such armed individuals. Intuitively, more guns within a community increases the likelihood of an armed victim or passerby, which in turn increases the risk associated with the commission of any given crime, ultimately reducing crime rates because the increased risk discourages some would-be criminals from committing crimes altogether. It is also possible that these two mechanisms reinforce one another; acts of self-defense are often noteworthy and publicized, thereby having a deterrence effect of their own.

The existence of these countervailing forces (criminal technology, self-defense, and deterrence) implies that the relationship between guns and crime rates cannot simply be deduced logically—this is necessarily an empirical question, because what matters is the relative magnitudes of these effects. If the deterrence and self-defense effects are bigger than the criminal technology effect, then guns reduce crime. If the criminal technology effect is bigger than the deterrence and self-defense effects, then guns increase crime. While there is considerable literature that looks at disentangling and quantifying the effect of each of these three forces, the focus here is simply to determine the net effect of the three forces combined.

But even if the goal is to simply quantify the net effect, looking just at correlations between gun prevalence and crime rates across different cities (or counties, states, countries, etc.) will inevitably lead to incorrect conclusions. For example, consider figure 9.2, which looks at the correlation between violent crime rates (measured as violent crimes per 100,000 population) (Federal Bureau, 2013) and gun ownership rates (the estimated percentage of

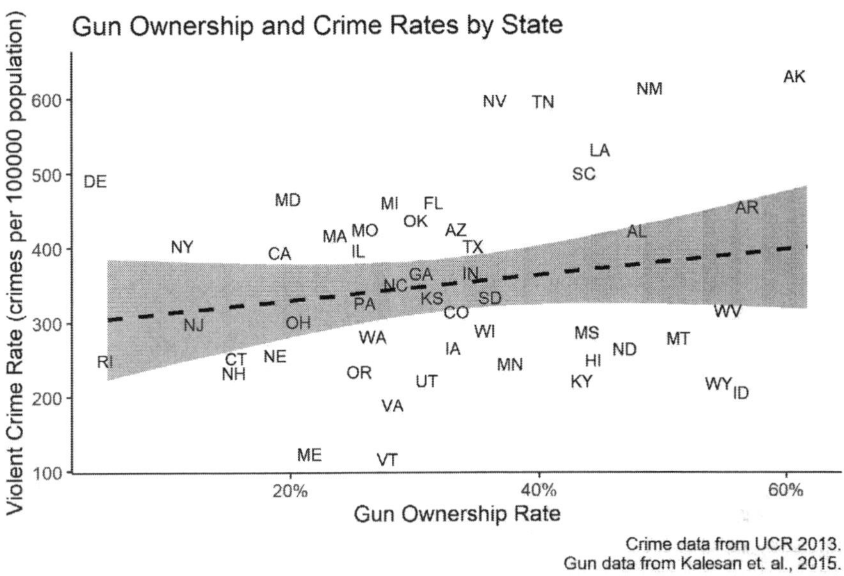

Figure 9.2. Gun Ownership and Crime Rates by State. ***Crime data from UCR 2013 Gun Data from Kalesan et al., 2016. Figure created by Matt Dobra.***

adults who are gun owners) (Kalesan et al., 2016), at the state level in 2013. The graph shows a positive (though not statistically significant) correlation between gun ownership and crime rates. Graphs of this ilk—showing simple correlations between some measure of gun prevalence and some outcome believed to be caused by guns—are commonplace in professional media, social media, infographics, and the like. But this graph, along with all graphs and studies based on correlational inference, is fundamentally flawed.

It is common to hear empirical researchers use the expression "correlation does not imply causation." Within the context of figure 9.2, "correlation does not imply causation" suggests that the mere relationship between states with higher gun ownership rates having higher violent crime rates does not imply that the higher gun ownership rate caused the higher violent crime rates. To establish causality—for example, to be able to say that *A* causes *B*—three conditions (Kenny, 1979) must be true. The first condition is that *A* must occur either before or at the same time as *B*. If *B* happens first, it cannot possibly have been caused by *A*. Second, *A* must be correlated with *B* with some degree of statistical significance. Finally, the relationship between *A* and *B* must not be *endogenous*, which is a term used in statistics that essentially means that the relationship between *A* and *B* cannot be explained by other causes that have not been accounted for in the analysis. If the final condition does not hold, and the relationship between *A* and *B* is endogenous, then any estimated correlation between *A* and *B* is meaningless. Generally speaking, the first condition for establishing causality—temporality—is fairly obvious, and the second condition is the relatively straightforward application of statistics. The third condition—endogeneity—is more complicated and a significant shortcoming of many analyses that examine the relationship between guns and crime. So, what causes endogeneity? In the case of the question being discussed at present—the relationship between rates of gun ownership and crime—there are three significant concerns: *omitted variables*, *simultaneity*, and *error in measurement* of the causal variable (in this case, guns) (Antonakis et al., 2010).

At the most basic level, omitted variable bias simply means that the analysis is not accounting for something that is also causing the phenomenon of interest. Consider again figure 9.2; a graph that plots gun ownership against crime rates implicitly assumes that the *only* factor that impacts crime rates is gun ownership. There is, however, considerable literature that crime rates have many causes. Every update of the FBI's Uniform Crime Report (Federal Bureau, 2011) since 2004 has included the following list of variables that affect crime:

- Population density and degree of urbanization.
- Variations in composition of the population, particularly youth concentration.
- Stability of the population with respect to residents' mobility, commuting patterns, and transient factors.
- Modes of transportation and highway system.
- Economic conditions, including median income, poverty level, and job availability.
- Cultural factors and educational, recreational, and religious characteristics.
- Family conditions with respect to divorce and family cohesiveness.
- Climate.
- Effective strength of law enforcement agencies.
- Administrative and investigative emphases of law enforcement.
- Policies of other components of the criminal justice system (i.e., prosecutorial, judicial, correctional, and probational).
- Citizens' attitudes toward crime.
- Crime reporting practices of the citizenry.
  (Federal Bureau, 2011)

Consider this list in light of the data presented in figure 9.3, which maps the crime rate data from figure 9.2 to the continental United States. It is certainly possible that many of the factors above contribute to the variation in crime rates across the states. For example, the FBI suggests that economic conditions influence crime rates. Nevada's crime rate was among the highest in the United States, but it also had the highest unemployment rate in the United States in 2013. The FBI suggests that climate influences crime rates; perhaps that explains, at least partially, why crime rates appear to be higher in southern states. If population density and urbanization matters, as stated by the FBI, that might explain why the five states with the lowest rates of urbanization (Maine, Vermont, West Virginia, Mississippi, and Montana) all appear to have lower than average crime rates. Failure to include these variables will almost certainly invalidate any inferences one might be tempted to draw from figure 9.2.

To one not trained in statistical analysis, the notion that the omitted variable issue might invalidate the entire analysis may seem rather extreme. Even if figure 9.2 does not include everything that influences crime rates, does it necessarily follow that the inference regarding guns is incorrect? The simple answer is almost certainly yes, and the statistical intuition is fairly straightforward.

Suppose, hypothetically, that crime rates are only influenced by one factor, climate, and that areas with warmer climates have higher crime rates. Further, assume that a statistical model incorporating both climate and gun ownership would find that only climate is positively correlated with crime. Finally, assume that people in warmer climates are more likely to own guns;

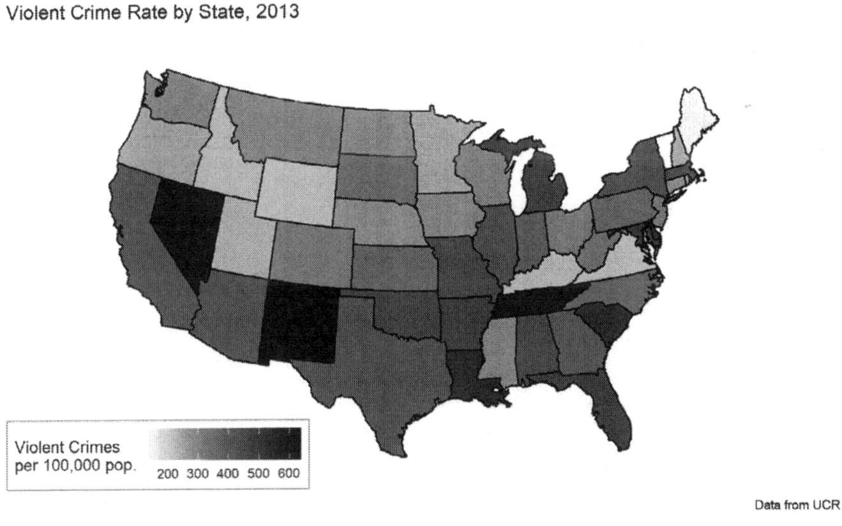

Figure 9.3. Violent Crime Rate by State, 2013. ***Crime data from UCR, 2013. Figure created by Matt Dobra.***

perhaps the warmer climate simply encourages more people to hunt, which is why they own more guns. If one were to estimate a statistical model that omits the climate variable, there is a high likelihood that it would show that gun ownership actually increases crime (which, by assumption, is false!) because gun ownership rates are correlated with the omitted variable. As climate is not included in the analysis, the statistical model for this hypothetical scenario cannot (correctly) attribute higher crime rates to warmer climates. However, since people in warmer places are more likely to own guns, there is a positive relationship between gun ownership and crime, not because guns cause crime, but rather because climate causes both crime rates and rates of gun ownership to be higher. As a result, the statistical model will erroneously attribute the effect of the climate on crime to gun ownership rates because gun ownership rates tend to be higher in warmer places.

Or suppose that crime rates are increased by exactly two factors: urbanization and gun ownership rates. Moreover, urbanization is correlated with gun ownership rates: a 2017 survey released by the Pew Research Center found that adults living in rural areas are more than twice as likely to own a gun than adults in urban areas (46% vs. 19%) (Parker et al., 2017). If one were to estimate a statistical model that omits the urbanization variable, as with the case above, the mathematics behind the analysis would again channel the effect of the missing variable (urbanization) through the variable with which it is correlated (gun ownership rates), again leading to incorrect results. In fact, not only would the impact of gun ownership be incorrectly estimated, but there is also a good chance that a statistical model would show that gun ownership actually reduces crime (which, by assumption, is false!) because gun ownership rates are negatively correlated with urbanization.

In short, omitted variable bias can lead to researchers finding statistical results that do not actually exist or failing to find results that do exist. Most careful, peer-reviewed studies in academic journals are acutely aware of this and attempt to account for omitted variables by either explicitly including them in their models or by careful data collection and sample selection. The types of statistical analysis often seen in the popular press, by contrast, are typically simple correlational studies and are likely to suffer from omitted variable bias, ultimately leading to deceptive and/or incorrect findings.

The second source of endogeneity, simultaneity, is also relatively straightforward to understand. Simultaneity simply refers to the idea that there might be a feedback loop in the data and is not uncommon when looking at data related to crime. One prominent example of this is in the relationship between police and crime. One might reasonably expect having more police officers would cause there to be less crime. But there is likely to be a feedback loop here, because one might also reasonably expect that having high crime rates would cause a city to hire more police officers. As a result, simple correlational analysis between the size of a police force and crime rates often finds that more police officers are correlated with higher crime rates (Levitt, 1997).

In the case of the relationship between gun ownership rates and crime, it is fairly clear that this relationship might exhibit simultaneity. If citizens believe that owning a gun is an effective form of self-defense, then the value of owning a gun is higher in areas with more crime, which ultimately encourages more people to acquire guns. Thus, regardless of the causal effect of guns on crime, there may be a causal effect of crime on gun ownership, establishing a feedback loop in the data. There are sophisticated statistical methods (Kovandzic et al., 2013) that are capable of "breaking" the feedback loop and separating the two effects. Again, these approaches are what one expects to see in peer-reviewed studies in academic journals and what tend to be absent in the popular press or social media.

The third source of endogeneity, measurement error, is probably the simplest source to understand but the hardest to deal with. In the foregoing discussion, it has been implicitly assumed that there exist accurate measures of gun ownership rates. Such measures simply do not exist. For example, in the United States, the 1986 Firearms Owners' Protection Act prohibits the federal government from creating a gun registry (Firearms Owners', 1986). Additionally, very few states have gun registries, and some states have laws barring state registries (Giffords Law, 2020). The Small Arms Survey estimated that, in 2017, there were roughly 393 million firearms in the United States, of which only 1 million were registered (Karp, 2018). Moreover, knowing how many guns exist is not the same thing as knowing how many people have access to guns, as many gun owners own more than one gun. The results of the 2004 National Firearms Survey suggested that roughly half of all gun owners owned at least four guns each (Hepburn et al., 2007), and the 1994 National Survey of Private Ownership of Firearms in the United States indicated that "the top 20 percent of gun owners [own] 55 percent of the total quantity" (Cook & Ludwig, 1996). Given the difficulty in using actual gun ownership data, empirical researchers are forced to rely on either survey data or *proxy variables*.

Survey data is simply data that comes from collecting responses to a survey. While survey methodologies are a common means by which gun data is collected, surveys have a number of drawbacks that limit their usefulness. Surveys on gun ownership are infrequent, and each survey uses different methodologies, making it difficult to compare the results of multiple surveys. For example, the gun ownership data from figure 9.2, mapped here to the continental United States in figure 9.4, resulted from a specific set of questions and a stratified matching sampling methodology. It is likely that the only time

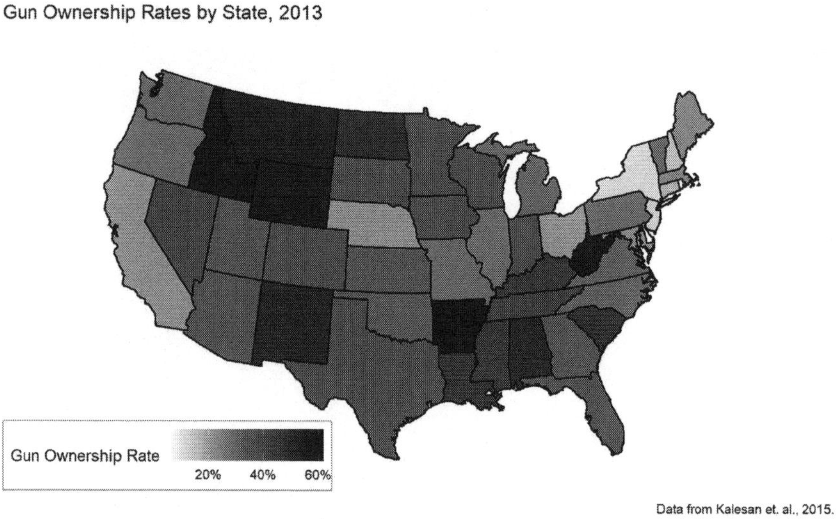

Figure 9.4. Gun Ownership Rates by State, 2013. *Data from Kalesan et al., 2016. Figure created by Matt Dobra.*

this particular set of questions and methodology was ever used was to collect gun ownership rate data for the Kalesan et al. (2016) paper. Additionally, many nationally representative surveys do not have a large enough sample size to make gun prevalence estimations at the sub-national level (e.g., state or county gun prevalence) with any degree of precision. Non-response bias is also a significant concern, particularly for more recent surveys; a 2019 paper found a marked increase in Americans refusing to answer gun ownership questions on surveys. This increase is sharpest among Republicans, a group one might expect to have higher-than-average gun ownership rates, implying that surveys might be severely undercounting gun ownership and thus "potentially skewing inferences about gun-related issues" (Urbatsch, 2019).

Ultimately, the discussion above implies that the usefulness of survey data in calculating gun ownership rates is both limited and has been declining significantly; this is causing researchers to lean more heavily on the use of proxy variables. A proxy variable is a variable that is expected to be highly correlated with the variable of interest; if the variable of interest is not available, the proxy is used in its place in statistical analysis. In the case of gun ownership, this means finding some variable that can be easily measured and is correlated with gun ownership rates. Despite typically being the best measure of gun ownership, proxies are still imprecise. Proxy variables often include various gun laws, such as concealed carry laws (Lott & Mustard, 1997) and gun bans (Lott, 2010), subscriptions to outdoor and gun magazines

Percent of Suicides by Gun, 2013

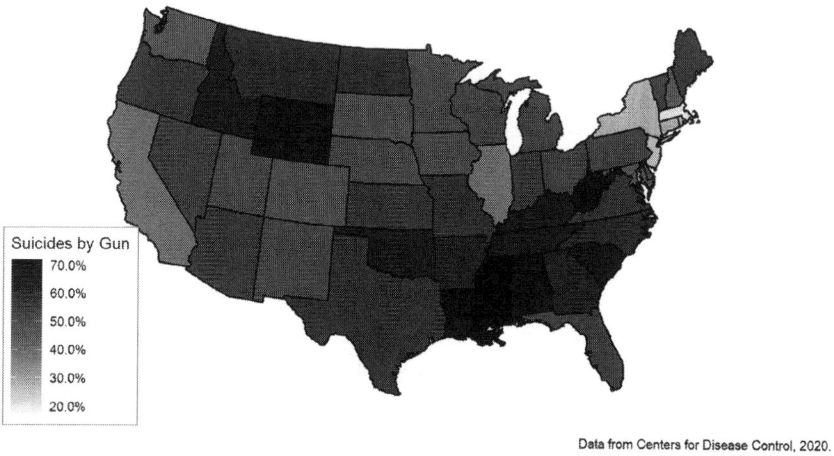

Figure 9.5. Percent of Suicides by Gun, 2013. ***Suicide Data from Centers for Disease Control, 2020.***

(e.g., *Field and Stream*, *Guns and Ammo*, *Outdoor Life*) (Kleck et al., 2006), or the percent of residents who are veterans (Cook & Ludwig, 1996). The variable that is widely viewed as the best proxy for gun ownership, and is used extensively in studies, is the percentage of suicides carried out with a gun (Kovandzic et al., 2013). Figure 9.5 shows the percentage of suicides by gun in each state in 2013 (Centers for Disease, 2020).

While figure 9.4 and figure 9.5 do not match exactly, figure 9.6 shows that the gun ownership survey data from figure 9.4 and the percentage of suicides by gun data in figure 9.5 are in fact highly correlated, which is why the percentage of suicides by gun is viewed to be a valid proxy for gun ownership data. Not only is the percentage of suicides by gun highly correlated with known measures of gun ownership, it has the added benefit of being data that is easy to obtain and calculate, is collected continuously and thus can be compared across regions and times, and is available at a variety of levels of observation (national, state, county, etc.).

While analysis with gun ownership proxies may seem inferior to surveys of gun ownership, survey data on gun ownership is not collected regularly enough for its meaningful use in data analysis. Additionally, the potential for response bias among Republicans on surveys likely makes their use in most data analysis dubious. As with the potential sources of bias discussed above, research found in high-quality, peer-reviewed journals is far more likely to

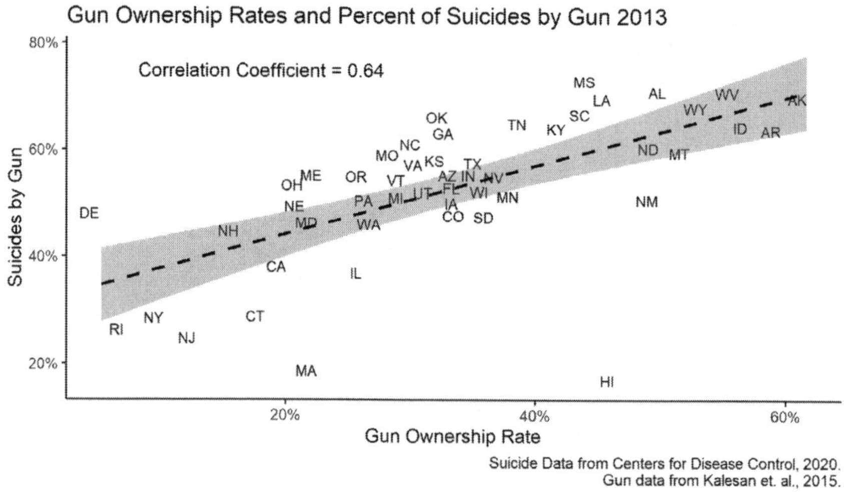

Figure 9.6. Gun Ownership Rates and Percent of Suicides by Gun 2013. ***Suicide Data from Centers for Disease Control, 2020. Gun Data from Kalesan et al., 2015.***

choose the correct measures of gun ownership (and other variables as well) than the mass media, investigative journalists, or social media.

CONCLUSION

While the question of whether or not America's high rate of gun ownership is the cause of America's high crime rates is straightforward, the purpose of this chapter has been to demonstrate that answering this question is by no means simple. The answer cannot be found through logic alone, as plausible countervailing forces exist that require looking at the data. But knowing that one must look at the data, and knowing how to look at the data, are vastly different propositions.

The purpose of this chapter has been to demonstrate that much of the data analysis surrounding the debate between guns and crime, particularly the research found outside of reputable, peer-reviewed journals, is prone to considerable statistical bias. Note that statistical bias is not an accusation of one-sidedness in analysis, or the researcher lying or falsifying data to achieve some predetermined outcome. This may happen, but statistical bias can happen even if the researcher is perfectly impartial. Statistical bias simply means that the way the data is collected or generated is likely to make even an impartial analysis of the data find an incorrect result.

While relying on the peer-review process to separate the good data analysis from the suspect, it is by no means perfect; occasionally poor data analysis slips in. Additionally, not all good data analysis appears in academic journals. Certainly, some reports of government agencies, think tanks, journalists, industry studies, and so on include careful data analysis. As a result, having the ability to evaluate the validity of data-driven research is a valuable skill, and the discussion above provides a solid foundation for thinking about the validity of data analysis in general. Ultimately, establishing a correlation is not the same thing as proving causation. A study that boils down to "when *A* is high, *B* is high, therefore *A* causes *B*" has not actually proven causality. There could be missing variables, reverse causation, or a whole host of other issues that a careful analysis should at least consider.

BIBLIOGRAPHY

Antonakis, J., Bendahan, S., Jacquart, P., and Lalive, R. (2010). On Making Causal Claims: A Review and Recommendations. *The Leadership Quarterly*, 1086–1120.

Centers for Disease Control. (2020). *CDC Wonder*. Retrieved from https://wonder.cdc.gov/.

Cook, P. J., and Ludwig, J. (1996). *Guns in America: Results of a Comprehensive National Survey on Firearms Ownership and Use.* Washington, DC: Police Foundation.

Federal Bureau of Investigation. (2011). *Variables Affecting Crime*. Retrieved from Uniform Crime Report: https://ucr.fbi.gov/hate-crime/2011/resources/variables-affecting-crime.

Federal Bureau of Investigation. (2013). *Uniform Crime Reports*. Retrieved from https://www.ucrdatatool.gov/index.cfm.

Federal Bureau of Investigation. (2020). *Quick Look: 277 Active Shooter Incidents in the United States from 2000 to 2018*. Retrieved from Federal Bureau of Investigation: https://www.fbi.gov/about/partnerships/office-of-partner-engagement/active-shooter-incidents-graphics.

Firearms Owners' Protection Act. (1986). *S.B. 99, 99th Cong.*

Giffords Law Center. (2020). *Registration*. Retrieved from Giffords Law Center: https://lawcenter.giffords.org/gun-laws/policy-areas/gun-owner-responsibilities/registration/.

Hepburn, L., Miller, M., Azrael, D., and Hemenway, D. (2007). The US Gun Stock: Results from the 2004 National Firearms Survey. *Injury Prevention*, 15–19.

Kalesan, B., Villarreal, M. D., Keyes, K. M., and Galea, S. (2016). Gun Ownership and Social Gun Culture. *Injury Prevention*, 216–220.

Karp, A. (2018). *Briefing Paper. Estimating Global Civilian-Held Firearms Numbers (Annexe).* Geneva: Small Arms Survey.

Kenny, D. A. (1979). *Correlation and Causality.* New York: Wiley.

Kleck, G., Kovandzic, T. V., and Schaffer, M. E. (2006). *Gun Prevalence, Homicide Rates and Causality: A GMM Approach to Endogeneity Bias.* CEPR Discussion Paper No. 5357.

Kovandzic, T., Schaffer, M., and Kleck, G. (2013). Estimating the Causal Effect of Gun Prevalence on Homicide Rates: A Local Average Treatment Effect Approach. *Journal of Quantitative Criminology*, 477–541.

Levitt, S. D. (1997). Using Electoral Cycles in Police Hiring to Estimate the Effects of Police on Crime. *American Economic Review*, 270–290.

Lott, J. R. (2010). *More Guns, Less Crime: Understanding Crime and Gun Control Laws, Third Edition.* University of Chicago Press.

Lott, J. R., and Mustard, D. B. (1997). Crime, Deterrence, and Right-to-Carry Concealed Handguns. *Journal of Legal Studies*, 1–68.

Parker, K., Horowitz, J. M., Igielnik, R., Oliphant, J. B., and Brown, A. (2017, June 22). *America's Complex Relationship with Guns*. Retrieved from Pew Research Center: https://www.pewsocialtrends.org/2017/06/22/americas-complex-relationship-with-guns/.

Urbatsch, R. (2019). Gun-shy: Refusal to Answer Questions about Firearm Ownership. *The Social Science Journal*, 189–195.

10

Guns in American Politics

Christopher Lee Cronin

Americans tend to speak about the government as if it were a living being separate from the people. This makes sense given how large modern governments are and how removed they can seem from everyday life. The fundamental purpose of a government, however, is to translate the will of the people. It is the machinery citizens use to take all the individual interests into account and measure them against a basic set of principles. The product of government is policy—the sum total of all parts of the political system. Policy is about what laws say, how laws are enforced, how court cases decide conflicts, and how all the other political pressures combine to affect day-to-day life. Gun policy is regulatory policy. Thus, the main political issue is the extent to which gun ownership should be regulated (Spitzer, 2016). Regulatory policy is difficult because it involves limiting what citizens can do. It also involves widespread benefits with specific costs. When the government regulates something, all citizens are safer in some small way, but those being regulated are not happy. Fining factories that pollute the air may make the air somewhat cleaner, but those factories face the costs. This makes for difficult environmental politics, and the same is true for policy about guns. America has a long cultural history with gun ownership but little political conversation about guns until the late twentieth century. Since then, national politics about private gun ownership has become some of the most contentious (Head, 2019).

COMPARATIVE POLITICS

Most nations in the world have converged on a single model for governance—Liberal Democracy. As the preeminent comparative political scientist, Howard Wiarda, used to say, "It's the only game in town" (Wiarda, 2009, p. 82). There are some nations that are not liberal democracies, but they are the outliers in today's world. The "liberal" part refers to the essential rights citizens have regardless of short-term changes in what the majority wants. The "democracy" part can be a little more complicated, but more or less refers to the people having the ultimate decision-making power. This combination of ideology and mechanism is not necessary, natural, or easy. In fact, the two pieces are often at odds. Balancing these opposing forces can be messy, but so far this is the best form of governance humanity has contrived. In the past, there were competing ideologies: classical conservatism, fascism, anarchism. There were also other forms of governance: tribal councils, oligarchies, monarchies. Our era is dominated by liberal democracies. Some argue this is the best we will ever come up with, while others theorize new forms that may follow. Nevertheless, this is the balancing act contemporary nations play when dealing with any particular policy issue—like guns.

There are constitutional rights to balance against the will of the majority. For instance, a citizen's right to life is protected no matter how much the majority might want to make a new law depriving that right. Fictional citizen "John" is constitutionally protected from any law the majority might make that singles out "Johns" for death. In this sense, rights are held to be more powerful than laws. Deciding which ideas to make rights and which to allow to fluctuate as laws is difficult and makes up a good portion of what the study of politics is all about. Guns are a classic policy issue for liberal democracies in the world. Each nation has a slightly different balance for what part of gun ownership will constitute a right and what part will be subject to the changing wishes of the majority. The big-picture story when comparing nations is that America has significantly different policy when it comes to gun ownership and gun control. For scholars who study policy among liberal democracies, this difference often gets labeled as "American Exceptionalism" (Lipset, 1997). When nations share basic structures and interests, policy analysts expect similar laws, regulations, and politics. In the case of guns, all nations share an interest in protecting citizens from gun violence while preserving individual rights of gun ownership. America tends to have far fewer restrictions on this ownership than other liberal democracies (Crifasi, 2018).

Liberal democracies around the world share the challenge of balancing individual rights with majority whims while dealing with the collective-action problem. This is a problem common to any democracy where the incentive to be involved in political issues is limited for any individual citizen who may benefit without effort. This is also known as the "free-rider" problem. There is no reason for a citizen to waste time advocating if other citizens might do it for them. This problem is not unique to America. Nearby nations, like

Canada, have faced similar societal hurdles and yet have seen significantly more gun control policy. The Coalition for Gun Control emerged in Canada to successfully lobby for the Firearms Act in 1995 while no such cohesion has been observed in America (Fleming et al., 2018).

There are many possible reasons why America has divergent gun policy. One argument has to do with history. It may be that guns are a key component of the American tradition due to a unique history (Spitzer, 2016). This history informs a gun culture in America that may be significantly different than other nations, and thus leads to different kinds of policy. There is a heavier cultural insistence on the right to keep and use guns, and this makes gun policy complex and uncertain (Head, 2019). There are structural reasons for the way gun policy works differently in America. The federal design of American government means there is competition and tension between the national level and state level. The federal system complicates things as does the presidential system (in contrast to a parliamentary system) that splits power between parts of the government (Kamal & Burton, 2018). These components are often lumped together under one term—political culture—to describe the way gun politics is different in America. This difference highlights some important parts of the American political system and extends beyond the effect on citizens (Mehalko, 2012). There are ways in which America behaves as an exception to the norm of liberal democracy that extend beyond any one policy area.

AMERICAN LIBERAL DEMOCRACY

The context for gun politics in America is a more individualized kind of democratic politics than other nations. Though all nations must balance individual interests and collective interests, most sociologists note that American collectivism is in decline (Celinska, 2007). This means that American politics leans toward the individual interest more than the collective interest across policy issues. In the case of gun ownership, this leads to a political culture more interested in preserving individual gun ownership than collective gun regulation. This may help explain on a cultural level why such regulations rarely come about, despite plenty of polling data suggesting Americans see value in further regulations.

There are many pieces of the political system that add up to deliver the rules a majority wants to see. Polls showing a majority of Americans (more than 50%) want new policy do not automatically lead to new policy. Eventually, some institutional change must occur. As mentioned, that might be a new law. Laws are passed by legislative bodies and are the general rules that guide day-to-day lives. Just as important as law is the executive enforcement of law. There may be a robust gun law in place, but if no one is being arrested for it, then the policy overall is weak or vice versa. Judicial decisions also play a role in policy when the laws or enforcement come in conflict with other constitutional issues. These are the three main pieces of our government and are the three places where institutional power is at work. For guns, there are laws in place at the national and state level that guide what citizens can do and own. There are executive orders and norms of law enforcement agencies that affect what practical gun ownership looks like, and there are important court decisions that determine how far regulation can reach. Beyond the institutions of government, there are the many intermediate pieces that affect policy. Public opinion, interest groups, the media, social movements, campaigns, and political parties all pressure the institutions to adapt to what the people want. Institutions adapt in ways that are limited by the rights spelled out in the Constitution.

CIVIL LIBERTIES AND FEDERALISM

The constitutional protections providing for individual rights are called "civil liberties." These are the protections an individual has from the power of the majority—as translated through the power of the government. There are civil liberties to be found sprinkled throughout the American Constitution, but the clearest list is found in the first ten additions to the original document—the Bill of Rights. The second addition, or amendment, is the one famously dealing with the constitutional right to own a gun. As is common with constitutional issues, much of the developing politics from the Second Amendment is about the language and intent of the authors. There are two main philosophies for how to interpret any part of the Constitution. One stresses the importance of sticking strictly to what is written. The other philosophy stresses the need to understand the intentions of the written words. This difference in philosophy makes it difficult for a united stance on constitutional gun policy to emerge (Head, 2019).

Compared to other policy areas, though, the court has been clear in the essential constitutional right, as written and interpreted, for citizens to own arms. Various cases have solidified the emphasis on individual ownership and the right to bear arms (Kamal & Burton, 2018). The interpretation of the constitutional protection will continue as future regulation arises, but the current judicial position on the national level is more consistent today than in previous eras. How much this judicial clarity will impact gun policy remains to be seen. The Second Amendment has been applied mainly to the federal (national) government. However, in many cases, the state governments have the primary responsibility for gun control (Head, 2019).

The fact that American government works through both national and state levels complicates the politics of guns. In many ways, the balance between national and state power reflects the balance between rights and majority will. Other major policy issues have seen political development over time that begins with allowing states to differ and ends with a national establishment of the issue as a right. Same-sex marriage passed through an era where the majority in each state could decide the legal status, and eventually through national constitutional rulings became established as a right. Marijuana policy currently resides at the state level, which means the issue is being decided mostly through majority will. For gun policy, America has clear national constitutional guidance, but sees variation on the state level. In fact, though change happens at both levels, gun laws change more frequently at the state level and often without the media attention that comes with national changes (Jacobs, 2019). One benefit of the federal system is that it allows states to reflect differences in local political culture. Different laws make sense for different areas of the nation. Many detailed studies of gun policy point to data that differs widely depending on which state the policy is in effect. For instance, Stand-Your-Ground Laws have had very different effects, and varied in the magnitude of those effects, in different states (Guettabi & Munasib, 2018).

The states have different political cultures, and the competition with the national level often depends on how that culture lines up with the politics in D.C. More progressive states tend to resist national policies in areas like immigration, tax reform, and marijuana policy. When it comes to gun policy, these states are more likely to fill the void of national action for gun control. On the other hand, more conservative state-level governments are often at work pre-empting their more progressive cities' policies (Rose, 2019). This is a reminder that aside from the constitutional balance between national and state levels, local and city governments wield power over their jurisdictions too.

PUBLIC OPINION AND MASS SHOOTINGS

In a democracy, the will of the people is an important driving force for policy. Early in American history the best way to know what the people wanted was the mechanism of elections. This mechanism is still the primary way that institutions adjust to the will of the people (every two years), but modern democracies have polling data readily available. Members of government now have daily numbers to track public opinion, and that opinion puts pressure on those members to adjust. Such polling data can be powerful depending on the policy area. For detailed gun policy public opinion is instrumental in driving and presenting gun matters in their context (Schildkraut, 2018). This is especially true when that context is mass shooting events.

Citizens come to have public opinions through a process known as political socialization. Many factors contribute to the process of forming a political identity, like family, income, education, experience, and major events. The most important major events for shaping public opinion in contemporary America are mass shootings. Mass shootings have some obvious effects and some less obvious effects on majority will. Mass shootings generate temporary surges in public opinion for more gun control. This support is related to individual citizens' proximity to such events. Research shows that people who live closer to where mass shootings happen have stronger reactions to the events. This strength of feeling is common for both Democrats and Republicans (Newman & Hartman, 2017). Overall, the effect on public opinion is for stricter gun regulations, but there are some ways in which political socialization shapes the data in more detail. There is evidence that mass shootings have polarizing effects that depend on citizens' background politics. Democrats who live near a mass shooting event become much more supportive of gun control, while Republicans who live nearby shift attitudes in a reactionary opposite direction (Barney & Schaffner, 2019).

This polarized response shows how contemporary America is divided and how that divide leads to different responses to major events. Once discussed as the "Culture War" (Huntington, 1996) and now more commonly discussed as "Voter Polarization" (Krasa & Polborn, 2014), there is a divide between progressive and conservative Americans. Sometimes these sides are represented by the colors of blue and red to signify cultural leanings. Research suggests that this divide has been growing (Abramowitz, 2010) and produces two divergent reactions to political news. In the case of mass shootings, blue America reacts with popular pressure for more gun regulation, while red America seeks to protect the individual right of gun ownership against any new regulation. This growing political divide leads to opposing responses to the same events or data.

Studies about the relationship between gun control and crime, violent crime, and freedom generate competing claims about the worth of further regulation. Worldwide, there is abundant data that shows gun control leads to fewer gun deaths. That conclusion is less overwhelming and decisive in the American context. However, when dealing with mass shootings in particular, there is basic scholarly agreement across the political spectrum. There is a negative relationship between a state's gun control strictness and the number of mass murders in that state. In other words, as gun control increases, mass murder incidents decrease, and there are fewer victims (Lewis, 2018). American public opinion is not united as to the proper response to mass shootings. There are other factors to consider. In the simplest sense, trying to decrease mass shootings is a policy outcome that must be balanced against the essential constitutional rights of gun ownership. The debate then shifts to the nature of the Second Amendment as well as arguments about how specific and rigid that right should be. The entire point of rights, after all, is to prevent majority will from changing the essential condition.

DEMOGRAPHICS AND POLARIZATION

Aside from the red state/blue state divide, demographics shape American sentiment on gun control. Gender is a persistent factor in gun crimes. Men are more likely to be both offenders and victims. This particular effect would seem to cancel itself out; nevertheless the gender divide is evident in public opinion (Rennison, 2009). Men (overall) are less in favor of gun control than women. The difference is less pronounced among Americans who identify as Democrats. Gun policy attitudes differ more based on gender among Republicans, with women reporting significantly more moderate views than men (Barnes & Cassese, 2017). Age is another demographic that affects public opinion on gun policy. Nearly every progressive political movement features a great deal of youth. The social energy behind recent surges in gun control advocacy has been led by the Millennial generation (Tzintzún, 2018). Following mass shootings, new waves of civic engagement from young people ebb. It remains to be seen how this engagement will translate to electoral outcomes. Young Americans are a common feature of movements for social change, but they are not so common on voting day—where turnout rates are always lowest for younger demographics. Larger demographic trends are often used to support optimistic future electoral outcomes for Democratic candidates. Growing urbanization, the growing Latino population, and youth engagement are pieces of this demographic change—but much like the youth vote, these shifts have yet to prove any meaningful long-term advantage.

Polarization persists in American public opinion and shapes the policy possibilities in national government. Legislators have found that despite polling data showing support for increased gun control, voter turnout can often trump those numbers. Polls show what people think and whom they would vote for on Election Day. When that day comes, however, all that matters is who actually shows up. Gun owners have high rates of voter turnout. These kinds of voters are often called "single-issue" voters. They are citizens who care most about one policy issue—rather than the sum total of candidates' positions on all policy. There are some American voters who vote solely based on abortion as an issue. There are some Americans who vote solely based on taxation. Gun owners are a reliable group of single-issue voters, which is an important factor when legislators consider gun policy. These legislators and other party elites have slowly increased their support for gun control over time. Democrats in power supported gun control at a rate of 30 percent in 1970 and today are closer to 85 percent. Republican elites showed support of just 5 percent in 1970 and are closer to 35 percent today (Lindaman & Haider-Markel, 2002). These are polarized numbers (85 is very different from 35) and that polarization is consistent among average citizens as well. The difference is that mass support for gun control is always higher than elite support—which speaks to the limitations of public opinion on institutional outcomes (Spitzer, 2016).

NEWS MEDIA

A free press is essential for any democracy. Citizens must be able to access information, form opinions, and see those opinions carried out by public servants. There are, of course, many factors that shape how this information is delivered. These factors can have an impact on how the issue of guns is framed in a political setting. Factual information was once hard to come by, and the primary purpose of news media was to discover and report on current events. This led for-profit journalism to model unbiased reporting in order to gain the largest amount of customers. Today, information is plentiful and the model for news media to make money has shifted away from such unbiased framing of issues. Breaking news is still consistent across networks and companies, but much of the delivery of news now caters to certain cultural demographics. Most citizens get their understanding of gun policy from the news media. The way in which it is covered has an important effect on public attitudes and beliefs (Surette, 2015).

American media coverage of mass shootings has closely mirrored the kind of framing common in other countries. For instance, when comparing such coverage in Canada and America, the media framed stories around mass shootings as indicative of the need for restrictive gun control about 78 percent of the time in both countries. American media coverage of gun politics in general, however, does not mirror the kind of framing common in other countries. When news is not event-driven (mass-shootings), the coverage tends to favor the gun rights frame (Fleming et al., 2018).

Aside from the political culture reasons discussed above, there are other factors that shape the framing of news in America. The news media is overwhelmingly a for-profit enterprise, so it needs to make money. The most attractive and most-watched news tends to be framed in narrative or story form. Telling an interesting story is more attractive than explaining statistics or social science. Thus, issues like gun control tend to be framed on the level of individual morality and individual decision-making rather than social functions. This framing suits individual rights better than social policy.

INTEREST GROUPS AND ELECTIONS

When politicians and activists talk about the ruinous effect of money on the political system, they are talking about interest groups. Perhaps the best-known interest group in the world is the National Rifle Association (NRA). The NRA is dedicated to gun rights issues and consistently ranks as one of the most influential interest groups. This is true because of two factors: resources and quality membership. An interest group is simply a private organization that wants to nudge policy in a certain direction. It can do this by spending money in different ways and by mobilizing members to put pressure on the government. The fact that interest groups can have a significant impact on policy can be seen as positive or negative. An interest group is, by definition, a subset of the total population. Thus, it is not the majority. When an interest group has an influence on policy, it is usually having an effect that counters the majority. Technically, this is undemocratic, but there are times when a small group of people having influence is good. One easy example is the influence an interest group can have that mirrors the majority will and is overcoming the collective action problem. If the Sierra Club, or any other environmentalist organization, has an effect on environmental policy, it is probably nudging the government in the way the general population desires. Its pressure is necessary because that general population is not putting enough direct pressure on government for change in that policy area. Interest groups can do the majority's will by mobilizing resources and membership. More often an interest group is pushing for policy that runs counter to majority will. While this may seem undemocratic, it can be a good way to balance the dangers of majority power. Majority public opinion can be fickle—it can change rapidly. Majority opinion can also run counter to basic rights. The mission of the NRA, for instance, is to safeguard the rights of gun owners despite fluctuations in majority public opinion. In this case, the NRA has been extremely effective in countering consistent public calls for further regulation. Its effectiveness is further highlighted by a lack of oppositional interest group strength. Many interest groups are counterbalanced by an opposing interest group working against the cause. Historically, the NRA has not had viable competition in this regard.

Interest group influence comes by way of a multitude of strategies. For the NRA it is also a case of magnitude, as the organization is one of the best-funded interest groups. One basic strategy is campaign contributions. Candidates for office need to raise large amounts of money. Over time, the NRA has given large amounts of money to members of both political parties. Campaign contributions to Republican lawmakers are not surprising, but consistent donations to Democratic candidates indicates a long-term strategy of influence. This strategy has been successful and has only recently shifted as the Democratic Party adjusts to public opinion trends. As recently as 2010, the NRA contributed to sixty-six Democratic incumbents. Those numbers have begun to shift with contemporary mass shootings reshaping the political possibilities for Democrats. By 2016, the NRA's contribution dropped to just four incumbent Democrats (Garcia, 2018).

Campaign contributions are just one tool for an interest group. Mobilizing members to protest, pressure, and vote in line with the organization can be just as effective. Sheer volume can be effective. One example is the AARP. They represent retired Americans, which is a large piece of the population. The organization has influence because of the size of its membership. Numbers alone are not as important as the quality of the membership. The NRA has both many members and quality members—meaning these members act politically based on gun rights issues and on the guidance of the NRA. The effectiveness of the NRA can be seen in positive campaign contributions and mobilization, but is even more evident in negative spending and mobilization. Candidates may or may not receive positive attention from the NRA, but need to avoid its negative attention. This effect is magnified on the local level and in primary elections where overall spending levels are low and the NRA's financial strength can be decisive. This is also true in districts/states where gun rights culture has deep roots and voters are easily mobilized on the issue. In these cases, underdog Democratic candidates use gun policy to help win primary elections (Gerber, 2018). Primary elections are within the party, so a Democratic candidate looking to separate from another Democrat can tap into the resources and easy mobilization on the issue.

Political scientists debate whether legislators' concerns for reelection outweigh their policy goals (Hurley, 2001). Of course, a policy-maker cannot make policy without holding office. The issue of gun control and gun rights is one of the most important single-issues in contemporary politics and is featured in campaign strategy and policy goals. Gun control mobilization has yet to have more of an effect than gun rights mobilization. Analysis of recent elections shows that being "anti-gun" can lose races for Democratic candidates. The 2000 presidential race is often cited as an example of a Democrat losing because of gun control issues (Barnes, 2007). Whether or not the single issue lost the race, it is clear the electoral perception weighs on Democratic candidates and their strategic policy positions.

The amount of time and resources spent on gun issues has risen dramatically in recent electoral cycles. The total percentage of candidates advertising on gun issues rose from 1 percent in 2012 to 8 percent in 2018. This shows the issue becoming more important to campaigns, and likely becoming a more competitive issue—the percent of content that was pro-guns dropped from 86 percent in 2012 to 45 percent in 2018 (Barry et al., 2020). This follows the similar trend of Democratic candidates receiving far less money from the NRA and signals a more competitive political environment for policy debate. This sets up future elections as an interesting testing ground for Democratic candidates. Historically, featuring gun control has not been a successful strategy. In fact, it has even hurt Democratic candidates with their own self-identified voters. Union members have long been an assumed part of Democratic coalitions. In recent presidential elections, single-issues, like gun ownership, have trumped union membership in mobilizing more than 40 percent of union members to vote Republican (Beachler, 2007).

POLITICAL PARTIES

Political parties serve to connect citizens to their government. Some scholars argue that political parties are bad for democracy (Michels, 1911). Other scholars argue parties play an integral role in making democracy work (Aldrich, 1995). Regardless of their relative benefit, they seem to be a natural party of democracies—no democracy exists without political parties (Schattschneider, 2009). America has a two-party political system. This is not to say there are no other parties aside from the Democrats and Republicans, but generally they do not win elections. This has a little to do with history and is carried on by campaign finance laws, but is mostly due to the way America runs elections. The map is divided into districts which feature a single representative per geographic area. The electoral contests are decided by winner-take-all plurality voting. These two features basically guarantee a system with only two main competitive parties as opposed to proportional representative systems that end up with many competitive parties. Having a two-party system affects how issues are discussed—or not discussed. Gun control has been largely ignored by the two parties until recently. It remains largely unaddressed because of voter polarization and the parties strategically choosing to "own" those polarized positions (Tatalovich, 2017). In general, it is harder for individual policies to go unaddressed in multiparty systems where the viability of many parties creates more room for different agendas.

The rest of the structure of American government tends to further slow the process of policy-making. The division of the legislature into House and Senate along with the separate institutional election of the presidency means party control is often divided. With divided control of government, policy change is difficult. This is in contrast to most democratic systems elsewhere, where coalition governance and party control leads to more unified policy change (Head, 2019). The two major parties in America are not especially cohesive, though, and this allows for major policy to pass in periods of divided government. However, this requires bi-partisan compromise which is unlikely on an issue like gun control where the politics are polarized. In terms of third-party politics, the most successful electoral non-major party is the Libertarian party. Libertarians favor reducing governmental regulations across all policy areas, and guns are no exception. Insofar as Libertarian candidates occasionally win local office, they pursue gun rights policy vs. gun control policy.

PARTY PLATFORMS

Every four years, the two major political parties put together statements that summarize their beliefs. These summaries are known as the party platforms. Platforms are a resource used to track ideology over time. They are not perfect indicators because the American political system is candidate-centered rather than party-centered. In early American politics, a candidate could not get elected without being loyal to the party—without adhering more-or-less to the party platform. Parties controlled the pathways to elected office. That is no longer true. Candidates do not need the party apparatus as much as they once did and so they vary in how much of their personal ideology matches the party's ideology. Platforms are also a place where parties send signals to their members that might not get sent by the particular presidential candidate. For instance, in 2016, the Republican platform featured more religious language than ever before. This was likely a strategic effort to balance out the candidacy of Donald Trump who was not a traditionally religious candidate (Cronin, 2020). There are reasons to temper conclusions drawn from any individual platform about party ideology and strategy. Over time, however, they are a good indicator for how individual policy issues are developed, emphasized, and featured. They are a way to track political messaging and agenda setting.

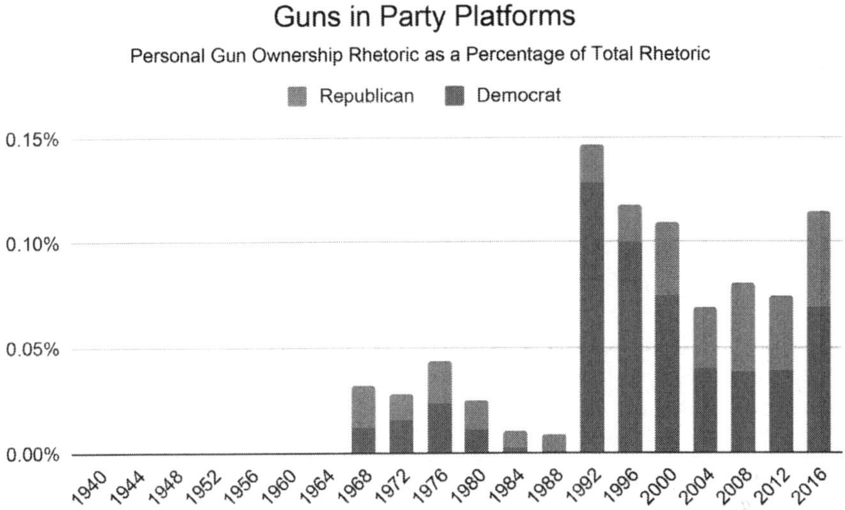

Figure 10.1. Guns in Party Platforms. ***Created by author.***

Platforms have drastically increased in size over time. In the early 1900s, they were about 3,000 words in length. Today's platforms are between 20,000 and 40,000 words in length. A lot more policy issues are addressed in detail. In the contemporary era, Democratic Party platforms present a vision for national identity based on toleration and the celebration of difference with emphasis on equality. Republican platforms provide a more direct sense of national identity based on American superiority, suspicion of government, and the protection of values (Stuckey, 2005). Platform rhetoric also devotes much more language to the dominant issues of the time. Cold War era platforms discuss foreign policy and nuclear weapons extensively while spending relatively less time on domestic policy. Discussion of personal gun ownership is basically nonexistent in platforms before the 1960s, which is evidence that gun control didn't emerge as an important policy issue until recent decades (Fleming et al., 2018). Figure 10.1 is a graph showing the number of times the political parties talked about gun rights and gun control in political platforms. Because the total amount of words has been increasing every year, the amount is shown as a percentage of the total platform. The trend for actual rhetoric looks the same with almost zero mention of anything having to do with gun policy before the 1960s and numbers rising to their highest totals in 2016. In that election year, Democrats referenced private gun ownership eighteen times and Republicans sixteen.

The emergence of gun policy on both platforms in the late 1960s and 1970s followed in the wake of high-profile shootings of President Kennedy, Martin Luther King Jr., and Robert Kennedy. On the heels of the 1968 Gun Control

Act, both parties discussed limiting firearms in general language—with the Democrats singling out mail-order firearm sales. In the 1980s, the Republican Party platforms pushed back against some aspects of the 1968 act, and began to speak about opposing federal restrictions. The spike for both party platforms in the 1990s came during the Clinton era. President Clinton pushed a sweeping crime bill that included a ban on assault weapons. Democratic leaders in Congress asked him to drop this part, fearing vulnerability in swing districts from the NRA (Barnes, 2007). In 1994, many of those Democrats were swept out of the House as Republicans won these swing districts.

In recent party conventions, Republican platforms have focused on law and order, highlighting shooting deaths of police officers as a way to show the need for individual citizens to be armed for personal protection (Rahman, 2016). The rhetoric about guns is primarily about keeping government restrictions at a minimum and picks up where the early 1980s platforms left off. Gun control is mentioned in the context of terrorism. Gun control restrictions to bar suspected terrorists from purchasing firearms come with detailed criteria that limit the level of governmental regulation. This balance of personal ownership and limitations for terrorists has significantly increased the total Republican rhetoric about gun policy. Some of the increase in rhetoric follows to counteract the increase in Democratic rhetoric in previous years. In particular, Republican platforms now feature the Second Amendment. There is no mention of that constitutional provision until 2000. Since 2000, the Second Amendment is featured an average of three times per platform (Fleming et al., 2018).

Following the Clinton years, the Democratic Party toned down the language about gun restrictions, essentially hoping to avoid alienating pro-gun voters in swing states (Rahman, 2016). However, gun violence took center stage at the Democratic Convention in 2016. The high profile for gun policy was also mirrored in the platform where gun rhetoric nearly doubled from the previous two platforms. Aside from language about the regulation of certain firearms, the platform includes a broader context. It states that the U.S. Centers for Disease Control and Prevention must have the resources required to study gun violence as a public health issue. This is an example of how the two parties' rhetoric differs in two ways. One is the tension between majority will and individual rights. The second is in how the parties treat the challenges of gun violence. The Republican Party focuses on individual actors and morality and the Democratic Party features rhetoric about how to address gun policy on a social level. Since the 1960s, Democratic platforms account for the vast majority of language about gun restrictions while Republican platforms account for the majority of language about gun rights. They overlap on language about punishing acts of gun violence (Fleming et al., 2018).

Analysis of platform rhetoric shows further evidence for trends in gun politics. It is a policy area receiving far more attention than ever before. It is also becoming more polarized as a political issue. America remains somewhat exceptional in comparison to other nations—with relatively minimal gun regulation. The classic tensions between majority will and individual rights are easily visible in discussions of gun control. The various levels of federal government compete as state and local governments look to regulate despite national and constitutional restraints. Public opinion surges behind calls for more gun control, especially in the wake of mass shootings—though that political energy has yet to translate into electoral outcomes. The news media's changing frames help to accentuate demographic and cultural divisions that exist in American society. Interest groups have a significant impact on gun policy agenda and on elections. A recent shift away from limited rhetoric puts Democratic candidates in a more direct confrontation with one of the most powerful interest groups—the NRA. The two major parties are escalating the rhetoric about gun policy and setting the future up for major clashes in a polarizing area of American politics.

BIBLIOGRAPHY

Abramowitz, Alan. (2010). *The Disappearing Center: Engaged Citizens, Polarization, and American Democracy*. Yale University Press.

Aldrich, John. (1995). *Why Parties?: The Origin and Transformation of Political Parties in America* (American Politics and Political Economy Series), First Edition. University of Chicago Press.

Barnes, J. A. (2007, Apr 21). "For Democrats, a Loaded Issue." *National Journal, 39*, 75–76.

Barnes, T. D., and Cassese, E. C. (2017). "American Party Women." *Political Research Quarterly, 70*(1), 127–141.

Barney, D. J., and Schaffner, B. F. (2019). "Reexamining the Effect of Mass Shootings on Public Support for Gun Control." *British Journal of Political Science, 49*(4), 1555–1565.

Barry, C. L., Bandara, S., Fowler, E. F., Baum, L., Gollust, S. E., Niederdeppe, J., and Hendricks, A. K. (2020). "Guns in Political Advertising over Four US Election Cycles, 2012–18." *Health Affairs, 39*(2), 327–333, 333A–333E.

Beachler, D. W. (2007). "Race, God, and Guns: Union Voting in the 2004 Election." *Working USA, 10*(3), 311–325.

Celinska, K. (2007). "Individualism and Collectivism in America: The Case of Gun Ownership and Attitudes toward Gun Control." *Sociological Perspectives, 50*(2), 229–247.

Crifasi, C. (2018). "Gun Policy in the United States: Evidence-Based Strategies to Reduce Gun Violence." *Applied Health Economics and Health Policy, 16*(5), 579–581.

Cronin, Christopher. (2020). Unpublished Dataset: Content Analysis of Gun Rhetoric in American Political Platforms over Time.

Fleming, A., McLean, D. S., and Tatalovich, R. (2018). "Debating Gun Control in Canada and the United States: Divergent Policy Frames and Political Cultures." *World Affairs, 181*(4), 348–371.

Garcia, E. (2018, Mar 6). "The Slow Breakup between Democrats and the NRA." *Roll Call.* https://www.rollcall.com/2018/03/06/the-slow-breakup-between-democrats-and-the-nra/.

Gerber, D. (2018, Mar 1). "Underdog Dems Look for Primary Traction in Gun Control." *Hotline—National Journal's Daily Briefing on Politics.*

Guettabi, M., and Munasib, A. (2018). "Stand Your Ground Laws, Homicides, and Gun Deaths." *Regional Studies, 52*(9), 1250–1260.

Head, Brian W. (2019) "Forty Years of Wicked Problems Literature: Forging Closer Links to Policy Studies." *Policy and Society, 38*(2), 180–197.

Huntington, Samuel P. (1996). *The Clash of Civilizations and the Remaking of World Order*. New York: Simon and Schuster.

Hurley, Patricia. (2001, Jun). "David Mayhew's 'Congress: The Electoral Connection' after 25 Years." *PS: Political Science and Politics, 34*(2), 259–261.

Jacobs, S. (2019, Oct 4). "State Gun Control in America: A Historic Guide to Major State Gun Control Laws and Acts." *The Libertarian Institute.* https://libertarian-institute.org/articles/state-gun-control-in-america-a-historic-guide-to-major-state-gun-control-laws-and-acts/.

Kamal, R. D., and Burton, C. (2018). "Policy Gridlock versus Policy Shift in Gun Politics: Comparative Veto Player Analysis of Gun Control Policies in the United States." *World Affairs, 181*(4), 317–347.

Krasa, Stefan, and Polborn, M. (2014, Feb). "Policy Divergence and Voter Polarization in a Structural Model of Elections." *The Journal of Law & Economics, 57*(1), 31–76.

Lewis, J. Scott. (2018). "The Relationship between Gun Control Strictness and Mass Murder in the United States: A National Study 2009–2015." *International Social Science Review, 94*(2), Article 4.

Lindaman, K., and Haider-Markel, D. (2002). "Issue Evolution, Political Parties, and the Culture Wars." *Political Research Quarterly, 55*(1), 91–110.

Lipset, S. (1997). *American Exceptionalism: A Double-Edged Sword.* W.W. Norton.

Mehalko, L. (2012). "This Is Gun Country: The International Implications of U.S. Gun Control Policy." *Boston College International and Comparative Law Review, 35*(1), 297–330.

Michels, Robert. (1911). *Political Parties: A Sociological Study of the Oligarchical Tendencies of Modern Democracy*. Werner Klinkhardt.

Newman, Benjamin J., and Hartman, Todd K. (2017). "Mass Shootings and Public Support for Gun Control." *British Journal of Political Science*, 1–27.

Rahman, R. (2016, Jul 27). "Victims, Families, Lawmakers Bring Firepower to Gun Control Fight." *Roll Call.* https://www.rollcall.com/2016/07/27/victims-families-lawmakers-bring-firepower-to-gun-control-fight/.

Rennison, C. M. (2009). "A New Look at the Gender Gap in Offending." *Women and Criminal Justice, 19*(3), 171–190.

Rose, S. (2019). "State Legislatures as National Actors." *PS, Political Science & Politics, 52*(3), 436–439.

Schattschneider, E. E. (2009). *Party Government.* Transaction Publishers. Third Edition. Original 1941.

Schildkraut, J. (2018). *Mass Shootings in America: Understanding the Debates, Causes, and Responses*. Santa Barbara, CA: ABC-CLIO, LLC.

Spitzer, Robert J. (2016). *The Politics of Gun Control.* New York: Taylor and Francis.

Stuckey, M. E. (2005). "One Nation (Pretty Darn) Divisible: National Identity in the 2004 Conventions." *Rhetoric & Public Affairs, 8*(4), 639–656.

Surette, R. (2015). *Media, Crime, & Criminal Justice: Images and Reality*, Fifth Edition. Pacific Grove, CA: Brooks/Cole.

Tatalovich, Raymond. (2017). "The Life Cycle of Moral Conflicts: Why Some Die, But Others Persist." *Journal of Policy History, 29*(4), 676–701.

Tzintzún, C. (2018, Summer). "Texas Millennials Move the Needle." *Dissent, 65*, 38.

Wiarda, H. (2009). "The Political Sociology of a Concept: Corporatism and the 'Distinct Tradition.'" *The Americas, 66*(1), 81–106. doi:10.1353/tam.0.0155.

11

Weapons of Mass Destruction

A Summary of Psychological Research on Gun Violence

Mark Kline

It is difficult to find a more politically contentious subject in the United States than guns and gun control. It is a continuous source of material for political campaigns and political talk shows. It neatly divides the country along political lines. Despite this, there is also one aspect about gun violence that almost all Americans agree on. The overwhelming majority of Americans, from the political left and the political right, believe that mental illness is a major factor at the root of gun violence (Pescosolido et al., 2019).

In 2017, 39,773 people died from gun-related injuries (Gramlich, 2019). Of these deaths, 60 percent were suicides and 27 percent were homicides. In 2017, 553 gun deaths were attributed to police and 77 percent of all homicides involved the use of a gun (Gramlich, 2019). In recent years, mass shootings such as those at Marjory Stoneman High School, Sandy Hook, and Las Vegas have turned public attention to issues of guns, gun control, and reasons for gun violence. It is widely reported and believed that the perpetrators of these shocking crimes are insane.

One prominent reason given for gun violence and mass shootings is mental health concerns. In public discussions on mass shootings, for example, the idea of limiting access to guns for those with mental health issues and of identifying those with mental health issues comes up on a regular basis. These topics arise so frequently that we thought it would be beneficial to include a chapter in this book on the links between mental illness and gun violence. This link is believed so deeply that it is believed equally by those on the political right and the political left.

In this chapter we will look at the links between mental illness and gun violence by examining the statistical relationship between mental illness and gun violence, the effects of mental health screening on gun violence, and possible pathways between mental illness and gun violence.

MENTAL ILLNESS AND GUN VIOLENCE

Imagine tuning your television to a news program at the end of the day. A tragedy has occurred: seventeen people were killed in a mass shooting incident at a local shopping center. Discussion panels of experts are convened to talk about the incident. What are the comments you are likely to hear? Do you expect there to be talk about the individual being deranged? Questions about how someone who is so clearly disturbed acquired a firearm? Calls for more stringent background checks to keep such mentally unhinged individuals from obtaining firearms? In all likelihood, these comments will form much of the discussion that takes place surrounding this issue, on the television shows as well as among the general public. Evidence indicates that the general public's belief that mentally ill individuals are prone to violence has increased over the years up to a high of 70 percent today (Pescosolido et al., 2019). A poll from the *Washington Post* (Craighill & Clement, 2019) demonstrates the scale of that belief.

From 1995 to 2014, over half of the news stories on gun violence mentioned mental illness as a potential cause (Beck, 2016). In 2019, over 73 percent of news stories linked mental illness with gun violence, even though mental illness is found to play a role in only 4 percent of cases of gun deaths (Swanson, McGinty et al., 2015). For any non-mental health professional, the idea that mental illness is important to understanding gun violence makes a certain sense. Most people do not engage in this type of violence, especially mass shootings, so there must be something wrong with the people who do these acts.

One of the ironies of this discussion is that gun violence is a major problem associated with mental illness but the main impact of mental illness on gun deaths seems to be associated with suicide risk. Mentally ill individuals commit suicide by firearm at four times the rate of those without mental illness (Swanson, Easter et al., 2016). In other words, one of the main influences of mental illness on gun violence concerns suicide much more than homicide. In terms of suicide, guns are much more lethal than other methods, such as poison, hanging, cutting wrists, and so forth. There are many types of psychological disorders associated with suicide, including depression, anxiety, bipolar disorder, schizophrenia, and borderline personality disorder. This category of gun deaths is often overlooked in public discussion of gun violence, but it represents the highest level of deaths due to gun violence around the world and accounts for approximately 60 percent of all gun deaths.

Table 11.1. Causes of Death for 2013

Heart disease	796,494
Malignant tumors	584,881
Diabetes mellitus	75,578
Kidney disease	47,112
Septicemia	38,158
Accidental poisoning	38,851
Car accidents	35,369
Firearms	33,383
Suicides	21,175
Murders	8,454
Manslaughter	2,001
Justifiables*	753

*Justifiables: Killing of felon, during commission of a felony, by LEO or citizen. 2014: Murders committed with firearms dropped 3.9% from 8,454 to 8,124.
Data obtained from CDC and FBI websites.

As shown in table 11.1, total deaths for 2013 from firearms was 33,383. Of these deaths, 21,175 were due to suicide. Since the presence of mental illness increases the risk for suicide by four times, effective screening for mental health issues would dramatically decrease the overall rate of firearms deaths every year. There is overall agreement between all parties on this data and it is in no way controversial. The real controversy comes when we start looking at homicides and mental illness. It turns out there is a great deal of disagreement between public perception and reported statistics concerning mental illness and homicide.

To explore these questions, we are going to look at studies on the topic of gun violence from several different perspectives. The short answer to the question of what percentage of gun violence is attributable to mental illness is 3 percent to 5 percent, according to the U.S. Department of Health and Human Services (2017). This statistic relies on all forms of violent behavior including acts of verbal, physical, gun-associated, and non-gun-associated violence. Even though this statistic is widely cited in any conversation on the effects of mental illness on gun violence, the sheer breadth of the definition of violence clouds the meaning we are able to attach to it. I think we can correctly interpret this number as suggesting that there are many different reasons for engaging in violent behavior and mental health is just one of many influences. When we are discussing gun violence and mental illness in the public, the situation is usually surrounding the latest mass shooting incident. For this reason, a more accurate set of statistics to look at would be mental illness as related to use of guns.

The MacArthur Violence Risk Assessment Study followed 951 severe mental illness patients after their release from treatment (Steadman et al., 2015). Of these, only 23 (2%) used guns to threaten or attack anyone during the follow-up period. So the numbers that indicate mentally ill individuals engage in violent acts at the rate of 3 percent to 5 percent seem to be accurate. If the focus of gun control policy is to limit rates of violent crime by addressing mental illness, it would likely not turn out to be very effective. The suicide statistics indicate that if we instead wish to reduce rates of gun-related death and injury, addressing mental illness may have a significant impact but primarily through decreasing suicide rates rather than appreciably impacting homicide rates.

When the question is reduced to mass shootings, we get a slightly different answer as to the impact of mental illness. A recent analysis of total number of victims per incident looked at several factors that related to the number of victims, and untreated mental illness was found to be the number one factor (Yelderman et al., 2019). There are several limitations to this study as it relied on media reports and interviews in determining the untreated mentally ill category (in other words, no mental health evaluations or formal diagnoses were available). The people who had a diagnosis did not contribute significantly to the model. In addition, studies that relied on media descriptions and interviews with acquaintances of mass shooters since the 1970s find that approximately 60 percent of mass shooters may have had problems with mental illness (Follman, 2012). Again, the overwhelming majority of these mass shooters were not being treated for or diagnosed with mental illness.

A broader definition of violence was used but there was an interesting relationship that has been borne out in many studies: Alcohol or substance use in conjunction with mental illness significantly increases the risk of violence. One of the theories of pathways to substance abuse problems is that of untreated mental illness. The theory is that individuals abuse drugs or alcohol in order to self-medicate their mental illness symptoms. This likely means that symptoms are not being addressed in therapy, leaving the person more likely to experience an increase in mental illness symptoms.

What do we make of this? Part of the difficulty in interpreting these findings is the discrepancy between the findings on the rate of violence in general among the mentally ill and the rates among mass shooters. One gives us a rate of violence of 3–5 percent, the other a rate of 60 percent. One reason for the discrepancy is the definition of violence being used: all violent behavior in the first case and mass shooting alone in the second. This narrowing of the definition would definitely be expected to decrease the ability to find a statistical relationship. This is because mass shootings are incredibly rare events, which leaves a very small sample of individuals to study.

The main problem seems to be the reliance on media reports and interviews in the latter case. In other words, the studies that find 60 percent of mass shooters showing evidence of mental illness tend to be based on third-party analyses of news reports and interviews (after the fact) with relatives and acquaintances.

It is likely that news reports are biased in favor of a mental illness interpretation. If we look at the statistics on media reports of mass shootings, then the percentage of stories that link mass shootings to mental illness suggests such bias. That bias is also seen in the public perceptions of a link between mental illness and violence. I would like to briefly explain how this bias in media and public perception could lead to the 60 percent statistics we see.

One reason could be selective memory at work in interviews of people who knew the shooters. Work by Elizabeth Loftus on eyewitness testimony could illustrate how this happens (Loftus & Palmer, 1974). Basically, our memory is constructed; it is not like a video. Past and present information can alter and interfere with our memories. In one study, subjects witnessed an automobile accident in which a car ran a stop sign. In one condition, subjects were asked how fast the car was going when it ran through the stop sign. In another, they were asked how fast the car was going when it coasted through the stop sign. Even though all subjects saw the same video, their estimates of the speed differed based on the question being asked. In a mass shooting, what are the questions being asked of the family and acquaintances of the shooter? Probably, they are hearing questions along the lines of "Did the individual show any signs of violence, instability, emotional instability," and so on. Could any of us have information brought up that might indicate, in hindsight, signs of mental instability? Ever? The point is that most people would remember every odd or eccentric behavior, which would then provide "evidence" of mental illness for the models being tested in the studies based on news reports.

Confirmation bias is another factor we really need to pay attention to in interpreting these findings. Confirmation bias is natural in humans. In fact, science was set up in large part to combat the influence of confirmation bias. All information that we receive is interpreted, not just received. As we saw with memory, information that is already present can alter or distort incoming information. This classic picture may help to explain. Do you see the old woman in the picture in figure 11.1?

Now look at it again. Do you see that it is really a young woman turning her head to the side? It is the same image, yet we see two different pictures because our prior information shapes how we interpret information and what information we pay attention to. It is these problems with memory and with confirmation bias that lead us to question the entire validity of the 60 percent

Figure 11.1. My Wife and My Mother-in-Law. They are both in this picture—find them. *Created by W. E. Hill, artist, November 6, 1915. LC-DIG-ds-00175, Illus. in AP101.P7 1915 (Case X) [P&P], Available from: Library of Congress, Accessed: 9/15/2021. https://www.loc.gov/pictures/item/2010652001/.*

estimate of people with mental illness committing mass shootings. And let us not forget that the very act of conducting a mass shooting is often taken as evidence of mental illness.

A final factor to keep in mind when looking at the 60 percent estimate is the low base rates of mass shootings. These events are very rare phenomena in general, so the statistics associated with them are likely to be biased and not a true reflection of propensity to violence in general.

A study conducted in Finland (Räsänen et al., 1998) can give us a stronger answer to the question because it is a "prospective" study. In a prospective study, a sample of the entire population is chosen and followed through to adulthood. They have no diagnoses or criminal history; they are just randomly chosen at birth. The researchers can then look at diagnoses and arrests for violence without preexisting bias in choosing subjects. The diagnosis that the Finnish researchers chose to look at is schizophrenia (Räsänen et al., 1998). This is a diagnosis that includes delusions (false beliefs), hallucinations, and irrational emotional states. This study (see table 11.2) found that 36.4 percent of schizophrenics who also had problems with alcohol use had been arrested for violent crimes. For schizophrenics without alcohol problems, 7.5 percent had been arrested for violent crimes. Those without a psychiatric diagnosis accounted for 2.2 percent of violent crimes. What is unique about this study is that it utilized a large, unselected birth cohort that was followed up at age twenty-six for the analyses. What is especially startling is that 20 percent of male schizophrenics were considered alcoholic before age twenty-seven during this study (Räsänen et al., 1998).

It should be noted that this study was not conducted in the United States and that it was based on a wide definition of "violence" that included verbal aggression and non-gun-related crimes. Still, it does inform our conversation. There certainly appears to be an increased risk for violent behavior due to mental illness, predominantly untreated mental illness, and especially when we look at the factor that drugs and alcohol play in gun violence, increasing the risk seven times above the baseline, whether someone is mentally ill or not (U.S. Department of Justice, 2014). A logical but impractical inference is that we could have an appreciable impact on gun violence by simply eliminating access to alcohol and other drugs. Of course, history has taught us that prohibition led to a black market in alcohol and the rise of the American Mafia. And attempts at eliminating the illegal drug trade have led more recently to the rise in Latin American drug cartels and gangs in the United States, all of which has led to rises in gun violence.

Most political attempts to address this issue revolve around gun control laws and measures that attempt to limit access to guns by people who are at high risk of committing violent acts. A study carried out by Duke University

Table 11.2. Male subjects convicted of violent crimes before the age of 27: The Northern Finland 1966 Birth Cohort

DSM-III-R diagnostics	*Subjects, n*	*Prevalence of violent offenders, n (%)*	*Odds ratios (95% CI)*	*p value (Fisher's exact test)*
Schizophrenia	51	7 (13.7)	7.0 (2.8–16.7)	0.0001
Schizophrenia with alcoholism[1]	11	4 (36.4)	25.2 (6.1–97.5)	<0.0001
Schizophrenia without alcoholism	40	3 (7.5)	3.6 (0.9–12.3)	0.06
Schizophrenia spectrum[2]	8	0 (0.0)	(0.0–0.0)	
Other psychoses[3]	27	4 (14.8)	7.7 (2.2–23.9)	0.003
All psychoses	86	11 (12.8)	6.5 (3.2–13.0)	<0.0001
No diagnosis	5,287	117 (2.2)	1.0 (reference)	

Note—C1 = confidence interval. DSM-III-R = Diagnostic and Statistical Manual of Mental Disorders. 3rd. ed. Revised (American Psychiatric Association 1987)

Source: Räsänen P, Tiihonen J, Isohanni M, Rantakallio P, Lehtonen J, Moring J. Schizophrenia, alcohol abuse, and violent behavior: a 26-year followup study of an unselected birth cohort. Schizophr Bull. 1998;24(3):437–441.

1. Alcoholism = alcohol abuse or dependence (DSM-III-R)
2. DSM-III-R diagnosis of schizophreniform disorder (295.40), schizoaffective disorder (295.70), delusional disorder (297.10), schizoid personality disorder (301.20), or schizotypal personality disorder (301.22).
3. DSM-III-R diagnosis of psychoses due to alcohol or psychoactive substance abuse, organic reasons, major depression, and psychotic disorder not otherwise specified (291–299, except 295 and 297).

researchers in Florida looked at the impact of these measures in a sample of 81,704 individuals who were diagnosed and treated for major mental illnesses and followed this group from 2002 to 2011 (Swanson et al., 2016). Guns were obtained and used for crimes by the study group at a rate of 13 percent, which can be compared to the national average of 24 percent in the general population. The suicide rate by gun for the study group was 20 percent, compared to 40 percent of suicides in the general population. Overall, the results indicate that policies to ban access to guns based on mental illness are not effective barriers.

Part of the problem is that we have not identified any good predictors or pathways from mental illness to violence. Theoretically, we can discuss pathways from anxiety and depression to suicide, and we know that suicide risk is high for those with these disorders. We can also hypothesize about psychotic symptoms, such as paranoid ideation and feelings of discrimination/persecution, as having the potential to lead to violent behavior. But the numbers, even for those with serious psychotic symptoms, just do not rise to levels that allow for statistical predictions. We can predict that persons with mental illness are far more likely to be victims of violence than perpetrators (approximately 65% to 130% higher victimization rates than the general public) (Brekke et al., 2001). Several articles report on studies that used statistical methods to try to identify pathways between mental illness and violence, but all point to similar, difficult-to-identify criteria such as substance abuse, prior history of violence, and prior history of being abused (Bruce & Laporte, 2015; Elbogen et al., 2016; Swanson et al., 2008).

A more successful approach to both problems would be to expand our mental health care capabilities in the United States. We hear this suggestion from both the political right and left in this country, but we never see any actual reforms to expand access to mental health care. If anything, we often see proposals to make cuts to Medicare and Medicaid that would make it more difficult to find treatment for those experiencing severe mental illness.

In terms of gun control, what we usually hear are calls to extend background checks to include more stringent measures for mental illness. The data presented here show the flaw in that argument. The overwhelming majority of violent acts perpetrated by the mentally ill are committed by people who have not been diagnosed. This would also explain why the majority of mass shootings have been conducted by perpetrators with legally obtained firearms. If someone has not been diagnosed with a mental illness, they will not be blocked from purchasing a firearm. In more everyday terms, the point of purchase is not an efficient place to execute mental health exclusions. The real impact can only come from identifying people with mental illness before the point of purchase of a firearm.

The sad truth is that the mental health system in the United States is completely inadequate when it comes to screening and identifying mental health issues. In America, we rely on a piecemeal system of mental health care based around private health insurance. Most private mental health providers only work with clients who have insurance. The majority of people with mental health issues are living in poverty and are uninsured. The public mental health system is overwhelmed by the need and does not have sufficient resources; this leads to chronic undertreatment and lack of diagnoses. In the United States, the identification and treatment of the chronically and seriously mentally ill has been relegated to the criminal justice system, where approximately 15 percent to 40 percent of inmates carry a mental health diagnosis. As you can imagine, this is less than ideal. Additionally, people with mental health problems tend to have difficulty maintaining employment and often end up impoverished and unable to afford treatment or medications. Most mental health issues do not materialize until people are in their late teens or early adult years. This means that current screening in the K–12 school system is inadequate for these needs. Those outside the K–12 system have to rely on either their own insurance or coverage received through their parents. Insurance has become ever more expensive, so many of these individuals are uninsured and incapable of navigating the public health system due to their symptoms. The data discussed here shows that the main problem with gun violence and mental illness concerns undiagnosed and untreated mental illness. We need to step up our efforts to increase access to mental health care in order to have any impact on mental-illness-related gun violence.

BIBLIOGRAPHY

Beck, J. (2016, June 7). Untangling gun violence from mental illness. *The Atlantic*. https://www.theatlantic.com/health/archive/2016/06/untangling-gun-violence-from-mental.

Brekke, J. S., Prindle, C., Bae, S. W., and Long, J. D. (2001). Risks for individuals with schizophrenia who are living in the community. *Psychiatric Services, 52*(10), 1358–1366. https://doi.org/10.1176/appi.ps.52.10.1358.

Bruce, M., and Laporte, D. (2015). Childhood trauma, antisocial personality typologies and recent violent acts among inpatient males with severe mental illness: Exploring an explanatory pathway. *Schizophrenia Research*, *162*(1–3), 285–290. https://doi.org/10.1016/j.schres. 2014.12.028.

Craighill, P. M., and Clement, S. (2019, April 26). What Americans blame most for mass shootings (Hint: it's not gun laws). *Washington Post*. https://www.washingtonpost.com/news/the-fix/wp/2015/10/26/gun-control-americans-overwhelmingly-blame-mental-health-failures-for-mass-shootings/.

Elbogen, E. B., Dennis, P. A., and Johnson, S. C. (2016). Beyond mental illness: Targeting stronger and more direct pathways to violence. *Clinical Psychological Science, 4*(5), 747–759. https://doi.org/10.1177/2167702615619363.

Follman, M. (2012, Nov. 9). Mass shootings: Maybe what we need is a better mental-health policy. *Mother Jones*. Retrieved July 23, 2014, from http://www.motherjones.com/ politics/2012/11/jared-loughner-mass-shootings-mental-illness.

Gramlich, J. (2019). What the data says about gun deaths in the United States. Pew Research Center, Washington, DC. https://www.pewresearch.org/fact-tank/2019/08/16/what-the-data-says-about-gun-deaths-in-the-u-s/.

Loftus, E. F., and Palmer, J. C. (1974). Reconstruction of automobile destruction: An example of the interaction between language and memory. *Journal of Verbal Learning and Verbal Behavior, 13*(5), 585–589. https://doi.org/10.1016/S0022-5371(74)80011-3.

Pescosolido, B. A., Manago, B., and Monahan, J. (2019). Evolving public views on the likelihood of violence from people with mental illness: Stigma and its consequences. *Health Affairs*, *38*, 1735–1743. https://doi.org/10.1377/hlthaff.2019.00702.

Räsänen, P., Tiihonen, J., Isohanni, M., Rantakallio, P., Lehtonen, J., and Moring, J. (1998). Schizophrenia, alcohol abuse, and violent behavior: A 26-year followup [*sic*] study of an unselected birth cohort. *Schizophrenia Bulletin, 24*(3), 437–441. https://doi.org/10.1093/ oxfordjournals.schbul.a033338.

Steadman, H. J., Monahan, J., Pinals, D. A., Vesselinov, R., and Clark Robbins, P. (2015). Gun violence and victimization of strangers by persons with a mental illness: Data from the MacArthur Violence Risk Assessment Study. *Psychiatric Services, 66*(11): 1238–1241. https://doi.org/10.1176/appi.ps.201400512.

Swanson, J. W., Easter, M. M., Robertson, A. G., Swartz, M. S., Alanis-Hirsch, K., Moseley, D., Dion, C., and Petrila, J. (2016). Gun violence, mental illness, and laws that prohibit gun possession: Evidence from two Florida counties. *Health Affairs, 35*(6), 1067–1075. https://www.healthaffairs.org/toc/hlthaff/35/6.

Swanson, J. W., McGinty, E. E., Fazel, S., and Mays, V. M. (2015). Mental illness and reduction of gun violence and suicide: Bringing epidemiologic research to policy. *Annals of Epidemiology, 25*(5), 366–376. https://doi.org/10.1016/j.annepidem.2014.03.004.

Swanson, J. W., Van Dorn, R. A., Swartz, M. S., Smith, A., Elbogen, E. B., and Monahan, J. (2008). Alternative pathways to violence in persons with schizophrenia: The role of childhood antisocial behavior problems. *Law and Human Behavior, 32*(3), 228. https://doi.org/10.1007/s10979-007-9095-7.

U.S. Department of Health and Human Services. (2017). *Mental health myths and facts*. https://www.mentalhealth.gov/basics/mental-health-myths-facts.

U.S. Department of Justice. (2014). A study of active shooter incidents in the United States between 2000 and 2013. Retrieved October 1, 2014, from http://www.fbi.gov/news/stories/2014/september/fbi-releases-study-on-active-shooter-incidents/pdfs/a-study-of-active-shooter-incidents-in-the-u.s.-between-2000-and-2013.

Yelderman, L. A., Joseph, J. J., West, M. P., and Butler, E. (2019). Mass shootings in the United States: Understanding the importance of mental health and firearm considerations. *Psychology, Public Policy, and Law, 25*(3), 212–223. https://doi.org/10.1037/law0000200.

12

Guns and the African American Community

Lisa G. Long

In 2019, the Cook County, Illinois, medical examiner's office reported 510 homicides. Of those homicides, 491 of them were reported as murders. Of those 491 murders, 315 of them were African American males between the ages of 15–40 years old. Forty-three of those murder victims were African American women between the ages of 18–70 years old. The most deadly incident was a shooting on the Northwest side, where the suspect opened fire on a condo building and killed five people (Charles, 2019). Conversations continue to spark concern and debate in regard to the gun violence in Chicago, particularly in predominantly African American communities.

In March 2020, Breonna Taylor, a Black female, was shot and killed in her home in Louisville, Kentucky. The Louisville Metro Police Department conducted a "no-knock" warrant at Taylor's house. According to police reports, the main target location of the investigation was miles away from Taylor's house (Oppel & Taylor, 2020). Taylor's boyfriend, Kenneth Walker, also Black, had a concealed carry permit. When police entered the house, Walker fired, claiming he thought they were being robbed. As Walker fired, police returned fire, killing Taylor. Walker was subsequently charged; however, the charges were dropped. This incident has received national attention and there are currently legislative actions in place to eliminate "no-knock" warrants. The Louisville Metro Council recently passed "Breonna's Law." This law bans the Louisville Metro Police Department from conducting any additional "no-knock" warrants. It also requires officers to use body cameras when executing a search warrant (Burke, 2020).

These two scenarios are just a couple of images that can be painted when discussing firearms in African American communities. This chapter will attempt to discuss a gamut of hot topics surrounding guns and African

American communities. We will address the history, the evolution of Black gun ownership, some of the pressing concerns surrounding firearms and the Black community, and then address the implications for the future. This chapter is not meant to be an all-inclusive guide or tutorial regarding African American communities and guns; rather, a thought-provoking and engrossing opportunity to create further conversations and discussions surrounding the future of guns and how they affect and impact the African American community in the United States.

HISTORY

When examining a historical context, Blacks have had varied relationships with firearms. As early as 1715, white colonists were known to have armed Black slaves to assist in the fight against Native Americans (Smallwood, 1999). During the 1760s, African slaves were also armed by the British in all thirteen original colonies. These armed slaves were mainly used in South Carolina and Georgia. Consequentially, Congress soon sanctioned the formation of four all-Black military units. These units were established on July 28, 1866, with the primary mission of serving during the Indian Wars from 1866 to 1880 (Smallwood, 1999). These units are now infamously known as "Buffalo Soldiers." There were two Calvary Regiments and two Infantry Units that were led by mostly white United States Army officers (National Museum, 2020). The soldiers serving in the 9th and 10th Cavalries and the 24th and 25th Infantries were typically handpicked because of their outstanding physical abilities and their high levels of intelligence (Smallwood, 1999).

While Congress felt that African slaves were fit to serve in battle and bear arms for the cause, other legislators took to implementing laws that prohibited Blacks from owning firearms. Many states created the Black Codes of 1865 (Constitutional Rights, 2020). These Black codes placed restrictions and limitations on Blacks' civil rights and oftentimes labor contracts and other freedoms and liberties. In most instances, these codes removed the rights of Black people to possess firearms, legally. South Carolina and Mississippi specifically enacted laws to accomplish such measures. Fears existed that armed African Americans may create slave rebellions or present armed opposition to Jim Crow laws (Trisler & Filindra, 2019).

While laws may have existed banning such ownership, many Black activists and freedom leaders encouraged African Americans to arm themselves for their own protection, particularly after the Emancipation Proclamation of 1863. Frederick Douglass was a very vocal proponent of African Americans arming themselves in protection of themselves and their families. Douglass also encouraged Blacks to enlist in the Union Army to make a political stance for their rights (Trisler & Filindra, 2019). In 1854, Douglass was quoted as prescribing: "A good revolver, a steady hand and a determination to shoot down any man attempting to kidnap" (Johnson, 2014, para. 3).

Ida B. Wells-Barnett, a Black female journalist, business owner, and activist was also known as a proponent for the Black community to arm themselves for their own protection. In 1892, Wells-Barnett was quoted as saying: "A Winchester rifle should have a place of honor in every black home and it should be used for that protection which the law refuses to give" (Constitutional Rights, 2018, para. 12).

While Douglass and Wells-Barnett encouraged African Americans to arm themselves in order to protect themselves and their homes in the era post–emancipation proclamation, this call for action did not end there. Moving ahead to 1964 in Jonesboro, Louisiana, the Deacons for Defense and Justice was established. This group consisted of mainly Black World War II veterans who were staunch supporters of armed self-defense. This group was active in providing protection and defense for protestors and marchers, particularly in Mississippi in 1966. Various chapters of the organization were spread across Louisiana, Mississippi, and Alabama to thwart attacks from the Ku Klux Klan (The United States National, 2020).

Early indications of gun usage among the Black community imply that citizens were encouraged to use firearms for protection against, in most cases, white racists. During the 1960s and 1970s Blacks were often encouraged to arm themselves to show a position of solidarity with the Black power movement. The Black Panther Party was founded in 1966 by Huey Newton and Bobby Seale. The original members of the party were armed in a stance to protect African Americans from police brutality in Oakland, California, and other large cities across the country. While the party was responsible for many social programs and positive movements within the Black community, they were also known for violence at times, more specifically, gun violence (History Channel, 2019).

A daunting Supreme Court decision should also be discussed in relation to the history of African Americans and firearms. In Tennessee v. Garner, 471 U.S. 1, Edward Garner was an unarmed fifteen-year-old African American male who was shot by the police (Patterson & Swan, 2016). In 1974, Garner was fleeing the scene of a robbery. He was seen climbing a fence. While climbing the fence, one of the responding Memphis Police Department officers shot Garner in the back of his head. The 6th Circuit Court of Appeals ruled that Garner's constitutional rights were violated by being shot in the back of the head (LoRusso & Davis, 2020). Ultimately, the Supreme Court set the following precedent, as it relates to police use of deadly force:

> The use of deadly force to prevent the escape of all felony suspects, whatever the circumstance, is constitutionally unreasonable. . . . Where the suspect poses NO immediate threat to the officer and no threat to others, the harm resulting from failing to apprehend him does not justify deadly force to do so. (LoRusso & Davis, 2020, para. 8)

A transition began to occur in Black communities, shifting the need for guns from protection from white racists and supremacists to feeling a need to protect themselves from each other. In 1996, a study was published providing the results from a nationwide survey of high school students. That study found that approximately 30 percent of high school males had carried a weapon to school, while only 8 percent of females had carried a weapon to school. A more alarming finding in this study was that African American students that were surveyed displayed more apprehension than any other ethnic groups when it came to a fear of being hurt by other students at school (Martin et al., 1996). These researchers also found that African American students were at a higher risk of violence based on the fact that they were more likely to experience high rates of poverty and be victims of racial discrimination. Some 36 percent of those students that were surveyed expressed concerns and fears that another student would injure or attack them while at school. This alarming shift in perceptions of weapons and use of weapons in the African American communities began to create serendipitous outcomes.

CURRENT GUN VIOLENCE IN AFRICAN AMERICAN COMMUNITIES

In 2014, the CDC reported that the leading cause of deaths among African Americans aged fifteen to twenty-four years was homicide. Most of those homicides occurred in urban areas and were directly related to a firearm discharge (Joseph et al., 2018). In 2018 the Bureau of Justice Statistics reported that approximately 644,710 African Americans were victims of violent crimes (Morgan & Oudekerk, 2019). The spread of gun violence in African American communities is creating everlasting effects on early childhood development and continues to have impacts that may not be seen for years to come (Fowler et al., 2017).

There are psychological and emotional effects on children living in African American communities with high rates of violence, specifically gun violence. Many African American children are living in economically disadvantaged communities, lending to the propensity for them to be exposed to a proliferation of firearms, a prevalence of gun violence, and community violence. The National Child Traumatic Stress Network defines community violence as being "the exposure to intentional acts of interpersonal violence committed in public areas by individuals who are not intimately related to the victim" (Joseph et al., 2018, p. 397). This exposure creates additional health risks and potential hazards on the brain development of African American adolescents. In some instances, adolescents that are exposed to extreme rates of violent crime may exhibit reduced cortisol levels as well as shortened telomere length. A telomere is the DNA protein structure that is found at the ends of each chromosome (Shammas, 2012). Telomere length plays a significant role in determining the lifespan of a cell or organism. The shortening of telomere may have an impact on the preservation of the information contained in genomes.

Additional exposure to community violence may also present other health concerns in African American adolescents, such as post-traumatic stress disorder, anxiety, aggression, and poor performance in school (Singleton, 2018). An exponential amount of research exists discussing the negative impacts and implications that gun violence and exposure have on African American adolescents. Urban African Americans are more likely to reside in communities that have higher rates of violence compared to whites (Khubchandani & Price, 2018). In 2008, a group of male and female high school students from the south side of Chicago participated in a qualitative study to determine the type of coping strategies that were present as well as the amount of violence, specifically gun violence, they had been exposed to (Voisin et al., 2011). The students were asked to comment about their level of exposure to gun violence and murders, physical attacks, fighting, and incidents involving police officers. Did they simply hear about it, did they witness it, or were they a direct victim of the violence? Parsing out the responses related to gun violence and murders, the respondents indicated that the most pervasive type of violence they had heard about was gun violence. Most of the male respondents indicated that they had seen people shot or killed by gunfire. Many respondents, male and female, indicated that they either knew several people that had been shot or heard about other shootings in the community (Voisin et al., 2011).

Several causes and reasons exist as to why urban African American communities are experiencing high levels of gun violence and gun exposure. Oftentimes, young people may be quick to resort to weapons to resolve disputes instead of simply fistfighting. In some violent communities, there is an abundance of firearms that are readily accessible to those who want them (Voisin et al., 2011). Knowing these things, it is important to examine coping strategies and mechanisms to keep African American adolescents safe.

Extreme exposure to community violence can be handled by victims in many ways. Voisin et al. offer different levels of involvement and coping strategies for adolescents in African American communities. The respondents in the study indicated that of all the levels of violence that they were exposed to, the most memorable form was gun violence because of the trauma that is experienced and the anxiety that may develop after the exposure. The first level of coping that may be exhibited by these adolescents is "getting through" (Voisin et al., 2011). This simply means that individuals that are exposed to the violence understand that their community is riddled with violence; however, they try to preoccupy their minds and time with other activities. They attempt to "forget about" the violence to simply maintain some level of normalcy.

The most common level of coping is "getting along" (Voisin et al., 2011). When an individual decides to "get along," they have determined that they need to associate with the "right people" in order to stay safe. Those people may be on the right side or the wrong side of the law. Another level is "getting away" (Voisin et al., 2011). Living in violent communities, adolescents begin to learn quick where they should and should not go to remain safe. "Getting away" entails individuals staying away from locations and people that may create or cause a violent situation to erupt. Oftentimes, individuals that select this level of coping experience feelings of loneliness and isolation. Finally, "getting back" (Voisin et al., 2011) is the last level of coping. This may be the most dangerous form of coping because the individual decides to actively resist the violence, normally by carrying a weapon or learning to fight.

Those methods of coping are frequent and apparent among African American adolescents who are dealing with regular community violence. An additional, oftentimes more productive method relies on the individual's ability to engage in school and their education. Research indicates that positive interaction and adequate performance in school is a likely protective factor for adolescents who are exposed to gun violence and firearm homicides within their community (Khubchandani & Price, 2018).

Discussing coping measures for adolescents is important, but it is also imperative to discuss the public health implications for African American communities in relation to gun violence in communities. Due to the sheer number of African Americans who are victims and perpetrators of gun violence, racial stereotyping exists. There is a school of thought that feels that there is "a small minority of extreme antisocial aberrants who manage to obtain guns whatever the level of gun ownership in the African American community" (Kates & Mauser, n.d., p. 377). In other words, no matter what level of gun control or gun ownership is in place, there will be members of the African American community who are deviant and possess a propensity to commit violent acts. Whether intentional or unintentional, this pervasive theme of racial stereotyping exudes into the public health agenda when trying to prevent and reduce gun violence among adolescents in African American communities (Levine et al., 2012). The effects of gun violence on the innocent victims in the community are being lost in the noise of punishing individuals who are actually pulling triggers.

From a public health perspective, gun violence prevention measures should address root causes of the issues. There are multiple protective factors that can be practiced and implemented to assist in the reduction of lasting effects of the trauma experienced by innocent victims of gun violence. Communities should see an increase in neighborhood programs and services that focus on good nutrition and health care. Prevention programs should be developed around the basis of encouraging school attendance and family connectedness. A well-rounded approach to provide better public service infrastructure in urban and impoverished communities will begin to address these root causes that have created and caused an increase in gun violence in African American communities.

THE SOCIETY OF BLACK ACADEMIC SURGEONS

In 1989, the Society of Black Academic Surgeons (SBAS) was formed to perpetuate a community of professional and intellectual Black surgeons and scientists (The Society, 2020). The SBAS has presented multiple concerns regarding gun violence among African Americans. The costs for gunshot injuries has increased over the years. Currently, the cost of a gunshot injury is approximately $430,000 (Joseph et al., 2018). This cost includes, but is not limited to, insurance claims processing, criminal justice costs, and loss of work.

Because African American males are disproportionately more likely to be victims of gun violence (National Institute, 2019), this has reduced the number of African American males who have been admitted to medical schools. The indirect or direct victimization may also create an effect on surgical services that are provided to Black patients because minority doctors are more likely to work in areas that have a large minority population (Joseph et al., 2018). SBAS has offered their own recommendations and advice for reducing these effects of gun violence in the Black community. They say gun violence must be researched nationally without any restrictions being placed on the types of questions that can be asked and studied. SBAS also recommends the elimination of gun-show loopholes. They recommend background checks be mandatory for all firearm purchases and transfers (Joseph et al., 2018).

AFRICAN AMERICAN PROPONENTS FOR FIREARMS

While staggering numbers exist indicating that of the number of children who suffered firearm injuries, the majority of them were African American male adolescents (Bachier-Rodriquez & Feliz, 2016), there has been a growing number of African American gun owners. Most gun owners state that they own a gun for protection (Gallup, 2016). In 2017, Pew Research Center conducted a survey about gun ownership. Approximately 33 percent of Blacks who were surveyed stated that someone had used a gun to threaten or intimidate their family (Pew Research, 2017). The survey also indicated that Blacks are more likely to have concerns about gun violence in their local communities (Pew Research, 2017). It is also clear that rural gun owners, regardless of their race, are more likely to own guns for the purposes of hunting or the sport of owning a gun. From 2012 to 2016 five states across the country showed an increase in Blacks with concealed carry permits. In those five states, permits were issued at a 30 percent faster rate for Blacks than Whites.

There are many organizations and groups that currently exist surrounding African Americans and gun ownership.

NATIONAL AFRICAN AMERICAN GUN ASSOCIATION

The National African American Gun Association was founded in 2015. Currently, there are more than seventy active chapters across the country with approximately 30,000 members. The group particularly targets its membership recruitment toward members of law enforcement and active and retired military members. According to their website, their mission is to "establish a fellowship by educating on the rich legacy of gun ownership by African Americans, offering training that supports safe gun use for self-defense and sportsmanship, and advocating for the inalienable right to self-defense for African Americans" (National African, 2020, para. 1). Currently, more than 60 percent of the registered members are women.

NAAGA also markets themselves as being a "pro 2nd amendment organization that focuses on the preservation of the community through armed protection and community building" (National African, 2020, para. 2). NAAGA is focused on providing a positive experience to gun ownership and the Black community.

BROTHERS AGAINST RACIST COPS

While little public information exists regarding this group, what is known is they are a radical minority group that is pro-firearms and pro–Second Amendment. They have been known to focus on learning as much as possible about police policies, the rights of citizens, and the laws. They practice physical fitness and training, hand-to-hand combat techniques, and weapons drills (Wilson, 2016).

HUEY P. NEWTON GUN CLUB

- It is important to mention that the Southern Poverty Law Center classifies this group as a hate group. While gun ownership of Black people is a part of the mission statement of this organization, they also market "self-preservation, self-defense and self-sufficiency through a militant culture" (Huey, 2020, para. 1). They indicate that they are aspiring to arm and educate Black people in the United States and abroad in regard to their Second Amendment rights (Huey, 2020).

NEW BLACK PANTHER PARTY

The Southern Poverty Law Center classifies this group as a hate group. The original Black Panther Party has rejected this group. They present as being an armed group of Black militants that believe Black Americans should have their own nation. The views of this group are anti-white and antisemitic. They feel that all Black prisoners should be released and that all Blacks should receive reparations for slavery. In March 2012, the group placed a bounty on the head of George Zimmerman, the accused killer of Trayvon Martin (Southern Poverty, 2020).

BLACK WOMEN AND GUN OWNERSHIP

Ultimately, gun ownership in Black communities is on the rise. As previously noted, the number of Blacks receiving concealed carry permits is on the rise. The percentage of African Americans who own guns is on the rise (Crime Prevention, 2017). The largest increase of gun ownership in the Black community is women. In North Carolina, the number of women holding a concealed carry permit increased from 21 percent in 2012 to 29 percent in 2017

(Mitchell, 2018). Black women contribute to that rise. In 2016, the American National Election Studies indicated that 6 percent of women that own guns are Black (Trisler & Filindra, 2019).

Just as seen in African American adolescents, Black women appear to be disproportionately vulnerable to become victims of violence. Oftentimes, women have seen or experienced some sort of community or interpersonal violence (Trisler & Filindra, 2019). Black women are feeling empowered to protect themselves. Owning firearms is seen as a way of empowering them (Price et al., 1994). It is important to note that owning the gun is only half the battle. Women must know how to use the gun safely in order to use it as a means of protection (Trisler & Filindra, 2019). There is a gun club in the Midwestern part of the country that was organized by and for Black women. Members feel that firearms are important for their protection and that "people kill people, not firearms" (Trisler & Filindra, 2019 p. 15).

Black women that own firearms may have experience in law enforcement and/or the military. In 2016, the Bureau of Justice Statistics reported that 2.7 percent of full-time sworn law enforcement officers in local police departments were Black females, while local sheriff's offices had 2.6 percent (Hyland & Davis, 2019). As of 2017, the Department of Veteran Affairs reported that 10 percent of the veteran population is female (Office of Data, 2017). Detective Sasha Graham of the Fayetteville Police Department in Fayetteville, North Carolina, discussed her experience as a gun owner. As a Black female, Graham stated that she grew up shooting guns, sometimes BB guns and sometimes real guns. She stated that her older brothers taught her a lot about guns, gun ownership, and gun safety. Graham remembered that growing up, she shot for fun, but now, as a single mother with a daughter, she feels that it is necessary for a woman to own a gun for protection. She said that recently, she has had many friends who have asked her lots of questions about buying guns and learning how to shoot. Graham shared that she has taught her daughter how to shoot and how to be comfortable with a gun. She stated that her career as a law enforcement officer has made her more comfortable with firearms. She also added that one of her bosses at the police department took her to purchase her first weapon (S. Graham, personal communication, June 14, 2020).

Ms. Raven Coleman is a United States Air Force Veteran, former state and federal probation officer, and currently a business owner and homeowner. As a single Black female, Coleman is an avid gun owner. While growing up, she was not exposed to guns for the means of protection. She said her father had a BB gun in the house for appearance, but not really for protection. Her first experience with firearms came when she enlisted in the United States Air

Force. From there, her subsequent jobs working in the criminal justice system required her to also operate a firearm.

"As a Black female business owner and a veteran, I think it is more imperative than ever in today's climate to be a legally licensed to carry and educated gun toting citizen," Coleman stated. Having said that, Coleman also feels that our country needs to have stricter gun control policies, regarding the types of guns individuals are allowed to possess. "I embrace the right to carry. The protection of self and survival is an innate characteristic that we all possess" (R. Coleman, personal communication, June 15, 2020).

Coleman and Graham are a small sample of the larger voice of Black females who are exercising their rights to carry guns and protect themselves. They echo the sentiments of the group of Black women in the Midwest who state that owning a gun is only half the battle. It is imperative for women to educate themselves about gun safety and how to use and maintain their weapon properly.

CONCLUSION

Firearms in the Black community is a complex issue. Early history indicates that there was a dichotomous relationship between the use of firearms against slaves and the encouragement of activists for slaves to arm themselves for protection. As shown in the communities and neighborhoods in Chicago, there is an increase in gun violence and homicides in Black communities. Recently, there has also been an increase in the number of Black women currently arming themselves for protection. There is nothing simple or trivial about the discussion of guns and gun ownership in the Black community.

A primary concern should be the reduction in the amount of Black adolescent males that are victims of homicides related to gun violence. The growing concern for young Black males living in Chicago and other urban areas across the country is dire. While many members of the African American community are arming themselves by legal means for protection, many young members of the African American community are fighting a losing battle against the gun violence occurring in their neighborhoods.

To continue strategies to reduce gun violence in urban areas, the public health agenda needs to address the underlying root causes and focus on removing racial prejudices and stereotypes when implementing gun violence prevention programs. Most prevention programs place a heavy importance on additional directed police patrols and are rooted in identifying hot spots of violent criminal activity. As such, young African American males often end up being targeted as suspects instead of being given tools and resources to find alternate courses of action in dealing with conflicts and disputes. As the Black community has evolved in its acceptance of legal gun ownership, additional research and conversations need to occur to level the playing field when it comes to the negative violent impacts of firearms in the Black community.

BIBLIOGRAPHY

Bachier-Rodriquez, M., and Feliz, J. F. (2016). Firearm injuries in a pediatric population: African-American adolescents continue to carry the heavy burden. *The American Journal of Surgery, 213,* 785–789.

Burke, M. (2020, June 13). *Breonna Taylor's death ignites debate on no-knock warrants as Louisville becomes latest city to ban them.* NBC News. https://www.nbcnews.com/news/us-news/breonna-taylor-s-death-ignites-debate-no-knock-warrants-louisville-n1208156.

Charles, S. (2019, December 30). With more than 500 homicides, Chicago's violent death total falls for 3rd straight year. *Chicago Sun Times.* https://chicago.suntimes.com/crime/2019/12/30/21043526/chicago-homicides-murders-2019-decline.

Constitutional Rights Foundation. (2018). *Ida B. Wells and her crusade for racial justice, 33(3).*

Constitutional Rights Foundation. (2020). *Southern Black Codes.* https://www.crf-usa.org/brown-v-board-50th-anniversary/southern-black-codes.html.

Crime Prevention Research Center. (2017, July 20). *Concealed carry permit holders across the United States: 2017.* https://ssrn.com/abstract=3004915.

Fowler, K., Dahlberg, L., Haileyesus, T., Gutierrez, C., and Bacon, S. (2017). Childhood firearm injuries in the United States. *Pediatrics, 140*(1). DOI: https:// doi. org/ 10.1542/ peds. 2016–3486.

Gallup. (2016). *Guns.* https://news.gallup.com/poll/1645/Guns.aspx.

History Channel. (2019, June 6). *Black Panthers.* https://www.history.com/topics/civil-rights-movement/black-panthers.

Huey P. Newton Gun Club. (2020, April 8). *Huey P. Newton Gun Club.* https://hueypnewtongunclub.org/about.

Hyland, S., and Davis, E. (2019 October). *Local police departments, 2016: personnel.* Bureau of Justice Statistics.

Johnson, N. (2014, January 28). Negroes and the gun: Slaves, fugitives, freemen, and citizens. *Washington Post.* https://www.washingtonpost.com/news/volokh-conspiracy/wp/2014/01/28/negroes-and-the-gun-slaves-fugitives-freemen-and-citizens/.

Joseph, K., Turner, P., Barry, L., Cooper, C., Danner, O., Enumah, S., Hayanga, J., James, I., Oppong, B., Gibson, C., Stanford, A., Thomas, Y., Weaver, W., Williams, M., Young, C., and Britt, L. (2018). Reducing the impact of violence on the health status of African-Americans: Literature review and recommendations from the society of black academic surgeons. *The American Journal of Surgery, 216,* 393–400.

Kates, D., and Mauser, G. (n.d.) Would banning firearms reduce murder and suicide? *Harvard Journal of Law & Public Policy, 30,* 649–694.

Khubchandani, J., and Price, J. (2018). Violent behaviors, weapon carrying, and firearm homicide trends in African American adolescents, 2001–2015. *Journal of Community Health, 43,* 947–955. https://doi.org/10.1007/s10900-018-0510-4.

Levine, R., Goldzweig, I., Kilbourne, B., and Juarez, P. (2012). Firearms, youth homicide, and public health. *Journal of Health Care for the Poor and Underserved, 23,* 7–19.

LoRusso, L., and Davis, K., (2020, March 26). Tennessee v. Garner: *The ensuring test of "objective reasonableness."* PoliceOne.com. https://www.policeone.com/legal/articles/tennessee-v-garner-the-enduring-test-of-objective-reasonableness-cYjlsV2eXSd7SbeV/.

Martin, S., Sadowski, L., Cotton, N., and McCarraher, D. (1996). Response of African-American adolescents in North Carolina to gun carrying school mates. *The Journal of School Health, 66*(1), 23–27.

Mitchell, M. (2018, July 13). *Gun ownership: Growing number of black women getting firearms, stats show.* WRAL. https://www.wral.com/gun-ownership-growing-number-of-black-women-getting-firearms-stats-show/17482447/.

Morgan, R., and Oudekerk, B. (2019). US Department of Justice. Bureau of Justice Statistics. *Criminal Victimization, 2018.* NCJ253043.29.

National African American Gun Association. (2020, June 14). About the NAAGA. https://naaga.co/about-us/.

National Institute of Justice. (2019, February 26). *Gun violence in America.* https://nij.ojp.gov/topics/articles/gun-violence-america.

National Museum of African American History and Culture. (2020, June 14). *Buffalo Soldiers: Legend and Legacy.* https://nmaahc.si.edu/explore/manylenses/buffalosoldiers.

Office of Data Governance and Analytics. (2017, February). *The Past, Present and Future of Women Veterans.* https://www.dvs.virginia.gov/wp-content/uploads/2017/05/VAMCWomen_Veterans_Feb-2017_Final.pdf.

Oppel, R., and Taylor, D. (2020, June 5). Here's what you need to know about Breonna Taylor's death. *New York Times.* https://www.nytimes.com/article/breonna-taylor-police.html.

Patterson, G., and Swan, P. (2016). Police shootings of unarmed African American males: A systematic review. *Journal of Human Behavior in the Social Environment, 26*(3–4), 267–278.

Pew Research Center. (2017, June 22). *Guns and daily life: Identity, experiences, activities and involvement.* https://www.pewsocialtrends.org/2017/06/22/guns-and-daily-life-identity-experiences-activities-and-involvement/.

Price, J., Kandakai, T., Casler, S., Everett, S., and Smith, D. (1994). African-American adults' perceptions of guns and violence. *Journal of the National Medical Association, 86*(6), 426–432.

Shammas, M. (2012). Telomeres, lifestyle, cancer and aging. *Current Opinion in Clinical Nutrition and Metabolic Care, 14*(1), 28–34.

Singleton, S. (2018, February 26). *As America debates gun control, remember the black community.* The Hill. https://thehill.com/opinion/civil-rights/375539-as-america-debates-gun-control-remember-the-black-community.

Smallwood, A. (1999). A history of Native American and African relations from 1502 to 1900. *Negro History Bulletin.*

The Society of Black Academic Surgeons. (2020, June). *Mission, vision and values.* https://www.sbas.net/about/.

Southern Poverty Law Center. (2020, April 8). *New Black Panther Party.* https://www.splcenter.org/fighting-hate/extremist-files/group/new-black-panther-party.

Trisler, B., and Filindra, A. (2019). *Black women gun enthusiasts: Computational propaganda in the United States.* Institute for the Future.

The United States National Archives and Records Administration. (2020 June). *The deacons for defense and justice.* https://www.archives.gov/research/african-americans/black-power/deacons.

Voisin, D., Bird, J., Hardestry, M., and Shiu, C. (2011). African American adolescents living and coping with community violence in Chicago's Southside. *Journal of Interpersonal Violence, 26*(12). DOI: 10.1177/0886260510383029.

Wilson, J. (2016, July 27). *It's a matter of survival: The black Americans fighting for gun rights.* The Guardian. https://www.theguardian.com/us-news/2016/jul/27/african-american-black-gun-rights-second-amendment.

Part IV

FIREARMS AND PUBLIC HEALTH

13

Applying Public Health Outcomes to the Culture of Gun Violence

Michelle L. Foster

INTRODUCTION AND CURRENT CLIMATE

In recent years, a review of violent crime data indicates that crime has gone down, and gun deaths have decreased as well. Many connect these two facts and say that the "problem" of guns has improved. On their face, connecting these data can yield an inaccurate picture. Research conducted by Jena, Sun, and Prasad (2014) demonstrated that deaths due to gun violence had only decreased because of changes in *procedures* when providing emergency care and treatment. This explanation is just one that is a far cry from the belief that gun violence had been reduced because persons were engaging in *less crime* with the *use* of guns. Understanding the whole picture of gun violence rather than the singular focus on guns can more accurately direct efforts of medical professionals, the criminal justice system, and other community stakeholders.

Gun deaths that occur by suicide, homicide, or accident are part of the public health crisis of the new millennium. During an eight-year period,

> From 2006 to 2014, the cost of initial hospitalizations for firearm-related injuries averaged $734.6 million per year. Medicaid paid one third and self-pay patients funded one quarter of the financial burden of these injuries. These figures substantially underestimate true health care costs. (Spitzer et al., 2017, section "Abstract: Conclusions")

Moreover, they underestimate the cost to society as a whole. Gun violence in communities affects the health of the residents and is linked to chronic illnesses, such as heart disease, cancer, stroke, obstructive lung disease, diabetes and hepatitis, mental illness, and barriers to educational achievement (Prevention Institute's, 2013).

Public health can play a role in understanding the physical and psychological impact of exposure to gun violence as a part of the multidisciplinary approach to change deeply ingrained beliefs. The main goal of public health is to improve the health of communities. Public health intersects with various disciplines and includes biology, chemistry, sociology, psychology, political science, and anthropology (Shi & Johnson, 2014). A few ways that the field of public health can contribute to address the issue of gun violence and homicides include gun safety approaches and changing cultural norms (Mozaffarian et al., 2013) through health promotion and health education.

Regarding safety approaches, communities can come together, and our government representatives can facilitate the passage of laws whereby persons need to wait longer to purchase a gun to enable a more thorough background check to be conducted on them. In our democracy, however, placing restrictions on any of these areas can be looked upon as an infringement of our civil liberties. Sometimes drastic measures need to be taken to solve large problems, so people need to be open to discussing effective options regardless of personal opinion. This issue is a significant problem affecting over 320 million people in the United States. While it might not be simple or even possible to reach a societal compromise on addressing gun violence, in a democratic republic such as ours, it is the government's responsibility to guide us and, in turn, them in these efforts (Shi & Johnson, 2014). A possible way to bridge the divide on this issue could be for those utilizing knowledge gained from the field of public health to take up the issue more aggressively to reduce gun injuries and homicides.

Exploring the issue of gun violence though the lens of public health is a fairly recent approach and has been tackled under the U.S. Department of Health and Human Services (HHS) Healthy People 2020 objectives. Background on this topic is covered in the first section of this chapter. There have been various models utilized for understanding gun violence, three of which connect with public health promotion and education. These models include Cure Violence, Biopsychosocial and Disease Model, and Group-Up Model. The Cure Violence model, developed by Gary Slutkin and colleagues, is just one public health approach dedicated to gun violence reduction. Another option that is receiving attention is viewing gun violence as a biopsychosocial disease whereby the Disease Model demonstrates that gun violence "follows predictable patterns just like infectious diseases and other illnesses" (Hargarten et al., 2018). A third model, the Group-Up Model, adopts the application of improving the community's environment. This chapter explores these three options along with how changing cultural norms facilitates increased health benefits for the public.

BRIEF BACKGROUND ON PUBLIC HEALTH

Core Functions and 10 Essential Public Health Services

Established in 1988, the Institute of Medicine (IOM) set forth three core functions that agencies must ensure are met to enable effective cooperation and distribution of public health services (Centers for Disease Control and Prevention [CDC], 2014b). Shown in figure 13.1, these three core functions include assessment, policy development, and assurance, and are designed along a continuum that outlines 10 Essential Services for public health. The 10 Essential Services were added later by the IOM in 1994 (Shi & Johnson, 2014).

The *assessment* function involves collecting and analyzing community-level data. There are two essential public health services in this group: (1) Monitoring the health status of communities and (2) diagnosing and investigating health problems within those communities (CDC, 2014b).

The next core function is *policy development*, which incorporates the application of science and what is known to be effective to the policy-making and decision-making processes (Santilli et al., 2017). Policy development includes the next three essential services:

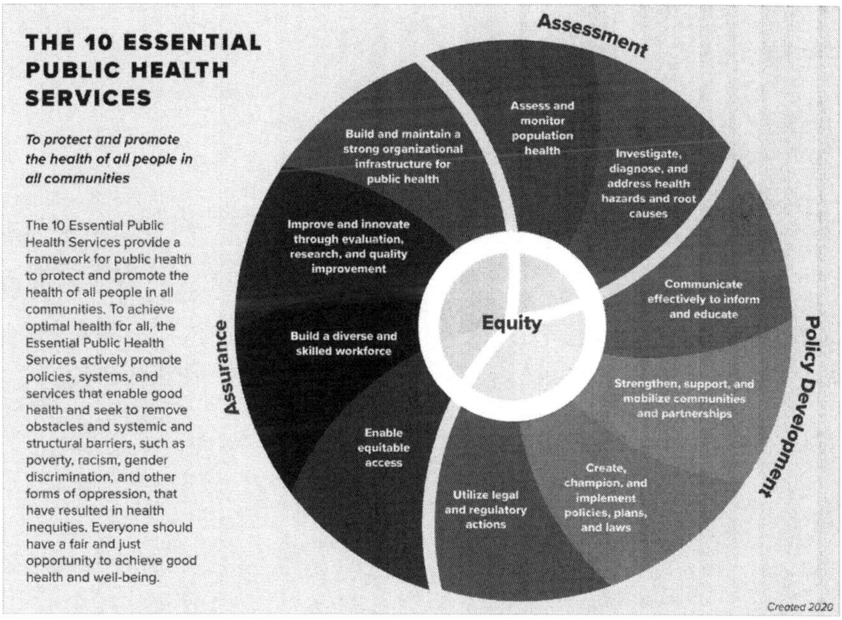

Figure 13.1. The Department of Health and the CDC integrate the Social Determinants of Health and the 10 Essential Services together. ***Source: https://www.cdc.gov/publichealthgateway/publichealthservices/essentialhealthservices.html.***

1. Informing, educating, and empowering individuals about health. This area often concerns itself with health inequities and racial disparities that affect the communities and health of those living within them.
2. Mobilizing community partnerships. Bringing together community leaders, groups, and school systems during information gathering while developing policies is clearly important because information about the practical application of the policy can be gleaned from those experienced in the field.
3. Developing policies designed to promote the health of the communities, which is evidence-based in research from data collected from the numerous sources encountered up to this point.

In other words, use what is learned to work and adjust what has shown to not be effective and led to unintended consequences/harms to others. Do not "reinvent the wheel"; rather, build upon the strengths.

The third and final core function is *assurance*. Assurance is, simply put, carrying out the services intended. Assurance incorporates the next four essential services:

1. Enforcing laws and regulations. Gun violence and homicides fall under this area of the model.
2. Linking people to the services they need and providing said services.
3. Ensuring competent public healthcare workers. Staff training, oversight, and licensing enables these efforts.
4. Evaluating the effectiveness of public policies.

Finally, at the center of all public health services is research, which is the tenth item on the 10 Essential Services and overlaps with the services mentioned above. As one can see, research and applying the knowledge gained is foundational and intersectional with the Essential Services in public health. With firearm deaths resulting in 30,000 people dying annually (Santilli et al., 2017), placing this issue in public health could consistently yield more informative and practical approaches than have been considered solely from a criminal justice stance.

Social Determinants of Health

One additional piece that needs to be covered before the topic of gun violence can be examined in the public health domain are the social determinants of health and their significance. The social determinants of health (SDOH) refer to the "conditions in the places where people live, learn, work, and play affect a wide range of health risks and outcomes" (Office of Disease Prevention and Health Promotion [ODPHP], 2020b). Under the secretary of HHS there is an advisory committee that reports health recommendations and the like every decade. The secretary's Advisory Committee on National Health Promotion and Disease Prevention published objectives that should be achieved by the years 2020 and 2030. With these objectives, advice on how to implement them are also contained in the reports. These reports, known as Healthy People 2020 and Healthy People 2030, are structured along the five main SDOH. The SDOH is a content section in the Healthy People 2020 report which "is designed to identify ways to create social and physical environments that promote good health for all" (ODPHP, 2020b). Thus, when examining issues from a public health perspective, one would be remiss not to incorporate SDOH in the planning and outcomes. The five areas of the SDOH include economic stability, education, social and community context, health and health care, and neighborhood and the built environment. Public health goals for agencies have been structured typically along these five main SDOH since their release in approximately 2008 and are similarly endorsed by the World Health Organization (WHO) (Hargarten et al., 2018).

"Crime and violence" is part of the focus of the SDOH's *Neighborhood and the Built Environment* topic, which has an outcome goal to reduce homicides in the Healthy People 2020 planning objectives. While the Healthy People 2030 report is still in its developmental stages as of this writing, these objectives are also anticipated to be included in the Healthy People 2030 report due to the continued concerns over increased firearm-related injuries and exposure to violence and other cultural issues. Including SDOH goals as part of problem evaluation and recommendations for solutions because the physical needs of the communities come into play, among others.

BACKGROUND OF FEDERAL POLICIES REGARDING PUBLIC HEALTH AND GUN VIOLENCE RESEARCH

In 1996, the Centers for Disease Control and Prevention (CDC) was banned from using federal funds for the purposes of gun control efforts due to the institution of the Dickey Amendment passed by the US Congress (Rostron, 2018). This amendment is believed to have come about as a type of blockage or control because the CDC suggests that, from a public health perspective, it should be involved with helping the government to explore efforts to control gun violence (Mozaffarian et al., 2013). Recognizing the need for continued research in the area, the National Institutes of Health (NIH) took up the task to promote research to understand the public health implications of gun violence and develop and advocate for recommendations to reduce the trend. However, after tragic events with the rise in school shootings, twenty-three executive orders were issued by President Barack Obama requiring the CDC and other federal agencies to focus their efforts toward understanding the issue(s) of gun violence. These executive orders superseded the Dickey Amendment's prohibition of the CDC engaging in the research. Therefore, the CDC was able to coordinate efforts with the NIH to get better data on the problem and suggest solutions. The Institute of Medicine, National Research Council (IOM/NRC) was subsequently directed by the CDC to begin this work. Since that time, public health experts have been evaluating this issue and making recommendations for policy change to reduce risk to communities. In March 2018, outcry from the public arose because of the rise in school shootings. As a result, the omnibus spending bill in 2018 explained provisions in the Dickey Amendment *did not* prohibit research to be conducted related to firearm violence (IOM/NRC, 2013). One caveat was made clear, however, and that was that none of the outcome recommendations could include gun control efforts as it would violate the conditions of the Dickey Amendment (Hargarten et al., 2018). Specifically, then, public health experts could conduct research on the subject and make recommendations for change to policy makers and policy entrepreneurs, but had to stop short of mentioning gun policy change itself. The likely main reason for this provision is the highly sensitive nature of individual rights interpreted under the Second Amendment. Policy can be difficult, and if recommendations included even hints at changing gun ownerships rights, then it is possible that important solutions would be objected to for that reason alone. Thus, if it seems odd to be slightly restrictive in outcome solutions, the approach still has merit.

PHYSICAL, MENTAL, AND DEVELOPMENTAL IMPACTS FROM EXPOSURE TO GUN VIOLENCE

Homicide by gun violence is the second leading cause of death for our nation's children. The risk of homicide is also "highly concentrated" among black males and in urban areas, which creates further problems for disadvantaged neighborhoods (Papachristos & Wildeman, 2014, section "Abstract: Conclusions"). These statistics are glaring as exposure to gun violence has potentially life-long consequences to the physical, mental, and developmental well-being of those affected. The below sections elaborate on these negative health impacts. Carried over from the Healthy People 2010 targets, the Healthy People 2020 targets include violent crime prevention objectives, including decreasing firearm- and non-firearm-related injuries and deaths and reducing the number of homicides in children, adults, and the elderly with a 10 percent improvement goal for each focus area (ODPHP, 2020c). Reductions in these areas enable the health conditions in the communities to improve, thus, increasing the health benefits to all members over time.

Chronic Illness

Chronic illnesses have been documented to occur in individuals suffering from exposure to gun violence. Health consequences include heart disease (2.2 times higher), cancer (1.9 times higher), stroke (2.4 times higher), obstructive lung disease (3.9 times higher), diabetes (1.6 times higher), and hepatitis (2.4 times higher) (Byrdsong et al., 2016). Often these conditions develop due to unhealthy coping behaviors that victims engage in as a means to adjust to their "new normal" post trauma. Negative coping behaviors consist of such actions as smoking, drinking, poor eating habits, impulsive thinking, and so forth. The coping behaviors become a regular crutch that increases the mortality and morbidity of individuals.

Mental and Psychological Illnesses

Communities that experience violence show increased anxiety, depression, hostility, fear among the members (Reid et al., 2017). They expressed powerlessness and hopelessness and signs of PTSD (Francis, 2018). Persons may be afraid to go outdoors and participate in regular, health-promoting activities. In the alternative, individuals may respond in the opposite way and become more aggressive or hypervigilant in protecting themselves while outdoors, which may lead to increasing negative emotions and worry (Byrdsong et al., 2016). From her study of gun violence exposure, Francis (2018) ascertained that some members learned to adapt to the threat of violence and view it as a part of life and something they just must endure. Even adaptive behaviors in this way carry long-term negative health consequences of stress, resentment, and the like. Becoming desensitized to gun homicide can lead to even more risk-taking behaviors and a continued cycle of trauma for the individual and others (Byrdsong et al., 2016). Substance abuse, especially with the younger population, is an especially concerning adaptive behavior that can occur among this group after witnessing or experiencing gun violence (Santilli et al., 2017).

Educational Barriers

When persons experience upheaval or threat in their lives, it becomes difficult to focus proper attention on regular daily life. When children experience the lack of safety and outbursts or constant threats of violence, a successful learning experience cannot be obtained (Prevention Institute's, 2013). Focusing on just "getting by" each day becomes the priority, and improving their future quality of life becomes secondary or nonexistent. Low high school graduation rates lead to various long-term problems in life. When individuals do not complete high school, they face the potential burdens of lower-paying jobs, job insecurity, family instability due to economic stress, and health-related issues due to the stress. Also lack of education prevents access to knowledge about additional life skills and individual health benefits. Higher education can lead to a longer life span as "on average, college graduates live nine years longer than those who didn't complete high school" (New York State, 2018, n.p.).

When they are unable to meet their primary need of safety, people, especially the young, distance themselves or become ingrained in a culture that provides that sense of security they are missing. These sources often lie at the fringes of society and consequently do not reinforce positive goals such as education or sustaining employment opportunities. The tendency to adopt behaviors such as these rises among those living in inner cities. Take, for example, Queens County, New York, where the quality of life ranking is 36th out of 62 counties in the state of New York (New York State, 2021a) and the violent crime rate is 621 per 100,000 (or almost two times higher than the entire state) (New York State, 2021b). Using the same time period for comparison, Queens County's high school graduation rate was 80 percent. This number was consistent across the state. Why? How can the graduation rate be so high while crime is high based on the previous statements above? The answer, or part of the answer, lies in the programs developed and put in place to help such at-risk youth. Prior to the institution of these programs—examples include Diplomas Now (2017) and NYGEAR UP (New York State, n.d.)—the graduation rates were half this number and the violent crime rate even higher. Alycia Santilli et al. (2017), who studied mass shootings and urban violence in New Haven, Connecticut, caution that planning approaches should ensure consideration for the needs of urban communities, thus reinforcing the need to take into account the social determinants of health, as indicated previously.

MODELS TO CHANGE CULTURAL NORMS WITH THE APPLICATION OF PUBLIC HEALTH

Cure Violence Model

Drs. Gary Slutkin and colleagues developed the Cure Violence ("CV") Model based on the idea that "changing individual and community attitudes and norms about gun-violence" is a necessary component to reduce firearm-related homicide (Butts et al., 2015). The CV Model, formerly called Chicago CeaseFire, focused on those at-risk and directed intervention efforts to reduce the likelihood of turning toward violence. This process included "interrupting transmission directly, identifying and changing the thinking of potential transmitters . . . and changing group norms regarding violence" (Butts et al., 2015, section "The Cure Violence Model"). Directly interrupting transmission of violence includes preventing shootings due to retaliation and encouraging conflict resolution (Rostron, 2018). The next two phases focused on changing the thought-process of at-risk persons so that they can learn how to more properly respond to violent behaviors. These persons consisted of gang members, drug dealers, youth and young adults ranging in age from sixteen to twenty-five, and former offenders. Various cities in addition to Chicago have implemented and evaluated the CV Model, including Baltimore, Brooklyn, New York City, Phoenix, and Pittsburgh, and have achieved mixed success. Barriers to implementation and the difficulty of measuring change appeared to be the largest issues faced by researchers at the varying sites (Rostron, 2018). The CV Model fits well with the guidelines established under the SDOH's *Neighborhood and the Built Environment.*

Disease Model

Drs. Steven Hargarten et al. (2018) applied the disease model to gun violence. They demonstrated how it followed a proper framework for prevention policy planning and implementation to address the issue within the model (Hargarten et al., 2018). To explain from a public health perspective, gun violence is understood to be a biopsychosocial disease. Biopsychosocial brings together biological and social aspects. This application is valuable given the complexity of human nature and societal influences. The biological component of this model includes the physical responses to stressors and trauma, along with mental health consequences due to exposure to violence. The Child Welfare League of America (CWLA) recommends "social, emotional, physical and mental health issues" jointly be considered in gun policies (Collins & Swoveland, 2014). A disease model can enable that goal. These ideas are guided by the overlapping dynamic of needing to focus on places rather than guns themselves to understand the multidimensional issue (Blais, 2019). This part is the social component, which must include the environment where individuals live. A focus on this concept changes the dynamic to strategies related to "managing places" where firearms violence is at the forefront. The conversation moves then from the contentious issue of gun control itself into a much broader scope.

Dr. Etienne Blais (2019) suggested that one way to manage places would be for communities to direct their attention to high crime places. Steps to address this idea would be "remediating blighted vacant lands" and enforcing regulations for homeowners to maintain private property (Blais, 2019, para. 1; Moyer et al. 2018) tested this approach as part of a study in Philadelphia, Pennsylvania. They found that remediating vacant land significantly reduced gun shootings in the surrounding areas. Further studies would be necessary to determine effectiveness; however, these results are promising and should be considered in a collaborative community design.

Ground-Up Model

Like the Cure Violence and Disease Models, the Ground-Up Model is also a multidisciplinary approach. The Ground-Up Model has as its main goal intervention incorporating prevention, rehabilitation, and development strategies (Santilli et al., 2017). Prevention promotes access to interventions that can lead to reduced gun violence in communities, such as counseling services for at-risk youth, curfew and truancy prevention, job training skills, and so on. Rehabilitation focuses on "violence diffusion" to help victims through their recovery and healing process, and includes such services as conflict mediation, addiction treatment, community reintegration, and mental health services. The development piece deals with "community enhancement" to revitalize businesses and social and recreational areas. This program was designed based on collaborative meetings with community members of Pittsburgh, Pennsylvania, in approximately 2014 and extensive research in the county (Byrdsong et al., 2016).

What is important about this study and program design is that it includes a qualitative piece where the researchers obtained information from the public, to assess the reasons for crime in the area, any public safety concerns, and stakeholder intervention options though numerous mechanisms, such as schools, churches, community groups, and town hall meetings (Byrdsong et al., 2016). Twelve key stakeholders were identified and included the following:

> (1) Peace Alliance Network, (2) Commission for Violence Reduction, (3) public officials (e.g., mayor, county executive, and elected public representatives), (4) community-based organizations, (5) faith-based organizations, (6) community residents, (7) local colleges and universities, (8) local businesses, (9) public schools, (10) health service institutions, (11) parents and guardians, and (12) youth and young adult residents. (Byrdsong et al., 2016)

Stakeholders provide knowledge about the issues of concern and can guide the public, which is why they are necessary to program design.

CONCLUSION AND FUTURE RECOMMENDATIONS

Community and constituency engagement are important initiatives to improve both the health status of populations and the health system. They are necessary because community representatives and constituents are considered to be part of the mobilization aspect of the 10 Essential Services in public health (Shi & Johnson, 2014). They assist in many areas because they can help achieve improvements in public health outcomes and services. Interventions need to be multifaceted for better outcomes, thus the need for involvement of all individuals and groups in localities. Leaders in public health and in the community can work together to identify and resolve firearm-related deaths and injuries that are area-specific, as what is a problem in one area may not be a problem in another area. Working with others provides the possibility to obtain "untapped" knowledge, opportunities, and resources, especially in diverse communities. Engaging in a dialogue with various people can achieve shared values and identify common interests. Active involvement increases transparency and establishes trust; therefore, these areas cannot be ignored to achieve the best outcome.

Ideas have been proposed that future work to reduce firearm-related injuries and deaths should include physicians in the models/programs; however, there are also counterbeliefs that to do so will put planning in the hands of the inexperienced. Therefore, the need for agencies to work together is all the more compelling. Piecemeal tinkering with personal health and lives of individuals is ineffective and irresponsible. Since law enforcement is reactive in nature (Cook, 2018), it would be appropriate for law enforcement policies to incorporate 10 Essential Services and social determinants as well. The place for physicians in the domain could be with the provision of patient education and public advocacy about gun violence (ODPHP, 2020c).

Effective planning and cooperation are paramount for awareness and possible prevention of as many negative, unintended consequences as possible. Since public health can be understood as being a multidisciplinary approach to provide improved health outcomes, processes, and procedures for populations (Shi & Johnson, 2014), the use of the CV Model, Disease Model, Ground-Up Model, or a combination of them would be an approach in the next phase of protecting the public and improving health. Cooperative relationships will be necessary in all fields to obtain change.

BIBLIOGRAPHY

Blais, E. (2019). Focusing on places rather than guns. *American Journal of Public Health, 109*(1), 25–26. https://doi.org/10.2105/AJPH.2018.304827.

Butts, J. A., Roman, C. G., Bostwick, L., and Porter, J. R. (2015). Cure violence: A public health model to reduce gun violence. *Annual Review of Public Health, 36*, 39–53. https://doi.org/10.1146/annurev-publhealth-031914-122509.

Byrdsong, T. R., Devan, A., and Yamanti, H. (2016). Ground-up model for gun violence reduction: A community-based public health approach. *Journal of Evidence-Informed Social Work, 13*, 76–86. https://doi.org/10.1080/15433714.2014.997090.

Centers for Disease Control and Prevention. (2014a). *Introduction to public health.* Retrieved from https://www.cdc.gov/publichealth101/public-health.html.

Centers for Disease Control and Prevention. (2014b). *The 10 essential public health services: An overview.* Retrieved from https://www.cdc.gov/publichealthgateway/publichealthservices/pdf/essential-phs.pdf.

Collins, J., and Swoveland, E. (2014). The impact of gun violence on children, families, and communities. *Children's VOICE, 23*(1), 10–13. Available from Child Welfare League of America at https://www.cwla.org/childrens-voice/.

Cook, P. J. (2018). Expanding the public health approach to gun violence prevention. *Annals of Internal Medicine, 169*(10), 723–724. https://doi.org/ 0.7326/M18-2846.

Diplomas Now. (2017). *Findings from the first decade and what's next.* Retrieved from http://www.tdschools.org/2017/02/16/new-report-findings-from-the-first-decade-and-whats-next.

Francis, M. (2018). A narrative inquiry into the experience of being a victim of gun violence. *Journal of Trauma Nursing, 25*(6), 381–388. https://doi.org/ 10.1097/JTN.0000000000000406.

Hargarten, S. W., Lerner, E. B., Gorelick, M., Brasel, K., deRoon-Cassini, T., and Kohlbeck, S. (2018). Gun violence: A biopsychosocial disease. *Western Journal of Emergency Medicine, 19*(6), 1024–1027. https://doi.org/10.5811/westjem.2018.7.38021.

Institute of Medicine and National Research Council. (2013). *Priorities for research to reduce the threat of firearm-related violence.* The National Academies Press. https://doi.org/10.17226/18319.

Jena, A. B., Sun, E. C., and Prasad, V. (2014). Does the declining lethality of gunshot injuries mask a rising epidemic of gun violence in the United States? *Journal of General Internal Medicine, 29*(7), 1065–1069. https://doi.org/10.1007/s11606-014-2779-z.

Moyer, R., MacDonald, J. M., Ridgeway, G., and Branas, C. C. (2018). Effect of remediating blighted vacant land on shootings: A citywide cluster randomized trial. *American Journal of Public Health, 109*, 140–144. https://doi.org/ 10.2105/AJPH.2018.304752.

Mozaffarian, D., Hemenway, D., and Ludwig, D. S. (2013). Curbing gun violence: Lessons from public health successes. *JAMA, 309*(6), 551–552. https://doi.org/10.1001/jama.2013.38.

New York State Department of Health. (2018). Differences in health outcomes within states by place and racial/ethnic groups. *State report county health rankings and roadmaps*. Retrieved from http://www.countyhealthrankings.org/explore-health-rankings/reports/state-reports/2018/new-york.

New York State Department of Health. (2021a). County demographics. Retrieved from https://www.countyhealthrankings.org/app/new-york/2018/rankings/queens/county/outcomes/overall/snapshot.

New York State Department of Health. (2021b). Violent crime. Retrieved from https://www.countyhealthrankings.org/app/new-york/2018/measure/factors/43/data.

New York State, Higher Education Services Corporation. (n.d.) NYGEAR UP. Retrieved from https://www.hesc.ny.gov/nygearup.

Office of Disease Prevention and Health Promotion. (2020a). Overview. *HealthyPeople.gov*. Retrieved from https://www.healthypeople.gov/2020/topics-objectives/topic/social-determinants-of-health.

Office of Disease Prevention and Health Promotion. (2020b). Social determinants of health. *HealthyPeople.gov*. Retrieved from https://www.healthypeople.gov/2020/topics-objectives/topic/social-determinants-of-health.

Office of Disease Prevention and Health Promotion. (2020c). Violence prevention. *Healthy People.gov*. Retrieved from https://www.healthypeople.gov/node/3497/objectives#4788.

Papachristos, A. V., and Wildeman, C. (2014). Network exposure and homicide victimization in an African American community. *American Journal of Health, 104*(1), 143–150. https://doi.org/10.2105/AJPH.2013.301441.

Prevention Institute's Urban Networks to Increase Thriving Youth. (2013). UNITY fact sheets: links between violence and chronic diseases, mental illness, and poor learning. Retrieved on March 26, 2020, from http://www.preventioninstitute.org/press/.

Reid, J. A., Richards, T. N., Loughran, T. A., and Mulvey, E. P. (2017). The relationships among exposure to violence, psychological distress, and gun carrying among male adolescents found guilty of serious legal offenses: A longitudinal cohort study. *Annals of Internal Medicine, 166*(6), 412–418. https://doi.org/10.7326/M16-1648.

Rostron, A. (2018). The Dickey Amendment on federal funding for research on gun violence: A legal dissection. *American Journal of Public Health, 108*(7), 865–867. https://doi.org/10.2105/AJPH.2018.304450.

Santilli, A., O'Connor Duffany, K., Carroll-Scott, A., Thomas, J., Greene, A., Arora, A., Agnoli, A., Gan, G., and Ickovics, J. (2017). Bridging the response to mass shootings and urban violence: Exposure to violence in New Haven, Connecticut. *American Journal of Public Health, 107*(3), 374–379. https://ajph.aphapublications.org/doi/full/10.2105/AJPH.2016.303613.

Shi, L., and Johnson, J. A. (Eds.). (2014). *Novick and Morrow's public health administration: principles for population-based management* (3rd ed.). Jones and Bartlett Learning.

Spitzer, S. A., Staudenmayer, K. L., Tennakoon, L., Spain, D. A., and Weiser, T. G. (2017). Costs and financial burden of initial hospitalizations for firearm injuries in the United States, 2006–2014. *American Journal of Public Health, 107,* 770–774. https://doi.org/10.2105/AJPH.2017.303684.

14

Guns and Public Health

Deborah Morris

The idea that a society bears responsibility for various aspects of the health of its public developed during the nineteenth and twentieth centuries, originating with an emphasis on preventing infectious diseases. This led to improvements in water supplies, management of sewage and waste, techniques of preventing disease transmission, including isolation and quarantine, immunizations for common diseases with a high burden of mortality and morbidity, and disease surveillance. The development of public health as a discipline led to great improvements in life span and quality of life by the middle of the twentieth century (Boston University School of Public Health, 2015).

During the second half of the twentieth century, with the decline of infectious diseases as a leading cause of death, the public health community began looking at other population health issues, including the health consequences of tobacco use, the societal burden of lifestyle-related chronic disease (such as heart disease, obesity, and diabetes), and the death and disability caused by motor vehicle accidents (MVA). Research provided evidence about both the societal costs of these problems in illness, disability, death, and dollars, and the potential to decrease these costs through public health interventions.

Many of these attempts to improve public health encountered opposition, often from industry and advocacy groups. The tobacco companies fought long and hard against federal efforts to decrease the impact of smoking on the public. Car companies resisted increasing their costs in adding safety equipment to motor vehicles. Processed food companies funded dubious research to counter the public health narrative that diets high in trans-fat, salt, and sugar created a public health problem. But with time, research, and effective strategies, progress was made, and research demonstrated the effectiveness of these public health measures in reducing deaths.

In the mid-twentieth century, when the medical community recognized the need to approach motor vehicle accident morbidity and mortality as a public health issue, a number of data-driven systems changes resulted in a decrease in death and injury resulting from MVAs. Laws and regulations triggered changes in car manufacturing, including safety measures like seat belts and airbags; changes in law enforcement, including tighter enforcement of laws around drunk driving; and changes in laws, including lower speed limits. Resources were devoted to public education about seatbelt use, car seat use, and impaired driving. These and other systemic measures contributed to significant decreases in motor vehicle-related deaths, which continue into the twenty-first century (Boston University, 2015).

During the last quarter of the twentieth century, the public health community began to look at the public health burden of gun violence in the United States. The Centers for Disease Control (CDC) had started to expand their focus to include injuries and accidents as well as diseases (Sleet et al., 2003). They began to monitor deaths from injuries, and statistics gathered from death certificates suggested high numbers of death from violence, homicides, and suicides. Violence was identified as a public health issue in the 1979 Surgeon General's report, and the CDC soon developed violence prevention objectives (CDC, 2020b). C. Everett Koop, Ronald Reagan's surgeon general, argued that violence was a "public health emergency" (Koop & Lundberg, 1992). Research and data analysis revealed that a high number of violence-related deaths and injuries resulted from firearms. Public health professionals in the CDC and in academia began to speculate that the gun violence problem could be mitigated by measures similar to those that had decreased MVA-related deaths.

The attempted assassination of Ronald Reagan in 1981, along with the wounding of his press secretary James Brady, led to calls for control of gun ownership, and ultimately to the Brady Bill, passed in 1993 with bipartisan support. The Brady Bill imposed a five-day waiting period and background check for the purchase of handguns and established the National Instant Criminal Background Check System. A year later, again with bipartisan support, a limited assault weapon ban was passed (Hulse, 2019).

In 1993 Dr. David Satcher became head of the Centers for Disease Control (CDC), the federal agency most identified with public health in the United States, continuing to support a broader view of public health including injuries and violence, particularly firearm-related injuries and violence, as public health issues. He is quoted as having said, concerning gun violence, "If it isn't a health problem, then why are all these people dying from it?" (Galea, 2019, para. 12, quoting Satcher). Along with infectious diseases, tobacco, teen pregnancy, and many other issues widely accepted as in the public health domain, he advocated for research on the impact of guns and gun violence on the public health (Applebome, 1993).

Guns and gun control have been a potent political issue since the 1980s, but the gun control laws passed in the early 1990s, along with the CDC's new attention to gun violence as a cause of death, galvanized the gun lobby into more political action. During the Nixon, Ford, Bush, and Reagan administrations, there was a good deal of bipartisan agreement over legislative issues related to firearms. The 1994 "Gingrich Revolution," shifted both the Senate and the House to the right. Speaker Gingrich said, "As long as I am Speaker of this House, no gun control legislation is going to move in committee or on the floor of this House and there will be no further erosion of their rights" (Gun Owners, 2011, para. 2, quoting Gingrich). Gun ownership became an issue strongly identified with the Republican party. Gun advocacy groups, particularly the National Rifle Association (NRA), increased their involvement in the politics of gun ownership through political contributions (Center for Responsive Politics, 2020).

In 1996 legislation was passed by Congress, as part of the omnibus funding bill, prohibiting the CDC and the federal government from engaging in or funding research on the issue of gun violence. This legislation is known as the Dickey Amendment after the legislator who introduced it (Rostron, 2018). While the CDC continued to monitor gunshots as a cause of injury and death, and while these injuries and deaths were similar in numbers to those caused by motor vehicle accidents (CDC, 1999), a problem that was improving from the public health perspective, most research on the issue of gun violence came to a halt. In 1998, when Dr. Satcher was appointed by President Clinton to be the surgeon general, he faced considerable congressional opposition. By then the NRA, with ties to gun manufacturing and lots of money, was heavily influencing the political discussions about guns and gun control through political contributions (Center for Responsive Politics, 2020).

The gun industry and gun owner lobbies successfully framed the debate as one over gun ownership. The NRA and other firearms advocacy groups equated the concept of gun control as an infringement on the right to bear arms. Then as now there were more civilian-owned guns in the United States than in any other country (Cook & Ludwig, 1997). Since the 1990s, the number of guns in civilian hands has continued to increase and is currently estimated at nearly 300 million guns in circulation, concentrated among a smaller number of people who own multiple firearms (Bangalore & Messerli, 2013).

Other surgeons general, including Vivek Murthy, appointed in 2015 by Barack Obama, and notably excepting Dr. Jerome Adams, appointed by President Trump in 2017, have continued to advocate for including measures to decrease firearm-related deaths in the CDC priorities, but, while statistics indicated increases in deaths related to guns, research languished, and most of the initiatives to use public health measures as a tool were opposed by the NRA. There are studies demonstrating that there has been far less research on the health consequences of firearm violence than on other leading causes of death (Stark & Shah, 2017). The Dickey Amendment was finally reversed in 2018, but the more than twenty-year hiatus in research means that, as a society, we have literally lost a generation of researchers focusing on these issues (Subbaraman, 2020).

The CDC (2020a) describes the public health approach to violence prevention as having four steps. The first is to define the problem and monitor it. This has been accomplished and has been ongoing for more than twenty years. As the next step it is important to identify the factors that either increase or decrease risk; this step uses data collection and analysis and is research based. A good deal of work has been done on identifying risks for gun violence, some of which we will discuss later in this chapter. The third step is to "develop and test prevention strategies." This step is also based in research and has been short-circuited by the research ban. While there has been some work done in this area, it has mostly been done using very limited private foundation money rather than with federal funds. The final step is to ensure that effective prevention strategies are widely adopted. The adoption of such strategies requires a multipronged approach—as demonstrated by the success in reducing MVA-related deaths and injuries through laws, regulations, changes in industry, public education, and so on—and requires resources (CDC, 2020a).

Dr. David Hemenway, one of the top advocates for the public health approach and a leading researcher in the area, frames the public health approach a little differently. Hemenway started his career as an expert in injury prevention and was drawn to working on the gun violence problem through the successes achieved in reducing MVA deaths. His approach has five components (Hemenway & Miller, 2013). First, the problem must be approached from a population, not an individual level. As an example, rather than making seat belts an option in cars, an individual decision, laws require them to be included in all cars and used by all drivers and passengers, the population most affected. The next component is focused on prevention, and ideally on changing the environment where the problem occurs rather than the individuals affected. Changing speed limit laws changes the environment in which the accidents that cause death and injury occur. Third is that the approach should be systems-based, creating systems in which it is harder for the problem to occur. Systems that make it harder for drivers to make mistakes that might result in an MVA decrease those mistakes and accidents. Hemenway and Miller then suggest that the approach has to be broad and include multiple possible interventions and constituencies. Using the MVA analogy, legislation, regulation, education, and engineering involving law enforcement, drivers, and industry all helped in achieving success. Finally, Hemenway and Miller (2013) emphasize that the focus should be on shared responsibility rather than on blame.

The public policy approach is more directed toward the criminal justice system, with an emphasis on removing perpetrators of gun violence from the streets, a strategy that has been shown to decrease the risk of those people committing additional acts of violence. This requires emphasis on enforcement, investigation, and successful prosecution of offenders. Successful implementation of these strategies decreases firearm violence (Decker, 2019). Because the focus of public policy is on individuals and not on populations, as well as on action that occurs after the violence has occurred rather than before, these public policy and criminal justice system interventions are not considered part of the public health approach. It is important to note that public health and public policy approaches to reducing gun violence are not necessarily the same, but are compatible. There is some conflict between the approaches regarding the amount of attention, and perhaps more importantly funding, that should be directed toward the different approaches, but the goals are similar (Decker, 2019).

Since this chapter focuses on using the public health approach to reducing gun violence, we need to start by defining the problem. According to the CDC there were 39,929 deaths from firearm violence in the United States in 2018, more than 100 a day (CDC, 2020c). Of these, 62.8 percent were suicide and 35.9 percent homicide. The CDC estimates 894,593 years of life lost. For persons aged fourteen to twenty-five, suicide and homicide by firearm are the second and third most common cause of death. Firearms account for more than half of suicides and have a bimodal distribution, most common as causes of death in adolescents and young adults, and in the elderly (CDC, 2020c). The vast majority of attempted gun suicides succeed, unlike other methods, where non-completed suicide is far more common (CDC, 2020a). There have been both decreases and increases in the rates of firearm violence over the past twenty-five years, but it is clear that injuries and death from guns are a significant problem in this country.

It is widely understood that, for many diseases, there are disparities in health status that are related to demographic differences such as age, sex, race, gender, socioeconomic status, and geography. There are certainly disparities in death and injury from gun violence (CDC, 2020c). Males are at higher risk across age ranges. Young Black males, particularly those who live in impoverished neighborhoods in cities and larger towns, are at the highest risk of the consequences of gun violence, as both victims and perpetrators.

10 Leading Causes of Injury Deaths by Age Group Highlighting Violence-Related Injury Deaths, United States – 2018

Rank	<1	1-4	5-9	10-14	15-24	25-34	35-44	45-54	55-64	65+	Total
	Age Groups										
1	Unintentional Suffocation 977	Unintentional Drowning 443	Unintentional MV Traffic 341	Suicide Suffocation 361	Unintentional MV Traffic 6,308	Unintentional Poisoning 15,353	Unintentional Poisoning 14,978	Unintentional Poisoning 13,620	Unintentional Poisoning 10,854	Unintentional Fall 32,522	Unintentional Poisoning 62,399
2	Homicide Unspecified 125	Unintentional MV Traffic 292	Unintentional Drowning 130	Unintentional MV Traffic 360	Unintentional Poisoning 4,245	Unintentional MV Traffic 6,886	Unintentional MV Traffic 5,068	Unintentional MV Traffic 5,328	Unintentional MV Traffic 5,629	Unintentional MV Traffic 7,697	Unintentional MV Traffic 37,991
3	Unintentional MV Traffic 80	Homicide Unspecified 152	Unintentional Fire/Burn 99	Suicide Firearm 202	Homicide Firearm 4,107	Homicide Firearm 4,348	Suicide Firearm 3,222	Suicide Firearm 3,787	Suicide Firearm 4,421	Suicide Firearm 6,375	Unintentional Fall 37,455
4	Homicide Other Spec. Classifiable 68	Unintentional Fire/Burn 123	Homicide Firearm 57	Homicide Firearm 134	Suicide Firearm 2,985	Suicide Firearm 3,429	Suicide Suffocation 2,688	Suicide Suffocation 2,481	Unintentional Fall 2,766	Unintentional Unspecified 4,607	Suicide Firearm 24,432
5	Undetermined Suffocation 45	Unintentional Suffocation 112	Unintentional Suffocation 30	Unintentional Drowning 86	Suicide Suffocation 2,237	Suicide Suffocation 3,117	Homicide Firearm 2,369	Suicide Poisoning 1,390	Suicide Suffocation 1,934	Unintentional Suffocation 3,793	Homicide Firearm 13,958
6	Unintentional Drowning 39	Unintentional Pedestrian, Other 70	Unintentional Other Land Transport 20	Unintentional Fire/Burn 52	Suicide Poisoning 454	Undetermined Poisoning 824	Suicide Poisoning 990	Homicide Firearm 1,382	Suicide Poisoning 1,491	Unintentional Poisoning 3,269	Suicide Suffocation 13,840
7	Homicide Suffocation 30	Homicide Other Spec. Classifiable 66	Homicide Unspecified 17	Unintentional Suffocation 43	Unintentional Drowning 431	Suicide Poisoning 753	Undetermined Poisoning 780	Unintentional Fall 1,131	Unintentional Suffocation 858	Adverse Effects 3,100	Unintentional Suffocation 6,701
8	Undetermined Unspecified 30	Homicide Firearm 54	Adverse Effects 16	Unintentional Other Land Transport 37	Homicide Cut/pierce 256	Unintentional Drowning 482	Unintentional Fall 502	Undetermined Poisoning 876	Homicide Firearm 802	Unintentional Fire/Burn 1,404	Suicide Poisoning 6,237
9	Unintentional Natural/ Environment 22	Unintentional Natural/ Environment 38	Unintentional Pedestrian, Other 15	Unintentional Poisoning 23	Undetermined Poisoning 224	Homicide Cut/pierce 455	Unintentional Drowning 414	Unintentional Drowning 456	Adverse Effects 766	Suicide Poisoning 1,133	Unintentional Unspecified 6,082
10	Two Tied 18	Unintentional Firearm 30	Homicide Other Spec. NEC 14	Suicide Poisoning 20	Suicide Fall 285	Unintentional Fall 345	Homicide Cut/pierce 340	Unintentional Suffocation 401	Undetermined Poisoning 704	Suicide Suffocation 1,614	Adverse Effects 4,604

Data Source: National Center for Health Statistics (NCHS), National Vital Statistics System.
Produced by: National Center for Injury Prevention and Control, CDC using WISQARS™.

Centers for Disease Control and Prevention
National Center for Injury Prevention and Control

Figure 14.1. Leading Causes of Injury Deaths by Age Group Highlighting Violence-Related Injury Deaths, United States—2018. ***Data downloaded from CDC WISQARS.***

Table 14.1. Violence Related Firearm Deaths by Race and Sex – 2018

Race	*Sex*	*Number of Deaths*	*Crude Rate*	*YPLL*
White	Males	23,749	18.82	450765
White	Females	4,329	3.37	87647
Black	Males	8,624	38.82	288618
Black	Females	1,152	4.79	37256

YPLL = Years of Potential Life Lost
(Date downloaded from CDC WISQARS)

For Black men between the ages of fifteen and thirty-four, homicide by firearm is the leading cause of death. Older White men are at highest risk of suicide by firearm (CDC, 2020c).

Death is, though, not the only outcome of gun violence. There are far more injuries, some with long-term consequent disability, and the cost in pain, productivity, and dollars is enormous. It has been estimated that gun violence costs the United States as much as $229 billion annually when all factors are considered: medical costs, lost work, cost of incarceration of perpetrators, and decreased quality of life for victims and families (Follman et al., 2015). There are also costs beyond monetary value. Children who live in communities plagued by gun violence suffer social and psychological consequences, and every school child in the United States, dealing with active shooter drills, pays a cost in time lost from school and, in many cases, increased anxiety.

However the costs are counted, they are enormous. In the last year that the federal government funded gun violence research at the CDC, 1994, the budget was $2.6 million dollars. These funds were not restored when the Dickey Amendment was reversed (Carswell, 2019). While the government does fund research into youth violence and youth violence prevention, the total spent, $75 million, is dwarfed by conditions with far less impact on years of life lost, such as dementia, $2.3 billion (National Institutes of Health, 2020).

Are there potential solutions? There has been a good deal of thought and some ongoing research on ways to improve individual and population safety from the threat of firearms. Arguments have been made by gun owners and firearm advocacy organizations that gun ownership contributes to the safety of one and one's family. Research suggests otherwise. A gun in a household increases the risk of suicide and less so the risk of homicide (Kellerman et al., 1998; Wiebe, 2003). A study of gun ownership and firearm-related deaths in twenty-seven developed countries showed a very strong correlation between guns owned per capita and firearm-related deaths, with the United States having the highest rates of both (Bangalore & Messerli, 2013). Laws supported by the gun lobby and gun owners, such as those allowing individuals to carry concealed firearms, and laws that promote the principle of "stand your ground," do not decrease the rates of homicide by firearm, but rather lead to modest increases in gun deaths (Santaella-Tenorio et al., 2016). Research has confirmed that firearms in the home do not contribute to the safety of the residents. According to research on how the risk of homicide and suicide is changed by the presence of firearms in homes, "For every time a gun in the home was used in a self-defense or legally justifiable shooting, there were four unintentional shootings, seven criminal assaults or homicides, and 11 attempted or completed suicides" (Kellerman et al., 1998, "Abstract"). Clearly, more guns will not decrease death and injury from gun violence.

While firearms are a political issue in our increasingly polarized society, the attempt to decrease firearm injuries needs to stay divorced from politics if it is going to be effective. Polling suggests that although a majority of Americans oppose "gun control," most support "gun safety" (Barry et al., 2018). There is research that demonstrates that even though there are two apparently deeply polarized "sides" in the societal argument about guns, there are actually some large areas of agreement among the partisans. Gun owners and non-gun owners agree on the importance of background checks prior to gun purchases, restriction of the licenses of gun dealers for record-keeping violations, testing and licensing for concealed carry, prohibiting serious criminals from gun ownership, and allowing the removal of guns from individuals with serious mental health issues (Barry et al., 2018).

The news is dominated by stories of mass shootings and urban gun violence, leading many to assume that homicide is the primary cause of gun-related deaths. Mass shootings account for less than 1 percent of firearm-related deaths, and suicide accounts for about 60 percent (CDC, 2020c). Mass shootings have tended to focus media attention on mental illness as it relates to firearm deaths, but the problem of firearm-related suicides is much more closely related to mental health issues than are mass shootings. In fact, the focus on the rare cases of mass shootings committed by people with apparent mental illness distorts the issue. Mass shootings, while both tragic and newsworthy, are a very small part of the gun violence problem.

However, a number of high-profile mass shootings in the past decade, including Sandy Hook, Miami, and Las Vegas, have reignited the desire among medical and public health professionals to take action to decrease gun violence. There is a lot of discussion in public health, medical, and legal literature about the need for action, as well as specific actions that might help to mitigate the death and disability resulting from gun violence (Branas et al., 2017; Bulger et al., 2019). If we define firearm-related deaths and injuries as a public health problem, what are measures that can be taken to reduce deaths and injuries from firearms? Framing an issue as a public health problem means looking at how efforts to reduce mortality and morbidity will benefit society as a whole. When taking a public health approach to any problem, remember that we need to focus on prevention as well as on populations rather than individuals.

Among measures that were introduced in the 1990s, intended to improve population safety, were recommendations for doctors to ask about gun ownership and assess the safety of guns in the home. This seemed especially important for pediatricians as a measure to prevent firearm-related accidents in children, a tragic and not uncommon problem. The American Academy of Pediatrics began recommending that providers ask about guns in the home and safe gun storage as part of the anticipatory guidance provided at well-child visits. In 2011, the Florida state legislature passed the Firearm Owners' Privacy Act (FOPA), a "physician gag law" prohibiting physicians from asking about guns in the home and gun safety measures (Rathore, 2014). Although there were immediate legal challenges, a number of other states introduced similar legislation. FOPA was finally overturned by the US Supreme Court in 2017 (Parmet et al., 2017).

The population disparities in gun violence, described earlier, provide some targets for intervention. Just as pediatricians are taught to ask about guns and gun safety in the home, providing guidance to keep children safe, other health care providers can intervene with populations at high risk. There have been interventions in some urban hospitals targeting young male victims injured by guns. Many gun homicide victims have previously been injured by firearms. Providing support, counseling, and at least temporary safe haven for this population of young men at risk has been shown to decrease their future risk of being killed by gun violence (Rich & Grey, 2005).

In an approach that provides an intersection between public policy and public health, efforts to improve relationships between the police and inner-city youth have proved helpful, especially when combined with the use of trained outreach workers and "violence interrupters." These individuals, not law enforcement officers, are familiar with the neighborhoods and the culture that promotes gun violence in urban neighborhoods, and they work with youth at high risk of carrying firearms and engaging in gun violence. The use of these strategies has been effective in several cities at reducing rates of gun homicide and firearm injury (Webster et al., 2013). Unfortunately, these interventions require considerable resources, and, when funding ceases, violence rates climb again (Carswell, 2019).

Screening older adults, particularly men, for suicidal intent, could be helpful in identifying individuals at risk of suicide who possess guns. Potentially this could lead to interventions such as mental health treatment, or even, in states with laws that allow this, temporarily removing the gun to decrease suicide risk. The United States Preventive Services Task Force (USPSTF), an organization of public health volunteers that makes public health recommendations (such as vaccine and screening test recommendations) based on research evidence, does not currently recommend such population-based screening because "the current evidence is insufficient to assess the balance of benefits and harms of screening for suicide risk in adolescents, adults, and older adults" (USPSTF, 2013). Again, we come back to the urgent need for research. It's not that such an intervention is ineffective; it's that we haven't investigated and therefore do not know.

Because of our unique history regarding gun ownership and gun use, the United States has a much higher rate of gun ownership along with higher rates of injury and death related to guns compared to other developed nations (Bangalore & Messerli, 2013). Efforts to impose "gun control" in a society that equates gun ownership with personal freedom are unpopular and have limited effectiveness. The effort must be framed differently if it is to succeed. Rather than focusing on limiting gun ownership, one newer approach is to emphasize gun safety, another area of agreement between gun owners and non-gun owners.

Improving background checks and enforcement of the laws governing gun sales could help to keep guns out of the hands of some people who are at risk of committing gun violence. Training and licensing of gun owners, using a model similar to licensing of drivers, might decrease accidental firearm deaths. There is research that handgun licensing laws have decreased gun homicides and decreased the number of illegal "straw" purchases of handguns that make it into criminal hands (Santaella-Tenorio et al., 2016). Some of the groups engaged in developing public health strategies to reduce gun violence are working with gun manufacturers to increase gun safety. Changing gun designs to only allow firing by the owner, so-called smart guns, is one of these strategies. Others include redesigning guns to ensure that they are "childproof," as are pill bottles (Hemenway & Miller, 2013).

Since many of the guns used in homicide are not legally purchased, and in fact many were stolen from legal purchasers, efforts to reduce gun theft could help reduce their use in crimes. This could include training gun owners in safe gun storage. Stricter enforcement of laws and rules concerning gun sales has been advocated. Removing dealers who circumvent background check laws and funnel guns into illegal markets could decrease guns available to criminals. Adding serial numbers that cannot be removed and otherwise personalizing newly manufactured firearms would make it easier to trace guns used in crimes (Hemenway & Miller, 2013).

In spite of a thirty-year history of approaching firearm violence as a public health issue, progress has been slow, likely because of the limited research that has been funded and conducted between passage of the Dickey Amendment and now. It will take years to restore the community of research professionals working on these problems, and more time to identify and test strategies that are effective in reducing gun violence. It will also take political will and a readiness to devote resources to both studying the problem and deploying effective strategies.

The pace of change is also slow because of ongoing political resistance to what are often considered "common sense" measures with broad approval. Spending by the gun lobby is at historically high levels and politicians who benefit—primarily Republican politicians from states with high gun ownership and specifically states in the South and the West, and states with primarily rural populations—are reluctant to support any legislation that potentially restricts access to guns (Hemenway, 2017). Of the $54 million spent by the NRA on political donations in 2016, more than $30 million went to the Trump campaign, and during his administration there was no movement toward imposing national background check legislation (Johnson, 2019).

Clearly, gun violence is not a problem that can be solved solely by government. The development and implementation of public health strategies to decrease firearm violence must be a collaborative effort involving the government, specifically the CDC and legislative bodies, the medical and legal professions, law enforcement, industry, and public health professionals both in the academic sphere and in state and local public health agencies. Ideally gun owners and advocacy groups should also be engaged.

There is a push for further research among many medical and public health professionals, but the combination of few researchers who have experience focusing on the issue and few public funds continues to slow the pace of progress. Without research to both define the causes and consequences of gun violence and to identify effective strategies to reduce it, we cannot expect the public health approach to yield results. With the will to act and funds for research and implementation, the CDC and public health agencies were able to successfully overcome the industry efforts to limit the changes that have brought about major decreases in deaths from motor vehicle accidents. Similarly, in spite of industry resistance, there have been major improvements in the public health regarding cigarette smoking and atherosclerotic heart disease. So far, the CDC, and our society as a whole, have made little progress in permanently reducing gun violence and death by firearm.

If the basis of the public health approach, first proposed more than thirty years ago, is research, then we have barely even begun to apply this approach to the ongoing serious health crisis caused by gun violence. While there have been some small steps and some identified strategies that appear effective, the barriers to ongoing research and the lack of funds for implementation of those strategies mean that we cannot yet say that the public health approach has value in decreasing death and disability from firearms.

BIBLIOGRAPHY

Applebome, P. (1993, September 26). Conversations/David Satcher; C.D.C.'s new chief worries as much about bullets as about bacteria. *New York Times.* Retrieved November 18, 2020, from https://nyti.ms/29dZj3Y.

Bangalore, S., and Messerli, F. H. (2013). Gun ownership and firearm-related deaths. *The American Journal of Medicine*, *126*(10), 873–876. https://doi.org/10.1016/j.amjmed.2013.04.012.

Barry, C. L., Webster, D. W., Stone, E., Crifasi, C. K., Vernick, J. S., and McGinty, E. E. (2018). Public support for gun violence prevention policies among gun owners and non-gun owners in 2017. *American Journal of Public Health*, *108*(7), 878–881. PubMed. https://doi.org/10.2105/AJPH.2018.304432.

Boston University School of Public Health. (2015). 20th century public health achievements. Retrieved November 18, 2020, from https://sphweb.bumc.bu.edu/otlt/mph-modules/ph/publichealthhistory/publichealthhistory9.html.

Branas, C. C., Flescher, A., Formica, M. K., Galea, S., Hennig, N., Liller, K. D., Madanat, H. N., Park, A., Rosenthal, J. E., and Ying, J. (2017). Academic public health and the firearm crisis: An agenda for action. *American Journal of Public Health, 107*(3), 365–367. https://doi.org/10.2105/AJPH.2016.303619.

Bulger, E. M., Kuhls, D. A., Campbell, B. T., Bonne, S., Cunningham, R. M., Betz, M., Dicker, R., Ranney, M. L., Barsotti, C., Hargarten, S., Sakran, J. V., Rivara, F. P., James, T., Lamis, D., Timmerman, G., Rogers, S. O., Choucair, B., and Stewart, R. M. (2019). Proceedings from the Medical Summit on Firearm Injury Prevention: A public health approach to reduce death and disability in the US. *Journal of the American College of Surgeons, 229*(4), 415–430.e12. https://doi.org/10.1016/j.jamcollsurg.2019.05.018.

Carswell, S. M. (2019). Have we surrendered to gun violence in urban America? Federal neglect stymies efforts to stop the slaughter among young Black men. *Race and Justice*. https://doi.org/10.1177/2153368719865306.

Center for Responsive Politics. (2020). Organization Profiles. OpenSecrets.org. Retrieved November 18, 2020, from https://www.opensecrets.org/orgs/national-rifle-assn/summary?id=d00000008.

Centers for Disease Control and Prevention (CDC). (1999). Nonfatal and fatal firearm-related injuries—United States, 1993–1997. *MMWR. Morbidity and mortality weekly report, 48*(45), 1029–1034. https://www.cdc.gov/mmwr/preview/mmwrhtml/mm4845a1.htm.

Centers for Disease Control and Prevention (CDC). (2020a). The public health approach to violence prevention. CDC Injury Center: Violence Prevention. Retrieved November 18, 2020, from https://www.cdc.gov/violenceprevention/publichealthissue/publichealthapproach.html.

Centers for Disease Control and Prevention (CDC). (2020b). Timeline of violence as a public health problem. CDC Injury Center: Violence Prevention. Retrieved November 18, 2020, from https://www.cdc.gov/violenceprevention/publichealthissue/timeline.html.

Centers for Disease Control and Prevention (CDC). (2020c). Web-based injury statistics query and reporting system (WISQARS). CDC Injury Prevention and Control. Retrieved November 18, 2020, from: www.cdc.gov/injury/wisqars.

Cook, P., and Ludwig, J. (1997). *Guns in America: National survey on private ownership and use of firearms*. National Institute of Justice, Research in Brief. https://nij.ojp.gov/library/publications/guns-america-national-survey-private-ownership-and-use-firearms-research-brief.

Decker, P. (2019). Understanding gun violence: The contribution of a public health framework. *Journal of Policy Analysis and Management, 38*(3), 787–804. https://doi.org/10:1002/pam.22144.

Follman, M., Lurie, J., Lee, J., and West, J. (2015, April 15). The true cost of gun violence in America. *Mother Jones*. Retrieved November 18, 2020, from https://www.motherjones.com/politics/2015/04/true-cost-of-gun-violence-in-america/.

Galea, S. (2019). Physicians' voices on gun violence and other important public health issues. *JAMA, 321*(2), 141–142. https://doi.org/10.1001/jama.2018.20754.

Gun Owners of America. (2011, November 22). Newt Gingrich on guns: A mixed record. Retrieved November 18, 2020, from https://gunowners.org/newtgingrich-2012/.

Hemenway, D. (2017). *Private guns public health.* [ebook]. University of Michigan Press.

Hemenway, D., and Miller, M. (2013). Public health approach to the prevention of gun violence. *The New England Journal of Medicine*, *368*(21), 2033–2035. https://doi.org/10.1056/NEJMsb1302631.

Hulse, C. (2019, September 7). How Congress passed an assault weapons ban in 1994. *New York Times*. Retrieved November 18, 2020, from https://www.nytimes.com/2019/09/07/us/politics/congress-assault-weapons-ban.html.

Johnson, L. (2019, August 21). NRA's 2016 donation to Trump's campaign pays off. *Fortune.* Retrieved November 18, 2020, from https://fortune.com/2019/08/21/how-much-did-nra-contribute-trump-campaign/.

Kellerman, A. L., Somes, G., Rivara, F. P., Lee, R. K., and Banton, J. G. (1998). Injuries and deaths due to firearms in the home. *Journal of Trauma, 45*(2), 263–267. https://doi.org/10.1097/00005373-199808000.

Koop, C. E., and Lundberg, G. D. (1992). Violence in America: A public health emergency: Time to bite the bullet back. *JAMA, 267*(22), 3075–3076. https://doi.org/ 10.1001/jama.1992.03480220093036.

National Institutes of Health. (2020, June 30). Estimates of funding for various research, condition, and disease categories. *NIH Research Portfolio Online Reporting Tools (RePORT)*. Retrieved November 18, 2020, from https://report.nih.gov/categorical_spending.aspx.

Parmet, W. E., Smith, J. A., and Miller, M. (2017). Physicians, firearms, and free speech—Overturning Florida's firearm-safety gag rule. *The New England Journal of Medicine*, *376*(20), 1901–1903. https://doi.org/ 10.1056/NEJMp1702516.

Rathore, M. H. (2014). Physician "gag laws" and gun safety. *Virtual Mentor*, *16*(4), 284–288. https://doi.org/10.1001/virtualmentor.2014.16.04.pfor2-1404.

Rich, J. A., and Grey, C. M. (2005). Pathways to recurrent trauma among young Black men: Traumatic stress, substance use, and the "code of the street." *American Journal of Public Health*, *95*(5), 816–824. https://doi.org/10.2105/AJPH.2004.044560

Rostron, A. (2018). The Dickey Amendment on federal funding for research on gun violence: A legal dissection. *American Journal of Public Health*, *108*(7), 865–867. PubMed. https://doi.org/10.2105/AJPH.2018.304450.

Santaella-Tenorio, J., Cerdá, M., Villaveces, A., and Galea, S. (2016). What do we know about the association between firearm legislation and firearm-related injuries? *Epidemiologic Reviews*, *38*(1), 140–157. https://doi.org/10.1093/epirev/mxv012.

Sleet, D. A., Hopkins, K. N., and Olson, S. J. (2003). From discovery to delivery: Injury prevention at CDC. *Health promotion practice*, *4*(2), 98–102. https://doi.org/10.1177/1524839902250750.

Stark, D. E., and Shah, N. H. (2017). Funding and publication of research on gun violence and other leading causes of death. *JAMA*, *317*(1), 84–85. https://doi.org/10.1001/jama.2016.16215.

Subbaraman, N. (2020). United States to fund gun-violence research after 20-year freeze. *Nature*, *577*(7788), 12. https://doi.org/10.1038/d41586-019-03882-w.

United States Preventive Services Task Force. (2013, December 18). *Final recommendation statement: Suicide risk in adolescents, adults and older adults: Screening.* Retrieved November 18, 2020, from https://www.uspreventiveservicestaskforce.org/uspstf/recommendation/suicide-risk-in-adolescents-adults-and-older-adults-screening.

Webster, D. W., Whitehill, J. M., Vernick, J. S., and Curriero, F. C. (2013). Effects of Baltimore's Safe Streets program on gun violence: A replication of Chicago's CeaseFire program. *Journal of Urban Health: Bulletin of the New York Academy of Medicine*, *90*(1), 27–40. https://doi.org/10.1007/s11524-012-9731-5.

Weibe, D. J. (2003). Homicide and suicide risks associated with firearms in the home: A national case-control study. *Annals of Emergency Medicine, 41*(6), 771–782. http://doi.org/10.1067/mem.2003.187.

15

The Social Construction of Mental Illness and Its Relation to Gun Control

J. Scott Lewis

INTRODUCTION

In the United States, in 2019, there were at least 21 mass shootings, totaling 124 fatalities. These catastrophic events were widely reported across the nation. In the shadow of these of mass shootings, many in which the perpetrator was alleged to have a mental illness, discussions of gun control have taken the form of limiting the ability of individuals who are deemed mentally ill to own guns. These discussions, popular on social and other media and among politicians eager to make their name are voraciously consumed by distraught citizens eager to make sense of tragic acts. Yet these discussions remain largely unexamined philosophically. Among key considerations are the ways in which conceptions of mental illness are socially constructed. Ideas about mental illness are rooted in intersecting ideas about race, social class, disability, and crime.

The purpose of this chapter is to explore the way in which ideas about mental illness are constructed as social narrative, and whether or not this construction warrants the abrogation or limitation of a fundamental Constitutional right. Many questions are manifest in such discussions. To ignore them or gloss them over in the name of safety is scientifically and socially irresponsible. It is essential to clearly understand the issues implicit in this discussion before racing toward social policy that seeks to limit or abrogate entirely the rights of an already marginalized group. It is the goal of this chapter to move toward clarity of thought in these discussions. The debate, of course, is not new. Researchers, practitioners, philosophers, and many others have long debated the efficacy of the concept of mental illness, and whether or not those diagnosed with mental illness should have access to guns (Rotenberg

& Sadoff, 1968). However, the debate seems to have taken on new urgency. With each mass shooting, the call to action grows louder. Accusations become more pronounced. Many state governments have already taken hasty action. Thus, the debate is particularly relevant in a time when society alleges to be expanding the rights of marginalized groups, while at the same time speaking of limiting the rights of those deemed to have a mental illness.

Chief among the questions that emerge in discussions of limiting access to firearms for people with mental illness is the foundational question of defining mental illness. Without a clear definition of what mental illness is, the debate seems shrouded in the arbitrariness of power and dominance. Yet, as we shall see, clear definition remains elusive.

THE SOCIAL CONSTRUCTION OF MENTAL ILLNESS

The first hurdle in any debate about whether or not the right to bear arms should be abridged or abrogated for those who are mentally ill is to clearly and objectively define what a mental illness is. As I hope to make clear, this is more easily said than done. If no proper, objective definition exists, what remains is the triumph of arbitrary power over individuals whose differences are used to marginalize, discredit, and stigmatize them in such a way that their rights are taken away. This, in short, is a form of social control.

What, then, is a mental illness? Does a credible objective definition exist? The first clue toward answering this question is to understand the social history of mental illness. Briefly, the history of mental illness can be summarized in three stages (Foucault, 1961). These correspond roughly to the stages of society identified by the founder of Sociology, Auguste Comte (Comte, 1830; 2010), outlining how he believed societies develop an understanding of their world. The earliest societies interpreted their world supernaturally. Spirits, gods, demons inhabit the world and the world is understood as being influenced or caused by these extra-human forces. Comte called this the theological stage. Gradually, as man's understanding evolved in response to that which theological thinking leaves unanswered, the world came to be understood metaphysically. Things in the world have a nature, and they tend toward that nature. Disassociations are explained as some variation or violation of that inherent metaphysics. Finally, human understanding reaches the age of science, and systematic thinking replaces metaphysical beliefs.

The earliest attempts at understanding and defining mental illness were theological. Behaviors that were considered socially deviant were explained through possessions or as a battle between the unseen forces of good and evil. Possessions were often linked to divine insight, and not always seen negatively. Indeed, many societies induced temporary psychosis or hallucinations through drug use as a way to approach communication with the spirits and gods (DeRios & Smith, 1977). To the degree that the mental aberration was seen as negative or disruptive, the individual was largely absolved of responsibility for their pathology because the possession was involuntary. Possession by demons, spirits, or other supernatural forces imposed themselves upon the unexpected victim. The possession was not chosen; it was rather something that happened to them.

Metaphysical explanations gradually replaced the long-dominant theological ones, stemming from observations of physical manifestations and observable causes of diseases. Explanations of mental illness in this tradition tended toward the biological. The body and mind have a nature (generally understood as some form of homeostatic equilibrium). Mental illness is seen as an aberration from this equilibrium state. In other words, the nature of the individual is disrupted in some way, thus disturbing the normal tendencies and balance of the individual. For example, for centuries a wandering womb was considered a physical dysfunction that caused hysteria in women. Once again, the pathology is something that happens to the individual. However, social response to this kind of deviance was punitive, locking away those who were troubled to keep them separate from the rest of society. Mental illness was, in essence, criminalized.

These early explanations of mental illness served important functions in those societies. As mentioned, religious significance was often attached to symptoms of mental illness. This might include interpreting visions, omens, or messages from the gods. These were considered forces acting on the individual from the outside, thus creating a sense of ablution of individual responsibility for the mental illness. This is consistent with the largely *gemeinschaft* values of these early cultures. The afflicted individual was seen either as set apart in such a way as to benefit society—such as in the case of a shaman—or reintegrated back into the society through tribal ritual. In stark contrast, modern societies, tending toward *gesellschaft* values, individualize and attribute mental illness to the afflicted individual. It is part of the identity of the individual, rather than the collective society.

Scientific ideas about mental illness generally take the form of seeing mental illness as having a specific etiology that is present within the individual. This is identified through behavioral symptoms that—in contrast to earlier societies—have been socially deemed as undesirable. The cause of the behaviors is presumed to have a scientific basis, even if that basis remains a mystery; and proper treatment is based in science. Pharmacological and clinical treatment are the new exorcisms and cleansing rituals for the mentally ill. Although clinical incarceration is no longer normative practice for treating patients with mental illness, remnants of the criminalization of mental illness remain in the social narrative through socially sanctioned stigmas that link mental illness to violence. As our conceptual understanding of mental illness has evolved, definition has proved increasingly elusive. As our evolution from a metaphysical understanding of mental illness to a more positivistic one, science has offered a myriad of related but distinct definitions for mental illness.

Angrist (1966) identifies at least four definitional positions that have historically been taken on mental illness. She argues persuasively that no one approach is empirically or theoretically adequate to completely understand mental illness. The first position identifies mental illness as a form of deviance. The second considers mental illness to be a pathological condition or disease. The third approach carves/categorizes mental illness as either deviant behavior or medical illness, depending on the criteria used and the specific disorder. The final approach calls for a focus on those who label certain behaviors or symptoms as unacceptable, as well as the way the judgments they make about behavior increases or decreases stigma on individuals being labeled.

There are many ways of defining a mental illness, all of which are encompassed in Angrist's typology: psychiatric, psychological, medical, sociological. None of these definitions are consistent. The American Psychiatric Association defines mental illnesses as "health conditions involving changes in emotion, thinking, or behavior (or a combination of these). Mental illnesses are associated with distress and/or problems functioning in social, work, or family activities" (American Psychiatric, 2020, para. 1). Psychologists rely on the DSM, which defines mental illness as a "clinically significant behavioral or psychological syndrome or pattern that occurs in an individual that is associated with present disease or disability or with a significantly increased risk of suffering death, pain, disability, or an important loss of freedom" (*Diagnostic and Statistical Manual*, 2013). Medical definitions vary, but include the broad representative definition of "disorders that affect your mood, thinking, and behavior" (Mayo Clinic, 2020, para. 1). Generally, sociologists view mental illness as a label imposed upon an individual by agents of power in society that creates limitations or which results in stigma of the individual.

Within disciplines such as psychology and psychiatry, varying definitional subtlety abounds, defying consensus. Each definition is encapsulated within the limitations of the respective discipline and subdiscipline, and amenable to criticism from without. Psychiatric definitions, for example, seem to include everything. As Horwitz and Wakefield (2007) persuasively argue, psychiatric definition ignores the relationship of symptoms to the context in which they emerge. The context of the health condition must be a relevant consideration. An impairment in functioning is not necessarily unjustifiable or abnormal merely because it is a change from what an individual would normally do. Believing otherwise assumes a homeostatic model of human behavior, rather than the more scientifically palatable allostatic one (Shulkin, 2003). For some disorders, V-codes have been added to the diagnostic criteria to indicate processes that are disruptive, yet do not qualify as mental illness (such as bereavement). For some disorders, context is removed entirely.

Conflating understandable temporary emotional states that change behaviors and limit functioning is to deny much of the variability in behavior that has helped humans adapt to a wide variety of environmental and social conditions. There are, at the end of the day, sound biological reasons for these adaptive behaviors that seem problematic to attribute merely pathology or deviance (Hagen, 2002). Even if these behaviors could be correctly and conclusively attributed to pathology, questions of ultimate causality remain problematic for mental health professionals. Behaviors cannot be separated from their context.

Psychological definitions are similarly problematic. Terms like "clinically significant" are subjective and require elaboration. Generally, it is defined in psychological parlance as the condition wherein the severity of the behavior is significantly different from the norm and indicates a strong possibility of a clinical problem. The choice of which behaviors are evaluated is largely subjective, as is the comparison with the norm. Comparison with a norm is tricky, because norms are averages, and by definition defy context. Any behavior is conditional and a product not only of internal factors but also of social and structural forces. These factors are highly individualized and nuanced. It is debatable to what degree such motivations and their accompanying behaviors can be generalized or compared. Additionally, identifying any behavior as significantly different from the norm is also judgmental in the sense that it implies moral superiority of normalcy over competing behaviors. The danger of such judgments is the pathologizing of behaviors that fall outside of the perceived norm. Radical expansion of the DSM from 60 mental illnesses in the inaugural edition to nearly 300 in the current edition testifies to the ever-shrinking window of what constitutes normal behavior and to the expanding scope of behaviors now seen as socially undesirable.

Medical definitions (separate from psychiatric ones) fare little better. To define a mental illness as a disorder, aside from being tautological, is to say something quite significant. Dis-order implies that which is not normal. But if an individual engages regularly in behavior that the rest of society perceives as deviant, it is normal to *them*. Thus, defining normalcy becomes the purview of the medical or legal professional, or of society more broadly. As already noted, what is normal is a construction of culture. What is normal is decided not by what people do, but rather by what experts and people in power consider to be important behaviors. It divests the individual both of responsibility and power. Edwards (1981) sees this medical imperialism as forcing more and more disapproved behaviors into the label of sick or deviant. Defining normalcy—and its correlate the process of defining what is not normal—is a means of social labeling and social control.

Advocates of the position known as anti-psychiatry, as advocated by Szasz (1960) and Leifer (1969), define mental illness not as something about the individual, but as rather something about the society in which the individual finds themselves (Sedgwick, 1972). Szasz notes that most mental illnesses are problematic in that they have no obvious point of origin. For example, a cold is caused by a virus. But what causes mental illness? Some mental illnesses, such as depression, have a known etiology—a chemical imbalance. However, Szasz interprets this and any such problem as a problem of the *brain*, rather than of the *mind*. For the remainder of mental disorders without a known etiology, Szasz argues that these equate only to problems of living, rather than of some inherent condition about the person. Szasz suggests that maintaining social narratives of mental illness as a real phenomenon serves a social function of maintaining social control over particular behaviors and the people who engage in them.

There are several criticisms of this approach. There does seem to be some qualitative difference between a problem of body that affects behavior (such as syphilis) and a disorder without an obvious physical cause that displays dysfunction of behavior. For instance, Ausubel (1961) suggests that mental diseases may be nonbiological in nature. Ausubel's criticism, however, seems to rely on a rather strict adherence to mind-body dualism. This approach is philosophically problematic for several reasons. Suggesting that the mind and body are separate and distinct from one another suggests that the immaterial (i.e., the mind) can cause action of a physical body. This needs philosophical elaboration. Similarly, how a physical entity (i.e., the brain) leads to an emergence of a mental event is largely unknown. Physicalism, the idea that all mental events can be reduced to physical ones (and thus that all mental problems are physical ones), seems much more consistent with scientific evidence in neuroscience (Tallis, 2011).

Perhaps a better criticism of Szasz is to reject the false dichotomy that emerges from his argument. Szasz seems to suggest that ideas of mental illness must either be something about society or something about the individual. It must be either a cause of human disharmony, or the result of it. We should be wary of such simplistic designations. In some sense, regardless of the etiology or symptoms, mental illness is a problem of living. It is a problem of living in a world which, as Foucault described, sees madness as embedded in a social structure that alienates man from his true self and places definitions of appropriate behavior in the hands of an extant power structure intent on controlling the behavior of individuals.

To the degree that sociologists discuss the definition of mental illness at all, they generally consider it a label that is imposed upon an individual by another individual or institution in power. The label has consequences in how that individual is thought of by other members of society, as well as how that individual thinks of herself. Consistent with the anti-psychiatry movement, the pathology is constructed rather than real. Sociologist Emile Durkheim, who studied patterns of suicide in Europe, concluded that suicide is due more to social and structural forces than to problems at the level of the individual (1897; 2013). In other words, suicide is the final resort for those with a problem of living, rather than a pathological mental disorder.

While philosophically useful as a foil to the other disciplines, anti-psychiatry and sociological views of mental illness threaten to abandon those who may really suffer from some issue of person that requires professional attention. On the other hand, ignoring this approach moves focus away from social structural problems such as poverty and substance abuse that may ultimately be more important for reducing violence than focusing on individuals. Given the link between mental illness and the demands for living in an increasingly complex postmodern world, it would seem that this approach would be more welcomed. Yet this approach is often ignored or not taken seriously by practitioners outside of the specific fields in which they are embedded. A most likely explanation for this is the relatively low social status of sociology and anti-psychiatry as disciplines relative to the more recognized psychology and psychiatry.

All of the definitions given are inherently value laden. They are shaped by the values of the specific discipline (Horwitz, 2003). They are shaped by the histories, educations, and experiences of those who research, practice, and teach within them. They also shape societal views on mental illness. Still, this is not to claim that mental illness does not exist. Sedgwick suggests that while the concept of mental illness is a social construct, it also reflects something real about the state of organisms. Organisms do exhibit dysfunctions in physical operation. In animals, those dysfunctions are typically limited to the physical. In humans, however, physical conditions can take mental states manifest as behavioral deviance. Thus, mental illness is both a construct, in the sense that it relies on societal norms and values to define certain behaviors as deviant or pathological, as well as something inherent in the functioning of the person. There are many examples. For example, the purported link between mental illness diagnosis and violence has changed over time. In the

1920s, schizophrenia was described as a mild and nonviolent form of mental illness that was merely an aberration in the way that an individual thinks and feels (Astbury, 2002). Psychiatric consensus at the time was that schizophrenics were harmless to society. Indeed, popular media portrayals of persons with schizophrenia at the time lauded schizophrenics like Louis Wain, Zelda Fitzgerald, Jack Kerouac, and Paul Goesch as innovative, expressive artists.

It was not until the 1960s that schizophrenia began to be associated with civil rights, and simultaneously with violence. Journals in psychiatry began to describe patients with diagnosed schizophrenia as having violent episodes. Although these were rare, they quickly found space in the broader social narrative. The Federal Bureau of Investigation began posting most-wanted lists in national newspapers, describing fugitives as schizophrenic killers, even when no diagnosis existed (Metzl & MacLeish, 2015). Television and movies also began to portray schizophrenics as violent offenders (Diefenbach, 1997; Signorielli, 1989). In 1968, the second edition of the *Diagnostic Statistics Manual* altered its description of schizophrenia to include incidence of frequent aggression, anger, and hostility.

It is unclear to what degree improvements in the science of mental illness drove the changing association of schizophrenia with violence, but it is clear that social circumstances had a major impact on the change. Many historical documents show that racial and gender associations underpin much of the association between schizophrenia and violence (Metzl, n.d.). Changes in beliefs about schizophrenia were formed in the crucible of social upheaval. The 1960s and 1970s were contentious times. Anti-war protests, women's rights protests, and civil rights protests divided America. An easy way to vilify individuals who sought to change the status quo was to associate them with mental illness and violence. Indeed, this appears to be exactly what happened. In the Archives of General Psychiatry, two scholars described "protest psychosis" in which the narrative of black power drove African American men to insanity, leading to interracial violence (Bromberg & Simon, 1968). Similarly, Raskin and colleagues (1970) suggested that African Americans with schizophrenia ranked higher than whites on a variety of "hostility variables" because of their belief that their civil rights were being compromised or violated.

An article in the *American Journal of Psychiatry* from 1968 argued that gun rights should be limited for individuals who threaten civil disorder (Rotenberg & Sadoff, 1968).

Criminal profilers for the Federal Bureau of Investigation diagnosed without basis leaders of civil rights protests as violent, pro-gun schizophrenics bent on overthrowing the government. Malcolm X was considered a "pre-psychotic paranoid schizophrenic" even though he met none of the clinical symptoms for such a diagnosis. Robert Williams, head of the NAACP in North Carolina, was also diagnosed by authorities as an armed and dangerous schizophrenic. This changing perception solidified in public memory in 1981 after John Hinkley Jr., a diagnosed schizophrenic, attempted to assassinate President Ronald Reagan in an attempt to impress an actress he had been stalking. Coverage of the shooting forever etched in the mind of America the crazed schizophrenic killer with delusional and dangerous tendencies. Today, schizophrenia is the mental illness most associated with violence in the minds of most Americans.

Similarly, conceptions of drug addiction as a mental illness have roots in social narratives rooted in race, gender, and social class. Where once caffeinism and smoking were considered mental illnesses due to their addictive qualities, they have since been removed from the DSM. However, substance abuse disorder, which includes alcoholism, addiction to heroin, cocaine, and other drugs, remains a cornerstone of the DSM. Despite the fact that nicotine ranks in the top five most addictive substances, it is typically not included in such diagnoses. The war on drugs increased criminal penalties for possession of crack cocaine over cocaine in powdered form. This was justified in the political narrative by associating powdered cocaine with upper-class white men and associating crack cocaine with poor, inner-city black men. Crack cocaine was portrayed as a drug that made black men violent and uncontrollable, rather than as mentally ill victims of addiction. Thus, addiction, like other mental illnesses, has been politicized. Black addicts are far more likely than white addicts to be put in prison, and far less likely to be placed in treatment (MacDonald et al., 2014).

Similar stories can be told for many other mental illnesses. Post-Traumatic Stress Disorder, once considered a benign mental illness, is now strongly associated with violent behavior and has become associated in the social narrative with returning soldiers unable to adapt to civilian life and who are now ticking time bombs waiting for the right moment to engage in a mass shooting. Soldiers returning from unpopular wars saw their sacrifices criticized and vilified as violent murderers who willingly and knowingly killed civilians. These images help to solidify the struggling soldier as someone to be feared rather than admired or pitied.

It is clear that conceptions of mental illness have become politicized in the debate about gun control. More importantly for our discussion, it is equally clear that representations of mental illness are subject to communal diagnosis. In other words, in discussions of gun control and mental illness, it is not out of the realm of possibility to envision assigning categories of mental illness to entire groups of people in order to marginalize them and abrogate their constitutional rights as a means of social control. The reality is that only about

4 percent of violence in the United States can be attributed to people with any diagnosed mental illnesses (Applebaum, 2006). The vast majority of those violent incidences are relatively minor acts of violence that do not involve guns. In fact, schizophrenics are far more likely be victims of violence than perpetrators of violence. Returning soldiers are more likely to take their own life than the lives of others.

THE CHANGING DSM

The DSM (*Diagnostic and Statistical Manual of Mental Disorders*) is the standard diagnostic text for psychology and psychiatry. Each edition entails international experts negotiating the addition, omission, and removal of perceived mental disorders. The original version of the DSM was published in 1952 and contained diagnostic criteria for about 60 distinct mental disorders. The most recent version has ballooned to nearly 300. Until very recently, the process by which disorders were added or removed, and the process by which diagnostic specifications were changed, was shrouded in secrecy. Prior to 2010, the APA was heavily criticized for the closed nature of the revision process. Responding to those criticisms, the APA became somewhat more transparent in their revision process. The APA published a brief outlining the process of revision, which involved more than 100 psychiatrists, 47 psychologists, 2 pediatric neurologists, and 3 statisticians. The task force oversees a variety of work groups to develop diagnostic criteria in respective subfields. More than 300 outside advisers were consulted to help. The APA then opened the revisions to public feedback, which received more than 11,000 comments. Some commented that the revisions added too many new disorders. Some commented on the diagnostic specifications for individual proposed disorders (Jabr, 2012).

Behaviors which are considered mental disorders are not fixed. Rather, they change with cultural values. Until 1973 homosexuality was considered a mental disorder. It was removed after competing theories, developed within the framework of changing sexual mores, challenged the consensus. This included criticisms from the anti-psychiatric movement as well as homophilic activists who began to change the social narrative regarding homosexuality (Drescher, 2015). With the gradual liberalization of sexual norms and social movements toward equality, perspectives changed that led to its removal from the DSM. Similarly, while the newest edition of the DSM eliminates Asperger's syndrome as a separate mental disorder, new disorders have recently been added. Among them are internet gaming disorder, intermittent explosive disorder, and oppositional defiance disorder. A closer look at the diagnostic specifications reveals more of the relativistic nature of mental illness and its subsequent diagnosis.

Oppositional defiance disorder is diagnosed through the following criteria:

- Often loses temper.
- Is often touchy or easily annoyed.
- Is often angry or resentful.
- Often argues with authority figures or, for children and adolescents, with adults.
- Often actively defies or refuses to comply with requests from authority figures or with rules.
- Often deliberately annoys others.
- Often blames others for his or her mistakes or behaviors.
- Has been spiteful or vindictive at least twice within the past six months.

Additional criteria include the persistence and frequency of these behaviors outside of what is considered normal; behaviors that are associated with more than one social context, such as work and school; and that the behaviors are not due to other mood or dysregulation disorders. Severity of symptoms, which in this case is described as the number of settings in which the symptoms manifest—one, two, or more than two—is also considered.

These criteria are fairly representative of mental health diagnostic criteria in the DSM. Of note is the subjective nature of the diagnostic criteria. How often is often? In what social and temporal context is the term often evaluated, and compared to what? Who is making the determination—patient, parent, psychiatrist? These questions cut to the heart of the matter. Diagnosis occurs with a specific setting, embedded within broad social values that shift and change over time. In a society which views deviance as a major social problem, conceptions of normalcy narrow. Negative behaviors are often remembered more accurately than positive behaviors (Kensinger, 2007). Additionally, patients are often diagnosed in a temporally narrow window. More recent behaviors will be remembered more accurately and more clearly than behaviors further in the past.

As a childhood disorder, the very notion of oppositional defiance disorder assumes that compliance to parental and other authority figures is normal and desirable and that staunch resistance is pathological. While in some situations deference to parental authority is warranted, in others it may not be. Context matters, and it is up to the individual mental health professional to determine the importance of context in each situation. Each individual diagnosis is rooted in the professional's perception of when resistance to authority is pathological or when it is warranted. One must ask, however, when dissent became pathological in any context, and who determined it to be so. Is the resistance of an African American child living in an oppressed society equivalent to the resistance of a rich member of the dominant class?

Certainly, a degree of subjectivity is necessary in the diagnostic process to accommodate the expansive variability of human behavior. What is considered normal for one person is not necessarily normal for another. Indeed, that is part of the point. The variability of human behavior is so great that imposing diagnostic constraints with the goal of labeling a person with a mental illness becomes rather tricky work. For that, we turn to professionals such as psychiatrists or psychologists. These people are empowered by society through social and legal means to make judgments about the behaviors of individuals. This is a significant assumption of power. The mental health professional is given special privilege in society that is often taken to be objective and research based. Some writers in the anti-psychiatrist movement suggest that mental illness is merely a categorization used by professionals to legitimate their positions and increase social and political power and control the population (Szasz, 1974).

The addition of disorders such as internet gaming disorder are also deeply rooted in cultural change. It represents a suite of behaviors that could not have existed prior to the popularization of the internet. Implicit in such diagnoses, as well, are comments about race and social class. The digital divide separates citizens who do not have reliable access to virtual technologies and services from those who do. Petry and O'Brien (2013) note that cross-cultural data for internet gaming disorder is lacking. It is likely that individuals who live in concentrated disadvantage or in areas with technological deficiencies are far less likely to engage in the diagnostic suite of behaviors that would comprise this disorder, thus confining it largely to middle-class or upper-class, largely white populations. The implications are clear. If, as some psychiatrists suggest, internet gaming disorder is comorbid with other disorders such as depression or anxiety, middle-class whites are far more likely to seek and receive diagnosis and treatment than their poor, black counterparts.

DEFINING VIOLENCE

Varshney and colleagues (2016) note that many of the studies linking mental illness with violence use disparate definitions of violence. Violence takes many forms, ranging from verbal to emotional to physical. Each of these categorizations includes a wide spectrum of behaviors. It seems reasonable to limit discussions of mental illness and gun control to incidences of gun violence. Yet studies often fail to limit themselves to this parameter. Studies linking mental illness to violence are often inappropriately generalized to gun violence, and to mass shootings specifically. According to Swanson (2011), mass shootings are extremely rare acts of violence with little to no predictive validity in relation to other forms of gun violence. Furthermore, violence and mental illness are often symptoms of broader social problems such as poverty, status threat, and substance abuse. Many longitudinal studies have established a strong relationship between substance abuse and violence (Boles & Miotto, 2003). Other studies show that many individuals with substance use disorders have underlying mental health conditions for which proper diagnosis and treatment are absent (Khantzian, 1985). Drugs often act as means of self-medication. It is often unclear whether it is the mental illness or the drug use that instigates the violence. Perhaps the proper causal attribution is something different altogether.

Gathering data on the relationship between mental illness and violence is also subject to cultural and social factors. Family and friends of a violent mentally ill individual may be reluctant to report incidences of violence in order to keep to the individual out of the criminal justice system. Others may be fearful of having their loved one labeled with a mental illness. In other cases, overreporting of violence may occur as a means of revenge or other vindictive behavior. A study by Phillips (1964) suggests that the nature of the source of help for the individual being labeled confers either more or less stigma upon the individual. Greater stigma is attached to the label of mental illness when given by psychiatric professionals than when given by medical professionals. It is likely that criminal justice and legal professionals will induce additional stigmas associated with incarceration and conviction.

ADDITIONAL QUESTIONS

Discussions of limiting firearms for people with mental illness generally fail to specify whether or not this limitation should apply to all mental illnesses or only some. The breadth of mental illnesses now identified through the DSM makes generalization of gun restriction difficult. Certainly, many identified mental illnesses, such as internet gaming disorder, have few if any empirical links to externalized violent behavior. Even among mental illnesses in which a link to violent behavior has been well established, wide variability among individuals exists. Conditions that create propensity for violence, such as concentrated disadvantage, social inequality, and abuse, vary from person to person and are largely absent in discussions of gun control for those with mental illness.

Many individuals with mental illnesses are successfully integrated members of society. Individuals who are being successfully treated, both in terms of proximate treatments such as symptom mitigation, as well as long-term treatments designed to remedy whatever pathologies exist, pose little danger unless the social and structural circumstances create conditions conducive to violence. In any discussion of mitigating fundamental rights for individuals with mental illness, a high degree of individuation is necessary. Additionally, since each mental illness may manifest in a myriad of ways, each diagnosed individual will likely need to be evaluated on a case-by-case basis. Indeed, this is the very assumption of red flag laws.

Red flag laws were hastily contrived legislation designed to allow designated institutional personnel, such as police, to petition the legal system for the temporary removal of firearms from an individual who is suspected of being a danger to themselves or to others. While this kind of legislation seems promising, several philosophical problems are evident. First, red flag laws place a significant burden on both the executive and judicial systems to determine to what degree an individual might be a danger. Cases involve the use of psychological personnel to establish the degree of danger—a considerable granting of social power—as well as the judgment of non-professionals to make determinations of potential violent intent. In many states, red flag laws are classified as civil matters, rather than criminal, thus depriving many defendants of adequate legal counsel during court proceedings.

Seventeen states have now adopted such laws, with varying degrees of strictness. While in most states, red flags can be raised by family or community members, in New York State red flag laws also give teachers the ability to begin the process. Given the number of school shootings and the publicity that they garner, giving teachers the ability to initiate legal proceedings against an individual suspected of violence seems problematic. Teachers are often politically liberal, favorable to gun control efforts, and are deeply concerned about gun violence. Therefore, they may err too often on the side of caution.

In most states, the laws are written to prevent "significant danger," with no real articulation about what constitutes a significant danger. As Sabella (2014) notes, there is a pervasive perception that the public needs to be protected from the mentally ill. Indeed, multiple studies have shown that the number of people who associate the mentally ill with violence has nearly doubled since 1950 (Pescodolido et al., 2011). Placed in the hands of mental health professionals who will examine the individual only in one moment in time, generally absent of context; put at the mercy of a judge often eager to enforce the law on the side of safety, the individual has little recourse. By their very nature, red flag laws presume that a person is guilty until they prove themselves innocent. How does one prove that they are not a danger to themselves or others? How does one prove the negative, particularly when compared to the expert testimony of mental health professionals?

Critics of red flag laws have also noted that these laws compromise due process. To restrict gun possession in a person who has not committed a crime for no other reason than they make a teacher, neighbor, family member, or judge uncomfortable does seem to warrant criticism. Contact with the criminal justice system, even if cleared of any wrongdoing, has significant social consequences that are often lifelong. Now, however, contact with the criminal justice system can be initiated on the mere suspicion of violence, where the accused individual is at the mercy of layers of definitional and diagnostic subjectivity. Some critics argue that psychiatric diagnosis is largely an observational tool rather than an extrapolative one. Some studies in fact show that psychiatrists using clinical guidelines fare little better than lay citizens in predicting which patients will engage in violence and which will not (Steadman & Cocozza, 1978).

MENTAL ILLNESS AS STIGMA

Individuals diagnosed with mental illness constitute a marginalized group in society. They are often seen as deviant or damaged in some way. Erving Goffman (1963), who wrote one of the most important works on the subject of stigma, describes a stigma as "a special kind of relationship between attribute and stereotype" (p. 4). He identifies three forms that stigma might take. First there are abominations of the body. This would include physical disabilities or deformities. There are also tribal stigmas, such as those ascribed to races, religions, or nationality. Finally, most relevant to our discussion, Goffman identifies stigmas of character. These include blemishes in the personal beliefs or behaviors of the individual that are perceived as deviant. Goffman specifically mentions mental illness as a stigma of character.

Goffman notes that "we believe the person with a stigma is not quite human. On this assumption we exercise varieties of discrimination, through which we effectively, if often unthinkingly, reduce his life chances. We construct a stigma-theory, an ideology to explain his inferiority and account for the danger he represents" (1963, p. 5). Constructing a narrative of the dangerous schizophrenic, the troubled soldier with PTSD, or the crazed student is easily used a justification for discrimination.

Individuals who have mental illnesses face a number of perceptions about their character. Aside from the ideological narratives that shape public perception, mental illness is often given a physical manifestation in society (Eisenhauer, 2008). For example, a popular Valentine's Day teddy bear wearing a straitjacket and carrying a commitment report with the label "Crazy for You!" sold out in 2005 despite criticism from mental health advocacy groups. This is part of a broader historical trend to visualize mental illness and create social perceptions that control behavior and protect normalcy. Indeed, many studies have shown a link between how the media portrays mental illness and attitudes toward individuals with mental illness. Specifically, negative media portrayals lead to negative perceptions of mental illness by members of society. One such study by Thornton and Wahl (1996) demonstrated the pervasive effect of media to shape perceptions. Subjects who read a newspaper article about an individual with a mental illness who committed a violent crime were more likely to evaluate mental illness in a negative way and more likely to favor restrictions of individuals who were diagnosed with a mental illness.

Non-print media has also been shown to shape societal views on mental illness. Signorielli (1989) analyzed television shows and measured the effects of perceptions of mental illness on people's perceptions of the mentally ill. She reports that mental illness appeared in approximately 20 percent of the programs surveyed and represented as afflicting about 3 percent of characters. Wilson and colleagues (1999) examined representation of individuals with mental illnesses in children's television shows. Nearly all of the representations of the mentally ill were in cartoons, and were represented through unruly hair and dress, rotting teeth widely spaced, frontal bossing with thick arched brows, and other stereotypical characteristics. The perceptions of the mentally ill in programs both child and adult are overwhelmingly negative (Diefenbach, 1997). Portrayals of these characters commonly made them out to be associated with violence—sometimes as victims, but most often as perpetrators. Portrayals of the mentally ill also included unemployment or failed employment. Analysis of Disney films revealed that 85 percent of films contained some reference to mental illness, with more than 20 percent of characters portrayed as being mentally ill. These portrayals were nearly universally used in a way that segregated and alienated the character, as well as created clear demarcations of the individual as somehow inferior (Lawson & Fouts, 2004).

Mass shooters get a lot of media attention. Given the specifics of the crimes committed, mass shooters are rightfully portrayed negatively in media. However, when they are portrayed as mentally ill, it adds to the extant stigma of all persons with mental illness by labeling members of this population as violent. This may put the cart before the horse. Goffman notes that "lacking the salutary feed-back of daily social intercourse with others, the self-isolate can become suspicious, depressed, hostile, anxious, and bewildered" (p. 13). In other words, the act of stigmatizing may create or exacerbate the very qualities that seems to be attributed to the stigmatized. A study by Elbogan and Johnson (2009) found that even while mental illnesses considered severe were not a valid predictor of future violence, there was a strong relationship between mental health issues, comorbid conditions—such as substance use, poverty, stigma—and violence.

This is consistent with literature that suggests status threat as a trigger for violence. Harrison and Bowers (2010) found that mass murders are often perpetrated by males who experienced some kind of status threat and who had a history of crime. Fox and Levin (1998) suggest that perpetrators of mass killings often have power or revenge as a motive for their actions. Stigmatized individuals certainly experience a disruption of status in society. For many people, this is manageable. However, for a person managing multiple stigmas, or with a history of social deprivation such as poverty or substance use, the results could be catastrophic. Thus, stigmatizing individuals with mental illnesses further by labeling them as potentially violent offenders simply adds to the problem.

Research also suggests that individuals with mental illnesses are more likely to be victims of violence than perpetrators of violence (Sells et al., 2003). Although this fact is sometimes portrayed in media representations of individuals with mental illness, it takes a backseat to the more negative and violent images of the mentally ill portrayed in various media.

CONCLUSION

According to legal standards, in order to limit the rights of citizens, the government must show a compelling interest in the removal of that right; and the restrictions must be narrowly tailored to restrict the right with as little diminution of the right as possible (Henderson, 2000). While discussions of gun control for those suffering with mental illness may meet the second criterion, it fails to meet the first. There is little reason to suggest that the mentally ill pose significant danger to society.

Among other things, mental illness is a social construct. The concept is embedded in a social reality that is fundamentally hierarchical. Individuals with mental illnesses exist in a highly stratified society that offers opportunity for some, and savagely curtails it for others. The concept of mental illness is a construct that serves many social functions, among them giving power to specific medical and legal professionals and defining the boundaries of normalcy for society. These enable control over behavior in order to gain compliance over deviant behavior. In other words, the label of mental illness is a way to remove opportunity from some segment of the population. Additionally, it offers a convenient group for scapegoating many of society's most pressing problems.

Even if it were possible to adequately define mental illness for the purpose of limiting rights; and if it were possible to identify the specific individuals with mental illnesses who are predisposed to violence, it is unlikely that forbidding them firearms would have more than a very negligible effect on rates of gun crime. It is far more likely that the stigma attached to psychiatric, psychological, and legal branding of an individual as mentally ill will do more harm than good. Stigmatizing labels rob individuals of their social power. It limits opportunity. It threatens the status and dignity of individuals who face challenges with coping in an increasingly postmodern world. There is great potential for abuse. Given the structures of the various definitions of mental illness, nearly any normal behavior could be considered a mental illness in some situation, or when completely removed from any context at all. The threat of communal diagnosis in a frightened world is no longer quixotic.

Public perceptions of individuals with mental illness as violent offenders are largely the product of media and politicians. Fear is a powerful tool to shape social perception. This is coupled with a sense of helplessness that citizens likely feel following the extreme violence of a mass shooting in ways that make the mentally ill scapegoats for violence rather than people in need of help. Science offers tools for understanding relationships between relevant variables; but it offers little comfort in the real lives of human beings devastated by images of violence repeated in the social narrative. Such fear dissuades rational discourse and leads to emotional cries for something to be done. But we do harm to those who are inevitably scapegoated for the crimes of another. We do not make the situation better by abrogating the rights of an entire group of people who are already marginalized and stigmatized in society.

Scapegoating the mentally ill shifts focus away from the more prevalent causes of violent crime, such as poverty, drug policy, contact with the criminal justice system, and other forms of social inequality. The problem is not of people, but of society. The solution to the problem of mass shootings is not the abrogation of rights, but rather the expansion of opportunity.

BIBLIOGRAPHY

American Psychiatric Association website. (2020). https://www.psychiatry.org/patients-families/what-is-mental-illness.

Angrist, S. S. (1966). Mental Illness and Deviant Behavior: Unresolved conceptual problems. *The Sociological Quarterly*, 7(4): 436–448.

Applebaum, P. S. (2006). Violence and Mental Disorders: Data and public policy. *American Journal of Psychiatry*, 163(8): 1319–1321.

Astbury, J. (2002). Mental Health: Gender bias, social position, and depression. *Engendering International Health: The challenge of equity*, Sen, George, and Ostlin, eds. Cambridge: MIT Press.

Ausubel, D. P. (1961). Personality Disorder Is Disease. *American Psychologist*, 16: 69–74.

Boles, S. M., and Miotto, K. (2003). Substance Abuse and Violence: A review of the literature. *Aggression and Violent Behavior*, 8(2): 155–174.

Bromberg, W., and Simon, F. (1968). The "Protest" Psychosis: A special type of reactive psychosis. *Archive of General Psychiatry*, 19(2): 155–160.

Comte, A. (1830; 2010). *The Course of Positive Philosophy*, vol. 1. Cambridge, MA: Cambridge University Press.

DeRios, M. D., and Smith, D. E. (1977). Drug Use and Abuse in Cross Cultural Perspective. *Human Organization*, 936(1): 14–21.

Diagnostic and Statistical Manual Mental Disorders V. (2013). American Psychiatric Association.

Diefenbach, D. L. (1997). The Portrayal of Mental Illness on Prime-Time Television. *Journal of Community Psychology*, 25(3): 289–302.

Drescher, J. (2015). Out of DSM: Depathologizing homosexuality. *Behavioral Sciences*, 5: 565–575.

Durkheim, E. (1897; 2013). *Suicide: A study in sociology*. New York: Snowball Publishing.

Edwards, R. B. (1981). Mental Health as Rational Autonomy. *The Journal of Medicine and Philosophy*, 6: 309–322.

Eisenhauer, J. (2008). A Visual Culture of Stigma: Critically examining representations of mental illness. *Art Education*, 61(5): 13–18.

Elbogan, E. B., and Johnson, S. C. (2009). The Intricate Link between Violence and Mental Disorder: Results from the National Epidemiological Survey on Alcohol and Related Conditions. *Archives of General Psychiatry*, 66: 152–161.

Foucault, M. (1961). *Madness and Civilization*. New York: Vintage.

Fox, J. A., and Levin, J. (1998). Multiple Homicide: Patterns of serial and mass murder. *Crime and Justice*, 23: 407–455.

Goffman, E. (1963). *Stigma: Notes on the management of spoiled identity*. New York: Touchstone.

Hagen, E. H. (2002). The Bargaining Model of Depression. *Genetic and Cultural Evolution of Cooperation*, Peter Hammerstein, ed. Cambridge: MIT Press.

Harrison, M. A., and Bowers, T. G. (2010). Autogenic Massacre as a Maladaptive Response to Status Threat. *Journal of Forensic Psychiatry and Psychology*, 21(6): 916–932.

Henderson, H. (2000). *Gun Control*. New York: Facts on File.

Horwitz, A. V. (2003). *Creating Mental Illness*. Chicago: University of Chicago Press.

Horwitz, A. V., and Wakefield, J. (2007). *The Loss of Sadness: How psychiatry transformed normal sorrow into depressive disorder*. New York: Oxford University Press.

Jabr, F. (2012, May-June). Redefining Mental Illness. *Scientific American Mind*: 29–35.

Khantzian, E. J. (1985). The Self-medication Hypothesis of Addictive Disorders: Focus on heroin and cocaine dependence. *American Journal of Psychiatry*, 142(11): 1259–1264.

Kensinger, E. A. (2007). Negative Emotion Enhances Memory Accuracy: Behavioral and neuroimaging evidence. *Current Directions in Psychological Science*, 16(4): 213–216.

Lawson, A., and Fouts, G. (2004). Mental Illness in Disney Animated Films. *The Canadian Journal of Psychiatry*, 49: 310–314.

Leifer, R. (1969). *In the Name of Mental Health: The social functions of psychiatry*. New York: Science House.

MacDonald, J., Arkes, J., Nicosia, N., and Pacula, R. L. (2014). Decomposing Racial Disparities in Prison and Drug Treatment Commitments for Criminal Offenders in California. *The Journal of Legal Studies, 43*(1), 155–187. https://doi.org/10.1086/675728.

Mayo Clinic website. (2020). https://www.mayoclinic.org/diseases-conditions/mental-illness/symptoms-causes/syc-20374968.

Metzl, J. M. *The Protest Psychosis: How Schizophrenia became a black disease*. Boston: Beacon.

Metzl, J. M., and MacLeish, K. T. (2015). Mental Illness, Mass Shootings, and the Politics of American Firearms. *Framing Health Matters*, 105(2): 240–249.

Pescodolido, B. A., Monahan, B. G., Link, A. S., and Kikuzawa, S. (2011). The Public's View of the Competence, Dangerousness, and Need for Legal Coercion of Persons with Mental Health Problems. *American Journal of Public Health*, 89(9): 1339–1345.

Petry, N. M., and O'Brien, C. P. (2013). Internet Gaming Disorder and the DSM-5. *Society for the Study of Addiction*, 108: 1186–1187.

Phillips, D. L. (1964). Rejection of the Mentally Ill. *American Sociological Review*, 29: 679–687.

Raskin, A., Crook, T. H., and Herman, K. D. (1970). Psychiatric History and Symptom Differences in Black and White Depressed Patients. *Journal of Consultative Clinical Psychology*, 43(1): 73–80.

Rotenberg, L. A., and Sadoff, R. L. (1968). Who Should Have a Gun? Some preliminary psychiatric thoughts. *American Journal of Psychiatry*, 125(6): 841–843.

Sabella, D. (2014). Mental Illness and Violence. *The American Journal of Nursing*, 114(1): 49–53.

Sedgwick, P. (1972). Mental Illness Is Illness. *Salmagundi* 20(Summer–Fall): 196–224.

Sells, D. J., Rowe, M., and Fisk, D. (2003). Violent Victimization of Persons with Co-Occurring Psychiatric and Substance Use Disorders. *Psychiatric Services*, 54: 1253–1257.

Shulkin, J. (2003). *Rethinking Homeostasis*. Cambridge: MIT Press.

Signorielli, N. (1989). The Stigma of Mental Illness on Television. *Journal of Broadcasting & Electronic Media*, 33(3): 325–331.

Steadman, H., and Cocozza, J. (1978). Dangerousness and the Repetitively Violent Offender. *Journal of Criminal Law and Criminology*, 69(2): 226–231.

Swanson, J. W. (2011). Explaining Rare Acts of Violence: The limits of evidence from population research. *Psychiatric Services*, 62(11): 1369–1371.

Szasz, T. S. (1960). The Myth of Mental Illness. *American Psychologist*, 15: 113–118.

Szasz, T. S. (1974). *The Myth of Mental Illness: Foundations of a theory of personal conduct.* New York: Harper & Row.

Tallis, R. (2011). *Aping Mankind: Neuromania, Darwinists and the misrepresentation of humanity*. Bristol, CT: Acumen.

Thornton, J. A., and Wahl, O. F. (1996). Impact of a Newspaper Article on Attitudes toward Mental Illness. *Journal of Community Psychology* 24(1): 17–25.

Varshney, M., Mahapatra, A., Krishnan, V., Gupta, R., and Deb, K. S. (2016). Violence and Mental Illness: What is the true story? *Journal of Epidemiology and Community Health*, 70(3): 223–225.

Wilson, C., Nairn, R., Coverdale, J., and Panapa, A. (1999). Mental Illness Depictions in Prime-Time Drama: Identifying the discursive resources. *Australian & New Zealand Journal of Psychiatry*, 33(2): 232–239.

Part V

FIREARMS AT WORK AND SCHOOL

16

Guns at Work

Management Considerations and Workplace Policies

Mark R. Regensburger

Senior management at most businesses in the United States consider the idea of guns at work infrequently, if at all. They are busy with other important questions: How can we better serve customers? How can we increase revenue and lower expenses? How can we equip our employees to be more productive, to provide better service? How will we replace critical skills if an employee leaves? When is the next health and safety inspection or report due? For many, guns only come to mind when something out of the ordinary happens. The evening news reports on a mass shooting somewhere. Online arguments break out between gun control activists and Second Amendment advocates. A local business is robbed. Perhaps there are several incidents of gun violence in their community. Any of these can cause management to stop and worry how guns might affect their business. They ask themselves: What if someone dies at my business? What can I do to prevent this?

In this chapter, we will look at the impact of guns in the workplace and culture, define possible workplace policies regarding guns, and discuss concerns management should consider in choosing and implementing these policies. A well-thought-out policy for guns in the workplace can help prevent tragedy and equip employees both to feel safer and to do their jobs better. This can help a business thrive and succeed, to the benefit of management, employees, and their community.

WORKPLACE FATALITIES

A workplace fatality is a traumatic event for any business, in part because it is a rare occasion for workplaces in the United States. On average, about

7,700 people die in the United States every day (National Center for Health Statistics, 2020); of these, 14 people die at work (Occupational Safety and Health Administration [OSHA], 2020a). This number reflects a vast improvement over the past five decades: in 1970, the workplace fatality rate was 38 per day (OSHA, 2020a). While daily averages are helpful to give a feel for the scope of the problem, fatality rates in the workplace are normally reported as annual deaths per 100,000 full-time equivalent workers. The overall workplace fatality rate in the United States is 3.27 per 100k; transportation incidents—primarily vehicle accidents—account for more than half of these fatalities, at 1.39 per 100k (U.S. Bureau of Labor Statistics, 2015). Falls, slips, and trips, at 0.54 per 100k, and contact with objects and equipment, at 0.49 per 100k, follow as second and third most frequent cause of death each year.

Gun deaths in the workplace are considerably less frequent, at 0.28 per 100k, and have been stable for most of the twenty-first century (Sabbath et al., 2020). Workers in the United States are nearly five times more likely to die in a work-related vehicle accident than to be killed by a gun at work. Excluding law enforcement officers killed on duty and deaths in extraordinary circumstances (accidental shootings, bystanders struck by stray bullets, mass shooting, or terrorism), workplace gun deaths occur in one of four specific circumstances (Doucette et al., 2019):

- Robberies—In 45 percent of cases, an employee or customer was killed by an outsider in the course of an armed robbery. Of these killers, 95 percent were not known to employees.
- Coworker conflict—In 18 percent of cases, a coworker killed another employee, either as part of an ongoing history of conflict or during an argument.
- Customer argument—In 10 percent of cases, an employee or a customer was killed during an argument between the employee and the customer.
- Personal relationship—In 10 percent of cases, an employee's personal relationship outside of work spilled over into the workplace.

Workplace safety programs have tended to focus on preventing vehicle accidents, slip or fall incidents, and struck-by-object incidents; these account for most fatalities—and the overwhelming majority of injuries—and their prevention is largely within the control of management and employees. Management in the past has tended to treat workplace violence, including gun fatalities, as a failure of disciplinary or security policies rather than as a safety issue, as an individual failing instead of an organizational failure. In the twenty-first century, there has been an increasing emphasis on promoting employee health and wellness, including mental health. This has led to a shift toward preventing workplace violence as a safety and health issue, and with this a shift toward understanding and planning for the impact of guns at work rather than treating their presence as a disciplinary or security failure (Miller, 1999; Runyan et al., 2000).

ONE NATION, TWO CULTURES

Confounding this historical tendency to treat guns at work as a disciplinary issue, rather than a manageable safety concern, is the cultural divide between two groups of people in the United States: those for whom guns are a normal part of their experience and those with little or no exposure to guns. For convenience, we can call them "gun people" and "non-gun people." There is no value judgment implied in these labels, simply a recognition of two different streams of life experience in our very diverse nation.

Gun people tend to grow up in a social gun culture, where guns are commonly used by many people for hunting, sport, and self-defense. Gun people are comfortable with the idea of guns and are far more likely to own their own guns (Kalesan et al., 2016). Of all U.S. adults, 42 percent live in a household with at least one gun (Gramlich & Schaeffer, 2019). Non-gun people grew up in cultural settings where guns were not common. They have little direct experience with guns, may never even have held one. They tend to think about guns only when they encounter media coverage of a shooting, crime, or other gun-related occurrence, and may thus have an overall negative perception of guns (Kalesan et al., 2016). These Americans make up the 60 percent who feel gun laws should be stricter; this view is especially pronounced among college graduates, with 72 percent of them favoring gun restrictions (Gramlich & Schaeffer, 2019). These two groups also tend to live in different parts of the country, with gun people in small cities, towns, and rural areas, and non-gun people in major metropolitan urban areas. For one group, guns are normal; for the other, guns are for police and for criminals. Bringing these two groups together in the same business setting requires a thoughtful and sensitive management approach.

POLICY APPROACHES TO WORKPLACE HAZARDS

The *General Duty Clause* of the Occupational Safety and Health Act of 1970 requires employers to provide employees with a job and a workplace that are "free from recognized hazards that are causing or are likely to cause death or serious physical harm" (Occupational Safety and Health Act, 1970, 29 USC sec. 654(a)(1)). This landmark U.S. legislation makes employers responsible for workplace safety, and the 63 percent reduction in workplace fatalities since it was enacted is a testimony to the powerful effectiveness of this simple General Duty Clause (OSHA, 2020a).

There are several approaches to providing a workplace free of recognized hazards: outright prohibition to eliminate a hazard; qualification, certification, and training to minimize hazards that are required to perform a given occupation; and workplace policies to control hazards that need to be reasonably accommodated for a business to function. Some concrete examples will serve to illustrate each of these three approaches.

Drugs and alcohol are a recognized workplace hazard. Multiple studies have established a strong connection between drug or alcohol abuse by employees and workplace injuries and fatalities (Ramchand et al., 2009). Businesses seeking federal contracts are required to have a drug-free workplace (Drug-Free Workplace Act, 1988). Because of this strong correlation, many businesses have adopted *prohibited-use* policies for alcohol on the job and for illegal drugs at any time. These are disciplinary policies, communicated during recruitment and hiring, and enforced by periodic medical testing, especially after accidents or other safety incidents. Most employers allow employees with substance abuse problems to self-refer for health and wellness treatment, but violations of workplace policies are handled as disciplinary matters, quite frequently with termination of employment as a zero-tolerance violation.

Vehicle accidents are a recognized workplace hazard; they are the leading cause of death in the workplace. However, many businesses need employees to operate motor vehicles in the course of their daily work. Driving is a "bona fide occupational qualification" for local delivery drivers, long-haul truckers, home healthcare aides, and countless other professions. A *required-use* approach recognizes that driving is both dangerous and essential, and mitigates the hazard by ensuring that drivers are appropriately qualified, currently licensed, and regularly trained on driving safety. An off-duty driving incident can lower an employer's trust in that employee's safety and capability, so personal driving records also impact employees' workplace qualification to drive as part of the job.

Even if not required in the course of daily duties, driving a vehicle to and from work is a societally accepted hazard: society accepts the significant dangers of motor vehicles as a necessary part of contemporary life. Most employers adopt a *permitted-use* workplace policy for allowing employees' privately owned vehicles on company property, with appropriately marked driveways and parking areas, safe driving policies in those areas, and potential loss of driving privilege on company property for safety violations or other disciplinary action.

These three approaches to managing known hazards in the workplace are based on the specific needs of the business and the past conduct of employees, and allow for changes based on future needs or conduct. They can provide a guideline for businesses to manage the hazards associated with guns at work.

POLICY APPROACHES TO GUNS IN THE WORKPLACE

Are guns a recognized hazard? Do guns cause death or serious physical harm? Clearly, guns can be a hazard in the workplace. However, guns also can serve a bona fide purpose in the workplace, and the right to self-defense is a societally accepted hazard, a basic right guaranteed to all Americans. What is the right policy approach to guns in the workplace? The answer varies from business to business and should be based on a risk analysis that includes business needs, safety needs, environmental analysis, and employee factors. The best policy for a suburban country club will be different from that for an urban investment banking firm, and a church preschool different from a rural bar and entertainment venue. What the right policy is varies widely from location to location. Management should always seek legal guidance as part of this risk analysis to ensure that workplace policies and training are in full compliance with federal, state, and local laws.

Prohibited Carry

Gun-free zone—the signs are seemingly everywhere. Some are legally mandated: Each of the fifty states has different laws, allowing or specifically prohibiting guns in K–12 schools, colleges and universities, movie theaters, government buildings, parks, banks, bars, places of worship, hospitals, daycares, amusement parks, or outdoor music festivals (Giffords Law Center, 2020). Each of the fifty states likewise allows or prohibits private businesses from limiting the self-defense right to carry guns. Qualified legal guidance can provide management with a thorough understanding of the legal environment for each business location.

A prohibited-carry policy specifies that no guns are permitted in the business. It applies to management, all employees, all customers, all suppliers and vendors, all sales representatives, law enforcement; everyone. If you want to delineate exceptions, these need to be specified. If you want no guns, but are glad to have police patronize your coffee shop, your policy should state so. The intent of a prohibited-carry policy is that no one has a gun in your business. However, the reality is that a prohibited-carry policy simply defines any guns in your business as unauthorized guns.

Adopting a gun-free zone means, by definition, that only "bad guys"[1] have guns—unauthorized guns carried by people who intend to do harm. Of the ten deadliest U.S. mass shootings in the twenty-first century, all were in gun-free zones, seven of those mandated by law, three by company policy (CNN Editorial Research, 2020). Unfortunately, prohibited-carry policies also prevent other individuals, who have cleared a law enforcement background check, obtained a concealed-carry permit, and are presumably trained and responsible gun owners, from carrying their guns. Though data is inconsistently gathered across states and local jurisdictions, there are definitely cases of "good guys" with legally carried guns thwarting criminal activity and saving lives in the workplace. A prohibited-carry policy either deprives businesses of the protection of trained and responsible gun owners, or turns them into "bad guys" if they decide to carry despite the policy.

Business adoption of prohibited-carry policies can also raise liability concerns. Libertarian and natural rights advocates present the argument that the Second Amendment merely prevents the government from depriving individuals of an already preexisting natural right to self-defense: If a business deprives an individual of this right to self-defense, is the business liable in cases where that individual is harmed? Legislation has been introduced in a number of states that would allow individuals deprived of their right to self-defense by a business's prohibited-carry policy to sue the business for damages if they are injured or killed (Gantert, 2019; Larimore, 2017; Li, 2016; McGaughey, 2016; Uren, 2020). This raises the reasonable question of whether a business has a general duty to protect customers and employees in a gun-free zone. One way to address this duty is through required carry of guns by employees to provide protection and security.

Required Carry

Armed security guards are a familiar sight in many business contexts. Just as employers may choose to make driving skills a bona fide occupational qualification, necessary to perform the required functions of a job, so they are also free to define competency with gun skills as necessary for the job of providing security in a business. Required carry of a gun becomes a part of that job. With this comes the employer's obligation to ensure employee competence and work performance.

Management may choose to outsource armed security through a security contractor whose employees provide this service, putting the obligation for staffing, training, and supervision on that contractor. For other business situations, it may be appropriate to contract individually with off-duty law enforcement personnel; this solution works well in many jurisdictions for small organizations with an intermittent requirement for security, such as worship services, athletic games, or community events. In all of these cases, required carry is limited to those employees or contractors directly providing security. Employers should definitely establish clear use-of-force workplace polices and require training to ensure that these are followed, whether required-carry personnel are employees or contractors.

Permitted Carry

Workplace policies regarding guns should be based on a thorough risk assessment. Thus far, we have explored prohibited-carry policy—treating the workplace a gun-free zone—and required-carry policy—arming employees or contractors to provide security as a paid agent of the business. The last option for management is permitted carry: allowing some people to have guns at work, other than paid and dedicated security. Management may set a business policy allowing individual employees, or others, to carry a gun in the workplace. This policy can take several forms.

Employees with a concealed-carry permit have already passed several local government checks and are credentialed as authorized to carry a concealed weapon. Permitting these employees to conceal carry in the workplace takes advantage of the security checks already completed, and gives employers more backing because of local government approval. Permitting concealed carry also keeps guns out of the view of other employees and customers, reducing the potential negative impact on non-gun people. Workplace policies can respect individual privacy by allowing employees to conceal carry without this being known to other employees; however, employers should require these employees to keep management informed when they are carrying. Employees who carry should be given clear guidance to define when they are acting in self-defense and when they are acting as an agent of the employer. Use-of-force policies and training are beneficial for permitted-carry employees, just as for required-carry personnel.

A business's management may decide to allow customers, suppliers, vendors, or other visitors to carry a gun, either concealed carry with a permit or open carry, depending on the risk analysis for that particular business. These outside individuals are clearly not acting as agents of the employer and are responsible for their own conduct. A management decision to not prohibit carry in a business does not automatically make them liable; individuals outside the employer's control remain responsible for their own actions. A number of major retailers allow concealed carry; only a few allow open carry where not prohibited by local government (Gangitano & Wong, 2019). Allowing customer carry, open or concealed, may also be a positive marketing strategy, targeting customers who place a high value on their Second Amendment rights.

The last option for permitted carry in the workplace is permitting open carry by employees, who do or do not have a concealed-carry permit. This policy may expose employers to a greater risk of liability for employees without government screened concealed-carry permits. There is also significant disagreement between open carry advocates who argue that the visible presence of guns helps deter crime (Frontier Carry, 2020) and others who believe that open carry easily identifies these individuals as the first target for criminals to neutralize (Ellifritz, 2018). In either case, a rational risk analysis will examine both options to determine what the best policy is for a given business.

Real World Policy: The Mixed-Carry Workplace

A thorough risk analysis gives management a solid basis to determine the appropriate policy for their specific workplace: *prohibited carry*, *required carry*, or *permitted carry*. In a real-world context, however, a particular business's policy results in a *mixed-carry* workplace. The presence of guns at work will be some mix of the policy chosen and the reality that shows up to work each day. Some of the possible permutations are as follows.

Gun-free zone + Unauthorized Carry. When management chooses to exclude all guns from the workplace, they are in reality excluding all guns except those carried by "bad guys." Those who bring guns into this workplace may be "good guys" with concealed-carry permits, who skirt workplace policies for self-defense; there are also those who bring guns into the workplace with intent to do harm.

Gun-free zone + Required Carry + Unauthorized Carry. This policy option is very common, especially for public sector locations that have statutory gun prohibitions with paid professional security. Educational institutions, both K–12 and higher education, are typical of this mix. These are also locations that have been particularly vulnerable to mass shootings (CNN Editorial Research, 2020), as the baseline assumption that only required-carry security personnel have guns may lead to complacency in overlooking threats.

Gun-free zone + Required Carry + Permitted Carry + Unauthorized Carry. This looks complicated, but is often the initial step for management seeking to empower ordinary employees. A retail or other customer-centric business has a weapons-free policy posted on the door, and employs armed security (required carry). Pressure from employees leads management to implement a policy allowing employees with permits to conceal carry. "Bad guys" walk in the door with a gun. Management needs to consider this scenario, with multiple actors armed and working in the same space. Workplace policies allowing employee concealed carry should have clear guidance for how these employees interact with required-carry security and unauthorized carry threats.

Full Permitted Carry. This is the broadest policy combination: permitted carry by employees (concealed or open), required-carry security, and permitted carry by customers and others (concealed or open), all in the same physical space. This allows for maximum individual freedom, but also greater potential for business liability. Clear workplace policies should spell out appropriate responses for security, ordinary employees, and others in the workplace. Appropriate policies should be combined with proactive human resource management—safety, training, staffing, and employee relations—to maximize workplace safety and minimize employer liability.

MANAGING SAFETY AND HEALTH IN THE MIXED-CARRY WORKPLACE

As discussed in this chapter, management must operate under the assumption that guns will be present in the workplace, whether authorized or not. Guns should therefore be treated as any other recognized workplace safety hazard. Safety and wellness programs are the primary management tool to prevent death, injuries, or illness in the workplace. An effective safety program focuses on mitigating *unsafe working conditions* and *unsafe employee actions* (OSHA, 2020b).

Creating a safer work environment is accomplished by identifying and eliminating physical hazards, and by designing processes to minimize hazards that cannot be eliminated. The first step is for management to identify all guns in the workplace. Managers on duty should know how many required-carry security personnel are at work, whether employees or contractors, and should know the specific guns each individual is carrying. These managers should also know any permitted-carry employees, and what guns they are carrying, at all times; even if business policy allows concealed carry while respecting individual privacy, management has a legitimate need to know in order to provide proper leadership and control in the workplace. Business processes should take the presence of guns into account, with simple procedures for authorized use-of-force based on clear situational criteria. Management should also consider how to ensure that unattended guns are handled safely to prevent accidental injuries.

Mitigating unsafe employee actions is also based on identifying hazardous behaviors. Earlier in this chapter, we identified the four major causes of workplace gun deaths: robberies, coworker conflict, customer arguments, and personal relationships. Each of these hazards can be addressed through workplace policies, procedures, and training. Employers should have clear procedures to guide employees safely in case of armed robberies, with defined roles for each employee, taking into consideration their carry status (required, permitted, or unarmed). Coworker conflict can be addressed through conflict resolution policies and training, and by active involvement of first-line managers in their employees' work. Conflict resolution policies and training can also equip employees for difficult customer arguments. Management support for employees dealing with difficult customers is also critical; there is a growing trend in customer service that the customer is not always right, that employees are valuable and should be backed up by management (Hawthorne, 2017; Mukherjee, 2018; Pozin, 2018). Reducing the negative effect of personal relationships on employees in the workplace requires management who are invested in and care for their employees. Access to wellness and mental health programs is also critical to empowering employees to deal with both personal relationships and workplace conflicts.

A thoughtful wellness program can also address the divide between gun people and non-gun people. Gun familiarization, education programs, and stress reduction can all help non-gun people to feel less excluded. Allowing employees from both groups to share their experiences and their personal journeys can reduce this cultural divide and can increase workplace camaraderie. Making mental health care available to all employees, including management involvement to destigmatize mental health concerns, can reduce stress, increase safety and wellness, and make for an overall more positive and supportive work environment for all employees.

TRAINING EMPLOYEES FOR THE MIXED-CARRY WORKPLACE

Well-designed workplace training equips employees with the knowledge, skills, and attitudes needed to perform effectively. Safety training, to mitigate workplace hazards and prevent unsafe employee actions, is essential with guns in the workplace. A thorough training program gives employees the tools they need to succeed, and the training process can create closer workplace cooperation and a feeling of belonging by including all employees from the first day of hire. Good training contributes to employee satisfaction and engagement, and to overall business success.

Training Required-Carry Employees

This brief section does not attempt to provide technical expertise on firearms training. Management should seek qualified professional guidance to ensure the proper technical training of armed employees. However, as a general workplace principle, all employees need to know how to safely operate all workplace equipment. Required-carry employees need to be proficient on the gun they will use at work; regular training might include weapons safety, range qualification, handling malfunctions, proper maintenance, and basic operator repairs.

Required-carry employees definitely need to be highly proficient in interpersonal skills, including conflict management and de-escalation, as they can expect to be drawn into any workplace robbery, argument, or conflict. Thorough knowledge of all workplace policies is essential, particularly relating to use-of-force, who is allowed to carry guns, concealed-carry policy, and interacting with other armed and unarmed employees and customers. Realistic situational scenario training is an essential part of training armed employees, contextualizing training to the particular work environment where employees will face challenges.

Management will need to carefully consider whether to require this level of training for permitted-carry employees. This is in part dependent on the employer's use-of-force policy. If permitted-carry employees are only to use personal guns for personal self-defense, less employer responsibility for training may be warranted. If these employees are authorized to use personal guns as an agent of the employer to thwart robberies or otherwise protect others, management may want to insist on ensuring their proficiency. Training considerations for permitted-carry employees should be discussed with legal counsel to reduce risk to the business.

Equipping All Employees for Success

All employees should be trained on the organization's workplace policies concerning guns. This begins from day one on the job. Onboarding should introduce policies, including who is authorized to carry, safety procedures for guns, and use-of-force policies. Reinforcing should also include equipping all employees to enforce workplace policies safely and effectively. Employee knowledge of policies should be incorporated into ongoing workplace training. This with customers, vendors, suppliers, contractors, and other outsiders, whether the business adopts a prohibited-carry "gun-free zone" policy, permitted concealed carry, or permitted open carry. This should include practical strategies to reassure non-gun people, in order to reduce their unease at guns in the workplace. Manager training should specifically equip supervisors to ensure consistent policy enforcement for everyone's safety.

Interpersonal skills, including conflict resolution, customer service, and argument de-escalation, are perishable skills, and require regular reinforcement through training. Situational scenario training is an effective means to equip employees for these interpersonal situations, and allow employees to have real input on shaping how workplace policies are carried out in their daily work. Basing scenarios on the four most common hazard situations—robbery, coworker conflict, customer argument, or personal relationship problem—can provide employees real-world skills and prepare them to handle these difficult situations should they arise in the workplace. Scenarios can also incorporate a variety of other soft skills: communication, cultural awareness, motivation, sales skills, and emotional intelligence are a few examples of skills that can be woven into situational scenario training. Throughout training, a sensitive acknowledgment of the divide between gun people and non-gun people can equip employees with greater understanding and empathy for coworkers.

Equipping all employees to deal with hazards in the workplace is essential. All employees should be trained on basic gun safety rules (NRA, 2020). Employees also need to know how to safely handle a gun they might encounter in the workplace; even in a gun-free zone, an unauthorized gun may be accidentally left behind. Training employees to assume that every gun is loaded can prevent accidental tragedy; equipping them to safely clear (unload) a gun lets them render their workplace safer. Off-site workplace training at a firing range facility, with hands-on opportunities for both gun people and non-gun people, can build knowledge, comfort, and confidence. Adding opportunities for employees to share their life stories about guns can make for stronger interpersonal relationships and more effective teamwork.

STAFFING THE MIXED-CARRY WORKPLACE

Decisions about workplace policies will affect staffing decisions. Choosing a policy that includes *required-carry* employees necessitates a thorough job analysis for these security positions to ensure clear definition of their role in the workplace and to establish proper criteria for gun proficiency as a bona fide occupational qualification. Alternately, management may decide to outsource this group of employees by contracting with an outside armed security provider. This solution allows management to focus on the core of their business, leaving it to the contractor to ensure that security personnel are qualified, certified, and regularly trained. This is a common solution for many businesses; however, outsourcing workplace security can complicate first-line managers' jobs. The contractor is normally free to send whatever personnel fit the contract requirements. Managers may be left dealing with a rotating roster of workers and may not be able to develop the same quality of relationship with contracted personnel as with employees. This situation also can cause complications when problems arise—robberies, conflicts, or arguments—as to who is in charge of use-of-force, the manager or the armed contractor. Contracted security may also be less integrated with the business's employees, again complicating crisis situations. Managers need to clearly and explicitly communicate expectations to the contractor and to contractor personnel and reinforce these expectations with each security contractor on the job.

Workplace gun policies will also impact recruitment and hiring of other employee positions. Management should make these policies readily available for potential recruits. Publicly available information about a business increases the likelihood candidates will be interested enough to apply for openings. Transparency throughout the recruitment and hiring process increases employees' perception that the business is fair, and contributes to employee performance (Jacksch & Klehe, 2016). A well-designed employment page on the business website should include an overview of major workplace policies; the business's policy toward guns should be among these. If the policy is a strict *prohibited-carry* gun-free zone, the hiring process should include a discussion of this to prevent "good guy" concealed carry in violation of policy. Conversely, if the policy includes any combination of *required carry* or *permitted carry*, hiring should include a discussion of this, with special attention to the concerns of non-gun people about guns in the workplace.

First-line managers' job descriptions should include explicit responsibility for overseeing and implementing whichever combination of carry policy the business has adopted. Manager training and promote-from-within policies should develop the supervisory skills necessary, including managing conflicts and arguments, and supervision of armed employees. Basic knowledge of gun safety is recommended, including safely clearing and handling guns; the first-line manager is often the one who must deal with such situations.

EMPLOYEE RELATIONS IN THE MIXED-CARRY WORKPLACE

A well-crafted workplace gun policy—based on a thorough risk analysis and consideration of the location, environment, customers, and type of business—provides employees with clear guidance in handling difficult workplace situations. Clear workplace policies that address real-world needs contribute to employee engagement. Equitable enforcement of these policies by competent managers increases employee job satisfaction.

Many workplaces have adopted disciplinary policies that include zero tolerance for workplace violence (Harlan & Thomas, 2017). These disciplinary policies make termination of employment the mandatory consequence for workplace violence. In the mixed-carry workplace, such policies must be explicit in defining what use of guns is authorized and what behaviors are considered workplace violence. Brandishing a weapon is a common example of workplace violence. Context, however, is critical: Brandishing a weapon in response to an armed robbery should be clearly defined as authorized by use-of-force policy; brandishing a weapon in an argument with a coworker or customer should be clearly prohibited as workplace violence. Verbal threats against coworkers by a permitted concealed-carry employee would be workplace violence; the same threat by an unarmed worker would also be workplace violence (Thelen, 2009). The presence of a gun does not automatically transform a given situation into workplace violence, and those managers who are tasked with enforcing zero-tolerance policies in the mixed-carry workplace need clear guidance from senior management for such situations.

A clear, well-defined employee disciplinary procedure helps management to maintain a work environment where misconduct is corrected and unacceptable behavior is not tolerated. A strong employee grievance procedure gives employees a safe mechanism for voicing concerns, with the assurance that their voices will be heard, and provides management a structured means of fairly resolving differences in the workplace. Evenly and equitably applied, disciplinary and grievance procedures allow management to maintain a positive, supportive work environment for all employees.

GUNS AT WORK FOR A BETTER WORKPLACE

Management must face the reality of guns in the workplace. Workplace policies should be rooted in clear risk analysis and the needs of that particular business. Clear policy guidelines help employees and management make the workplace safer. Comprehensive training equips them to respond to unexpected situations. And thoughtful staffing and employee relations help create greater employee engagement and job satisfaction, leading ultimately to better products, better customer service, and business success.

NOTE

1. The word "guy" is used in this context as a gender-neutral word, based on current socially accepted usage. "Good guy" and "bad guy" have established and readily recognized meanings in U.S. culture. A thorough scholarly analysis of the gender-neutral use of "guy" is addressed in Foubert, O., and Lemmens, M. (2018), Gender-biased neologisms: The case of man-X, *Lexis – Journal in English Lexicology, 12,* https://doi.org/10.4000/lexis.2453.

REFERENCES

CNN Editorial Research. (2020, May 3). *Mass shootings in the US fast facts.* https://www.cnn.com/2019/08/19/us/mass-shootings-fast-facts/index.html.

Doucette, M. L., Bulzacchelli, M. T., Frattaroli, S., and Crifasi, C. (2019). Workplace homicides committed by firearm: Recent trends and narrative text analysis. *Injury Epidemiology, 6*(5). https://doi.org/10.1186/s40621-019-0184-0.

Drug-Free Workplace Act, 41 U.S. Code § 8102 (1988).

Ellifritz, G. (2018, September 24). *Friends don't let friends open carry.* Active Response Training. https://www.activeresponsetraining.net/friends-dont-let-friends-open-carry.

Frontier Carry. (2020). *Open carry.* https://www.frontiercarry.org/open-carry.html.

Gangitano, A., and Wong, S. (2019, September 7). Here are the gun policies for America's largest retailers. *The Hill.* https://thehill.com/policy/finance/460336-here-are-the-gun-policies-for-americas-largest-retailers.

Gantert, T. (2019, September 27). Lawmaker wants to make gun-free zones liable if someone hurt. *Michigan Capital Confidential.* Mackinac Center for Public Policy. https://www.michigancapitolconfidential.com/lawmaker-wants-to-make-gun-free-zones-liable-if-someone-hurt.

Giffords Law Center to Prevent Gun Violence. (2020). *Location restrictions.* https://lawcenter.giffords.org/gun-laws/policy-areas/guns-in-public/location-restrictions/.

Gramlich, J., and Schaeffer, K. (2019, October 22). *7 facts about guns in the U.S.* Pew Research Center. https://www.pewresearch.org/fact-tank/2019/10/22/facts-about-guns-in-united-states.

Harlan, E., and Thomas, A. G. (2017, December). Strategies for creating and implementing a zero-tolerance workplace violence policy. *Lexis Practice Advisor Journal.* https://www.lexisnexis.com/lexis-practice-advisor/the-journal/b/lpa/posts/strategies-for-creating-and-implementing-a-zero-tolerance-workplace-violence-policy.

Hawthorne, J. (2017, April 13). 7 reasons why your customers are NOT always right. *Business 2 Community.* https://www.business2community.com/customer-experience/7-reasons-customers-not-always-right-01816088.

Jacksch, V., and Klehe, U-C. (2016). Unintended consequences of transparency during personnel selection: Benefitting some candidates, but harming others? *International Journal of Selection and Assessment, 24*(1), 4–13. https://doi.org/10.1111/ijsa.12124.

Kalesan, B., Villarreal, M. D., Keyes, K. M., and Galea, S. (2016). Gun ownership and social gun culture. *Injury Prevention, 22*(3), 216–220. http://dx.doi.org/10.1136/injuryprev-2015-041586.

Larimore, J. (2017, January 3). Bill would hold business owners liable in shootings if they prohibit weapons. *Joplin Globe*. https://www.joplinglobe.com/news/local_news/bill-would-hold-business-owners-liable-in-shootings-if-they-prohibit-weapons/article_c32e8a15-5e8f-5954-8f6a-1cbf5ce0b36f.html.

Li, O. (2016, January 28). Can't bring your gun inside? This state might let you sue the store owner. *The Trace*. https://www.thetrace.org/2016/01/tennessee-gun-free-zones-bill/.

McGaughey, L. (2016, August 8). Texas businesses that ban guns should be liable if unarmed patrons are hurt, Dallas senator says. *Dallas News*. https://www.dallasnews.com/news/politics/2016/08/08/texas-businesses-that-ban-guns-should-be-liable-if-unarmed-patrons-are-hurt-dallas-senator-says/.

Miller, L. (1999). Workplace violence: Prevention, response, and recovery. *Psychotherapy, 36*(2), 160–169. http://dx.doi.org.ezp.waldenulibrary.org/10.1037/h0087694.

Mukherjee, B. (2018, February 5). 5 reasons why the customer is not always right. *Entrepreneur*. https://www.entrepreneur.com/article/308548.

National Center for Health Statistics, Centers for Disease Control. (2020). *FastStats: Death and mortality*. https://www.cdc.gov/nchs/fastats/deaths.htm.

NRA. (2020). *NRA gun safety rules*. https://gunsafetyrules.nra.org/.

Occupational Safety and Health Act, 29 U.S. Code § 654 (1970).

Occupational Safety and Health Administration (OSHA). (2020a). *Commonly used statistics*. https://www.osha.gov/data/commonstats.

OSHA. (2020b). *Recommended practices for safety and health programs*. https://www.osha.gov/shpguidelines/hazard-prevention.html.

Pozin, I. (2018, May 7). The customer isn't always right—Here's when. *Inc*. https://www.inc.com/ilya-pozin/the-customer-isnt-always-right-heres-when.html.

Ramchand, R., Pomeroy, A., and Arkes, J. (2009). *The effects of substance use on workplace injuries*. Rand Center for Health and Safety in the Workplace. https://www.rand.org/pubs/occasional_papers/OP247.html.

Runyan, C. W., Zakocs, R. C., and Zwerling, C. (2000). Administrative and behavioral interventions for workplace violence prevention. *American Journal of Preventive Medicine, 18*(4), 116–127. https://doi.org/10.1016/S0749-3797(00)00147-1.

Sabbath, E. K., Hawkins, S. S., and Baum, C. F. (2020). State-level changes in firearm laws and workplace homicide rates: United States, 2011 to 2017. *American Journal of Public Health, 110*(2), 230–236. https://doi.org/10.2105/AJPH.2019.305405.

Thelen, J. B. (2009, December 1). Is that a threat? An employer's response to threats by employees can prevent workplace violence. *HR Magazine*. Society for Human Resources Management. https://www.shrm.org/hr-today/news/hr-magazine/pages/1209legal.aspx.

Uren, A. (2020, February 18). GOP bill would allow gun owners to sue "gun-free zone" business in event of injury. *Bring Me the News—Minnesota.* https://bringmethenews.com/minnesota-news/gop-bill-would-allow-gun-owners-to-sue-gun-free-zone-businesses-in-event-of-injury.

U.S. Bureau of Labor Statistics. (2015). *Census of fatal occupational injuries (final data): Industry by event or exposure.* https://stats.bls.gov/iif/oshcfoi1.htm.

17

Rational-Based Policies and Irrational Actors

An Examination of Recent Tragedies at Domestic Military Installations, Houses of Worship, and Schools

David A. Mackey

The debate over the efficacy of gun-free zones has intensified in recent years. The issue might, quite possibly, have been one of the major political issues for the 2020 election but for the onset of a global pandemic and massive civil unrest following the death of George Floyd. On one end of the continuum, some individuals believe that declared gun-free zones convey a sense of safety based on the assumption that people are rational human beings who would be deterred or at least limited in their physical ability to carry out violence upon others due to a firearm prohibition. In this view, firearms are instruments of destruction in the hands of the public (while some individuals would also include the police [Luebbert, 2019]) and the mere presence of firearms poses an existential threat (Turner, 2016). Individuals would therefore be safer without the presence of firearms in the specific location. On the other end of the continuum, some individuals believe areas designated as gun-free zones can produce the disastrous unintended consequence of removing the ability of citizens to defend themselves from individuals bent on causing harm and injury. Consequently, individuals and communities are safer due to the presence of lawful firearms possession (Turner). This chapter examines several recent tragedies associated with gun-free zones with attention to domestic military installations, houses of worship, and schools with a focus on the assailant's underlining mental health factors.

There is no standard set by agreed definition related to the physical size or scope of area for a gun-free zone. These can include a single school building or multibuilding school campus, military installation, federal building, houses of worship, and private venues. Some of the settings are narrowly defined with limited public access points while others can extend over multiple buildings accessible by traversing semipublic and public space, to include city streets and sidewalks, as is the case with some urban-based institutions of higher education. Adding to the complexity, some gun-free zones are created by the government through law while others are created by nongovernmental entities such as houses of worship, any level of private school, hospitals, theaters, and a variety of businesses, restaurants, and bars. The prohibition often impacts employees as well as patrons and other visitor classifications. In addition, the Rand Corporation (2018) notes that federal law currently prohibits firearms on some of its property, such as that belonging to the U.S. Department of Veterans Affairs and the U.S. Postal Service. Likewise, there are over 400 national park sites comprised of over eighty million acres (National Park Service, 2020), and the National Park Service notes national parks follow the law for firearms possession of the state in which the specific park is located. Alternatively, carrying concealed on the twelve million acres managed by the U.S. Army Corps of Engineers currently requires written permission from the district commander (McCombie, 2020).

The Rand Corporation (2018) also notes the variations across states in firearm prohibition in bars and restaurants; some prohibitions for firearms in restaurants depend on the percentage of revenue generated by alcohol sales. The Giffords Law Center to Prevent Gun Violence (2021) details other locations states have deemed gun-free zones. For instance, a number of states have laws that prohibit firearms at any athletic event not related to firearms. The Giffords Law Center notes that some states add the provision that the athletic event is sponsored by a school or college while others add the condition that it is a professional athletic event. A firearms ban was upheld by the Texas Attorney General's Office at the Fort Worth Zoo because—although the zoo is on city property and would not usually be legally permitted to prohibit firearms—it is operated by a private entity (National Rifle Association, 2016).

Likewise, legitimate questions remain as to the effectiveness of gun-free zones to provide the blanket security that advocates of the concept would anticipate, while Cooke (2020) describes their anticipation as "idle aspiration" (para. 8). Writing in the National Rifle Association (NRA) publication *America's 1st Freedom*, Cooke identifies a very narrow application of the gun-free zone concept that he would describe as proper and reasonable, where "the 'zone' in question is small in size, sensitive in nature, entirely contained within an established perimeter and already being protected by men bearing arms" (para. 2). Restricted public access and extensive physical screening for weapons would reduce the likelihood of weapons being introduced into the area. Beyond the very narrow applications, most locations designated as gun free may fall well short of effective screening procedures and limited access to ensure the absence of weapons. In its review of research on the impact of gun-free zones, the Rand Corporation (2018) found no qualifying studies—that is, using research designs with sufficient methodological rigor—that determined whether such zones increased or decreased key outcomes.

SOCIAL CONTROL THEORY AND DETERRENCE THEORY

Gun-free zones draw from a particular view of human nature, and a number of criminological perspectives can provide some insight into gun-free zones and gun violence. Social control theory and deterrence theory share some similar characteristics in terms of their view of basic human nature although they depart in terms of the nature of social control necessary to constrain criminal behavior. Social control theory and deterrence theory take the view that individuals are motivated to naturally pursue their self-interest rather than act out of altruistic motives. In this hedonistic view, people are assumed to pursue self-benefit potentially at the expense of other individuals. Deterrence theory relies on the threat of formal punishments to keep people restrained while social control theory emphasizes the role of informal controls such as family, friends, career, and community standing. Both theoretical frameworks incorporate the view that people are rational and are able to contemplate the risks and rewards of their actions. Negative mental health factors can negatively impact rational decision-making and negate the deterrent aspects of formal sanctions and even the influential power of informal social control. As detailed below, several individuals responsible for firearms-related attacks in areas designated as gun free suffered from mental health concerns.

Another aspect of the gun-free zone issue is the negative impact a gun-free designation may have on otherwise law-abiding individuals, placing them in the dilemma of choosing to obey a law or policy, or exercising their Second Amendment right. This was the situation with the twenty-two-year veteran teacher who was also a sworn police reserve officer. He was suspended for having his service weapon in a locked cabinet in his California classroom (NRA, 2019). Consequences of gun-free zones can be more tragic, as was the case of Nicole "Nikki" Goeser (Dixon, 2020). Although she had a concealed handgun permit, Tennessee state law prohibits firearms in restaurants serving alcohol. A man who had been stalking her shot her husband seven times, killing him. Cooke (2020) contends that law-abiding citizens are negatively impacted by the gun-free designation more so than the violent offender. Lawful gun owners, as a lot, are more apt to follow applicable state and federal laws regarding purchasing, possession, and use of firearms. Individuals bent on committing violent crime, to include murder, may remain undeterred by laws restricting the mere spatial possession of a firearm. They may already be prohibited possessors due to felony convictions, drug use, domestic violence, and/or mental health preclusions to legal firearm ownership. The protection of human life hinges on the mere designation of an area being a gun-free zone; however, for the ill-intentioned actor, possessing a firearm in a gun-free zone may be only one of multiple statutes violated on his or her way to commit murder. Cooke sums this point up by stating, "The good people who try to follow the law, and who do not want to be convicted of a crime . . . are made into easier targets by their compliance" (para. 6).

SCHOOLS

Weapon possession by students in school negatively impacts school climate and the perception of safety in school. Students are likely to possess firearms due to fear of victimization associated with gangs, drugs, and victimization. The federal Gun-Free Schools Act of 1994 is particularly relevant to the discussion. The Gun-Free Schools Act requires that every state receiving federal funds under the Elementary and Secondary Education Act enact a state law requiring any student who brings a firearm to school to be expelled for not less than one year (Rand Corporation, 2018), as well as prohibiting the possession of a firearm within 1,000 feet of a school, with the exception of individuals licensed under state law. Political sentiments have shifted across several states, as Lott (2017) notes: twenty-five states now allow teachers and staff to carry concealed firearms at school.

The legality of concealed firearm possession on college campuses has been a debate for over a decade, marked with landmark legal decisions in the Oregon Court of Appeals and the Colorado State Supreme Court to allow concealed-carry holders the lawful ability to carry a concealed firearm on campus (Grasgreen, 2012). Cramer (2014) notes that the basis for firearm prohibition on campus may likely be the philosophy of *in loco parentis*, with an emphasis on policies "the system" would determine best serve the health and safety of its students. Legalizing firearms on campus is certainly not without criticism and concern. Cramer states that "[i]f an insane person walks onto a University of Oregon campus with a rifle, he will not be technically outside the law" (para. 2). The Bureau of Alcohol, Tobacco, Firearms, and Explosives (BATF) notes that a person adjudicated as a mental defective would be legally prohibited from possessing a firearm. Likewise, in Oregon, a commitment to a mental health facility or determination to be mentally ill with a court order barring firearms possession would result in the person being legally prohibited from purchasing or possessing a firearm. While

Idaho and Colorado allow students, staff, and faculty to legally carry a concealed firearm, Oregon has implemented its firearm ban on campus through a contract (Cramer, 2014). In effect, a vote of the majority to accept the contract and barter away their rights impacts the rights of the minority.

MILITARY INSTALLATIONS

Army Regulation 190–14 (1993) governs the possession of firearms for military law enforcement and security functions. The regulation also pertains to the use of force and training requirements for less-than-lethal weapons. The Army regulation clearly restricts firearms possession by Army personnel, civilians, and contractors. It also prohibits carrying non-government issued weapons or ammunition. The regulation applies to active Army, the U.S. Army Reserve, the Department of the Army civilian police and security forces. It applies to Army National Guard personnel only when called or ordered to active duty in a federal status. The regulation is intended to institute a universal policy, and local exceptions are not authorized without specific approval from the Department of the Army. Law enforcement, military operations, and authorized security functions are specifically addressed in the policy. Weapon possession for personal protection is granted on a limited case-by-case basis. (Some changes to this policy may be forthcoming [Crime Prevention Research Center, 2020]). Restrictions are imposed on military personnel and contractors who are taking prescription medication that would impair judgment or have consumed alcohol within eight hours from firearms possession. Army regulation 109-14 states that the "authorization to carry firearms will be issued only to qualified personnel when there is a reasonable expectation that life or Department of the Army (DA) assets will be jeopardized if firearms are not carried" (Section 1-5(a)).

At the time of this writing, recent shootings on military installations have occurred at the Naval Air Station Pensacola and at the Pearl Harbor Naval Shipyard. Hutchinson (2019) notes these events were recorded as the third and fourth attacks on a domestic U.S. base during 2019. Potential explanations for the four incidents in 2019 include domestic violence, retaliation, mental health issues, and potential terrorism. Hutchinson notes that, due to military budget decisions, the duties of security and first responders have increasingly been outsourced to private contractors as well as civilian law enforcement rather than military personnel. Threat assessments for military installations must include both external and internal threats. Gate security functions include controlling physical access to the facility to prevent unauthorized access and reducing the threat posed by external sources. While violence can be perpetrated by individuals who breach the perimeter of the facility, the internal threat to military personnel, contractors, and military dependents can be perpetrated by military personnel or individuals with legitimate access to the facility.

For instance, Mohammed Alshamrani, a Saudi Arabian airman who was on the Pensacola Naval Air Station for training, opened fire in a classroom at the base and killed four U.S. Naval airmen and wounded several others. Per Department of Defense policy, only security personnel are allowed to carry a weapon at the facility (Zarrell et al., 2019). Hutchinson (2019) notes that the violent event came to conclusion through the response of county sheriff personnel who responded to the scene and shot and killed the shooter. Hutchinson and Francescani (2019) note that, although he was a foreign national, the shooter was legally permitted to purchase a firearm due to what was described as a loophole in existing federal law. Investigations would reveal Alshamrani had extensive contacts with al-Qaida while in the United States, even up to the day before the attack (Tucker, 2020).

Shootings at military installations have been perpetrated by non-military personnel with legitimate access to the facility, such as government contractors and Department of Defense personnel. Illustrating this type of internal threat, in September 2013 Aaron Alexis shot and killed twelve people and injured four others at the Washington Navy Yard. NBC Washington (2013) attributed the violence to mental health issues, quoting "authorities" who said the shooter "held a delusional belief that he was being controlled or influenced by extremely low frequency, or ELF, electromagnetic waves" (para. 8).

There have been several firearms-related mass casualty events on military installations perpetrated by uniformed military personnel. For example, Camden (2014) reported that recently discharged airman Dean Mellberg opened fire at the Fairchild Air Force Base killing four people and injuring twenty-three. He was shot and killed by responding security personnel. Mellberg had been previously diagnosed with mental health conditions both during his initial training and during his duty assignment. He was eventually involuntarily discharged due to mental health concerns without a plan of mental health care. Camden reports that Mellberg returned to the hospital at Fairchild Air Force Base and began his rampage with targeted individuals who had diagnosed his mental health conditions while he was stationed there. Although he had been discharged, he was able to access the base hospital as it was outside the perimeter fence for the installation (Camden). The perimeter fence was later moved to encompass the base hospital.

Just over one year later, the military experienced another shooting with mental health connections. Smothers (1995) reports that, in 1995, Sergeant William J. Kreutzer Jr. set up ambush on nearly 1,300 unarmed soldiers of the

82nd Airborne Division as they set off on a four-mile run at Fort Bragg, North Carolina. The soldiers, wearing running shorts and T-shirts, were targeted as they exited a stadium in formation for their run. Kreutzer shot nineteen soldiers, killing one soldier, before he was subdued by soldiers who, like the shooter's intended targets, were unarmed. Kreutzer, who faced the death penalty, was later sentenced to life in prison. Brooks (2009) notes that Kreutzer had previously made threatening comments while on deployment, even citing the future location of the shooting, and that he was even nicknamed "Crazy Kreutzer," "Wild Bill," "Hannibal Lecter," or "Falling Down Bill." (*Falling Down* is a 1993 movie starring Michael Douglas.) Kreutzer attempted to reach out to superiors and a mental health professional the night before the shooting. His threats were not seen as credible, although some soldiers were briefed about the threat prior to the run. Brooks noted that armed military police officers arrived at the scene fifteen minutes after shooting commenced.

On November 5, 2009, Major Nidal Hasan, a U.S. Army psychiatrist, opened fire during a mobilization event at the Soldier Readiness Center at Fort Hood. Soldiers at the base were scheduled to deploy to Iraq and Afghanistan the following month. Gerhart and Rupar (2014) state, "Soldiers on all military installations, including Fort Hood, are not armed while on post, nor are they permitted to carry any privately owned firearms. Only law enforcement and security personnel are allowed to have weapons on post" (para. 1). Service members needed to have their privately owned weapons registered on post and secured in the arms room. Writing about the incident for the *Washington Post*, Hewitt et al. (2009) report that Hasan shot fifty-one people, killing thirteen. Hasan himself was shot and taken into custody. Police sergeant and SWAT member Kim Munley was shot twice in Hasan's apprehension. Hasan, who is Muslim, was in contact with an American-born Muslim cleric in Yemen. The investigation revealed Hasan had previously praised suicide bombers, and he had previously received an official reprimand for attempting to convert soldiers to Islam during counseling sessions for PTSD. He is also believed to have written online posts praising suicide bombers (Hewitt et al.). Speculation was raised as to why Hasan was not discharged from the military amid concerns about his mental stability and allegiance. Wolverton (2010) states that "directors of the program were concerned that any disciplinary action could be interpreted as discriminatory and motivated by religious intolerance and profiling" (para. 10). Wolverton notes that Hasan also delivered an inappropriate presentation at Walter Reed Army Medical Center; rather than on a medically relevant topic per the assignment instructions, he presented on the dangers of forcing U.S. soldiers who are Muslim into overseas conflict in Muslim nations. Roselle (2010) briefly describes the "under reaction" of authorities in both the Army and the FBI to the pattern of concerning behavior of Hasan leading up to the shooting.

Fort Hood was also the scene of another deadly shooting just a few years later. *Washington Post* reporter Lamothe (2015) notes that, in 2014, Specialist Ivan Lopez shot fifteen people, killing three and wounding twelve, before taking his own life as military police officers responded to the scene about ten minutes after shooting began. Lamothe reports that financial stress, recent familial deaths, and potential contradictory statements about previous military duty-related injuries impacting a potential disability claim were viewed as possible motivating factors.

Military recruiting centers present additional challenges due to facility vulnerabilities unlike traditional military bases. External threats to facilities and personnel are amplified since a recruiting center needs to be accessible to the public. In 2009, Abdulhakim Mujahid Muhammad opened fire at the Army-Navy Career Center in Little Rock, Arkansas, killing one service member and injuring another. A subsequent report by the U.S. Secret Service's National Threat Assessment Center (2015) identified Abdulhakim Muhammad as an ideologically motivated violent extremist and noted the correlations with his prior concerning behavior, to include disturbing patterns of communication prior to his violent outbursts. The Threat Assessment Center also noted that Abdulhakim Muhammad had two previous weapons-related contacts in the criminal justice system, including a "second weapons charge after he was found in possession of a loaded SKS rifle, two shotguns, a switchblade, and a small amount of marijuana" (section "Applying a Community-Level Investigative Approach"). This event was expunged from his record months later, and his first weapons offense, as a juvenile, was sealed. Therefore, he did not have an official criminal record for the two firearms events. Corroborative interviews conducted after the shooting noted the change in his personality, habits, and interests after his conversion to Islam. The investigation revealed that he reportedly smoked an ounce of marijuana a week around the time of his second weapons charge, and his conversion to Islam followed soon after his second weapons offense. He had previously traveled to Yemen where his stated intent was to learn Arabic, but the investigation revealed that he also experienced further radicalization, including learning about making explosives. He fired fifteen shots at two soldiers standing outside the recruiting center, striking both and killing one. He was taken into custody twelve minutes later, still in the possession of the weapons, ammunition, and Molotov cocktails. Two of the three weapons in his possession were purchased through private sales, and all three purchases occurred after his return from Yemen (National Threat Assessment Center). He was convicted of capital murder and several additional charges, and received twelve life sentences for the convictions. In another incident, in 2015 Muhammad Youssef Abdulazeez opened fire at a recruiting center in Chattanooga, Tennessee, killing five military personnel and wounding two others before being killed by police (NBC Washington, 2013). NBC Washington reported that the shooter had previously downloaded al-Qaeda materials.

HOUSES OF WORSHIP

Houses of worship in some states have been designated as gun-free zones by state statute. Baker (2018) notes that as of 2018 only two states had a prohibition on firearms possession in a house of worship while seven states and the District of Columbia required both a permit and permission of the pastor in order to lawfully carry a concealed weapon. Baker identifies the importance of training and preparation to thwart an active shooter, which certainly includes armed, trained parishioners. A number of law enforcement agencies have conducted concealed-carry training connected to protecting houses of worship. In 2012, Georgia's state statute prohibiting the possession of firearms in places of worship and in bars was upheld on appeal in the Eleventh Circuit Court of Appeals in the case of *GeorgiaCarry.org* (2012). In its decision, the court stated, "A place of worship's right, rooted in the common law, to forbid possession of firearms on its property is entirely consistent with the Second Amendment"(*GeorgiaCarry.org,* p. 35). Further, the court noted that "[w]e conclude that the Second Amendment does not give an individual a right to carry a firearm on a place of worship's premises against the owner's wishes because such right did not pre-exist the Amendment's adoption" (*GeorgiaCarry.org,* p. 40).

One recent event captured the essence of the right to armed self-defense and the concept of the good guy with a gun. On Sunday December 29, 2019, Keith Kinnunen opened fire during a church service at the West Freeway Church of Christ in White Settlement, Texas. Services at the church were live streamed, which provided a video and photographic account of the events. Reports indicated that five armed members of the congregation confronted the gunman within seconds of his first shot; two parishioners were killed; one parishioner shot and killed the assailant literally within moments of the first shot (Off Grid Survival, 2019). Kinnunen had a previous conviction for aggravated assault with a deadly weapon. Fedschun (2019) reported on Fox News that a Texas law was enacted during the same year that reaffirmed the legal right to carry firearms in houses of worship unless specifically prohibited by the specific location.

Another tragic incident occurred just a few years earlier in Texas on November 25, 2017, when gunman Devin Kelley opened fire at congregants at the First Baptist Church of Sutherland Springs, killing twenty-six people and wounding twenty others (Darrah, 2017). The shooter was previously court-martialed in 2012 for assaulting his wife and child, and was discharged from the U.S. Air Force. Stephen Willeford responded to the sounds of gunfire at the church from his home near the church. The shooting continued for so long that Willeford retrieved his firearm, loaded a magazine, and responded on foot. Arriving at the scene, Willeford yelled out to the shooter, who was still inside the church, deliberately calling him out of the church; by that time Kelley had fired fifteen 30-round magazines at unarmed parishioners. The active shooter was wearing body armor which provided protection from Willeford's first two rounds, which hit him center mass in the body armor. Willeford's next shots were placed to avoid the body armor protection. Writing in *Texas Monthly*, Mooney (2018) provides a rich description of Willeford's faith and character. Willeford was later an invited guest at the State of the Union address and also spoke at the NRA annual convention, where he stated, "We are the people that stand between the people that would do evil to our neighbors" (Mooney, p. 67).

The shooting at the First Baptist Church of Sutherland Springs by Devin Kelley led to an investigation and report by the Office of Inspector General (OIG) (2018) of the Department of Defense. The weapon Kelley used to commit the murders was purchased from a federal-firearms-licensed dealer although Kelley had previously been convicted by general court-martial of assault on his wife and stepson. This conviction for domestic assault should have disqualified Kelley from purchasing or possessing a firearm under federal law, but the conviction was never reported by the Air Force to the FBI for inclusion in the National Crime Information Center (NCIC) database. The OIG found that, in addition to the court-martial, Kelley had previously received thirteen disciplinary actions within a nine-month period. His Air Force service was marked by outpatient mental health counseling and two brief periods of in-patient mental health treatment stays, including an unauthorized absence during his second hospitalization. The investigation revealed allegations that he perpetrated acts of physical violence including threats with a handgun, sexual abuse, mental abuse, and both homicidal and suicidal threats. A Military Protection Order was issued during the investigation, preventing contact and communication with his wife except through his First Sergeant, but since the order was issued by his military unit and not by a court, the order would not have been entered into the NCIC database if submitted (OIG). At his court-martial, Kelley entered into an agreement to plead guilty to assault charges (wife and stepson) in return for dismissal of the firearms charge, a recommendation for sentencing, and a bad conduct discharge from the Air Force. He was sentenced to one year of incarceration, including time already served in pretrial detainment.

The investigation revealed four process points to submit his fingerprints to the FBI as well as two process points to submit his final disposition report to the FBI; each was missed (OIG, 2018). Allegations of sexual assault and criminal threats followed this conviction as well as a civilian conviction for cruelty to animals. The investigation revealed that four of his six weapons were purchased after his military conviction. The transactions were not flagged because his military conviction had never been submitted to the FBI. The OIG investigation concluded that 20 percent of the required fingerprint cards and nearly one-third of final disposition reports were not submitted as required to the FBI. The government later implicated the retailer Academy Sports as a responsible third party in a lawsuit since Colorado had a ban on magazines that hold more than fifteen rounds (Frame, 2019). Kelley used his Colorado driver's license to purchase the firearm in Texas. His widow stated that he was first rejected by another retailer due to the lack of state-issued ID (Associated Press, 2019).

PUBLIC SETTINGS: MALLS, THEATERS, BARS, AND HOSPITALS

Malls, theaters, bars, and hospitals can also be designated gun-free zones. Florida state law prohibits firearms in any establishment serving alcohol (Giffords Law Center, 2021). Omar Mateen disregarded the state law prohibiting firearms in night clubs. As a lone gunman, he shot and killed forty-nine people and wounded over fifty more. The timeline of the prolonged attack is detailed in the Community Oriented Policing Services (COPS) report (Straub et al., 2017). Writing for the Future of Freedom Foundation, LaRosa (2016) states, "He reloaded several times, made at least 16 telephone calls, and checked and even posted to his Facebook page numerous times!" (para. 2). The COPS report notes, "According to survivors, . . . he stood over the individuals lying on the floor and fired additional rounds into them at point-blank range without regard for whether they were alive or already dead" (p. 2). Omar Mateen called 911 and a local cable channel to "take credit" for the attack and proclaim his allegiance to Abu Baghdadi and ISIS.

RIGHT TO SELF-DEFENSE

Unfortunately, there are many other firearms-related instances of violence not detailed here. The assailants' motives are varied. The Crime Prevention Research Center (2020) compiles cases where concealed permit holders have stopped violent offenders during the commission of their crimes; the list is admittedly incomplete since events may not generate national news coverage. In very limited contexts, gun-free zones are reasonable and practical. These exceptions require extensive access control, screening, and security. These conditions are not likely to be available for most malls, theaters, and restaurants. Gun-free zones present obvious obstacles to the legal exercise of the inalienable right to self-defense (See et al., 2021). As noted above, there are instances of a "good guy with a gun" terminating an active shooter event more quickly than a law enforcement response to the scene. Likewise, lawful concealed carry also becomes the great equalizer benefitting women's right to self-defense. Lawful firearms provide the legal ability to fight back against those with evil intentions.

Law enforcement's specific duty to protect citizens from harm is not always a legal requirement for the police as confirmed by the United States Supreme Court (*Town of Castle Rock*, 2005). While civil cases have examined the role of manufacturers and sales of firearms used in crime, states' courts have also grappled with civil governmental liability for shootings in a gun-free zone. "[T]he Constitution does not require the government to protect citizens from privately created danger. It may, however, demand protection if the state disables people from protecting themselves; having rendered someone helpless, the state must supply the sort of defenses that the person could have provided on his own" (*Sandage et al.,* 2008).

REFERENCES

Army Regulation 190–14. (1993). Carrying of firearms and use of force for law enforcement and security duties. Headquarters Department of the Army. https://armypubs.army.mil/epubs/DR_pubs/DR_a/pdf/web/r190_14.pdf.

Associated Press. (2019, November 1). Church shooter's widow says 1st retailer denied him a gun. *CBS Austin*. https://cbsaustin.com/news/local/church-shooters-widow-says-1st-retailer-denied-him-a-gun.

Baker, B. (2018). *Concealed carry in church and houses of worship.* USA Carry. Retrieved from https://www.usacarry.com/concealed-carry-church-houses-worship/.

Brooks, D. (2009, March 18). Testimony: Threats by Kreutzer preceded shootings. *The Fayetteville Observer* (NC). Retrieved from https://www.fayobserver.com/news/.

Camden, J. (2014, June 15). In one week 20 years ago, Fairchild Air Force Base saw its darkest hours. *The Spokesman-Review* (Spokane, WA). https://www.spokesman.com/.

Cooke, C. C. W. (2020). Gun-free zones are victim zones. *America's 1st Freedom*, *21*(5), 24–26. National Rifle Association. https://www.americas1stfreedom.org/articles/2020/4/27/gun-free-zones-are-victim-zones/.

Cramer, C. E. (2014). Guns on campus: A history. *Academic questions: A publication of the National Association of Scholars*, *27*(4), 411–425. https://link.springer.com/journal/12129/volumes-and-issues/27-4.

Crime Prevention Research Center. (2020, January 4). Some Marines are now allowed to carry concealed on base. Crime Prevention Research Center.

Darrah, N. (2017, November 5). At least 26 killed in mass shooting at Texas church. Fox News. https://www.foxnews.com/us/at-least-26-killed-in-mass-shooting-at-texas-church.

Dixon, M. (2020, January 9). Nikki Goeser highlights the danger of "gun-free" zones in new book. *America's 1st Freedom*. National Rifle Association. https://www.americas1stfreedom.org/articles/2020/1/9/nikki-goeser-highlights-the-danger-of-gun-free-zones-in-new-book/.

Fedschun, T. (2019, December 31). Texas church shooting gunman grew angry in past over money requests, visited "multiple" times, minister says. Fox News. https://www.foxnews.com/us/texas-church-shooting-gunman-cash-requests-anger-vists-minister.

Frame, C. (2019, October 17). Federal government implicates Academy Sports in Sutherland Springs mass shooting. *All Things Considered: Texas Public Radio*. https://www.tpr.org/post/federal-government-implicates-academy-sports-sutherland-springs-mass-shooting.

GeorgiaCarry.org, Inc., The Baptist Tabernacle of Thomaston Georgia, Inc., Edward Stone, Jonathan Wilkins v. The State of Georgia, Upson County Georgia, Governor of Georgia, County Manager Kyle Hood. No. 11-10387. (11th Cir., 2012). Appeal [decision on appeal to 11th Circuit]. https://law.justia.com/cases/federal/appellate-courts/ca11/11-10387/11-10387-2012-07-20.html.

Gerhart, A., and Rupar, T. (2014, April 2). Here are the rules on carrying firearms on Fort Hood. *Washington Post*. https://www.washingtonpost.com/news/post-nation/wp/2014/04/02/here-are-the-rules-on-carrying-firearms-on-fort-hood/.

Giffords Law Center to Prevent Gun Violence. (2021). *Location restrictions: State by state*. https://lawcenter.giffords.org/gun-laws/state-law/50-state-summaries/location-restrictions-state-by-state/.

Grasgreen, A. (2012, March 6). Campus gun ban struck down. *Inside Higher Ed*. https://www.insidehighered.com/news/2012/03/06/state-supreme-court-rules-colorado-regents-cant-ban-guns.

Hewitt, B., Bartolomeo, J., Atlas, D., Dennis, A., Keating, S., Bass, S., Lang, A., Braiker, B., and Rodriguez, B. (2009, November 23). Massacre at Fort Hood.

People, 72(21), 58. https://people.com/archive/massacre-at-fort-hood-vol-72-no-21/.

Hutchinson, B. (2019, December 11). Fatal shootings at US military bases highlight unexpected and growing threat—Insiders with access badges. ABC News. https://abcnews.go.com/US/fatal-shootings-us-military-bases-highlight-unexpected-growing/story?id=67597032.

Hutchinson, B., and Francescani, C. (2019, December 10). Saudi pilot used gun loophole to buy murder weapon used in shooting at Pensacola air base, FBI says. ABC News. https://abcnews.go.com/US/saudi-pilot-gun-loophole-buy-murder-weapon-shooting/story?id=67630953.

Lamothe, D. (2015, January 23). Army details the strange, downward spiral of Fort Hood shooter Ivan Lopez. *Washington Post.* https://www.washingtonpost.com/news/checkpoint/wp/2015/01/23/army-details-the-downward-spiral-of-the-fort-hood-shooter-ivan-lopez/.

LaRosa, B. D. (2016, October 1). Lessons of the Orlando massacre. *The Future of Freedom Foundation*. https://www.fff.org/explore-freedom/article/lessons-orlando-massacre/.

Lott, J. R., Jr. (2017, May 18). Shooting down myths of "gun-free zones" in schools. *Orange County Register*. https://www.ocregister.com/2017/05/18/shooting-down-myths-of-gun-free-zones-in-schools/.

Luebbert, L. A. (2019, October 20). Anti-gunners create broad fear of firearms—Even of armed police. *America's 1st Freedom.* National Rifle Association. https://www.americas1stfreedom.org/articles/2019/10/20/anti-gunners-create-broad-fear-of-firearms-even-of-armed-police/.

McCombie, B. (2020, May 5). U.S. Army Corps of Engineers needs to hear from you about its firearms policy. *America's 1st Freedom.* National Rifle Association. https://www.americas1stfreedom.org/articles/2020/5/5/us-army-corps-of-engineers-needs-to-hear-from-you-about-its-firearms-policy/.

Mooney, M. J. (2018, November). The hero of the Sutherland Springs shooting is still reckoning with what happened that day. *Texas Monthly.* Retrieved from https://www.texasmonthly.com/articles/stephen-willeford-sutherland-springs-mass-murder/.

National Park Service. (2020). *Frequently asked questions.* Retrieved on June 7, 2020, from https://www.nps.gov/aboutus/faqs.htm.

National Rifle Association. (2016, December 2). Texas AG: Fort Worth Zoo can continue banning carry. *America's 1st Freedom.* https://www.americas1stfreedom.org/articles/2016/12/2/ftf/texas-ag-fort-worth-zoo-can-continue-banning-carry/.

National Rifle Association. (2019, May 15). Teacher/hero survivor of mass shooting suspended for having concealed carry in locked cabinet. *America's 1st Freedom.* https://www.americas1stfreedom.org/articles/2019/5/15/hero-survivor-of-mass-shooting-suspended-for-having-concealed-carry-in-locked-cabinet/.

National Threat Assessment Center, United States Secret Service. (2015). *Investigating ideologically inspired violent extremists: Local partners are an asset, a case study on Abdulhakim Mujahid Muhammad.* U.S. Department of

Homeland Security, United States Secret Service. Retrieved from https://www.hsdl.org/?view&did=788760.

NBC Washington. (2013, September 16; updated December 6, 2019). *A history of shootings at military installations in the U.S.* https://www.nbcwashington.com/news/local/a-history-of-shootings-at-military-installations-in-the-us/1953672/.

Off Grid Survival. (2019, December 29). *Church mass shooting in Texas stopped by good guy with gun.* https://offgridsurvival.com/church-mass-shooting-in-texas-stopped-by-good-guy-with-gun/.

Office of Inspector General, U.S. Department of Defense. (2018, December 6). *Report of investigation into the United States Air Force's failure to submit Devin Kelley's criminal history information to the Federal Bureau of Investigation: Report no. DODIG-2019-030.* https://www.oversight.gov/report/dod/report-investigation-united-states-air-force%E2%80%99s-failure-submit-devin-kelley%E2%80%99s-criminal.

Rand Corporation. (2018). *The effects of gun-free zones.* Retrieved from https://www.rand.org/research/gun-policy/analysis/gun-free-zones.html.

Roselle, B. (2010). Caution under-reaction: Lessons from Ft. Hood. *T+D*, *64*(4), 50–52.

Sandage, et al., v. Board of Commissioners of Vanderburgh County, et al. No. 08-1540. 2008.

See, E. S., Bellas, C. M., and See, S. A. (2021). The firearm debate: The legality, morality, and ethics of firearms ownership. In D. A. Mackey, and K. M. Elvey (Eds.), *Society, ethics, and the law: A reader,* 93–103. Jones and Bartlett.

Smothers, R. (1995, 28 October). Sniper kills 1, wounds 18 at army base. *New York Times*, p. 11. https://www.nytimes.com/1995/10/28/us/sniper-kills-1-wounds-18-at-army-base.html.

Straub, F., Cambria, J., Castor, J., Gorban, B., Meade, B., Waltemeyer, D., and Zeunik, J. (2017). *Rescue, response, and resilience: A critical incident review of the Orlando public safety response to the attack on the Pulse Nightclub.* Critical Response Initiative, Office of Community Oriented Policing Services, Department of Justice. https://cops.usdoj.gov/RIC/Publications/cops-w0857-pub.pdf.

Town of Castle Rock, Colorado v. Gonzales, et al., 545 U.S. 748 (2005). https://supreme.justia.com/cases/federal/us/545/748/.

Tucker, E. (2020, May 18). FBI: Shooter at Pensacola Navy base coordinated with al-Qaida. *Military Times.* https://www.militarytimes.com/news/your-military/2020/05/18/official-fbi-finds-link-between-pensacola-gunman-al-qaida/.

Turner, C. (2016, June 2). The vulnerability index: What's your VX at the NRA annual meetings? *America's 1st Freedom.* National Rifle Association. https://www.americas1stfreedom.org/articles/2016/6/2/the-vulnerability-index-whats-your-vx-at-the-nra-annual-meetings/.

Wolverton, J., II. (2010). Major Nidal Malik Hasan: An officer and a jihadist. *New American, 26*(2), 21–23. The John Birch Society. https://thenewamerican.com/major-nidal-hasan-an-officer-and-jihadist/.

Zarrell, M., Martinez, L., Margolin, J., and Katersky, A. (2019, December 6). 4 dead in shooting incident at Pensacola naval base; suspect was Saudi national, officials say. ABC News. https://abcnews.go.com/US/active-shooter-naval-base-ensacola/story?id=67542409.

18

The Effect of School Mass Shootings

Should We Be Arming Our Teachers and Students?

Nicole A. Shoenberger

The media has helped perpetuate the myth that schools are unsafe for kids. It is true that some of the deadliest mass shootings have occurred within the last thirteen years (e.g., Las Vegas, Orlando, Newtown, etc.) (Kaysiyannis et al., 2018). It is also true that students are more likely to be killed outside of school than inside one (Cornell, 2018). Violence in schools is not a new phenomenon; however, the mass shooting at Columbine High School in Colorado in 1999 made school shootings a mainstay in the media. A consequence of our everyday induction to school violence is to stretch how far schools will go with reactionary solutions. Reactions to school shootings have led to zero-tolerance policies, metal detectors, security cameras, police resource officers, locker searches, active shooter drills, see-through backpacks, and bulletproof backpacks.

A controversial argument has been made to arm teachers. These efforts are becoming a reality for schools. After the Parkland shooting, Marjory Stoneman Douglas High School Public Safety Commission pushed for arming teachers in efforts to increase school safety (Smart, 2019). In response to the Parkland shootings, President Trump suggested that teachers who know how to use guns should be able to receive a permit to carry a concealed firearm. He further indicated he would mark federal funding to train teachers who were qualified to carry a firearm (Proulx, 2018). In Wisconsin, a bill was introduced to allow anyone who has a concealed firearm license to carry a firearm inside private schools (WTMJ-TV, 2018). A sheriff in Ohio has offered to hold training for teachers who are interested in learning how to use firearms; he states he has received multiple applications from teachers (Sparling, 2018). An Ohio group called the Buckeye Firearms Association has created a program, Faster Saves Lives, after the mass shooting at Sandy

Hook. This program exists in eleven states and has trained over 1,300 school-related workers in firearm use (Saul, 2018). According to the Education Commission of the States (2019), ten states have passed legislation that allows for concealed carry of firearms on school property. The push for arming teachers is not new, nor is it fading away. However, questions remain. Would arming teachers reduce school shootings? Is it safe to arm teachers? Do teachers, educational associations, parents, or students support the idea?

These questions are difficult to answer. Simply, there is not much data on armed teachers inside schools. Though some schools allow guns on the premises of the school, this does not mean teachers are carrying guns into their classrooms. This chapter reviews some of the information we do know. Specifically, this chapter starts with what we know about arming everyday citizens and whether or not it deters gun violence from occurring. Do right-to-carry permits decrease violent acts of crime, and are people using guns in self-defense to protect those they love? This chapter will also review reports by the Federal Bureau of Investigation concerning active shooters in the United States and whether having an armed citizen stops mass shootings from occurring. Evidence of current school resource officers and teachers mishandling guns while in school, potential suicides, and trauma will also be addressed. Finally, the chapter will review whether or not teachers, students, and parents want teachers to be armed. Overall, the information presented in this chapter does not support arming teachers inside schools.

GOOD GUYS WITH GUNS

Gun rights activists often state that "good guys with guns" reduce crime, make our society safer, and could stop a mass shooting from occurring (Ayres & Donohue, 2003). Given that criminals will carry guns whether it is legal or not, gun activists feel gun control laws only protect criminals and hurt law-abiding citizens by stripping their ability to protect themselves (Ayres & Donohue). The theory is that, if citizens cannot carry weapons, criminals will be less fearful to commit crime and therefore crime will increase; however, if the good guy has a gun, criminals will be less likely to commit crime out of fear that the victim is armed (Ayres & Donohue). According to this line of thinking, not allowing teachers to carry firearms in school will make those who might consider committing an act of crime on a school campus less fearful to do so because no one could retaliate or stop them.

Gun activists often point to studies conducted by John R. Lott Jr., a gun researcher, who has argued that crime rates, specifically homicides by guns, have decreased at the same time concealed carry permits increased in the 1990s (Lott, 1997, 1998). Lott contends crime rates in states that passed right-to-carry laws experienced even bigger decreases in crime than states without right-to-carry laws (Lott, 1997, 1998; Lott & Mustard, 1997). These drops in crime are argued to be a direct deterrence effect from criminals being more fearful of committing crime in right-to-carry states (Lott, 1997, 1998). Bartley and Cohen (1998) agree with Lott and Mustard's assessment. They argue that even though there is model uncertainty (a major critique of the work: see Black and Nagin [1998]), the deterrence effect of right-to-carry laws cannot be dismissed in their findings (Bartley & Cohen, 1998). The National Rifle Association (NRA) and gun rights activists have used the work of Lott to argue for the need to expand right-to-carry laws while attempting to push legislators to allow guns on school premises (see, e.g., NRA, 2015).

Though Bartley and Cohen (1998) provide support for Lott, far more researchers have critiqued the argument of good-guys-with-guns than support it. Most researchers argue that Lott's analysis not only fails to properly account for the reduction of crime but also that many of Lott's assertions do not make criminological sense. Alschuler (1997) points out that some of Lott's arguments are counter to standard arguments about crime. For instance, Alschuler observes that Lott and Mustard (1997) argue both rural and urban counties were negatively associated with crime. The typical assumption is that urban counties have higher crime rates compared to rural counties; this makes the finding of both urban and rural counties being negatively associated with crime suspect. Further, according to Lott and Mustard, young Black men were negatively associated with property crime. Again, when using UCR data, we tend to find young Black men positively associated with property crime. Lott and Mustard argue that stranger killings increased while domestic killings decreased. However, the assumption that your everyday citizen was carrying a gun would make Lott's argument stronger if stranger killings decreased rather than increased.

One of the harder-hitting critiques of Lott's work comes from Black and Nagin (1998). Black and Nagin disaggregate Lott's data to analyze crime patterns by state. They illustrate that in six out of seven categories tested by Lott and Mustard (1997), crime increased for some states, while in other states there was a decrease. Black and Nagin argue that if right-to-carry laws were effective, they should have a consistent effect in all states. To further the argument, the data do not show immediate negative effects in the states that see a decrease. Black and Nagin reveal a delayed effect of almost four years. If one parses out the data past the years that Lott and Mustard analyze, one sees decreases in states that did not adopt right-to-carry laws (Ayres & Donohue, 2003). And, if one removes Florida from Lott and Mustard's analysis, there is no statistically significant effect in six of the seven categories tested against right-to-carry laws (Black & Nagin, 1998).

Ayres and Donohue (2003) flip the assumption that arming everyday citizens would decrease crime. Instead, they argue that, if criminals know citizens are carrying weapons, they might also start carrying weapons. In theory, armed criminals may discharge the weapon more quickly if they fear threatened by a potential victim who may or may not have a gun. Further, Ayres and Donohue argue people might interject guns more into everyday arguments if everyday citizens possess a firearm (see also Zimring & Hawkins, 1997). In an actual case, a person fighting with his roommate over rent discharged his firearm into the back of his roommate's head, killing him in the process (Ayres & Donohue, 2003). Not only could guns be used in regular disputes, but also if more people have guns because of more permits, these guns could also be stolen and used by criminals (Ayres & Donohue), misused by kids in the home, or used by a person who might want to commit a mass shooting in a school. In theory, having more guns in homes could increase crime.

Crime rates are also very fickle things. Crime trended upward from the 1970s to the 1990s. In the 1990s the United States experienced an overall decrease in crime. However, there were flutters. Robbery, for instance, increased in the late 1970s, then decreased at the beginning of the 1980s and increased again until the mid-1990s (Ayres & Donohue, 2003). This interesting pattern for robbery cannot be explained by the many factors attributed to crime patterns, and it is difficult to attribute this pattern to the addition of right-to-carry laws (Ayres & Donohue). Ayres and Donohue note that the largest dip in robbery rates between 1977 to 1999 occurred in states that did not adopt right-to-carry laws. They are not claiming that it is because these states did not adopt such laws. Their argument, however, illustrates that the decrease in crime rates for various crimes can be attributed to other factors.

In 2005, a report issued by the National Research Council (NRC) stated one could not reasonably argue right-to-carry laws increased or decreased crime (Wellford et al., 2005). Aneja, Donohue, and Zhang (2011) extended the NRC's research on right-to-carry laws by six years. They found no statistical support for the argument that right-to-carry laws decreased crime. Instead, Aneja and colleagues found aggravated assault increased in right-to-carry states. Further, they argue right-to-carry laws may increase gun assault by 33 percent. Looking at 1999–2010, these researchers found that models also indicated a possible increase in murder due to right-to-carry laws. Though Aneja et al. found associations with increases in robbery and murder, Phillips et al. (2015) found no correlations between right-to-carry laws and crime—in both directions; instead, they argue increases in gun dealers affect increases in crime rates.

Though right-to-carry laws are not specific to teachers, we can extrapolate from the data. Past research illustrates that giving a good guy a gun has not deterred violent crime. In fact, crime patterns have changed for various reasons over time, regardless of whether the state has extended right-to-carry laws. If there is no solid evidence to show that a good guy with a gun deters people from committing crimes such as assault, robbery, or murder, how is it possible to argue that arming teachers would stop an assault at a school?

EVIDENCE OF GOOD GUYS USING THEIR GUNS TO STOP ACTIVE SHOOTERS

Much of the information offered so far has been research on crime patterns and right-to-carry laws. But what about the good guys who do have guns? Do they use them in self-defense, and have they used them to stop an active shooter? Kleck and Getz (1996) surveyed 5,000 participants and showed that 66 percent of respondents stated they had used firearms defensively. Just as Lott and Mustard (1997) became the standard for right-to-carry laws, Kleck and Getz's paper became the standard evidence touted by the National Rifle Association (NRA) for the need for more guns in ordinary citizens' hands. The NRA (2015) claims there are at least 760,000 defensive gun uses per year in the United States, and it uses research provided by Kleck and Getz to support arming ordinary Americans.

Though the research by Kleck and Getz (1996) sounds plausible, Hemenway (1997) refutes the research for two reasons. First, Hemenway argues that Kleck and Getz's research is subject to social desirability. Specifically, he argues those who purchase a gun because they feel they will use it for self-defense will be more likely to state this is exactly what has happened. In such a manner, the gun owner will be commended for his purchase and use of his firearm. This argument is then compounded when Kleck and Getz somehow find the ability to research the "needle in a haystack" (p. 1431): Kleck and Getz claim to have found enough respondents who had used a gun in self-defense to estimate a general pattern of self-defense gun use. Previously, researchers had only been able to cite the incidence of self-defense gun use at 1 percent, not 66 percent (Hemenway, 1997; Hemenway & Solnick, 2015). In a report from the National Research Council, Reiss and Roth (1992) agree that Kleck and Getz's arguments are exaggerated, and they argue that questions about self-defense in Kleck and Getz's study would not be defined as such by others. Further, data pulled from law enforcement, media, and government sources and aggregated into the Gun Violence Archive (2019) simply do not provide gun use data that could verify the claims of Kleck and

Getz. In sum, Kleck and Getz drew near impossible conclusions about self-defense with guns from their survey.

In 2014, researchers for the Federal Bureau of Investigation (FBI) studied active shooter incidents in the United States from 2000–2013 (Blair & Schweit, 2014). In their study for the FBI, Blair and Schweit pinpointed 160 cases defined as active shooter incidents. The report stated that 90 of the occurrences stopped due to the shooter initiating the end of the event by either committing suicide, stopping shooting, or fleeing the scene. In 21 of these events, the shooter was stopped by an unarmed citizen; two of these unarmed defenders were off-duty police officers. Of the 21 cases stopped by unarmed citizens, 11 were stopped by principals, teachers, or school staff who were able to confront the shooter toward the end of the shooting spree. In 5 incidents, the shooting ended with an armed individual exchanging fire with the shooter; however, only one of these individuals used a concealed-carry firearm (Blair & Schweit).

The FBI researchers Blair and Schweit (2014) also examined the various locations of the active shooter incidents. The largest group (46%) of shootings occurred in areas defined as commercial, such as businesses and malls. Educational environments were the second most common site (24.4%) of active shootings. Though second in occurrence, educational settings had the highest fatality rates. Of the shootings that occurred at higher education institutes, five shooters were arrested by police, four committed suicide, two were killed by police who arrived on the scene, and one shooter left the location and was arrested by police at a secondary location. Shootings that occurred in both high school and middle school involved shooters being apprehended by police arriving at the school after employees of the school detained the shooter without the use of a firearm. When reviewing the FBI report, we see that out of all of these active shootings at schools, not one of the shooters was detained by an armed guard or an armed citizen. In the report, Blair and Schweit direct attention to learning how to prevent these active shootings from occurring and do not offer the advice to arm teachers or personnel inside schools.

One common but incorrect assumption about active shootings at schools is that no one on the school premise was armed. If there were an armed officer or employee, it is assumed that the active shooter would have been stopped. Klarevas (2016) examined 111 active school shooting attempts from 1966 to 2015. Of these shootings, Klarevas found that only 18 took place at a school where firearms were *not* allowed on the premises. This means 93 of the 111 active shooter situations took place at a school where firearms were legally allowed for certain personnel, and this fact alone did not deter the active shooter from engaging in the shooting.

Livingston, Rossheim, and Hall (2019), analyzing data from 1999–2018, conclude that having an armed guard at a school was not associated with reducing the severity of the school shooting. Although active shootings occurred at schools that had trained armed guards on the premises, such as Marjory Stoneman Douglas High School in Florida and Santa Fe High School in Texas, the armed guards were unable to stop the armed shooter from attacking students and school personnel (Livingston et al.). Further, Klarevas (2016) observes that most of the shootings he reviewed ended within ten minutes from the start, providing evidence that an active shooter does not need much time to inflict mass casualties and that many public spaces such as schools are difficult to defend regardless of the presence of an armed defender.

Although the NRA claims that people need guns to protect themselves, data on gun use in the United States does not demonstrate self-defense use of guns. Kleck and Getz (1996) found that people were likely to use their firearms in self-defense; however, most researchers dismiss these findings (see Hemenway, 1997; Hemenway & Solnick, 2015; Gun Violence Archive, 2019; Reiss & Roth, 1992). Further, the FBI researchers Reiss and Roth have shown that, in active shooting situations, most shooters are not subdued by a good guy with a gun: the shooter either commits suicide, stops shooting, or flees the scene. Lastly, even looking at active shootings that occurred in schools, we see that active shooters have knowingly attacked schools with armed personnel and have succeeded. In many cases, it has been unarmed teachers and staff who have stopped the attack. The biggest point to highlight is the fact that even trained, armed guards or personnel did not stop an active shooting inside a school. If they are unable to do so, how can we make the assumption that untrained or inexperienced gun owners (teachers) would be able to stop an active shooter?

COLLATERAL CONSEQUENCES OF GUNS IN SCHOOLS

When we think of guns in schools, we tend to concentrate on the good guy being able to stop an attack at a school. However, when we only concentrate on the perceived benefit of guns in schools, we may neglect the possibility that guns and those who possess the guns may have collateral consequences on the kids who attend those schools. The question to ask is this: If data show guns probably do not stop active shooters, are the unintended negative consequences of having guns in the school worth it?

Just as with truancy and other status offenses, having armed guards and other protective factors makes parents feel safer about their children. This is based on the perception that having an armed guard automatically makes the school safer. Intrabartola (2019) reports the analysis by a Rutgers University professor, Matthew Mayer, who argues that policies such as armed guards, cameras, metal detectors, and armed teachers merely give the impression that a school has a hardened stance on violence inside the schools, when in truth these measures result from the university administration checking off security measures from a list instead of addressing the real issues behind school violence. This wrong impression, that our schools are safer because of armed guards or teachers, indirectly steers us away from concentrating on issues in the home and in underfunded schools, and the reasons that students may feel the need to attack schools in the first place. As Lankford (2015) has asserted, active shootings inside schools are a uniquely American phenomenon. He argues that shooters tend to attack social systems in which they feel failed or mistreated in some way. Lankford attributes this strain to the pressure on adolescents to achieve the American Dream and the failure to do so in the school system. By putting the focus of violence prevention on armed teachers and guards, we neglect the issue of why a student might feel wronged by a school and feel the only way to right that wrong is through a mass shooting (Lankford).

Though it is believed that armed officers know what to do, their actions with their firearms in some schools have come into question. A Giffords report showed both teachers and armed guards mishandling their firearms while in school (Giffords Law Center, 2021). The report noted 100 cases in which guns were mishandled or misplaced by adults in schools (Giffords Law Center, 2021). Below are a few of the reported cases of adults mishandling their responsibility of having a gun while at a school (Giffords Law Center, 2021):

- One teacher dropped their gun while doing a cartwheel.
- A student was able to grab a gun from an officer while the officer was subduing another student.
- A teacher accidentally discharged a firearm in class while conducting a safety demonstration.
- A resource officer left his gun in a bathroom where a student found it.
- One district employee did not notice that his gun fell out of the holster on a bus seat. It was later found by a student.
- A student picked up a purse that contained a gun and bullets on a school bus.
- A Transportation Director who has been trained and allowed to carry a gun on school property left an unlocked case with a gun near her desk.
- A firearm was stolen from a teacher by two students.

If mishandling guns was not enough, in multiple incidents a school employee brought a firearm to a school to commit suicide (Giffords Law Center, 2019). One school employee barricaded himself inside of a bathroom with a handgun and threatened to kill himself; ten hours later, he surrendered to the police (Ritchie, 2017). Another teacher shot himself in his classroom before students arrived and sought help from fellow faculty members (Park, 2017). Lastly, a school resource officer in Baltimore County fatally shot himself in the basement of the school in the middle of the day; no students witnessed the shooting, but faculty were the ones who found him (Campbell & Anderson, 2018). Though students did not witness these events, they all could cause emotional and psychological trauma for students and faculty. The very reason for allowing guns in schools is to reduce violence; however, events like these increase the risk of violence in schools.

OTHER FACTORS TO CONSIDER

If guns are allowed in schools, training and experience with firearms need to be a top priority. Matthew Mayer, the Rutgers professor, argues that at least veteran police officers (who are sometimes hired as armed guards at schools) are trained in how to think in a dangerous and chaotic situation (Intrabartola, 2019). He points out that teachers, however, are trained to teach. They are not trained for these types of situations. Even if they receive firearms training, they have minimal firearms experience and could act on emotion instead of calculated risk. Mayer argues that it is a possibility that a teacher could accidentally shoot an innocent bystander, faculty member, or student (Intrabartola).

Secondly, it would be a failure not to address the possibility of bias in the teacher-student relationship. Studies show teachers are more likely to discipline students of color—either through detention, suspension, or expulsion (Blake et al., 2015; Gregory & Weinstein, 2008). If teachers are expected to carry a firearm into their classrooms and a disagreement or escalation of an issue starts, we have no evidence to show that a teacher with a racial bias (overt or implicit) would not use the weapon inappropriately in the classroom. In the current policing climate in which the United States is addressing this very issue with police, it would be negligent to expect teachers to know how to better handle behavioral de-escalation situations while carrying a firearm.

Some politicians may feel that arming teachers is a good solution to violence in schools; however, parents, students, and the teachers do not agree. The Giffords Law Center (2019) reports that 70 percent of students and 70 percent of parents are in opposition to arming teachers in schools. In response to the Trump administration's proposal to arm teachers, President Lily Eskelsen García of the National Education Association stated that arming teachers would be "ill-conceived, preposterous, and dangerous" (Gonzales, 2018). García argues that arming teachers does not prevent violence and that teachers would feel uncomfortable with guns in schools. García also asserts, "Teachers should be teaching, not acting as armed security guards, or receiving training to become sharpshooters" (Gonzales).

The National Education Association also surveyed teachers across the United States (Gonzales, 2018). The majority of teachers (82 percent) said they would not carry a firearm. This included teachers who own a gun. More than half (64 percent) stated they would not feel safe if teachers or other personal carried guns to school. Furthermore, 69 percent felt that arming teachers is an ineffective strategy for preventing gun violence in schools (Gonzales).

If schools decide to arm teachers, teachers will have a firearm in possession while traveling to and from the school. They would also be responsible for proper gun safety in the home. Teachers with a gun at home could increase the risk of the gun being used improperly in the home (e.g., being found by a child), as evidence shows that guns in the home increase the risk of gun death for all household members (Anglemyer et al., 2014; Hemenway, 2011). In one study, people who possessed a gun were 2.55 times more likely to be shot in an assault than those who did not possess a gun; people who possessed a gun were also 3.54 times more likely to be fatally shot (Branas et al., 2009). In opportunities where the victim had a chance to resist, those who had a gun were 2.92 times more likely to be shot (Branas et al.). Branas and colleagues speculate that possessing a gun may falsely empower the person to escalate a situation; furthermore, those who carry a firearm might enter into riskier situations, which they might have avoided if they were not carrying a firearm. The researchers also suggest that those who carry a gun into a situation that would otherwise be gun-free could have their weapon used against them (Branas et al.).

Lastly, it is also important to address the fact that kids are safer inside schools than outside them. In the last twenty years, 1,480 students have been killed outside schools (Cornell, 2018). Students are 67 times more likely to be murdered outside a school than inside it; although there have been 300 school shootings since 2012, there been approximately 275 shootings outside of schools *per day* since 2012 (Cornell). Though the media portrays school shootings as everyday occurrences, on average a schoolchild in the United States more likely to be a victim of a shooting at a restaurant, a public park, home, or a shopping center (Cornell; Borum et al., 2010).

CONCLUSION

School shootings are devastating, and the United States experiences active shooters in schools more than other countries (Lankford, 2015). The ways in which schools in America have dealt with school shootings and violence have mostly been reactionary. We have added metal detectors and armed guards/police, implemented zero-tolerance policies, conducted locker sweeps, funded active-shooter drills, and advised students to invest in bulletproof backpacks. Arming teachers is another avenue that has been pursued by some schools but caught fire as the Trump administration stated it would support trainings for teachers. Given that teachers are abundantly present in our schools, arguments for arming teachers to stop active shooters have raised a loud chorus. After all, aren't teachers the good guys we would want to give guns to?

Schools should make students feel safe. There is little evidence that putting guns in the hands of teachers would increase school safety or make students feel safer while at school. Coupled with the fact that active shooter incidents are overwhelmingly rare, there is not much information out there that supports arming teachers. On the contrary, it might be more warranted to increase mental health access for students and to increase support for teachers so that they can teach and be a mentor for students who may need help.

REFERENCES

Alschuler, A. W. (1997). Two guns, four guns, six guns, more guns: Does arming the public reduce crime? *Symposium on Juvenile Crime: Policy Proposals on Guns & Violence, Gangs, & Drugs*, *31*(2), 365–373. https://scholar.valpo.edu/vulr/vol31/iss2/3/.

Aneja, A., Donohue, J. J., III, and Zhang, A. (2011). The impact of right to carry laws and the NRC report: Lessons for the empirical evaluation of law and policy. *American Law and Economics Review*, *13*(2), 565–632. https://www.jstor.org/stable/42705603?seq=1#metadata_info_tab_contents.

Anglemyer, A., Horvath, T., and Rutherford, G. (2014). The accessibility of firearms and risk for suicide and homicide victimization among household members: A systematic review and meta-analysis. *Annals of Internal Medicine, 160*(2), 101–110. https://doi.org/10.7326/M13-1301.

Ayres, I., and Donohue, J. J. III. (2003). Shooting down the "more guns, less crime" hypothesis. *Stanford Law Review*, *55*(4), 1193–1313. https://www.jstor.org/stable/i252797.

Bartley, W. A., and Cohen, M. A. (1998). The effect of concealed weapons laws: An extreme bound analysis. *Economic Inquiry*, *36*(2), 258–265. https://doi.org/10.1111/j.1465-7295.1998.tb01711.x.

Black, D. A., and Nagin, D. S. (1998). Do right-to-carry laws deter violent crime? *Journal of Legal Studies*, *27*(1), Article 8, 209–220. https://chicagounbound.uchicago.edu/jls/vol27/iss1/8/.

Blair, J. P., and Schweit, K. W. (2014). *A study of active shooter incidents, 2000–2013.* Texas State University and Federal Bureau of Investigation, U.S. Department of Justice. https://www.fbi.gov/file-repository/active-shooter-study-2000-2013-1.pdf.

Blake, J. J., Butler, B. R., and Smith, D. (2015). Challenging middle-class notions of femininity: The cause of black females' disproportionate suspension rates. In D. J. Losen (Ed.), *Closing the school discipline gap: Equitable remedies for excessive exclusion,* 75–88. Teachers College Press.

Borum, R., Cornell, D. G., Modzeleski, W., and Jimerson, S. R. (2010). What can be done about school shootings?: A review of the evidence. *Educational Researcher*, *39*, 27–37. https://doi.org/10.3102/0013189X09357620.

Branas, C. C., Richmond, T. S., Culhane, D. P., Ten Have, T. R., and Wiebe, D. J. (2009). Investigating the link between gun possession and gun assault. *American Journal of Public Health*, *99*(11), 2034–2040. https://doi.org/10.2105/AJPH.2008.143099.

Campbell, C., and Anderson, J. (2018, November 12). Baltimore county school resource officer fatally shot himself at school Monday, police say. *Baltimore Sun.* https://www.baltimoresun.com/maryland/baltimore-county/bs-md-co-school-officer-medical-emergency-20181112-story.html.

Cornell, D. G. (2018). *The prevention of gun violence in schools and communities: Written statement for the Forum on School Safety (March 20, 2018)*. Committee on Education and the Workforce, U.S. House of Representatives. https://education.virginia.edu/sites/default/files/images/YVP/Cornell Hearing Statement 3–2.

Education Commission of the States. (2019). *50-state comparison: K–12 school safety*. https://www.ecs.org/50-state-comparison-k-12-school-safety/.

Giffords Law Center. (2021). Every incident of mishandled guns in schools. https://giffords.org/lawcenter/report/every-incident-of-mishandled-guns-in-schools/

Giffords Law Center to Prevent Gun Violence. (2019). *The truth about school shootings.* https://lawcenter.giffords.org/wp-content/uploads/2019/02/The-Truth-About-School-Shootings-Report.pdf.

Gonzales, M. A. (2018, March 13). *New NEA national survey: Educators overwhelmingly reject proposals to arm teachers* [press release]. National Education Association. https://www.nea.org/about-nea/press/press-releases/new-nea-national-survey-educators-overwhelmingly-reject-proposals.

Gregory, A., and Weinstein, R. S. (2008). The discipline gap and African Americans: Defiance or cooperation in the high school classroom. *Journal of School Psychology, 46*(4), 455–475. https://doi.org/10.1016/j.jsp.2007.09.001.

Gun Violence Archive (2019). *Past summary ledgers*. https://www.gunviolencearchive.org/past-tolls.

Hemenway, D. (1997). Survey research and self-defense gun use: An explanation of extreme overestimates. *Journal of Criminal Law and Criminology, 87*(4), 1430–1445. https://scholarlycommons.law.northwestern.edu/jclc/vol87/iss4/5/.

Hemenway, D. (2011). Risks and benefits of a gun in the home. *American Journal of Lifestyle Medicine, 5*(6), 502–511. https://doi.org/10.1177/1559827610396294.

Hemenway, D., and Solnick, S. J. (2015). The epidemiology of self-defense gun use: Evidence from the National Crime Victimization Surveys 2007–2011. *Preventive Medicine, 79,* 22–27. https://doi.org/10.1016/j.ypmed.2015.03.029.

Intrabartola, L. (2019, September 4). Back to school in the era of gun violence. *Rutgers Today*. https://www.rutgers.edu/news/back-school-era-gun-violence.

Kaysiyannis, A., Whitford, D., and Parks Ennis, R. (2018). Historical examination of United States intentional mass school shootings in the 20th and 21st centuries: Implications for students, schools, and society. *Journal of Child and Family Studies, 27*(8), 2562–2573. https://link.springer.com/article/10.1007/s10826-018-1096-2.

Klarevas, L. (2016). *Rampage nation: Securing America from mass shootings*. Prometheus Books.

Kleck, G., and Getz, M. (1996). Armed resistance to crime: The prevalence and nature of self-defense with a gun. *The Journal of Criminal Law and Criminology (1973–), 86*(1), 150–187. https://doi.org/10.2307/1144004.

Lankford, A. (2015, August 23). Mass shootings, firearms, and social strains: A global analysis of an exceptionally American problem. The American Sociological Association 110th Annual Meeting, Chicago, IL.

Livingston, M. D., Rossheim, M. E., and Stidham Hall, K. (2019). A descriptive analysis of school and school shooter characteristics and the severity of school shootings in the United States, 1999–2018. *Journal of Adolescent Health, 64*(6), 797–799. https://www.sciencedirect.com/journal/journal-of-adolescent-health/vol/64/issue/6.

Lott, J. R., Jr. (1997). *More guns, less crime: Understanding crime and gun control laws*. University of Chicago Press. https://www.academia.edu/35305054/More_Guns_Less_Crime_Jhon_R_Lott_Jr.

Lott, J. R., Jr. (1998). The concealed handgun debate. *Journal of Legal Studies, 27*(1), 221–243. https://www.journals.uchicago.edu/doi/abs/10.1086/468020.

Lott, J. R., Jr., and Mustard, D. B. (1997). Crime, deterrence, and right-to-carry concealed handguns. *Journal of Legal Studies, 26*(1), 1–68. http://www.journals.uchicago.edu/JLS/lott.pdf.

National Rifle Association. (2015, February 25). *Researcher affirms: At least 760,000 defensive gun uses a year.* National Rifle Association, Institute for Legislative Action. https://www.nraila.org/articles/20150222/researcher-reaffirms-at-least-760-000-defensive-gun-uses-a-year.

Park, C. (2017, August 17). Teacher shoots self at Lithia Springs High School. *NBC 11 Alive News*. https://www.11alive.com/article/news/local/teacher-shoots-self-at-lithia-springs-high-school/85-465045529.

Phillips, C. D., Nwaiwu, O., Lin, S., Edwards, R., Imanpour, S., and Ohsfeldt, R. (2015). Concealed handgun licensing and crime in four states. *Journal of Criminology, 2015*, 1–8. https://doi.org/10.1155/2015/803742.

Proulx, N. (2018, February 23). Should teachers be armed with guns? *New York Times*, Student Opinion. https://www.nytimes.com/2018/02/23/learning/should-teachers-be-armed-with-guns.html.

Reiss, A. J., Jr., and Roth, J. A. (1992). *Understanding and preventing violence* (Vol. 1). Panel on the Understanding and Control of Violent Behavior, National Research Council. National Academy Press. https://psycnet.apa.org/record/1992-98885-000.

Ritchie, E. I. (2017, April 23, updated May 17, 2017). Barricaded school employee with handgun at El Modena High surrenders. *Orange County Register*. https://www.ocregister.com/2017/04/23/school-employee-at-el-modena-barricaded-with-gun/.

Saul, S. (2018, February 21). An armed principal detained a campus gunman but he's against arming school staff. *New York Times*. https://www.nytimes.com/2018/02/21/us/school-shootings-teachers.html.

Smart, G. (2019, February 14). A year after Parkland school shooting, should we be arming teachers already? *USA Today*. https://www.usatoday.com/story/opinion/voices/2019/02/14/school-shootings-show-need-arm-teachers-column/2849291002/.

Sparling, H. K. (2018, February 20). Butler county sheriff Richard K. Jones on arming teachers: This is for my grandkids. *Cincinnati.com—The Enquirer*. https://www.cincinnati.com/story/news/education/2018/02/20/butler-county-sheriff-richard-k-jones-arming-teachers-my-grandkids/354298002/.

Wellford, C. F., Pepper, J. V., and Petrie, C. V. (Eds). (2005). *Firearms and violence: A critical review*. National Research Council, National Academies. The National Academies Press. https://www.nap.edu/read/10881/chapter/1.

WTMJ-TV Milwaukee. (2018, February 19). Proposed bill would allow concealed weapons in Wisconsin's private schools. *WTMJ-TV Milwaukee, Local news*. https://www.tmj4.com/news/local-news/proposed-bill-would-allow-concealed-weapons-in-wisconsins-private-schools.

Zimring, F. E., and Hawkins, G. (1997). *Crime is not the problem: Lethal violence in America*. Oxford University Press.

19

The Tragedy of Firearms in American Schools

Student Voices, Perspectives, and Experiences

Bertha Llamas, Madeline Yeung, Mikaela Brosh, Kayla Birmingham, Robert Szewczyk

Although there were school shootings prior to Columbine, April 20, 1999, marks the beginning of the school shooting era for most Americans. That day and that event have been seared into the public conscience. Since that day, the *Washington Post* has estimated that 240,000 students at 249 schools have been affected by gun violence (Cox et al., 2018). The *Post* also determined that 147 people have been killed and 310 have been injured during these incidents (Cox et al., 2018). As of this writing, Columbine took place over 21 years ago, and society as a whole seems no closer to solving the problem of school shootings.

While we have heard from pro- and anti-gun politicians, from the NRA and gun control groups, an important group of voices has been left out: the students who have grown up and attended school in the post-Columbine generation. To begin to fill that gap, this chapter features the voices of five diverse undergraduate students who grew up and attended school in the post-Columbine era, and includes military veterans and those who had never held a gun until they began working on this chapter.

These five students chose these topics themselves. In this chapter they directly address their fellow students who are reading and using this text. The five students offer their voices, their perspectives, and their research on the issues of firearms and schools, as well as insights and research on topics such as school policy, school training, the glorification of school shooters, technology and school defense, and issues affecting college campuses. Their perspective, which has been ignored for too long, developed as a result of growing up and attending school in an environment they did not create, did not ask for, and had no control over: The Post-Columbine World.

SCHOOL POLICIES, MADELINE YEUNG

Since the 1990s, school policies have shifted. From zero-tolerance policies to active-shooter scenarios, schools have taken increasingly proactive steps to prepare students for emergent situations. Initial policies included prohibiting firearms in school zones and expelling "problem students." However, school shootings continued, so schools have turned to resource officers, security management, and active-shooter drills with law enforcement to secure the safety of students.

The Gun-Free School Zones Act of 1990 (GFSA) was the first of two notable acts to be passed by the United States Congress concerning guns in schools. In the wake of violence spurred by weapons, gang activity, and drug offenses, the GFSA set forth a zero-tolerance policy for schools nationwide (Gun-Free School, 1990). Initially, zero-tolerance mandated predetermined punishments for specific offenses, a practice intended to show that certain behaviors would not be tolerated in schools (Skiba & Knesting, 2001). However, schools soon expanded zero-tolerance practices to include punishing students for alcohol and tobacco use, as well as for general violence in schools. In 1994, the GFSA was revised to include an addendum requiring that students violating the act be suspended for a mandatory period of one year (Gun-Free Schools, 1994). The act set a standard of intolerance toward activities that schools deemed dangerous or inappropriate for students.

These policies resulted in unexpected consequences, such as discriminatory practices. Although zero-tolerance is meant to punish all offenses equally, studies have found discrepancies in how zero-tolerance is applied, particularly when it comes to subjective offenses such as behavioral issues. Students with disabilities, including emotional disabilities, are particularly at risk for exclusionary practices. Minority students have also been disproportionately affected. One study in 2016 reported a 32/100 rate of removal for African Americans in Illinois, as compared to a 5/100 rate of removal for Caucasian students (Moreno & Scaletta, 2018). This study indicates that, instead of providing additional protections for all students and preventing gun violence in schools, zero-tolerance policies have harmed minority and disadvantaged students. In general, zero-tolerance policies are regarded as ineffective in achieving the desired goal of preventing gun violence on school grounds.

Despite efforts to reduce school shootings with zero-tolerance policies, school shootings continued to happen, and schools started shifting to different policies. This shift is evident in a document titled "State Regulation of Private Schools," published by the United States Department of Education in 2009, when it mentioned Illinois's policy regarding active-shooter scenarios and bomb threats (U.S. Department of Education, 2009). Although the regulatory document laid out the legal requirements for starting a private school in each of the fifty states, the document also included noncompulsory recommendations and shows the shift from zero-tolerance to active-shooter drills.

Schools also began working in conjunction with law enforcement and equipping their schools with school resource officers (SROs). Since 2003, the National Center for Education Statistics has surveyed schools across America on the factors of crime and violence. The center pulls results from a nationally representative stratified random sample of 3,000 to 4,000 schools each time it produces a report. In these surveys, an SRO is typically defined as a sworn law enforcement officer with arrest authority who has specialized training and works in collaboration with school organizations. SROs working in schools typically carry a firearm, wear a body camera, and carry chemical aerosol sprays (National Center, 2016).

In 2003–2004, while schools were surveyed on whether they utilized SROs, the schools produced no data about SROs. Somewhat similarly, in 2005–2006, respondents answered questions about SROs less than 85 percent of the time (National Center, 2006). While the survey was also conducted in the years following, it was not until 2015–2016 that SRO data was noted as a highlight. That year, 77 percent of schools in which 1,000+ students were enrolled had an SRO present at least once a week. This percentage dropped to 47 percent when student enrollment numbered 500–999, 36 percent when student enrollment numbered 300–499, and 24 percent when student enrollment numbered less than 300. This data shows that SRO presence is more likely when student enrollment is higher. In 2018–2019, schools reported even higher percentages of SRO presence. Schools with less than 300 students saw the highest increase across the board with their SRO presence reaching 34 percent. The use of SROs has been on the rise for the past few years, but determining whether their presence helps stop school violence may necessitate more targeted studies over a longer period of time.

In addition to increasing SROs, schools also began incorporating the "run-hide-fight" model into emergency procedures. Currently, this model is the most common safety practice that schools utilize in the event of an active school shooter. This prevalence makes run-hide-fight a de facto policy. The model is mostly self-descriptive and is often used in conjunction with code-name announcements to inform students of what is occurring on school grounds. In contrast to the sequence in the run-hide-fight model, some K–12 school districts recommend "hide-run-fight" as the order of response.

According to the 2019–2020 emergency guide of Cumberland County schools, hiding is the recommended course of action (Cumberland County, 2020). Teachers should lead students to a location where the active shooter is less likely to find them, and all should remain there until the school is given back to the jurisdiction of the principal. Running is the second course of action, recommended when students are instructed to do so by law enforcement or first responders. In cases of imminent threat, teachers should lead students to evacuate the premises, tell them which route to take, and ensure student safety. As a last resort, students are told to fight, which includes throwing items, improvising weapons, and yelling or shouting to distract or frighten the shooter. Teachers are also instructed to engage the active shooter in order to allow students to safely escape.

From Columbine to now, policies have changed and shifted. The GFSA and zero-tolerance policies were the first attempts at preventing gun violence. Equipping schools with SROs is the most recent practice that attempts to stop school shootings before they start. The commonly employed run-hide-fight model aims to increase student survivability should an active-shooter situation occur. Current suggestions on improving school security include training teachers on thinking tactically in high-stress situations. Another recommendation is that schools evaluate their school warning systems in order to identify and fix key flaws before they become a fatal weakness.

STUDENT TRAINING, MIKAELA BROSH

During my time in public school, I was no stranger to active-shooter drills. While they were more common during my elementary school years (2004–2010), the drills eventually dwindled until they were nonexistent in my high school years. These "lockdown drills," as they were called, consisted of nothing more than the teachers locking the classroom door, turning the lights off, closing the blinds, having us students hide in the back corner of the room, and making us be quiet. Looking back at my experience, these lockdown drills were never taken very seriously, but how could they be: we were children, and no one had ever explained to us why we did these drills. We had always been told that we needed to know them and practice them for our safety. It wasn't until middle school that someone explained to us that we did them because of the Columbine shooting.

I find it interesting to juxtapose the active-shooter drills when I was in school and the ones that some students go through now. When I was a kid, the scariest thing to happen during one of the active-shooter drills was that the administration might have had a teacher walk down the halls and yank on the doors to make sure they had been locked properly, as the drill guidelines said they should be. Sometimes adults wouldn't tell us that there was to be a drill, or wouldn't tell us until the drill was complete that we were only practicing.

Now, however, schools are performing "realistic active-shooter drills." Some of these drills include fake blood, blank bullets, and "dead bodies" to simulate a real-life scenario. Alongside this, students are being taught the run-hide-fight method, whereas everyone my age was taught to just run-and-hide.

Within the past two decades, the strategy taught to students has shifted from the previously used "run-and-hide" active-shooter drill training to the newer run-hide-fight model, which was originally meant to be used in workplace settings instead of in schools (O'Regan, 2019). With this shift in responsive methods, companies have introduced newer, more realistic active-shooter training. Previously, the main tactic of reaction in "run-and-hide" drills was that teachers and students locked the doors of the classroom, drew the blinds, and hid, whereas in run-hide-fight training, gunshots, fake blood, and fake dead bodies are sometimes used to create a realistic scenario to "prepare" students in the case of a real-life emergency taking place.

During one run-hide-fight training session at Meadowlawn Elementary School in Monticello, Indiana, teachers reported being shot during several of the training exercises, sometimes execution-style, and were not warned beforehand (Zraick, 2019). Teachers were left with welts and bruises after being shot with pellets. In addition to the physical injuries, the teachers also claimed that this training was frightening and insulting. They "recognized the need for safety training but [felt] that the risks of venturing so far into realism outweighed the benefits" (Zraick, 2019, para. 9). The White County Sheriff's Office, which conducted the training, is said to have routinely run safety drills using the ALICE training methods.

One of the main companies involved in this new type of realistic active-shooter training is the ALICE Training Institute. The ALICE method stands for alert, lockdown, inform, counter, and evacuate. The creator of ALICE was a law enforcement officer in the Dallas–Fort Worth area, who believed that the lock-the-door and hide tactic was the reason behind the abnormally high number of killed and wounded in the mass shootings of the 1990s (ALICE, 2020). The ALICE Training Institute has adopted the run-hide-fight tactic with the belief that the more passive run-and-hide method does more harm than good. These proactive methods include counter methods and even mock shootings, which many people believe go too far and are far too traumatic for students.

The possible psychological impact of this realistic approach has brought into question whether training methods such as ALICE are worth it. According to the study "Mass Shootings in America," there is extensive documentation that school shootings were more frequent in the 1990s than today and approximately 98–99 percent of violent deaths of children occur outside of school in our homes and communities (Fox & Delateur, 2014). The National

Association of School Psychologists (NASP) states that schools should have their psychologists present during the planning and involved during active-shooter training drills (National Association, 2018). The association also recommends that psychologists take into consideration participants' and students' trauma history, and provide accommodations when and if needed (Erbacher & Poland, 2019). In addition, the ALICE Training Institute suggests a trauma-informed approach that consists of (a) carefully planned and integrated drills before which students are informed and reminded of the training, (b) an avoidance of titles and codes such as Code Red, and (c) a statement from the administration that the exercise is indeed a drill. The NASP also suggests that, during these training drills, schools should work alongside first responders. This approach will help determine if full-scale drills are too traumatic. Full-scale drills, including "simulated bullet wounds, students pretending to be deceased, real guns shooting blanks, and students banging on classroom doors during a lockdown drill begging to be let in," can end up doing more harm than good (Erbacher & Poland, 2019, p. 10).

Interestingly enough, numerous articles say active-shooter drills are stress-, anxiety-, and trauma-inducing. I always remember the drills I went through, and most of the time, they were just something we had to do that got us away from whatever boring thing we were being taught. However, these new realistic active-shooter drills have become psychologically damaging to some extent because they simulate a real-life scenario, complete with real-life emotion, drama, and fear. Not all students are able to view this event as merely a drill. One 2019 article, titled "Active Shooter Drills Stress Kids but Are Needed, Experts Say," recommends that a mental health professional should be present and involved in every step of the active-shooter drill planning (Cohan, 2019). What does that say about the drills being created? Another article, which was published the same year by *HuffPost* and titled "The Company behind America's Scariest School Shooter Drills," states that this realistic method was never meant for schools, but instead was meant to be geared toward businesses. In addition, the idea of fighting the shooter can readily be romanticized by students because of the hero status that is conferred on individuals who charge toward gunmen to stop them. I think that the "realistic" drills and the encouragement for students to fight an active shooter, compiled together, can brew trauma in students.

GLORIFICATION, KAYLA BIRMINGHAM

Adolescents can easily be influenced, which can result in copycat behaviors. Growing up, I was influenced by family and community. My mother is a deeply religious woman who constantly reminded my siblings and me to put our faith first. She often made me feel as though she did not think my siblings and I were fully devoted. Due to this, I tried to live and show my faith in every way I could. I attended church and youth groups, listened only to Christian music, and wore my faith proudly printed on T-shirts and engraved on jewelry in hopes that no one would question my devotion.

In 1999, I was in sixth grade and moved from a school in Detroit with bag checks and metal detectors to a small town in Minnesota where people seldom locked their doors. I do not remember having any conversations about Columbine until I was in the seventh grade and read *She Said Yes: The Unlikely Martyrdom of Cassie Bernall* and *Rachel's Tears: The Spiritual Journey of Columbine Martyr Rachel Scott.* I learned about the first book from kids in my class, but learned about the second one at a church-led event. The books were about two of the young women murdered during Columbine. The central theme was their faith and both were considered martyrs. Discussions about Columbine primarily took place at church or church-led events; however, the primary focus of those discussions was Cassie's and Rachel's spiritual journeys and the question of where church members were in their own journeys.

I remember going to a church-sponsored event in which Rachel's father was one of the speakers. Again, the discussions revolved around living one's faith. At the time, I was still young, in seventh or eighth grade, and after reading the books and listening to the discussions about Cassie and Rachel, I considered them heroes. I began hoping and praying that I, too, could become a martyr for my faith like them; I thought this would prove my devotion.

Later, when I considered how much I was affected by these books, and how I wanted to be a copycat of these martyrs, it made me wonder how shooters are influenced and if these influences may cause copycat behavior. When it comes to mass shootings, chances are readers have all seen breaking news reports when information is first developing. These reports are not always correct, causing the release of misleading information. Moreover, mass shootings are often played on a constant loop and repeated across all forms of media. In the past, the coverage has included everything from the perpetrator's name and face to the victim count, and as a result, many have called for the media to put more focus on the victims. However, social media and the livestreaming of shootings pose a challenge as mass shooters are taking the power of media into their own hands.

The media's portrayal of the shooters, whether it is accurate or not, can influence copycat behaviors. The shooting on May 20, 1999, at Heritage High School in Conyers, Georgia, occurred exactly one month to the day from Columbine (Sullivan & Guerrette, 2003). After his arrest, the shooter claimed that he had just gotten the idea from the shooting at Columbine High School, and some of his previous declarations claimed his attack was "for the sake of my brothers and sisters related to the trench coat mafia" (Sullivan & Guerrette, 2003, p. 50). During the coverage of Columbine, the media reported that the Columbine shooters were members of a student group called the trench coat mafia, outsiders who were targeting jocks and other groups (Langman, 2018). The media also reported that "[m]embers of the 'Mafia' don't socialize with other students" and that "[t]hey hate the popular school jocks, and, in turn, are teased and ridiculed by members of the football and wrestling teams. Their uniforms are black trench coats under which they wear head-to-toe black" (Trench Coat, 1999, paras. 3–5). The media focused on the shooters' involvement with the trench coat mafia without fact checking. However, it turns out the media's portrayal of the Columbine shooters was inaccurate. The shooters were average or above-average students who were involved in sports or other extracurricular activities, and they were not part of the trench coat mafia (Langman, 2009). Had the media taken the time to get the facts right, perhaps the Heritage shooter would not have seen two people he could relate to and draw inspiration from.

The amount of media coverage given to mass shootings can also influence copycats. A study done by criminologist Grant Duwe (2000) shows that the amount of media coverage that mass shootings receive is out of proportion to the amount received by other forms of homicide. Duwe goes on to point out that the higher the death count the more coverage the incident receives (Duwe, 2000). A blog written in 2009 by the Umpqua Community College shooter, who killed nine people, spoke about the level of influence the media coverage had. He wrote about a shooter in Roanoke, saying, "So many people like him are all alone and unknown, yet when they spill a little blood, the whole world knows who they are," and goes on to say, "[h]is face splashed across every screen, his name across the lips of every person on the planet, all in the course of a day. Seems the more people you kill, the more you're in the limelight" (Harper-Mercer, 2015, para. 3). Another example of a shooter wanting to gain notoriety was the Virginia Tech shooter, who prepared his own writings, videos, and photographs and sent them to MSNBC before murdering thirty-two people, showing that he expected the media to share his message, and indeed they did (Johnson, 2007). In addition, psychologist Peter Langman, known for his studies of mass shootings, lists nine shootings, including the two mentioned, that occurred between 1999 and 2017, in which the perpetrators' influences included seeking fame (Langman, 2018). The media's extensive coverage of mass shootings has had an unintended effect of influencing copycats who hope to gain a similar level of attention.

Calls have been made by various campaigns, such as "Don't Name Them" and "No Notoriety," for the media to bring more attention to the victims. In 2018, Lankford and Madfis, inspired by such campaigns, released their own proposal with four guidelines: (1) to not name the shooter(s); (2) to not use any images or likenesses of the shooter(s); (3) to no longer use past shooters' names and images; and (4) to report everything else with as much detail as the media chooses (Lankford & Madfis, 2018). However, the existence of social media poses a challenge for such proposals and campaigns.

Social media, especially the use of livestreaming, shifts the power of the media to the shooters who are able to share videos or any other content in real time for all to see. An example of this occurred in New Zealand, on March 15, 2019, when a perpetrator livestreamed on Facebook the shootings of over fifty people during his attack on two mosques (Tamkin, 2019). Before the mass shooting, he had posted a link on the online forum 8chan to his Facebook page, where he began the livestream (Garsd, 2019). Facebook did not take the video down until after the feed ended and the video had already gone viral on YouTube and Twitter (Garsd, 2019). Another incident, this time in Thailand, occurred February 8–9, 2020. The shooter livestreamed during a rampage that left twenty-nine people dead (Soldier Live-streams, 2020; Thai Soldier Kills, 2020). In the video, the shooter claimed to be tired and unable to pull the trigger anymore while doing a trigger motion with his hand (Soldier Live-streams, 2020; Thai Soldier Kills, 2020). The shooter continued to post photos and comments until Facebook disabled his account about six and half hours after the first shots (A Thai Soldier, 2020; Olarn & Sullivan, 2020; Soldier Live-streams, 2020; Thai Soldier Kills, 2020). Facebook later defended its reaction time, stating that no direct violence was depicted in the posts (A Thai Soldier, 2020).

When it comes to why youth are influenced by media, the deep mechanics are not fully understood, but it has been suggested that it could be due to the adolescents' still-developing brains (Hummer, 2015). Tom A. Hummer, an assistant research professor of psychiatry, writes, "Given the significant evidence associating greater media violence exposure with both short- and long-term increases in aggressive thoughts, feelings, and behaviors, there is a strong need to understand the mechanisms underlying emotional and behavioral control and how these mechanisms are influenced by media violence" (Hummer, 2015, p. 1797). In particular, it is mentioned that "attention, inhibitory control, and emotion or behavior regulation, are particularly vulnerable during adolescence" (Hummer, 2015, p. 1794). However, the researchers caution that further studies are still needed to better understand the effects of media on the developing brain and that media is not a lone factor in an individual's behaviors (Hummer, 2015).

While it is difficult for me to admit my own experiences as an adolescent, I now realize how my hope of dying for my faith was connected, in large part, to the profound influences my family, church community, and the two books about Cassie and Rachel had during that time in my life. I feel now that those influences romanticized the idea of martyrdom. Similarly, there is a danger that the amount of media attention given to active shootings can result in copycats wanting to gain a similar level of recognition. Both the media and social media should be cautious on how they portray active shooters to avoid glorifying and romanticizing their actions.

TECHNOLOGY, ROBERT SZEWCZYK

I grew up in a military household in which my family moved often, and I attended many different schools. I went to three different high schools, two in Georgia and the last in Colorado. During my years in high school, everyone had a fear of firearms in schools, thanks to the Columbine shooting and similar incidents. I remember that the view of our neighbors was that you either liked firearms or were afraid of them. My family did not actually have weapons in the household, but we did not have any fear of them either. The major difference between my friends and me was that my stepfather was insistent that my family always be prepared for any danger, like a car accident or natural disaster. As a result, I had combat lifesaver training numerous times and was a member of the Boy Scouts. So, in middle and high school, when there was a big push for "safety drills," I already had an idea of what I thought that should look like.

In high school, the active-shooter drill was simple and not taken seriously. Code words were given over the intercom. Students were unaware of the situation, but teachers knew to commence the drill. Then the instructor locked the door, turned off the lights, and told everyone to be silent until the drill was complete. The code words used over the intercom were "unidentified adult" or "possible bomb threat," except we knew that neither was the case. If the bomb threat had been real, we would have evacuated, and if an unknown individual had actually posed a threat, turning the lights off and locking the door would have done little to protect us. Every time we went through the drill, students talked, and the teacher fussed at us to be quiet; no one took the drills seriously at all.

I thought the standard for school safety was ridiculous then, but now the standards are even worse. Students today are subject to drones, turnstiles, bulletproof backpacks, bulletproof whiteboards, smoke cannons in ceilings, and security teams running drills to test the school's response. Most of these measures were not even a thought back in 2010, let alone seen as mandatory for students' safety. In fact, research indicates that schools have not become so much more dangerous as to warrant this escalation of security so rapidly. Policy makers and school administrators need to take the emotion out of security planning around school shootings and approach the problem with a more logical, rational, and effective framework. Current trends in school security and the related research—indicated by both the *Final Report* of the Safe School Initiative, which was produced by the Secret Service, and *A Comprehensive Report on School Safety Technology*, prepared for the Department of Justice's National Institute of Justice—show that the build-up of physical defenses is misguided and that school personnel should focus more on better communication and outreach to students (U.S. Department, 2016; Vossekuil et al., 2002).

Security companies have been pushing schools for years to buy more and more products in an attempt to "harden" defenses (Dunklin & Pritchard, 2018). These tools can be as straightforward as locking devices for doors, metal detectors, and fencing, or they can be as obscure and complicated as bulletproof whiteboards, smoke cannons installed in ceilings, and even unmanned aerial vehicles, more commonly referred to as drones. However, according to FBI statistics, school shootings are not nearly as common as society is led to believe (Federal Bureau, n.d.), and analysis by the Secret Service has shown that the shootings are predominantly confined to certain characteristics (Vossekuil et al., 2002). The *Final Report* on the Safe School Initiative identified thirty-seven separate school shootings from 1974–2000 (Dunklin & Pritchard, 2018). By analyzing these incidents, the agency concluded that only 27 percent of the shootings were stopped through law enforcement and that 47 percent of all attacks lasted fifteen minutes or less (Vossekuil et al., 2002). Regardless of prompt response times given by high-tech sensors or alarms, the benefits of more technology are likely nonexistent given the nature of these incidents. However, after every incident, there is a spike in demand to do something different, and security companies are always there ready to sell another tool. Nonetheless, the rational conclusions of federal agencies—when combined with costs of acquisition, concerns about product effectiveness, and conflicts of interest with the security companies that advocate and sell these devices—make it unlikely that these tools will provide any benefits. The current approach is not yielding the desired results, and school systems need to find an approach that is effective, cost-efficient, and not directed by those with a conflict of interest.

Funding is a major factor when it comes to active-shooter safety. Most schools cannot afford the price tag attached to many of the products being promoted, but administrators feel they cannot sit idle as school shootings are given more media coverage. These conflicting pressures result in many schools settling for more obscure defenses, such as the Pennsylvania school district that purchased 500 sixteen-inch bats for faculty and staff at a cost of $1,800 (DeMarche, 2018). Another Pennsylvania school district resorted to putting five-gallon buckets of river stones in 200 classrooms (Johnson, 2018). A majority of school districts are unable to afford the new school safety technology, which has resulted in less expensive and questionable solutions, like the buckets of river stones and miniature bats found in Pennsylvania.

New security measures come with varying levels of effectiveness and their own problems. For example, in assessments of 18" x 20" bulletproof whiteboards, experts suggest that due to the white boards' lack of coverage and therefore low effectiveness, the safety budget should be used on other more practical alternatives, such as overall training for staff to recognize potentially violent students (U.S. Department, 2016). *A Comprehensive Report on School Safety Technology*, prepared for the U.S. Department of Justice, concluded that ballistic tests performed by manufacturers on handheld bulletproof whiteboards do not predict how well the product will perform in an actual incident (2016). The tests failed to protect against either certain weapons, repeated attempts to breach the material, or different angles and distances, while also failing to provide full coverage for the individuals defending themselves (U.S. Department, 2016). The study ultimately concluded that the term "Bullet resistant" is far more accurate than the advertised label "Bullet proof."

While this author found no statistics to indicate the effectiveness of bullet-resistant protective devices for students, a national survey of body armor used by police officers reported that nearly 60 percent (306) of the 521 officers shot during the years 1997 to 2006 were killed while wearing body armor (U.S. Department, 2016). Most deaths were the result of being shot in an area not protected by the armor, such as the head or neck or where side and shoulder panels connect (U.S. Department, 2016). If most deaths from being shot in body armor are from nonprotected areas, the effectiveness of an 18"x 20" bullet-resistant shield is questionable. It is also worth noting that some defense technology, such as door jams, may not be in compliance with local, state, or federal laws that address concerns with disability or fire safety (U.S. Department, 2016). If the technology does not work or cannot be implemented, then society needs to find a better approach.

Our current approach has created a school safety market spearheaded by the very people who sell the products. Education security revenue in the United States was roughly $2.5 billion in 2017, with "best practices" setting a steep price of up to $11 billion, according to the nonprofit group Secure Schools Alliance (Dunklin & Pritchard, 2018). The Secure Schools Alliance does not advertise that the organization was created and funded by Allegion plc, a publicly traded corporation that specializes in doors, locks, and entry systems. These security companies are setting not only the safety standards but also the prices. The Consolidated Appropriations Act of 2018 provided $25 million immediately for school security technology (Consolidated Appropriations, 2018) and the Students, Teachers, and Officers Preventing School Violence Act, commonly known as the STOP School Violence Act, authorized nearly $85.3 million in funding for Department of Justice school safety grants in 2019 (Department of Justice, 2019). The security companies have not only set the price tag and encouraged demand, but have also effectively lobbied the federal government to create a market in school security. Mason Wooldridge, a security consultant who assesses vulnerabilities in school districts, has been reported to have said, "School safety is the wild, wild West. Any company can claim anything they want" (Dunklin & Pritchard, 2018, para. 8). School safety has become an arena riddled with conflict of interest; seeking advice from those who set the standards and the price tag is a mistake.

School safety is a controversial issue with many wanting drastic changes and a fix-all solution. However, the data do not support the fear-mongering narrative that the only solution to school shootings is more safety technology. The *Final Report* of the Safe School Initiative concludes, "The use of a threat assessment approach may be a promising strategy for preventing a school-based attack" (Vossekuil et al., 2002, p. 41). Teachers and parents should be communicating with students who are known to be struggling with problems. In most school shootings, not only did the attackers' peers know the attack was going to occur, but also most shooters were not "invisible" and were already a concern to people in their lives (Vossekuil et al., 2002). Minding the *Final Report* on the Safe School Initiative and focusing on threat assessments and better communication with students is more beneficial than listening to those who profit from the situation with expensive and ineffective solutions.

COLLEGES, BERTHA LLAMAS

Lockdown drills were not uncommon in all the schools I attended prior to college. We had them about once per month, but no one took them seriously. The procedure was simple, and every teacher had it memorized: lock all doors, cover every window, turn the lights off, lay low, and keep the students away from any possible viewpoint. If a student was in a bathroom or hallway, he or she found the nearest classroom and stayed there until the drill was over.

In elementary school, we did not fully understand the purpose of the drills. We had never experienced an active-shooter incident and had not heard of anything like that happening. Most of the students followed procedure out of fear of being punished for not doing what they were told. Even then, some students would still act up, joke, and squirm around while they were supposed to be quiet. The only times when everyone sat still were when we heard footsteps and voices in the hallway. The resource officers would try to turn the classroom doorknob, pretending to be someone trying to break in. It was not violent, just a turn or two of the handle, and then they would move on, but we knew we were being tested.

In middle school, we did not think an active-shooter situation would happen. We did not live in a place like that. Yes, we had the different cliques and the outcasts, but we could not picture anyone walking in and pulling a gun or any weapon on us or a teacher. However, around this time, I distinctly remember our drills being modified. The principal no longer stated we were under lockdown. Instead, the drills were masked with the phrase, "Swim team practice is cancelled for the evening," which was chosen because our school did not have a swim team. Administrators did not consider an active-shooter situation in which the perpetrator could be a student. Regardless of the intention, we all found the code phrase to be silly and joked about it.

When I first entered high school, most students still thought our lockdown drills were a joke. However, that changed after the fall semester of my freshman year when one student was suspended. Rumors began to spread that he had been arrested for talking about bringing firearms to school and threatening to bring a bomb. The school began to lock all doors at all times, including the ones leading to the courtyard, which most students used as a shortcut between two buildings, and every door in the school stayed locked for the rest of that year.

The following month, we had multiple lockdown drills, which no one joked about. During these drills, officers would shake the door handles and push and pull as if trying to force their way in. Occasionally, students would be pulled from a classroom prior to the drill to see what teachers would do if students were missing. This made some of us nervous, but no one was overly concerned; we all knew that it was just a drill.

When I was a junior at my second high school, a student's truck was found in the parking lot with multiple firearms. The student had forgotten to put away his hunting gear, but it could have been a different situation. Our drills did not change, and students shrugged the incident off like it was nothing. Their attitudes surprised me, but none of them had been there at my other high school where the threat felt real.

Now that I am in college, security feels even more lax. When students drive visitors onto my university campus, no record is kept of who is being brought in and no questions are typically asked about the visitor's identity.

Only one of our possible points of entry/exit has a security guard, while the other point blocks vehicle entry but remains open to anyone who wishes to walk onto campus. This resembles most colleges in the United States, where it is impossible to cover every point of entry. As someone who learned to always keep my back to the wall, it makes me nervous to see that the gate security allows any familiar face onto campus with a smile and a wave. Some of those familiar faces do not attend our university or have a permit to park on campus, yet they are allowed to pass the gate without question.

Protecting and securing college campuses is different from protecting an elementary, middle, or high school. There are multiple factors to consider, including campus size, the practicality of security measures, security personnel, and campus firearm regulations. Flaws in these areas of security can be detrimental in emergency situations, as demonstrated by the outcome of the 2007 Virginia Tech shooting, which resulted in security reforms at many colleges and universities.

One distinct difference between grade school security and college-campus security is the physical space that must be accounted for. While grade schools tend to be more compact, colleges and universities tend to have multiple buildings spread out over larger areas. The significance of this difference was evident in the University of Texas at Austin shooting in 2010. During this incident, a student of the 350-acre university boarded a city bus with a wrapped AK-47 in his backpack and made his way onto campus. He fired eleven rounds in one of the busiest areas of the university, then entered a campus library and shot himself in a cubicle before many even knew there was a shooter on campus (University of Texas, 2010). In a single-building grade school, it would not take several minutes for students and staff to be made aware of an active-shooter situation, and school resource officers would likely be able to access the scene much sooner.

Another important aspect of college campus security is the practicality of the safety measures implemented. While colleges should strive to keep their campuses safe, security measures should be appropriate for the risk. Between 2000 and 2018, institutions of higher education accounted for about 26 percent of the total active-shooter incidents in educational environments, significantly less than the estimated 75 percent that occurred in grade schools (Federal Bureau, 2019). Though the percentage for university shootings is lower, this does not mean campus security should be lax. In a 2009 nationwide study, 95 percent of colleges recommended the creation of an all-hazards emergency response plan (ERP) and the adoption of a mass emergency communication system, but less than half those colleges recommended regularly updating their emergency plans, and less than 30 percent recommended regularly testing the mass notification system (Fox & Savage,

2009). Having an ERP and a mass emergency notification system can be effective, but only if they are up to date.

The security personnel and their role protecting a campus are crucial to the overall safety of a university, but there is controversy about whether or not campus security should be armed. A 1995 Bureau of Justice Statistics report shows that 64 percent of all four-year college campus security agencies used armed, sworn officers (Reaves & Goldberg, 1996). However, an updated report from 2011–2012 shows only a 5 percent increase in universities with armed officers over a seventeen-year span, despite an over 800-university increase (Reaves, 2015; Snyder et al., 2019). This indicates that events like the Virginia Tech shooting have not caused a significant increase in the use of armed officers on college campuses, and nearly one-third of colleges and universities do not believe that campus security officers should carry a firearm.

The topic of student and faculty access to firearms on campus is another important security factor that has been debated since the Virginia Tech shooting. Immediately after the shooting, at least one well-known campus-carry advocacy group was created: the Students for Concealed Carry. Composed of university professors, college students, parents, and other community members, the organization pushes state legislators and university administrators around the country to permit concealed-carry license holders to possess firearms on campus (About, 2020). Members of the organization believe that students and faculty should be allowed to use their firearms for protection during an active-shooter situation, instead of having to run, hide, and wait for campus officers to arrive at the scene. On the other side of this debate are groups like the American Association of State Colleges and Universities, which asserts that the increased access to student- and faculty-owned firearms on campus increases the risk of successful suicide attempts, gun theft, and firearm misuse (Harnisch, 2008). This group supports laws banning concealed carry on college campuses, as its members believe that allowing licensed students and faculty to possess firearms on college campuses only increases the risk of injury and loss of life.

To further complicate the debate over the appropriate measures for campus security, protecting campuses poses unique challenges. The overall safety of colleges and universities is dependent on the physical campus size, the security measures in place, the security staff, and a college or university's firearm restrictions. The Virginia Tech shooting in 2007 showed the United States that the security systems of colleges and universities are generally reactive, when the focus of security should be on having preventative measures. However, not all universities are the same, and they should therefore determine what security measures are best suited for them. Although it may come with a financial price and a perceived restriction of freedom, and while it is important that universities continue to be a welcoming environment to the community, the safety of students, faculty, and staff must ultimately be a university's number one priority.

CLOSING THOUGHTS

This chapter examined the issues of guns in schools through the eyes of students who walked the halls in the post-Columbine world. These are the very students who learned the code words, practiced the drills, and hoped that violence would never come to their schools. Theirs is a perspective that has been missing from the rhetoric around school violence until now. In this chapter they spoke directly to students across the country, contributing their personal stories as well as the conclusions of their research on various aspects of school gun violence. The five students have added a valuable perspective to the academic literature.

These students are ready to take their next steps, this time not as middle or high school students, but as soon-to-be college graduates. They will serve as part of the next generation of criminal justice professionals, policy makers, and academics. Unless a real solution can be found to the problem of school violence, many of these student authors, as well as the students they wrote this chapter for, will also take on the roles of concerned parents, hoping and fearing for the safety of their children in the public and private middle schools, high schools, colleges, and universities of this nation.

BIBLIOGRAPHY

About. (2020). *ConcealedCampus.org*. Students for Concealed Carry. https://concealedcampus.org/about/.

ALICE. (2020).Training for violent intruder events. *ALICEtraining.com*. www.alicetraining.com/our-program/.

Cohan, A. (2019, August 19). Active shooter drills stress kids but are needed, experts say. *Boston Herald*. https://www.govtech.com/em/safety/Active-Shooter-Drills-Stress-Kids-but-are-Necessary-Experts-say.html.

Consolidated Appropriations Act, 2018 (H.R. 1625). (2018). https://www.congress.gov/bill/115th-congress/house-bill/1625.

Cox, J. W., Rich, S., Chiu, A., Muyskens, J., and Ulmanu, M. (2018, April 20). Analysis: More than 240,000 students have experienced gun violence at school since Columbine. *Washington Post*. https://www.washingtonpost.com/graphics/2018/local/school-shootings-database/.

Cumberland County Schools. (2020). *2019–2020 Cumberland County Schools Emergency Guide.*

DeMarche, E. (2018, April 11). Pennsylvania school district arms teachers with baseball bats: Report. *FoxNews.com.* https://www.foxnews.com/us/pennsylvania-school-district-arms-teachers-with-baseball-bats-report.

Department of Justice, Office of Justice Programs. (2019, October 21). Fact sheet: Department of Justice invests about $85.3 million in grants to address school violence. *OJP.gov.* https://www.ojp.gov/sites/g/files/xyckuh241/files/archives/press-releases/2019/factsheets/FINAL_FY19%20STOP%20School%20Violence%20Grant%20Awards_FACT%20SHEET.pdf.

Dunklin, R., and Pritchard, J. (2018, October 2) . Firms sell school "hardening" as mass shooting solution. *APnews.com.* https://apnews.com/4a5c1bde535a43adab51bcc9a121cb97.

Duwe, G. (2000). Body-count journalism: The presentation of mass murder in the news media. *Homicide Studies, 4*(4), 364–399. doi:10.1177/1088767900004004004.

Erbacher, T. A., and Poland, S. (2019). School psychologists must be involved in planning and conducting active shooter drills. *Communique, 48*(1), 10–13. National Association of School Psychologists. static1.squarespace.com/static/5d63fedcb8c88e00011779a1/t/5d66b7892d18f0000121bda5/1567012749149/School Psychologists Must Be Involved in Planning and Conducting Active Shooter Drills PDF.pdf.

Federal Bureau of Investigation. (n.d.). *2000 to 2018 Active Shooter Incidents*. https://www.fbi.gov/file-repository/active-shooter-incidents-2000-2018.pdf/view.

Federal Bureau of Investigation. (2019). *Active shooter incidents: Topical one pagers, 2000–2018.* https://www.fbi.gov/file-repository/ active-shooter-one-page-summaries-2000-2018.pdf.

Fox, J. A., and Delateur, M. (2014). Mass shootings in America. *Homicide Studies, 18*(1), 125–145.

Fox, J. A., and Savage, J. (2009). Mass murder goes to college: An examination of changes on college campuses following Virginia Tech. *American Behavioral Scientist, 52*(10), 1465–1485. https://doi.org/10.1177/0002764209332558.

Garsd, J. (2019, March 15). Social media companies struggle to pull live streamed video of mass shootings. *NPR, All Things Considered.* Washington, DC. http://ez-proxy.methodist.edu:2048/login?url=https://search.proquest.com/docview/2191957711?accountid=12408.

Gun-Free Schools Act of 1994. (1994). 20 U.S. Code § 7961.

Gun Free School Zone Act of 1990. (1990). 18 United States Code § 922.

Harnisch, T. L. (2008). *Policy matters—Concealed weapons on state college campuses: In pursuit of individual liberty and collective security*. American Association of State Colleges and Universities. www.aascu.org/policy/publications/policymatters/2008/gunsoncampus.pdf.

Harper-Mercer, C. (2015). Chris Harper-Mercer's blog. *SchoolShooters.info,* Peter Langman [website manager]. https://schoolshooters.info/sites/default/files/harper-mercer_blog_1.0.pdf.

Hummer, T. A. (2015). Media violence effects on brain development: What neuroimaging has revealed and what lies ahead. *American Behavioral Scientist, 59*(14), 1790–1806. doi:10.1177/0002764215596553.

Johnson, A. (2007, April 19). Gunman sent package to NBC News. https://www.nbcnews.com/id/wbna18195423.

Johnson, R. J. (2018, March 23). Bucket of rocks are last defense against school shooters in Pennsylvania. *iHeartRadio.com.* https://www.iheart.com/content/2018-03-23-bucket-of-rocks-last-defense-against-school-shooters-in-pennsylvania/.

Langman, P. (2009). *Why Kids Kill: Inside the Minds of School Shooters*. New York: Palgrave Macmillan.

Langman, P. (2018). Different types of role model influence and fame seeking among mass killers and copycat offenders. *American Behavioral Scientist, 62*(2), 210–228. doi:10.1177/0002764217739663.

Lankford, A., and Madfis, E. (2018). Don't name them, don't show them, but report everything else: A pragmatic proposal for denying mass killers the attention they seek and deterring future offenders. *American Behavioral Scientist, 62*(2), 260–279. doi:10.1177/0002764217730854.

Moreno, G., and Scaletta, M. (2018). Moving away from zero tolerance policies: Examination of Illinois educator preparedness in addressing student behavior. *International Journal of Emotional Education, 10*(2), 93–110.

National Association of School Psychologists. (2018). *School safety and crisis—Mitigating negative psychological effects of school lockdowns: Brief guidance for schools.* https://www.Nasponline.org/resources-and-publications/resources/school-safety-and-crisis/ mitigating-psychological-effects-of-lockdowns.

National Center for Education Statistics. (2006). *Crime, violence, discipline, and safety in U.S. public schools: Findings from the School Survey on Crime and Safety: 2005–06.* NCES 2007–361. https://nces.ed.gov/pubs2007/2007361.pdf.

National Center for Education Statistics. (2016). *Crime, violence, discipline, and safety in U.S. public schools: Findings from the School Survey on Crime and Safety: 2015–16.* NCES 2017–122. https://nces.ed.gov/pubs2017/2017122.pdf.

Olarn, K., and Sullivan, R. (2020, February 9). One gunman, four locations, 29 dead: How the mass shooting in Thailand unfolded. *Reuters.com.* https://www.reuters.com/ article/us-thailand-shooting-timeline-idUSKBN2030FQ.

O'Regan, S. V. (2019, December 17). The company behind America's scariest school shooter drills. *HuffPost.* www.huffpost.com/entry/alice-active-shooter-drills-do-they-work_n_5df397e5e4b0deb78b530940.

Reaves, B. A. (2015). *Campus law enforcement, 2011–12.* United States Bureau of Justice Statistics. NCJ 248028. https://www.bjs.gov/index.cfm?ty=pbdetail&iid=5216.

Reaves, B. A., and Goldberg, A. L. (1996). *Campus Law Enforcement Agencies, 1995.* NCJ-161137. United States Bureau of Justice Statistics. https://www.stetson.edu/law/conferences/highered/archive/2008/Bureau_of_Justice_Statistics.pdf.

Skiba, R., and Knesting, K. (2001). Zero tolerance, zero evidence: An analysis of school disciplinary practice. *New Directions for Youth Development, 92*(92), 17–43. doi: 10.1002/yd.23320019204.

Snyder, T. D., de Brey, C., and Dillow, S. A. (2019). *Digest of Education Statistics, 2018*. U.S. Department of Education. NCES 2020–009. https://files.eric.ed.gov/fulltext/ED601992.pdf.

Soldier live-streams shooting rampage in Thailand, kills at least 21 people. (2020, February 8). *CBSNews.com*.

Sullivan, M., and Guerette, R. T. (2003). The copycat factor: Mental illness, guns, and the shooting incident at Heritage High School, Rockdale County. In National Research Council (Ed.), *Deadly Lessons: Understanding Lethal School Violence*, 25–69. Washington, DC: National Academies Press.

Tamkin, E. (2019, March 18). After live-streamed New Zealand shooting, firms push platforms to change by threatening to pull ads. *Washington Post.*

A Thai soldier has killed at least 20 people in a shooting spree, authorities say. He may be at a mall. (2020, February 8). *CNN.com.* https://www.cnn.com/2020/02/08/asia/thai-soldier-shooting-intl/index.html.

Thai soldier kills 20 during live-streamed gun rampage. (2020, February 9). *Sunday Telegraph*. London, England. http://ez-proxy.methodist.edu:2048/login?url=https://search.proquest.com/docview/2352396281?accountid=12408.

Trench coat mafia is just plain "weird." (1999, April 21). *New York Post*. https://nypost.com/1999/04/21/trench-coat-mafia-is-just-plain-weird/.

University of Texas at Austin Police Department. (2010, September 28). *Active Shooter/Suicide After Action Report*. https://police.utexas.edu/sites/police.utexas.edu/files/utpd_after_action_report.pdf.

U.S. Department of Education. (2009). *State regulation of private schools.* www2.ed.gov/admins/comm/choice/regprivschl/regprivschl.pdf.

U.S. Department of Justice, National Institute of Justice. (2016). *A Comprehensive Report on School Safety Technology, prepared by the Johns Hopkins University Applied Physics Laboratory*. No. 250274. https://www.ncjrs.gov/pdffiles1/nij/grants/250274.pdf.

Vossekuil, B., Fein, R. A., Reddy, M., Borum, R., and Modzeleski, W. (2002). The final report and findings of the Safe School Initiative: Implications for the prevention of school attacks in the United States. Washington, DC: U.S. Secret Service and U.S. Department of Education.

Zraick, K. (2019, March 22). Indiana teachers were shot with pellets during active-shooter drill, union says. *New York Times*, www.nytimes.com/2019/03/22/us/indiana-teachers-shot.html.

20

Weapons Prohibited

An Examination of Issues Regarding Possession of Firearms on College Campuses

Haley Lapcevich, Jason Simon, Amanda Moreschi, Courtney Platt, Justin Shaughnessy

"COME AND TAKE IT."

With an AR-10 rifle strapped over her shoulder and resting on her back, Ohio native Kaitlin Bennett (Bennett et al., 2012) sparked intense national conversation when her graduation picture showed her cap decorated with the words "COME AND TAKE IT." Since the beginning of her controversy, Bennett, now referred to as the "Kent State Gun Girl," has branded herself as an advocate for the Second Amendment. She centers much of her advocacy and protests on college campuses; specifically, ones that she believes lack the freedoms and rights afforded to students by her interpretation of the "right to bear arms" found in the Second Amendment of the U.S. Constitution. She has visited numerous college campuses, including the University of Akron, Kent State, Youngstown State, Ohio University, the University of Kentucky, and Rutgers (Bennett et al., 2012). While on these campuses, Bennett typically engages in conversation with students on a range of topics including abortion, taxes, racism, and politics; however, conversations ultimately tend to end in debates over gun laws, the right to bear arms, and campus carry (Jones & Horan, 2019). Her videos tend to show the students, faculty, staff, or administration that disagree with her views and the way they present themselves in debate.

Bennett (Bennett et al., 2012) began a group called "Liberty Hangout," which focuses its time and advocacy on economic and firearms policies as well as publishing editorials related to politics and current events. She uses this platform to promote her agenda for "Peace, Prosperity, and Property Rights" (Moldow, n.d.). Aside from her advocacy, she is also well "followed" on nearly all social media platforms where she posts videos promoting her stance on prevalent issues. It is not uncommon for Bennett to participate in fiery debate with users on Twitter and other social media outlets.

While her unique approach is a more recent example of gun advocacy, specifically on college campuses, gun carrying has been an ongoing issue that many gun supporters have been addressing. With the current political climate focusing heavily on school shootings (Gius, 2018) and gun rights provided under the Second Amendment, there has been serious discussion on law and policy changes that would support, or prevent, the carrying of weapons on colleges and universities in the United States, often referred to as "campus carry" (Jones & Horan, 2019). When examining such a controversial issue, some considerations to take into account are: crime on campuses, legal precedent, state law and university policies, and public opinion. Moreover, there should also be consideration given on how the carrying of firearms on campus would be implemented. These are just some of the issues discussed in this chapter.

SEMINAL SCHOOL SHOOTINGS

The August 1, 1966, shooting at the University of Texas is the first mass shooting that took place on a college campus (Somers & Phelps, 2018). The shooter took fifteen lives and wounded thirty-one others. May 18, 2018, saw another tragic day in Texas when eight students and two teachers were killed and thirteen others wounded at Santé Fe High School near Houston (Goebel, 2019). It was because of these tragedies that nearly fifty-three years after the first shooting, Texas passed Senate Bill 11 to "legalize the carrying of concealed handguns with a chambered round by licensed permit holders in most academic, administrative, and residential spaces, including most classrooms and many offices, at public colleges and universities" (Somers & Phelps, 2018).

While the students at the University of Texas (Somers & Phelps, 2018) lived an unimaginable nightmare, no one could have predicted in 1966 just how "routine" school shootings (Gius, 2018) would come to be in America. To date, the massacre at Virginia Tech (Thrower et al., 2008) in Blacksburg, Virginia, ranks as the deadliest school shooting on any grade level. Thirty-two students' lives were taken on April 16, 2007, along with the shooter's life through suicide. The shooter perpetrated this crime with two handguns, a .40 caliber Smith and Wesson (S&W) pistol and a .22 caliber pistol, neither of which is an uncommon concealed weapon.

The tragedy at Sandy Hook Elementary School in Newtown, Connecticut, on December 14, 2012, was the second-deadliest school shooting where twenty-six young children and teachers were killed with an AR-15 sporting rifle and a 10mm handgun—again, common firearms in the United States (History.com Editors, 2019). Just over five years later, another large-scale school shooting made headlines when seventeen people were killed, and as many wounded, at Marjory Stoneman Douglas High School in Parkland, Florida, in February 2018 (History.com Editors, 2020).

"The U.S. has had 1,316 school shootings since 1970 and these numbers are increasing. 18% of school shootings have taken place since the tragedy at Sandy Hook Elementary School in December 2012" (Gius, 2018). Gun violence is an important issue that has a profound impact on the educational system in the United States, from elementary school to college. The aforementioned devastations are, sadly, not all-inclusive of the lives of students, teachers, and employees lost to gun violence at schools. Still, debate ensues regarding what measures can be taken to eliminate such calamities.

One commonly discussed method of reducing gun violence on campuses is more rigorous gun control laws (Gius, 2018), and research has been done to examine how these gun control policies affect school shootings (Gius, 2018). Research indicates that most gun control policies, such as concealed carry laws, private sale background checks, and federal dealer background checks, have no significant correlation with school shootings (Gius, 2018). One gun control policy that did have a statistically significant effect on the number of school shooting victims was the "assault weapons ban," formally known as the Public Safety and Recreational Firearms Use Protection Act (United States Congress, n.d.). "When the assault weapons ban (state or Federal) was in effect, the number of school shooting victims was 54.4% less than when the assault weapons ban was not in effect, holding all other factors constant" (Gius, 2018).

VIOLENT CRIME ON COLLEGE CAMPUSES

Of the 4,300 colleges and universities in the United States, there is an estimate of over 30,000 violent crimes annually on campuses directed against students (Thompson et al., 2013). However, the number of college campus homicides are less than twenty-five a year, with a homicide rate of .07 per 100,000 persons (Thompson et al., 2013). Additionally, "Past studies found the rate of violent crime on college grounds to be around two percent" (Thompson et al., 2013).

Statistical data provided by the U.S. Department of Education and Office of Postsecondary Education, through mandatory reporting requirements under the Jeanne Clery Disclosure of Campus Security Policy and Campus Crime Statistics Act and the Higher Education Opportunity Act (Clery Center, 2020) (commonly known as the "Clery Act"), provides a comprehensive national perspective on campus crime. Using their "Campus Safety and Security Data Analysis Cutting Tool," the authors analyzed criminal offenses from 2001–2018 with the following information concerning crimes on campus grounds and in student housing facilities that were collected from 5,581 public or private, small to large institutions across all fifty states plus Washington, DC (Campus Safety and Security, n.d.). Results showed that of the 904,137 offenses reported during that time period, murder, non-negligent manslaughter, and negligent manslaughter accounted for 401 (0.00044%) of those incidents. The data analytics tool did not disclose further details regarding the cause of death. Though firearm-related deaths and mass shootings in educational institutions at any level are a cause for concern and have immeasurable lasting effects on the lives of students, faculty, and family, the evidence shows that the frequency of such events is, in fact, very rare.

Opponents against carrying on campus suggest that allowing individuals on college campuses to conceal carry would result in more deaths, those in addition to what would have already taken place when mass shootings or individual acts of violent crime do occur. However, others believe that allowing individuals to carry on campus could contribute to a deterrent effect and result in lower crime rates or at least reluctance on the part of a perpetrator to engage in the crime at the outset, because he/she is unaware of who on campus is carrying. A few studies have examined the effects of campus carry laws on campus crimes (Jones & Horan, 2019). These studies found no significant effects on campus crime (Gius, 2019). A more recent study was done using state-level rather than institutional data and found that campus carry laws are not significantly associated with violent crime (Gius, 2019). Research also indicates that allowing firearms on campuses makes other violent crime worse and not better (Gerstmann, 2019). A study of three states that changed their laws to allow concealed weapons on college campuses found that sexual assaults increased after those laws were passed and further found that there is a strong link between gun ownership and suicide (Gerstmann, 2019).

SUPREME AND STATE COURT CASES

Several legal challenges have been brought involving the issue of guns on college campuses, potentially setting new legal precedent. At the highest level, the decision made by the Supreme Court of the United States in the landmark case of *District of Columbia v. Heller* (U.S. Supreme Court, 2008) has led to much debate surrounding the specific places where firearms should and should not be allowed. College campuses are often at the center of this debate due to the inconsistent nature of school policies and state laws.

The decision in *Heller* declared that "the Second Amendment protects an individual's right to possess a firearm, unconnected with militia service, and the right to use firearms for traditionally lawful purposes, including self-defense, within the home" (Wasserman, 2011). This case is significant where the Supreme Court declared a law (in this case, from the District of Columbia) as being in violation of the Second Amendment. *McDonald v. City of Chicago* (Wasserman, 2011), a subsequent Supreme Court case, extended the Second Amendment protection to apply not only to states but localities as well. The court found the right to self-defense to be a fundamental right deeply rooted in the history of the United States. The *Heller* and *McDonald* rulings provided individuals with broader rights involving the use of firearms by allowing people to carry and use guns for self-defense.

The majority opinion in *Heller*, however, acknowledged that the rights established by the Second Amendment are not absolute, stating that "nothing in our opinion should be taken to cast doubt on longstanding prohibitions on the possession of firearms by felons and the mentally ill, or laws forbidding the carrying of firearms in sensitive places such as schools and government buildings" (U.S. Supreme Court, 2008). It is clear the Supreme Court does not intend for its decision in *Heller* to grant individuals free reign with respect to the manner and location in which one exercises his/her Second Amendment right. There are exceptions, although not clearly established, as to the type of firearm allowed for self-defense and the location in which they are allowed. Problems arise, however, when policy language never describes in precise detail what exact locations are to be considered a "sensitive place," leaving this open to interpretation by lower courts.

Another case, *University of Utah v. Shurtleff* (U.S. District Court for the District of Utah, 2003), is one example of a lower court interpreting the policies that dictate the legality of carrying a gun on a college campus. In this case, the university sued the state attorney general who was seeking a declaration that the university's firearms policy violated the state's firearm statutes (U.S. District Court for the District of Utah, 2003). The state of Utah claimed that the university had abused the power delegated to it by passing its own legislation controlling guns on campus. In contrast, the University of Utah argued that the state was infringing on its institutional autonomy by trying to control its campus policy on guns. Moreover, the university claimed that its firearm policy was critical to the operation of the campus as an academic institution. Judge Dale Kimball acknowledged in the opinion of the court that the University of Utah's policy is consistent with policies of other universities in the country. He asserted that "the purpose of such policies include (1) the preservation of academic freedom, (2) the protection of students, faculty, and staff from gun-related accidents, crime, and suicides, and (3) the preservation of the educational process" (U.S. District Court for the District of Utah, 2003). Such stated purposes are commonly referenced in arguments throughout other court cases regarding guns on college campuses. There is undoubtedly concern throughout the nation that the presence of guns on a college campus will have a devastating effect on universities' ability to perform its desired academic functions, as schools may be more focused on tempering lectures by instructors and stifling heated debates in the classroom, knowing that firearms may be present, which could create a deadly situation.

The legal issue of firearms on a college campus can also be seen in *The Regents of the University of Colorado v. Students for Concealed Carry* (Colorado Supreme Court, 2012). In this case, students at the university challenged the Colorado Board of Regents campus firearm prohibitions on both statutory and constitutional grounds (Colorado Supreme Court, 2012). Similar to the argument provided by the university in *Shurtleff*, the university claimed the policy was necessary to ensure the school was able to reach its academic mission to educate students without interference. As stated in the opinion by the Supreme Court of Colorado, the university expressed concern stating that firearm possession "threatens the tranquility of the educational environment in an intimidating way" (Colorado Supreme Court, 2012). This is an example of a case where the court ruled in favor of those seeking to carry on campus, further complicating what is meant by the phrase "sensitive place" as used in *Heller* (U.S. Supreme Court, 2008; Wasserman, 2011). Colorado had enacted the Colorado Concealed Carry Act (CCA) with the intent to create a uniform standard throughout the state regarding carrying concealed handguns. Being that the goal of the CCA was to implement a statewide, uniform policy and that it "did not specify public universities in its list of exceptions, the Court concluded that the student/plaintiff's allegations against the Regents that they met the CCA's permit requirements and Policy 14-I violated the CCA" (Wasserman, 2011).

Extensive examination of case law throughout the nation showcases the "differences among the state level constitutions, statutory laws and regulations of the 50 states, that have created a hodge-podge of guidelines that affect the legality of carrying guns on campus" (Birnbaum, 2013). Many cases have been brought to court as a result of the vague language in *Heller* (U.S. Supreme Court, 2008; Wasserman, 2011), but the nation still lacks uniform legislation specifically dictating if and where an individual is able to carry a firearm on a college campus, leaving such decisions to state legislators and university boards. The cases mentioned here are just a few of the many instances in which it has been left up to the judicial system to interpret the legality of various gun control policies in different jurisdictions across the United States. Any policies made at the federal level in the future, whether it be further restricting or permitting the carrying of firearms on college campuses, will certainly carry significant weight and may trickle down to the states.

STATE CAMPUS CARRY LAWS AND UNIVERSITY POLICIES

In recent years, gun violence has received increased attention on college campuses. This has prompted debate if students, professors, or staff should have the right to carry on their campuses.

As of 2018, there are sixteen states that ban carrying a concealed weapon on a college campus and twenty-three states where the decision to ban or allow campus carry is made by each college or university individually (National Conference of State Legislatures [NCSL], 2018). Ten states have provisions allowing the carrying of concealed weapons on public, postsecondary campuses, and the state of Tennessee allows faculty members with concealed weapon permits to campus carry (NCSL, 2018). The only state that allows concealed weapon permit holders to carry on campuses with a statute that specifically forbids public colleges and universities from banning that right is the state of Utah.

If permitted by state law, many colleges have their own restrictions on allowing firearms on campuses. For example, Youngstown State University (YSU) in Youngstown, Ohio, states (Ohio Admin. Code, 2012):

3356-7-03 Possession of weapons on campus.

A. Policy statement. Youngstown state university prohibits carrying, displaying, or usage of any firearm and/or other weapon by all persons while on university property.
B. Purpose. This policy is designed to create and maintain an environment that sustains the general health and well-being of students, employees, and visitors.

YSU chose to exercise its option under Ohio Revised Code 2923.126, which, in part, leaves the authorization for a licensee to carry a concealed handgun on campus grounds in the hands of the board of trustees for the college (Ohio Rev. Code, 2019).

PUBLIC OPINION ON CAMPUS CARRY

When examining the desire, or purported need for guns on college campuses, one should always consider the attitude and atmosphere such an environment would bring about not only on the campus, but the community as a whole. A study by Thompson et al. (2013) revealed that 94 percent of the public does not support the carrying of concealed handguns on college campuses. While advocates for campus carry (Jones & Horan, 2019) cite the Second Amendment interpretation of the "right to bear arms" as their defense, some of those in opposition to carrying on campus actually look to the First Amendment of the U.S. Constitution, focusing on academic freedom. According to the American Association of University Professors' 1940 *Statement on Principles of Academic Freedom and Tenure,* academic freedom is defined as "giving professors the freedom to research and teach in their academic disciplines without interference" (Somers & Phelps, 2018). While academic freedom takes its form in a myriad of ways depending on the educator and institution, a common theme consistent with the First Amendment's freedoms of speech and expression is being allowed to do so without the fear of violent repercussions.

The university setting is touted as being an ideal environment to initiate difficult and often controversial conversations without the fear of being ridiculed or dissuaded from freely speaking. These exchanges are essential for the expansion and development of knowledge. As such, moral, ethical, and political debates are typically a component of the curriculum for most majors. Some faculty have indicated that the presence of a weapon in the classroom would discourage, and perhaps even tacitly forbid, productive discourse on these controversial subjects. The fear that a student's opinion may offend or challenge another's opinion to the point of driving one to violent means infringes on the principle of academic freedom discussed previously.

Public safety is always of great concern on both sides of the gun debate. Those who support guns on campus argue more weapons in the hands of trained and responsible individuals will prevent those with bad intentions from harming students at their university. Meanwhile, those who oppose guns on campus argue that having firearms on campus diminishes the safe atmosphere of learning. One way to gauge the setting within a college campus is by surveying the faculty and administration. In a study by Bennett, Kraft, and Grubb (2012) and published by the *Journal of Criminal Justice Education*, faculty and administration were surveyed at a university in southeastern Georgia. The survey, titled "University Faculty Attitudes Toward Guns on Campus," included 287 individuals (159 men and 128 women; 55% response rate). The survey asked if participants supported a proposed piece of legislation that would allow carrying guns in all parks, historic sites, and other public locations in Georgia. Following this question, the faculty/administration was asked two questions regarding their views on extending this piece of legislation to college campuses. Accordingly, 72.4 percent of the faculty and administration stated that they would "strongly oppose" such an amendment to this bill (Bennett et al., 2012).

When it comes to students, the level of concern is relatively proportional. In a 2018 study published by the *Journal of Social Psychology*, when asked, "How safe would you feel if others carried a gun [on campus]?," it was found that 63.1 percent of the 11,804 college students surveyed stated they would feel "unsafe" (Shepperd et al., 2018). Interestingly, only 34.7 percent of the same 11,804 students stated they would feel safe if they themselves were carrying a gun (Shepperd et al., 2018). Examining these results, one of the reasons some of the students may feel unsafe is due to the unease they have when they do not know who has and does not have a gun. If a student is personally armed, they are fully aware of their own purposes; however, if a student witnesses or thinks another person may be armed with a weapon, they are uncertain of the other person's intentions.

Such unease may also pose a safety risk to the faculty members who decide the grades (and ultimately, the future) of students. The fear of an irate student meeting one-on-one with a professor while possibly being armed is a concern of some faculty (Somers & Phelps, 2018), and further consideration would be warranted before policy should be made whether guns would be allowed in professors' personal offices during office hours, if allowed on the campus at all. A faculty member under the pseudonym of John who was interviewed about the issue once said, "I found myself pulling back more and more from what I would commit to talk about or do and my whole mindset was 'just don't escalate'" (Somers & Phelps, 2018).

A 2019 study suggested the majority of students from surveyed colleges and universities are opposed to allowing guns on their campuses (Esthappan et al., 2019). Research in the state of Kansas, which was based on interviews with college and university administrators and a survey of students, found that the perceptions of the Kansas law allowing guns on campuses are predominantly negative (Esthappan et al., 2019). This negative perception is driven by safety concerns, given the potential for the mishandling of firearms that could have lethal consequences. The research further suggested that many believe by allowing firearms on college campuses, it changes the climate and social interactions of those on campus, decreases people's sense of safety on campus, increases the potential for gun-related injuries, and strains already tight security budgets (Esthappan et al., 2019). However, a paradigm shift may be on the horizon. According to an article published in

Communication Education by communication professionals at both Rutgers and Fairfield Universities, "Researchers have argued that support for campus carry has increased in recent years due to increases in gun violence" (Jones & Horan, 2019). Additionally, more states are passing campus carry laws each year. First on the list was Utah, which passed a campus carry law back in 2004, followed in subsequent years by ten more states. As of 2019, twenty-three concealed-carry provisions have been passed for specific universities and college campuses (Jones & Horan, 2019) that permit some form of concealed carry by students and/or faculty.

RESPONSIBILITY AND MATURITY OF THE STUDENT BODY

Numerous psychological studies have been conducted regarding the level of brain maturity and its correlation with chronological age in traditional college students. The National Institute of Mental Health sponsored a longitudinal study on brain development, which determined that the human brain is not fully mature until at least age twenty-five (Midgen, 2017). In particular, the frontal lobes of the brain, which are responsible for high-level reasoning and decision making, are not fully matured until the mid-twenties (Midgen, 2017). One fear is that college students, who lack full decision-making capabilities, may use a firearm to resolve intrinsic or extrinsic personal problems that turn lethal. Around 24,000 college students in the United States attempt suicide with a firearm each year, and around 1,100 of those students are successful (Clery Center, 2020). Additionally, Thompson et al. (2013) pointed out that "researchers have also shown that where there are more guns present, there are more accidental gun deaths." College campuses are most often occupied by younger individuals, who, it can be argued, are more impulsive and are more prone to making foolish, impetuous decisions. Young adults are often figuring out who they want to be, what they want for a career, and struggle with juggling schoolwork, family obligations, friendship issues, and serious romantic relationships, some for the first time.

Furthermore, accidents are inevitable when large groups of young adults are in one location for long periods of time, sometimes under the influence of alcohol and/or other substances. With respect to carrying weapons, the Crime Prevention Research Center has compiled a list of accidental shootings on K–12 and college campuses by permit holders and only eight such cases were found (Lott, 2018). Nevertheless, hearing a gun shot in a residence hall or building could be traumatizing for many students. Even this small sample shows that even someone who has received training and a legal license to carry could make a fatal mistake and put many people in danger. This poses thoughtful questions for legislators and university officials alike: Could these types of accidents be prevented? Do these incidents suggest that the training required for a concealed weapons license fail to adequately ensure proper handling? How severe should the consequences be for students who do not handle their weapons responsibly even if there are no injuries?

FACULTY AND CAMPUS CARRY

If colleges do not allow their students to carry a firearm, should they allow their professors or other employees to carry? Viewpoints, as one would imagine, are divided. Some argue that a professor's focus should be on teaching students and not having to concern themselves with the responsibility to potentially deploy lethal force in the event of an incident. This could theoretically cost colleges more in terms of funding because the school would have to implement training programs in order to arm their professors. In addition, there would be a likely increase in liability insurance for the campus. Colleges might be further ahead by putting their efforts into training to help identify students who are dealing with mental health problems in order to prevent acts of violence from occurring in the first place.

Although where a shooting incident may begin can vary, research by the Federal Bureau of Investigation has shown that the response rate by police to the scene of an active shooter was three minutes (FBI Law Enforcement Bulletin, 2017). Though quick by law enforcement standards, one could argue that arming professors, employees, or even students, would allow for an even faster response to an active shooter situation.

TRAINING

Thompson et al. (2009) found that out of the 97 percent of college campuses nationwide that had a policy prohibiting firearms, less than one-third of their faculty were regularly trained on active shooter situations, identifying troubled students, or knowing whom they should inform about troubled students. Training is an issue when deciding whether to allow individuals to carry firearms on campus. Although it varies by jurisdiction, concealed weapon holders do not necessarily have to qualify with the particular firearm they use to take their certification course. Additionally, civilians do not necessarily have the extensive legal, situational, operational, and tactical training that police officers do. Hence, individuals engaging in campus carry (Jones & Horan, 2019) would not likely have the preparation to effectively mitigate a situation with an active shooter. Another potential pitfall is that by allowing individuals to carry on campus, in the event that an active shooter situation occurs, it would become more difficult for police and other responders to differentiate between the threat and the armed Samaritan trying to assist.

If campus carry (Jones & Horan, 2019) were to be permitted at nearly all colleges and universities, states and universities could help mitigate gun violence at school by following in the footsteps of Arkansas, which requires additional training to individuals who would like to carry concealed weapons on campuses. In Arkansas, those who wish to campus carry must have additional training to obtain their Enhanced Concealed Handgun Carry License (ECHCL). The additional eight hours of training includes self-defense and proper use of deadly force, techniques for weapon retention, emergent situations in public locations, issues related to campus carry, and other practical and legal considerations (Arkansas State Police, 2018). This additional training is intended to give persons carrying on campus some skills to deal with the complexities of a public, active-shooter situation.

A counterargument to the additional training would be the likelihood of concealed carriers, who are traumatized by the events, to make effective and timely interventions in an active-shooter situation. For example, in October 2015, a shooting occurred at the Umpqua Community College in Oregon (Cegavske, 2017). The shooting began at 10:38 a.m. and ended with law enforcement engaging the shooter at 10:46 a.m. (Cegavske, 2017). Their campus allowed for concealed carry; however, no one intervened to stop the shooting in the long eight minutes of the incident. Although it is unknown how many persons may have been carrying weapons that day, or where those people were at the time of the shooting, this incident illustrates that carrying a weapon does not guarantee intervention by the student or faculty body. When individuals are faced with a deadly threat, absent proper training in tactics and mind-set, many will choose the option of "flight" rather than "fight."

A December 2019 shooting that occurred at the West Freeway Church of Christ in White Settlement, Texas (Aguilera et al., 2019), seems to counter the Umpqua incident. A video taken from security footage went viral following the tragedy. While graphic to view, this video provides unique insight into the split-second decisions that occur during a shooting. The offender can be seen standing up in the crowded church while the congregation has their heads bowed in prayer. Thankfully, not everyone present was looking down at the time. The shooter drew his concealed shotgun and fired several times in various directions. However, in seconds churchgoers subdued the perpetrator, several of whom were functioning as plain-clothes security, as they fired back in defense and killed the shooter.

The events and timeline that unfolded in the church that day are indisputable thanks to the released footage. It is clear that the presence of civilians who had concealed weapons were instrumental in quickly neutralizing the situation and minimizing the loss of life. However, the brave parishioners who drew their weapons were far older than the average college student, with arguably more experience with firearms.

How responsible are gun users who in fact hold permits? A study of revocation rates of gun owners with permits was conducted by the Crime Prevention Research Center. Lott, Whitley, and Riley (2014) found that "Michigan and Texas, which provide permit revocation data on the permit holder's year of age, show college age permit holders are responsible or even more responsible than older permit holders." From 2009 to 2013, Texan permit holders ages 18–22 saw a revocation rate of .04 percent. This is quite small compared to those ages 25–34 at .26 percent (Lott et al., 2014).

> Although 4 out of 5 campus police officers believed that they should play the lead role in minimizing firearm violence on college campuses and all respondents agreed that they should be called and included when dealing with an active shooter on campus, one fourth were not qualified annually on the use of deadly force. (Thompson et al., 2009)

CONCLUSION

The right to carry a concealed firearm on a college campus is a controversial issue. Much of the dispute stems from numerous high-profile gun-related deaths at schools, which is why policy makers and universities continue to seek ways to eliminate such mishaps and to improve safety while preserving the liberties of the students, staff, and faculty. However, states and universities vary on their approach. Some states recognize the university's autonomy while others have legislation addressing whether campus carry (Jones & Horan, 2019) is within their university's purview. The nation still lacks uniform legislation specifically outlining if and where an individual is able to carry a firearm on a campus. Nevertheless, more states are passing campus carry laws each year, but the public, student, and faculty viewpoints are still divided. Some worry that allowing firearms on campuses will affect the classroom setting that fosters learning by discouraging controversial conversations. The maturity of the individuals that these laws would allow to carry on campus, as well as the innumerable pressures they face, are also debatable. Lastly, training is a fundamental issue when discussing whether to allow individuals to carry in such dynamic and crowded environments since civilians do not have the extensive legal or tactical training compared to police officers. The right to carry a concealed firearm on a college campus is a disputed matter that shows no signs of waning. Like the "living, breathing document" which has been used to describe the U.S. Constitution, so too will this issue continue to evolve with societal viewpoint and legal interpretation.

REFERENCES

Aguilera, J., Gunia, A., and Law, T. (2019). Parishioner who volunteered for Texas church's security team killed gunman in shooting. Here's what to know. *Time*. https://time.com/5756485/white-settlement-church-texas-shooting/.

Arkansas State Police. (2018, January 23). *Enhanced concealed handgun carry license syllabus for enhanced training*. State of Arkansas. https://static.ark.org/eeuploads/asp/ECHCL_Training_Instruction_Manual_(minimum_requirements_for_ECHCL).pdf.

Bennett, K., Kraft, J., and Grubb, D. (2012). University attitudes toward guns on campus. *Journal of Criminal Justice Education, 23*(3), 336–355. https://doi.org/10.1080/10511253.2011.590515.

Birnbaum, R. (2013). Ready, fire, aim: The college campus gun fight. *University of Maryland, 45*(5), 6–14.

Campus Safety and Security. (n.d.). *Campus safety and security data analysis cutting tool*. Department of Education. https://ope.ed.gov/campussafety/#/.

Cegavske, C. (2017, September 8). Report gives timeline of events day of Umpqua Community College shooting. *News-Review*. https://www.nrtoday.com/news/crime/ucc_shooting/report-gives-timeline-of-events-day-of-umpqua-community-college-shooting/article_02210734-669d-5f7b-8bf5-fb7fbe585778.html.

Clery Center. (2020). *Summary of the Jeanne Clery Act*. Clery Center. https://clerycenter.org/policy-resources/the-clery-act/.

Colorado Supreme Court. (2012). *The Regents of the University of Colorado v. Students for Concealed Carry on Campus, No. 10SC344*. Justia. https://law.justia.com/cases/colorado/supreme-court/2012/10sc344.html.

Esthappan, S., Jagannath, J., Reimal, E., and Thompson, P. (2019). *Guns on college campuses students' and university officials' perceptions of campus carry legislation in Kansas*. Urban Institute. https://www.urban.org/sites/default/files/publication/100963/guns_on_college_campuses_1.pdf.

FBI Law Enforcement Bulletin. (2017, April 11). *Police response time to active shooter attacks*. U.S. Department of Justice. https://leb.fbi.gov/image-repository/police-response-time-to-active-shooter-attacks.jpg/view.

Gerstmann, E. (2019, January). Allowing concealed weapons on campus is not the solution to campus sexual assault. *Forbes Media LLC*. https://www.forbes.com/sites/evangerstmann/2019/01/16/allowing-concealed-weapons-on-campus-is-not-the-solution-to-campus-sexual-assault/#48ebd7a147c8.

Gius, M. (2018). The effects of state and federal gun control laws on school shootings. *Applied Economics Letters*, *25*(5), 317–320. https://doi.org/10.1080/13504851.2017.1319555.

Gius, M. (2019). Campus crime and concealed carry laws: Is arming students the answer? *The Social Science Journal*, *56*(1), 3–9. https://doi.org/10.1016/J.SOSCIJ.2018.04.004.

Goebel, E. (2019, July 31). *Guide to Texas SB 11: What you need to know*. PublicSchoolWORKS. https://corp.publicschoolworks.com/blog/guide-to-texas-sb-11-what-you-need-to-know/.

History.com Editors. (2019, December 11). *Sandy Hook school shooting.* A&E Television Networks. https://www.history.com/this-day-in-history/gunman-kills-students-and-adults-at-newtown-connecticut-elementary-school.

History.com Editors. (2020, February 13). *Teen gunman kills 17, injures 17 at Parkland, Florida high school*. A&E Television Networks. https://www.history.com/this-day-in-history/parkland-marjory-stoneman-douglas-school-shooting.

Jones, H. E., and Horan, S. M. (2019). Guns on campus: Campus carry and instructor–student communication. *Communication Education*, *68*(4), 417. https://doi.org/10.1080/03634523.2019.1643899.

Lott, J. L. (2018, March 14). *UPDATED: Accidental shootings on K-12 and university property by permit holders.* Crime Prevention Research Center. https://crimeresearch.org/2018/03/accidental-shootings-on-k-12-and-university-property-by-permit-holders/.

Lott, J. L., Whitley, J. E., and Riley, R. C. (2014). *Concealed carry revocation rates by age.* Crime Prevention Research Center. https://crimeresearch.org/wp-content/uploads/2014/08/Concealed-Carry-Revocation-rates-by-age.pdf.

Migden, S. E. (2017). The injustice of a felony conviction for offenders under age twenty-one: A new option for the courts to save our youths' futures. *Family Court Review*, *55*(2), 292–306. https://doi.org/10.1111/fcre.12278.

Moldow, J. (n.d.). *Peace. Prosperity. Property rights*. Liberty Hangout. http://libertyhangout.org/.

National Conference of State Legislatures (NCSL). (2018). *Guns on campus: Overview*. National Conference of State Legislatures. https://www.ncsl.org/research/education/guns-on-campus-overview.aspx.

Ohio Admin. Code. (2012). *33 Ohio Admin. Code § 3356-7-03*. LAWriter. http://codes.ohio.gov/oac/3356-7-03.

Ohio Rev. Code. (2019). *29 Ohio Rev. Code. § 2923.126*. LAWriter. http://codes.ohio.gov/orc/2923.126.

Shepperd, J. A., Pogge, G., Losee, J. E., Lipsey, N. P., and Redford, L. (2018). Gun attitudes on campus: United and divided by safety needs. *Journal of Social Psychology*, *158*(5), 615–624. https://doi.org/10.1080/00224545.2017.1412932.

Somers, P., and Phelps, N. (2018). Not chilly enough? Texas campus carry and academic freedom. *AAUP Journal of Academic Freedom, 9*, 1–7. https://www.aaup.org/sites/default/files/SomersPhelps.pdf.

Thompson, A., Price, J., Dake, J., Teeple, K., Bassler, S., Khubchandani, J., . . . Stratton, C. (2013). Student perceptions and practices regarding carrying concealed handguns on university campuses. *Journal of American College Health, 61*(5), 243–253. https://search.ebscohost.com/login.aspx?direct=true&db=s3h&AN=88212504&site=eds-live.

Thompson, A., Price, J., Mrdjenovich, A., and Khubchandani, J. (2009). Reducing firearm-related violence on college campuses—Police chiefs' perceptions and practices. *Journal of American College Health, 58*(3), 247–254. https://doi.org/10.1080/07448480903295367.

Thrower, R. H., Healy, S. J., Margolis, G. J., Lynch, M., Stafford, D., and Taylor, W. (2008). *Overview of the Virginia Tech tragedy and implications for campus safety: The IACLEA blueprint for safer campuses*. International Association of Chiefs of Police. https://www.theiacp.org/sites/default/files/all/i-j/iacleablueprint.pdf.

United States Congress. (n.d.). *H.R.4296 - Public safety and recreational firearms use protection act*. Congress.gov. https://www.congress.gov/bill/103rd-congress/house-bill/4296/text.

U.S. District Court for the District of Utah. (2003). *University of Utah v. Shurtleff, No. 2:02 CV 212 DAK*. Justia. https://law.justia.com/cases/federal/district-courts/FSupp2/252/1264/2424820/.

U.S. Supreme Court. (2008). *District of Columbia v. Heller, No. 07–290*. Justia. https://supreme.justia.com/cases/federal/us/554/570/.

Wasserman, L. M. (2011). Gun control on college and university campuses in the wake of *District of Columbia v. Heller* and *Mcdonald v. City of Chicago*. *Virginia Journal of Social Policy & the Law, 19*(1), 1–57.

Part VI

UNDERSTANDING THE ROLE OF FIREARMS IN LEGAL AND INVESTIGATIVE ISSUES

21

Investigation of Firearm-Related Crimes

Mark Vecellio and Steve Downs

Firearms are involved in a wide variety of crimes, including violent crimes. This chapter provides a look inside the tactics, techniques, and methods used by seasoned homicide detectives, crime scene investigators and reconstructionists, and forensic scientists who are involved in the investigation of gun-related crimes.

Violent crime, particularly gun-related crime, preoccupies the mind of Americans (Gallup, 2019). From movies, to novels, to television shows, to the constant flux of news, Americans are confronted every day with a barrage of gun-related violent crime. While much of this exposure is sensationalized, actual news stories seem to have an effect. A relatively recent poll showed that over a third of Americans reported they were afraid, because of the prevalence of violent crime, to simply walk alone in areas near their homes (Stats about All, n.d.).

The total number of violent crimes committed within the United States has steadily and dramatically risen over the past sixty years, from approximately 288,460 in 1960 to an astounding 1,206,836 in 2019 (FBI, n.d.-b). Bear in mind, however, that the actual rate of violent crimes, a measurement that incorporates the increase in population size within the United States, has fluctuated over this time, and peaked nearly thirty years ago (FBI, n.d.-a). In the early to mid-1990s, the violent crime rate began to decline, a trend that lasted nearly twenty years. The rate has stabilized over the past eight years at a rate about half that of the peak. Despite the downward trend in violent crime rates, public attention, interest, and fear remains high.

Firearms are directly involved in a significant percentage of violent crimes within the United States, estimated at 26 percent of the total number of violent victimizations (Perkins, 2003). One study showed that between 1993 and 2011, annual firearm-related homicides ranged from approximately 18,253 in 1993 to 11,101 in 2011 (Planty & Truman, 2013). When nonfatal events are included, these numbers climb dramatically, to a range of 421,600 to over 1,500,000 (Planty & Truman, 2013). Consider also that the number of firearm-related incidents is probably much higher as estimates reveal that nearly 40 percent of nonfatal events are unreported (Planty & Truman, 2013). In 2018, in the United States, firearms accounted for approximately 38 percent of 282,061 robberies, 26 percent of over 800,000 aggravated assaults, and 72 percent of over 16,000 homicides (Federal Bureau, Crime in the U.S.). Furthermore, in 2017, firearms were involved in approximately 23,854 suicides and 486 accidental deaths (Kochanek et al., 2019). To add some perspective to these statistics, among high-income nations, the United States ranks highest in the world in firearms violence, has a firearms suicide rate ten times higher than average, a homicide rate nearly twenty-five times higher than average, and accounts for nearly 84 percent of all firearm deaths (Grinshetyn & Hemenway, 2019; Monuteaux et al., 2015).

Given the high volume of firearm-related violence, law enforcement personnel must be trained and equipped to thoroughly investigate firearm-related incidents. Though many standard techniques used across an array of investigations are utilized in firearm-related casework (i.e., interviewing), incidents involving firearms often require specialized methods and tactics. This chapter will describe the most common methods used to investigate firearm-related incidents, as well as describe some fascinating techniques used by highly trained scientists and reconstructionists.

INVESTIGATIVE TECHNIQUES AND METHODS

An effective investigation of shooting incidents requires a combination of general investigative tactics as well as specialized techniques that specifically relate to firearms, ammunition, and firearm discharges. Those charged with conducting these investigations must always focus on the fact that the evidence they collect could ultimately go in front of the trier of fact, a judge and/or a jury, and as such their work should be unbiased and simply follow the trail left behind by the evidence collected. Let's first review some of the more common investigative tactics that apply to a wide range of criminal investigations.

INTERVIEWS

Interviews are performed in all types of investigations and serve as the means of obtaining testimonial evidence from victims, witnesses, and suspects. Investigators conduct interviews to gather facts germane to the investigation. In shooting investigations, interviews can help to examine motive; explore what people saw, heard, or otherwise sensed; and gain insight into a wealth of other information that may be relevant to the incident. Though interviews may seem to be a relatively uncomplicated process involving talking and listening, the truth is that successful interviewers are highly trained professionals, who understand, through education and experience, that following prescribed procedures and methodologies enables them to maximize the extraction of reliable information.

One interview method in particular is well known for its ability to enhance memory recall. This method is known as cognitive interviewing and was developed by researchers over thirty years ago (Geiselman et al., 1986). This method relies upon a series of prescribed memory retrieval methods, such as the cognitive reinstatement, in which the interviewer, essentially, mentally guides the witness back to the event through activation of various senses (Fisher & Geiselman, 2010; Geiselman et al., 1986). The cognitive method has been shown to reliably increase the recollection of memories while decreasing confabulations (Köhnken et al., 1999).

Another interview method relevant to shooting investigations and violent crime is the trauma-informed interview, which is still emerging as a best-practice technique for interviewing victims of traumatic crime. This type of interview protocol is followed when interviewees suffer psychological trauma that disrupts normal cognition and memory formation processes. Victims who survive gun-related crimes and witnesses to these crimes often fall into this category and this interview technique tends to be extremely beneficial to obtain vitally needed information to solve the crime. The technique requires the interviewer to adopt a victim-centered approach, thus reducing pressure for the victim to recall information which may fragmented. The interviewer, who should not be concerned with obtaining information in a traditional, logical sequence, instead guides the traumatized interviewee in recalling information through a variety of sensory stimulation. This technique is believed to result in more reliable information and less confabulations (Barlow, 2019).

In many types of criminal cases, investigators often find it useful to perform cursory interviews of large numbers of people with the goal of identifying those who may have witnessed the crime or possess knowledge that may otherwise help investigators. This process is called canvass interviewing and is widely known among seasoned detectives to be one of the most effective means of solving homicide cases (Wellford & Cronin, 2000). Investigators and police patrols often perform canvass interviews in neighborhoods, but they can also be conducted at places of employment, business locations, or wherever investigators determine people with relevant information may be found. Investigators should approach the canvass interview process in a methodical manner, being sure to ask a set of predetermined questions and performing this technique at suitable times to ensure witnesses can be located. These suitable times include the same time of day that the crime occurred, the same day of the week, and also other times when the majority of potential witnesses will be home. Insiders in the field of criminal investigations know that those detectives who expend the extra energy and sacrifice their own time by performing canvass interviews on nights and weekends are often the most successful.

Suspect Interviews/Interrogations

The purpose of interviewing suspects, in addition to the standard fact-gathering agenda associated with any interview, is to obtain admissions and ultimately a confession. Admissions can be looked at as partial confessions and may provide valuable investigative leads, confirm or refute other evidence gathered in the investigation, and lead to a full confession. A confession, obviously, is an extremely valuable piece of testimonial evidence. Investigators should always plan for suspect interviews by being fully knowledgeable about all aspects of the criminal investigation as well as the background of the suspect. Most suspects do not readily confess to crime; thus, investigators use a variety of techniques to guide the process (Adcock & Chancellor, 2013). Investigators must also be mindful of various rules and legal guidelines that govern interrogations. Suspects who are in custody and are being questioned must be advised of their Miranda Rights and investigators must be sure that any confession obtained meets legal standards of voluntariness (Warren & Supreme Court of the United States, 1965; Marcus, 2006). These rules, generated by the U.S. Supreme Court, should not be viewed as hindrances to investigators, but rather as guidelines that help ensure better-quality testimonial evidence. Admissions and confessions must be investigated thoroughly to substantiate the information provided by the suspect much as a denial of participation in the crime or alibi(s) and independent evidence gathered to confirm or refute the information provided by the suspect.

SHOWUPS, PHOTOGRAPHIC LINEUPS, AND PHYSICAL LINEUPS

Victims of violent crimes often are familiar with their offender(s) and provide that knowledge to investigators; however, in other instances victims and eyewitnesses may not know the identity of the offender(s). When this is not the case, law enforcement must find other ways to quickly identify the suspect. Depending on the jurisdiction involved, if a person matching the physical description of the suspect is located quickly near the crime scene, that person may be brought to the victim or eyewitness to conduct a showup in order to limit the time that suspect is detained by law enforcement. This process allows an innocent citizen who just happened to be at the wrong place at the wrong time to be let go instead of being taken to jail as a suspect. It is vital to follow the proper procedures to inform the victim or eyewitness that the person may not be the actual offender and prevent the victim or eyewitness from hearing or seeing anything that would indicate law enforcement has caught the actual offender. This person is then shown to the victim or eyewitness and asked if they recognize the person and if so, how do they recognize that person. Leading questions and statements must be strictly avoided to prevent a misidentification. Some agencies have an officer not involved with the investigation conduct the showup. Another common investigative technique is a photographic lineup. Law enforcement shows victim(s) and eyewitness(es) a series or set of photographs that include the suspect along with other people that closely resemble the suspect. The same questions are asked of the victim(s) and eyewitness(es) while no leading questions or statements are made. Some agencies have an officer not involved with the investigation conduct the lineup. Physical lineups are the last type of this investigative step. In these that are similar to a showup, law enforcement shows the victim(s) and eyewitness(es), who are usually behind a two-way mirror, a group of usually at least six people including the suspect standing in a room together and that are all dressed similarly and all having the same basic appearance. In some instances, the people in the lineup are instructed to say a certain phrase or words that the victim(s) or eyewitness(es) heard the suspect say before, during, or after the crime. In cases where the suspect is at large and unknown, it is common for law enforcement to ask the victim(s) and eyewitness(es) to notify an investigator or 911 immediately if they happen to run into the person whom they witnessed commit the crime.

DETECTING THE SOUND OF GUNSHOTS

The ability to detect gunshots using acoustic sensors is a relatively recent technology that has offered law enforcement agencies the opportunity to be alerted to gunshots that may not be reported by citizens. The most employed detection system is known as ShotSpotter. ShotSpotter has received rave reviews from many law enforcement agencies across the United States (Home-ShotSpotter, n.d.). According to the ShotSpotter website, the technology functions through placement of acoustic sensors in a designated coverage area. Upon an occurrence of gunfire, the sound is detected, triangulated to determine a specific location, and analyzed by employees of ShotSpotter. Once the sound is confirmed as gunfire, the law enforcement agency is alerted. This process takes less than one minute. According to ShotSpotter claims and one independent study, the technology and notification system has improved police response time to shooting incidents (Home-ShotSpotter, n.d.; Choi et al., 2013). ShotSpotter claims that the technology has been accepted in over 100 court cases and has survived several legal challenges (Home-ShotSpotter, n.d.).

The effectiveness of this technology, despite the anecdotal claims offered by both ShotSpotter and customers, has yet to be thoroughly studied. Numerous testimonial reports from customers of ShotSpotter claim positive results, such as reductions in shooting incidents and homicide rates. However, one must be cautious in interpreting this, or any, crime data since numerous factors may be involved. In fact, the one study published to date, in St. Louis, Missouri, revealed that the technology failed to show impact on reported gun crimes (La Vigne et al., 2019). Despite the lack of formal study supporting the ShotSpotter's ability to reduce gun-related crime, the technology appears to be a practical method of rapidly detecting gunshots, and therefore should presumably and logically aid in investigative efforts (La Vigne et al., 2019). The total cost of ShotSpotter includes the initial setup of the system and an annual fee thereafter, and some critics say the results do not warrant the cost or worry the system may infringe on the privacy of citizens (Vaughn, 2019).

SHOOTING SCENE INVESTIGATION BASICS

Shooting scene investigations only begin after the shooting ends and the scene is secured by the responding patrol officers. These investigations are often fast paced with multiple simultaneous actions being required in order to appropriately and accurately complete the investigation. Investigators must obtain the appropriate authorization to conduct a crime scene investigation through a warrant or consent to search from the person with the authority to provide such consent. This is of critical importance as any evidence not obtained legally will not be allowed in court and any derivative evidence will most likely not be admissible in court. There are various exceptions to the Fourth Amendment including exigent circumstances such as continuing an active pursuit of a suspect or search for additional victims who may be saved by not waiting for a warrant, but investigators must not rely on such exceptions when the crime scene investigation will take hours or even days to complete an obtain a warrant or consent to search.

The preservation of life is always the highest priority for law enforcement, and as such any victim who potentially can be saved must be provided immediate first aid, be removed from the scene, and transported to the nearest medical facility with the capabilities to treat the patient. Officers must respond to each and every medical facility utilized to treat the wounded to both ensure they know exactly who each victim is and what their injuries are. Most states require medical facilities to protect the privacy and safety of their patients and to provide an alias for the victim of criminal violence. Simply calling these facilities may lead to confusion and inaccurate information. Shooting victims were eyewitnesses and should be interviewed as soon as possible. The unfortunate reality, in some cases, is that victims and witnesses may refuse to cooperate with the investigation and seek to exact revenge for themselves. In these instances, investigators must be prepared to be extra vigilant and innovative in order to find other ways to solve these cases.

Investigators must locate and collect any clothing worn by the victim(s) as they may have bullet holes in them, various items of potential trace evidence, as well as any projectiles or shrapnel removed from the victims. Medical personnel who spoke with any victim during the process should be identified and interviewed as the statements made to them by a victim may be admissible in court under a medical exception to the hearsay rules (Exceptions to the Rule Against Hearsay, n.d., Rule 803). The unfortunate reality of some shooting scenes is that it results in the death of the victim(s). These victims must be checked for any signs of life, but when medical personnel pronounce them dead, they should be considered a unique crime scene in and of itself and therefore be processed for evidence prior to being removed from the scene. When a body is placed in a body bag, minute trace evidence can be lost as well as various other severe negative impacts on the possibility of finding critical evidence on the body and the clothing. After the victim(s) is processed thoroughly at the scene, the body is then placed in a body bag that is tagged and sealed in a unique manner that is documented to preserve the chain of custody of the body all the way through that process a complete forensic autopsy begins. Many law enforcement agencies require deceased homicide victims to be escorted by an appropriate officer to the morgue to witness the chain of custody.

Shooting scenes are often larger than first thought, and as soon as possible after the safety of all parties is secured, the scene must be cordoned off using both crime scene barrier tape and personnel to enforce the restrictions being imposed on the public not to cross that barrier. It is highly recommended to consider immediately expanding the crime scene boundaries moving the crime scene barrier tape outward further and adding a second crime scene barrier tape even further out to protect potential evidence and providing room for evidence and equipment to be safely and securely maintained throughout the crime scene processing. Locating any shell casings at the scene is a vital step in the process, and once located, they must be protected until the scene is thoroughly processed. A common method to protect these valuable pieces of evidence is to place a scene number marker over the shell casing to protect it from inadvertent movement or being stepped on.

A crime scene entry log should also be initiated and maintained throughout the scene processing in order to document who was allowed into the crime scene and for what purpose. No matter the gravity, scope, or depravity found at the scene of a shooting, responding officers and crime scene investigators cannot forget the basic foundation of all good crime scene investigations: notes, photographs, and sketches. These must begin as soon as possible in order to fully document the investigation and all of the investigative findings. All of the information obtained during the crime scene examination, coupled with other evidence collected from the victim(s), eyewitnesses, and other sources, may be utilized later to complete a shooting scene reconstruction. An excellent approach to avoid bias and predetermination of a case is to treat every unattended death as a homicide and should be investigated until it is proven otherwise, such as a suicide or accident, including all shooting deaths. Following all of the evidence free of bias and conducting a thorough investigation following all of the investigative leads to their logical conclusions is the best method to ensure that the results are correct and will stand the test of a trial and public scrutiny. Any alibi should be investigated thoroughly to determine its validity and whether or not it has any impact on the ability of a person to have been involved in the crime or not.

Weapons located at a shooting scene, found in a suspect's possession, or found during any subsequent search must be considered loaded and must be immediately cleared as soon as police physically seize it. The weapon should be carefully unloaded and the officer or investigator unloading it must record the absence or presence of ammunition, the quantity of ammunition, and manufacturer markings on the base of the ammunition. In the case of revolvers, the officer or investigator must note the position in the chambers of where each bullet is located and if there are firing pin impressions on the base of each round. Depending on the jurisdiction and agency policies, some officers or investigators are required to unload any magazine and should also count the ammunition present in the magazine, and manufacturer markings on the ammunition.

WEAPON OWNERSHIP

Determining ownership of a firearm and if a firearm is stolen or not is often a first step in firearm-related investigations. The Gun Control Act of 1968 required all manufacturers of firearms engrave every firearm made or imported into the United States with the manufacturer's identity—for example, Smith & Wesson—and then a unique serial number (Identification Markings, 2001). Some of the oldest firearms manufacturers in the United States began this voluntarily as early as the mid-1800s (Winchester Firearms, n.d.). Officers locating a firearm with a serial number present can determine if the firearm has been reported as stolen to law enforcement by checking the National Crime Information Center (NCIC) database or a variety of local and state databases that contain information on property reported stolen including firearms. Some criminals illegally try to remove or alter the serial number by various means by filing or scraping it off as a way to try to make a firearm untraceable. When law enforcement finds such a firearm, it is illegal to possess under 18 U.S.C. § 922(k) which carries a maximum of up to five years in federal prison (Public Law 90-618, 1968). These firearms should be sent to the servicing forensic lab that will attempt to retrieve the serial number and any other information that was obliterated through a process, including the use of various chemicals such as acids that will allow the forensic examiner to visualize the information that had been thought to have been removed.

A 2018 proficiency test of obliterated serial numbers was sent to 296 forensic examiners around the world and found that 92 percent of the examiners recovered the obliterated serial number completely, 7 percent recovered five out of the six characters, 2 percent recovered four out of six characters, with the remaining 1 percent recovered three out six characters (Serial Number Restoration, 2018). Firearms whose required markings have been altered or removed should be reported to the Bureau of Alcohol, Tobacco, Firearms, and Explosives' (ATF) Obliterated Serial Number Program to aid in the tracking of organized illegal firearms trafficking patterns on a national and global level (Bureau of Alcohol, Tobacco, Firearms, and Explosives [ATF], Tracing, n.d.). The ATF has multiple programs designed to aid law enforcement in the investigation of firearms-related investigations. The ATF has a firearms tracing program that allows law enforcement to determine the first person who purchased a firearm legally in the United States and is an excellent starting point for law enforcement to track the firearm to the last known person who legally owned the firearm (ATF, Tracing, n.d.). This information can be vital in firearms investigations and often leads to the possible identity of the last person with the firearm and who a shooter was in some cases.

CRIME SCENE PROCESSING

Investigators document the characteristics and conditions of crime scenes using three primary methods: notes, photographs, and sketches. To properly record one's observations of the scene, along with nuances which may be present, the investigator will take detailed and copious notes. These notes can be later used to help generate formal reports, analyze various aspects of the scene, or refresh the investigator's testimony before court hearings. Note-taking, however, is inherently subjective since one's observations are influenced by past experiences, training, and cognitive biases. Photographs, or digital images, serve to offset some of the objectivity associated with note-taking. When taken properly, photographs serve to be valuable aids in later investigative and reconstruction efforts and may provide a courtroom jury the chance to view the scene and/or key items of evidence. Sketching is the third primary documentation method. A sketch serves to display the layout of the scene with an emphasis on spatial relationships of important items. Investigators often include measurements depicting specific locations of key items of evidence within sketches. Sketches may range from hand-drawn, rough sketches made at the scene to sophisticated, software-generated drawings to scale.

Another alternative is the use of a three-dimensional scanning system which can produce intricately detailed and precise three-dimensional images of the scene. Because these systems tend to be expensive and require substantial training, the use of this equipment varies across investigative agencies. Three-dimensional models of a scene are sometimes produced at the request of attorneys to augment courtroom presentations. These models are often produced by highly skilled individuals including those at the FBI Laboratory at Quantico, Virginia. They are produced in similar fashion as architectural models or can be printed by 3-D printers. These models provide a scaled-down version of the crime scene that can be taken into the courtroom to allow the trier of fact to see the spatial relationships they may otherwise not be able to visualize through photographs and traditional sketches.

Crime scene processing is a time-consuming process that is very much unlike what is portrayed on television and movies. A cost-benefit analysis of conducting a crime scene examination is often conducted as it is often determined that a CSI or investigator spending several hours at a $20 larceny is simply cost prohibitive. However, in a murder, the decision is often very different with CSIs and investigators spending as much time as needed to process the scene. Shooting scenes add additional tasks to crime scene processing that are not needed in other scenes and should also be processed for the basic crime scene staples such as trace evidence (i.e., hairs, fibers, other materials, etc.), biological evidence (i.e., blood, semen, other body fluids), 2-D and 3-D impression evidence (i.e., fingerprints, shoe impressions, bitemarks, etc.), drug evidence, questioned document evidence, and digital evidence. Digital evidence in the form of surveillance videos and photographs should be sought out quickly before that evidence can be destroyed or overwritten by a business surveillance system routine purging of data.

FORENSIC LABORATORY TESTING

The firearm should be sent to the servicing laboratory or testing facility for a function's test to ensure the firearm is functioning properly to counter any claims that the firearm discharged accidently due to a malfunction. Firearm examiners at the lab will also conduct test fires of the weapon using the same ammunition used in the commission of the crime under investigation if at all possible. The firearm will be fired into a water tank or similar apparatus designed to safely slow down and stop the projectile without causing any deformations. The shell casings and projectiles will then be examined for various markings and striations caused during the firing process. These markings and striations are then most often compared using a comparison microscope, allowing the firearms examiner to match or exclude the firearm being tested as the firearm that fired the rounds in the case under investigation. Additional tests that should be conducted by the forensic laboratories include the examinations by other forensic disciplines such as latent prints and DNA.

It is a common belief that a shooter's DNA will be located on a firearm, spent or unspent cartridge, or on a magazine in the case of a semi-automatic firearm. A study published in 2017 found that in the best scenario a DNA profile was only found 26 percent of the time using a set of specific procedures (Fan et al., 2017). The extreme heat and pressures created during the firing process along with lubricants and how a weapon actually functions makes obtaining positive DNA results challenging (Fan et al., 2017). A promising study found the most likely places to locate viable DNA on a firearm to be on the grip, and for semi-automatic firearms on the slide, both surfaces being generally rougher and thus the likelihood of skin cells being present (Gosch et al., 2019). These same issues make locating viable latent prints equally challenging.

NATIONAL INTEGRATED BALLISTIC INFORMATION NETWORK (NIBIN)

NIBIN is a federal program administered by the ATF that began in 1999 which aids law enforcement in firearm-related investigations. By the end of 2019, NIBIN partnered with 220 state and local law enforcement agencies to provide ease of entering evidence into the system in a timely manner (ATF, Fact Sheet, n.d.). This program compares markings on both projectiles and shell casings from other incidents entered into the program and often leads to links to other unsolved crimes. According to the ATF, over 4.2 million items of ballistic evidence have been entered in the system, producing nearly a quarter of a million investigative leads, with over 67,000 investigative leads in 2019 alone (ATF, Fact Sheet, n.d.). This database of shell casings and projectiles is run by qualified and trained NIBIN technicians and can provide invaluable clues that link firearms incidents together faster than traditional forensic laboratory examinations. As in all investigations, close coordination with the prosecuting attorney should be maintained and in some cases the evidence submitted to NIBIN should be examined by a qualified forensic firearm examiner at the law enforcement agency's servicing forensic laboratory for forensic confirmation of the NIBIN results.

The National Institute of Standards and Technology (NIST) began a 3-D database of firearms evidence in 2016 that seeks to improve the results of traditional forensic firearm examinations (2020). Instead of comparing 2-D views of the traditional evidence submitted in firearms cases such as shell casings and projectiles, this process will produce a 3-D view that will provide additional verification of the significance of forensic testing results (NIST, 2020). Forensic science disciplines including firearms and toolmarks constantly seek to improve their abilities and results to ensure the rights of the accused while protecting the rights of the victims through scientific applications to physical or digital evidence in a criminal investigation.

Gunshot Residue (GSR) Testing

GSR consists of partially burned and unburned gunpowder particles, primer residue, and residues from projectiles. The presence of GSR on a person, especially a shooting hand, has historically and generally been considered relevant evidence in firearm-related investigations. However, because the presence of the three base components of GSR (barium, antimony, and lead) are naturally occurring elements and are present in the environment, some disagreement exists regarding the value of this evidence. Most of the original GSR tests involved using a swab on the hands of a suspect or victim. If the test was positive it was not scientifically possible to determine if the person actually had handled or shot a firearm as there was no discrimination from the natural occurrence of the three elements. However, with the advent of the scanning electron microscope (SEM), the ability to discriminate and produce a result that has potential investigative value. In a 1977 study conducted at the direction of the US Department of Justice, it was determined that the SEM examination of potential GSR was able to determine if barium, antimony, and lead are present in the basic form of a sphere which does not occur in nature and occurs in the manufacture of gunpowder and can be successfully retrieved for up to twelve hours following a shooting (Wolten et al., 1977). If GSR is found on a person involved in a shooting investigation, it must be determined if that person had lawfully handled a weapon or worked in an environment that produces similar compounds that would logically explain the presence of that compound. The 1977 study cited above provides an exhaustive list of the types of locations, work environments, and occupations that they determined should be considered as potential sources of these compounds (Wolten et al., 1977).

When GSR testing is determined to be used in an investigation, investigators must take the appropriate steps to avoid cross-contamination. If the investigator has recently handled a weapon and/or ammunition, the investigator must thoroughly wash their hands and put on clean gloves that could not have any GSR on them. The hand of all suspects and victims should be processed for GSR as soon as possible following the initial notification of a shooting. SEM GSR test kits come with all of the supplies needed along with instructions on the suggested methods to follow in most circumstances. As with all criminal investigations, the investigator must be prepared to adapt to the particular situation in order to have the opportunity to collect any evidence that may be present. An exciting advancement in GSR testing at a crime scene setting versus a laboratory setting is being developed utilizing Laser Induced Breakdown Spectroscopy (LIBS) (Fernandez et al., 2018). The ability for an investigator or CSI to test for the presence at the scene would speed up their investigation and lead to additional investigative leads quickly and thus potentially speed up the successful resolution of a shooting investigation. LIBS has been found to be a viable tool in the field for the identification of GSR on surfaces that cannot be removed from the scene as well as on clothing with blood surrounding the suspected bullet hole (Pyl et al., 2020). A novel approach to locating two of the components in GSR, antimony and barium, is through nasal samples of suspects (Merli et al., 2016). This method supposes that a shooter will ingest some of the GSR in their nasal cavities when firing a firearm. One study found scientifically significant amounts of antimony and barium in suspects who fired a firearm within the first three hours after the shooting occurred (Merli et al., 2016).

FORENSIC AUTOPSY

Shooting incidents that result in loss of life require an autopsy, normally performed by a forensic pathologist. (See figure 21.1.) A forensic pathologist is a medical doctor, trained and educated to specifically perform forensic autopsies—those autopsies that have legal implications. A primary objective of a forensic autopsy is determination of the cause and manner of death. The cause of death in shooting cases is often the gunshot wound itself, though other contributing causes may be observed. The manner of death in shooting cases may be homicide, suicide, accident, or undetermined, depending on the circumstances of the death. Police investigators often work closely with forensic pathologists and medical investigators who specialize in death investigations. These investigators are referred to as "medicolegal death investigators." They

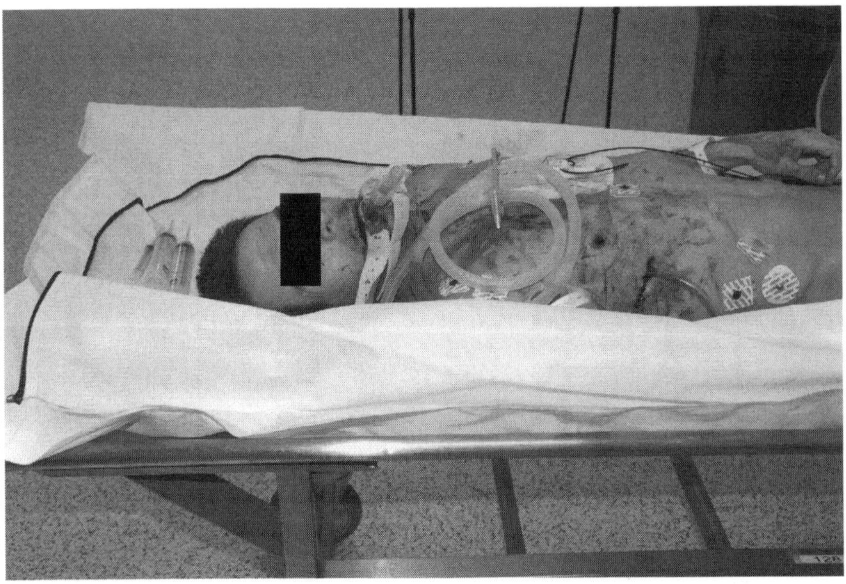

Figure 21.1. A forensic autopsy is an integral portion of any shooting death investigation. ***Image courtesy of Erick Bryant, Colorado Bureau of Investigations.***

receive specialized training in various aspects of forensic pathology. Medico-legal death investigators are employed by medical examiner's offices and are not law enforcement officers.

Another purpose of an autopsy is to identify the victim. This usually involves fingerprint, dental, and/or DNA comparisons with records that existed prior to the person's death. In cases involving decomposed remains and skeletons, a forensic anthropologist, a "bone expert," may be consulted. Forensic anthropologists help develop physical profiles for unidentified skeletal remains by determining the approximate age, sex, and possibly race of the victim. In the eyes of a skilled forensic anthropologist, the skeleton can provide other interesting clues such as whether victims suffered from unusual bone disease or disorders, provide insight into a variety of skeletal injuries, help determine the time of death, and even be used to help identify a person's previous occupation.

The forensic autopsy begins with an external examination of the decedent's body. Gunshot wounds and any other injuries are carefully analyzed, annotated, and photographed. In addition, features such as scars and tattoos will also be documented. X-rays of the body are routinely obtained, especially in gunshot cases, and are of immense help in locating bullets and bullet fragments which have been imbedded within the body.

After the external examination, incisions are made allowing the pathologist to examine internal aspects of the body, including the organs. Injuries, abnormalities, evidence of disease or other factors that may have contributed to the death are carefully analyzed during this internal examination process. The head and brain are thoroughly examined as well. Bullet wound tracks are identified, examined, and photographed. The bullet path through the body is identified and articulated on reports. Trajectory rods are sometimes used to illustrate the bullet path (see figure 21.2). The trajectory through the body may be important to investigators when reconstructing the scene as it may help reveal the position and location of the victim at the time of the shooting. Various fluids, such as blood, urine, and vitreous humor are obtained for later toxicological testing.

Though forensic autopsies generally take a half to full day to complete, the final autopsy findings and report may not be published for several weeks. Forensic pathologists perform numerous autopsies and must also wait for other examinations, such as microscopic examination of tissues and toxicology, to be completed, analyzed, and synthesized with other findings and case facts. Once the final autopsy report is obtained, it should be reviewed for any potential investigative leads or steps that should be completed to follow all of the evidence to its logical conclusion(s).

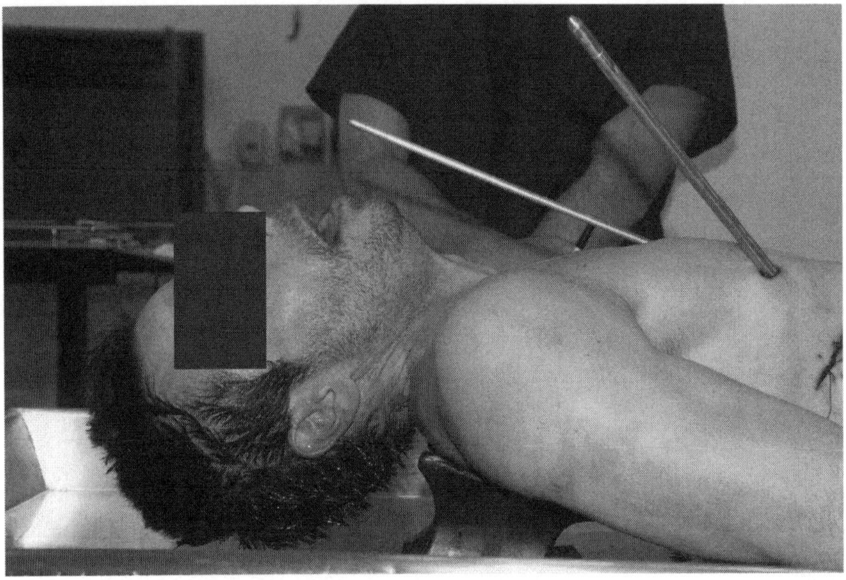

Figure 21.2. Forensic pathologists may use trajectory rods to help visualize the trajectory of the bullet through the body of a decedent. *Image courtesy of Erick Bryant, Colorado Bureau of Investigations.*

Gunshot Wound Analysis: The Basics

Close examination of gunshot injuries occurs at autopsy but is also completed at the crime scene or other locations prior to the autopsy. The initial hours after the crime are widely known as a critical time for investigators to gather evidence and identify suspects. Therefore, analysis of the injuries early in the process is advantageous. Analyzing gunshot injuries can aid investigators in a multitude of ways. By examining injuries, investigators may be able to obtain useful information concerning the type of ammunition used, the type of weapon, directionality of the bullet path through the body, range of fire, or whether the bullet struck an intermediary target.

Gunshot wounds are generally first categorized as entrance or exit wounds. Entrance wounds from rifled barrel weapons are typically circular in shape, but atypical wounds can occur when bullets ricochet or pass through intermediate targets, causing the bullet to tumble. A common misconception is that exit wounds are always larger than entrance wounds; this is not actually the case. Exit wounds may have a variety of shapes and sizes, depending on a variety of factors including the type of weapon, ammunition, and bullet pathway through the body, and exit site. Since numerous variables affect the exit wound appearance, investigators at the scene must be extremely cautious interpreting the injuries. The most reliable method of distinguishing an exit from entrance wound is examining the injuries for the presence of soot deposits from the burnt and unburnt gunpowder discharge. Entrance locations may also show signs of burning, small abrasions known as stippling caused by gunpowder residue particles, and a superficial injury around the perimeter of the injury known as an abrasion collar. The presence of any of these characteristics indicate the wound is an entry wound since exit wounds will not exhibit these features. Examination at the scene is often difficult, however, because blood, hair, clothing, or other items may obscure the injury. Since the injury will not be cleaned until the autopsy, in these instances, investigators will wait until autopsy to interpret the injuries.

Entrance wounds are subclassified as contact, near-contact or loose-contact, intermediate, and distant or indeterminate. This classification is based upon the distance of the muzzle from the body at the time of discharge. Contact gunshot wounds are commonly observed in suicides and most often occur on the head (Blumenthal, 2007; DiMaio, 2015). A contact gunshot wound means the weapon's muzzle was pressed against the body at the time of discharge. Because the barrel is hot, the muzzle often leaves an imprint on the skin. Hot gases and gunpowder are discharged directly into the wound tract causing burning, searing, and blackening inside of the wound. In cases in which the weapon was not placed firmly against the skin, some of the gases and gunpowder can be visualized around the margin of the wound. Many experts refer to this type of gunshot wound as loose contact.

Intermediate gunshot wounds are injuries in which the muzzle was not pressed tight against the skin, but still close enough to allow gunpowder residue to be deposited on skin and/or superficial injuries to occur near the gunshot wound. Intermediate gunshot wounds are characterized by the presence of stippling. Stippling may be caused by unburned gunpowder particles and when so, is termed powder tattooing (DiMaio, 2015). Stippling, unlike soot depositions, cannot be washed away. The specific range of fire cannot be determined solely by visual examination, because gunpowder and other materials causing stippling are affected by a variety of variables, including the weapon and ammunition. Thus, the term "intermediate" is a general one that describes a range from near contact up to a few feet (Denton et al., 2006). The presence of soot, however, is indicative of a closer range of fire.

In general terms, the closer the muzzle to the skin, the more condensed the stippling pattern. This pattern may sometimes allow pathologists to determine the direction the bullet was traveling upon impact with the body. Gas discharges from compensators, flash suppressors, gas ports, and vents may also leave characteristic soot patterns which can provide useful information regarding the range of fire, and possibly position of the weapon in relation to the injury (DiMaio, 2015). Pathologists and investigators must be cautious with any range of fire interpretation because the weapon, ammunition, intermediary targets, and clothing will affect the deposition of soot and stippling (Denton et al., 2006). Investigators must rely upon forensic testing using the weapon and same type of ammunition to obtain more reliable range of fire estimates. Intermediate range gunshot wounds often result from homicidal killings but are seen in suicides as well (Blumenthal, 2007; DiMaio, 2015).

Distant gunshot wounds occur when the range of the muzzle to skin exceeds the distance at which stippling or soot deposits occur (DiMaio, 2015; Denton et al., 2006). Forensic pathologists cannot provide an estimate of the range of fire upon inspection of distant wounds; the injuries appear the same whether the shot was fired at 5 feet or 500 feet. An abrasion ring may be visible. Also, a dark circle referred to as bullet wipe may be visible. Bullet wipe is caused by transfer of oil and other residue from the bullet to the skin as it passes through. Both the abrasion ring and bullet wipe may be seen at closer distance shots but are often obscured.

Shotgun injuries often present distinctive characteristics from those caused by rifled barrel guns. Shotguns fire shells that contain numerous pellets or single slugs. Injuries arising from slugs are somewhat similar in appearance to injuries arising from rifled barrel guns; however, injuries caused by pellets differ dramatically. In general, shotguns have shorter effective ranges of fire than rifled weapons, thus mortality rates decrease significantly at longer distances (Cassidy, 2000; Spitz, 1993). Close contact shotgun injuries to the head usually result in massive devastation to tissue with exit wounds often completely removing portions of the skull. Shots from close and intermediate distances result in the pellets penetrating the body and deposition of soot around and in the wound. The wad may penetrate the body at closer ranges or strike and deflect off the skin at further distances. Wad deflections usually leave impression marks that would be helpful to investigators. Distant shots result in the pellets striking the body over a wider area and causing contusions and abrasions on the skin at the impact sites. Exit wounds often are not present in intermediate and distant range shotgun shootings. Though a range of factors are involved in the spread of pellets, in general terms, the further the shooting distance, the larger the pellet pattern on the body. A generalized rule of thumb is that one-third of the spread of shot in centimeters equals the range of fire in meters (Knight, 1996). Just as with shootings involving rifled barrel weapons, forensic firearms examiners should test-fire weapons to obtain more accurate and reliable range of fire estimates. A reader who wishes to delve deeper into shotgun injuries, or gunshot injuries in general, may consider *Gunshot Wounds: Practical Aspects of Firearms, Ballistics, and Forensic Techniques*, Third Ed., by Vincent J. M. DiMaio.

CRIME SCENE RECONSTRUCTION

Crime scene reconstruction is a commonly misunderstood and misapplied term, often confused with terms such as reenactment and recreation. Reconstruction is a scientific process involving an analysis of case circumstances along with forensic and investigative findings, whereas reenactments and recreations are used in many different contexts but are often subjective in nature and unscientific. The term recreation, itself, suggests that one explicitly "creates" the information. This, of course, should be avoided by all measures. Reenactments, on the other hand, involve a demonstration, or model, of the crime being performed again. Reenactments are sometimes used in trial but should be based on an actual reconstruction of the events performed by forensic professionals trained in the crime scene reconstruction process.

The specific purpose of crime scene reconstruction, according to the Association for Crime Scene Reconstruction, is "to gain explicit knowledge of the series of events that surround the commission of a crime using deductive and inductive reasoning, physical evidence, scientific methods, and their interrelationships" (n.d.; para. 1). Reconstruction may occur in a variety of ways: a specific fact regarding the commission of a crime may be analyzed (for example, a suspect handled a weapon, based on fingerprint evidence) or an event, series of events, or entire incident may be analyzed or sequenced (for example, a victim was shot in a bedroom [1], then moved to the living room [2] before collapsing [3]).

Crime scene reconstruction involves assimilation of findings from a variety of forensic and investigative disciplines. Forensic scientists in fields such as biology/DNA, chemistry, toxicology, questioned documents, digital evidence, footwear, and fingerprints, depending on the evidence identified and collected in the investigation, may analyze evidence and provide scientific conclusions to investigators. Investigators then integrate and assimilate those findings with information gathered from interviews, analysis of the crime scene, the forensic autopsy, and other investigative activity, to perform the actual reconstruction process. The reconstruction should follow the scientific method and be free of cognitive or other biases. The reconstruction of shooting incidents often involves the use of several unique techniques and analysis of evidence unique to shootings.

SHOOTING INCIDENT RECONSTRUCTION TECHNIQUES

Shooting incident reconstruction is essentially a subset of crime scene reconstruction that includes various methods and analytical techniques which apply specifically to shootings. Some of these methods include analyzing bullet holes and bullet impact sites; determining the flight path, or trajectory, of the bullet; and analyzing cartridge case ejection patterns. Information gleaned from these activities, when synthesized with forensic examinations and general investigative findings, can often help determine the most probable sequence of events, positions of victims and shooter(s) at various junctures during the event, and help answer specific investigative questions that may arise during the investigation.

Bullet Impact Site Analysis

A few things can happen when a bullet strikes an object at a crime scene: the bullet may perforate the target forming entry and exit sites, it may penetrate the target but not exit, or it may strike the target but not penetrate it. Which of these occurs is based on the bullet characteristics, the velocity of travel, and the composition of the target. Some objects, such as sheetrock, are easily penetrable, while others, such as concrete, are much more difficult to penetrate. Bullets that strike objects without penetrating may provide some clues to investigators. The force of the impact results in the bullet creating distinguishing impressions on the target that may be used to help identify the type of bullet.

Bullets that do not penetrate targets often ricochet. A ricochet angle, defined as the angle at which the bullet travels after impacting the target surface, is affected by the angle at which the bullet struck the surface, called the incident angle; the bullet characteristics; and the target surface. The incident angle at or below which a bullet will ricochet is referred to as the critical angle. Researchers have extensively studied various ammunition and materials to determine critical angles (Burke & Rowe, 1992). Known critical angles for various ammunition and surfaces, of course, is very useful for the reconstructionist.

The sites of impact at ricochet points can often provide valuable information. The bullet impact on a painted surface will compress, or pinch, the paint resulting in marks that allow directionality of the bullet to be ascertained by a trained reconstructionist. Likewise, lead-in marks and depositions of partially vaporized lead may be present that also allow directionality to be gleaned. Depending on how the bullet strikes the surface, a unique mark, known as a chisum trail, may be found on smooth, unyielding surfaces. The marks are typically longer on either the left or right sides and are strong indicators of the bullet's twist.

When bullets penetrate a target, the characteristics of the bullet hole itself may help investigators understand a variety of things concerning the shooting, such as direction of travel, angle of impact, and whether the hole is an entry or exit site. Bullet hole characteristics are dependent upon the bullet, velocity, and the target itself. Common materials struck by bullets at crime scenes include sheet rock, sheet metal, wood, glass, rubber, plastic, asphalt, and fabric. Bullets penetrating these materials will have very different characteristics and appearances; thus, it is important for the reconstructionist to be familiar with contemporary research regarding these interactions. Since there are so many variables involved in the bullet hole formation, estimating the caliber of the bullet that passed through the hole may be imprecise. For example, wood, some plastics, and rubber result in bullet holes being smaller than the diameter of the bullet. Wood particles may become embedded in the nose of the bullet inhibiting it from expanding while the smaller holes in rubber are due to rubber's elastic nature.

Bullet holes in glass create unique characteristics which may allow investigators to determine the bullet's direction of travel and the sequence in which the bullets passed through the glass. All glass, however, is not the same, and the type of glass will determine whether these exams can be performed. Glass panes that are standard in homes and businesses are considered plate glass. When a bullet passes through plate glass, the cavity widens, creating a larger exit than entrance. This phenomenon is called beveling or coning and is commonly examined to determine the direction of a bullet hole as an entrance or exit site. When bullets pass through plate glass, the forces will cause the glass to bend, resulting in a series of radial fractures that extend outward from the bullet hole. When additional bullet holes are formed, and radial fractures generated, those fractures cannot travel across other preexisting fractures. This phenomenon allows investigators to determine the sequence of shots by examining locations where radial fractures intersect.

Unfortunately, this technique is not always viable for glass on motor vehicles. Windshields are composed of laminated glass, which is actually two pieces of glass with a layer of polyvinyl butyral between them. When bullets pass through laminated glass, additional stress fractures are known to occur from vehicle movement or thermal changes. Because these fractures may be unpredictable and unable to be distinguished from those caused by the stresses of the bullet penetration, bullet sequencing should be attempted with caution. Laminate glass does, however, cause beveling, and thus the direction of travel can be ascertained.

Motor vehicle passenger and rear windows are composed of tempered glass, which is designed to fragment into small cubes when enough force is applied. The first bullet that passes through tempered glass will cause fractures and essentially shatter the glass. If subsequent bullets pass through, they will knock out chunks of already shattered glass. The first shot passing through the glass will always be the one that caused the visible fractures. In very high-profile cases, crime scene investigators may need to collect as many of the small pieces of glass as can be located and send them to their servicing forensic laboratory to have them put back together to determine where the first bullet went through the glass and if the bullet came from outside or inside of the vehicle.

Bullet Path/Trajectory

One of the most valuable and insightful techniques investigators employ at shooting scenes is bullet path analysis. A bullet's trajectory, which falls under the broad category of external ballistics, is affected by two main factors: air resistance and gravity (Heard, 1997). Upon leaving the barrel, the bullet will travel in parabolic fashion in a general downward curved path. Factors such as muzzle velocity, barrel angle and elevation, velocity, bullet shape, and bullet density all affect the specific trajectory path (Heard, 1997). In most instances, however, shootings involve relatively short distances, and the actual trajectory is estimated using straight line methods as gravity has not had the opportunity to affect the trajectory of a projectile in any meaningful manner, hence the commonly used terminology "bullet path analysis." In cases involving longer-range shots, advanced mathematical calculations are required in order to generate an accurate bullet trajectory.

Whenever a bullet passes through a surface and strikes or penetrates a second surface, reconstructionists can use trajectory rods to generate an accurate straight-line estimate of the bullet path. Trajectory rods are wooden or metal rods that reconstructionists place into the actual bullet hole(s). The rod, itself, is representative of a straight-line trajectory. Reconstructionists usually use lasers or string to illustrate the straight-line path through space. This method, when documented with advanced photographic techniques, allows a full visualization of the straight-line pathway of the bullet and can be immensely helpful in identifying positions of shooters, victims, and other objects at the scene. Both vertical and horizontal angles of the bullet's impact point are obtained and recorded in order to produce an accurate record of the bullet impact angle. These angles, along with the straight-line trajectory, result in a reconstructed bullet path that yields a +/- 5 degrees accuracy rate (Hueske, 2016). When trajectory rods are not practical, a geometrical equation may be used to generate an estimate of the impact angle. This method, though useful in helping to establish shooter and victim positions at the scene, is less precise than the trajectory rod method, with a generally accepted error rate of +/- 10 degrees (Hueske, 2016).

The investigative power of bullet path analysis lies in the reconstructionist's ability to integrate their findings with other facts of the investigation. Taken alone, the bullet's impact angle and bullet path are useful, but when analyzed along with information from interviews, scientific examinations, crime scene analysis, and medical examiner reports, this technique allows the reconstructionist to obtain a deeper understanding of many aspects of the shooting incident. This method becomes even more insightful when integrated with the analysis of bloodstains.

Bloodstain Pattern Analysis

Bloodstain evidence is one of the more interesting, and insightful, types of physical evidence that can be found at a crime scene. The volume and depth of information that can be obtained from blood is astounding. Consider that a trained analyst may determine the positions of suspects, victims, or objects at a scene; direction a specific blood drop was traveling at its impact point with a surface; an approximate angle of that impact; the nature of force involved in the incident that caused the bleeding; an approximate number of blows struck during an incident; and a sequence of events (Bevel & Gardner, 2001). A full analysis of a scene with bloodstains can render a story of what unfolded, though not quite in the same manner as many television shows portray. In actuality, it is more fragmented, but one with several known pieces of data. For example, a trained analyst, from a single smeared blood drop, could determine the approximate direction in which the drop fell, and gain understanding of a general sequence of events that must have occurred. First, the injury must have occurred causing bleeding. Second, the victim must have been positioned in a certain area relative to the bloodstain. Third, the blood drop struck the surface. Lastly, something came in contact with the blood on the surface, causing the blood to smear. Again, the analyst can generate all of this from a single drop of blood! Imagine what a trained analyst can do with a heavily bloodstained crime scene.

With specific regard to shooting scenes, the analysis of small individual stains created by a penetrating injury and the resulting projection of blood is known as area of origin determination. Analysts can examine impact spatter patterns and determine an approximate origin of the individual stains, or in other words, determine an approximate position of the victim when he or she was shot. This information, when combined with the shooting incident reconstruction techniques, especially bullet path analysis, is a powerful analytical tool, one that elucidates the analytical and integrative portions of the reconstruction process.

ACTIVE SHOOTER INVESTIGATIONS

A statistically rare occurrence is active shooter cases in which large numbers of victims are present at one time. According to the Federal Bureau of Investigation, there have been 305 active shooter cases between 2000 and 2019, creating an average of 15.25 cases per year in the United States (Federal Bureau of Investigation, Quick Look: 277 Active Shooter Incidents, n.d.; Active Shooter Incidents in the United States, n.d.). The FBI reported that in 2019 there were 28 active shooter incidents, almost double this average, continuing the decade-long overall increase in the frequency of these incidents (Active Shooter Incidents in the United States, n.d.). Of the 30 active shooters in the 28 incidents in 2019, 15 died—by suicide (5), killed by law enforcement (9), or killed by a bystander (1)—and the remaining 15 were arrested by law enforcement (Active Shooter Incidents in the United States, n.d.). Between 2000 and 2018, approximately 20 percent of all active shooter incidents occurred in an educational setting, and in 2019 only approximately 11 percent of the active shooter incidents occurred in an educational setting (Quick Look: 277 Active Shooter Incidents, n.d.; Active Shooter Incidents in the United States, n.d.).

An active shooter investigation begins the same way that every other firearm-related incident occurs—after the shooting stops. Every law enforcement officer involved with an actual active shooter situation has to focus on stopping the shooter(s) and caring for the wounded, including the shooter(s) as applicable. Once the shooting stops, the similarities to other smaller shooting investigations remain, but the complexity and size of the tasks required is enormous with tremendous pressure placed on any law enforcement agency responsible for the investigation. With the exception of a very few of the very largest law enforcement agencies in our country, it is extremely wise for the vast majority of law enforcement agencies to seek and/or accept help from other law enforcement agencies and form a temporary investigative task force to complete the investigation as quickly and as thoroughly as possible. The pressure of both national and international news media is immense as these cases draw worldwide attention, headlines, and news programs that are dedicated to the incident. State and federal legislative bodies often hold hearings on these incidents seeking out ways in order to prevent future ones.

Processing these crime scenes often takes weeks to accomplish, and in some instances the site is maintained by law enforcement until the trial in the event the jury requests to visit the scene in person. These cases are often given the highest priority over every other investigation in the country by the FBI forensic laboratory as well as other state or federal forensic laboratories. Law enforcement is well served to be trained, equipped, and prepared to face the many challenges these incidents create. Having established relationships and memorandums of agreement or assistance (MOA) between multiple law enforcement agencies that train and prepare together so that they are ready to work together seamlessly often helps both the response and the subsequent investigation.

CONCLUSION

Violent crime induces fear and a great deal of intrigue among U.S. citizens. Though violent crime rates have fluctuated over time, the raw number is at an all-time high. A significant percentage of violent crime and suicides in the United States involves the use of firearms. The investigation of firearm-related incidents, therefore, should be of particular importance. A wide range of investigative and forensic techniques, from basic interviewing to advanced crime scene reconstruction specializations, are often utilized to better understand firearm-related incidents. This chapter has provided an overview of investigative tactics, forensic science techniques, and novel technologies that are commonly used in firearm-related investigations.

BIBLIOGRAPHY

Adcock, J. [2019, August 19]. Can new NIJ 'best practices' solve the 'cold case crisis'? Retrieved from https://thecrimereport.org/2019/08/19/can-new-nij-best-practices-solve-the-cold-case-crisis/.

Adcock, J. M., and Chancellor, A. S. [2013]. *Death Investigations*. Burlington, MA: Jones & Bartlett Learning.

Association for Crime Scene Reconstruction. [n.d.]. ACSR – Association for Crime Scene Reconstruction. Retrieved February 6, 2020, from https://www.acsr.org/.

Barlow, B. [2019, March 27]. When "just the facts" doesn't work. Retrieved December 5, 2019, from https://www.w-z.com/2019/03/27/when-just-the-facts-doesnt-work/.

Bevel, T., and Gardner, R. M. [2001]. *Bloodstain Pattern Analysis: With an Introduction to Crime Scene Reconstruction, Second Edition [Practical Aspects of Criminal and Forensic Investigations]* [Second ed.]. Amsterdam, Netherlands: Amsterdam University Press.

Blumenthal, R. [2007]. Suicidal gunshot wounds to the head. *The American Journal of Forensic Medicine and Pathology*, *28*[4], 288–291. https://doi.org/10.1097/paf.0b013e318148bdca.

Bureau of Alcohol, Tobacco, Firearms and Explosives [n.d.]. Fact Sheet – National Integrated Information Network. Retrieved from https://www.atf.gov/resource-center/fact-sheet/fact-sheet-national-integrated-ballistic-information-network.

Bureau of Alcohol, Tobacco, Firearms and Explosives [n.d.]. National Tracing Center. Retrieved from https://www.atf.gov/firearms/national-tracing-center.

Burke, T. W., and Rowe, W. F. [1992]. Bullet ricochet: A comprehensive review. *Journal of Forensic Sciences*, *37*[5], 13312J. https://doi.org/10.1520/jfs13312j.

Cassidy, M. [2000]. "Smooth-bore firearm injuries." Chapter 5, in J. K. Mason and B. N. Purdue [Eds.]. *The Pathology of Trauma*, Third Ed. Arnold Publishers.

Choi, K.-S., Librett, M., and Collins, T. J. [2013]. An empirical evaluation: Gunshot detection system and its effectiveness on police practices. *Police Practice and Research*, *15*[1], 48–61. https://doi.org/10.1080/15614263.2013.800671.

Denton, J., Segovia, A., and Filkins, J. [2006]. Practical pathology of gunshot wounds. *Arch Pathol Lab Med*, *130*[9], 1283–1289. https://doi.org/10.1043/1543-2165.

DiMaio, V. J. M. [2015]. *Gunshot wounds: Practical aspects of firearms, ballistics, and forensic techniques, Third Edition [Practical aspects of criminal and forensic investigations]* [3rd ed.]. Boca Raton, FL: CRC Press.

Fan, G., Li, W., and Zhang, Q. [2017, December]. An evaluation of the performance of DNA recovered from fired firearms and cartridge cases using microdialysis filtration. *Forensic Science International: Genetics Supplement Series.* Retrieved from https://doi.org/10.1016/j.fsigss.2017.09.096.

Federal Bureau of Investigation. [n.d.]. Active shooter incidents in the United States in 2019. Retrieved June 1, 2019, from https://www.fbi.gov/file-repository/active-shooter-incidents-in-the-us-2019-042820.pdf/view.

Federal Bureau of Investigation. [n.d.]. Crime in the U.S. 2018. Retrieved December 5, 2019, from https://ucr.fbi.gov/crime-in-the-u.s/2018/crime-in-the-u.s.-2018.

Federal Bureau of Investigation. [n.d.]. Quick look: 277 active shooter incidents in the United States from 2000 to 2018. Retrieved June 1, 2019, from https://www.fbi.gov/about/partnerships/office-of-partner-engagement/active-shooter-incidents-graphics.

Federal Bureau of Investigation. [n.d.-b]. Uniform Crime Reporting [UCR] Program. Retrieved December 5, 2019, from https://www.fbi.gov/services/cjis/ucr.

Federal Bureau of Investigation. [n.d.-a]. Uniform Crime Reporting Statistics. Retrieved December 5, 2019, from https://www.ucrdatatool.gov/Search/Crime/State/RunCrimeStatebyState.cfm.

Fernandez, A., Gimeno, I., Toribio, P., Fernandez, E., Snachez, F., and Gonzalez, A. [2018, November]. Real-time detection of GSR particles from crime scene: A comparative study of SEM/EDX and portable LIBS system. *Forensic Science International*, *292*, 167–175. Retrieved from https://doi.org/10.1016/j.forsciint.2018.09.021.

Fisher, R. P., and Geiselman, R. E. [2010]. The cognitive interview method of conducting police interviews: Eliciting extensive information and promoting therapeutic jurisprudence. *International Journal of Law and Psychiatry*, *33*[5–6], 321–328. https://doi.org/10.1016/j.ijlp.2010.09.004.

Gallup, Inc. [2019, November 20]. Crime | Gallup Historical Trends. Retrieved December 5, 2019, from https://news.gallup.com/poll/1603/crime.aspx.

Geiselman, R. E., Fisher, R. P., MacKinnon, D. P., and Holland, H. L. [1986]. Enhancement of eyewitness memory with the cognitive interview. *The American Journal of Psychology*, *99*[3], 385. https://doi.org/10.2307/1422492.

Gosch, A., Euteneuer, J., Wossner, J., and Courts, C. [2019, December]. Analysis of DNA transfer to firearms considering relevant alternative handling scenarios. *Forensic Science International: Genetics Supplement Series*. Retrieved from https://doi.org/10.1016/j.fsigss.2019.10.041.

Grinshteyn, E., and Hemenway, D. [2019]. Violent death rates in the US compared to those of the other high-income countries, 2015. *Preventive Medicine*, *123*, 20–26. https://doi.org/10.1016/j.ypmed.2019.02.026.

Heard, B. J. [1997]. *Handbook of Firearms and Ballistics*. Hoboken, NJ: Wiley.

Home-ShotSpotter. [n.d.]. Retrieved March 5, 2020, from https://www.shotspotter.com/.

Hueske, E. [2016]. *Practical Analysis and Reconstruction of Shooting Incidents, Second Edition*. Boca Raton: CRC Press, https://doi.org/10.1201/b19092.

Identification Markings Placed on Firearms (98R-341P). [2001, August 3]. Federal Register. Retrieved from https://www.federalregister.gov/documents/2001/08/03/01-19418/identification-markings-placed-on-firearms-98r-341p#p-6.

Knight, B. [1996]. *Forensic Pathology*, Second Ed. London, UK: Taylor and Francis.

Kochanek, K., Murphy, S., Xu, J., and Arias, E. [2019]. National vital statistics report: Deaths final data for 2017 [68–69]. Retrieved from https://www.cdc.gov/nchs/data/nvsr/nvsr68/nvsr68_09-508.pdf.

Köhnken, G., Milne, R., Memon, A., and Bull, R. [1999]. The cognitive interview: A meta-analysis. *Psychology, Crime & Law*, *5*[1–2], 3–27. https://doi.org/10.1080/10683169908414991.

La Vigne, N., Thompson, P., Lawrence, D., and Goff, M. [2019, October 1]. Implementing gunshot detection technology. Retrieved from https://www.urban.org/sites/default/files/publication/101161/implementing_gunshot_detection_technology_recommendations_for_law_enforcement_and_municipal_partners.pdf.

Marcus, P. [2006]. It's not just about Miranda! Determining the voluntariness of confessions in criminal prosecutions. *Valparaiso University Law Review*, *40*[3], 601–644. Retrieved from https://ssrn.com/abstract=1789004.

Mares, D., and Blackburn, E. [2012]. Evaluating the effectiveness of an acoustic gunshot location system in St. Louis, MO. *Policing*, *6*[1], 26–42. https://doi.org/10.1093/police/par056.

Merli, D., Brandone, A., Amadasi, A., Cattaneo, C., and Profumo, A. [2016, May 14]. The detection of gunshot residues in the nasal mucus of suspected shooters. *International Journal of Legal Medicine, 130*, 1045–1052. https://doi-org.ez-proxy.methodist.edu/10.1007/s00414-016-1375-7.

Monuteaux, M. C., Lee, L. K., Hemenway, D., Mannix, R., and Fleegler, E. W. [2015]. Firearm ownership and violent crime in the U.S. *American Journal of Preventive Medicine*, *49*[2], 207–214. https://doi.org/10.1016/j.amepre.2015.02.008.

National Institute of Standards and Technology. [2020, January 3]. NIST Ballistics Toolmark Database. Retrieved from https://www.nist.gov/programs-projects/nist-ballistics-toolmark-database#:~:text=The%20NIST%20

Ballistics%20Toolmark%20Research,and%20cartridge%20case%20toolmark%20 data.&text=ease%20the%20transition%20to%20the,topography%20data%20 in%20firearms%20identification.

Perkins, C. [2003]. National crime victimization survey, 1993–2011: Weapon use and violent crime [NCJ 241730]. Retrieved from https://www.bjs.gov/content/pub/pdf/wuvc01.pdf

Planty, M., and Truman, J. [2013]. Firearms violence, 1993–2011 [NCJ 241730]. Retrieved from https://www.bjs.gov/content/pub/pdf/fv9311.pdf.

Public Law 90-618. [1968, October 22]. 18 United States Code, Chapter 44.-FIREARMS. Retrieved from https://www.govinfo.gov/content/pkg/STATUTE-82/pdf/STATUTE-82-Pg1213-2.pdf#page=1.

Pyl, C., Morris, K., Arroyo, L., and Trejos, T. [2020, June]. Assessing the utility of LIBS in the reconstruction of firearm related incidents. *Forensic Chemistry, 19*. Retrieved from https://doi.org/10.1016/j.forc.2020.100251.

Rule 803. Exceptions to the Rule Against Hearsay. Cornell Law School. Retrieved from https://www.law.cornell.edu/rules/fre/rule_803.

Serial Number Restoration Test No. 18-5250 Summary Report. [2018, April 16]. Retrieved from https://cts-forensics.com/reports/38250_Web.pdf.

Spitz, W. U. [Ed.]. [1993]. *Spitz and Fisher's Medicolegal Investigation of Death – Guidelines for the application of pathology to crime investigation*, Third Ed. Charles C. Thomas Publishers.

Stats about all US cities. City Data. Website. (n.d.). https://city-data.com/.

Vaughn, D. [2019, March 8]. Leaders weigh pros and cons of ShotSpotter in Durham, N.C. Retrieved from https://www.govtech.com/biz/Leaders-Weighs-Pros-and-Cons-of-ShotSpotter-in-Durham-NC.html.

Warren, E., and Supreme Court of the United States. [1965]. *U.S. reports: Miranda v. Arizona, 384 U.S. 436*. [Periodical]. Retrieved from the Library of Congress, https://www.loc.gov/item/usrep384436/.

Wellford, C., and Cronin, J. [2000]. Clearing-up homicide clearance rates. *National Institute of Justice*, 2–7. Retrieved from https://www.ncjrs.gov/App/Publications/abstract.aspx?ID=181728.

Winchester Firearms Manufacturing Dates by Serial Number and Year 1866 through the Early 1990s. [n.d.]. Retrieved from https://www.winchesterguns.com/content/dam/winchester-repeating-arms/support/faq/serial-number-reference/Winchester-Manufacture-Dates-by-Year-2012-Scanned-Documents.pdf.

Wolten, G., Nesbitt, R., Calloway, A., Loper, G., and Jones, P. [1977, September]. Final report on particle analysis for gunshot residue detection. Retrieved from https://www.ncjrs.gov/pdffiles1/Digitization/43632NCJRS.pdf.

22

Patterns in Homicide

Revisited

Mary G. Wilson and Michelle L. Foster

"No other modernized country comes close to the United States in terms of gun-related homicides" (Walsh & Jorgensen, 2018, p. 248). This shocking fact warrants examining more closely the theoretical components that can yield a better understanding as to why the United States is failing to protect its citizens from violent homicides. Marvin Wolfgang and Franco Ferracuti's 1967 work provides a viable explanation of these causes that are still applicable today. Their idea lies with the subculture of violence and reinforcing structure of the surrounding environment to which individuals are regularly exposed. Informal social controls stemming from norms within the subculture reinforce persons engaging in violent acts. Guns play a complex role in our lives. Guns provide protection, security, and even food for those who hunt. Guns also are used in violent crimes to threaten or take advantage of others or to murder persons. Guns are even used in accidental shootings and suicides. Guns are to blame for a lot that has gone wrong in our world today. However, if blame must be placed on someone or on something, then the fault lies with the people who use guns improperly. It lies with society. In the teachings of Emile Durkheim, it is the normlessness or the breakdown of social ties and social order that creates divisions in society. These moments of lawlessness and/or distrust can drive persons to seek alternative measures for safety. For some, guns provide that sense of safety. The watchful eye of law enforcement cannot be everywhere and all of the time.

Homicides accounted for 14,545 of the 19,510 gun deaths in 2017 in the United States (Centers for Disease, n.d). This number, while substantially lower than the number of deaths that occurred by accidental injury (169,936) or automobile crashes (38,659) (Walsh & Jorgensen, 2018), could be reduced with many of the deaths preventable losses (May, 1999). Over a six-year period, homicide by handguns has steadily increased since 2014 (at 15,208 in 2019) with the only exception being in 2018 when the number decreased slightly (14,789), but this number is far greater than it needs to be (Gun Violence Archive, 2020). In this chapter, homicides by gun violence are evaluated by applying criminological theories of violence. Understanding how violence can erupt into a homicide enables the criminal justice system to ensure that more appropriate resources are in place for community members who are experiencing stressors and to more easily identify signs of growing strain.

DEFINITION (OFFICIAL) OF HOMICIDE

The FBI's Uniform Crime Reporting (UCR) Program defines murder and non-negligent manslaughter as the willful (non-negligent) killing of one human being by another (Uniform Crime, 2018).

SOURCES OF HOMICIDE DATA

Firearm homicides are the second leading cause of death for persons ages 15–19 (May, 1999). When viewed through the lens of race, firearm homicides are the leading cause of death among African American males ages 10–34 (Centers for Disease, n.d.). These statistics reveal an unfortunate disproportionality for persons of color.

In 2018, the vast majority of murder victims were killed with firearms (73%) followed by stabbing weapons (11%), other dangerous weapons (12%), and manual weapons (hands and feet, 5%). Over 6,600 murders were committed with handguns, rifles, and shotguns in that order. Of the roughly 31,000 murders that were committed from 2014 to 2018 with handguns in the United States, 70 percent of the cases involved a gun (Giffords Law, 2020b). The murder rate in the United States is much higher than that of other countries with similarly developed societies and economies. By comparison to the rest of the world, only 60 percent of homicides outside of the United States are committed with firearms (Dammer & Albanese, 2014). Western and Central Europe in 2011 reported very low figures of gun homicides, while South America had the highest in the world. "The US gun homicide rate is 25 times that of other high-income countries" (Giffords Law, 2020b). The United States has fewer restrictions on gun ownership than many countries in the world, which may account for fewer gun homicides in those countries.

Circumstances of Homicides

Circumstances were known for 61 percent of murders for which supplementary details were reported in 2018. Understanding the circumstances leading up to a homicide can yield important information for prevention. The majority of murder victims were killed by an acquaintance in 2018 (n=2,692). Of those victims, 39.4 percent were murdered during *arguments* arising from *alcohol* or drug usage, over money or property, or other unspecified reasons (May, 1999). The other unspecified *arguments* constitute the largest circumstances among acquaintance homicides. Handguns were the primary weapon used in these unspecified *argument* homicides (n=1,516) followed by money, drugs, and alcohol (May, 1999). Over the period from 2014 to 2018 homicides arising from unspecified *arguments* accounted for 15,000 murders (May, 1999). In contrast during that same time period *alcohol* fueled killings accounted for 436 murders (May, 1999).

In an effort to catalog the number of homicides in a given location, the *L.A. Times* newspaper created the Homicide Report (2020). Los Angeles county has a high number of homicides. The county accounted for 4 percent of all the homicides in the United States in 2012 and 32 percent of homicides in California. The report was created in 2007 to provide information beyond simply numerical findings. The *L.A. Times* sought to describe more fully the life story of the victim. It is an interactive database and blog. The interactive software allows the public to map out the locations of the homicides in a given year. The database contains detailed information on homicides committed in L.A. County dating back to 2000. The searchable database allows the public free access to view detailed reporting on location of the homicide, demographic details of the victim(s) including race, ethnicity, and gender, along with case status. The report found that 350 people in L.A. County were killed by guns (non-police involved) in 2019. Conversely, "gun homicides are concentrated in cities, with roughly half of all gun homicides taking place in urban areas that contain just a quarter of the total US population" (Giffords Law, 2020b).

THEORIES OF HOMICIDE

Social Disorganization

Social disorganization occurs in "places where various social problems coincide with crime. That occurs most often in the toughest areas of a central city" (Felson & Eckert, 2018, p. 245). Social problems cover a wide range of issues, including economic and job strain, lack of urban renewal or upkeep, poor educational opportunities, and so forth. Clifford Shaw and Henry McKay's theory about social disorganization stems from a study conducted in their city of Chicago to explain how crime clusters within inner-city areas. They refer to these areas as "delinquency areas" (Dammer & Albanese, 2014). Shaw and McKay find delinquency areas include three main problems, which are disorganized neighborhoods, lack of connection with community members, and highly disadvantaged groups of persons (Dammer & Albanese, 2014). Thus, within these urban spaces serious issues such as the physical breakdown of the buildings, disrepair of streets, and lack of comfortable and shareable community spaces arise, along with losses of communication and interconnectedness among the persons. Further, there is lack of trust that builds among the members living within and around the communities and economic distress is high. There may be a wide range of criminal activity that occurs in the open or in secret, such as drug sales and property theft, that arises to help financially compensate for the loss of available jobs. Drug sales themselves can initiate violence, and when the violence is witnessed more commonly by others in their daily lives, further violent behavior can arise within a community (Dammer & Albanese, 2014).

The theory of social disorganization begs the question, Is it the *place* or is it the *people* that "cause" crime. To address this question further, Shaw and McKay evaluated the juvenile delinquency records from 1900 to 1933 in Cook County, Illinois (Dammer & Albanese, 2014). They determined that the impact the environment had on juveniles was stronger than ethnicity in poor residential areas. Therefore, the transitional nature of persons in urban areas can lead to an imbalance in the roles and expectations of others, thereby leading to the lack of stable informal controls within the community members themselves. Bonds between persons are likewise broken down and crime would be more prone to occur. Of course, there are arguments that indicate people themselves lead to the criminogenic behavior rather than the impact that places have on individuals. However, not surprisingly, the answer to this question is that it is *both* persons and places. To be sure, not all persons from poor urban areas will turn to crime, but the likelihood that they will do so is higher when there is a lack of protective factors in place (Wikstrom & Loeber, 2000). Protective factors include a financially stable home and a two-parent household. The same problems can be found in rural areas. D. Wayne Osgood and Jeff M. Chambers looked at rural areas in four states (Florida, Georgia, Nebraska, and South Carolina) and found residential instability, ethnic diversity, and family disruption were related to criminal behaviors (Gun Violence Archive, 2020). All three of these variables are types of protective factors and when missing increase criminal tendencies. Female-headed households saw a 33 percent increase with homicide and a 75 percent increase in weapon offenses (Osgood & Chambers, 2003). In communities that experience delinquency areas of social disorganization, one can see how a subculture of violence can form as a response to these pervasive environments. Subcultures can become a protective factor for individuals as a way to adjust to what is lacking in a community. Subculture of violence is explored in the next section below.

Social Interaction: Patterns in Criminal Homicide

Subculture of Violence

Criminologists Marvin Wolfgang and Franco Ferracuti (1967) are still viewed as the leading theorists in understanding how violence plays a role in society (Cao et al., 1997). A subculture consists of a group of persons who have differing beliefs and values than society as a whole. Within this subculture, violence can become part of the group dynamic when they reinforce these differing beliefs and values which are viewed by the larger society as negative. Negative behaviors become legitimized by the group when others within the group (i.e., subculture) model the same behaviors or dismiss and normalize any negative behaviors or violent acts. Violence is a culturally learned way of dealing with life (Wolfgang, 1958). Victims of homicide are actively involved in the event. The victim in fact was often the first actor to brandish a weapon (gun) or use deadly force in the encounter. Wolfgang, in 1958, identified three other salient factors present in the fatal encounters including: the consumption of alcohol, a verbal dispute or argument between the participants, which escalated into physical violence prior to the homicide (Wolfgang, 1958).

Code of the Street

Elijah Anderson's 1999 *Code of the Street* research on the code is distinguished from Wolfgang and Ferracuti's 1967 subculture of violence theory. The code, unlike the subculture, is less specific and does not identify norms that encompass an entire community. The code on the other hand reflects the public behavior of persons residing within a stratum of distressed communities. The code does not apply to everyone equally. The "code" is a set of informal rules governing interpersonal public behavior, including violence (Wolfgang, 1958).

Respect is at the heart of the code. The code is not a strictly American phenomenon. It is universal according to Anderson. The code can be traced back to ancient Rome, communities of color and heritage, and other regions with access to firearms. It is the access to guns among urban young males. The ability to acquire a gun for protection, to engage in commerce, and maintain street cred is vital. Commerce in the form of the drug trade requires protection, and nothing protects like a gun. Though it is not only drug transactions where guns are present. The use and availability of guns to carry out street robberies or "stick-ups" is also quite common (Wolfgang, 1958).

According to Anderson, "guns can have a personality and status" (Anderson, 1999, p. 119). Guns also have a history that can be identified through the serial number, presuming it has not been altered. The gun's history can be revealed in the number of crimes associated with it, including homicide. The presence of a gun to commit a crime is the great equalizer (Wolfgang, 1958). Kauffman and Koontz further assert that "everyone speaks gun" and "everyone understands gun" (Kauffman & Koontz, 2013, p. 22). The introduction of a gun into a criminal interaction elevates the level of seriousness of the situation but more importantly shifts the balance of power dramatically. The level of understanding is arguably universal (Wolfgang, 1958).

In fact, the presence of the gun is transformative. The person with the gun holds all the power vis-à-vis "your money or your life" (Wolfgang, 1958). Inherent within the code is the understanding that a gun is another tool, a powerful one, which permits better maintenance of street cred, including the possibility of death. In economically disadvantaged areas where the civil law is weak, street justice becomes normative. In these locations, "quite a primitive form of social exchange" occurs or a self-policing mechanism develops to thwart rule violators and dispense justice (Wolfgang, 1958). There is an apparent functionalism aspect. The policing of the neighborhood by the neighborhood occurs because of a lack of trust with our criminal justice system. It is more than just "no snitching." The normative understanding is not to call the police. Thus, it is encouraged to settle the dispute yourself. It is further understood that such communities have not only been disenfranchised but have been abandoned by the mainstream society—almost written off. Consequently, the code emerges as a means of fending for yourself; hence, the need for and development of "street cred" (Stewart & Simons, 2006).

Persons in affected communities are alienated from mainstream society on many levels, including social, economic, and political. They have limited access to Kingdon's problem, policy, or political streams that might draw attention to and thus alleviate the need for the code (Kingdon, 1995). Many dream of a decent family or life. They are not necessarily proud of the street life. Many have experienced a loss of hope and thus have no stake in conformity (Hirschi, 1969). The yearning for something better is juxtaposed with the desire to have and be respected by one's peers. In the mind-set of a young adult who lacks opportunities, respect is currency. The currency is traded upon and must be maintained. The maintenance of street cred comes at a high price. The price is the cause of much violence, especially gun violence. The source of gun violence is located in verbal disputes or arguments (Comcast Cable, 2012). Such disputes lack substance or are over perceived slights including but not limited to disrespect. These disputes escalate leading to a gun homicide. The use of gun violence to solve problems or respond to threats, real or imagined, is quite common. The response is predicated on the belief or assumption that the use of violence will ward off would-be threats and you will be left alone. Street cred requires a good deal of social maintenance and is cyclical in nature. There may be a correlation with street cred and homicide rates along with other crimes, including the drug trade. For some, the correlation to the drug trade is evidenced by survival. The trafficking in drugs is a means to an end for many street families. Robert K. Merton in 1938 identified such individuals as "innovators" or "rebels" (Merton, 1938). Non-conforming persons or decent families who cannot achieve the "American Dream" will seek alternative means to success. Such individuals will use tools such as guns to protect their commercial, albeit illegal, activities.

> Although Anderson presents an interesting and compelling explanation for the high rates of violence among African American adolescents, the major claims of his code of the street thesis have not been extensively tested beyond his ethnographic work in Philadelphia. (Stewart & Simons, 2006, p. 4)

Neuroscience and evolutionary biology can help explain how the subculture forms and persists (Walsh & Hemmens, 2019). Neuroscientists describe the modeling process that develops by an individual as the individual replicating the actions of others. Regular interactions within the subculture "rewire" the brain by imprinting on the brain violent experiences that become normal, acceptable behaviors by the group. Evolutionary biology, likewise, evaluates how regular exposure in an environment impacts the brain to create reinforcing behavior. If surrounded by violent actions, violence becomes normalized by the repetitive exposure to such behavior (Merton, 1938). Protective factors can come into play here and reduce the likelihood of criminal tendencies for violence.

Regional Culture of Violence

Raymond D. Gastil (1971) studied patterns in murder rates in support of his Regional Culture of Violence theory. He found that murder rates were higher in the southern United States than in other regions (Doerner & Lab, 2015). He attributed the differences to regional culture. The culture dates back to before the U.S. Civil War and reflects a personal honor code that is intolerant of disrespect, similar to Anderson's Code of the Streets. The need to preserve one's honor with violence, if necessary, is viewed as acceptable within the culture of the south. Other features of the southern culture can be traced to the institution of slavery, gun ownership, settling feuds with violence, some element of doing masculinity, as well as a distrust of government.

The regional theory of homicide has been evaluated. Loftin and Hill's work from 1974 asserts that the use of region as a marker for southern culture does not fully capture the complexity of the culture. Their study included economic indicator variables as well as regional. The economic variable produced more robust explanations for murder rates than region alone. Subsequent analysis of regional culture of violence theory were unable to substantiate any significant link between the south and murder rates.

Golden Hour

A more modern explanation for homicide rates has been examined through the lens of medical science and trauma response to mortal violence (Braga & Pierce, 2005). Mortal violence is defined as an injury sustained from a traffic accident, workplace accidents, overdoses, stabbings, and gunshots (Braga & Pierce, 2005). From the time that an individual is mortally wounded, there is a finite period of time, generally the first 60 minutes or the "golden hour," for which survivability is likely. Survivability is impacted by a number of factors. Several factors have been identified as increasing the likelihood of surviving a mortal wound, including the location of the nearest trauma center, the celerity of transportation, coupled with the experience and skill-set of the medical staff. Absent some or all of these factors, the odds of surviving may be reduced, but surviving even in the most specialized trauma centers is not guaranteed (Braga & Pierce, 2005). The variation in homicide rates and medical services across regions warrants further research.

LEGISLATION AND POLICY AIMED AT REDUCING FIREARM HOMICIDES

Operation Cease-Fire

Operation Cease-Fire was established in various U.S. cities in the 1990s (Boston, Chicago, and Cincinnati) (City of Cincinnati, 2020). It is a problem-solving police strategy using a "pulling levers" strategy that seeks to "pull every lever" to legally reduce gang violence, illegal gun possession, and gun violence in communities (Engel et al., 2013). In Boston, gun violence was concentrated among serious, youthful offenders (Braga, 2003). The Boston

Project specifically focused on reducing firearm homicides of young people (Braga & Pierce, 2005).

A National Institute of Justice (NIJ)–sponsored evaluation found that the Cease-Fire intervention was associated with a 63 percent reduction in Boston youth homicide and similar large reductions in nonfatal serious gun violence (Braga et al., 2001). By aggressively reducing the demand for firearms, many lives were undoubtedly saved as guns used in the commission of crimes including homicide dropped during the period of the project.

The Cincinnati Initiative to Reduce Violence (CIRV) began in 2007 (University of Cincinnati, 2020). The partnership comprises multi-justice system agencies and community organizations similar to Operation Cease-Fire in Boston (Braga et al., 2001). An evaluation by Engel et al. (2013) found that gang or group member homicides with firearms declined significantly upon implementation of the CIRV. In addition, there was a decline in general violent firearm incidents. The Initiative was able to expediently and dramatically reduce gun-violence and associated homicides, with sustained reductions over time.

The city of Oakland launched a program to reduce gun violence and homicides in 2012 (Giffords Law, 2020a). Similar to Boston and Cincinnati, Oakland Ceasefire is an ongoing partnership between community members, social service providers, and law enforcement officials who work together to reduce violence, build police-community trust, and improve outcomes for high-risk individuals (Giffords Law, 2020a). Oakland has been able to reduce gun homicides by 50 percent since 2012.

The federal government initiated legislation to address gun violence in and around schools. The Gun Free Schools Zones Act of 1990 amended the federal criminal code to increase penalties for crimes committed with a firearm in a school zone (primary and secondary) (Gun-Free Schools, 1990). In addition, the Gun-Free Schools Act of 1994 prohibits students from possessing firearms on school grounds and schools must expel any student in violation for at least one full year or face financial penalties (Gun-Free Schools, 1994). A study by the Rand Corporation (2018) found no evidence that such zones increase or decrease the use of firearms at schools (Rand Corp, 2018).

Passed during the Clinton administration in a further effort to curtail gun violence, the 1997 Violence Against Women Act and subsequent reauthorization in 2005 requires that any person who is the subject of a protect order receive notification concerning their firearms (Violence Against, 1997). The person who is ordered to stay away must relinquish their guns to the local law enforcement or dispose of them for the period of the protection order. Notification to both parties listed in the order and law enforcement is to be provided in-person (at the time of the hearing) and written (within the court order). The person subject to the order may not own or possess, purchase, sell, order, or transport firearms during the pendency of the protection order. The subject of the order may request the return of the firearm at the end of the protected period.

A number of states added penalty enhancements for homicides committed with a firearm. Indictments would reflect a specification that the homicide was committed with a gun to distinguish from non-gun cases. These legislative enactments were used as part of a deterrence strategy. The idea being that additional prison time would deter individuals from committing a homicide or any other crime with a gun. Persons convicted of homicides with guns received an additional sentence. The gun specification sentence would be served consecutively to any prison time received for the homicide.

In addition to penalty enhancements, states and the federal government have issued prohibitions on firearm ownership by convicted persons. Individuals convicted of a felony crime, or even certain misdemeanor offenses such as domestic violence, are prohibited from owning a firearm (*Voisine et al.*, 2016). Legislatures have developed statutory language to address persons convicted of illegally possessing a firearm or having a weapon under disability. The disability is the prior conviction that bars the convicted person from legally owing, purchasing, or selling a firearm. The possession of a firearm by a convicted person may be incarcerated or placed on community control.

CONCLUSION AND FUTURE RESEARCH RECOMMENDATIONS

There is a clear relationship between guns and homicide in the United States. Guns are used in homicides more frequently than other types of weapons. A number of researchers have explored the salient variables associated with guns and homicide. These variables were first observed by Wolfgang in his 1958 work. Judging by the UCR Homicide Data report of 2018, Wolfgang's findings remain important. Future research in this area should evaluate more robustly the Code of the Street as proposed by Anderson in 1999. Research-identified variables must continue to be explored as their presence often precipitates gun homicides—including disputes, often over trivial matters; the presence or usage of alcohol; maintaining street reputation or honor; committing other violent crimes; and trafficking of narcotics. Gun homicides and the "Golden Hour" should be examined through the lens of public health. Medical and technological improvements have reduced the number of gun homicides dramatically in the United States. Finally, the use of cease-fire initiatives in urban communities has demonstrated reductions in gun homicides.

These programs should continue to be evaluated for purposes of implementation and replication.

BIBLIOGRAPHY

Anderson, E. (1999). *Code of the Street*. New York: W.W. Norton and Company Inc.

Braga, A. (2003). Serious Youth Gun Offenders and the Epidemic of Youth Violence in Boston. *Journal of Quantitative Criminology*, *19*(1): 33–54.

Braga, A. A., and G. L. Pierce. (2005). Disrupting Illegal Firearms Markets in Boston: The Effects of Operation Ceasefire on the Supply of New Handguns to Criminals. *Criminology & Public Policy, 4*(4): 717–748.

Braga, A. A., D. M. Kennedy, E. J. Waring, and A. M. Piehl. (2001). Problem-Oriented Policing, Deterrence, and Youth Violence: An Evaluation of Boston's Operation Ceasefire. *Journal of Research in Crime and Delinquency, 38*(3): 195–225.

Cao, L., A. Adams, and V. Jensen. (1997). A Test of the Black Subculture of Violence Thesis: A Research Note. *Criminology*, *35*, 367–369.

Centers for Disease Control and Prevention. (n.d.). Retrieved from https://www.cdc.gov/nchs/fastats/homicide.htm. Downloaded on March 25, 2020.

City of Cincinnati. (2020). The Cincinnati Initiative to Reduce Violence (CIRV). Retrieved from https://www.cincinnati-oh.gov/police/community-involvement/cincinnati-initiative-to-reduce-violence/.

Comcast Cable Newsmakers. (2012). Podcast. 2012 U.S. Conference of Mayors Winter Meeting. Retrieved from https://www.youtube.com/watch?v=ZTLX9hl14O0).

Dammer, H. R., and J. S. Albanese. (2014). *Comparative Criminal Justice Systems*, Fifth ed., 28–30 and 31–32. Belmont, CA: Wadsworth Cengage Learning.

Doerner, W, G., and S. P. Lab. (2015). *Victimology*, Seventh ed. Anderson Pub.

Engel, R. S., M. Skubak Tillyer, and N. Corsaro. (2013). Reducing Gang Violence Using Focused Deterrence: Evaluating the Cincinnati Initiative to Reduce Violence (CIRV). *Justice Quarterly, 30*(3), 403–439. http://dx.doi.org/10.1080/07418825.2011.619559.

Felson, M., and M. A. Eckert. (2018). *Introductory Criminology*. New York: Routledge Taylor & Francis Group.

Gastil, R. J. (1971). Homicide and Regional Culture of Violence. *American Sociological Review*, *36*, 412–427.

Giffords Law Center. (2020a). A Case Study in Hope. Retrieved from https://lawcenter.giffords.org/wp-content/uploads/2019/04/Giffords-Law-Center-A-Case-Study-in-Hope-Lessons-from-Oaklands-Remarkable-Reduction-in-Gun-Violence.pdf.

Giffords Law Center. (2020b). Fact Sheet. Violence Statistics. Retrieved from https://lawcenter.giffords.org/facts/gun-violence-statistics/.

Gun Violence Archive. (2020). GVA Six-Year Review. Retrieved from https://www.gunviolencearchive.org/.

Hirschi, T. (1969). *The Causes of Delinquency*. Berkeley: University of California Press.

H.R. 3757 Gun Free Schools Zones Act of 1990.

Kauffman, R., and H. Koontz. (2013). Preparing Students of Criminal Justice for Restorative Justice Practice. In *Restorative Justice Today Practical Applications*, K. van Wormer and L. Walker, 21–30. Thousand Oaks, CA: Sage Pub.

Kingdon, J. W. (1995). *Agendas, Alternatives, and Public Policies*, Second ed. Addison-Wesley Educational Publishers, Inc.

Loftin, C., and R. H. Hill. (1974). Regional Subculture and Homicide: An Examination of the Gastil-Hackney Thesis. *American Sociological Review*, *39*, 714–724.

Los Angeles Times. (2020). The Homicide Report. Retrieved from https://homicide.latimes.com/

May, D. C. (1999). Scared Kids, Unattached Kids, or Peer Pressure: Why Do Students Carry Firearms to School? *Youth and Society, 31*(1), 100–127.

Merton, R. (1938). Social structure and Anomie. *American Sociological Review*, *3*, 672–682.

Osgood, D. W., and J. M. Chambers. (2003, May). Community Correlates of Rural Youth Violence. *OJJDP Juvenile Justice Bulletin*.

Rand Corp. (2018). Analysis of Gun Free Zones. Retrieved from https://www.rand.org/research/gun-policy/analysis/gun-free-zones.html.

Stewart, E. A., and R. L. Simons. (2006). Structure and Culture in African American Adolescent Violence: A Partial Test of the "Code of the Street" Thesis. *Justice Quarterly*, *23*(1), 1–34.

Uniform Crime Reports. 2018. Expanded Homicide Data. Retrieved from https://ucr.fbi.gov/crime-in-the-u.s/2018/crime-in-the-u.s.-2018/tables/expanded-homicide-data-table-8.xls.

United States Code, Title 20, Section 7961 of the Gun-Free Schools Act of 1994.

University of Cincinnati Institute of Crime and Violence. (2020). The Cincinnati Initiative to Reduce Violence (CIRV). Retrieved from https://www.uc.edu/ics/projects/violencereduction.html.

Violence Against Women Act (1997).

Voisine et al., v. U.S., 2016.

Walsh, A., and C. Hemmens (2019). *Introduction to Criminology*, Fourth ed. "Gun Violence," 393–395. Thousand Oaks, CA: Sage Publishing.

Walsh, A., and C. Jorgensen. (2018). *Criminology: The Essentials*, Third. ed., Sage Publishing.

Wikstrom, P., and R. Loeber. (2000). Do Disadvantaged Neighborhoods Cause Well-Adjusted Children to Become Adolescent Delinquents? A Study of Male Juvenile Serious Offending, Individual Risk and Protective Factors and Neighborhood Context. *Criminology*, *38*, 1109–1142.

Wolfgang, M. E. (1958). *Patterns in Criminal Homicide*. Montclair, NJ: Patterson-Smith.

Wolfgang, M.E., and F. Ferracuti (1967). *The Subculture of Violence: Towards an Integrated Theory in Criminology*. London and New York: Tavistock Publications.

23

Stand Your Ground Laws and the Evolution of Self-Defense in the United States

Christopher M. Bellas

> "Detached reflection cannot be demanded in the presence of an uplifted knife."
>
> (*Brown v. United States*, 256 U.S. 335, 343, 1921)

In the 2019 movie *Joker*, there is a scene where the primary character, Arthur, was minding his own business on a subway station car when several persons approached him to not only provide ridicule but to physically assault him. As each person took turns kicking Arthur while he was lying on the ground, he finally had enough, pulled out a gun, and shot them multiple times. The scene was based on the famous New York case of Bernhard Goetz (New York Courts, 1986). On December 22, 1984, Goetz was on a New York subway when four people approached him. Two of the four had screwdrivers to use to break into coin boxes, but no gun. Goetz had gotten on the subway with an unlicensed .38 caliber handgun when one of the four asked Goetz for five dollars. Goetz took out his gun and shot all of them, with one ending up paralyzed. When questioned, Goetz stated he was afraid of being "maimed" by the men, even though he admitted that he knew they did not have a weapon (New York Courts, 1986). Goetz was found not guilty by a jury on all charges except for a weapons violation.

Although Stand Your Ground (SYG) Laws did not exist during the 1980s in the United States, the belief one should be able to protect oneself from violent people who may cause harm, especially in a high-crime city, like New York at the time, made sense to most. Was Goetz right in defending himself? Had New York at the time had a SYG law, would that have prevented Goetz from even being charged? This chapter explores the evolution of self-defense law in the United States, specifically focusing on SYG laws.

In criminal law, there are two ways in which one can defend themselves to a criminal act they have performed; one is an excuse, the other is one of justification. An excuse for one's criminal behavior means that what the person did was in fact wrong, but he or she is not responsible for their actions. Legal insanity is one type of excuse because although the act was wrong, the person who committed it could not be held responsible due to a mental illness or defect. The other defense is one of justification. A person is justified in his or her actions when what the person did was not wrong, given the circumstances at the time (Dressler, 1999). One justification to having committed a crime is that of self-defense, which is closely linked to two other criminal law defenses, necessity and provocation.

Self-defense has the following three major elements: necessity, proportionality, and reasonableness (Dressler, 1999). The first is that of necessity, that the person who is using self-defense is doing so because he or she has no other means to protect themselves. Here, the harmful actions of the perpetrator are *imminent*; therefore, the victim must act in the moment to save themselves or someone else from impending harm. The second element is proportionality, where the victim can only use that amount of force necessary in order to propel the attack or threat. Certainly, one is not justified in using deadly force against a perpetrator caught in a minor property crime (i.e., trespassing), but only a far more serious crime. Finally, the last element is one of reasonableness. The victim must reasonably believe at the time of using self-defense that he or she is in grave danger, and most states require that the reasonableness requirement meet the objective test of an "ordinary person" standard, although, as will be examined below, states like Ohio have swayed back and forth on the objective versus subjective legal standard (Sweeney, 2016). A subjective test is looking at the events, circumstances, and prior experiences of the person claiming self-defense and his/her thinking at that moment. An objective test is based on a reasonable person's belief given the circumstances at the time of the incident. The former is based on the individual's mind-set while the latter is based on societal expectations.

The jurisprudence of self-defense is intertwined with what is known as the Castle Doctrine (Ward, 2015). The Castle Doctrine is the legal principle that a law-abiding person confronted with life-threatening danger, has no duty to retreat *in his/her own home*, and may *stand his/her ground* to defend themselves or their home (U.S. Supreme Court, 1963; Drake, 2008). The term "castle" is important because the location of the danger aimed at the alleged victim matters, since the exception to the "duty to retreat" bears on where the harmful event occurred, here, in the victim's residence. The Castle Doctrine implies the sanctuary of one's residence is the place where one should feel the safest and preservation of such a sanctuary is of utmost importance.

HISTORY OF THE CASTLE DOCTRINE

The Castle Doctrine genesis began in English Common Law dating back to the seventeenth century (Ward, 2015). English Common Law did not permit persons to take the law into their own hands especially if doing so could take the life of another. The Castle Doctrine, however, permitted a person to take the law into his/her own hand IF their "back was to the wall" in a life-or-death situation. It is this phrase, "back to the wall," that has been repeated in numerous court cases over the years that became the foundation for the Castle Doctrine. Edward Coke, a well-known legal jurist, stated that a person was well justified in using deadly force, if threatened with imminent danger or grave bodily injury *for which the defendant bore no blame*. The last part of the statement is important. In the self-defense justification we use today, the defendant cannot successfully claim self-defense if he or she was the "initial aggressor" in the event, unless that aggressor withdraws from their provocation (Samaha, 2017).

The motivation behind English jurists scowling at any individual who might seek to take another's life is debatable. Was it that England wanted to maintain its dominance over the use of deadly force in the country or was it born out of true respect for the value of all human life (Levin, 2010)? It appears that the government was reluctant to give any power of killing to individual people unless it was in the interest of the state. As time progressed and a new American culture emerged revolving around individualism and the need to protect one's property interests, the relaxation of a "retreat to the wall" standard evolved. Where there is little disagreement between English Common Law and present legal doctrine is the preservation of self-defense as a legitimate justification to protect one's home. Most readers are familiar with the adage "A man's home is his castle," and we have always given a great amount of reverence to the privacy and sanctity in one's residence. For example, the Fourth Amendment to the U.S. Constitution has important safeguards to protect citizens from governmental intrusion in recognition of the high value placed on the home (United States Congress, 1992). Except for the home, state laws have historically mandated (prior to those states that developed SYG laws) that one should retreat, whenever possible, if their life is in danger. The duty to retreat requirement can be seen in the Model Penal Code.

The rationale underlying the retreat requirement was succinctly stated by the drafters of the Model Penal Code (American Law Institute, 1985):

> It rests, of course, upon the view that the protection of life has such a high place in a proper scheme of social values that the law should not permit conduct that places life in jeopardy, when the necessity for doing so can be avoided by the sacrifice of the much smaller value that inheres in standing up to an aggression.

> To the argument that retreat is cowardly and dishonorable, the answer embraced has been that of Beale: "A really honorable man, a man of truly refined and elevated feeling, would perhaps always regret the apparent cowardice of a retreat, but he would regret ten times more, after the excitement of the contest was past, the thought that he had the blood of a fellow-being on his hands."

Therefore, the Model Penal Code has balanced the duty to retreat and the view of a hurtful pride, with the regret at taking a human life.

Whether or not a claim of self-defense is going to be successful is often left up to the jury should the case make it to trial. Therefore, jury instructions on self-defense and SYG laws are important. In the state of Ohio, the courts have used both an objective reasonableness standard and a subjective standard when reviewing the mental state of the person claiming self-defense (Giannelli, 1988). Some have argued that the true standard for what the defendant believed should be somewhere in the middle, as cited in a Case Western Reserve University Law School faculty publication by Giannelli in 1988, who proclaimed this intermediate position is perhaps best captured in Ohio Jury Instruction 411.33(2) (Giannelli, 1988):

> In determining whether the defendant had reasonable grounds for an honest belief that he/she was in imminent danger, you must put yourselves in the position of this defendant, with his characteristics, his knowledge or lack of knowledge, and under the circumstances and conditions that surrounded him at that time. You must consider the conduct of [the victim] and determine if his acts and words caused the defendant to reasonably and honestly believe that he was about to be killed or to receive great bodily injury.

The law school publication goes on to provide examples of just how a self-defense claim might play out in the courtroom, showing the state of mind of the defendant. One way would be for the accused to provide evidence of threats made to him/her by the perpetrator, which would go a long way in helping the trier of fact decide on the mental state of the person claiming self-defense. For example, what if the person who is about to attack had made life-threatening comments in the past that were not only detailed but highly plausible? When looking at persons making threatening comments, one often turns to the specificity of what was said as a measure of the probability the threats would be carried out. Another way of getting to the state of mind of the person claiming self-defense would be if the accused could demonstrate that he/she was aware, at the time of the killing, that the victim had a known history of violent acts (Giannelli, 1988). If the person who utilized self-defense had knowledge that the person who is threatening him has harmed others or had a known history of violent behavior, that is certainly a reasonable factor to take into consideration in deciding whether you are in immediate danger.

These are the factors one could present to a court to establish whether the conduct was in fact reasonable.

Court Cases

In one of the leading U.S. Supreme Court cases on self-defense, the court supported the Castle Doctrine. In *Beard v. U.S.* (U.S. Supreme Court, 1895), the court stated that a man assailed on his own grounds, without provocation, by a person armed with a deadly weapon, is not obligated to retreat, but to stand his ground and defend himself as long as what he is doing is necessary to save his own life. There are some important caveats in the court's opinion. First is that the person using self-defense is on his own property, not anywhere else. Second, the element of nonprovocateur is important and makes sense that one cannot claim self-defense if he started the attack or in fact continued the aggression. Finally is the necessity element, meaning the person had no other choice but to use deadly force.

In 1896, the court heard the case of *Alberty v. U.S.* (U.S. Supreme Court, 1896). Again, the court stood firm in supporting the no retreat rule. The court proclaimed that a man who finds another trying to enter the bedroom of his wife through a window may utilize as much force as necessary to prevent the attack and has no duty to retreat. This case suggests the importance of *proportionality*, stressing whatever a person must do to protect the welfare of not only himself, but a close loved one, has no duty to retreat, but to stand his ground. Finally, with respect to the reasonableness standard, in *Brown v. U.S.* (U.S. Supreme Court, 1921) where a defendant was approached by a man with a knife who had made previous threats to him, the court argued for a subjective standard to be applied. The court said, "The right of a man to stand his ground and defend himself when attacked depends upon whether he reasonably believes that he is in imminent danger of death, not upon a detached test of a reasonable man" (U.S. Supreme Court, 1921).

Courts at the state level have also weighed in on self-defense and SYG protections. In *Erwin v. State*, the Ohio Supreme Court wrote (Ward, 2015):

> Does the law hold a man who is violently and feloniously assaulted responsible for having brought such necessity upon himself, on the sole ground that he failed to fly from his assailant when he might have done so? . . . *[A] true man*, who is without fault, is not obliged to fly from an assailant, who, by violence or surprise maliciously seeks to take his life or do him enormous bodily harm.

In this case, the court identified a "true man" standard, and many have taken this phrase to support the position that people should not have to resort to coward-like behavior in their own home, but rather be able to stand up for themselves. However, the "true man" phrase has also been characterized as an honorable person who is doing what needs to be done to protect him- or herself from imminent danger. Although in a much more recent Ohio case, *State v. Williford* (Supreme Court of Ohio, 1990), the court noted that in "most circumstances, a person may not kill in self-defense if he has available a reasonable means of retreat from the confrontation."

Two state cases more recently focused on the immunity provision under state SYG laws. In 2016, a Kansas court ruled that immunity under a SYG law could be invoked at any time prior to sentencing. The case was *Kansas v. Barlow* (Supreme Court of the State of Kansas, 2016), where the defendant, Barlow, placed a gun to a man's head in order to prevent him from continuing a rape of an unconscious woman. The judge granted him immunity under the SYG defense of "others" under Kansas law. In another state, North Carolina, a defendant had his second-degree murder conviction reversed because the trial judge omitted in his jury instruction that a person who is confronted with deadly force has no duty to retreat but can stand his ground (Court of Appeals of North Carolina, 2016). The appellate court ruled the omission was not harmless and had it been told to the jury, there could have been a different verdict.

WHAT IS STAND YOUR GROUND?

SYG laws can be spelled out differently among the state jurisdictions that have them on the books, to date well over twenty-five (Ferraro & Ghatak, 2019). This is in addition to states that have other forms of self-defense laws. State laws profess that a person is justified in the use of deadly force and does not have a duty to retreat IF he or she *reasonably* believes that such force is necessary to prevent *imminent* death or great bodily harm to him/herself or another (American Bar Association, 2015). What extends the self-defense claim beyond the Castle Doctrine is the location of the predicament to outside places, an important element in SYG laws. In SYG jurisdictions, a person can use deadly force in places outside the home and in some places wherever a person has a legal right to be, such as a vehicle, a grocery store, or a bank.

Florida . . . Florida . . . Florida

During the 2000 U.S. presidential election, it was said by a well-known political journalist, Tim Russert, that winning the presidential election all comes down to one state, "Florida, Florida, Florida," which proved to be the case (Tsujimoto, 2016). Florida took center stage once again for passing the very first and somewhat controversial SYG law in 2005. On April 26, 2005, the then governor of Florida, Jeb Bush, signed into law Florida Senate Bill 436 that expanded the right to use deadly force in the state of Florida while at the same time putting an end to the "duty to retreat" doctrine. SYG laws were fueled in the political arena by one of the largest and most powerful interest groups in the United States, the National Rifle Association (NRA) (Ferraro & Ghatak, 2019). The NRA gave significant contributions to many Republican lawmakers in the state of Florida to push for SYG legislation (State of Florida, 2019). In fact, "more than one-third of the 114 Floridian lawmakers who co-sponsored the passage of the SYG legislation received NRA money" (Bell, 2019). Florida was the first state to enact the legislation in October 2005; by 2008, there were twelve states with SYG laws, and in 2012 the number rose to twenty-five (Ferraro & Ghatak, 2019).

Today, Florida §776.012 currently reads (State of Florida, 2019):

> (1) A person is justified in using or threatening to use force, except deadly force, against another when and to the extent that the person reasonably believes that such conduct is necessary to defend himself or herself or another against the other's imminent use of unlawful force. A person who uses or threatens to use force in accordance with this subsection does not have a duty to retreat before using or threatening to use such force.
> (2) A person is justified in using or threatening to use deadly force if he or she reasonably believes that using or threatening to use such force is necessary to prevent imminent death or great bodily harm to himself or herself or another or to prevent the imminent commission of a forcible felony. A person who uses or threatens to use deadly force in accordance with this subsection does not have a duty to retreat and has the *right to stand his or her ground* if the person using or threatening to use the deadly force is not engaged in a criminal activity and is in a place where he or she has a right to be.

Laws in at least 30 states and Puerto Rico allow that there is no duty to retreat from an attacker in any place in which one is lawfully present. (Alabama, Alaska, Arizona, Arkansas, Florida, Georgia, Idaho, Indiana, Iowa, Kansas, Kentucky, Louisiana, Michigan, Mississippi, Missouri, Montana, Nevada, New Hampshire, North Carolina, North Dakota, Ohio, Oklahoma, Pennsylvania, South Carolina, South Dakota, Tennessee, Texas, Utah, West Virginia, and Wyoming.) At least ten of those states include language stating one may "stand his or her ground." (Alabama, Florida, Georgia, Idaho, Kansas, Kentucky, Louisiana, Oklahoma, Pennsylvania and South Carolina.) (National Conference of State Legislatures, 2022, para. 3).

It would be impossible to detail all the state statutes within the limits here, but below is a sample of some.

Arizona

Arizona's §13-405 SYG reads as follows (State of Arizona, n.d.):

> **A.** A person is justified in threatening or using deadly physical force against another:
>
> 1. If such person would be justified in threatening or using physical force against the other under § 13-404, and
> 2. When and to the degree a reasonable person would believe that deadly physical force is immediately necessary to protect himself against the other's use or attempted use of unlawful deadly physical force.
>
> **B.** A person has no duty to retreat before threatening or using deadly physical force pursuant to this section if the person is in a place where the person may legally be and is not engaged in an unlawful act.

Arizona, like all states, does not allow one to claim any type of self-defense if they were the one in fact to start or provoke the attack. Also, in the state, one is not allowed to use deadly force to resist an arrest, lawful or not, by a law enforcement officer. Finally, verbal threats, no matter how serious, are not covered under the statute.

Ohio

In April 2021, Ohio implemented a new SYG law which expanded the existing statute that limited its use to residences and vehicles. The new law justifies standing your ground, to *any* place in which the person has a right to be. Also, now in Ohio the burden rests with the state to prove that self-defense was *not* justified.

O.R.C. §2901.09 (State of Ohio, 2021) reads as follows:

> A. As used in this section, "residence" has the same meaning as in section 2901.05 of the Revised Code.
> B. For purposes of any section of the Revised Code that sets forth a criminal offense, a person has no duty to retreat before using force in self-defense, defense of another, or defense of that person's residence if that person is in a place in which the person lawfully has a right to be.
> C. A trier of fact shall not consider the possibility of retreat as a factor in determining whether or not a person who used force in self-defense, defense of another, or defense of that person's residence reasonably believed that the force was necessary to prevent injury, loss, or risk to life or safety.

New York

New York law has two statutes related to the Castle Doctrine, one has to do with defense of person and the other with defense of property, especially during the commission of a burglary. New York Penal Law §35.15 outlines the justification defense of the use of physical force in defense of a person (State of New York, n.d.a):

> Subsection 2: A person may not use deadly physical force upon another person . . . unless the actor reasonably believes that such other person is using or about to use deadly physical force . . . The actor is under no duty to retreat if he or she is . . . in his or her dwelling and not the initial aggressor.

New York Penal Law §35.20 outlines the justification defense of the use of physical force in defense of premises and in defense of a person in the course of burglary (State of New York, n.d.b):

> Subsection 3: A person in possession or control of, or licensed or privileged to be in, a dwelling or an occupied building, who reasonably believes that another person is committing or attempting to commit a burglary of such dwelling or building, may use deadly physical force upon such other person when he or she reasonably believes such to be necessary to prevent or terminate the commission or attempted commission of such burglary.

The New York statute is mentioned to highlight the second part of the justification of self-defense. In New York, you can use deadly force if you reasonably believe it is necessary to prevent not a violent crime, but the property crime of burglary. Someone could argue, what if one's life is not in danger? What if a burglar had no intention of causing death or grave bodily injury to the person(s) within the dwelling? Most likely all the homeowner has to say is that he/she was in fear, and that would be enough for the self-defense claim to work.

Vermont

Some states are more likely to have a standard justifiable homicide statute such as the one in Vermont. One could argue that you do not need a separate SYG or Castle Doctrine statute because it is already covered. Vermont law, **§2305.** Justifiable homicide, reads (State of Vermont, 2012):

> If a person kills or wounds another under any of the circumstances enumerated below, he or she shall be guiltless:

(1) in the just and necessary defense of his or her own life or the life of his or her husband, wife, parent, child, brother, sister, master, mistress, servant, guardian, or ward; or

(2) in the suppression of a person attempting to commit murder, sexual assault, aggravated sexual assault, burglary, or robbery, with force or violence; or

(3) in the case of a civil officer; or a military officer or private soldier when lawfully called out to suppress riot or rebellion, or to prevent or suppress invasion, or to assist in serving legal process, in suppressing opposition against him or her in the just and necessary discharge of his or her duty. (Amended 1983, No. 23, §2.)

It is important to know that facts matter. How juries and judges take in the totality of the circumstances will determine the outcome of a case, should it ever make it that far.

STAND YOUR GROUND LAWS AND PUBLICITY

Although self-defense laws have always created a debate in American Criminal Law, it was a Florida case in 2012 that had several factors that made SYG laws rise to the national spotlight. On February 26, 2012, seventeen-year-old Trayvon Martin, a resident of Sanford, Florida, was shot and killed by another condominium tenant and neighborhood watch volunteer, then twenty-eight-year-old George Zimmerman (Sofastaii, 2013). The exact facts of what happened that night are still unknown, which made determining what specifically happened a difficult task for the jury in the case. What is known from a 911 call is that George Zimmerman reported to police that there was a suspicious guy "up to no good" lurking in the neighborhood (Sofastaii, 2013). What Zimmerman did not do was listen to police who told him not to go outside and pursue the alleged suspect. He antagonized Trayvon Martin and a confrontation ensued. Trayvon, unarmed and walking home from a convenience store with candy, was shot in the chest (Sofastaii, 2013). The case went to trial and during closing arguments, Zimmerman's defense attorney presented before the jury a slab of concrete and illustrated how that slab became the weapon used by Trayvon Martin against George Zimmerman, who was allegedly in fear for his life, and thus Zimmerman was only defending himself when he fired at Trayvon. The Trayvon Martin case was a case, much like the O. J. Simpson case, which brought racial tension within the criminal justice system back to the forefront. Zimmerman had made racial remarks about African Americans prior to the conflict, and the acquittal of Zimmerman only solidified beliefs to many that the criminal justice system was racist.

Defenders of the Zimmerman verdict believe that the jury did follow the law as constructed by the state of Florida. Many argued that whether Zimmerman should have followed Trayvon is irrelevant to the ultimate battle that ended Martin's life. What is relevant is what George Zimmerman was thinking during his confrontation with Trayvon given the circumstances at the time. For all the media attention surrounding race (George Zimmerman was White, and Trayvon Martin was Black), the actual defense that George Zimmerman invoked was one of self-defense and not technically one of SYG. The jury, based on post-trial interviews, mentioned Florida's SYG law because that was included as part of the jury instructions; yet if we are to believe Zimmerman's version of events, there was no option for him to "retreat" from Trayvon Martin because he had no chance to do so—allegedly his head was being slammed against the concrete.

Trayvon Martin is not the only case that has raised concerns over SYG laws. In a 2012 article in *Propublica*, the news outlet identified several cases that raised concern across the United States that took place soon after the killing of Trayvon Martin that include (Lee, 2012):

1. A Texas man who shot and killed two suspecting burglars on *his neighbor's property*, after calling police and telling them he was aware of Texas law giving him the right to do so. He was not indicted.
2. A twenty-one-year-old in the state of Louisiana who spotted an SUV full of teens potentially dealing marijuana, fired into the vehicle because he said someone could have jumped out with a gun and caused him harm, despite the fact the SUV allegedly was driving away. He claimed he was standing his ground. A grand jury did not indict him.
3. A homeowner in Wisconsin shot and killed someone who was on his porch who he thought might burglarize him. The twenty-year-old victim was evading police on a noise complaint.
4. A twenty-two-year-old Cordell Jude shot and killed Daniel Adkins Jr., a pedestrian who walked in front of Jude's car just as Jude was pulling up to the window of a Taco Bell drive-thru in Arizona. Jude claimed Adkins had waved his arms in the air, wielding what Jude thought was a metal pipe—it was a dog leash. Jude shot the twenty-nine-year-old Adkins, who was mentally disabled, once in the chest.

What these cases suggest is that the publicity from SYG laws enables persons with hot tempers to take minor arguments at times to deadly extremes. This line of thinking is only fueled by a current culture of gun ownership, which continues to grow in the United States.

State statutes, although similar in most jurisdictions, do have important even if minor distinctions. If a statute has a necessity element, then the expectation is that the person who exercised self-defense did so because there was an immediate threat of death or great bodily harm. Yet imagine no necessity language in the statute, but only language of "no duty to retreat." You could have a case that slips away from the withdraw exception discussed earlier in this chapter. If the initial aggressor no longer possesses an imminent threat to the defendant, does that defendant still have a right to use deadly force? It may not be necessary, but if necessity is not a statutory requirement, then the defense is likely to succeed (Sweeney, 2016).

While self-defense laws are already controversial when used at trial, defendants often do not even get to trial. Pretrial motions are now starting to shift the affirmative defense burden to the state instead of the defendant. For example, at least up until 2017 in the state of Florida, the defense had the burden of showing that standing one's ground was necessary, but in 2017 an amendment to the SYG law in Florida shifted the burden to the government (Woodall, 2017).

Arguments for Stand Your Ground Laws

While SYG laws have many opponents, there is a view that such laws are a success not just in legal terms, but psychologically as well. Madison Fair (2014) points out several reasons why SYG laws are positive for our criminal justice system. First, it supports the value of dignity for crime victims. It can be argued that there is nothing more degrading than having to "run away" from an intruder in your own home or wherever you have a right to be. It may be that a victim does want to flee in a dangerous situation, or it may be that he/she wants to stand their ground and not bear the humiliation of retreat. At best, the nonaggressor should be given that option. The second justification for SYG laws is that relying on police presence to defuse a situation may be too little too late. We know police officers cannot be everywhere; their jobs are too demanding. Furthermore, public confidence in the criminal justice system providing the security one needs in a time of crisis has been tested over time with questionable satisfaction. With SYG laws in place, citizens feel a sense of ownership of their own lives, the lives of family and friends and do not have the fear of having to rely on a potentially unresponsive law enforcement reply to a situation of deadly force, when every second matters in a life or death situation.

There is also a potential deterrent effect from the criminals' point of view. The argument is often used with concealed carry laws that criminals will be deterred from targeting persons who may be armed. Even further to this point,

SYG laws are more aggressive in giving potential victims legal permission to resort to deadly force in cases where he or she reasonably feels their life is at stake. According to Fair (2014), there is a psychological component to SYG laws for both the offender and the victim. The victim now has the power to act, given to him or her by the state, and the offender knows it if SYG laws are in place. The empowerment such SYG laws give to law-abiding citizens is positive, many argue, despite opposition labeling such empowerment as vigilante justice.

Arguments against Stand Your Ground Laws

While SYG laws are viewed by many as imparting victim empowerment, the flip side could be that victims are given too much power. Individuals are not only the victim, but also the judge, jury, and executioner (Bell, 2019). Another problem is the mechanics of invoking the SYG defense. As noted at the beginning of this chapter, self-defense is a justification defense and more importantly, an affirmative defense. In an affirmative defense, the defendant is obligated to show by a "preponderance of the evidence" that self-defense was justified. Yet in six states where law enforcement are given the sole responsibility for the initial determination of criminal immunity (Alabama, Florida, Kansas, Kentucky, Oklahoma, and South Carolina), police are prohibited from making an arrest unless there is evidence to demonstrate that the shooter was not acting in a reasonable manner. In these six states, it is presumed that when shots were fired by the defendant, that it was done because the victim reasonably believed their life or the life of another was in imminent danger (Weaver, 2008). In most cases, the police are going to have only one witness at the scene to establish the facts because one party is dead. Hence, law enforcement is going to base their decision to make an arrest, solely on the word of one person who has an obvious self-interest. Where jurisdictions allow for the law to presume reasonable fear, SYG laws in these locations switch the burden of proof required in other areas of criminal law (Holliday, 2012).

Research on Stand Your Ground Laws

It has been suggested that SYG laws have a deterrent effect. Criminals will think twice before engaging in violent criminal conduct against someone for fear that that person may have a weapon and have permission from the state to use that weapon in a deadly manner in order to protect themselves. This theory raises numerous assumptions. First, it assumes that criminals are aware of the law. Do criminals have a basic knowledge of criminal law, and assuming they do, are they aware of what states do and do not have SYG legislation in place? Second, the same can be said for law-abiding citizens. Does the average citizen know if they are in a SYG state, and if so, are they familiar with the elements of such a statute? We also are assuming, as we do with any deterrence policy, that those in such an altercation are rational actors. We know many homicides are premediated, but many are not. Do offenders and victims rationally act in situations where SYG confrontations come into play? It may be these faulty assumptions that explain the research findings as to whether SYG states do in fact deter crime.

Several studies have indicated that SYG laws do not deter crime (Morral & Smart, 2019). Chamlin (2014) found that Arizona's SYG law had no effect on aggravated assaults but ironically had an increased effect on armed and unarmed robbery. More troubling is the fact that Chamlin found that such laws increased suicides. Similarly, Cheng and Hoekstra (2013) found SYG laws did not deter burglary, robbery, or aggravated assault but led to an 8 percent increase in the numbers of murders and non-negligent homicides. Finally, Gius (2016) found that states with SYG laws had robbery rates that were 5.25 percent higher than non-SYG states. He (Gius, 2016) concluded that "states with SYG laws either have higher crime rates than non SYG states, or they have crime rates that are not statistically different from those of non-SYG states." It appears that demographic and socioeconomic factors have a greater impact on crime trends. Humphreys, Wiebe, and Ukert (2018) found disparity in Florida at the county level where the SYG law was associated with increases in homicide in counties that were safer, more rural, and where economic conditions are more hazardous. Bell (2019) cited research studies showing that between the year the first SYG law was enacted (2005) to 2007, the number of "justifiable" homicides increased as follows: 200 percent in Florida, 54 percent in Texas, 83 percent in Georgia, 24 percent in Arizona, and 725 percent in Kentucky.

The American Bar Association 2015 Task Force Report (American Bar Association, 2015) recommended the elimination of SYG laws, which is unlikely to happen anytime soon. The conservative culture of gun ownership, coupled with the idea of being able to protect oneself, far outweigh the potential risk factors from incorrectly applying SYG laws. Still, the Task Force did recommend some policies that would be useful for knowing what happened as well as identifying any racial disparities in the exercising of these laws. First is creating a national database for the detailed tracking and investigation of self-defense cases. The tracking would incorporate all the stages of the case, from the initial call and arrival by police to the disposition of the case. Second, better-trained law enforcement would be helpful so that they could recognize the signs of a legitimate claim of self-defense in those cases that appear ambiguous. Third, the Task Force recommended that jury instructions be clearer. These instructions are already notorious for imparting confusion among jurors. These jurors may not understand the subjective versus objective standard to apply, and they may also be confused on the difference between the traditional self-defense option versus a specific SYG statute. Finally, public education is important. If citizens are going to be able to use firearms for the purpose of killing without any legal consequences, the public should know under what circumstances that is able to happen.

REFERENCES

American Bar Association. (2015). *National Task Force on Stand Your Ground Laws*. American Bar Association. https://www.americanbar.org/content/dam/aba/administrative/corej/StandYourGroundReport.pdf.

American Law Institute. (1985). *Model penal code: Official draft and explanatory notes: Complete text of model penal code as adopted at the 1962 annual meeting of the American Law Institute at Washington, D.C., May 24, 1962*. American Law Institute Philadelphia, PA, United States.

Bell, V. (2019). The "White" to bear arms: How immunity provisions in stand your ground statutes lead to an unequal application of the law for black gun owners. *Fordham Urban Law Journal*, *46*(4), 902.

Chamlin, M. B. (2014). An assessment of the intended and unintended consequences of Arizona's self-defense, home protection act. *Journal of Crime & Justice*, *37*(3), 327–338.

Cheng, C., and Hoekstra, M. (2013). Does strengthening self-defense laws deter crime or escalate violence? Evidence from expansions to the castle doctrine. *Journal of Human Resources*, *48*(3), 821–854.

Court of Appeals of North Carolina. (2016). *State of North Carolina v. Lee 789 S.E.2d 679*. Find Law. https://caselaw.findlaw.com/nc-court-of-appeals/1889782.html.

Drake, D. M. (2008). The Castle Doctrine: An expanding right to stand your ground. *St. Mary's Law Journal*, *39*, 573–574.

Dressler, J. (1999). *Cases and materials on criminal law. American casebook series*. West Group.

Fair, M. (2014). Dare defend: Standing for stand your ground. *Law & Psychology Review*, *38*, 153–176.

Ferraro, V., and Ghatak, S. (2019). Expanding the castle: Explaining stand your ground legislation in American states, 2005–2012. *Sociological Perspective*, *62*(6), 907–928.

Giannelli, P. C. (1988). Self-Defense. *Public Defender Reporter*, *18*(2), 409. https://scholarlycommons.law.case.edu/faculty_publications/409.

Gius, M. (2016). The relationship between stand-your-ground laws and crime: A state-level analysis. *The Social Science Journal*, *53*(3), 329–338. https://doi.org/10.1016/j.soscij.2016.01.001.

Holliday, W. (2012). "The answer to criminal aggression is retaliation": Stand-your-ground laws and the liberation of self-defense. *University of Toledo Law Review, 43*(2), 407.

Humphreys, D. K., Wiebe, D. J., and Ukert, B. (2018). Regional differences in the impact of the "stand your ground" law in Florida. *Preventive Medicine, 115*, 68–75. https://doi.org/10.1016/j.ypmed.2018.08.010.

Lee, S. (2012, June 8). *Five 'stand your ground' cases you should know about*. Pro Publica Inc. https://www.propublica.org/article/five-stand-your-ground-cases-you-should-know-about.

Levin, B. (2010). A defensible defense? Reexamining castle doctrine statutes. *Harvard Journal on Legislation, 47*(2).

Morral, A. R., and Smart, R. (2019, September 12). *'Stand your ground' laws may be causing more harm than good*. The RAND Blog. https://www.rand.org/blog/2019/09/stand-your-ground-laws-increase-violence.html.

New York Courts. (1986). *People v. Goetz, 68 NY2d 96*. New York State Unified Court System. http://www.courts.state.ny.us/reporter/archives/p_goetz.htm.

Samaha, J. (2017). *Criminal law* (12th ed.). Cengage.

Sofastaii, M. (2013). Trayvon Martin case provokes justice and race debate. *PBS NewsHour Extra*. https://www.pbs.org/newshour/extra/2013/07/trayvon-martin-case-provokes-justice-and-race-debate/.

State of Arizona. (n.d.). *Arizona Revised Statutes Title 13. Criminal Code § 13-405. Justification; use of deadly physical force*. Find Law. https://codes.findlaw.com/az/title-13-criminal-code/az-rev-st-sect-13-405.html.

State of Florida. (2019). *Florida Statutes Title XLVI. Crimes § 776.012. Use or threatened use of force in defense of person*. Find Law. https://codes.findlaw.com/fl/title-xlvi-crimes/fl-st-sect-776-012.html.

State of New York. (n.d.a). *New York Consolidated Laws, Penal Law - PEN* §35.15: *Justification; use of physical force in defense of a person*. Find Law. https://codes.findlaw.com/ny/penal-law/pen-sect-35-15.html.

State of New York. (n.d.b). *New York Consolidated Laws, Penal Law - PEN* §35.20: *Justification; use of physical force in defense of premises and in defense of a person in the course of burglary*. Find Law. https://codes.findlaw.com/ny/penal-law/pen-sect-35-20.html.

State of Ohio. (2021). *29 Ohio Rev. Code. § 2901.09 No duty to retreat in residence or vehicle*. LAWriter. http://codes.ohio.gov/orc/2901.09v1.

State of Vermont. (2012). **§** *2305. Justifiable homicide*. Justia. https://law.justia.com/codes/vermont/2012/title13/chapter53/section2305/.

Supreme Court of Ohio. (1990). *State v. Williford, 49 Ohio St. 3d 247*. Case Text. https://casetext.com/case/state-v-williford.

Supreme Court of the State of Kansas. (2016). *Kansas v. Barlow, 368 p. 3d 331*. Case Text. https://casetext.com/case/state-v-barlow-60.

Sweeney, D. (2016). Standing up to "stand your ground" laws: How the modern NRA-inspired self-defense statutes destroy the principle of necessity, disrupt the criminal justice system, and increase overall violence. *Cleveland State Law Review, 64*(3), 714–746.

Teigen, A. (2022, February 9). *Self Defense and "Stand Your Ground"*. National Conference of State Legislatures. Retrieved February 16, 2022, from https://www.ncsl.org/research/civil-and-criminal-justice/self-defense-and-stand-your-ground.aspx.

Tsujimoto, B. (2016, November 8). Tim Russert was right: 'Florida, Florida, Florida.' *The Buffalo News*. https://buffalonews.com/2016/11/08/tim-russert-right-florida-florida-florida/.

United States Congress. (1992). United States of America 1789 (rev. 1992). Constitution Project. https://www.constituteproject.org/constitution/United_States_of_America_1992.

U.S. Supreme Court. (1895). *Beard v. United States, 158 U.S. 550*. Justia. https://supreme.justia.com/cases/federal/us/158/550/.

U.S. Supreme Court. (1896). *Alberty v. United States, 162 U.S. 499*. Justia. https://supreme.justia.com/cases/federal/us/162/499/.

U.S. Supreme Court. (1921). *Brown v. United States, 256 U.S. 335*. Justia. https://supreme.justia.com/cases/federal/us/256/335/.

U.S. Supreme Court. (1963). *Lombard v. Louisiana, 373 U.S. 267, 275*. Justia. https://supreme.justia.com/cases/federal/us/373/267/.

Ward, C. (2015). "Stand your ground" and self-defense. *American Journal of Criminal Law*, *42*, 89–138.

Weaver, Z. L. (2008). Florida's "stand your ground" law: The actual effects and the need for clarification. *University of Miami Law Review*, *63*, 395–418.

Woodall, B. (2017, June 9). *Florida governor signs bolstered 'stand your ground' law*. Reuters. https://www.reuters.com/article/us-florida-guns/florida-governor-signs-bolstered-stand-your-ground-law-idUSKBN19033X.

24

Guns and Domestic Violence

When Home Isn't So Sweet

Monica Merrill

INTRODUCTION

Intimate partner violence specifically and domestic violence more broadly remain large problems in our society. Domestic violence (DV) refers to violence that happens in any familial relationship (parent-child, siblings, grandparent-grandchild, etc.), while intimate partner violence (IPV) focuses on violence within an intimate relationship (spouses or dating partners). Both DV and IPV are long-term crimes where the offender's goal is to get and maintain power and control over the victim. The violence lasts for weeks, months, and even years. The offender's control over the victim becomes more comprehensive over time, making it harder for the victim to remove themselves from the situation. Firearms often play a critical role in the maintenance of this control.

Researchers and professionals in the field rely on unofficial estimates of DV since these crimes are notoriously underreported due to victim fear, lack of resources, belief in being able to save the intimate relationship, and a variety of other factors. The Centers for Disease Control estimates that twelve million Americans experience some form of DV at some point in their lives (Centers for Disease, 2010). Current estimates put the rate of IPV victimization at 540 per 100,000 people for females and 50 per 100,000 people for males (Office for Victims of Crime, 2018). To put this in context, the highest homicide rate we have had in the last sixty years was in 1980 where the rate was 10.2 homicides per 100,000 people (Uniform Crime, 2020). These numbers show the pervasiveness of IPV in American society.

Firearms interact with DV in many ways. They are used as a tool to maintain power and control over a victim. Firearms are also the most common weapon used when victims of DV are killed by their abusers (Campbell et al., 2003). Also, those who have a history of DV are more likely to engage in mass shootings than those who do not (Zeoli & Paruk, 2020). Recent high-profile shootings where the offender has had a history of DV have opened up discussions about using DV convictions as an exclusionary factor in firearm purchase or possession. In this chapter, legislation trends related to mass shooting and DV prevention are discussed as well as some of the consequences of the different forms of prevention legislation.

NONFATAL FIREARM USE IN INTIMATE PARTNER VIOLENCE

Studies about the use of firearms in nonfatal IPV cases are sparse. Typically, the bulk of the research on the relationship between firearms and IPV comes when there are fatalities involved. What limited research there has been on nonfatal firearm use in IPV has provided mixed results (Sorenson & Schut, 2016). One thing we do know is that the presence of weapons is often used as a way to control behavior (Sorenson & Wiebe, 2004). We see this in international affairs, such as the way countries continually develop bigger and better weapons to control other countries that are within their range. The same logic applies to how offenders use weapons in IPV. The knowledge that a firearm is in the home may be enough to control the behavior of a victim. An abuser can strategically decide when to display a firearm. If they do so in the middle of an argument, this display sends a message to the victim that their life may be in danger should the argument continue, leading them to acquiesce to the offender's wishes. The law recognizes this acquiescence by coercion in robbery statutes, meaning that the presence of a weapon is enough to convince the cashier to hand over the cash in the register without question. The display of a weapon is enough to elevate the criminal charge because it is an implied threat of violence. When a gun is simply displayed in an IPV incident, the threat is often not taken as seriously by law enforcement as it would be in the case of a robbery.

When there is a firearm present in a household experiencing IPV, the threat is experienced differently by the victim. In a robbery, the presence of the firearm and the threat that goes along with it is a one-time event. With IPV, the presence of a firearm is an ongoing concern. The firearm does not even have to be present in the IPV incident. Just knowing that the offender could get a firearm at any time is enough to affect the behavior of the victim. The ever-present threat that a firearm is always readily available results in coercive control (Stark, 2013). This is a pattern of offender behavior where a consistent stream of low-level physical and sexual abuse is employed, coupled with various tactics that otherwise serve to isolate and control a victim. It could be as simple as cleaning a firearm on the kitchen table when asking about the victim's whereabouts during the day. Or shooting holes in victim's clothes that the offender finds inappropriate. Or brushing the hair from a victim's face with the barrel of a gun while asking for sexual favors. Offenders are often creative with the ways in which they employ coercive control, but having firearms in the home makes it more likely a firearm will be used to strike fear in the victim (Myhill & Hohl, 2016).

The goal of IPV is to exert control over the victim. Threatening harm to anything of value to a victim is a common way to maintain this control. Offenders may increase the threat level by pointing the firearm at someone, or something. The object at the end of the barrel does not necessarily have to be the victim in order to control the victim's behavior. Other possible targets can be a car, piece of furniture, pet, a child living in the home, or the offender themselves. Once the offender makes the jump from simply displaying the weapon to actively aiming it with purpose, the risk of a fatality is escalated (Campbell et al., 2003).

FIREARM FATALITIES

While IPV affects both male and female victims, females have often borne the brunt of IPV victimization. This imbalance is more apparent in IPV cases where firearms have been used. Over half of all female homicide victims are killed by a current or former partner (Petrosky et al., 2017); the majority of these homicides are committed with firearms (Sorenson & Wiebe, 2004). This is likely because the majority of gun owners are male. Traditional gender norms show that males are also more likely to be comfortable being around firearms and have experience shooting them, which further emphasizes the power imbalance in a home experiencing DV. Scholars estimate that 4.5 million U.S. women alive today have been threatened by an intimate partner with a firearm (Sorenson & Schut, 2016).

Abusers' access to firearms has been associated with an increased risk of fatality for IPV victims (Campbell et al., 2003). In fact, the presence of a firearm in a domestic violence situation increases the risk of fatality by 500 percent (Campbell et al., 2003). Women in the United States are sixteen times more likely to be killed with a gun compared to women in other high-income countries (Grinshteyn & Hemenway, 2016).

The prevalence of guns in DV fatalities mirrors that of violent crimes overall. More homicides are committed with firearms, handguns specifically, than any other weapon combined (Uniform Crime, 2020). The increase in fatality risk associated with firearms can be explained by the sheer lethality of guns. Also, an offender does not have to be in close proximity (for example, within arm's length) to use a firearm to kill someone effectively. This is not true for most other weapons such as knives, blunt instruments, and so on.

There are often other lives lost than the original victim of IPV. Homicides that are IPV related are often coupled with an offender suicide (Van Wormer & Roberts, 2009). Offender suicide happens in around 60 percent of IPV-related homicides (Smucker et al., 2018), and firearms are the weapon of choice for the majority of these suicides. Offenders can also be shot and killed by responding law enforcement in order to prevent further loss of life. Suicide by cop is another phenomenon that is often seen with IPV homicides (Lord, 2014), and those numbers are not included with technical suicides.

There may be other corollary victims who lose their lives such as children living in the home, romantic competitors, friends, neighbors, bystanders, or police responding to the DV incident. Research has shown that if an intimate partner homicide is committed with a firearm, the offender is twice as likely to kill multiple victims than if any other type of weapon was used (Smucker et al., 2018). This means that the additional victims are likely those inside the home such as children or other family members. Recent work is showing that DV may be a warning sign for other mass fatalities such as mass shootings outside of the home as well.

FIREARMS, IPV, AND MASS SHOOTINGS

Although mass shootings in public places dominate the media, most incidents that meet the congressional definition of a mass killing, the killing of three or more people in a single incident, occur within families (Office for the Victims of Crime. 2018b). Note that the Federal Bureau of Investigation (FBI) does not have an actual definition for mass killings, but only for active shooters. The FBI definition specifies that the shooting must be taking place in a public area, while the congressional definition is inclusive of violence that happens in private spaces such as homes (Mass Casualty, 2018). One effect of these different definitions is that it makes clear that the FBI is not tasked with violence or fatalities that happen in homes, where they are most likely to occur.

About 61 percent of mass shootings occur in a home with another 10 percent occurring partially in the home and partially in a public space (Everytown, 2018). The victims in these shootings are often family or intimate partners of the shooter. The average person may not know that the majority of deaths resulting from mass shootings actually happen within the family unit, as the media focus on mass shootings tends to be on high-profile incidents that happen in public spaces.

Coverage of familicide, the killing of one's own family, is not typically seen in the media, particularly when the incident ends with the offender committing suicide, as they do about 60 percent of the time (Smucker et al., 2018). The media does use statistics that include familicides, but typically when they are covering a mass shooting in a public place leading the viewers to believe that the tally of mass shootings reflect the circumstances of the cases that they are covering.

We now know that those who engage in mass shootings outside of the home often have a history of DV (Zeoli & Paruk, 2020). Studies estimate that roughly 30 percent of mass shootings were committed by someone who was, at the very least, known to law enforcement as being involved with domestic violence. This number likely underrepresents the true relationship between mass shootings and DV as we know DV is not regularly reported to law enforcement.

High-profile examples of this relationship include the Sutherland Springs shooting committed by Devin Kelley. Kelley had a documented history of IPV. In 2012 he was brought to a general court-martial, where he pleaded guilty to two counts of assault, one against his wife and one against his stepson (Dwyer, 2017). It was documented that he had used firearms to threaten his then wife on multiple occasions. Kelley was sentenced to twelve months of confinement and lost his rank in the Air Force. Kelley was dismissed from the Air Force in 2014 with a bad conduct discharge, which should have prevented him from legally purchasing firearms (Brook, 2018). In 2017, Kelley fatally shot twenty-six people in a Texas Baptist church, wounding twenty others. Kelley's mother-in-law was a parishioner at this church (Dwyer, 2017). It was since discovered that the Air Force did not enter Kelley's convictions into the National Crime Information Center database, which meant that he was not flagged when he purchased the firearm he used in the Sutherland Springs shooting (Brook, 2018).

Cedric Ford took a rifle into his workplace in Heston, Kansas. He killed three colleagues and injured fourteen more before he was shot and killed by a responding police officer. Ford had a documented history of domestic violence against his girlfriend and was served with a protection order at his place of employment ninety minutes before the shooting began (Wang et al., 2016).

Adam Lanza was the perpetrator behind the tragedy in Newtown, Connecticut, where twenty-six people, many of them children, were killed. Lanza had threatened to kill his mother years before and did, in fact, kill her in their home before heading to the school on the day of the shooting (Salam, 2017).

The above examples are documented, straightforward cases where mass shooters had a history of DV. There are other examples of mass shooters who did not have documented histories of domestic violence, but their past intimate partners have now come forward about their abuse. Sitora Yusufiy, the ex-wife of the Pulse nightclub shooter Omar Mateen, told media outlets how Mateen would physically abuse her, verbally demean her, and demand sole access to her finances (Snyder, 2018). This abuse was not officially documented by law enforcement but does speak to the trend of mass shooters having past histories of DV or IPV.

Other high-profile shooters have not necessarily had documented histories of IPV or DV but have demonstrated a deep hatred for women that could also be considered a relevant factor to this discussion. Elliot Rodger, the offender behind the Isla Vista killings in 2014, is a good example of this connection. He was active in internet communities that were vocal about their misogynistic views of women. Rodger wrote out his plans for what he called his Day of Retribution, the second phase of which was titled War on Women. Here he detailed how he wanted to punish women for depriving him of sex. Rodger states, "I cannot kill every single female on earth, but I can deliver a devastating blow that will shake all of them to the core of their wicked hearts" (Winton et al., 2014, p. 1). Rodger would eventually put his plan into motion killing six people and wounding fourteen others in a combination of stabbings, shootings, and striking pedestrians with his vehicle. One of Rodger's main targets was a sorority house which, according to him, housed the most beautiful girls on the campus where he attended school. Rodger ended his life after engaging the police in a shootout (Nagourney et al., 2014). This incident took place in California, which has some of the most restrictive gun laws in the country. These deaths were some of the many high-profile incidents that reinvigorated the discussion about firearm legislation.

FIREARM LEGISLATION AS PREVENTION

Legislators are taking a closer look at firearm restrictions from DV convictions to see how they can be used to both prevent further DV and also possibly serve as prevention for mass shootings. Research has consistently shown those states that have legislation restricting access to firearms after a domestic violence conviction have lower IPV homicide rates than states that do not have this type of legislation (Vigdor & Mercy, 2006). These findings show the importance of identifying high-risk situations where fatalities are likely and allowing law enforcement to act.

Under existing federal law, both the 1994 Violence Against Women Act and the 1996 Lautenberg Amendment prohibit persons with past convictions of domestic violence or those that are under current protection orders from purchasing or possessing firearms. This means for the past twenty-six years it has been acknowledged that the increased risk or amplified levels of abuse, even fatalities, exists when firearms are present in homes experiencing IPV. While this shows that this relationship exists, researchers, practitioners, and legislators are still struggling with the best way to combat it. The most recent attempts involve "red flag" laws, or "extreme risk protection orders."

Federal law has two main mechanisms to prevent DV offenders from legally obtaining or possessing firearms. The first is the Domestic Violence Restraining Order (DVRO), which disallows an individual under a DVRO to purchase or possess a firearm. The second is a conviction of a misdemeanor crime of domestic violence (MCDV). This means that while all felonies prevent access to firearm ownership for the offender, the crime of domestic violence needs only to be committed at the misdemeanor level to make the offender ineligible for firearm possession. However, the relationship requirement to meet these federal mandates is limited. The victim–offender relationship between the petitioner and the respondent must be that of a current or former spouse or cohabitant or have had a child together. Some states have expanded this requirement to include dating partners.

Of course, the structure of the system is only effective if implemented properly. Private sales of firearms still occur. These are likely happening without buyer background checks, even in those states with a background check requirement (Miller et al., 2017). In recent years, internet sales of firearms between private parties have become popular. Social media platforms such as Facebook have attempted to police the sale of firearms on their platform; however, this has proven quite difficult. Individuals are still finding ways to sell guns to one another off the record. These ways involve changing group names, disbanding of groups and re-forming under a new name, or even speaking to each other in "code" on the sale page, referring to guns as puppies or kittens or any other nonthreatening object. Gun shows and flea markets are other venues for private parties to buy and sell firearms without background checks. Inheriting property is another concern when it comes to firearm possession. An individual who may be prohibited from purchasing a firearm may inherit one from a family member, leaving legislation aimed at restricting purchasing firearms totally moot.

Removal of firearms once there is a "red flag" is another area of legislation that focuses on DV. Some experts advocate red flag laws as an answer to the perceived increase in mass shootings. As of this writing, there are thirteen states that have some type of red flag law. Eight states out of the thirteen passed these laws in 2018 (Kohrman & Stephens, 2020). A large contingent of supporters of red flag laws became quite vocal as a result of the Parkland, Florida, school shooting on February 14, 2018, possibly leading to the influx of states legislating red flag laws.

Nicholas Cruz, the shooter in the Parkland case, evidenced a number of what could potentially be considered red flags. These include a long history of domestic violence against his brother and mother that necessitated eighteen separate law enforcement responses during his adolescence, proven access to firearms, placing those firearms against the head of his mother and brother, an Instagram post insinuating plans for a school shooting, expulsion from school, and self-harm behavior (Fausset & Kovaleski, 2018). Any number of these things could now trigger a red flag clause in Florida where authorities could remove a firearm from a home if need be. Red flag laws are also often discussed when there is a highly publicized DV fatality involving a firearm and a long, documented history of abuse.

In thirteen states (California, Connecticut, Delaware, Florida, Illinois, Indiana, Maryland, Massachusetts, New Jersey, Oregon, Rhode Island, Vermont, and Washington) law enforcement has the power to petition the court for an emergency removal of an individual's firearms (Wang et al., 2016). Vermont is the only state that requires this petition be filed at the state level by the attorney general's office. All others can be filed by local law enforcement. Eight states (California, Delaware, Illinois, Maryland, Massachusetts, New Jersey, Oregon, and Washington) all agree that some version of a family member (ranges include immediate family only to all household members) can file a petition to remove a firearm from someone. Maryland is the only state that extends this option to health professionals. Maryland is also unique in that it is the only state that recognizes the petitioner as the one to fall under potential harm (Wang et al., 2016). All other states include some variation of a broad statement like "hurting themselves or others."

All thirteen states that have "red flag laws" on the books allow for Extreme Risk Protection Order (ERPO) removals. The ERPO can be filed without notice of a hearing for the respondent. The ERPOs can last anywhere from seven to fourteen days, depending on the state. Once an ERPO is granted, another hearing is held where the petitioner is required to present evidence showing that the respondent meets the criteria for removal in the state (Everytown, 2020). The standard of proof here varies. All states' laws but two are written to require clear and convincing evidence that the respondent may cause harm to themselves or others. Washington and Massachusetts, two of the more recent additions, require the higher preponderance of evidence standard. California is unique in that it also requires documentation that less restrictive measures have been tried before they will grant an ERPO (Giffords Law, 2018).

The red flag laws do have flaws. Namely, in states without mandatory gun registration there is no way for authorities to know if and/or how many guns are in a home. Past work has examined this question and found that over half of DV offenders (52%) kept at least one gun in the home after they had been required by law to turn their guns over to authorities because of a protection order (Webster et al., 2010).

One glaring problem with this approach to prevention is that DV and IPV are notoriously underreported crimes. This means that the criminal justice system can only help in the cases of which they are aware. If law enforcement and the court system aren't involved, any tools they have for prevention cannot be utilized. The majority of existing laws and discussions about changes to purchasing firearms, red flag laws, and ERPOs necessitate either a past DV conviction or an active protection order. Victims may be reluctant to report their victimization for a variety of reasons: fear, not wanting the offender to be arrested, embarrassment, lack of faith in the criminal justice system, and so on. This means that victims who do not report are often left to work out their own prevention and safety plans. Alternatively, victims may also place too much stock in our system's ability to protect them, as often seen with protection orders.

Protection orders are legal tools, nothing else. They provide a mechanism to charge an offender for violating the terms listed in the protection order, but they do little to actually protect the victim. In fact, the serving of a protection order is often a trigger point for an offender to commit more violence against their victim. Roughly 11 percent of the victims killed in DV or IPV incidents had an active protection order against their killer. Of those victims, 20 percent are killed within two days of the protection order being issued (Vites & Sorenson, 2008).

If prevention measures are being triggered by protection orders, those involved with procuring a protection order need to be sure that victims understand what they are, how they work, and the potential retribution they may face when granted one. A protection order is not an armed guard or a bulletproof vest, it is a piece of paper that is most useful once it is violated. If we are using protection orders as a precursor to prevention measures, it would be in the best interest of the victims filing for these orders to engage in safety planning in conjunction with their application.

Recent efforts to improve legislation include training officers to encourage voluntary relinquishment of firearms on the scenes of IPV incidents (Giffords Law, n.d.). The logic is that if the officer can voluntarily remove the firearm from the scene, then the chances of a serious injury or fatality are minimized. This policy has the potential to be effective, but only if the offender and victim agree to relinquish *all* of the firearms in the home on scene. There also needs to be a clear process by which the offender and/or the victim can easily regain access to the firearm.

GUN OWNERSHIP FOR VICTIMS AS A MEANS OF PROTECTION

IPV victims arming themselves is a topic that often surfaces in the ongoing debate between gun rights and gun control advocates. The argument for firearm ownership states that a victim of IPV would not be able to be victimized if they had access to their own firearm. That they would assert themselves and use the firearm as a means of protection. The push to arm victims of IPV is consistent with gun rights activists' logic that if all people were armed, violent crime would drop because the potential victims would be able to defend themselves against offenders.

Research here is mixed; arming potential victims may or may not be effective at preventing violent crime outside the home (Hamill et al., 2019). However, arming victims as an IPV prevention strategy evidences a clear ignorance of the complexities of IPV. A victim owning a firearm, in and of itself, would not automatically end their victimization. Nor would a victim necessarily be likely to use it against their offender. Power and control are critical components of IPV. So much so that victims often lose their own sense of power or self-efficacy. Victims may also not use a firearm against their offender because they depend on that offender for certain things (income, shelter, transportation, etc.).

Despite there being no clear evidence that arming victims of IPV would protect them from harm, several states have passed legislation granting temporary firearm permits to victims of IPV who successfully obtained a protection order from their abuser. These laws come and go based on the political landscape. For example, in 2014 Kentucky passed a bill that allowed a person who has an active protection order to get an expedited temporary concealed carry permit (Ky. Rev., 2014). The permit would be processed within twenty-four hours to ensure that the victim could legally carry firearms as a protection mechanism and do so quickly. Incidentally, this temporary permit requires no training or safety courses like the actual concealed carry permit does in Kentucky. Other states such as Michigan have tried to pass extensions to where victims with protection orders and existing concealed carry permits can legally carry their weapons in what would normally be considered gun-free zones (i.e., bars, college campuses, etc.). As of this writing, these expansions have not yet passed into law in any state.

While some victims of IPV say that they would *feel* safer with a firearm in the home, evidence shows that they may actually not *be* safer. The victim bringing a firearm into the home ensures that the offender has access to a firearm. This can actually facilitate the death of the victim. Research shows that an IPV offender's direct access to a gun increases the likelihood of the death of the victim by eleven times (Spencer & Stith, 2018). The victim owning a firearm may also increase the likelihood that they would kill the offender, which they may not want to do. Even throughout an abusive relationship, the victim often retains feeling for the offender and may also be dependent on them for income, transportation, shelter, childcare. Lastly, purchasing a firearm for self-defense means that a victim needs to have quick and easy access to the firearm. This likely means strategically placing the firearm within the home and leaving it loaded. This poses a danger to the victim, the offender, and children living inside the home. Accidental shootings and injuries occur in the United States at a rate of ten times higher than in other countries (Richardson & Hemenway, 2011). This is especially true for homes with children in them. There is also a concern that a child would use the weapon to defend a parent, victim, or offender in a DV incident.

When victims of IPV were asked about using a weapon to defend themselves from their intimate partner, only 5.5 percent thought that it could possibly improve their situation. Sixty-eight percent, however, believed having their own gun would make their situation worse (Sorensen & Wiebe, 2004). Not all victims of DV feel this way. There have been cases where a firearm has been used successfully by the victim to defend themselves against the offender, although research on this phenomenon and how it relates specifically to firearms has been limited.

CONCLUSION

Often, well-meaning researchers, legislators, and practitioners get caught up in addressing only one aspect of a social issue. When we discuss the relationship between firearms and DV, we focus on the coercive behavior and the increased risk of fatality. These are obviously important components to DV, but they are symptoms of the underlying problem. Domestic violence is about control. Offenders will use whatever means necessary to get that control, whether that includes firearms or not. In a qualitative study done with victims of IPV, some victims expressed concerns that if their offender did not have access to firearms, they would harm them in another way. For example, one victim is quoted as saying, "He tried to run me over with the car. Whether or not he had guns made no difference to me whatsoever. I wouldn't feel comfortable just because he doesn't have a gun." The victims also reported that they do not think removing offender's firearms would make victims any safer. They cited knives, frying pans, and other various household items that could potentially be used (or in some cases, were used) to abuse or even kill victims (Lynch, 2020, p. 7). Additionally, the seizure of an offender's firearms may feel like a loss of control to that offender who may then retaliate against the victim. This could potentially be a fatal retaliation.

While firearms are often used as tools in DV, it is a mistake to think that all DV will disappear without them. Firearms are just the tool of choice used by many offenders to maintain power and control over victims.

BIBLIOGRAPHY

Brook, T. V. 2018. Air force failed four times to prevent Sutherland Springs church killer from buying guns. *USA Today*. Retrieved from https://www.usatoday.com/story/news/politics/2018/12/07/air-force-failed-four-times-prevent-sutherland-springs-shooter-gun-purchase/2237400002/.

Campbell, J. C., Webster, D., Koziol-McLain, J., Block, C., Campbell, D., Curry, M. A., and Laughon, K. 2003. Risk factors for femicide in abusive relationships: Results from a multisite case control study. *American Journal of Public Health*, *93*: 1089–1097.

Centers for Disease Control. 2010. National intimate partner and sexual violence survey findings. Retrieved from https://www.cdc.gov/ViolencePrevention/pdf/NISVS_FactSheet-a.pdf.

Dwyer, C. 2017. Texas shooter may have been motivated to kill by "domestic situation." National Public Radio. Retrieved from https://www.npr.org/sections/thetwo-way/2017/11/06/562299408/texas-church-shooter-may-have-been-motivated-to-kill-by-domestic-situation.

Everytown for Gun Safety. 2020. Extreme risk laws save lives. Retrieved from https://everytownresearch.org/documents/2019/09/extremerisklaws-appendix-b.pdf/.

Everytown for Gun Safety. 2018. Mass shootings in America. Retrieved from https://everytownresearch.org/massshootingsreports/mass-shootings-in-america-2009-2019/.

Fausset, R., and Kovaleski, S. 2018. Nicholas Cruz, Florida shooting suspect, showed every red flag. *New York Times*. Retrieved from https://www.nytimes.com/2018/02/15/us/nikolas-cruz-florida-shooting.html.

Giffords Law Center. 2018. Extreme risk protection orders. Retrieved from https://lawcenter.giffords.org/gun-laws/policy-areas/who-can-have-a-gun/extreme-risk-protection-orders/.

Giffords Law Center. N.d. Domestic violence and firearms. Retrieved from https://lawcenter.giffords.org/gun-laws/policy-areas/who-can-have-a-gun/domestic-violence-firearms/.

Grinshteyn, E., and Hemenway, D. 2016. Violent death rates: The US compared with other high-income OECD countries, 2010. *The American Journal of Medicine*, *129*: 266–273.

Hamill, M. E., Hernandez, M. C., Bailey, K. R., Zielinski, M. D., Matos, M. A., and Schiller, H. J. 2019. State level firearm concealed-carry legislation and rates of homicide and other violent crime. *Journal of the American College of Surgeons*, *228*: 1–8.

Kohrman, M., and Stephens, Alain. 2020. States are embracing red flag laws for gun owners. Here's how they work. The Trace. Retrieved from https://www.thetrace.org/2020/02/states-are-embracing-red-flag-laws-for-gun-owners-heres-how-they-work/.

Ky. Rev. Stat. Ann § 403.754. 2014.

Lord, V. B. 2014. Police responses in officer-involved violent deaths: Comparison of suicide by cop and non-suicide by cop incidents. *Police Quarterly, 17*(1): 79–100.

Lynch, K. 2020. Female firepower: Gun ownership for self-protection among female intimate partner violence victims. *Violence and Gender*, *7*: 19–26.

Miller, M., Hepburn, L., and Azrael, D. 2017. Firearm acquisition without background checks: Results of a national survey. *Annals of Internal Medicine, 166*(4): 233–239.

Myhill, A., and Hohl, K. 2016. The "golden thread": Coercive control and risk assessment for domestic violence. *Journal of Interpersonal Violence*, *34*(21–22): 4477–4497.

Nagourney, A., Cieply, M., Feuer, A., and Lovett, I. 2014. Before brief, deadly spree, trouble since age 8. *New York Times*. Retrieved from https://www.nytimes.com/2014/06/02/us/elliot-rodger-killings-in-california-followed-years-of-withdrawal.html.

Office for Victims of Crime. 2018a. Intimate partner violence. Retrieved from https://ovc.ncjrs.gov/ncvrw2018/info_flyers/fact_sheets/2018NCVRW_IPV_508_QC.pdf.

Office for Victims of Crime. 2018b. Mass casualty shootings fact sheet. Retrieved from https://ovc.ncjrs.gov/ncvrw2018/info_flyers/fact_sheets/2018NCVRW_MassCasualty_508_QC.pdf.

Petrosky, E., Blair, J. M., Betz, C. J., Fowler, K. A., Jack, S. P., and Lyons, B. H. 2017. Racial and ethnic differences in homicides of adult women and the role of intimate partner violence—United States, 2003–2014. *Morbidity and Mortality Weekly Report*, *66*, 741–746.

Richardson. E. G., Hemenway, D. 2011. Homicide, suicide, and unintentional firearm fatality: Comparing the United States with other high-income countries, 2003. *Journal of Trauma and Acute Care Surgery*, *70*: 238–243.

Salam, M. 2017. Adam Lanza threatened Sandy Hook killings years earlier, records show. *New York Times.* Retrieved from https://www.nytimes.com/2017/10/26/us/adam-lanza-sandy-hook.html.

Smucker, S., Kerber, R. E., and Cook, P. J. 2018. Suicide and additional homicides associated with intimate partner homicide: North Carolina 2004–2013. *Journal of Urban Health*, *95*: 337–343.

Snyder, R. L. 2018. Was the wife of the Pulse shooter a victim or accomplice? *The New Yorker*. Retrieved from https://www.newyorker.com/news/news-desk/the-wife-of-the-pulse-night-club-shooter-goes-on-trial.

Sorenson, S. B., and Schut, R. 2016. Non-fatal gun use in intimate partner violence: A systematic review of the literature. *Trauma, Violence & Abuse, 19*(4): 431–442.

Sorenson, S. B., and Wiebe, D. J. 2004. Weapons in the lives of battered women. *American Journal of Public Health, 94*: 1412–1417.

Spencer, C., and Stith, S. 2018. Risk factors for male perpetration and female victimization of intimate partner homicide: A Meta-Analysis. *Trauma, Violence, and Abuse, 21*(3): 527–540.

Stark, E. 2013. The dangers of dangerousness assessment. *Family & Intimate Partner Violence Quarterly, 6*: 13–22.

Uniform Crime Report. 2020. Uniform crime reporting statistics. Retrieved from https://www.ucrdatatool.gov.

Van Wormer, K., and Roberts, A. R. 2009. Death by domestic violence: Preventing the murders and murder-suicides. In *Women and families at risk: An overview*, 1–20. Westport, CT: Praeger; 2009.

Vigdor, E. R., and Mercy, J. A. 2006. Do laws restricting access to firearms by domestic violence offenders prevent intimate partner homicide? *Evaluation Review, 30*(3): 313–346.

Vites, K. A., and Sorenson, S. B. 2008. Restraining orders among victims of intimate partner homicide. *Injury Prevention, 14*(3): 191–195.

Wang, Y., Moyer, J. W., and Bever, L. 2016. Something "real off" about him: Portrait of Kansas shooter Cedric Ford emerges. *Washington Post*. Retrieved from https://www.washingtonpost.com/news/morning-mix/wp/2016/02/26/alcoholic-violent-depressed-portrait-of-kansas-shooter-emerges/.

Webster, D. W., Frattaroli, S., Vernick, J. S., O'Sullivan, C., Roehl, J., and Campbell, J. C. 2010. Women with protective orders report failure to remove firearms from their abusive partners: Results from an exploratory study. *Journal of Women's Health, 19*: 93–98.

Winton, W., Rosanna, X., and Rong-Gong, L., II. 2014. Isla Vista shooting: Read Elliot Rodger's graphic, elaborate attack plan. *The Los Angeles Times*. Retrieved from https://www.latimes.com/local/lanow/la-me-ln-isla-vista-document-20140524-story.html.

Zeoli, A., and Paruk, K. 2020. Potential to prevent mass shootings through domestic violence firearms restrictions. *Criminology and Public Policy, 19*: 129–145.

25

Guns and the Dark Web

How Technological Advances Easily Facilitate Access to Firearms and Other Weaponry

Sabrina Koncaba and Karla Weinbrenner

INTRODUCTION

Prior to the advancement of the Internet, gun sales were primarily conducted offline. One could either go to a private seller or a gun show to obtain a firearm of choice. Now with advances in technology, gun ownership has become easier than ever—whether the purchase is conducted legally or illegally. Technologies such as encryption, cryptocurrencies, and steganography make it easier than ever for individuals to remain anonymous through the process of purchasing and/or trafficking firearms. In addition, "dark webs" are being used to make it harder for police to identify, capture, and prosecute criminals. Criminals are getting more adept at employing these technologies to evade capture and provide anonymity along with transactional privacy.

In this chapter, we will explore the following:

- How guns are purchased legally through the Internet
- How "Dark Webs" work
- How guns are purchased through cryptomarkets on the Dark Web
- How other technologies are used to facilitate underground purchases of guns and other weaponry
- Challenges and issues posed by law enforcement in policing and prosecuting gun crimes

INTERNET/SURFACE WEB GUN PURCHASES*

In order to buy a gun online, an individual must first identify a gun store that is also a Federal Firearm Licensee (FFL). This ensures that a background check will be satisfied to determine if a firearm can be transferred to the purchaser in person. The purchaser fills out an ATF (Alcohol, Tobacco and Firearm) form, called Form 4473. This form is then used by the FFL to conduct a background check as it requires information about the identity of the purchaser, and it requires answers to a series of questions to ensure that an individual is not a prohibited person.

Assuming that the purchaser passed the background check, the purchaser then goes online and chooses the gun that they want to purchase. As part of the online check-out process, the FFL's license must be provided so that the online gun store can verify their legitimacy. The gun is then paid for by the purchaser.

Once the online store has verified the FFL provided by the purchaser, the gun is then shipped to the FFL location. The purchaser is then notified to come and pick up their firearm. The purchaser then provides a government-issued identification (ID) that has a picture and current address, and the purchaser takes possession of the firearm.

Purchasing weapons has become easier with the Internet; however, there is a significant loophole when it comes to background checks. Federal law requires licensed gun dealers to perform background checks on prospective purchasers; it does not require unlicensed sellers to perform background checks (Miller et al., 2017). The Internet has made it increasingly easy for all types of people to take advantage of the private-sale loophole by arranging gun sales with unlicensed sellers in online chat rooms, social media, auctions, and classified ads. The online market has become a good place to purchase weapons for people who cannot pass a background check at a licensed store.

In a recent survey, it was found that 45 percent of gun owners who acquired a gun online in the past two years did so without any background check (Miller et al., 2017). Almost one in nine of the people who purchased a firearm through a major web platform, Armslist.com, would not have passed a background check (Unchecked: Over 1 Million, 2020). In 2018 alone, there were 1.2 million advertisements on Armslist.com for firearms sales where no background check was required (Unchecked: Over 1 Million, 2020).

Armslist.com operates similarly to other online classified platforms where a seller posts an ad that includes price, description, and a photo.

* *Note that firearm purchase rules vary from state to state and also whether or not the purchase is from a gun store/dealer or private party transaction.*

Armslist.com allows firearms ads to be posted by both licensed (called "premium vendors") who are required to conduct a background check on all gun sales and unlicensed sellers (called "private parties") who are not covered by the federal requirement. The sales are completed offline after e-mail, phone, text, and in-person communications (Unchecked: Over 1 Million, 2020).

LAYERS OF THE INTERNET

Before we can discuss purchasing a firearm in a cryptomarket on the "dark web," one must identify and understand the Internet along with its various layers. In figure 25.1, you will notice that the Internet is comprised of the following layers:

- The World Wide Web (WWW)
- The Internet
- The Surface Web
- Deep Web
- Dark Web
- Dark Net

THE INTERNET

The Internet as shown in the image is the largest circle and encompasses all of the layers to include the "deep" and "dark webs." Most average users consider the dark part of the web a separate entity from the Internet; however, the Internet comprises every single server, computer, and device that is connected together in a network of networks. The Internet is actually divided into two elements: The Surface Web and the Deep Web (Chertoff, 2017).

The World Wide Web and Surface Web

The World Wide Web (WWW) is the graphical interface of the Internet that is accessible through a web browser such as Microsoft Edge, Google Chrome, or Mozilla Firefox. It includes "pages" that are connected to each other by hyperlinks—i.e., electronic connections that link related pieces of information or other pages in order to allow a user easy access to them. These pages are indexed by search engines like Google, Yahoo!, and Bing and are easily accessed through standard browsers and Internet protocols (Chertoff, 2017).

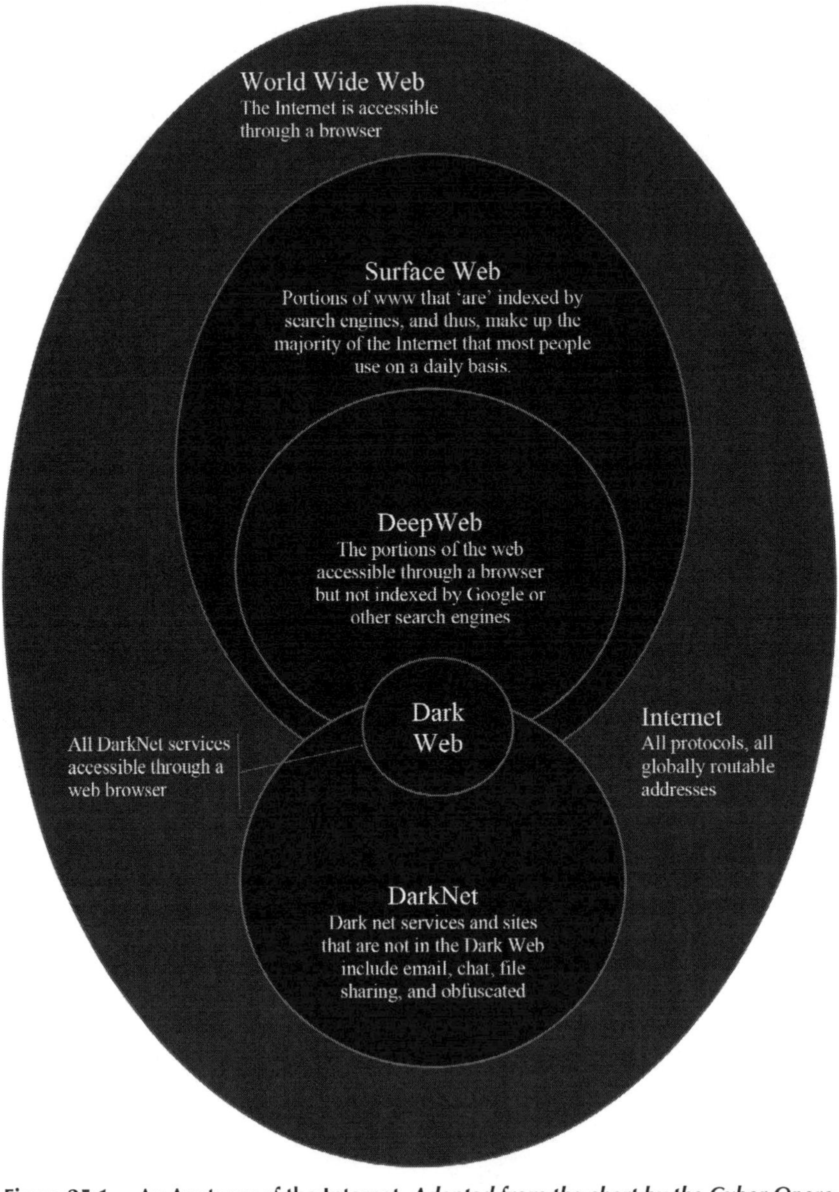

Figure 25.1. An Anatomy of the Internet. *Adapted from the chart by the Cyber Operations, Analysis, and Research department of Argonne National Laboratory.*

This may seem like a vast quantity of information, but the Surface Web is the smallest part of the overall Internet.

Although the Surface Web is growing, there are fluctuations that make it difficult to determine the overall size of the World Wide Web. According to Verisign, there were a total of 366.8 million domain name registrations across all top-level domains (TLDs) during the first quarter of 2020 (Verisign, 2020). As of January 2020, there are over 1.7 billion websites (Internet Live Stats, 2020).

The Deep Web

The term Deep Web is often used interchangeably with Dark Web, but the definitions are actually different. The Deep Web is part of the overall Surface Web; however, it cannot be accessed by traditional search engines such as Google because the content in this area of the Internet is not indexed. These pages are also not "static" and linked to other pages as information on the Surface Web. One can get to these pages by some type of action which includes: putting in username and password, checking out your cart, paying to access specific information, and so on. Information on the Deep Web equally includes back-end data for most of the worlds' biggest websites and platforms, as well as encrypted information stored on private networks and cloud servers. Examples include:

- Password-protected pages that require usernames and passwords
- Shopping Cart pages
- Pages that allow you to "input" information such as web forms
- Pages that allow you to create content
- Private Networks
- Corporate Databases

The Dark Net

The Dark Net is part of the Internet that we utilize through application interfaces and services to include e-mail (through an e-mail client such as Microsoft Outlook), chat (such as Microsoft Teams, Discord, and Mattermost), and file sharing (Dropbox, OneDrive, Google Drive) along with obfuscated routing. These platforms are also accessible by a web browser such as Google Chrome but also as specific stand-alone applications (apps) that can be downloaded to a tablet or smart device.

The Dark Web

The Dark Web, by contrast, is a very small portion of the Deep Web. It accounts for approximately 4.5 percent of the total sites on the Internet: There are around 80,000 unique Dark Web Sites and hundreds of millions of regular ones (Internet Live Stats, 2020; Holmes, 2020).

Unlike the various "webs" above, a specialized browser such as The Onion Router (TOR) must be used in order to access sites that are hosted on the Dark Web. Once accessed and if a user knows where to look, a viewer can find and buy anything: drugs, weapons, stolen art, credit card numbers, pornography (adult and child), hackers for hire, and people (for human trafficking).

The Dark Web can also facilitate a wide variety of criminal transactions where a range of malicious actors—from drug and arms dealers to terrorists to hackers for hire leverage the secrecy and anonymity afforded by tools such as TOR and Invisible Internet Project (I2P) to facilitate conversation, coordination, and action (Finklea, 2017).

How the TOR Network Works

Above, we discussed using TOR as a browser; however, TOR can also be used to run the network of computers that manages the TOR connections (Estes, 2013). TOR's users connect to websites "through a series of virtual encrypted tunnels rather than making a direct connection, thus allowing both organizations and individuals to share information over public networks without compromising their privacy" (TOR Overview, 2020). Users route their web traffic through other users' computers such that the traffic cannot be traced to the original user. TOR essentially establishes layers (like layers of an onion) and routes traffic through those layers to conceal users' identities (Estes, 2013). To get from layer to layer, TOR has established "relays" on computers around the world through which information passes. Information is encrypted between relays and "all TOR traffic passes through at least three relays before it reaches its destination" (What Is a Tor Relay?, 2020). The final relay is called the "exit relay" and the IP address of this relay is viewed as the source of the TOR traffic. When using TOR software, users' IP addresses remain hidden. As such, it appears that the connection to any given website is "coming from the IP address of a TOR exit relay, which can be anywhere in the world" (What Is a Tor Relay?, 2020, para. 2).

Accessing the TOR Network and Dark Web Sites

In order to access the Dark Web, one must have access to one of three browsers: TOR, I2P, or FreeNet. Because TOR is the most popular of the three,

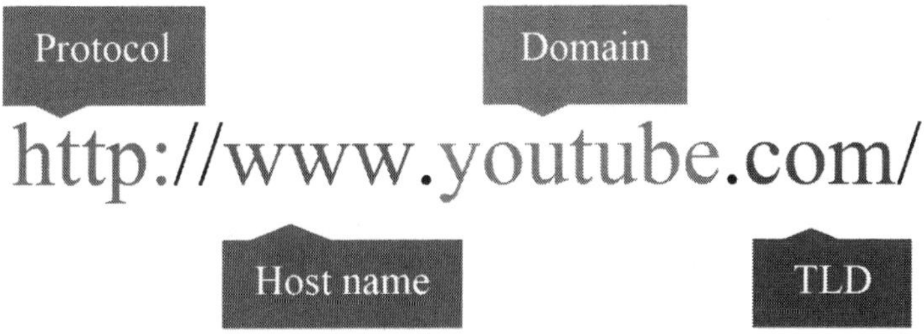

Figure 25.2. Uniform Resource Locator Breakdown. ***Figure created by author.***

we will focus on this browser. A user visits the TOR Project website (https://www.torproject.org/) and clicks the link to *Download Now*. The operating system that you will be installing the TOR browser on should be selected. The website will then begin downloading the executable file. Once you have downloaded the file, install based upon the directions of the specific operating system that will be utilized. After installation, go to the icon and double-click. After doing so, you will be presented with the graphic of the TOR browser.

One can use TOR to surf the Surface Internet/World Wide Web. So in order to do so, we open up the TOR browser and type in the Uniform Resource Locator (URL) or web address of where we would like to visit. In this example we will use YouTube (www.youtube.com).

TOR presents you with the YouTube web site. Now, before we start looking at sites on the Dark Web, we need to analyze the URL that we typed in. The URL for the Dark Web will follow the same format; however, it will look completely different, and you will need to understand this before proceeding to use Dark Web URLs.

The URL in our example has four parts (figure 25.2): the protocol, host name, the Domain Name, and the Top Level Domain (TLD).

The protocol, HTTP, which stands for HyperText Transfer Protocol is the portion of the URL that tells the computer how to format the data so that it can communicate with the remote server. The WWW, which stands for World Wide Web, is the host name of the Domain Name System (DNS) Server. Once the request is received, the DNS Server either resolves IP Address and

Figure 25.3. Dark Web URL. ***Figure created by author.***

sends the webpage to the requesting computer or the DNS Server forwards the request to resolve the TLD and the requested Domain.

In accessing the Dark Web through TOR, the resolution works very similarly; however, the URLs look very different. See figure 25.3.

You will notice that the URL has the protocol, host name, and the TLD. But what is most apparent is that the host name is not "friendly" or easily remembered and is randomly generated from the TOR browser software. The TLD is an *.onion top level domain that is only reachable by the TOR browser on the TOR network. (The asterisk represents the name of the Top Level domain on the onion network.)

After conducting a Google search on the Internet, one is easily able to find websites that can be visited to gain access to the type of content that you are looking for. A simple Google search about guns can yield a wide variety of results to include pages dedicated to selling firearms and ammunition. These websites include but are not limited to pistols, semi-automatic, and automatic rifles, and in some instances explosives as well.

What Can Be Found on the Dark Web?

The Dark Web is generally synonymous with illegal or criminal activity. Anything the heart desires can be found on the Dark Web. In 2019, Dr. Michael McGuires at the University of Surrey, showed that the number of Dark Web Listings that host illicit content has risen by 20 percent since 2016 (Moore, 2016). Categories of illegal activities for hire are shown in table 25.1.

Famous Cryptomarkets

Cryptomarkets are online marketplaces that sell multiple items that are categorized for the user and require the use of cryptocurrency for payment. Cryptomarkets can sell a variety of items such as firearms, drugs, credit cards, digital documents, fake identifications, hacker services, hitman services, pornography, people. The Silk Road, "also known as the Amazon of drugs and vice," is one of the best-known examples of a successful and lucrative online criminal marketplace. Known as the first modern Darknet market, it was launched in 2011 and offered every possible illicit product imaginable, neatly presented by category with customer reviews, high-resolution photos, and descriptions. It offered, "stolen bank accounts, counterfeit currency, AK-47s, armor piercing rounds, stolen credit cards, computer viruses, keystroke loggers, compromised Facebook accounts, tutorials with step-by-step instructions on hacking ATMs and other point of sale machines, child pornography and even hitmen for hire" (CASEFILE, 2018). Silk Road accepted only

Table 25.1. Categories of Websites in the TOR Network

Category	*Details*
Arms	Trading of firearms and weapons
Drugs	Trade or manufacture of illegal drugs, including illegally obtained prescription medicine
Extremism	Content espousing extremist ideologies, including ideological texts, expressions of support for terrorist violence, militant how-to guides, and extremist community forums
Finance	Money laundering, counterfeit bills, trade in stolen credit cards or accounts
Hacking	Hackers for hire, trade, or distribution of malware or DDoS capabilities
Illegitimate pornography	Pornographic material involving children, violence, animals, or materials obtained without participants consent
Nexus	Websites primarily focused on linking to other illicit websites and resources within the dark net
Other illicit	Materials that did not easily fit into the other categories but remain problematic, such as trade of other illegal goods and fake passports or IDs
Social	Online communities for sharing illicit material in the form of forums, social networks, and other message boards
Violence	Hitmen for hire, and instructional material on conducting violent attacks
Other	Non-illicit content, such as ideological or political content, secure drop sites, information repositories, legitimate services
None	Websites which were either completely inaccessible or otherwise had no visible content, including websites which hosted only placeholder text, indicating that their operation had yet to generate indicative content.

Moore, 2016

Bitcoin payments and relied on Bitcoin's anonymity capabilities to prevent exposure of criminal activity. Furthermore, only those who used an untraceable Internet browsing network (TOR, FreeNet) were able to access the site. It took the government over two years to uncover the individual behind Silk Road. Eventually the FBI shut down the cryptomarket after successfully identifying Ross Ulbricht as the owner and operator. On October 1, 2013, the government apprehended Ulbricht and charged him with narcotics trafficking and money laundering conspiracies through creating and operating Silk Road (Huang, 2015).

AlphaBay was another online cryptomarket that operated on the TOR network. It was officially launched in December 2014. The cryptomarket saw steady growth within the first ninety days of operation. Almost a year after it launched, AlphaBay was recognized as the largest online dark net crypto market and had over 200,000 users ("AlphaBay," 2020). AlphaBay was estimated to have sales in the hundreds of millions of dollars annually, making it "many times" larger than Silk Road. In July 2017, AlphaBay was seized by the U.S. government and shut down. Its developer, Alexandre Cazes, was apprehended on July 5, 2017. At the time of his capture, he was worth US$23 million including $12.5 million in properties and vehicles. The rest was in cash and in cryptocurrencies (Bellemare, 2017). Cazes was found dead in a Thai jail a week later, on July 12, 2017. U.S. Justice officials said he took his own life.

What is most interesting about how Cazes was caught is that authorities were able to find him through his Hotmail address that was sent unencrypted to new AlphaBay users who had just joined the platform (Bellemare, 2017).

The Armory was another site that primarily sold weapons in the dark net market. It was established in 2012. However, due to lack of demand, it was shut down.

Other Dark Markets that have either been seized or shut down include:

- Agora
- Dream Market
- Project Black Flag
- Black Market Reloaded

It is imperative to note that most sites on the Dark Web do not have longevity. Although Silk Road and AlphaBay lasted years, this is not the norm. Most dark web sites generally last for up to three months. At this point, the sites are moved and/or shut down to evade being seized by government entities.

Is the "Dark Web" All Bad or Illegal?

Initially, the original purpose of the "Dark Web'"was to provide an overlay of online protection. It was developed in the 1990s by the Naval Research Laboratory (NRL) as a means for military personnel to communicate abroad anonymously. At that time, only the military was utilizing the TOR network. In 2002, the TOR browser was released to the public so that one could have lots of encrypted traffic so that it would not look like that only the military was the sole consumer of services. With TOR's traffic encryption methodology, it makes all users look the same and it confuses the outside observers. In addition, with TOR's network of volunteers it is almost impossible to find anyone's real identity when they access a site using the TOR browser.

Although TOR is used as a way to view sites on the Dark Web, it can also be used to securely browse the Surface Web without divulging one's IP address. Privacy advocates generally promote the use of TOR to maintain free speech, privacy, and anonymity (7 Things You Should Know About Tor, 2014). There are several ways how TOR can be used for anonymity and privacy purposes:

- *Anti-Censorship and Political Activism.* TOR may be used as a "censorship circumvention tool, allowing its users to reach otherwise blocked destinations or content" (TOR Overview, 2020). Because individuals may rely upon TOR to access content that may be blocked in certain parts of the world, some governments have reportedly suggested tightening regulations around using TOR. Some have purportedly blocked access to it at times (PHW, A Closer Look, 2014). Political dissidents may also use TOR to secure and anonymize their communications and locations, as they have reportedly done in dissident movements in Iran and Egypt (Sullivan, 2011). In July 2017, the Russian Federation Council approved a bill that would outlaw the use of virtual private networks, the TOR network, anonymous mobile messaging services, and Internet Proxy services in general (Seals, 2017).
- *Sensitive Communication.* TOR may also be used by individuals who want to access chat rooms and other forums for sensitive communications—both for personal and business uses. Individuals may seek out a safe haven for discussing private issues such as victimization or physical or mental illnesses. They may also use TOR to protect their children online by concealing the IP addresses of children's activities (Tor Project, 2020). Businesses may use it to protect their projects and help prevent spies from gaining a competitive advantage (TOR Overview, 2020). TOR can also be used by abused women who are seeking shelter/refuge from abusive partners (LeVines, 2014).
- *Leaked Information.* Journalists may use TOR for communicating "more safely with whistleblowers and dissidents" (TOR Overview, 2020, para. 3). The *New Yorker*'s Strongbox, for instance, is accessible through TOR and allows individuals to communicate and share documents anonymously with the publication (TOR Overview, 2020). In addition, Edward Snowden reportedly used Tails (an "operating system optimized for anonymity")—which automatically runs TOR—to communicate with journalists and leak classified information on U.S. mass surveillance programs (Finley, 2014). Among the documents leaked by Snowden was a top-secret presentation outlining National Security Agency (NSA) efforts to exploit the TOR browser and de-anonymize users (Schneier, 2013).

It is important to note that the vast majority of TOR's users are not necessarily accessing the Dark Web for illegal purposes. They may be using it to browse the Surface Web anonymously, often because they are located in a country that does not have free and open access to the Internet. It may also just be because these individuals are privacy minded and want to protect their anonymity.

The ATF and Prohibited Persons

As we have discovered, buying a weapon on the surface web is simple and background checks can easily be circumvented. However, let us take a look at who is unable to purchase a firearm legally. The ATF identifies those who are unable to purchase a firearm as *prohibited person.* A *prohibited person* is someone who fits the following criteria (Bureau of Alcohol, Tobacco, Firearms and Explosives, 2020).

- A person convicted in any court of a crime punishable by imprisonment for a term exceeding one year
- an individual who is a fugitive from justice
- an individual who is an unlawful user of or addicted to any controlled substance
- an individual who has been adjudicated as a mental defective or has been committed to any mental institution
- an individual who is an illegal alien
- an individual who has been discharged from the Armed Forces under dishonorable conditions
- an individual who has renounced his or her United States Citizenship
- an individual who is subject to a court order restraining the person from harassing, stalking, or threatening an intimate partner or child of the intimate partner; or
- an individual who has been convicted of a misdemeanor crime of domestic violence.

So, other than *prohibited persons* as described by the ATF, who else buys firearms on the dark web? Other individuals that use the dark web to procure firearms include terrorists, career criminals, and those who purchase for personal reasons—which can include mass murder, murder for hire, family protection (Ubbink, 2019).

Gun Purchases, Cryptocurrency, and the Dark Web

In order to purchase firearms on the dark web, an understanding of cryptocurrency is needed. Cryptocurrency is just another form of currency; it can be used to buy goods and services. Unlike other currencies, cryptocurrencies are digital and use cryptography and encryption to provide secure online transactions.

So, how does one go about purchasing a gun on the dark web?

Before one can buy any goods or services, the user must have a virtual cryptocurrency such as Bitcoin (BTC) or Monero (XMR) readily available.

In order to obtain Bitcoin, one can do the following (Coin Trader, 2020).

- *Use a Bitcoin exchange.* There are businesses that will help you buy Bitcoin using your bank account. This allows you to exchange paper currency for virtual currency.
- *Use a Peer to Peer (P2P) Directory.* One browses a directory in order to find a seller who will sell you Bitcoin for a cost. This cost includes the Bitcoin conversion plus whatever fees are assessed by the seller.
- *Use a Bitcoin Automatic Teller Machine (ATM).* Using a Bitcoin ATM allows an individual to sell or buy their digital currency for cash. Additional fees may be assessed.
- *"Mine" for Bitcoin.* Bitcoin miners are paid in bitcoins for executing complicated computations that are essential for implementing Bitcoin transactions. Bitcoin miners download a software program that allows them to connect to the Bitcoin network (Huang, 2015).

Once an individual has obtained Bitcoin virtual currency, then this currency must be transferred to a cryptowallet. Cryptowallets can either be hardware that one plugs into the computer or software that is installed into the operating system. Well-known cryptowallets include (Rosenberg, 2020):

- Coinbase
- Trezor
- Ledger
- SoFi
- Robinhood
- Edge
- Exodus

Once the Bitcoin is stored in the wallet, then one is ready to purchase on the dark web. The individual would then choose a cryptomarket or a website that sells the firearm of choice. Depending on how the site is set up, the user may click on the button to *Add to Cart.* Once the item is in the cart, the individual proceeds to check out. The seller then provides the address of their cryptowallet so that the user can transfer the Bitcoin directly. Once the Bitcoin is received, then the seller then ships out the firearm (or other good). It is also possible that the money can be held in escrow until the item is received by the buyer. The buyer then contacts the seller and the monies are then disbursed to the seller's cryptowallet. The transaction is transparent to the user and is encrypted. One would be able to view that the transaction occurred but would not be able to tell whom the transaction was associated with (Kirkland, 2017).

There are sites on the dark web that are not automated like those on the Surface Web. There are no *Add to Cart* buttons or *Checkout* buttons. If this is the case, the individual must conduct the transaction by email. The buyer still transfers the cryptocurrency to the seller's cryptowallet, but the buyer must then *trust* the seller that they will make good on shipping the item. Because of the nefarious nature of Dark Web markets, this is problematic for the buyer.

Assuming the transaction completed successfully, the seller will contact the purchaser with additional information on their shipping process. This can include advice on how to avoid detection and how to feign surprise if their package is held up in customs. Some vendors will even go so far as to tell the buyer how their products will be shipped—that is, in computer devices, air freshener cans, books, shoes, flour bags, Coke bottles, and the like (Copeland, 2019). Once this communication has occurred, the seller then ships out the item either to specific GPS coordinates or a predetermined address. Generally, the shipping address is *not* to the buyer's home as this could lead law enforcement to potentially identify the buyer and seize the shipments.

Arms Trade

Arms trade on the dark web is relatively small in volume compared to other products trafficked online; even though it is small, it has a large impact on international security (International Arms Trade, 2020). RAND Europe and the University of Manchester partnered to conduct a study commissioned by the Economic and Social Research Council through the Partnership for Conflict, Crime and Security Research. The purpose of the study was to explore the worldwide illegal arms trade, with a focus on the role played by the dark web.

The project had seven objectives:

1. To understand the methods of buying and selling firearms and related products on the dark web.
2. To consider the viability of dark web markets for the selling of firearms, and more specifically, the extent to which these sellers may engage in scamming by taking payment for products they do not deliver or may not possess.

3. To estimate the size and scope of the trade in firearms and related products on cryptomarkets, including the number of dark web markets listing firearms and related products and services for sale, and the range and type of firearms and related products advertised and sold on cryptomarkets.
4. To estimate the value of the trade in firearms and related products on cryptomarkets.
5. To identify shipping routes and the most common shipping techniques for firearms and related products sold on cryptomarkets.
6. To identify the potential impact of dark web enabled arms trafficking on the overall arms black market.
7. To identify the potential implications of dark web enabled arms trafficking for law enforcement agencies and policy makers, at both national and international levels (International Arms Trade, 2020).

According to the study conducted by RAND Europe, the dark web is increasing the availability of better performing, newer firearms for the same or lower price compared to what would be available on the street. Out of the different types of firearms, pistols were the commonly listed firearm (84 percent), followed by rifles (10 percent), and submachine guns (6 percent). It is surprising to find that the common firearms purchased on the dark web are handguns and not the "exotic or rare firearm" (Brooks, 2019). Of all of the countries studied, the United States appeared to be the most common *source* country in that 60 percent of the firearm listings are associated with products that originate from the United States.

The overall value of arms trade on the dark web, based on twelve different cryptomarkets, is estimated to be around US$80,000 per month, with firearms generating about 90 percent of all revenue (International Arms Trade, 2020). However, RAND Europe claims that the dark web is unlikely to become the method of choice to fuel conflicts because firearms are not traded on a large enough scale and because there are potential limitations on infrastructure and services that reside in a conflict zone (International Arms Trade, 2020).

Other Technologies Used to Facilitate Obtaining Weaponry

Throughout this chapter, we have primarily focused on the dark web and the use of cryptocurrency and cryptomarkets to facilitate the sale of illegal firearms. However, we would be remiss if other technologies that facilitate firearms purchasing and trafficking were not discussed.

Steganography

The word steganography comes from the Greek *steganos* (covered or secret) and—*graphy* (writing or drawing) and literally means covered writing. Its main purpose is to pass information in a way that leaves the casual observer unaware (Kellen, n.d.). The way that this is accomplished is that a person would take an image file and then use a steganographic tool to then embed text or another picture inside the original image. Once the image is hidden, it tricks the casual observer into thinking that there is no message that is being exchanged. They would just assume that the original picture file was just that—a picture file.

So, for example, a seller has a lot of assault rifles that he wants his buyer to see an image of so that the buyer would know exactly what he is paying for. The seller could use the contents of an original text-based file such as the image of an American flag, and with the use of a steganographic tool embed the following text document:

Textbox 25.1: Embedded Text Document

Mr. Bashar al-Assad,
I have found the lot of assault rifles that you are looking for. There are 500 in the lot and the seller, Shahrukh al-Habib is willing to sell them for $110,000 US American Dollars or 9 BTC. This can be sent to the following 18PnKsP1f3mVnKg32aS4TMHXmCMg99RGf8

AWS

Textbox 25.2: StegoDoc.text embedded into flag.jpg file

```
C:\steghide>steghide embed +cf flag.jpeg +ef StegoDoc.txt
Enter passphrase:
Re-Enter passphrase:
embedding "StegoDoc.txt" in "flag.jpg" ...done
   1 [main] steghide 183168 handle_exceptions: exception: STATUS_ACCESS_VIOLATION
   593 [main] steghide 183168 open_stackdumpfile: Dumping stack trace to steghide.exe.stackdump

C:\steghide>
```

Using a steganographic tool such as StegHide, I can embed the document in figure 25.2 into the American Flag picture.

If the flag.jpg image file were viewed after running StegHide, you would not be able to tell that there was a text file embedded into the document.

This file would then be attached to an email and sent to its intended recipient. In order to access the text document, the email recipient would have to use the same steganographic tool that was used to embed the text document (i.e., StegHide) and know that passcode to be able to open it.

Cryptography

Cryptography is associated with the process of converting ordinary plain text into unintelligible text (The *Economic Times*, "Cryptography", n.d.). It changes the contents of a file or message in such a way that is not readable by someone who is not the intended recipient. The intended recipient would have a key that would allow the encrypted file to be unlocked and viewed as planned by the sender.

The challenge comes when both cryptography and steganography are used simultaneously. The encryption provides a layer of protection so that the file contents cannot be read (Kellen, n.d.). If the correct key were obtained to decrypt the file, the user would then need to be able to unhide the message that the steganographic file contains. Using these two technologies together make it virtually impossible for the messages to be deciphered and read; thus making this method a secure communication channel.

So, if we use the example above, we have a seller who has embedded a text file into a picture file of an American flag. The intermediary in this case would then attach the image to the email. Once this has happened, the intermediary would then encrypt the document so that no one would be able to decipher the contents unless they had the key (i.e., passcode) to open the file. The key decrypts the message so that the recipient can read the email and see the flag. However, without the passcode to the steganographic image and the tool used, the text file is unobtainable.

Note: If using a web-based platform such as Yahoo! or Gmail, the messages are already encrypted using Secure/Multipurpose Internet Mail Extensions (S/MIME) and Transport Layer Security (TLS).

Social Media

The Internet has always been a useful tool for arms traffickers to connect with prospective customers. The rise of social media has made that even easier, with arms traffickers increasingly turning to platforms like Facebook, Instagram, and Snapchat to market their illegal goods (From Gun Trafficking, 2019). In January 2018, the U.S. Bureau of Alcohol, Tobacco, Firearms and Explosives discovered a trafficking ring led by a twenty-two-year-old Nevada resident, Anthony Reed. Along with two of his associates, Reed purchased hundreds of semi-automatic pistols through private party transactions and smuggled them into California. He then used Snapchat to advertise the weapons by posting photos and videos of himself holding the guns to his own account. Reed eventually was approached by an undercover ATF agent who bought 35 handguns for more than $30,000 over the course of 11 months. Reed's trafficking ring managed to sell more than 100 firearms in the San Francisco Bay area before they were finally arrested (From Gun Trafficking, 2019).

In 2015, *Telegraph*, a social media networking site much like Twitter, rolled out channels within its platform. In just a few days after Telegraph launched its new channel features, a massive migration of users from other social networking sites started using Telegraph as their primary communications platform. Since Telegraph's messages use encryption, one is unable to decipher the dialogue that occurs to facilitate gun purchases or arms trafficking (Weinmann, 2016).

Forums

In early 2016, Facebook took a stand and prohibited private gun sales on its website (Drange, 2020). When gun enthusiasts found out, they started moving into the social network's discussion forums and then into various groups to hide. In addition, they changed their vernacular so that when their bots scanned for keywords, they were unable to find minimal advertisements and/or conversations related to firearm sales. Facebook then tried to shut down the sales on Instagram, but the users quickly found work-arounds, with sellers posting photos of a gun with accompanying language designed to shift the sales conversation to private messaging (Drange, 2020).

Reddit, a popular forum site has specific forums that are related to firearms. Reddit updated their content policy to prohibit transactions involving *some goods and services* (Musil, 2018). This policy affected subreddits that discussed firearms, ammunition, and explosives along with other goods and services. Nonetheless, users still found work-arounds to advertise and link to other sites for private gun sales.

General Digital Products

The trade in arms-related digital products poses an additional layer of complexity. These products are often guides that provide tutorials for a wide range of illegal actions, ranging from the conversion of replica/alarm guns into live weapons, to the full manufacture of homemade guns and explosives, and also include models that can be turned into fully functioning firearms through 3-D printing. Firearms can easily and inexpensively be printed in their disassembled state and sent to buyers for reassembly and use.

3-D Printing

A new type of technology that is growing in popularity is the 3-D-printed gun space. There are people around the world who are actively developing 3-D-printed gun technology. These individuals, through niched websites, communicate across digital platforms such as Twitter, Inter-relay chat (IRC), and Discord. They critique each other's work, exchange 3-D gun CAD (Computer Aided Drafting) files, offer advice, and collaborate on future blueprints (Hanrahan, 2019).

For anyone who is interested, free CAD files are uploaded to the Internet so that anyone with a FDM (Fused Deposition Modeling) 3-D printer and some hand tools can make a workable handgun. After the user downloads the CAD file, it is opened in a program that translates it into instructions that the 3D printer can understand. Once the 3-D printed parts are ready, they can be assembled into a fully workable gun (Hanrahan, 2019).

In an effort to combat 3-D printed technology, states have sued the federal government to stop the process of uploading CAD files to the Internet for download. In addition, states such as New York have passed legislation to ban 3-D printed guns entirely. As homemade guns gain in popularity, it will become increasingly difficult to monitor and control their distribution since 3-D printed guns are untraceable and require no background checks.

SMART GUNS

While not a consumption-based technology, smart guns are not a new concept or technology; they have been around for almost two decades (Nguyen, 2018). Smart guns work by using either biometrics or RFID (Radio Frequency Identification) technology. This allows for the firearm to only be discharged when the owner has been identified—either by a wearable device such as a ring or watch or through fingerprint technology.

A Johns Hopkins 2016 Survey states that 60 percent of Americans favor smart guns; however, due to political pressure from gun rights proponents and a lack of investment in their development, most smart guns in the United States are still in prototype form (Nguyen, 2018). Two major U.S. gun manufacturers, Colt and Smith & Wesson, agreed in 2000 to become leaders and signed a partnership agreement to create government-sponsored smart guns to prevent accidental shootings and gun deaths. However, gun owners boycotted them and nearly drove them out of business (Nguyen, 2018). To date, the major gun manufacturers have not invested in smart gun technology.

Fearmongering toward personalized guns has stunted consumer access in the U.S. gun market. Smart guns have faced enormous blowback from the National Rifle Association, which rejects smart gun technology as costly, unreliable, and an expansion of government control over firearms. Hacking smart guns exists and RFID guns struggle to shake off the stigma of unreliability (Heubl, 2020). There are vendors, such as Ignis-Kinetix and Identilock, that manufacture smart guns and smart gun technology; however, gaining access to funding has been difficult—and they have yet to bring a smart firearm to market.

POLICING CRIMINAL ACTIVITY

Because criminals employ multiple technologies to mask their illegal activities such as arms trafficking, policing Internet crimes has become extremely difficult. Jurisdictional issues pose a huge problem since the concept of borders is evolving to include both physical and cyber borders.

- *Physical Borders.* For law enforcement purposes, jurisdictional boundaries have been drawn between nations, states, and other localities. Within these territories, various enforcement agencies are designated authority to administer justice. When crimes cross boundaries, a given entity may no longer have sole responsibility for criminal enforcement, and the laws across jurisdictions may not be consistent (Richman, n.d.). Criminals have long understood these phenomena—and exploited them (Finklea, 2017).
- *Physical—Cyber Borders.* The relatively clear borders within the physical world are not always replicated in the virtual realm. High speed Internet communication has not only facilitated the growth of legitimate business, but it has bolstered criminals' abilities to operate in an environment where they can broaden their goal of potential targets and rapidly exploit their victims. Frauds and schemes that were once conducted face

to face can now be carried out remotely from across the country or even across the world. For instance, criminals can rely upon botnets to target victims across the globe without crossing a single border themselves (Finklea, 2017).

- *Cyber Borders.* While cyberspace crosses physical borders, boundaries *within* cyberspace—both jurisdictional and technological—still exist. Some web addresses, for instance are country specific, and the administration of those websites is controlled by particular nations. Another barrier in cyberspace involves the lines between the Surface Web and the Deep Web. Crossing these boundaries may involve subscriptions or fee-based access to particular website content. Certain businesses—news sites, journals, file-sharing sites, and others—may require paid access. Other sites may only be accessed through an invitation (Finklea, 2017).

Local police can often be the first to learn of a cybercrime but often lack the capacity and jurisdiction to act effectively. National law enforcement usually has the capacity and jurisdiction to act effectively but can lack knowledge that a particular cybercrime is occurring. The knowledge of local police should be paired with national law enforcement; however, this rarely occurs.

In addition to jurisdictional issues, law enforcement officers are understaffed and undertrained to meet the challenges of investigating cybercrime. Most police departments have limited capability and are unable to meet the demands since many more crimes are now shifting online or have some technology-based component to be examined. If digital evidence is identified, law enforcement must contact the appropriate vendor so that data pertinent to their cases can be retrieved (Nakashima, 2018). Since there is a distrust between law enforcement and tech companies, tech companies are deliberately seeking to bar access to data, even when the agency has a warrant or other legal order. If companies do comply, they are slow to respond and/or data is usually turned over in formats that made it difficult for law enforcement to parse the information to get any type of meaningful results (Nakashima, 2018).

Another limitation that can occur for police departments is believing a crime has actually occurred when it only exists in the cyber realm. A physical burglary or violent crime in a jurisdiction will be recorded accurately and quickly in most cases. A cybercrime of harassment or theft is far less likely to be counted. The primary reason is that it is harder for local police to address these crimes, given resources, capacity, and the jurisdiction in which they work (Jardine, 2015).

Lastly, criminals are very adept at changing strategies or techniques to hide their illegal dealings. This makes it difficult for law enforcement to keep up. Depending upon the complexity of the change, the law enforcement officer needs a tool that has yet to be developed and/or training in order to spot potential flags that can lead to the criminal activity (Rhumorbarbe et al., 2017)—both of which are difficult to obtain due to availability of financial and personnel resources.

CONCLUSION

Technology has facilitated not only how we do business, but also how we buy, learn, and communicate. This also holds true for obtaining firearms. Despite efforts to regulate the sale of firearms, there are multiple avenues that can be bypassed in order to purchase weapons on the Internet. One of these avenues is the "Dark Web." While not the proliferated marketplace, the Dark Web does contribute to a small portion of overall gun sales and arms trafficking. The majority of sales still come from the Surface web and private party sales using technologies such as forums and social networking sites. Also, criminals and those who are unable to pass a background check typically use a combination of technologies discussed in this chapter in order to obtain a firearm. In either way, policing becomes extremely difficult due to increased challenges and limitations.

BIBLIOGRAPHY

"AlphaBay," [Online]. Available: https://en.wikipedia.org/wiki/AlphaBay. [Accessed 29 June 2020].

Bellemare, A. 2017, July 23. "The Secret Life of Alexandre Cazes, Alleged Dark Web Mastermind." CBC. [Online]. Available: https://www.cbc.ca/news/canada/montreal/alexandre-cazes-millionaire-cars-property-alphabay-1.4215894. [Accessed 29 July 2020].

Brooks, C. 2019, April 24. "People Are Secretly Buying Handguns on the Dark Web." Michigan State University. [Online]. Available: https://www.futurity.org/guns-dark-web-2044652/. [Accessed 28 June 2020].

Bureau of Alcohol, Tobacco, Firearms and Explosives. "Identify Prohibited Persons." [Online]. Available: https://www.atf.gov/firearms/identify-prohibited-persons. [Accessed 28 June 2020].

CASEFILE, "Case 76: Silk Road Part 1." 2018, February 11. [Online]. Available: https://casefilepodcast.com/case-76-silk-road-part-1/. [Accessed 28 June 2020].

Chertoff, M. 2017, March 13. "A Public Policy Perspective of the Dark Web." *Journal of Cyber Policy*, vol. 2, no. 1, pp. 25–38.

"Coin Trader," [Online]. Available: https://coinatmradar.com/. [Accessed 28 June 2020].

Copeland, C. W. 2019, March 30. "Assessing the Practices and Products of Dark Web Firearms Vendors." *Deviant Behavior*.

Drange, M. 2020, February 12. "Facebook Tried to Ban Gun Sales 4 Years Ago. It's Still Trying." *Protocol*. [Online]. Available: https://www.protocol.com/facebook-gun-sales-ban. [Accessed 29 June 2020].

Estes, A. 2013, August 30. "Tor: The Anonymous Internet, and If It's Right for You." [Online]. Available: https://gizmodo.com/tor-the-anonymous-internet-and-if-its-right-for-you-1222400823. [Accessed 26 June 2020].

Finklea, K. 2017. "Dark Web." Congressional Research Service.

Finley, K. 2014, April 14. "Out in the Open: Inside the Operating System Edward Snowden Used to Evade the NSA." Wired.com. [Online].

"From Gun Trafficking Social Media Accounts to AI Deepfakes—Crime Is Going High-Tech." 2019, December 11. [Online]. Available: https://www.richardvanhooijdonk.com/blog/en/from-gun-trafficking-social-media-accounts-to-ai-deepfakes-crime-is-going-high-tech/.

Hanrahan, J. 2019, May. "3D Printed Guns Are Back, and This Time They Are Unstoppable." *Wired*. [Online]. Available: https://www.wired.co.uk/article/3d-printed-guns-blueprints. [Accessed 29 June 2020].

Heubl, B. 2020, June 5. "Will Smart Guns Hit Their Target This Time?" [Online]. Available: https://eandt.theiet.org/content/articles/2020/06/us-smart-gun-tech-start-ups-to-bring-personalised-weapons-to-market/. [Accessed 30 June 2020].

Holmes, A. 2020. "The Dark Web Turns 20 This Month. From Black Market Hotspots to Facilitating the Arab Spring, Here's How It Changed the World."

Huang, A. 2015, December 1. "Reaching within Silk Road: The Need for a New Subpoena Power That Targets Illegal Bitcoin Transactions." *Boston College Law Review,* vol. 56, no. 5, pp. 2093–2125.

"International Arms Trade on the Dark Web." [Online]. Available: https://www.rand.org/randeurope/research/projects/international-arms-trade-on-the-hidden-web.html. [Accessed 22 June 2020].

"Internet Live Stats." [Online]. Available: https://www.internetlivestats.com/. [Accessed 25 June 2020].

Jardine, E. 2015, September. The Dark Web Dilemma: Tor, Anonymity and Online Policing. (G. C. Governance, Ed.) *Global Commission on Internet Governance Paper Series*, 24. doi:10.2139/ssrn.2667711.

Kellen, T. N.d. "Hiding in Plain View: Could Steganography Be a Terrorist Tool?" SANS. [Online]. Available: https://www.giac.org/paper/gsec/1411/hiding-plain-view-steganography-terrorist-tool/102638.

Kirkland, J. 2017, December 27. "Okay, Here's What You Actually Need to Know about Bitcoin." *Esquire*. [Online]. Available: https://www.esquire.com/lifestyle/money/a14500146/beginners-guide-bitcoin-what-is-bitcoin/. [Accessed 29 June 2020].

LeVines, G. 2014, May 12. "As Domestic Abuse Goes Digital, Shelters Turn to Counter-Surveillance with Tor." Thomson Reuters Foundation News. [Online]. Available: http://cms.trust.org/item/20140509204741-lok65. [Accessed 28 June 2020].

Miller, M., Hepburn, L., and Azrael, D. 2017. "Firearm Acquisition without Background Checks." *Annals of Internal Medicine*.

Moore, D. 2016. "Cryptopolitik and the DarkNet." *Survival* 58, no. 1, pp. 7–38.

Musil, S. 2018, March 21. "Reddit Removes Several Firearms-Related Forums." CNET. [Online]. Available: https://www.cnet.com/news/reddit-removes-several-firearms-related-forums/. [Accessed 29 June 2020].

Nakashima, E. 2018, July 18. "Encryption? Law Enforcement's Biggest Obstacle to Digital Evidence Is More Basic, Study Finds." [Online]. Available: https://www.washingtonpost.com/world/national-security/encryption-law-enforcements-biggest-obstacle-to-digital-evidence-is-more-basic-study-finds/2018/07/24/32bcbc40-8e19-11e8-bcd5-9d911c784c38_story.html. [Accessed 23 June 2020].

Nguyen, N. 2018, March 18. "Here's What's Up with 'Smart Guns' — And Why You Can't Buy One in the US." [Online]. Available: https://www.buzzfeednews.com/article/nicolenguyen/what-is-smart-gun-technology. [Accessed 30 June 2020].

PHW. 2014, October 6. "A Closer Look at the Great Firewall of China." Tor Project Blog. [Online]. Available: https://blog.torproject.org/closer-look-great-firewall-china. [Accessed 28 June 2020].

Retzkin, S. 2018. Hands-On Dark Web Analysis, Packet, p. 32.

Rhumorbarbe, D., Werner, D., Gillieron, Q., Staehli, L., Broseus, J., and Rossy, Q. 2017, March 10. "Characterizing the Online Weapons Trafficking on Cryptomarkets." *Forensic Science International*, no. 283, pp. 16–20.

Richman, D. N.d. "The Changing Boundaries between Federal and Local Law Enforcement." In *Boundary Changes in Criminal Justice Organizations*.

Rosenberg, E. "Best Bitcoin Wallets." The Balance. [Online]. Available: https://www.thebalance.com/best-bitcoin-wallets-4160642. [Accessed 28 June 2020].

Schneier, B. 2013, October 4. "Attacking Tor: How the NSA Targets Users' Online Anonymity." *The Guardian*. [Online].

Seals, T. 2017, July 25. "Russia Passes Bill Banning Tor, VPNs." [Online]. Available: https://www.infosecurity-magazine.com/news/russia-passes-bill-banning-tor-vpns/. [Accessed 26 June 2020].

"7 Things You Should Know about Tor." 2014, July 1. Electronic Frontier Foundation. [Online]. Available: https://www.eff.org/deeplinks/2014/07/7-things-you-should-know-about-tor. [Accessed 26 June 2020].

Sullivan, J. 2011, March 22. "2010 Free Software Awards Announced." Free Software Foundation. [Online]. Available: https://www.fsf.org/news/2010-free-software-awards-announced. [Accessed 28 June 2020].

The Economic Times. "Cryptography." [Online]. Available: https://economictimes.indiatimes.com/definition/cryptography.

"TOR Overview." [Online]. Available: https://2019.www.torproject.org/about/overview.html. [Accessed 26 June 2020].

"Tor Project." [Online]. Available: https://2019.www.torproject.org/about/torusers.html.en. [Accessed 28 June 2020].

Ubbink, J. 2019. "Characterization of Illegal Dark Web Arms Markets."

"Unchecked: Over 1 Million Online Firearm Ads, No background Checks Required." [Online]. Available: https://everytownresearch.org. [Accessed 25 June 2020].

Verisign. "The Verisign Domain Name Industry Brief." [Online]. Available: https://www.verisign.com/en_US/domain-names/dnib/index.xhtml. [Accessed 25 June 2020].

Weinmann, G. 2016, June. "Terrorist Migration to the Dark Web." *Perspectives on Terrorism*, vol. 10, no. 3, pp. 40–44.

"What Is a Tor Relay?" Electronic Frontier Foundation. [Online]. Available: https://www.eff.org/pages/what-tor-relay. [Accessed 26 June 2020].

Index

About the Contributors

Josiah R. Baker is Nimocks Professor of International Business and Professor of Financial Economics at Methodist University near Fort Bragg in Fayetteville, North Carolina. For nearly twenty-five years, Dr. Baker has taught college courses in Kentucky, Florida, the Washington, DC, area, and North Carolina. In Washington, DC, he completed his dissertation on the economic history of the construction of Sweden's welfare state. He has also lived in six countries (including Norway, Japan, Bolivia, Russia, Sweden) and studied six languages (French, Norwegian, Spanish, Japanese, Swedish, and Russian). Dr. Baker has over sixty academic publications, not including dozens of newspaper and magazine articles.

Christopher M. Bellas is associate professor of criminal justice and Graduate Program Coordinator in the Department of Criminal Justice and Consumer Sciences at Youngstown State University in Ohio. His areas of research primarily centers on juries and the death penalty. Bellas holds a BA and MA in political science, MS in criminal justice, and PhD in political science. He received a paralegal certificate from Kent State University's ABA Program. Besides teaching full time at YSU, he has taught at Kent State University and Penn State in the areas of law and criminology.

Joseph Binns is currently chief of police for the Garner Police Department. He is a police firearms instructor and former Special Response Team leader. Chief Binns is a graduate of the 261st F.B.I. National Academy and a graduate of the MJA program at Methodist University.

Kayla Birmingham graduated summa cum laude from Methodist University's Justice Studies Digital Forensics and Cyber Security Program. She received the Undergraduate Research Award in Justice Studies from Methodist University for her contribution to the research for this volume's chapter 19, "The Tragedy of Firearms in American Schools: Student Voices, Perspectives, and Experiences." While writing, she pulled from her own past experience as an adolescent after the Columbine High School massacre. She currently works and resides in North Carolina.

Mikaela Brosh was born in Fayetteville, North Carolina, but due to a military upbringing she has lived in many different places. She is currently attending Methodist University where she is studying for a double major in applied forensic science and criminal justice. She is also a member of the Alpha Delta Pi sorority chapter at Methodist University.

Chris Cronin is professor of political science at Methodist University. He writes about religion and politics and party politics. Previous works include *The Cross, the Fall, and the Resurrection: The Social Gospel Movement and the Democratic Party*, and *Mormons in American Politics: From Persecution to Power*.

Matt Dobra holds a PhD and MA in economics from George Mason University, a graduate certificate in higher education from Monash University, and a BA in history from Loyola University, New Orleans. He is currently professor of economics and the Nimocks Endowed Professor of Business in the Reeves School of Business at Methodist University in Fayetteville, North Carolina. His primary research interests lie in the fields of resource economics, public economics, and political economy.

Dr. Steve Downs retired as a CW5 from the US Army where he served for nearly thirty years as an MP and as a supervisory special agent and forensic science officer for the United States Army Criminal Investigation Command (CID). During his long and illustrious career in CID he investigated and led the investigation of thousands of felony cases, many of which were high-profile cases including the 2009 attack on Fort Hood, Texas, by Nidal Hasan. After his retirement from the Army, he taught forensic science and law enforcement courses at the Federal Law Enforcement Center at Glynco, Georgia. He now is associate professor at Methodist University where he teaches forensic science and criminal justice courses, where he shares his vast knowledge and experience with the future generations of forensic scientists and law enforcement leaders.

Michelle L. Foster is associate professor at Kent State University. She teaches criminology and justice studies courses in the Department of Sociology for three campuses at the university. She also teaches American government courses for the Political Science Department at the Kent State Salem Campus.

Dr. Mark Kline is associate professor and department chair of psychology and sociology at Methodist University. Dr. Kline received his PhD in psychology from Indiana University and has been at Methodist University since 2011 and has specialized in research on trauma/PTSD and alcohol abuse.

Dr. Paul Knudson is associate professor and chair of sociology at Methodist University. Dr. Knudson earned his PhD in sociology in 2011 from the State University of New York at Albany. His research focuses on urban and metropolitan affairs, urban schools and families, and race and ethnic relations. His latest project examined upper-middle-class families who have chosen to remain in a struggling central-city public school district despite having the resources to relocate to suburban schools or enroll their children in private schools. Another recent project examined African American parents' views of charter schools in New York State. For his dissertation research, Knudson examined how nongovernmental organizations, including environmental groups, worked with local governments in the Hudson River Valley of upstate New York to promote regional planning and sustainable land use practices.

Sabrina Koncaba is a passionate reader and piano player who has a genuine love and curiosity of technology and information security. She designed, built, and implemented the Digital Forensics and Cyber Security Program at Methodist University and serves as the Educational Program Director. She has been employed with Methodist University for eight years and currently resides in Sanford, North Carolina.

Haley M. Lapcevich is a graduate student at Youngstown State University. She is earning a master of science and has a bachelor of science in criminal justice with summa cum laude honors. Haley is proudly serving as a sergeant in the U.S. Army Reserves and is a current law enforcement officer. She has internship experience with the United States Marshal Service, Mahoning County Prosecutor's Office, and Whalen Duffrin LLC law firm. Haley enjoys traveling with her fiancé and taking their two dogs on walks.

J. Scott Lewis received his PhD in sociology from Bowling Green State University. He is currently associate teaching professor of sociology and coordinator of the sociology program at Penn State Harrisburg. He is the author of several articles, book chapters, and a textbook. Research interests are varied, and include pedagogy, biosociology, and the philosophy of social science.

Bertha Llamas is a third-year undergraduate student at Methodist University. She is a criminal justice, applied forensic science, and digital forensics and cybersecurity major. Ms. Llamas is a Lowdermilk award recipient. She intends to graduate in May 2022.

Lisa G. Long is criminal justice adjunct professor at North Carolina A&T State University (Greensboro, NC), Elizabeth City State University (Elizabeth City, NC), and Greenville University (Greenville, IL). Lisa earned her PhD in criminal justice with a concentration in behavioral science from Nova Southeastern University. Lisa worked as a criminal intelligence analyst for the Fayetteville (NC) Police Department. While at FPD, Lisa was instrumental in the formation of the Crime Information Center at the Fayetteville Police Department, which is a real-time crime center, providing live closed-circuit camera feeds and intelligence data to police officers in the field.

David A. Mackey is professor of criminal justice at Plymouth State University. He earned his PhD in criminology from Indiana University of Pennsylvania. His recent publications include *Society, Ethics, and the Law*, coedited with Kathryn Elvey, and "Making methods relevant: Undergraduate research methods and the content analysis project," coauthored with Kevin E. Courtright.

Monica Merrill is assistant professor in the Department of Criminal Justice and Consumer Sciences at Youngstown State University. Her research interests include criminology, inequalities, violence, and the scholarship of teaching. Her current work focuses on domestic violence-related fatalities.

Amanda J. Moreschi is a junior at Youngstown State University, working toward her bachelor of science in criminal justice. She is an honors student with aspirations of pursuing a career in the legal field. She serves on the executive board of both her sorority, Alpha Omicron Pi, and Greek Campus Life. Amanda works as a leader for Girls Leading Our World, a summer camp that empowers young women and teaches them valuable life skills.

Deborah Morris, MD, is professor of clinical medicine at the Methodist University Physician Assistant Program in Fayetteville, North Carolina, where she has taught since 2007. She graduated from the Yale University School of Medicine Physician Assistant Program in 1982 and from the University of North Carolina School of Medicine in Chapel Hill in 1992, and spent her medical career working in urgent and primary care settings. She has an interest in writing, especially creative nonfiction, and has been published in the *Journal of Physician Assistant Education*, *Blood and Thunder: Musings on the Art of Medicine*, and *The Examined Life Journal*.

Courtney Platt graduated from Youngstown State University in May 2020 with a bachelor of science in criminal justice. She graduated magna cum laude and was a member of the Honors College during her time at YSU. Courtney is currently pursuing a juris doctor at the University of Toledo College of Law.

Michael Potts is professor of philosophy at Methodist University in Fayetteville, North Carolina. His areas of specialization include professional ethics and philosophy of religion. He is the author of numerous peer-reviewed articles and book chapters. He is the editor-in-chief of *Beyond Brain Death: The Case against Brain-Based Criteria for Human Death*.

Mark R. Regensburger has over thirty years of management experience across a broad variety of industries. He served in combat with the U.S. Army; has led nonprofit and for-profit organizations; and has taught management and HR for more than ten years. Regensburger is currently assistant professor of management for the Reeves School of Business at Methodist University, Fayetteville, North Carolina.

Eric S. See holds a PhD in criminology and is professor and chair of the Department of Criminal Justice at Methodist University in Fayetteville, North Carolina. He has published on a variety of topics including: the right to own and carry firearms, police use of force, terrorism, methamphetamine abuse, and the mentally ill in the criminal justice system. He won the Distinguished Professor of the Year award at Methodist University in 2012.

Sarah A. See is assistant professor at Methodist University in the Department of Criminal Justice. She received her bachelor's degree in psychology and a master's degree in criminology from Indiana University of Pennsylvania. Her previous research has been focused on the mentally ill in our jail and prison systems, carry conceal, and police use of force.

Raised in Northeast Ohio, **Justin Shaughnessy** served as the 2020–2021 student body president at Youngstown State University. Justin has received a bachelor's degree in criminal justice with a special interest in the legal process and is working toward his MSEd in College Counseling at Youngstown State. He has a passion for government, higher education, and appropriate criminal justice reform.

Nicole Shoenberger is assistant professor of sociology at Loyola University Maryland. She received her PhD from Bowling Green State University. She teaches courses on criminal justice, juvenile delinquency, serial killing, mass murder, deviance, social problems, and research methods. Her research interests focus on criminological theory, disproportionate minority contact in the criminal justice system, and positive deviance.

Jason Simon is a twenty-year veteran of the Youngstown Police Department in Youngstown, Ohio, holding the rank of captain. He is a graduate of Youngstown State University and holds bachelor's and master's degrees in criminal justice, has attended Johns Hopkins Executive Leadership and Management training, and is a graduate of the FBI National Academy (Session #264). Much of Capt. Simon's work has centered on the successful merging of academic research, community engagement, and practical law enforcement application. He teaches at both Youngstown State University and Eastern Gateway Community College.

Kevin Swift is a veteran of broadcast news in many capacities. He worked as a writer/producer and reporter for several TV and radio stations in the Youngstown, Ohio, and Pittsburgh, Pennsylvania, areas (WBZY, WKBN, WTAE, and several cable stations). He also served as an anchor/reporter for the award-winning news team at WVLK News in Lexington, Kentucky. Swift has worked extensively as a voice-over artist for organizations such as the Red Cross, NPR/Health Beat, Ford, and hundreds of local TV and radio spots. Before joining the faculty at Methodist University, Kevin taught at Catholic University, the University of Maryland, and Missouri State University. His research interests include FCC policy and media literacy.

Robert Henry Szewczyk is a junior at Methodist University majoring in digital forensics and cyber security. He is a retired sergeant of the U.S. Army after serving four years and five months as an Information Technology Specialist. He was born in Fort Bragg, North Carolina, on April 13, 1994.

Currently a lecturer at North Carolina State University, **Dan Trigoboff** was a journalist for many years prior to becoming an academic. He previously was on the faculties at Elon and Methodist Universities. He holds a JD from the University of San Diego and a PhD from N.C. State University.

Mark Vecellio retired from the U.S. Army Criminal Investigations Command, where he supervised and performed criminal investigations spanning the globe. Mark's specializations include crime scene processing/reconstruction, forensic photography, sexual assault investigations, death investigations, and cold cases. Mark has a master's degree in forensic sciences from the George Washington University, a master's in public administration–criminal justice from City University of Seattle, and a completed fellowship in forensic medicine with the Armed Forces Medical Examiner's Office. Mark has published several research and technical articles and coauthored a book in the field of crime scene investigations. Mark is a member of numerous forensic science and criminal investigations organizations, including the American Academy of Forensic Science and the International Association for Identification. Mark is currently professor of applied forensic science at Methodist University in Fayetteville, North Carolina.

Karla Weinbrenner is Computer Forensic Analyst at CACI and adjunct professor at Methodist University within Digital Forensics and Cyber Security program, in Fayetteville, North Carolina. Karla also forward deployed numerous times conduction investigations on items that came off the battlefield to include digital and mobile investigations. Karla currently holds CFCE, ACE, CCO, CCPA, and Security+ certifications.

Dr. Mary Wilson is professor of criminal justice in the Department of Sociology, Criminology and Justice Studies at Kent State University Trumbull Campus. She has a PhD in political science with a specific concentration in justice studies, and a MA in criminal justice administration.

David Wulff retired as a major from the Cary Police Department, Cary, North Carolina. He served in various roles as the criminal investigations division commander, training director, and firearms instructor. He also coordinated the development and construction of the Cary Police Department Firearms Training Center. He has a bachelor's degree from Campbell University, and a master's in justice administration from Methodist University. Major Wulff is currently a college professor and a deacon in the Roman Catholic Church for the diocese of Raleigh, North Carolina.

Madeline Yeung is a senior at Methodist University majoring in applied forensic science and justice studies. She is an inducted member of Phi Kappa Phi and an academic enthusiast. Madeline is working on her master's degree in public administration.